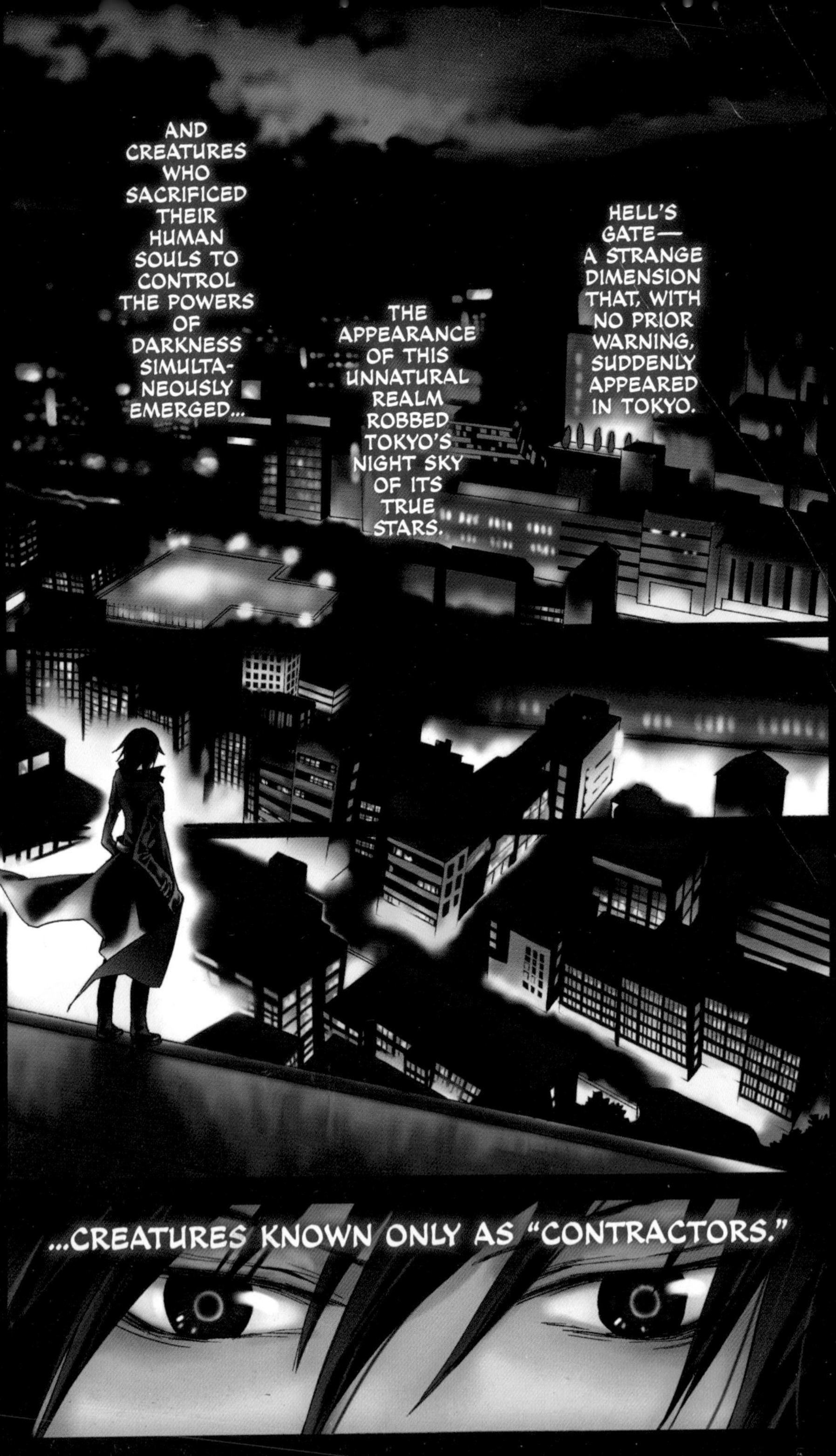
HELL'S GATE—A STRANGE DIMENSION THAT, WITH NO PRIOR WARNING, SUDDENLY APPEARED IN TOKYO.
THE APPEARANCE OF THIS UNNATURAL REALM ROBBED TOKYO'S NIGHT SKY OF ITS TRUE STARS.
AND CREATURES WHO SACRIFICED THEIR HUMAN SOULS TO CONTROL THE POWERS OF DARKNESS SIMULTA-NEOUSLY EMERGED...
...CREATURES KNOWN ONLY AS "CONTRACTORS."

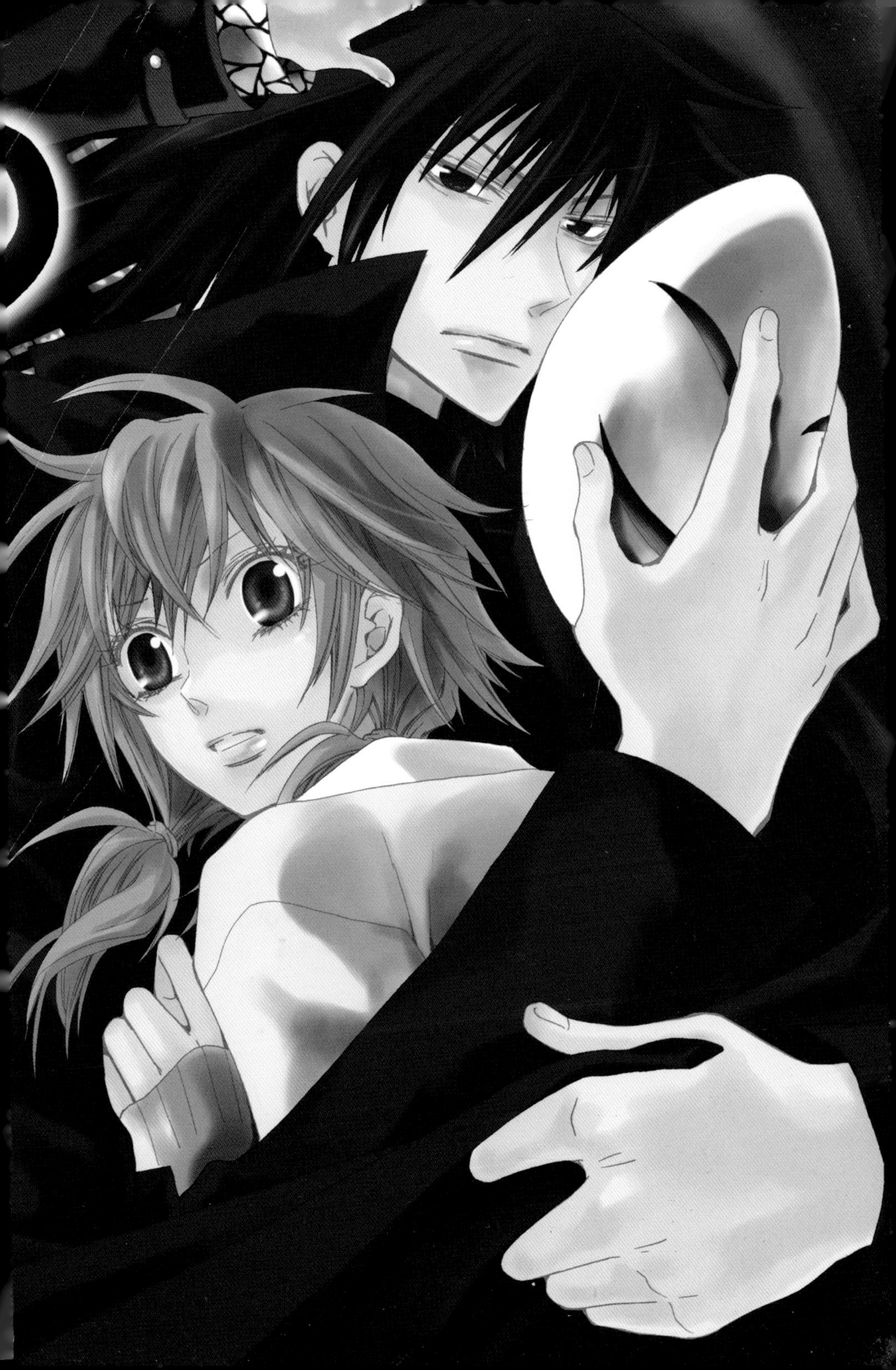

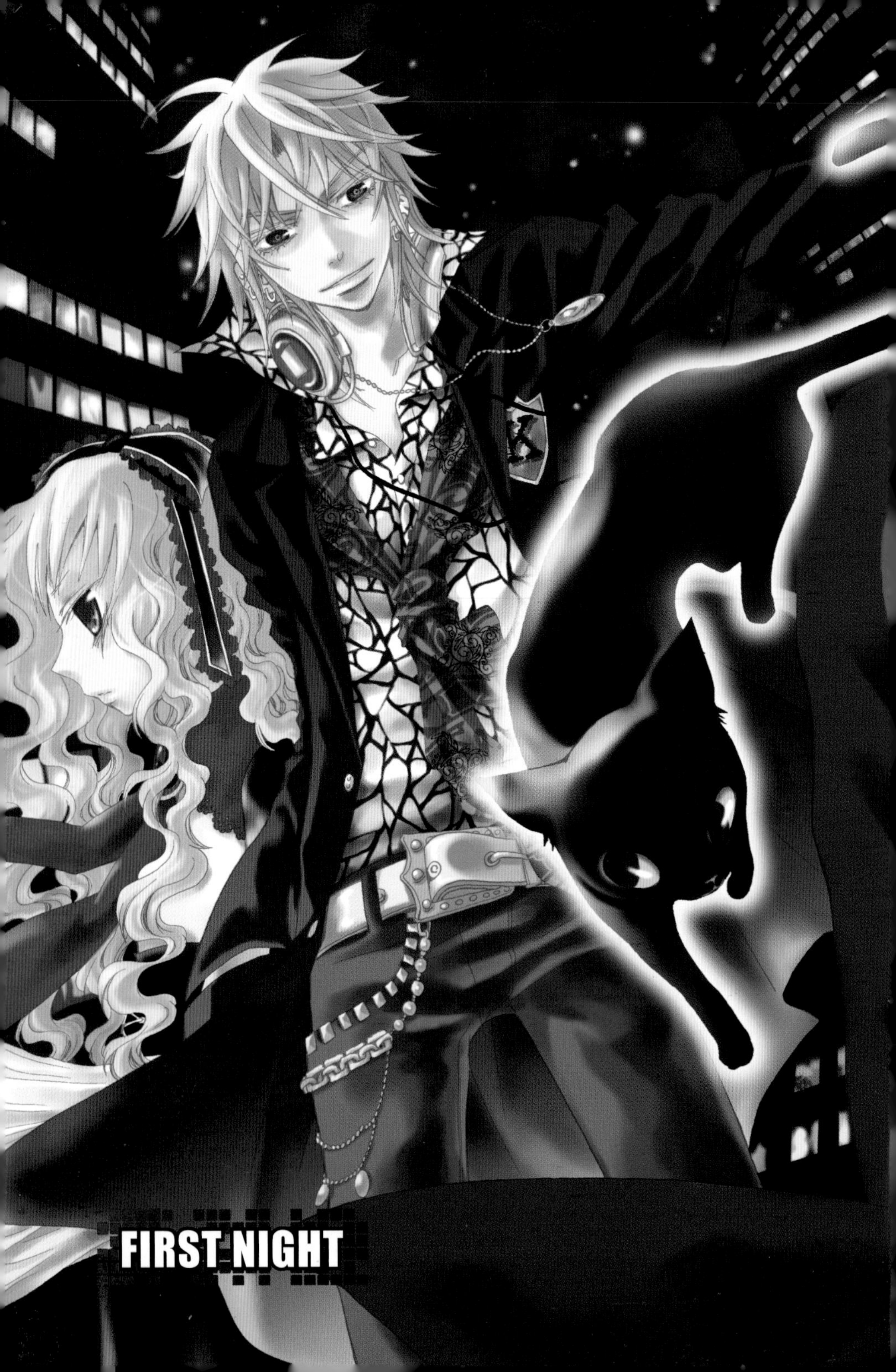
FIRST NIGHT

Contents

DARKER THAN
BLACK

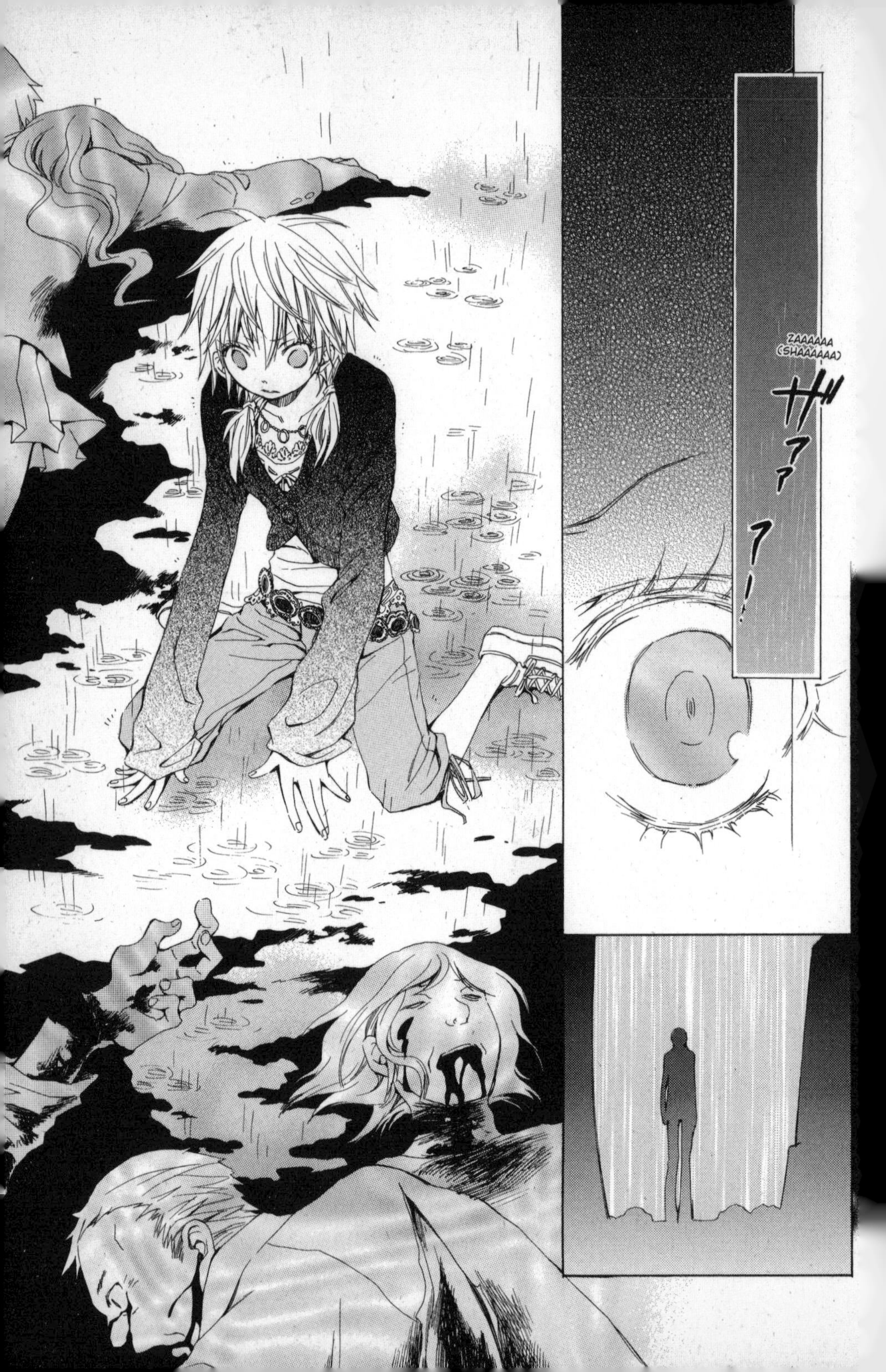
ZAAAAAA (SHAAAAAA)
ザァァァー!

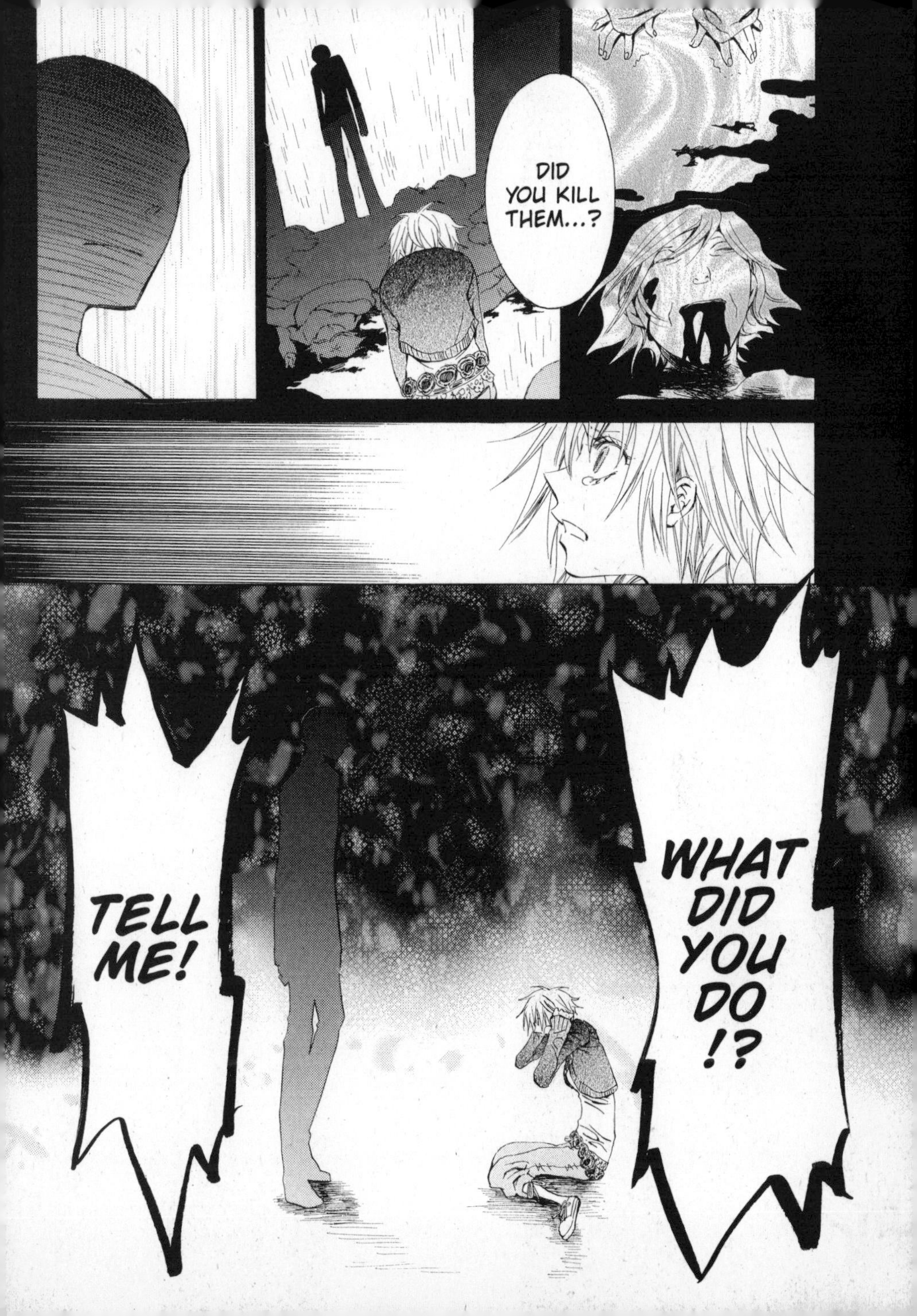
DID YOU KILL THEM...?
WHAT DID YOU DO!?
TELL ME!

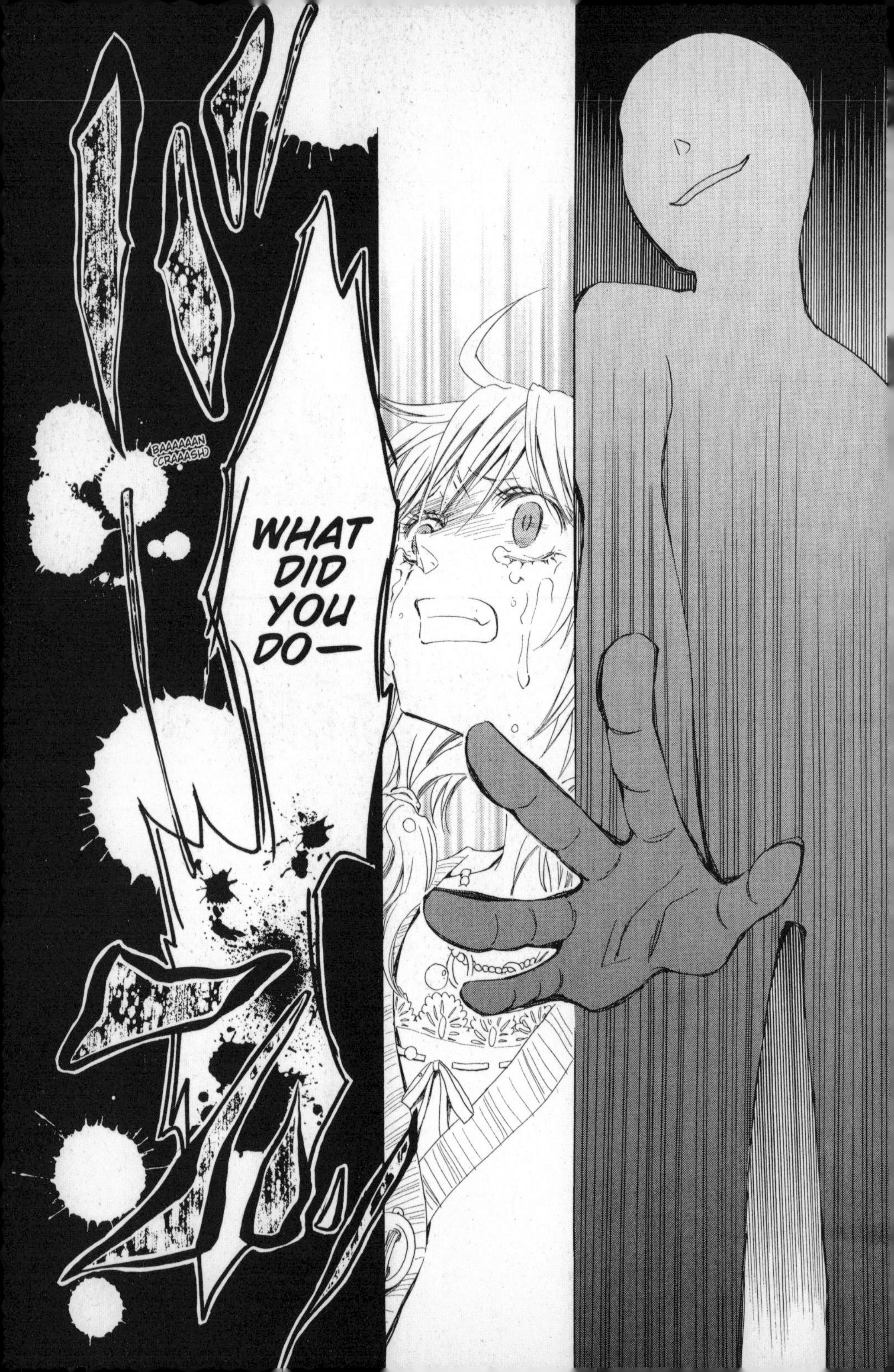
BAAAAAAN (CRAAASH)
WHAT DID YOU DO—

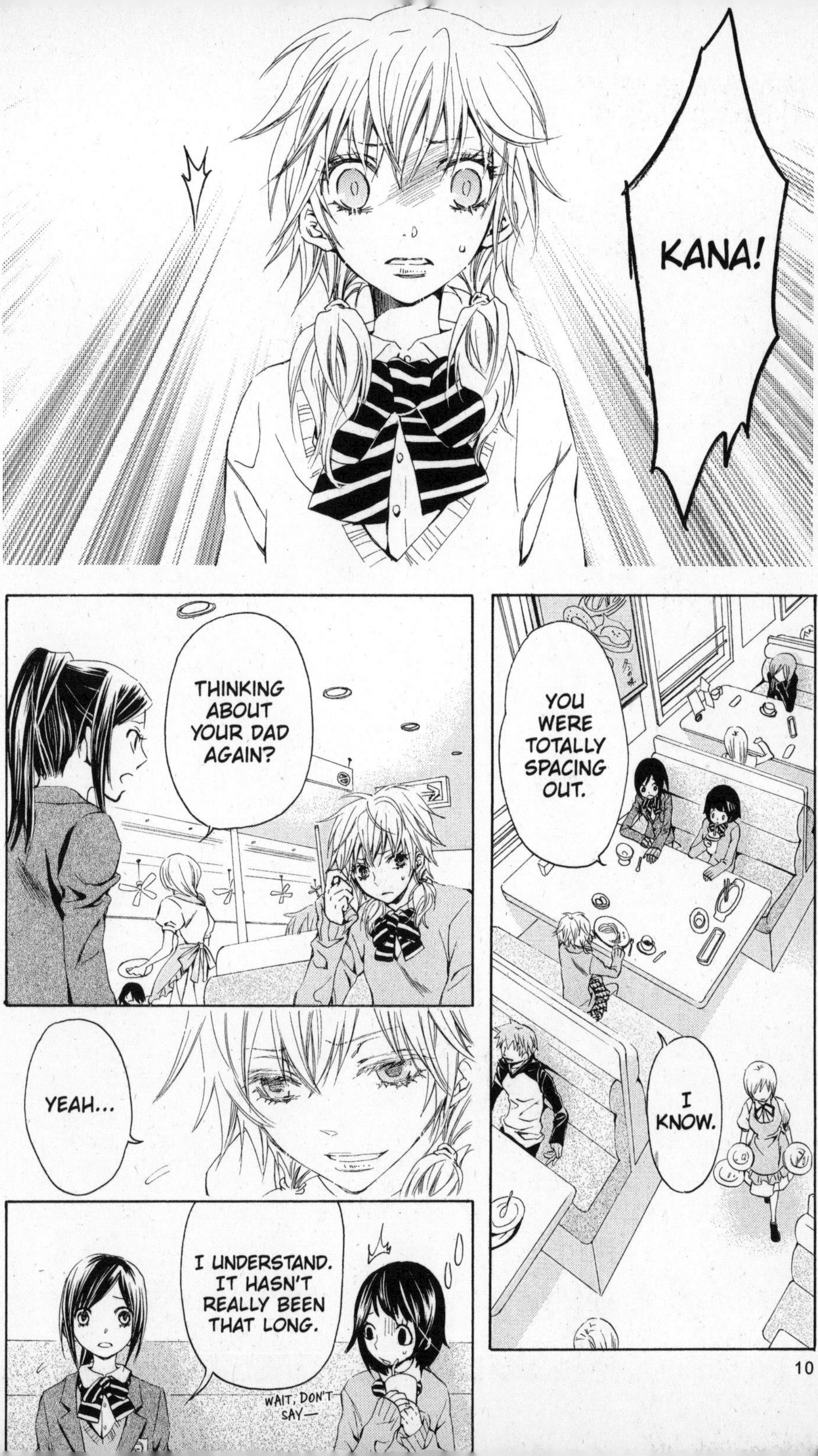

KANA!
YOU WERE TOTALLY SPACING OUT.
I KNOW.
THINKING ABOUT YOUR DAD AGAIN?
YEAH...
I UNDERSTAND. IT HASN'T REALLY BEEN THAT LONG.
WAIT, DON'T SAY—

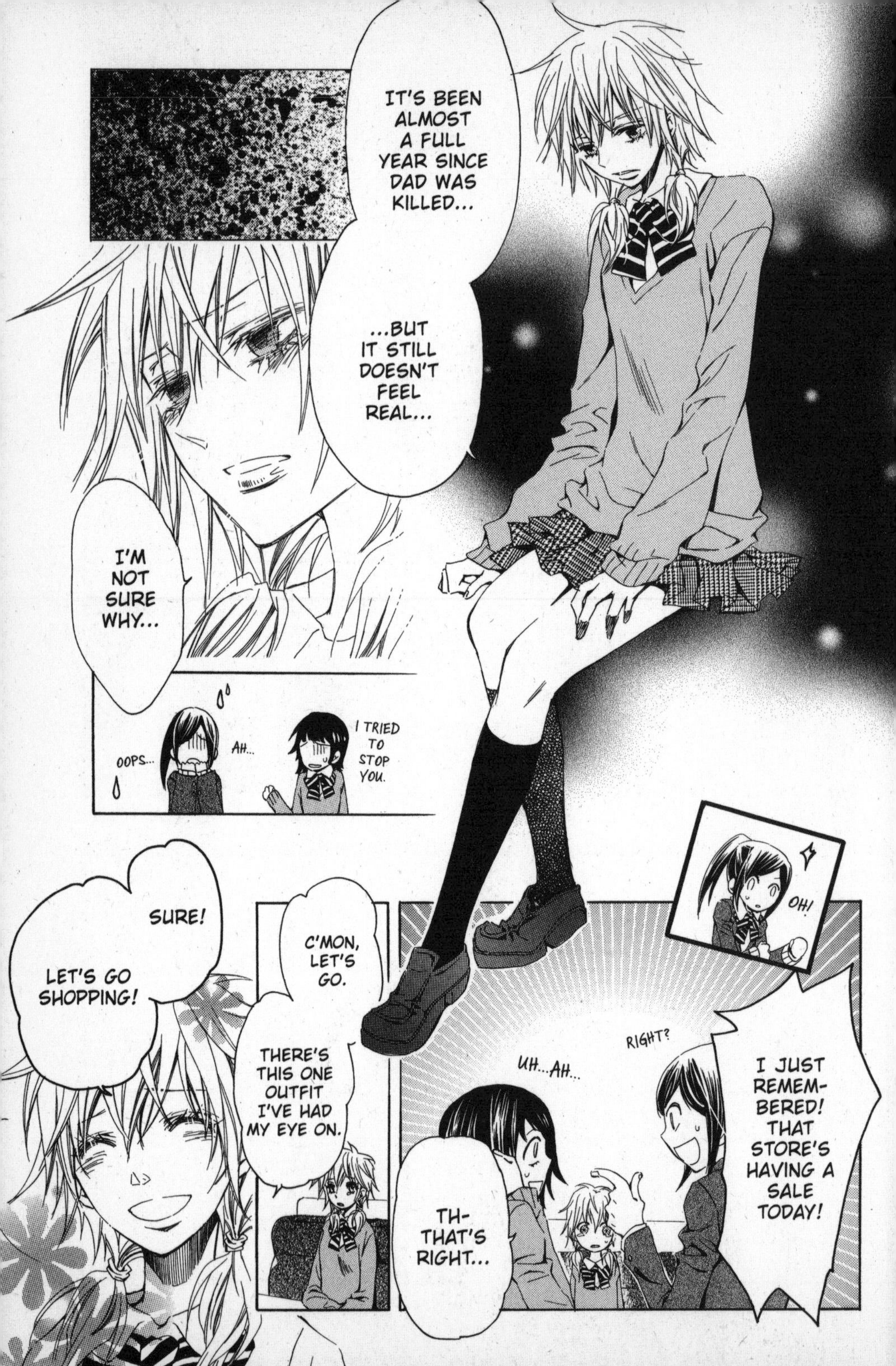
IT'S BEEN ALMOST A FULL YEAR SINCE DAD WAS KILLED...
...BUT IT STILL DOESN'T FEEL REAL...
I'M NOT SURE WHY...
I TRIED TO STOP YOU.
AH...
OOPS...
OH!
I JUST REMEM-BERED! THAT STORE'S HAVING A SALE TODAY!
RIGHT?
UH...AH...
TH-THAT'S RIGHT...
C'MON, LET'S GO.
THERE'S THIS ONE OUTFIT I'VE HAD MY EYE ON.
SURE!
LET'S GO SHOPPING!

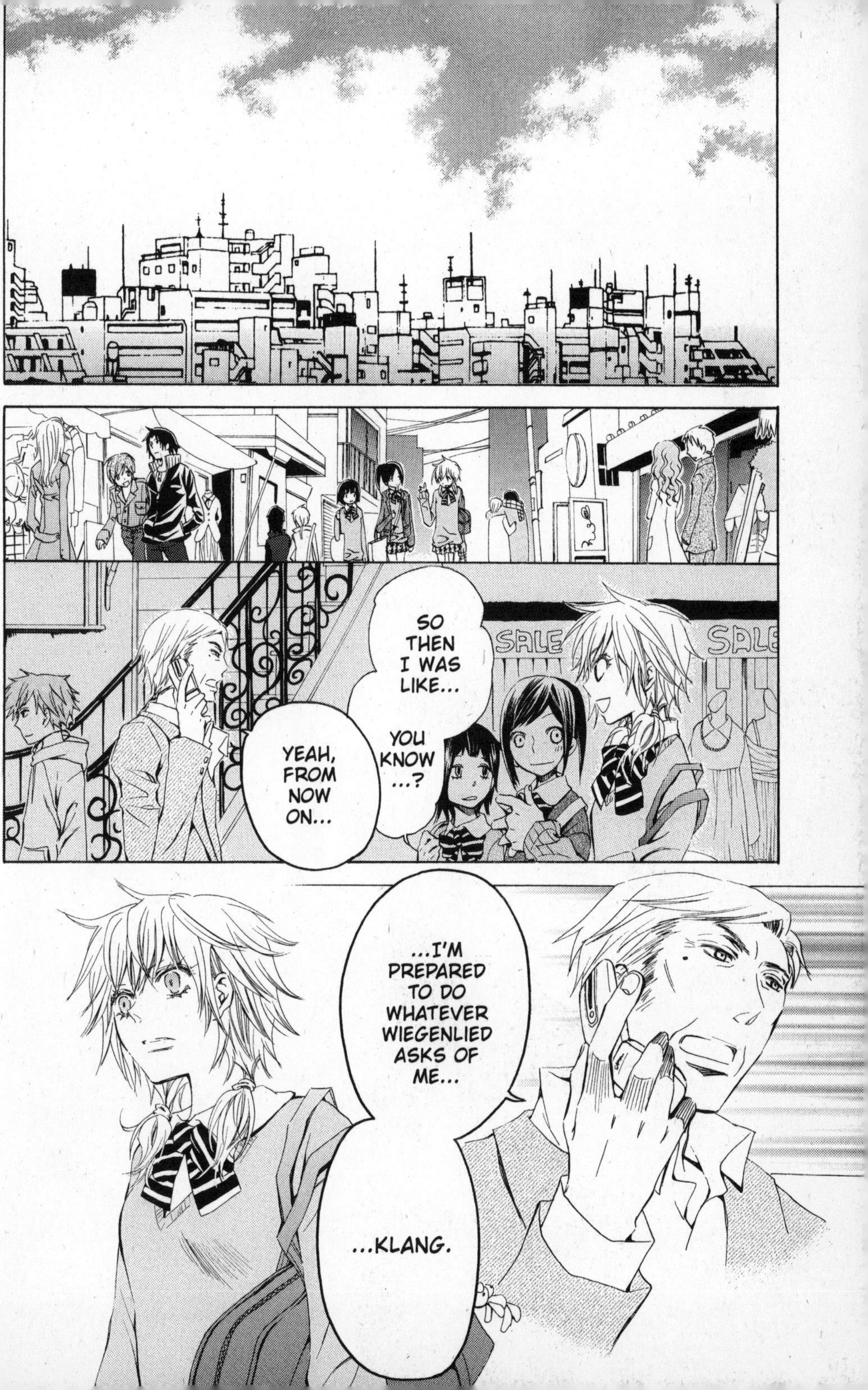
SALE
SALE
SO THEN I WAS LIKE...
YOU KNOW...?
YEAH, FROM NOW ON...
...I'M PREPARED TO DO WHATEVER WIEGENLIED ASKS OF ME...
...KLANG.

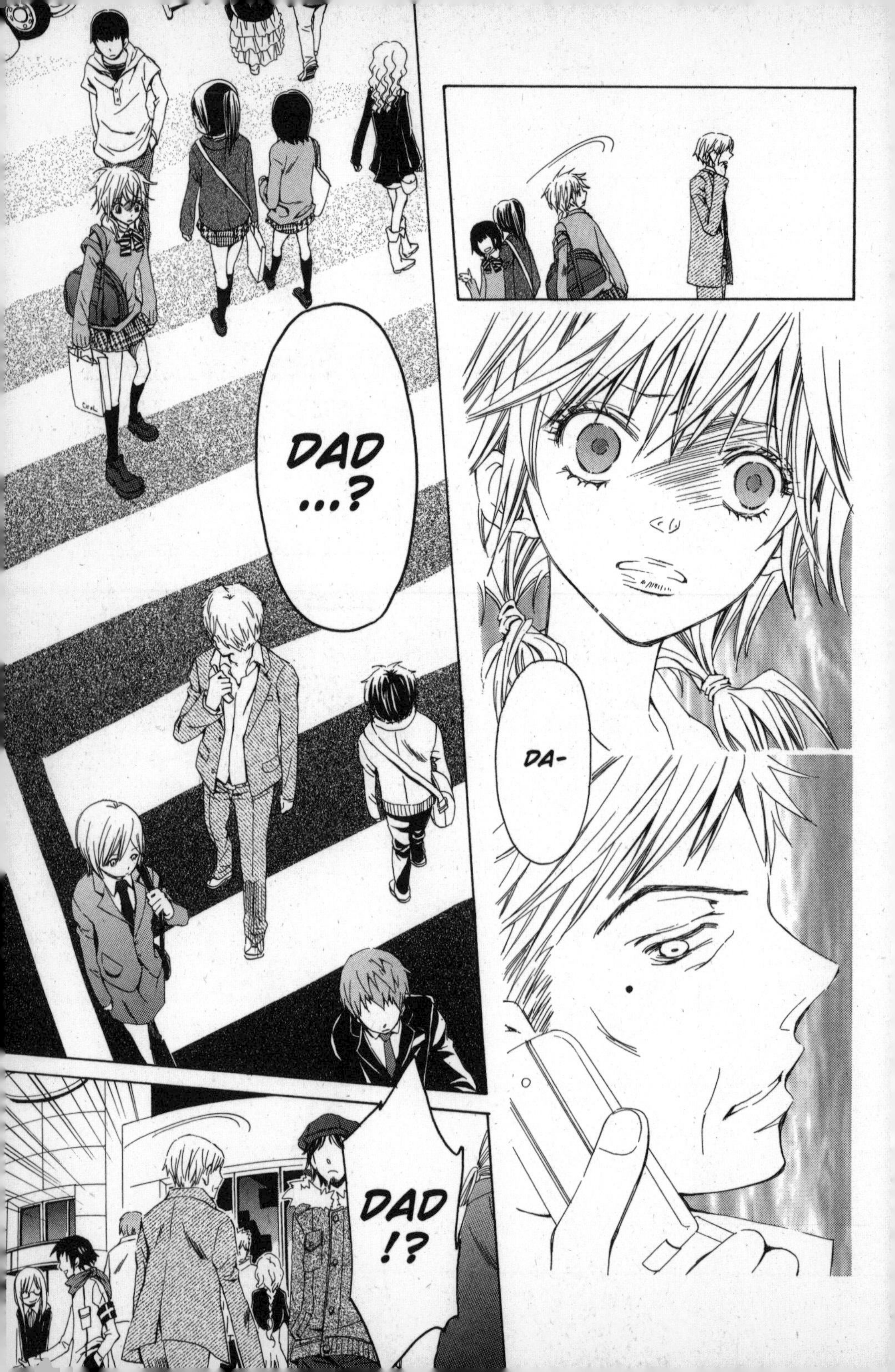
DA-
DAD ...?
DAD !?

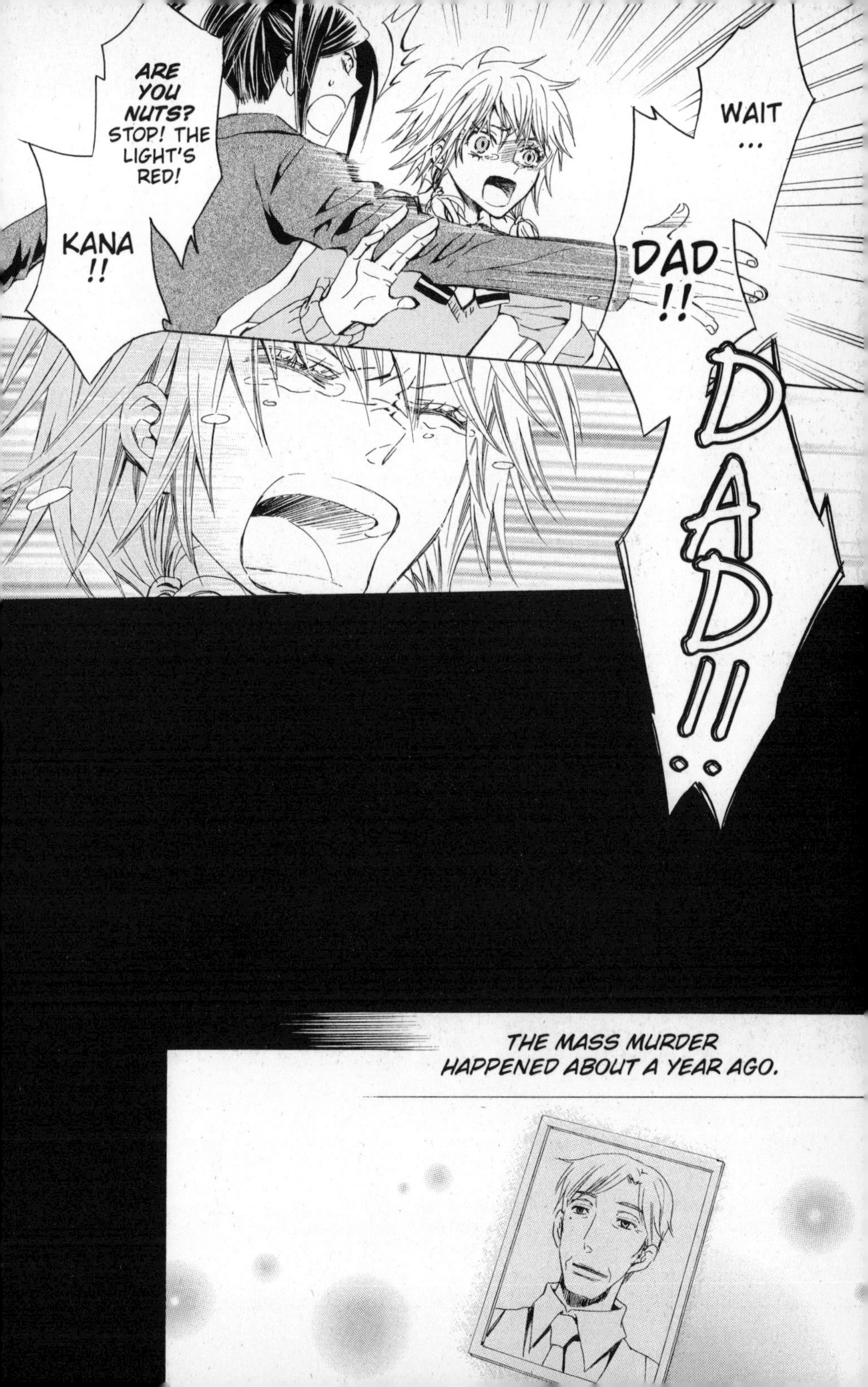
WAIT ...
DAD!!
ARE YOU NUTS? STOP! THE LIGHT'S RED!
KANA!!
DAD!!
THE MASS MURDER HAPPENED ABOUT A YEAR AGO.

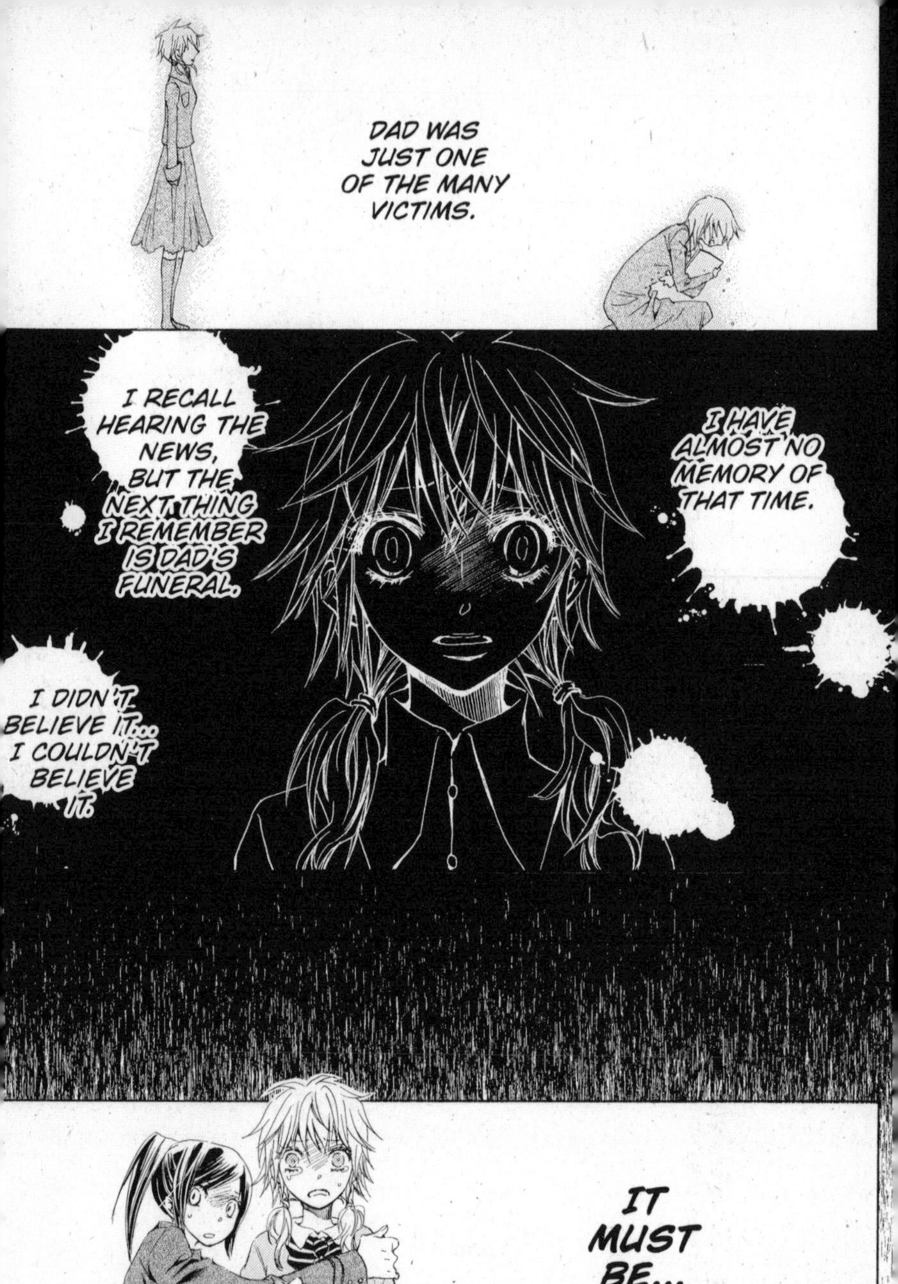
DAD WAS JUST ONE OF THE MANY VICTIMS.
I HAVE ALMOST NO MEMORY OF THAT TIME.
I RECALL HEARING THE NEWS, BUT THE NEXT THING I REMEMBER IS DAD'S FUNERAL.
I DIDN'T BELIEVE IT... I COULDN'T BELIEVE IT.
IT MUST BE...

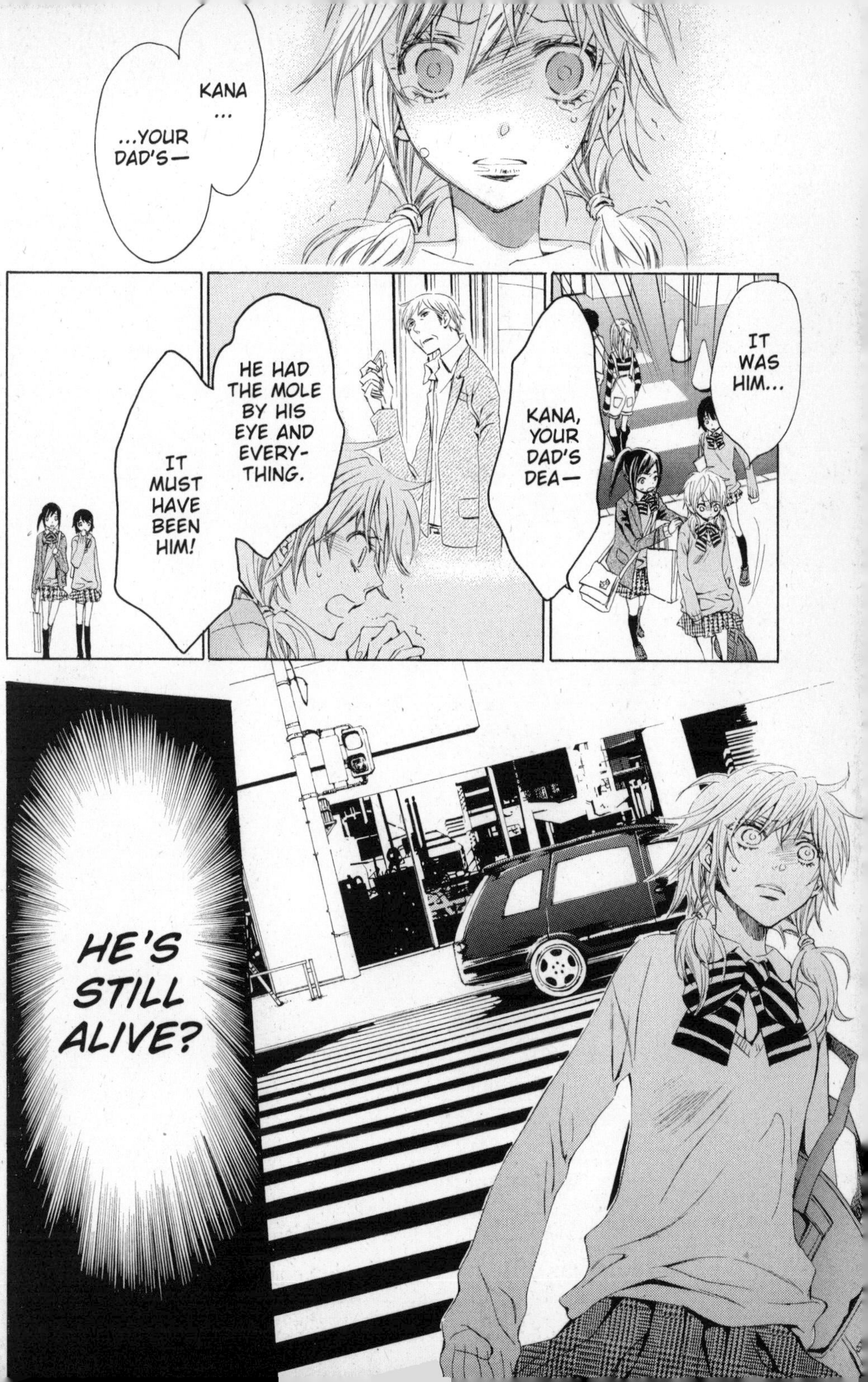
KANA ... ...YOUR DAD'S—
IT WAS HIM...
KANA, YOUR DAD'S DEA—
HE HAD THE MOLE BY HIS EYE AND EVERY-THING.
IT MUST HAVE BEEN HIM!
HE'S STILL ALIVE?

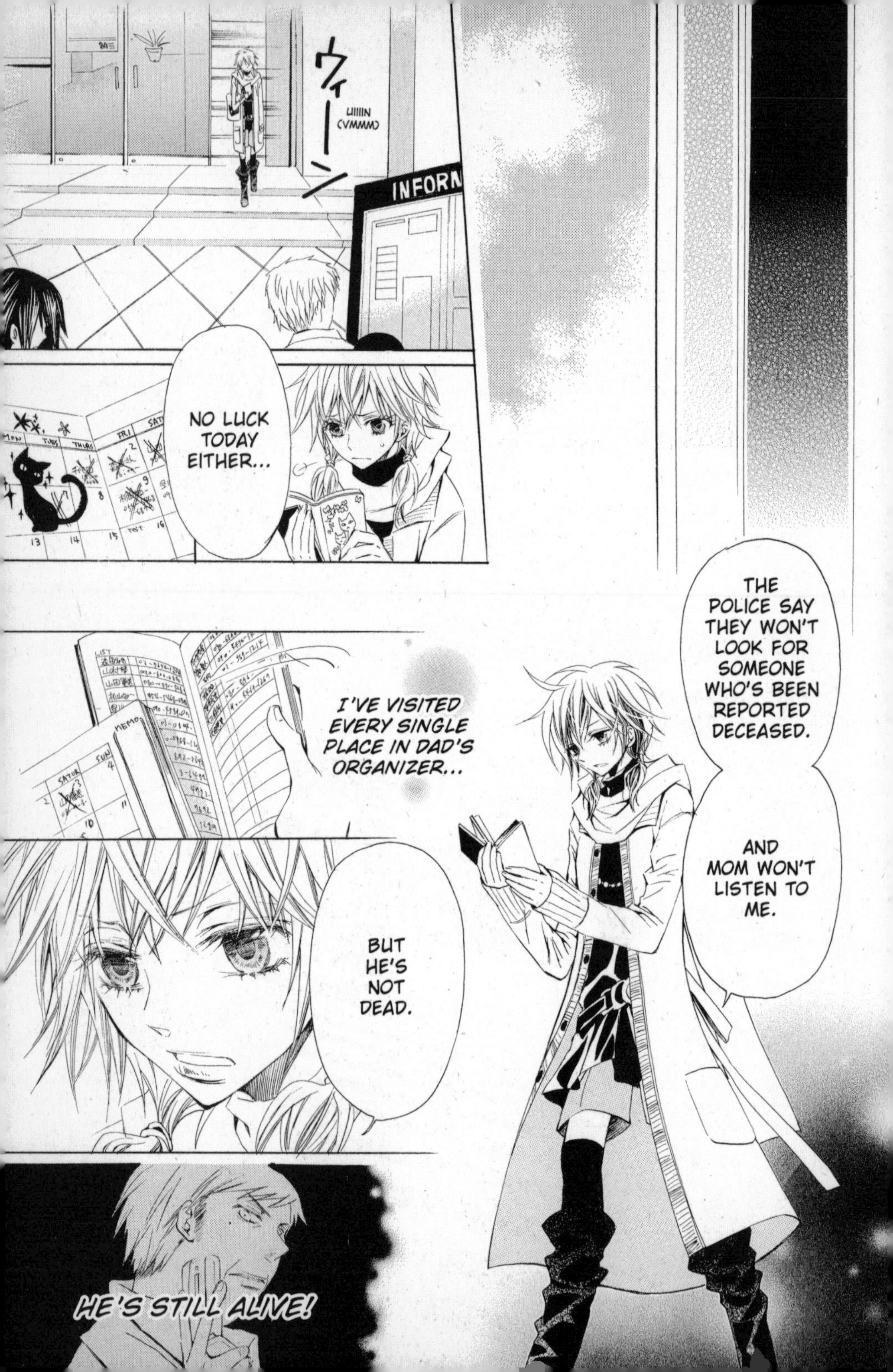
ウィーン
UIIIIN (VMMM)
INFORM
NO LUCK TODAY EITHER...
THE POLICE SAY THEY WON'T LOOK FOR SOMEONE WHO'S BEEN REPORTED DECEASED.
AND MOM WON'T LISTEN TO ME.
I'VE VISITED EVERY SINGLE PLACE IN DAD'S ORGANIZER...
BUT HE'S NOT DEAD.
HE'S STILL ALIVE!

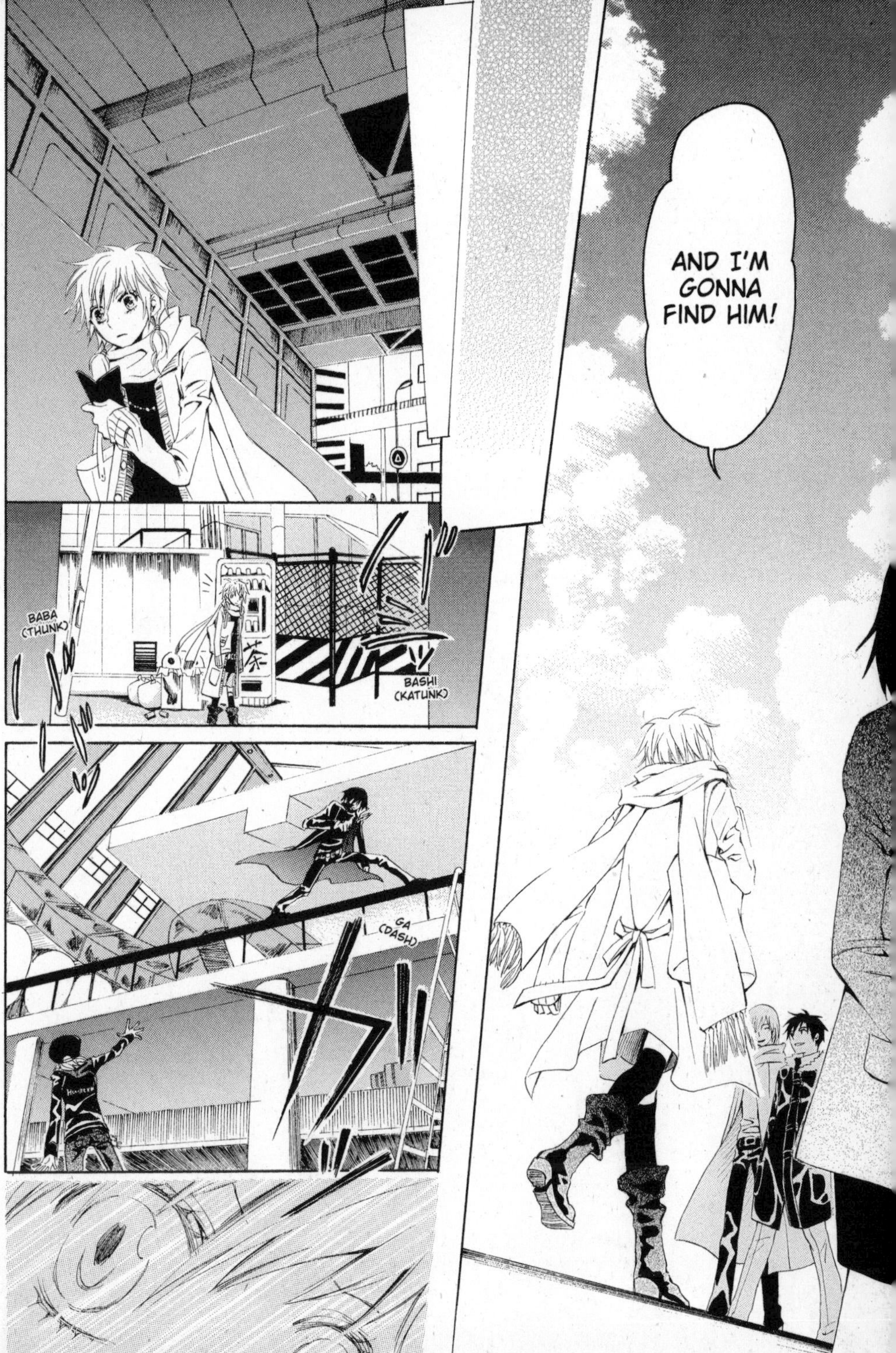
AND I'M GONNA FIND HIM!
BASHI (KATUNK)
BABA (THUNK)
GA (DASH)

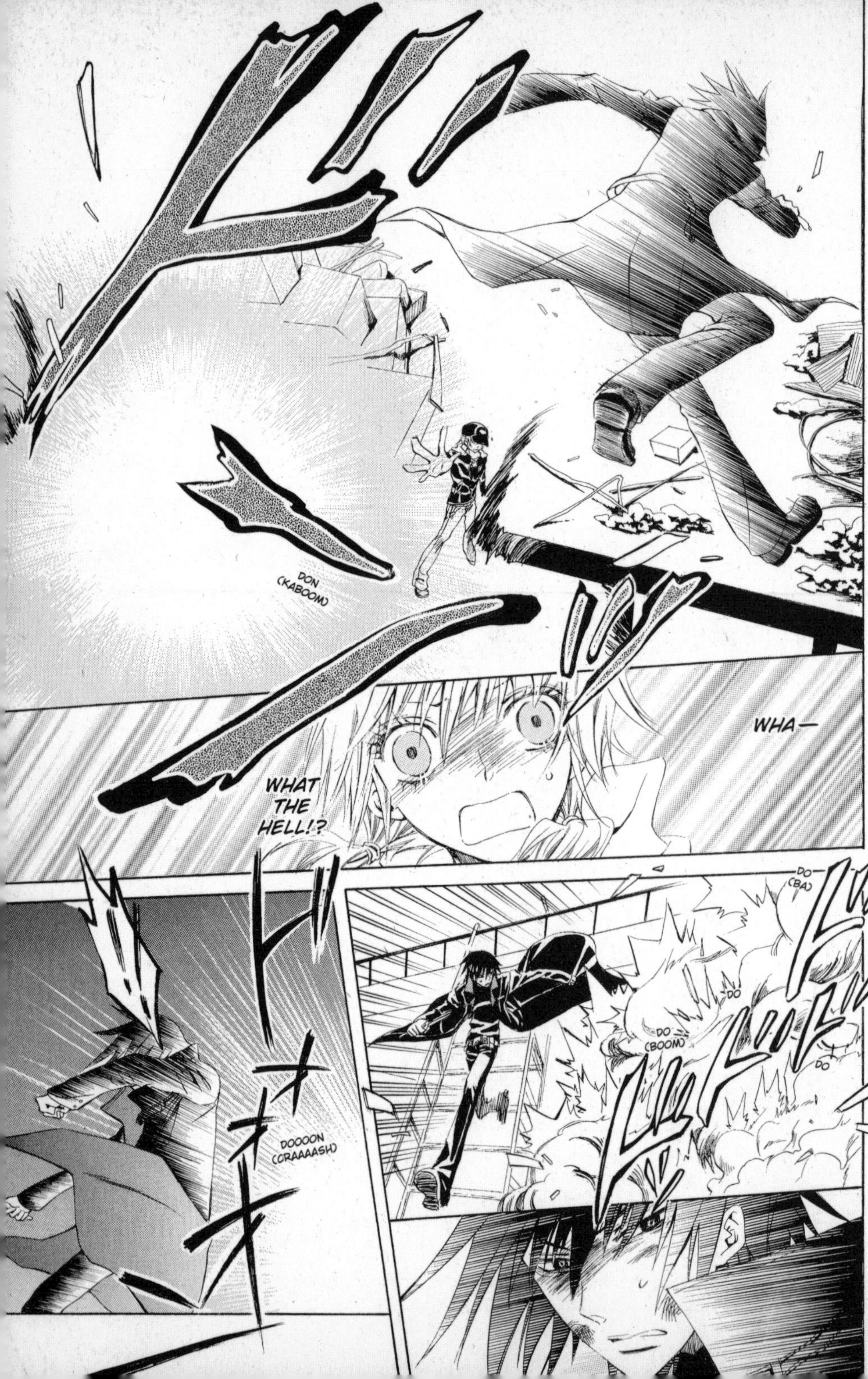
DON
(KABOOM)
WHA—
WHAT THE HELL!?
DO
(BA)
DO
DO
(BOOM)
DO
DOOOON
(CRAAAASH)

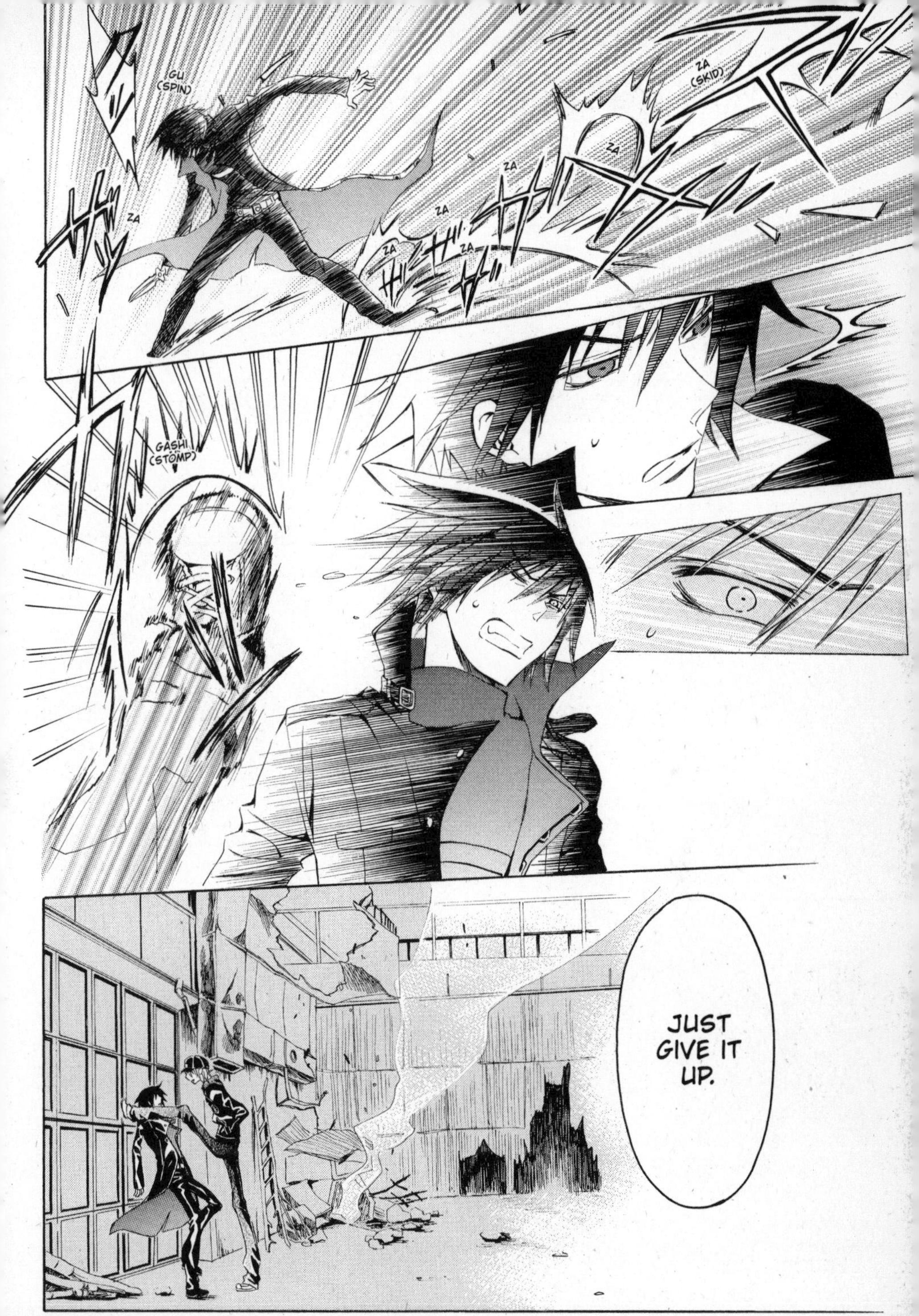
ZA (SKID)
ZA
ZA
ZA
ZA
ZA
GU (SPIN)
ZA
GASHI (STÖMP)
JUST GIVE IT UP.

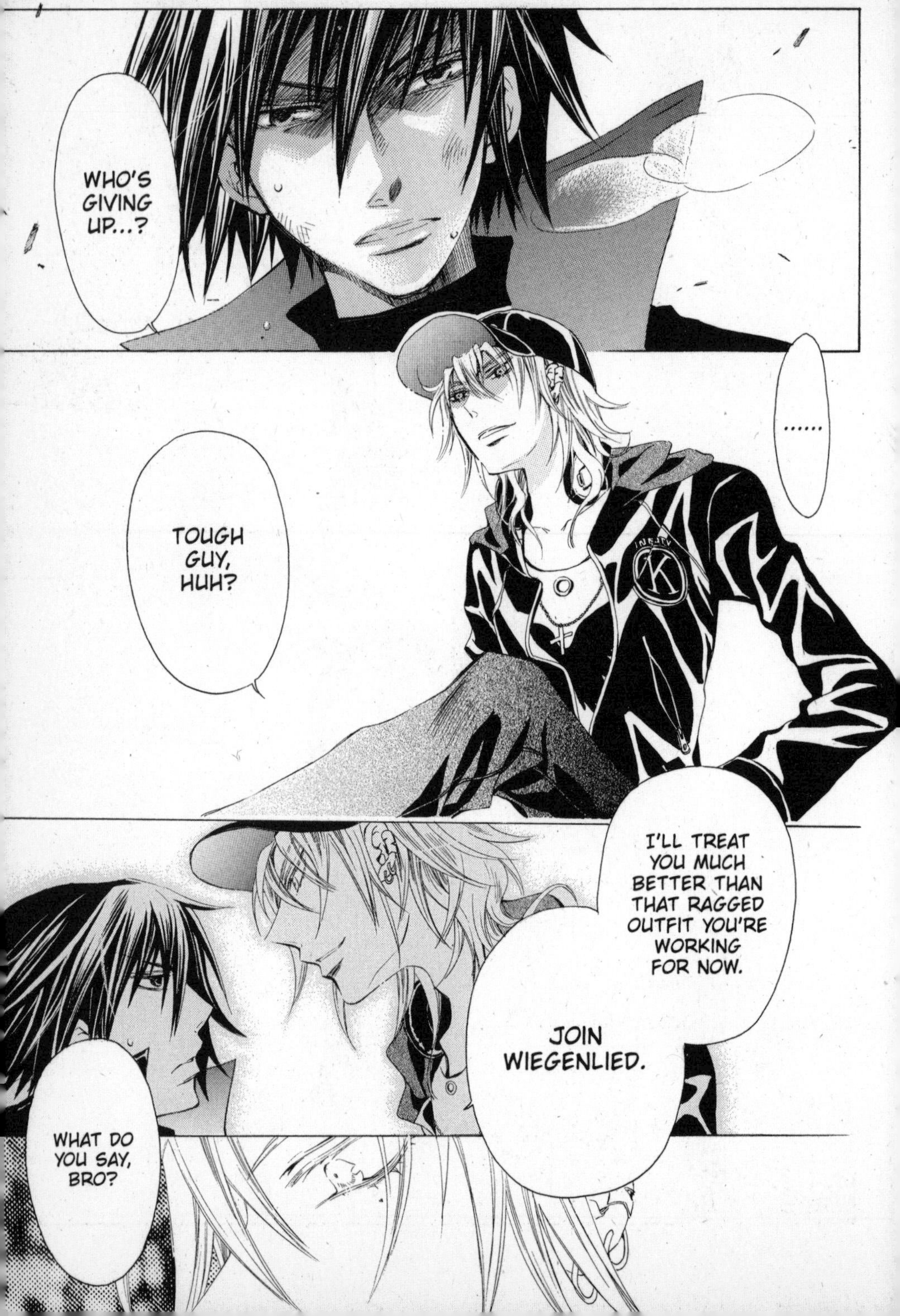
WHO'S GIVING UP...?
......
TOUGH GUY, HUH?
I'LL TREAT YOU MUCH BETTER THAN THAT RAGGED OUTFIT YOU'RE WORKING FOR NOW.
JOIN WIEGENLIED.
WHAT DO YOU SAY, BRO?

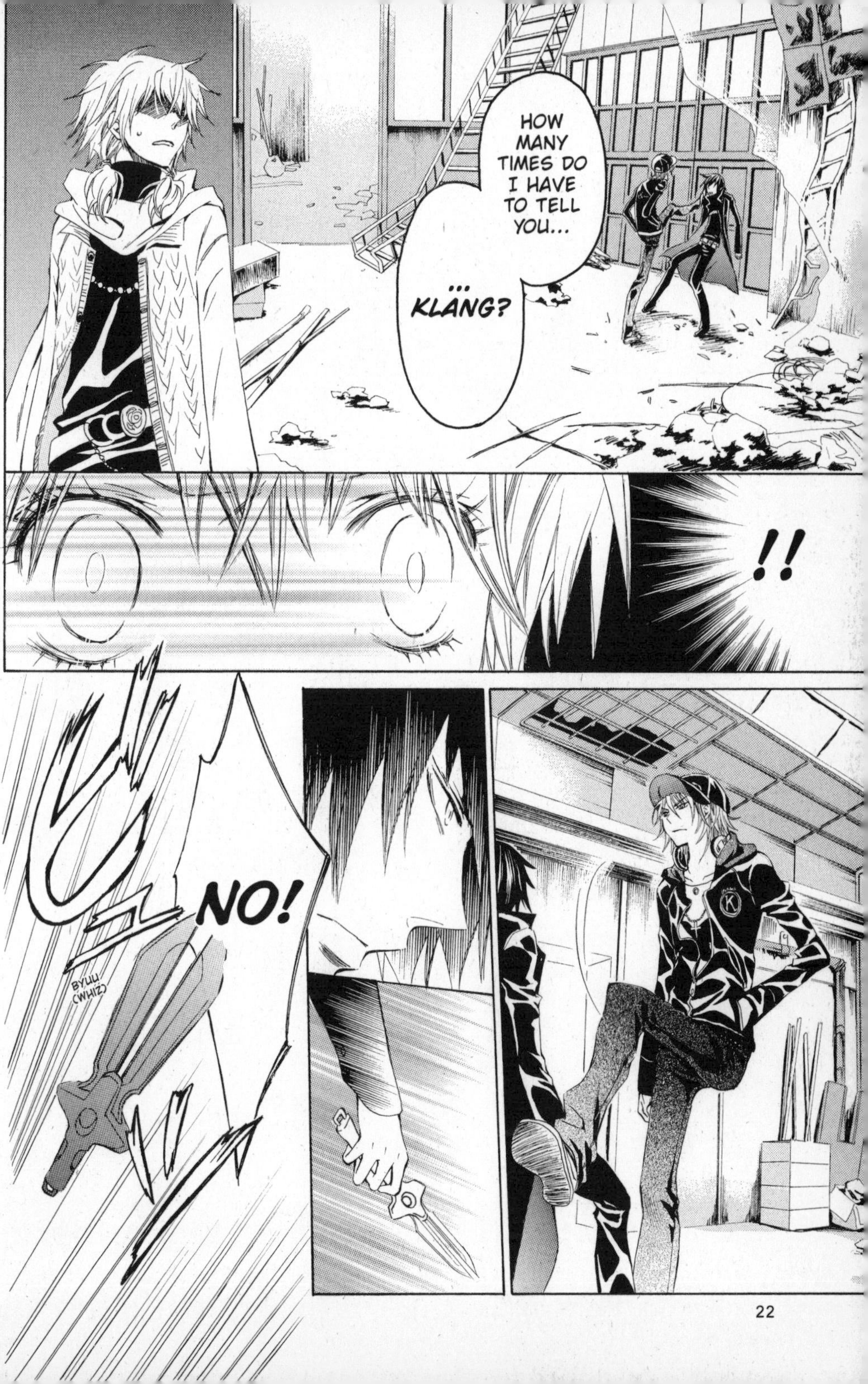
HOW MANY TIMES DO I HAVE TO TELL YOU...
...KLÄNG?
!!
NO!
BYUU (WHIZ)

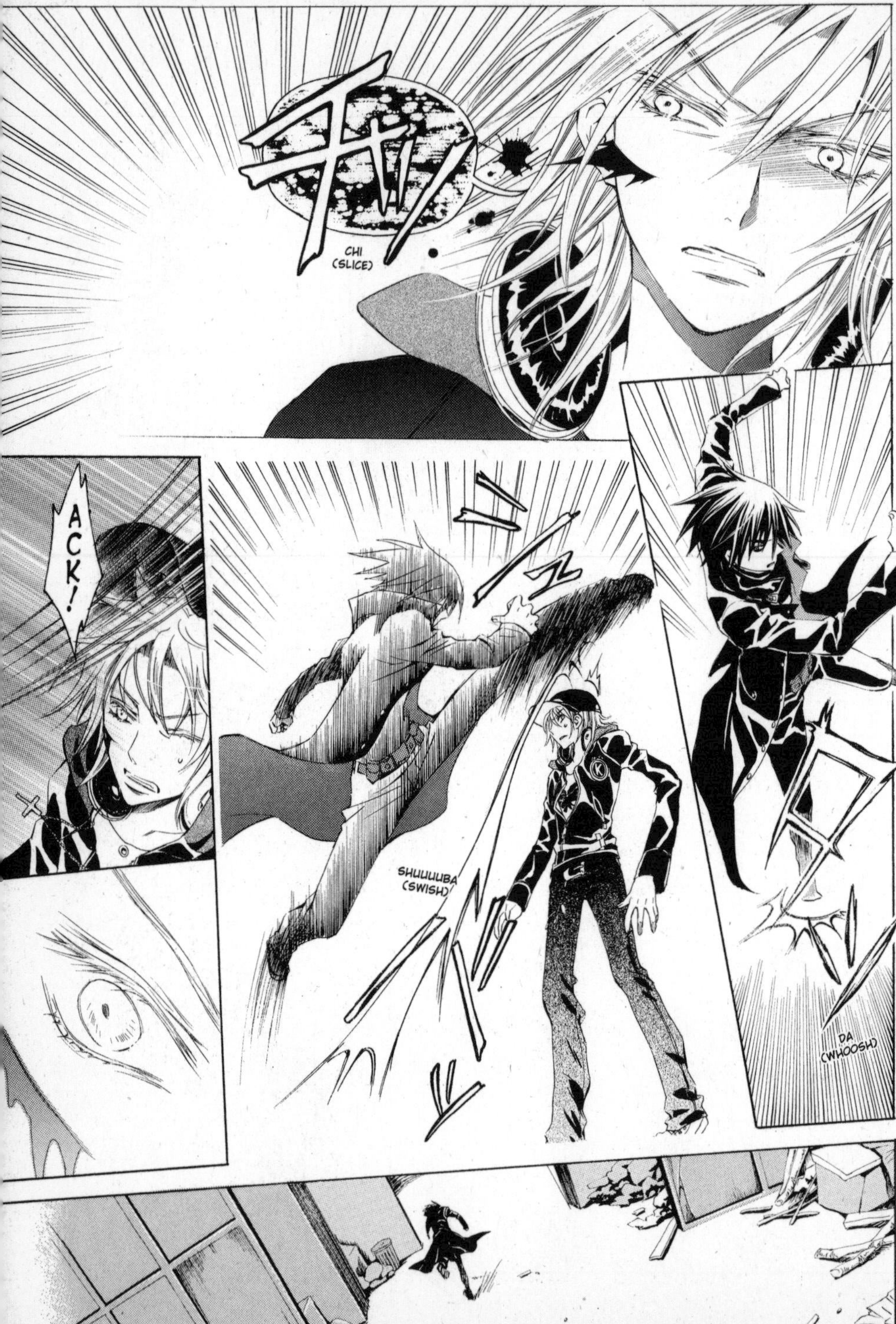
CHI
(SLICE)
DA
(WHOOSH)
SHUUUUBA
(SWISH)
ACK!

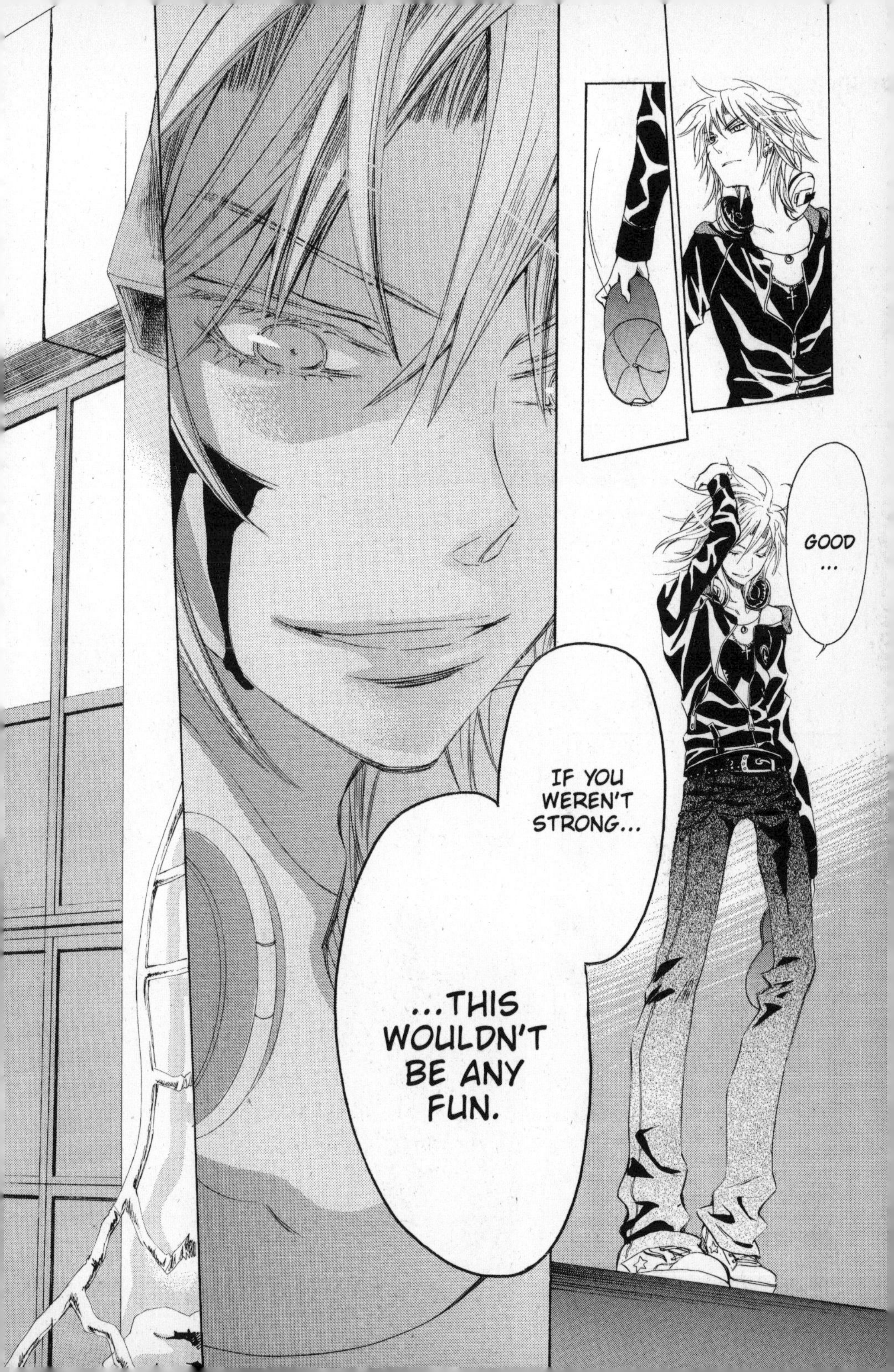
GOOD ...
IF YOU WEREN'T STRONG...
...THIS WOULDN'T BE ANY FUN.

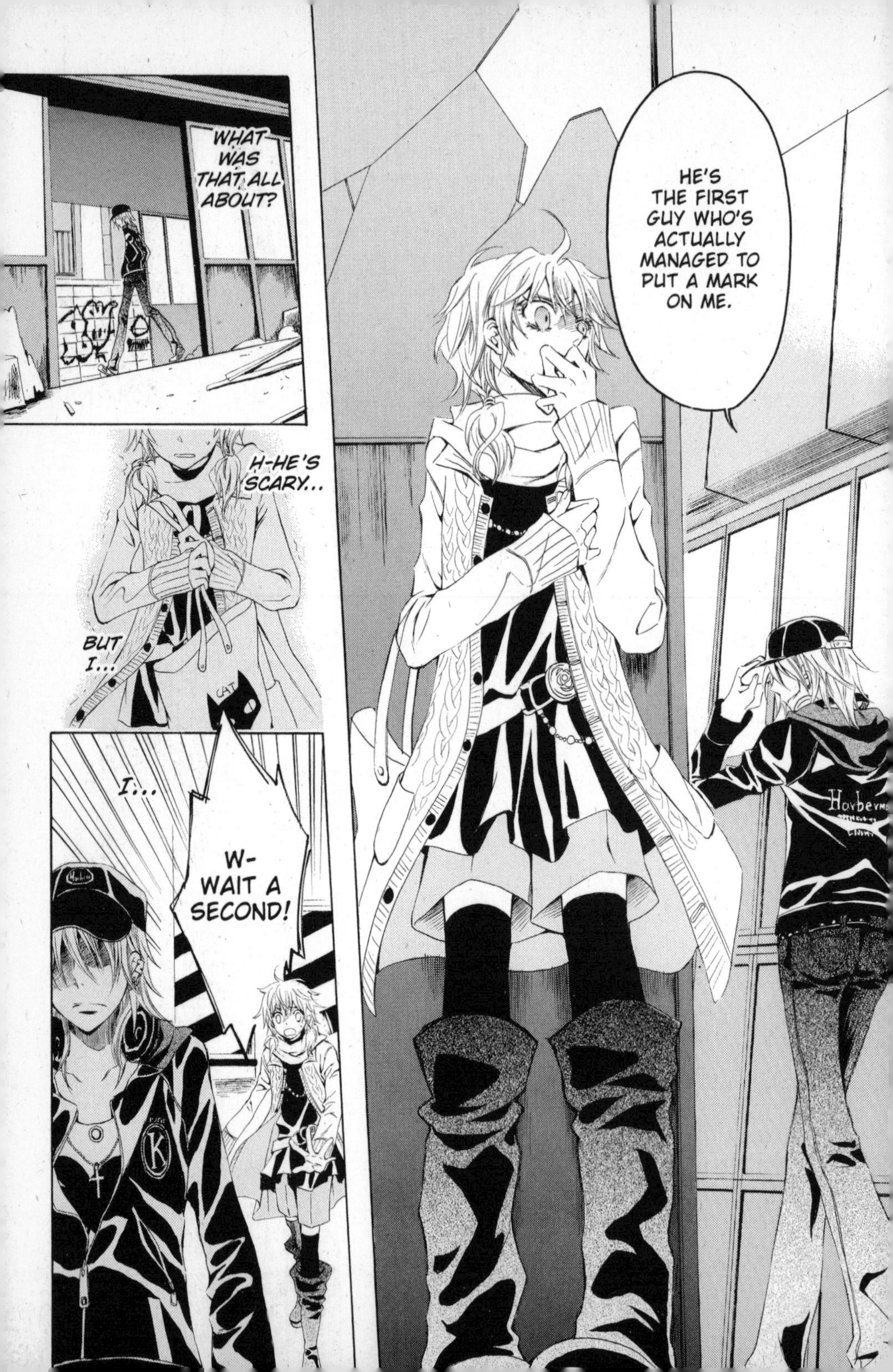
HE'S THE FIRST GUY WHO'S ACTUALLY MANAGED TO PUT A MARK ON ME.
WHAT WAS THAT ALL ABOUT?
H-HE'S SCARY...
BUT I...
I...
W-WAIT A SECOND!

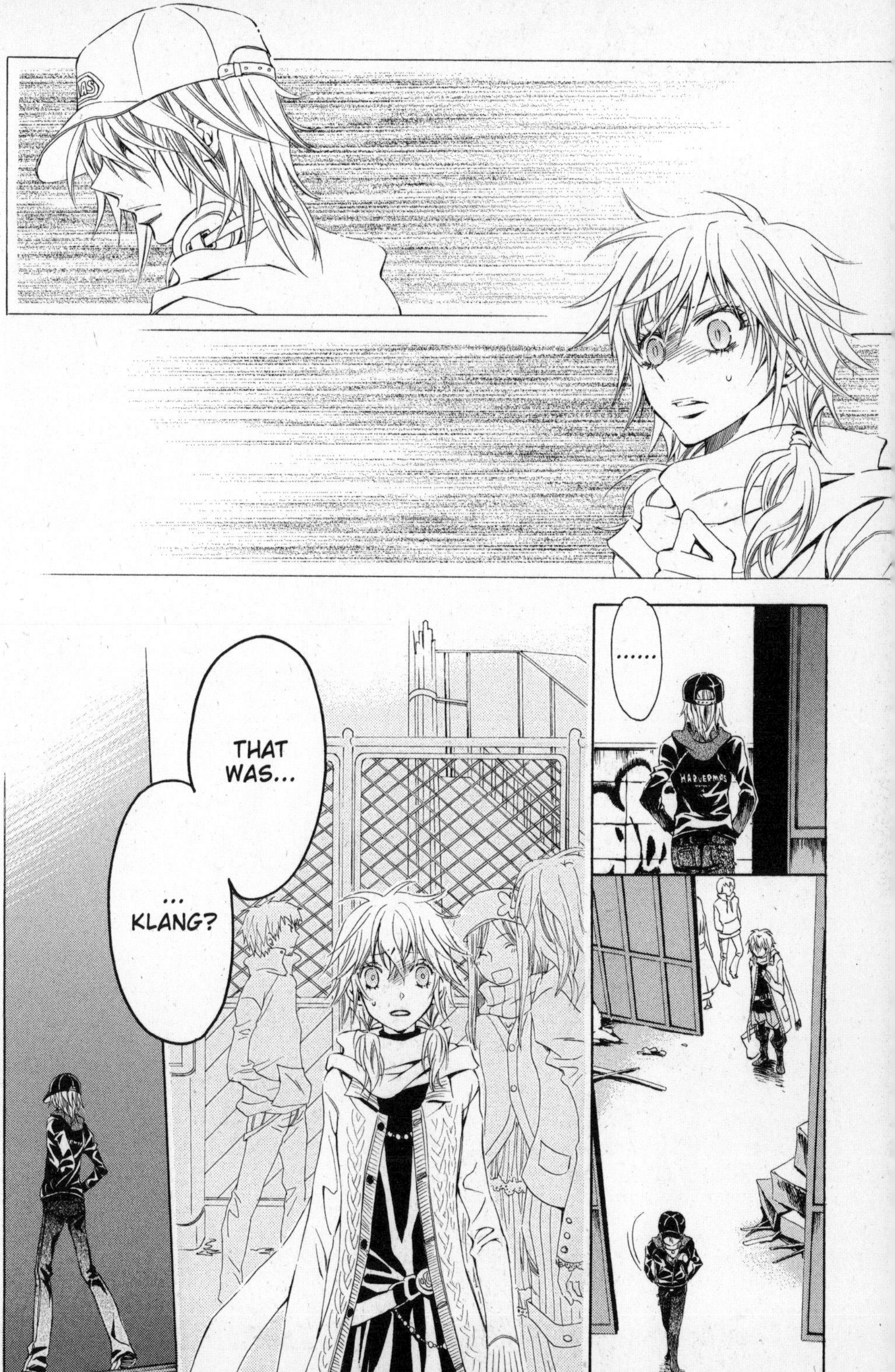
......
THAT WAS...
... KLANG?

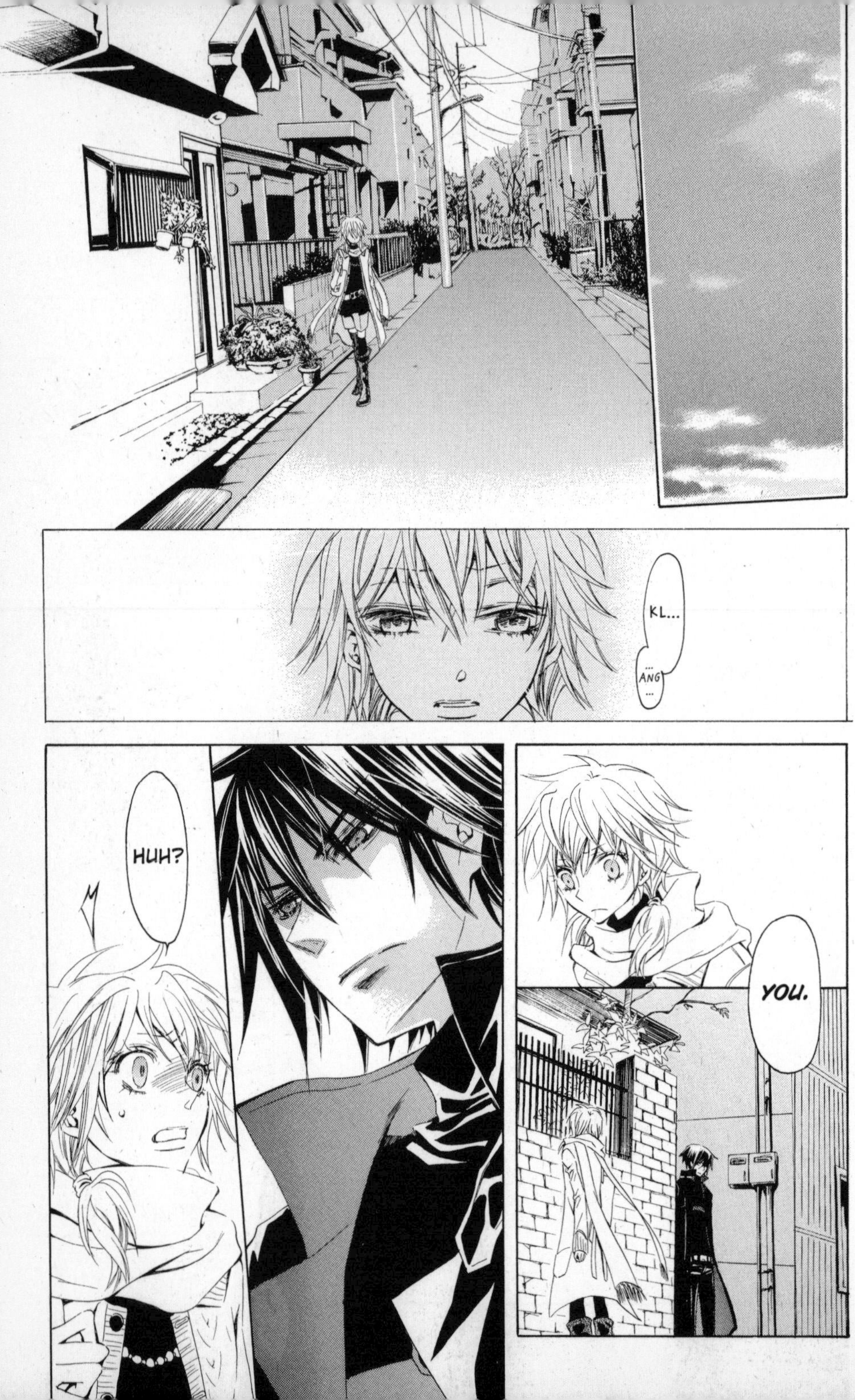

KL...
...ANG...
YOU.
HUH?

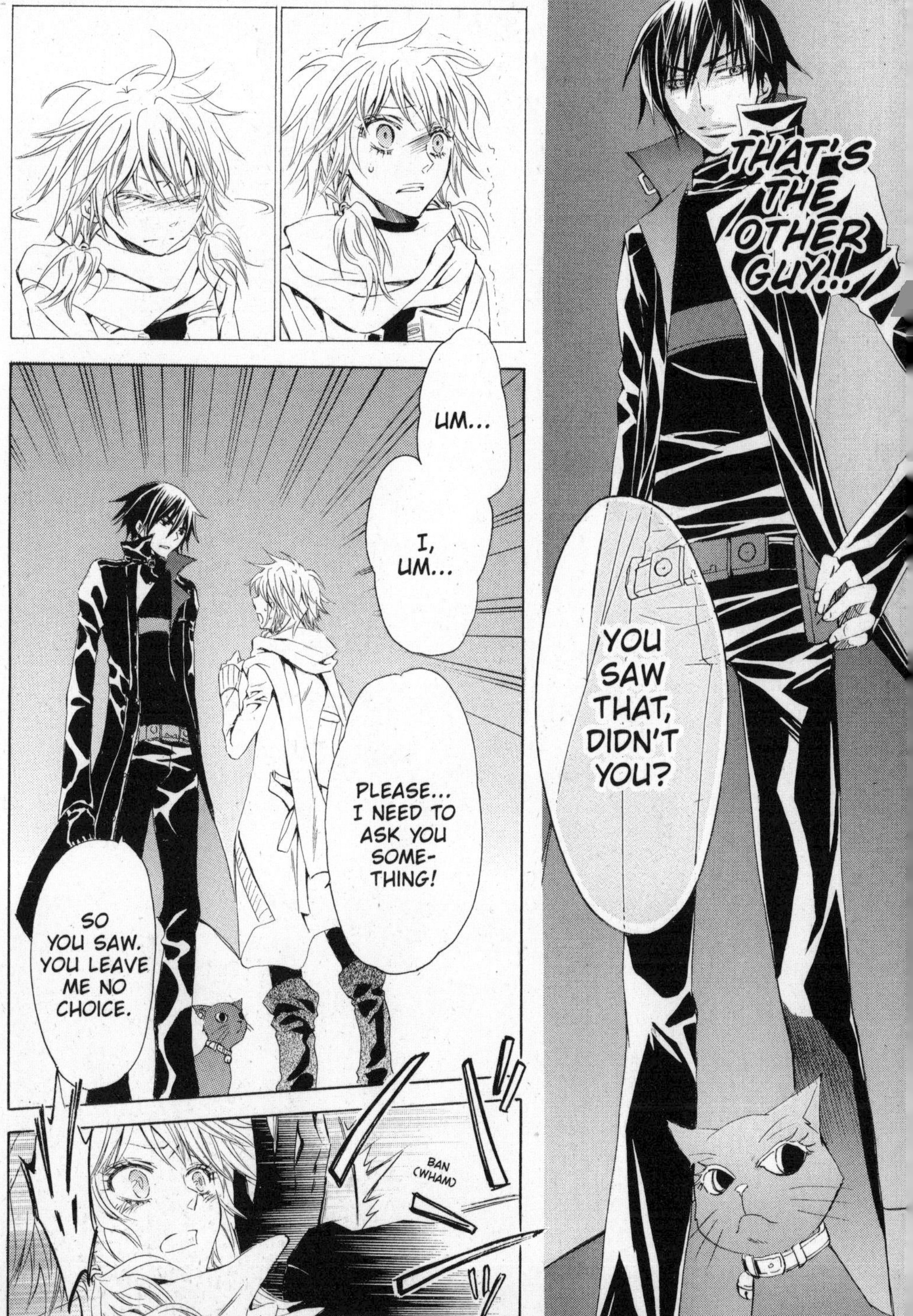
THAT'S THE OTHER GUY..!!
YOU SAW THAT, DIDN'T YOU?
UM...
I, UM...
PLEASE... I NEED TO ASK YOU SOME-THING!
SO YOU SAW. YOU LEAVE ME NO CHOICE.
BAN (WHAM)

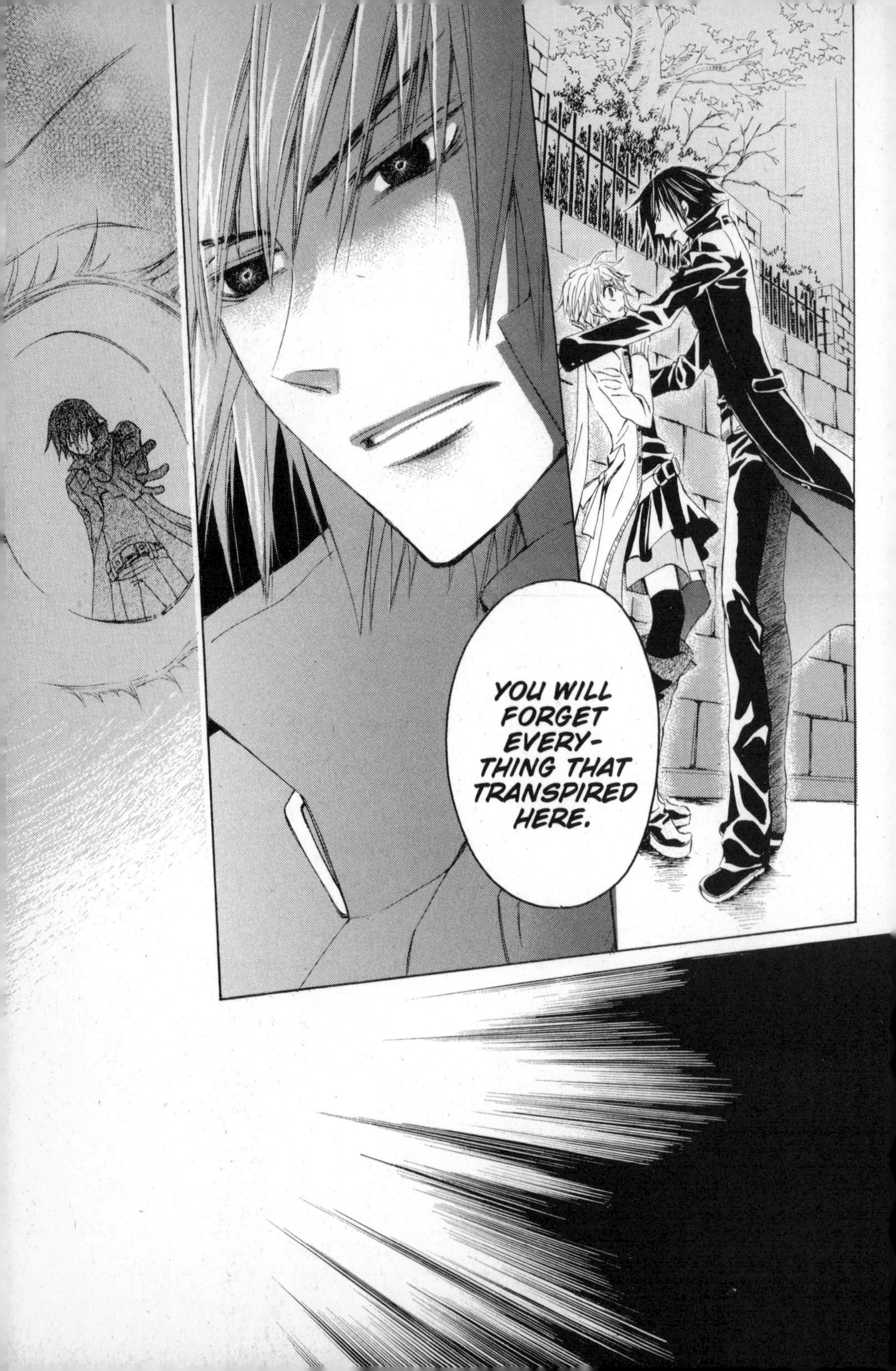
YOU WILL FORGET EVERYTHING THAT TRANSPIRED HERE.

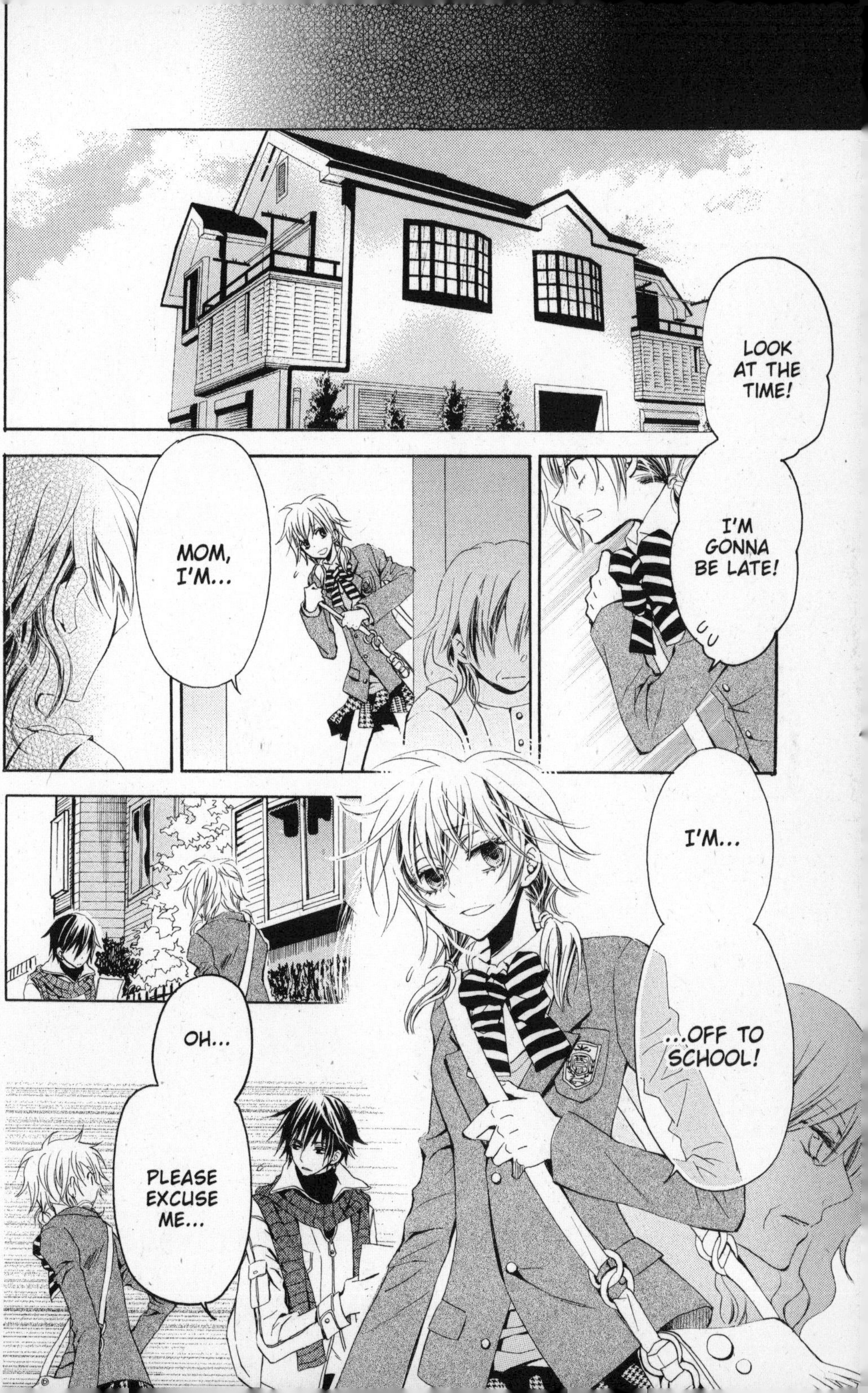
LOOK AT THE TIME!
I'M GONNA BE LATE!
MOM, I'M...
I'M...
...OFF TO SCHOOL!
OH...
PLEASE EXCUSE ME...

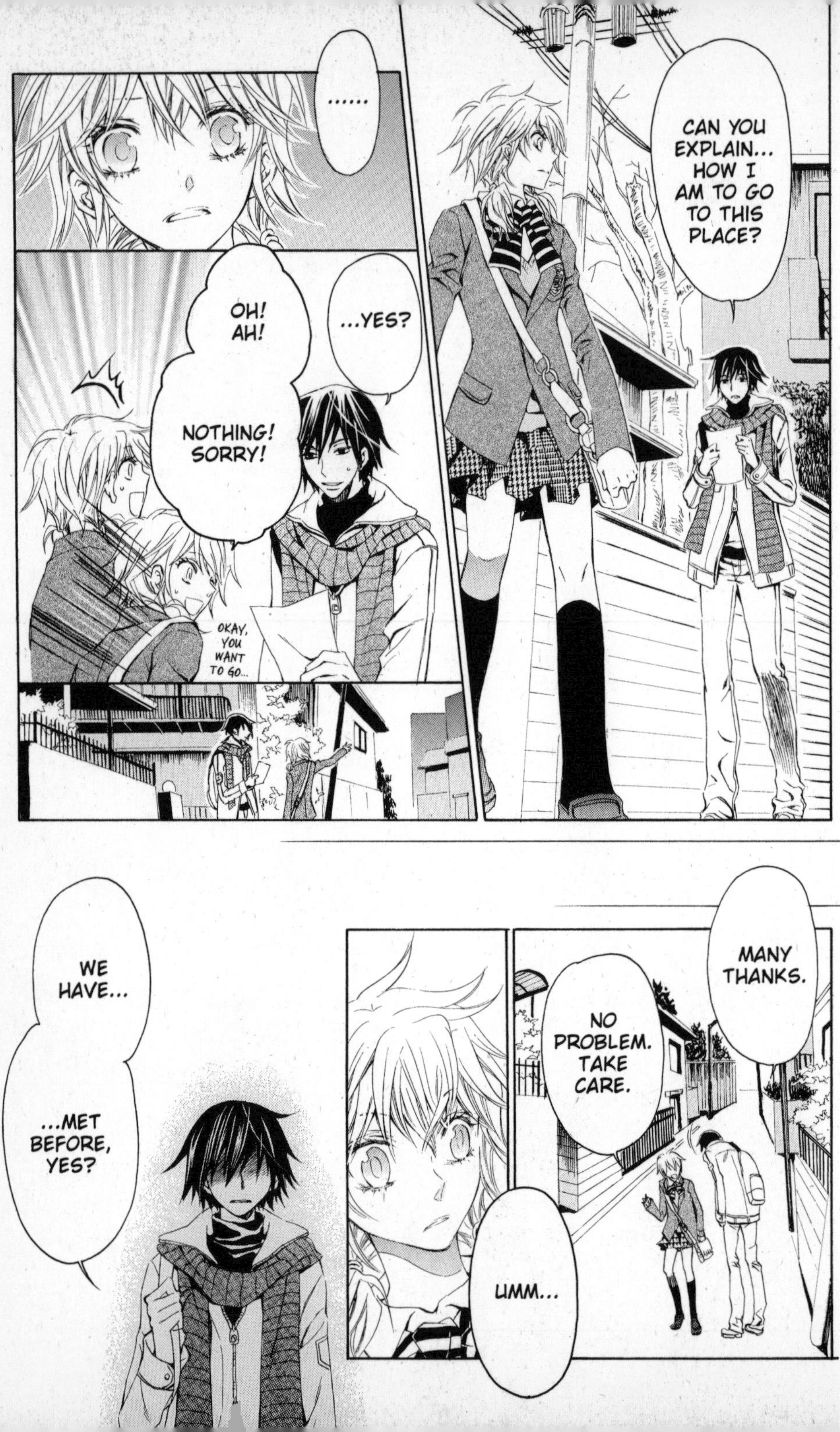
CAN YOU EXPLAIN... HOW I AM TO GO TO THIS PLACE?
......
...YES?
OH! AH!
NOTHING! SORRY!
OKAY, YOU WANT TO GO...
MANY THANKS.
NO PROBLEM. TAKE CARE.
UMM...
WE HAVE...
...MET BEFORE, YES?

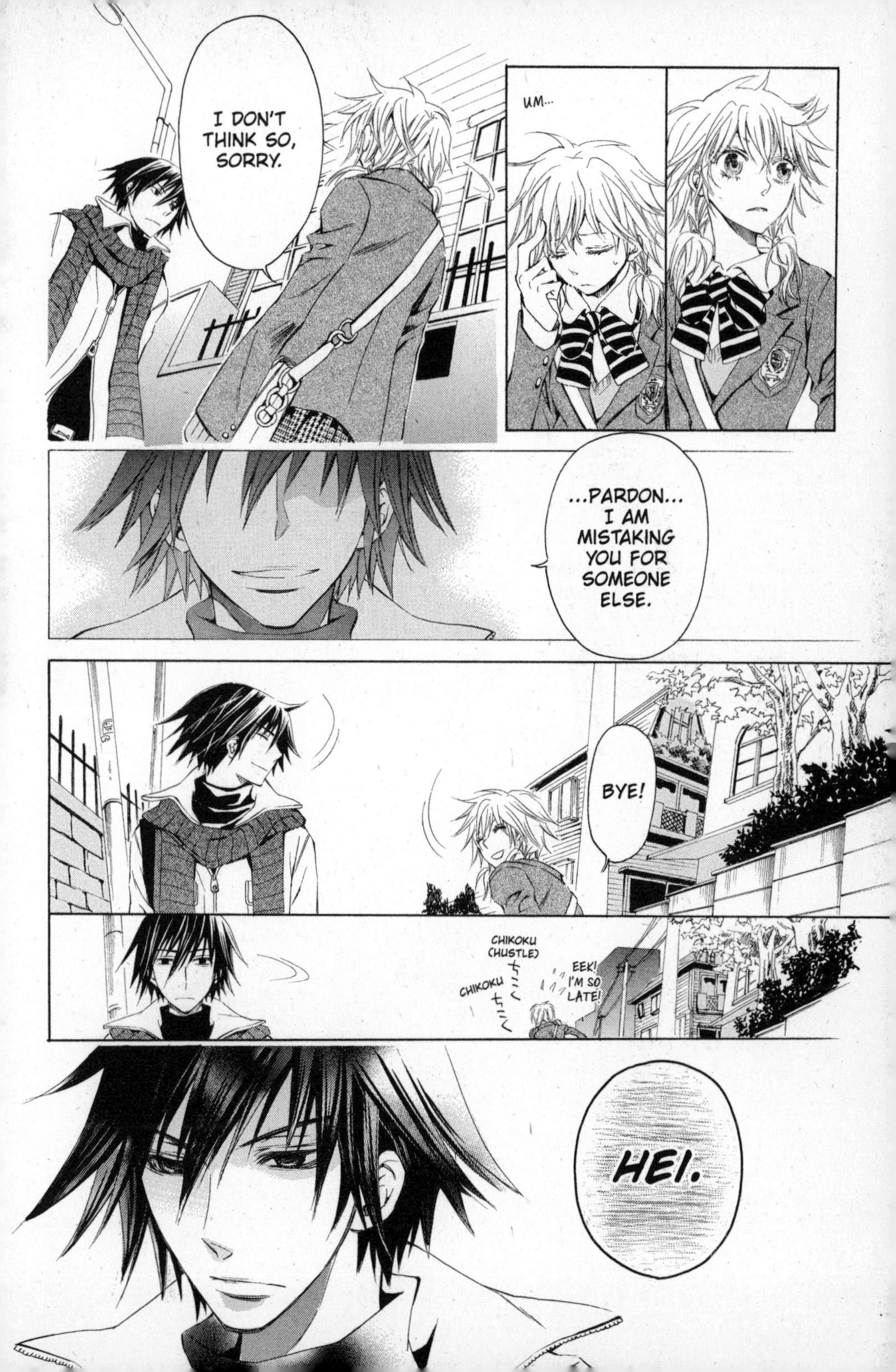
UM...
I DON'T THINK SO, SORRY.
...PARDON... I AM MISTAKING YOU FOR SOMEONE ELSE.
BYE!
EEK! I'M SO LATE!
CHIKOKU (HUSTLE) ちこく
CHIKOKU ちこく
HEI.

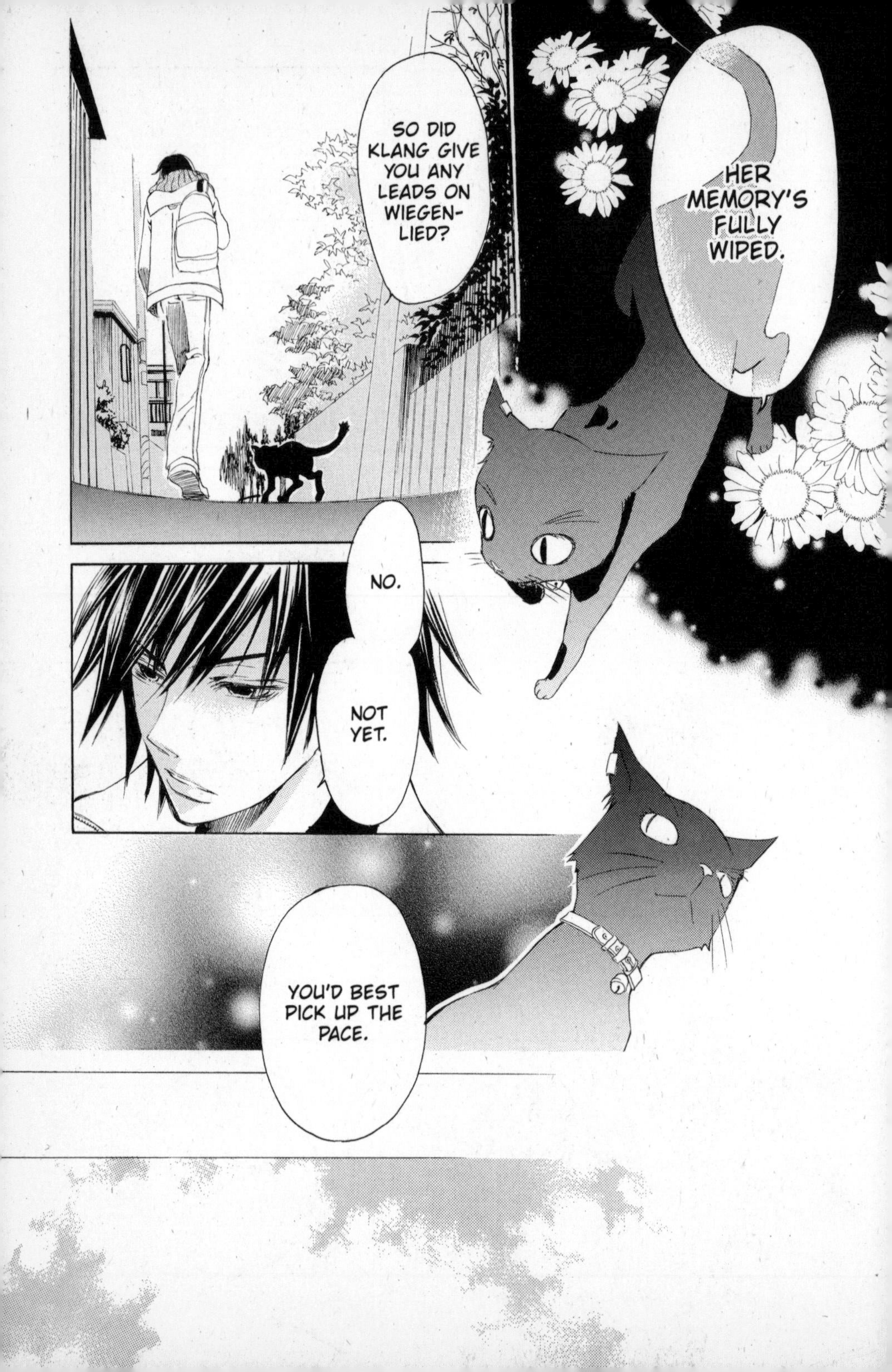
HER MEMORY'S FULLY WIPED.
SO DID KLANG GIVE YOU ANY LEADS ON WIEGEN-LIED?
NO.
NOT YET.
YOU'D BEST PICK UP THE PACE.

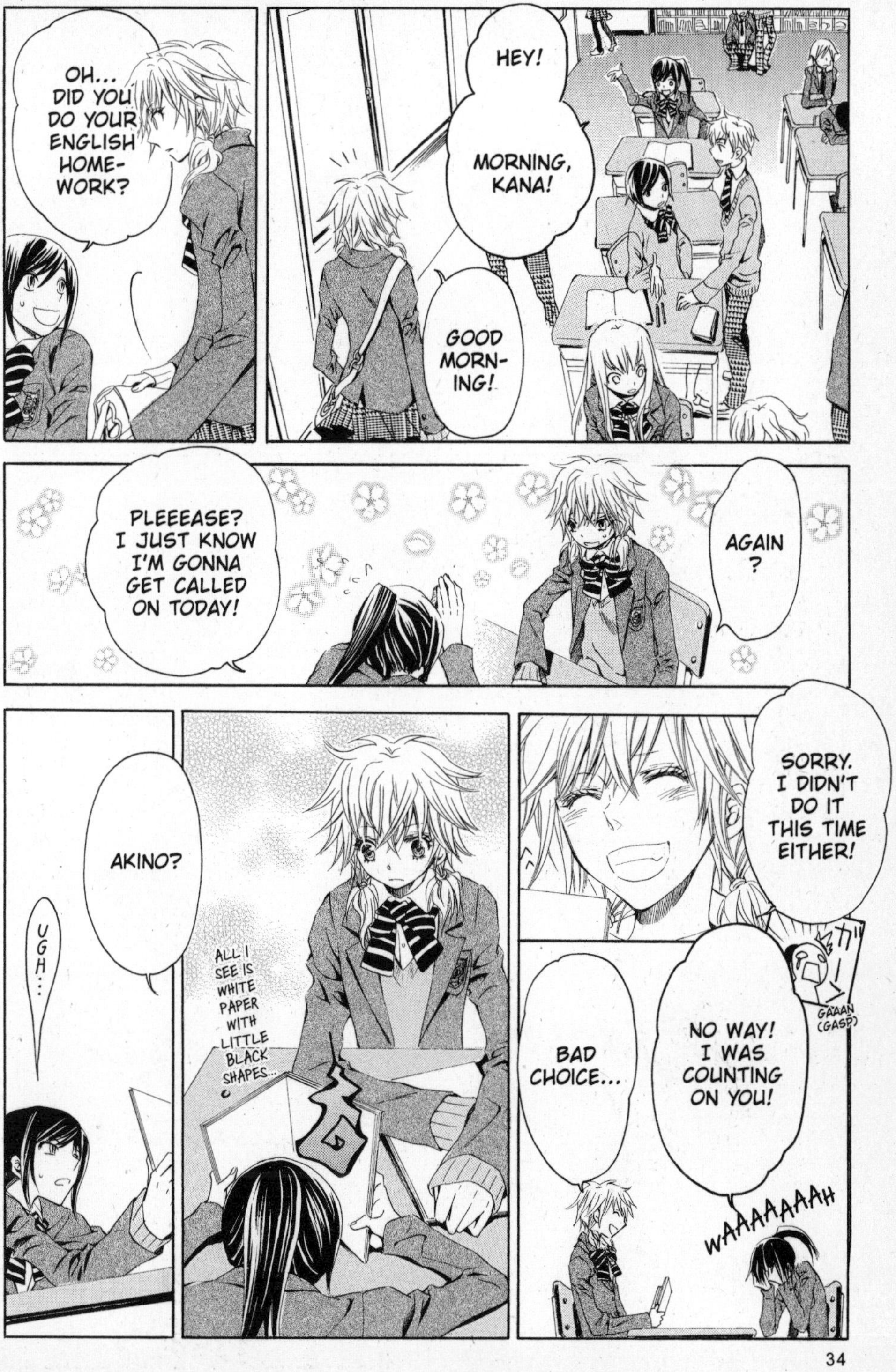
HEY!
MORNING, KANA!
GOOD MORNING!
OH... DID YOU DO YOUR ENGLISH HOME-WORK?
AGAIN?
PLEEEASE? I JUST KNOW I'M GONNA GET CALLED ON TODAY!
SORRY. I DIDN'T DO IT THIS TIME EITHER!
GAAAN (GASP)
NO WAY! I WAS COUNTING ON YOU!
BAD CHOICE...
WAAAAAAAH
ALL I SEE IS WHITE PAPER WITH LITTLE BLACK SHAPES...
AKINO?
UGH...

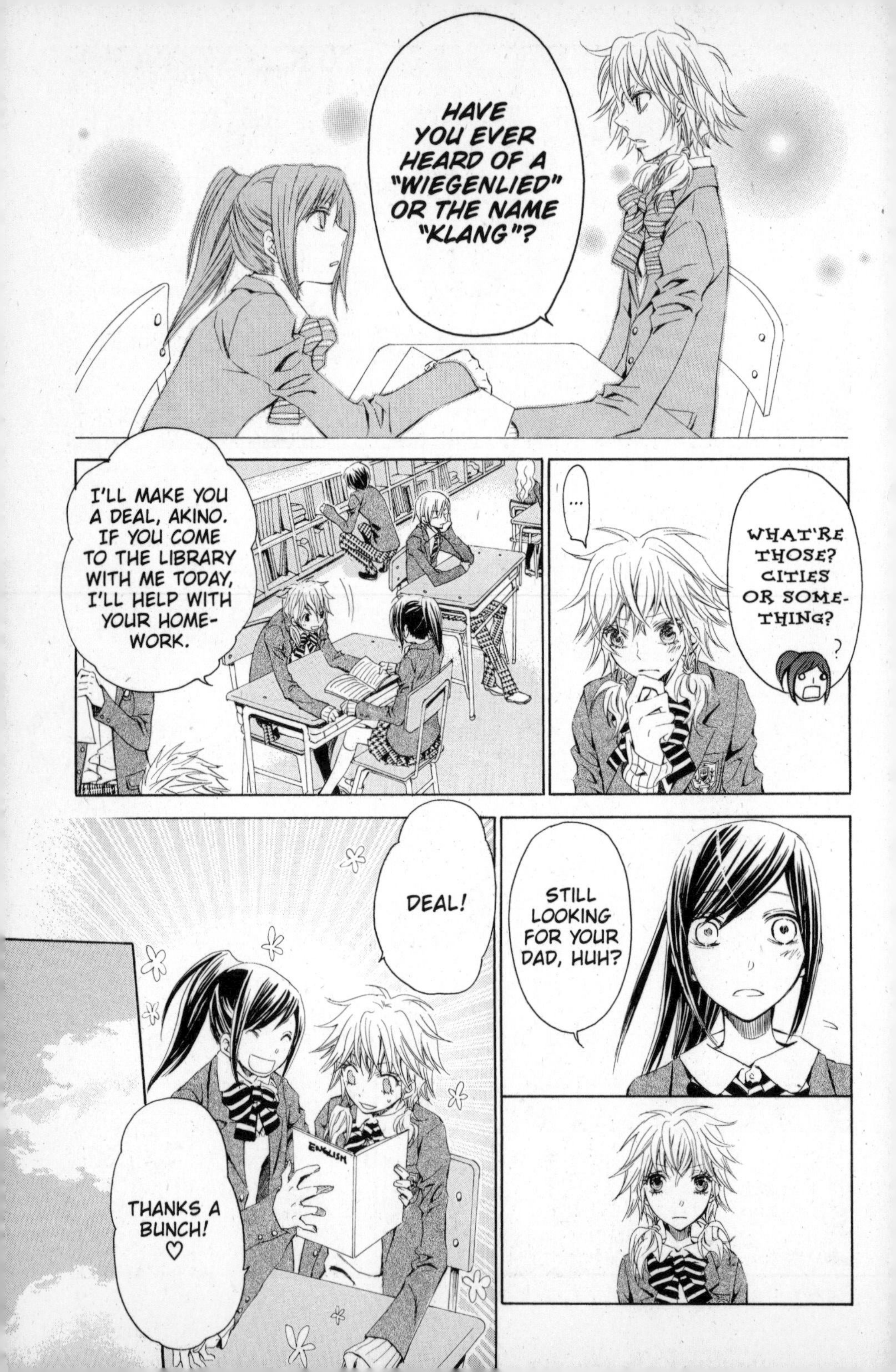
HAVE YOU EVER HEARD OF A "WIEGENLIED" OR THE NAME "KLANG"?
WHAT'RE THOSE? CITIES OR SOME-THING?
?
...
I'LL MAKE YOU A DEAL, AKINO. IF YOU COME TO THE LIBRARY WITH ME TODAY, I'LL HELP WITH YOUR HOME-WORK.
STILL LOOKING FOR YOUR DAD, HUH?
DEAL!
ENGLISH
THANKS A BUNCH! ♡

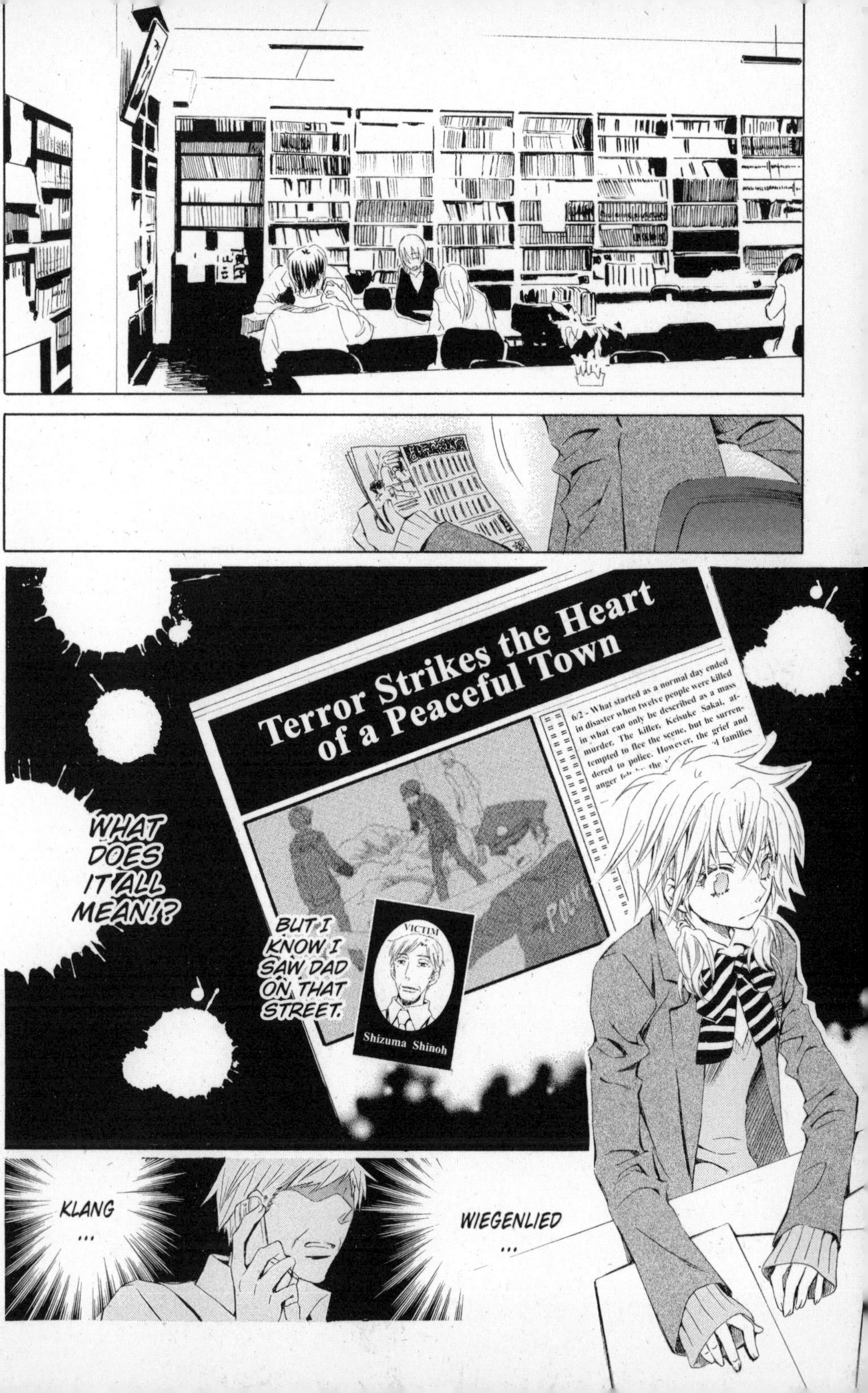
Terror Strikes the Heart of a Peaceful Town
6/2 - What started as a normal day ended in disaster when twelve people were killed in what can only be described as a mass murder. The killer, Keisuke Sakai, attempted to flee the scene, but he surrendered to police. However, the grief and
VICTIM
Shizuma Shinoh
BUT I KNOW I SAW DAD ON THAT STREET.
WHAT DOES IT ALL MEAN!?
WIEGENLIED ...
KLANG ...

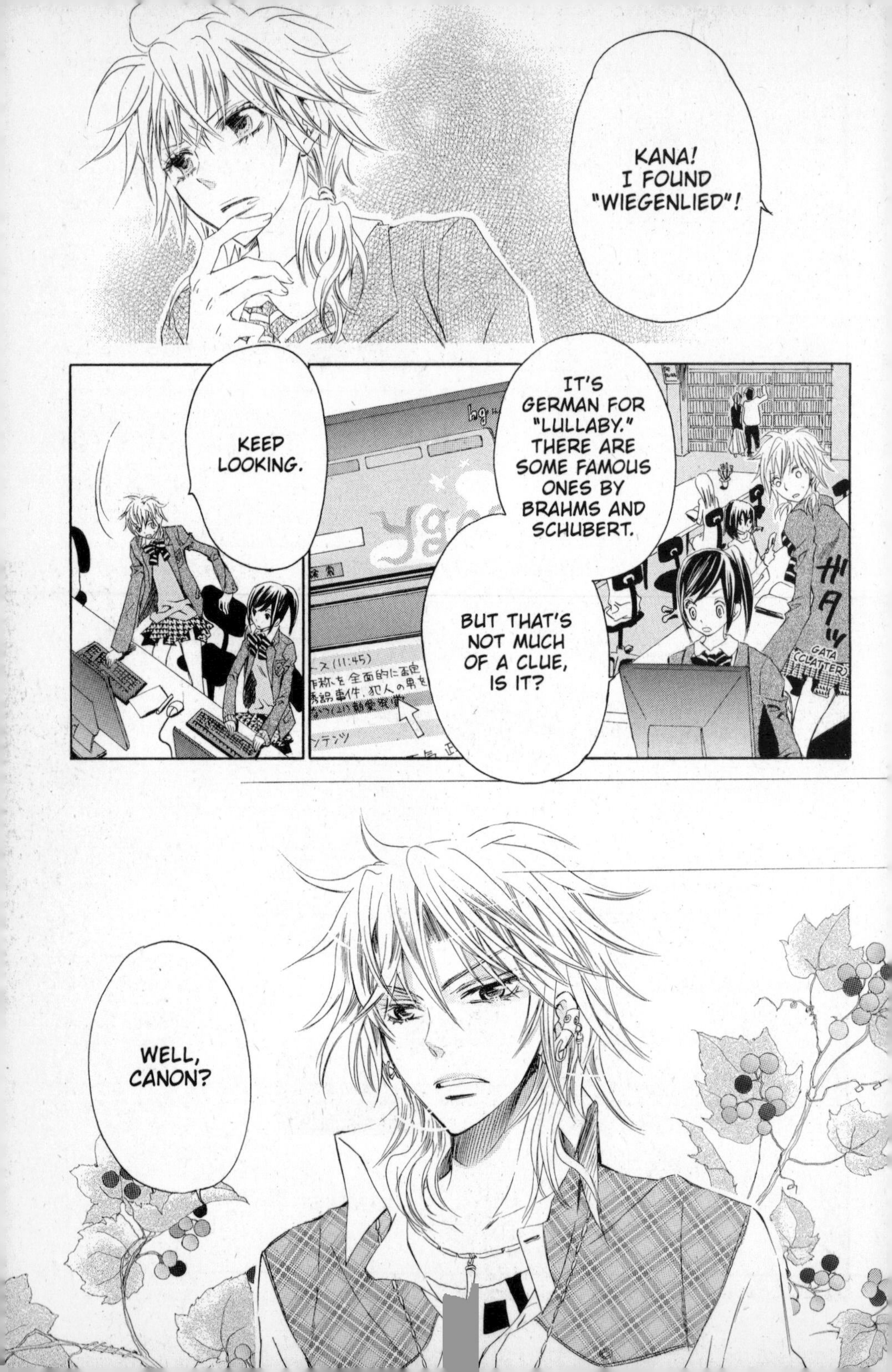
KANA! I FOUND "WIEGENLIED"!
IT'S GERMAN FOR "LULLABY." THERE ARE SOME FAMOUS ONES BY BRAHMS AND SCHUBERT.
BUT THAT'S NOT MUCH OF A CLUE, IS IT?
ガタッ
GATA (CLATTER)
KEEP LOOKING.
WELL, CANON?

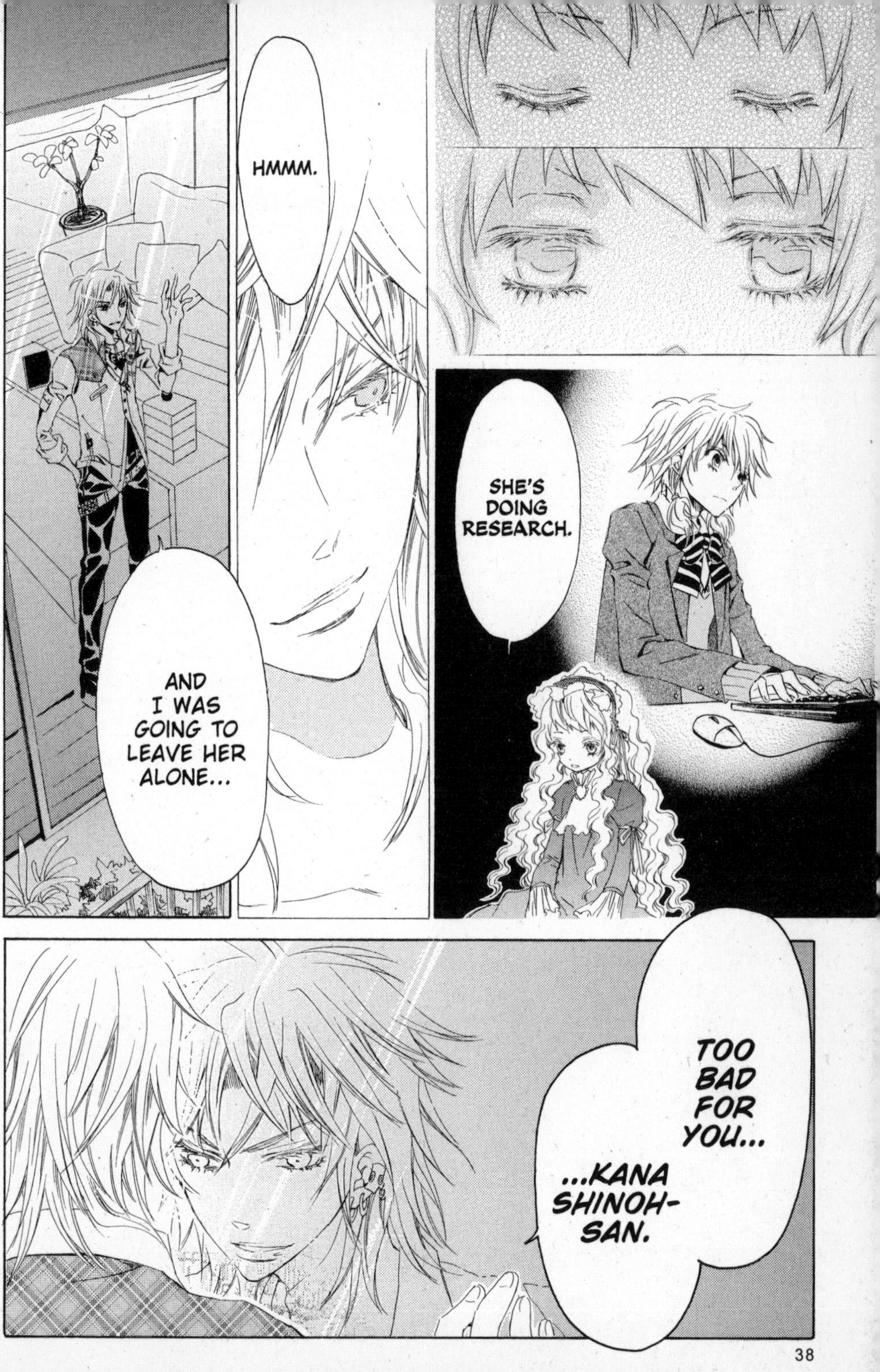
SHE'S DOING RESEARCH.
HMMM.
AND I WAS GOING TO LEAVE HER ALONE...
TOO BAD FOR YOU...
...KANA SHINOH-SAN.

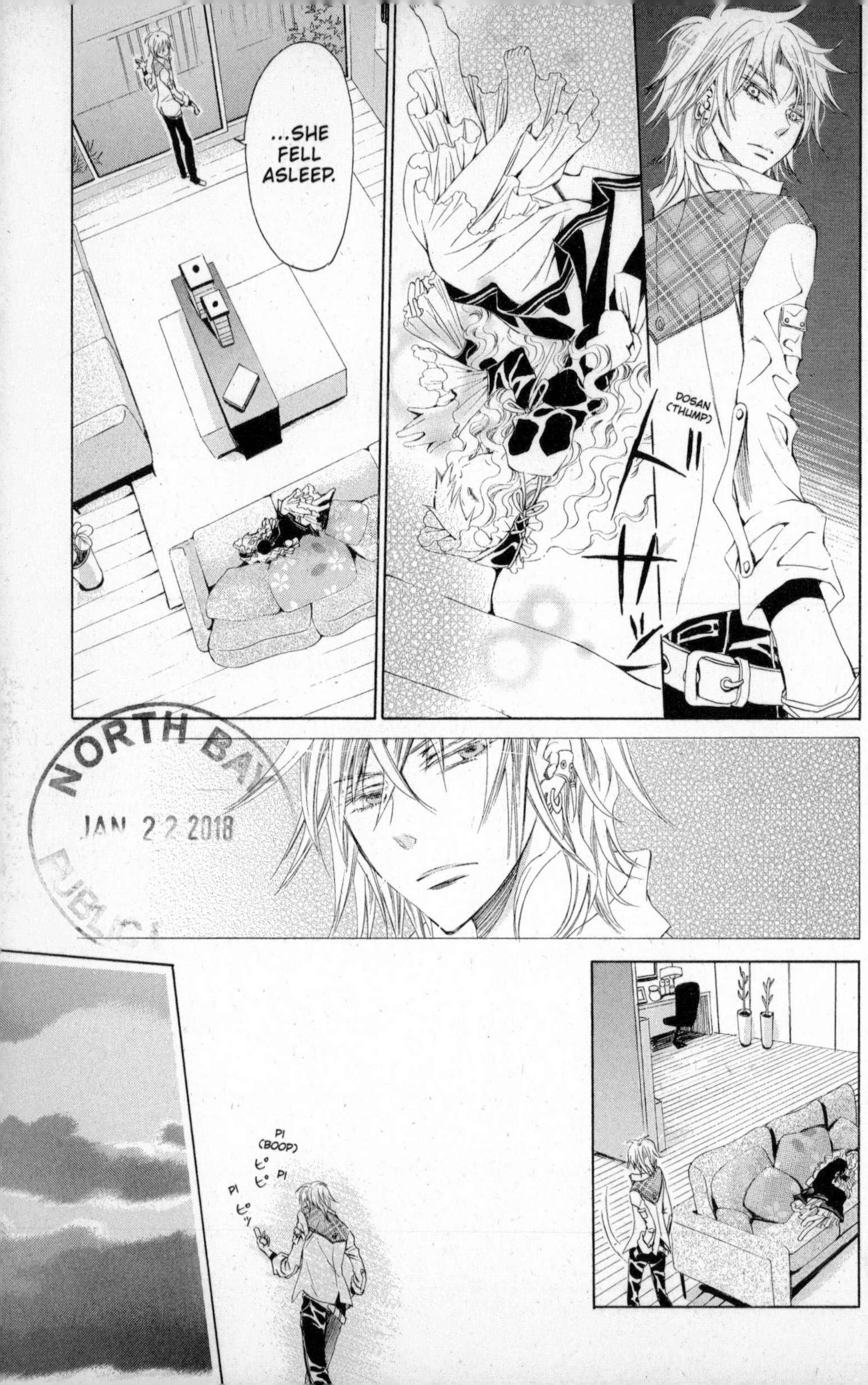
DOSAN (THUMP)
...SHE FELL ASLEEP.
PI (BOOP)
ピ
PI
ピ
PI
ピッ

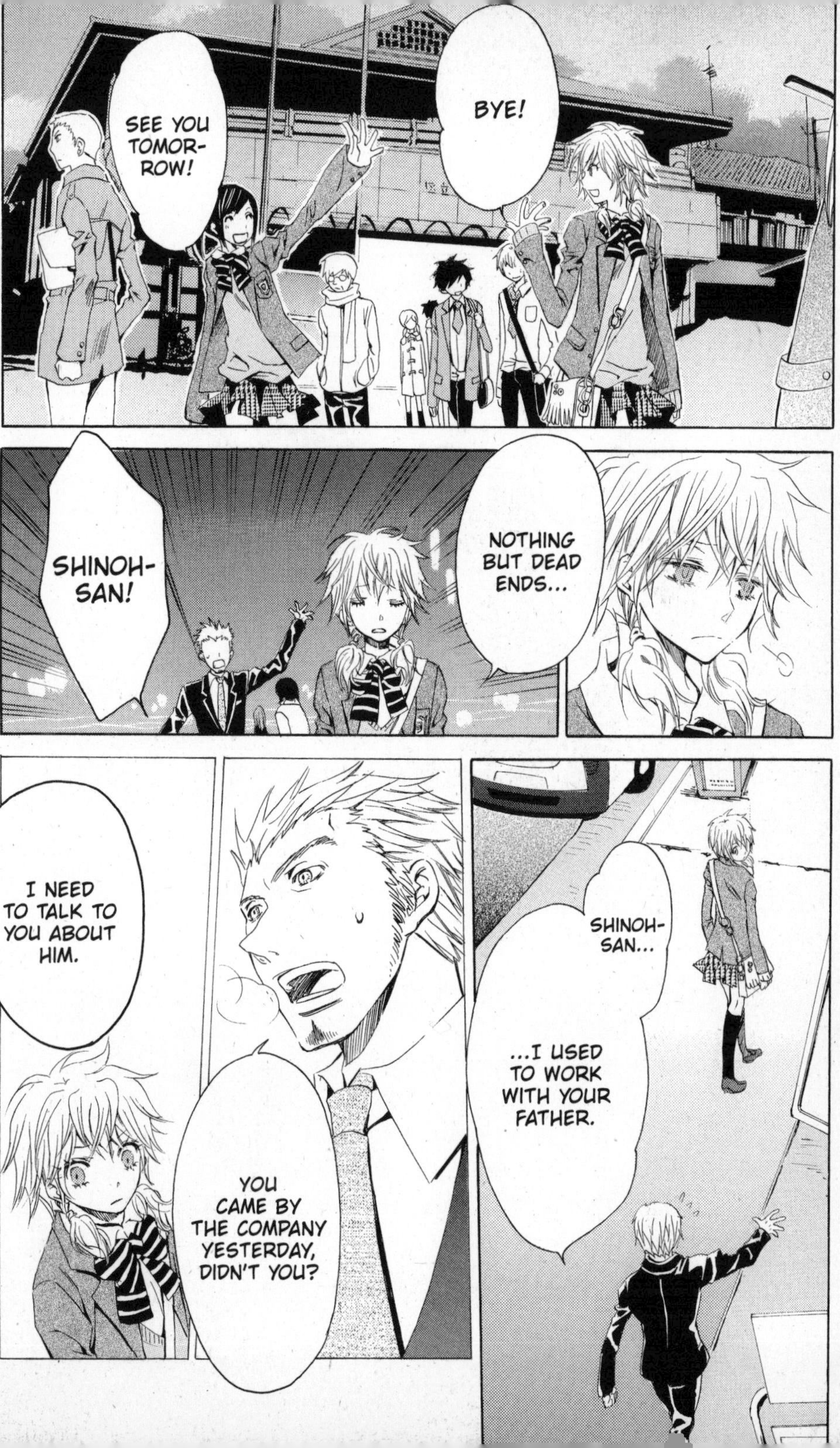
BYE!
SEE YOU TOMOR-ROW!
NOTHING BUT DEAD ENDS...
SHINOH-SAN!
SHINOH-SAN...
...I USED TO WORK WITH YOUR FATHER.
YOU CAME BY THE COMPANY YESTERDAY, DIDN'T YOU?
I NEED TO TALK TO YOU ABOUT HIM.

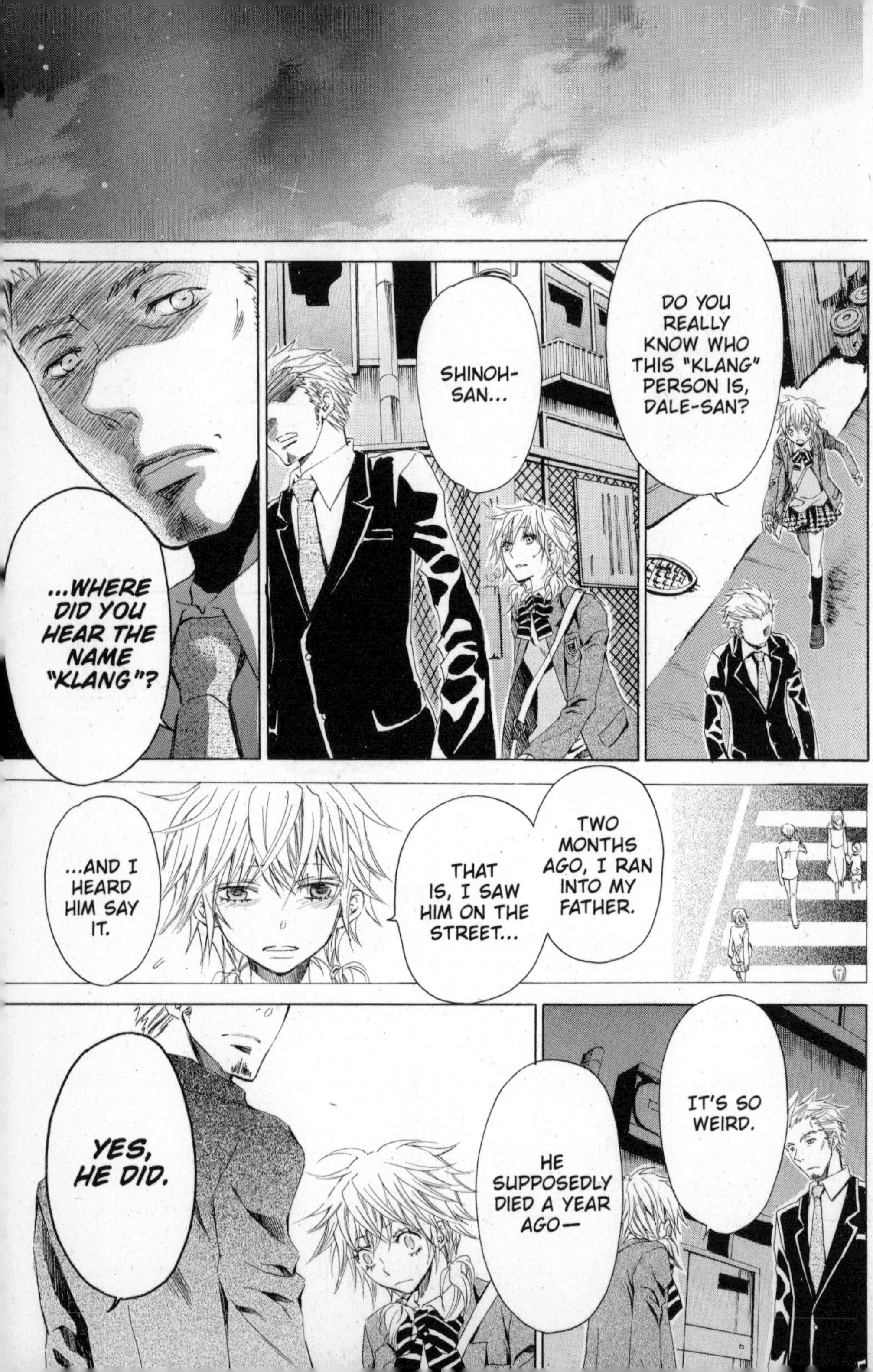
DO YOU REALLY KNOW WHO THIS "KLANG" PERSON IS, DALE-SAN?
SHINOH-SAN...
...WHERE DID YOU HEAR THE NAME "KLANG"?
TWO MONTHS AGO, I RAN INTO MY FATHER.
THAT IS, I SAW HIM ON THE STREET...
...AND I HEARD HIM SAY IT.
IT'S SO WEIRD.
HE SUPPOSEDLY DIED A YEAR AGO—
YES, HE DID.

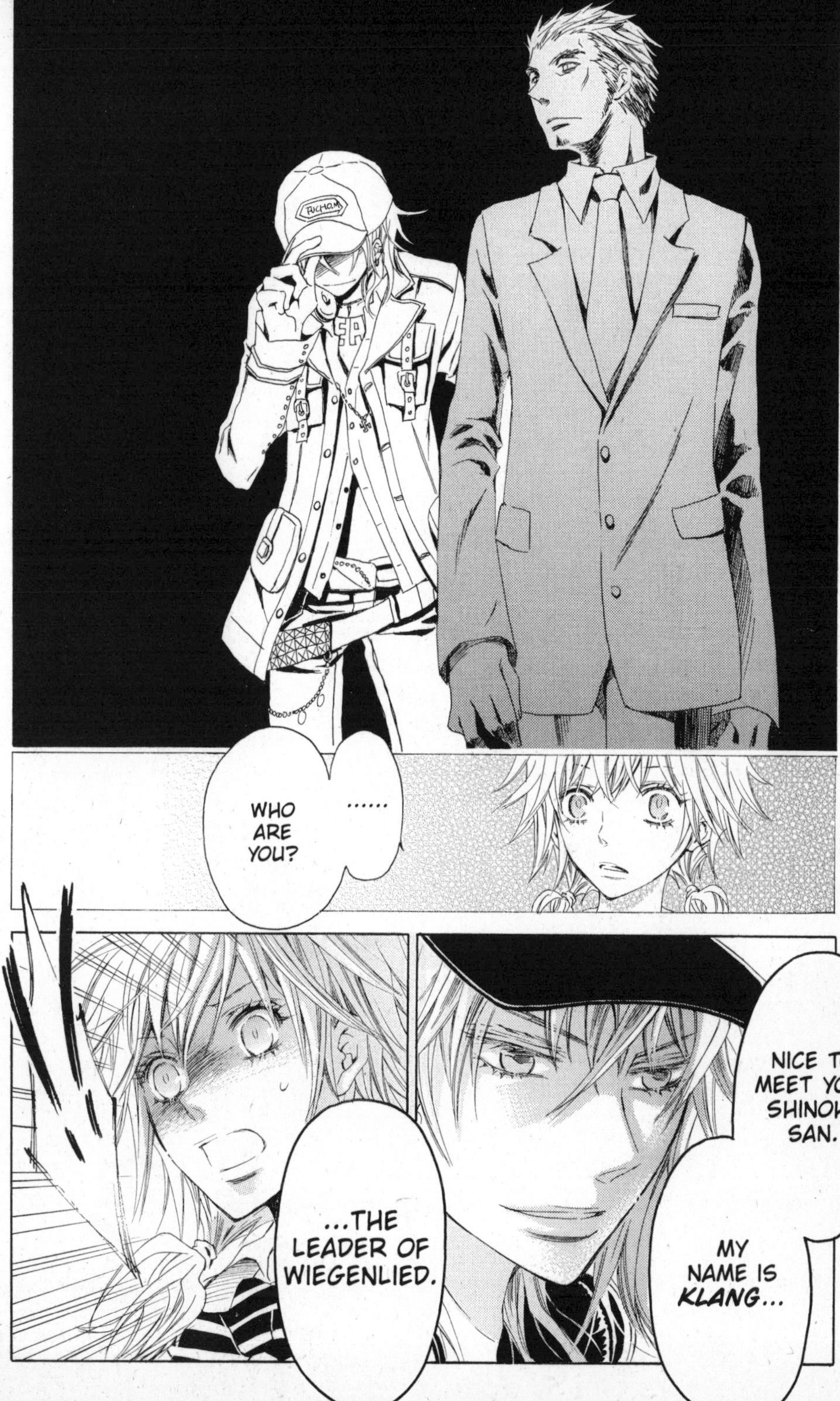
......
WHO ARE YOU?
NICE TO MEET YOU, SHINOH-SAN.
MY NAME IS *KLANG*...
...THE LEADER OF WIEGENLIED.

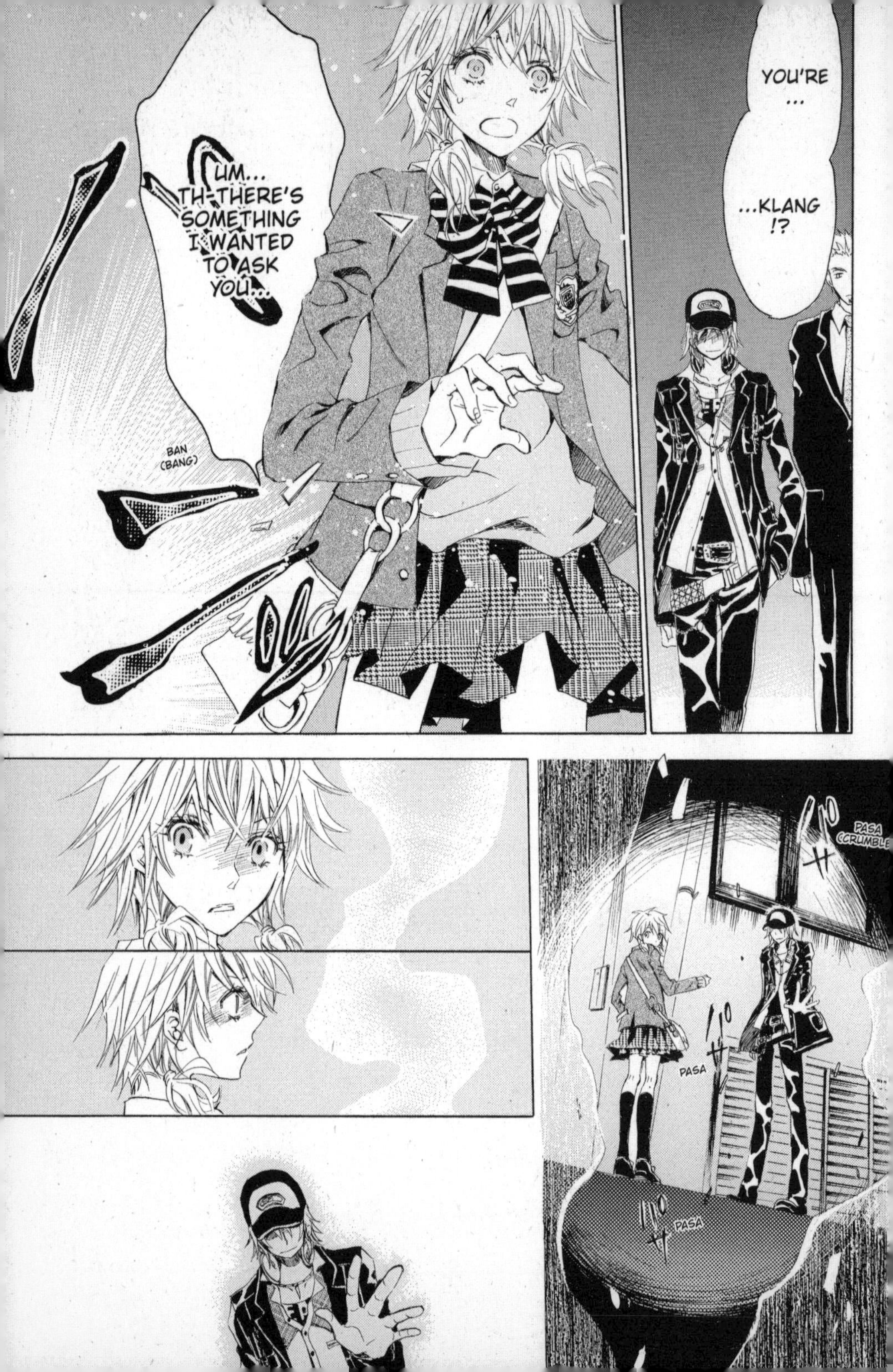
YOU'RE ...
...KLANG !?
UM... TH-THERE'S SOMETHING I WANTED TO ASK YOU...
BAN (BANG)
PASA (CRUMBLE)
PASA
PASA

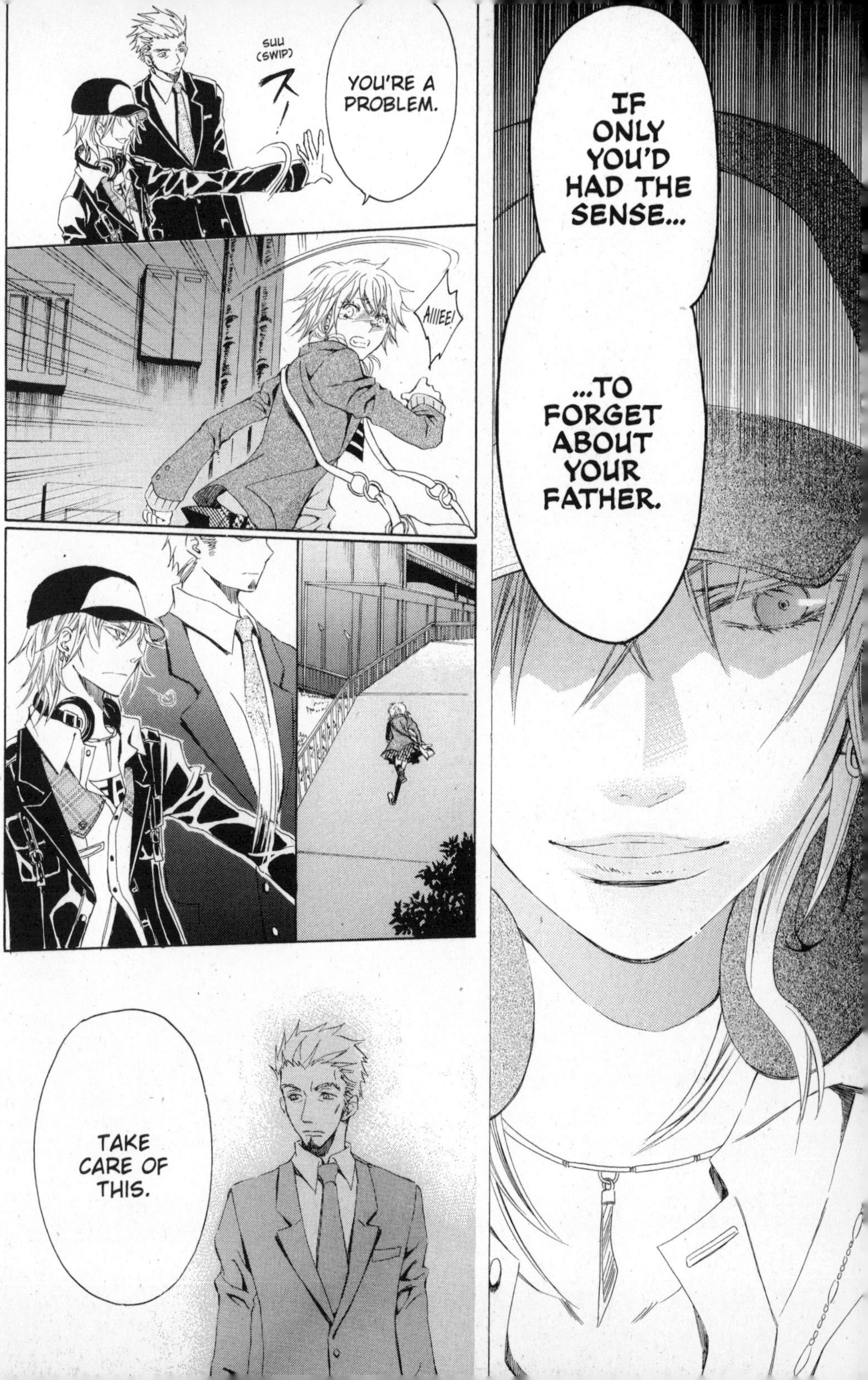
IF ONLY YOU'D HAD THE SENSE...
...TO FORGET ABOUT YOUR FATHER.
YOU'RE A PROBLEM.
SUU (SWIP)
AIIIEE!
TAKE CARE OF THIS.

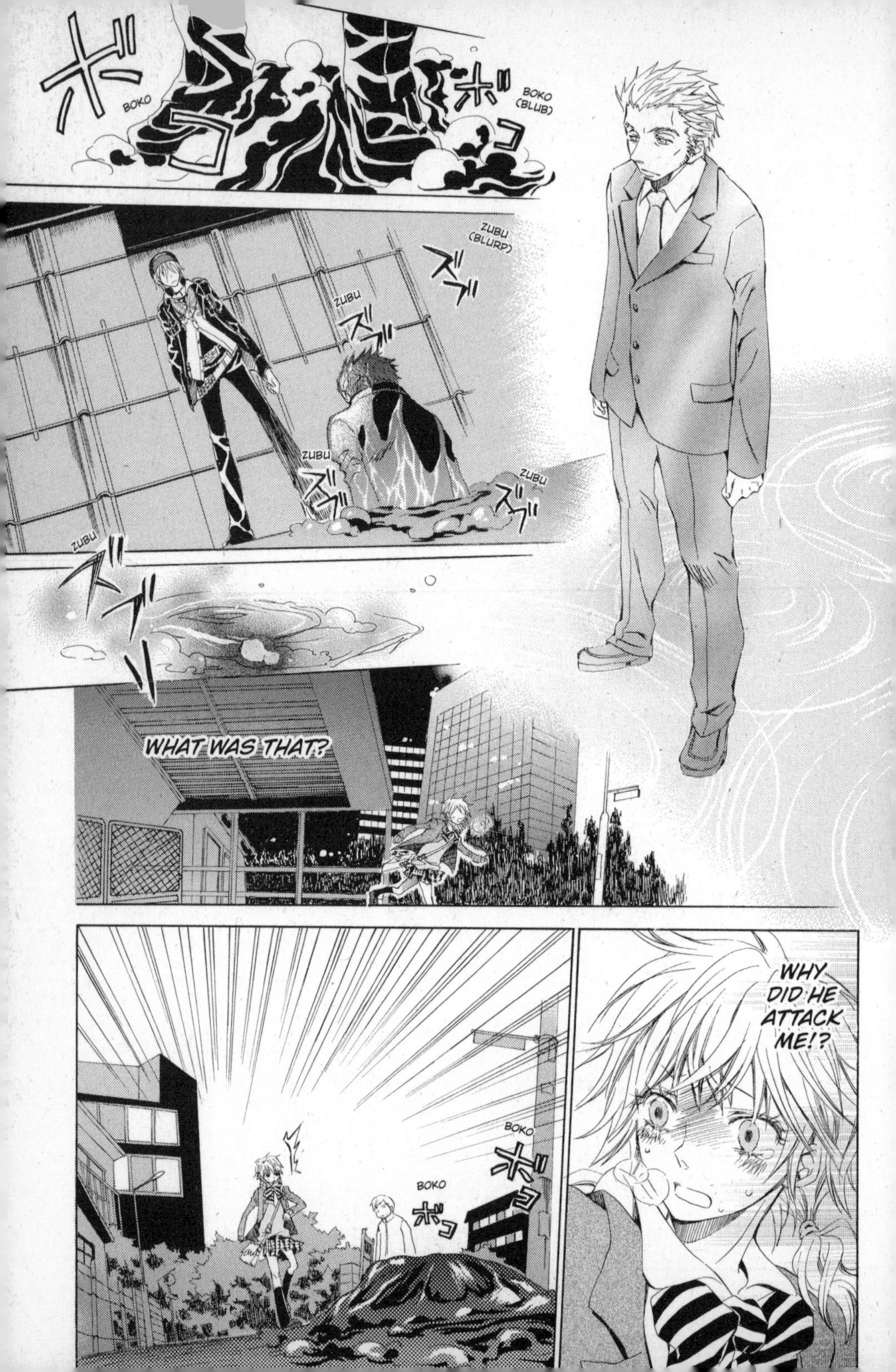
BOKO (BLUB)
BOKO
ZUBU (BLURP)
ZUBU
ZUBU
ZUBU
ZUBU
WHAT WAS THAT?
WHY DID HE ATTACK ME!?
BOKO
BOKO

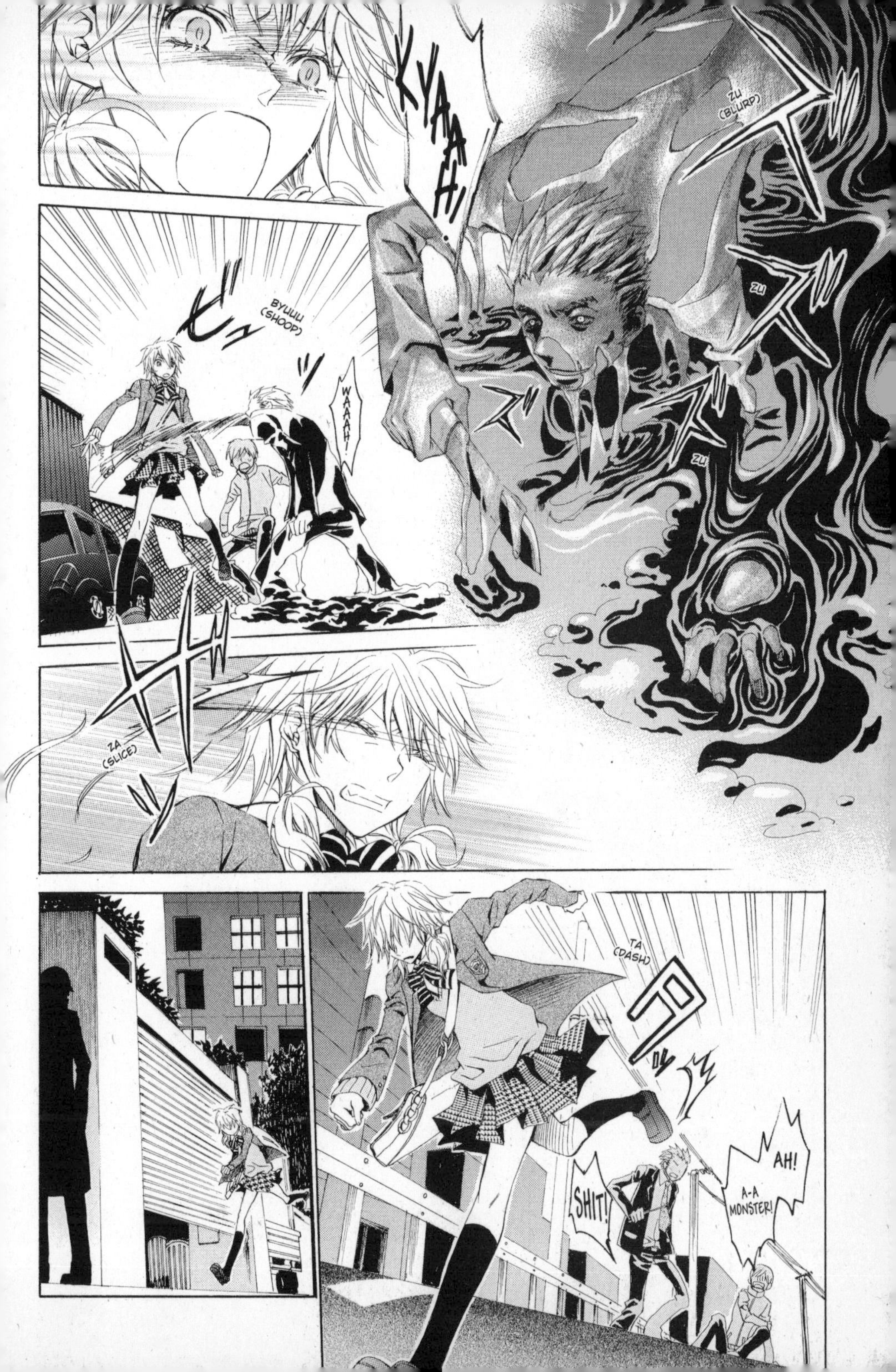
KYAAAH!
ZU
(BLURP)
ZU
ZU
BYUUU
(SHOOP)
WAAAAH!
ZA
(SLICE)
TA
(DASH)
AH!
A-A
MONSTER!
SHIT!

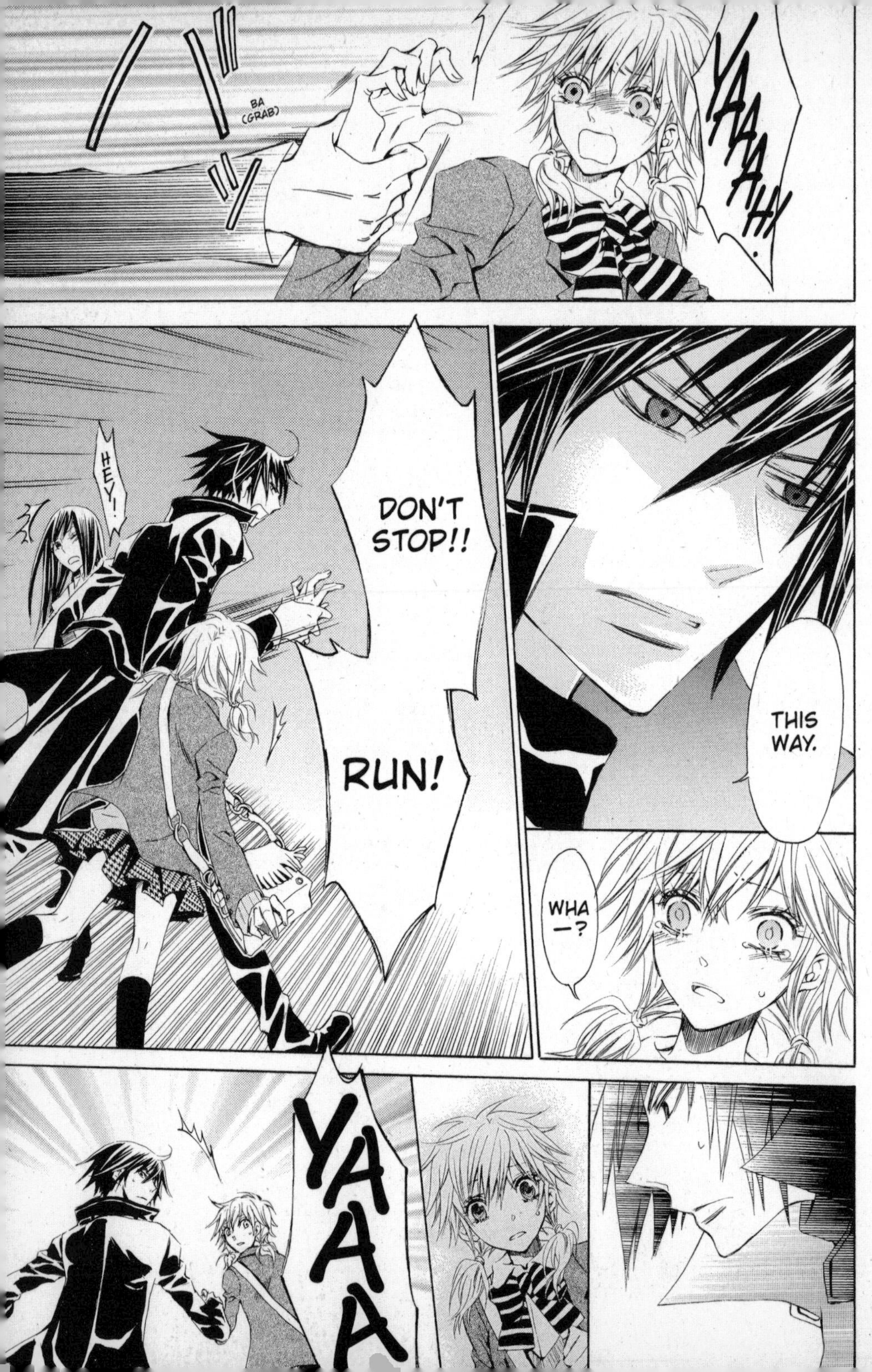
YAAAAH!!
BA (GRAB)
THIS WAY.
WHA—?
DON'T STOP!!
RUN!
HEY!
YAAA

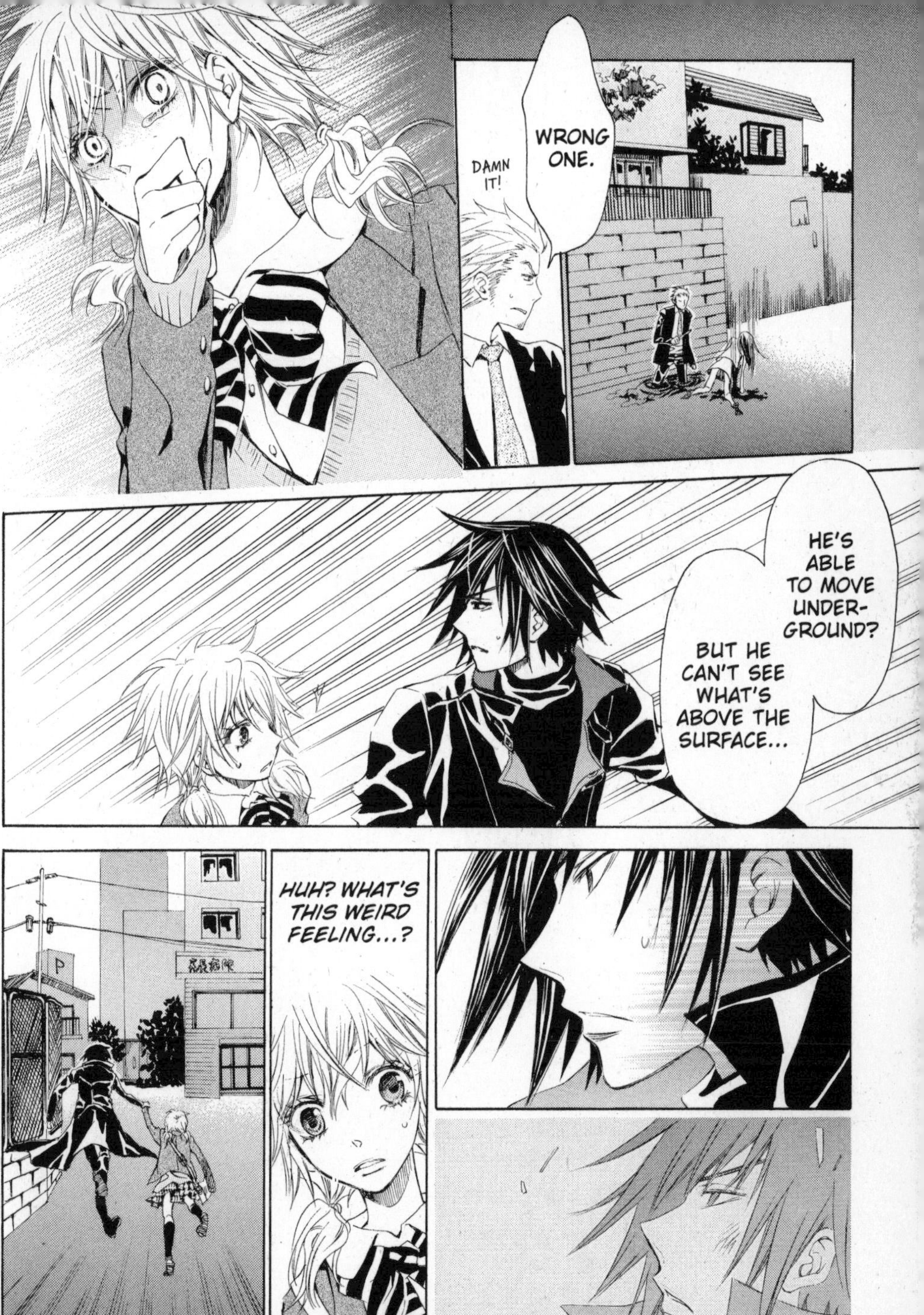
WRONG ONE.
DAMN IT!
HE'S ABLE TO MOVE UNDER-GROUND?
BUT HE CAN'T SEE WHAT'S ABOVE THE SURFACE...
HUH? WHAT'S THIS WEIRD FEELING...?

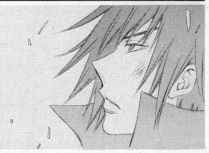

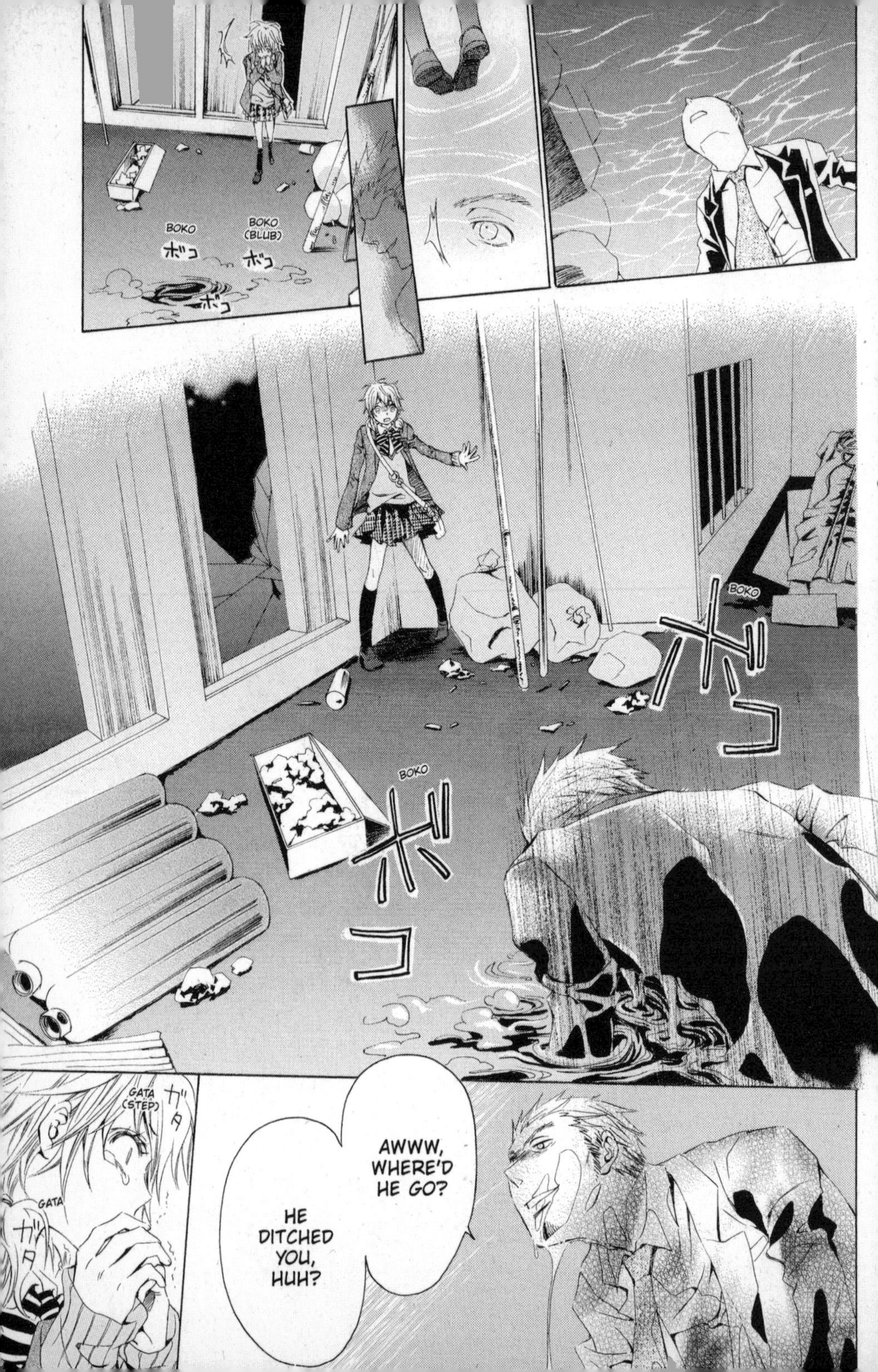
BOKO (BLUB)
ボコ
BOKO
ボコ
ボコ
BOKO
ボコ
BOKO
ボコ
AWWW, WHERE'D HE GO?
HE DITCHED YOU, HUH?
GATA (STEP)
ガタ
GATA
ガタ

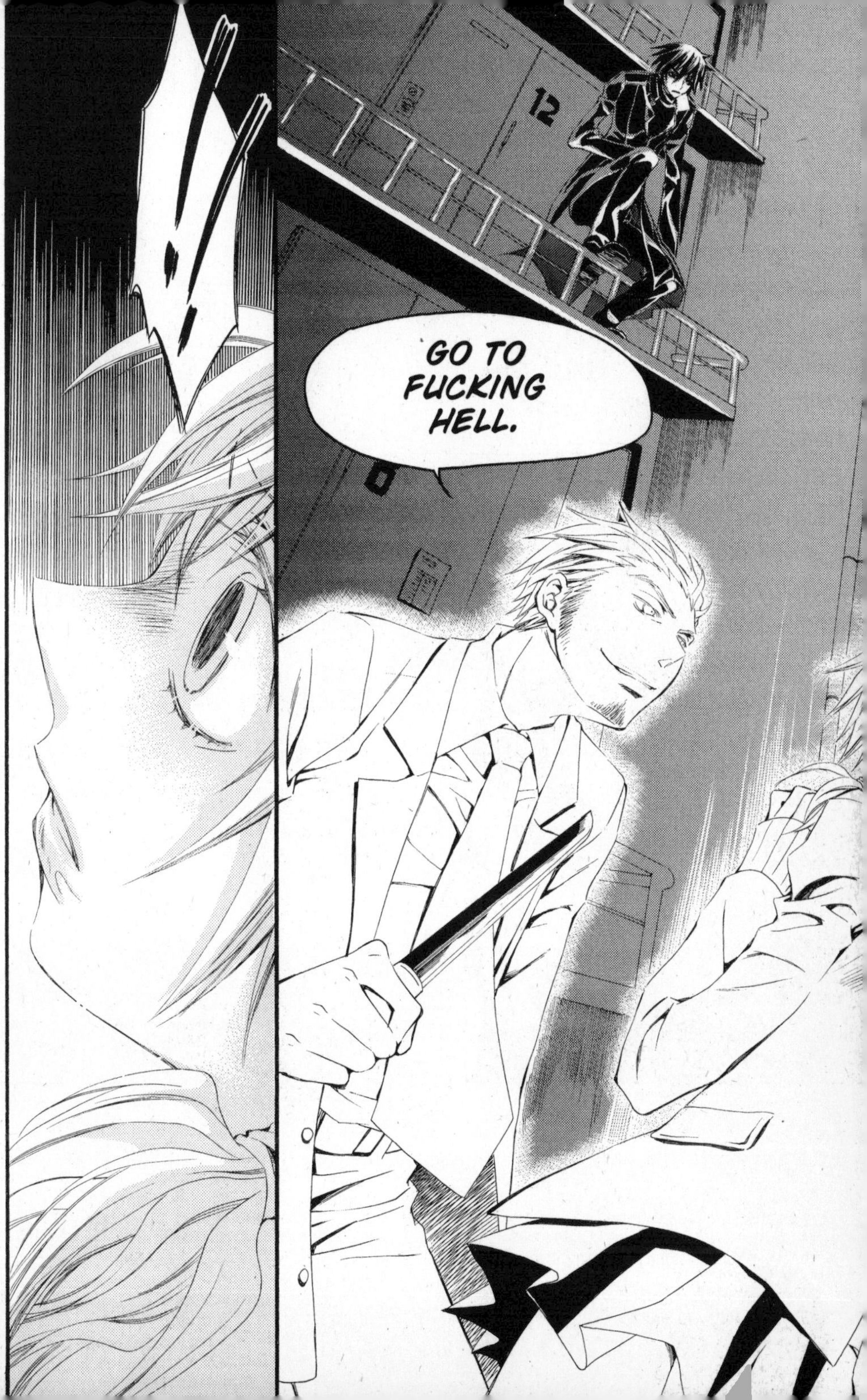
GO TO FUCKING HELL.

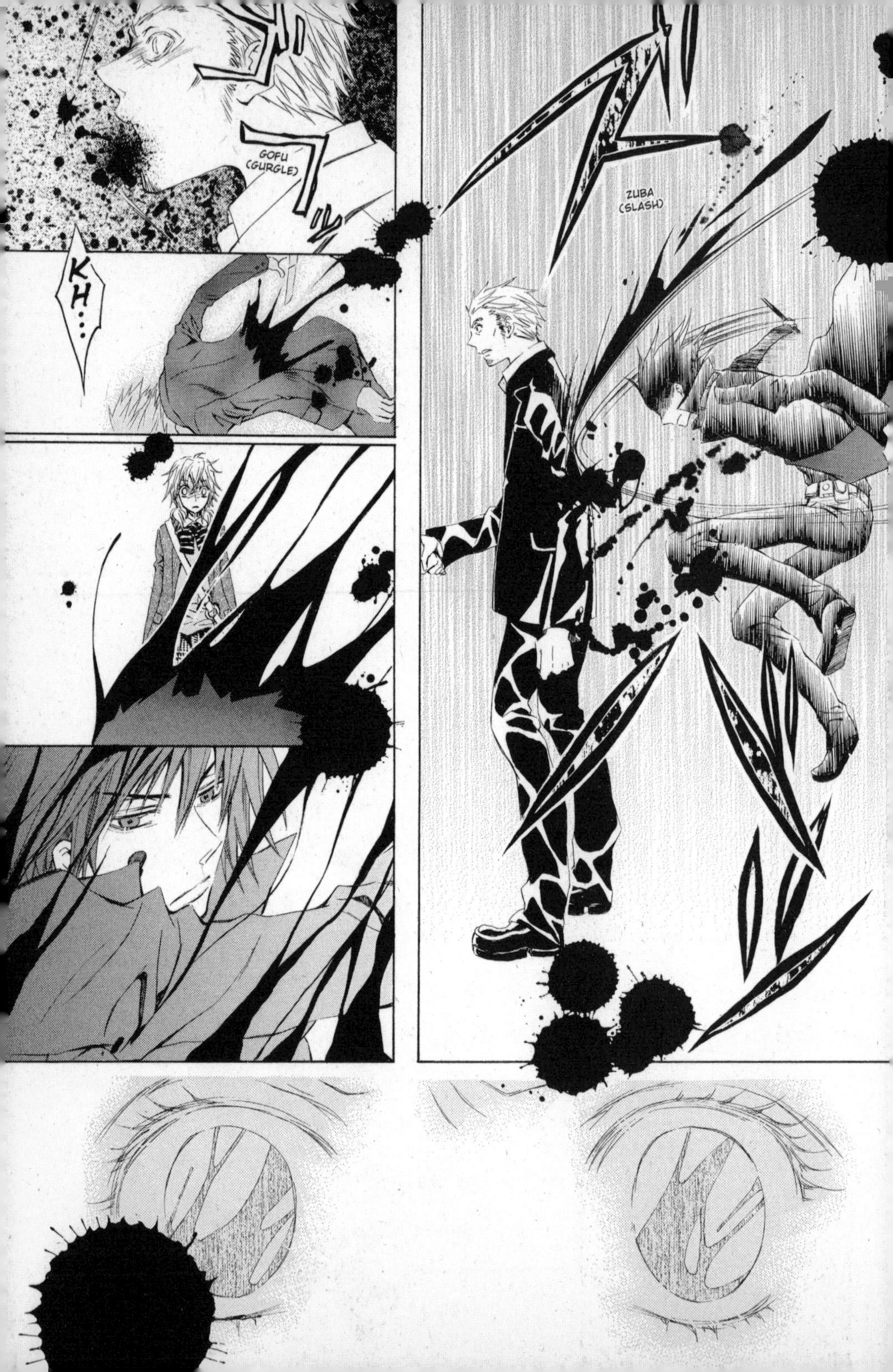
ZUBA
(SLASH)
GOFU
(GURGLE)
KH...

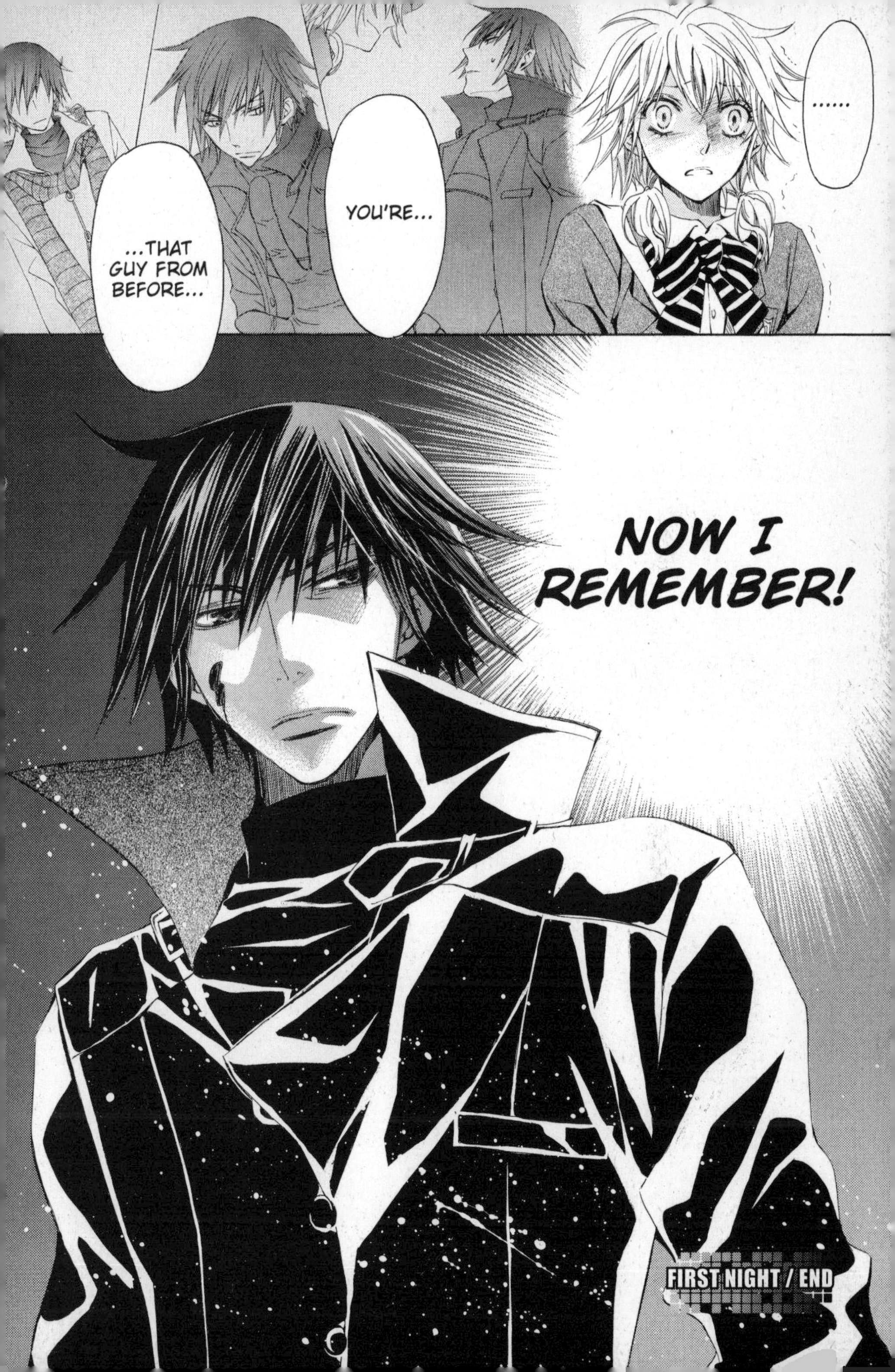
......
YOU'RE...
...THAT GUY FROM BEFORE...
NOW I REMEMBER!
FIRST NIGHT / END

SECOND NIGHT

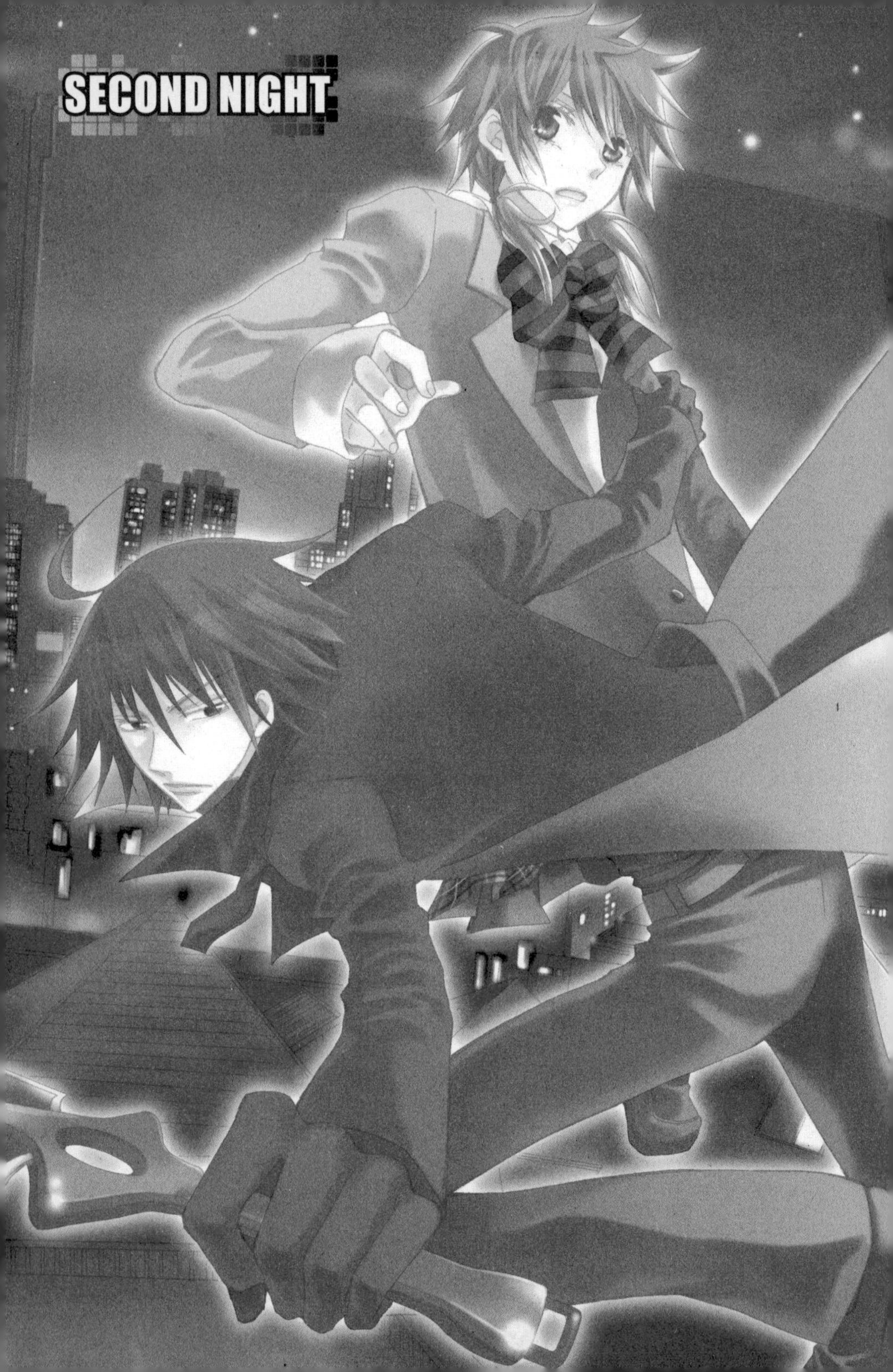

DARKER THAN BLACK
THE BLACK CONTRACTOR

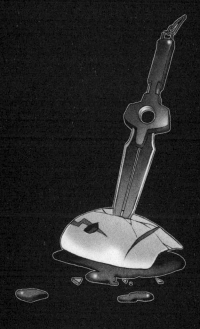

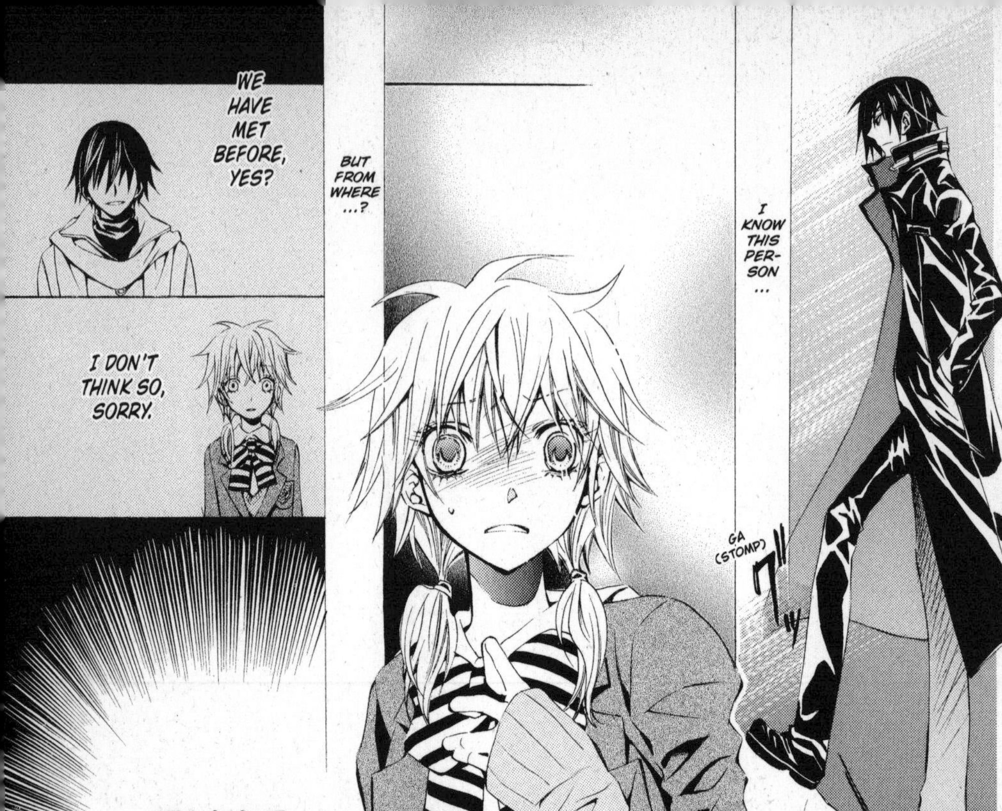
I KNOW THIS PERSON...
BUT FROM WHERE...?
GA (STOMP)
WE HAVE MET BEFORE, YES?
I DON'T THINK SO, SORRY.
THAT WAS HIM!?

You really should read the whole series before you look at this...

IMPOSSIBLE COMIC STRIP (1)

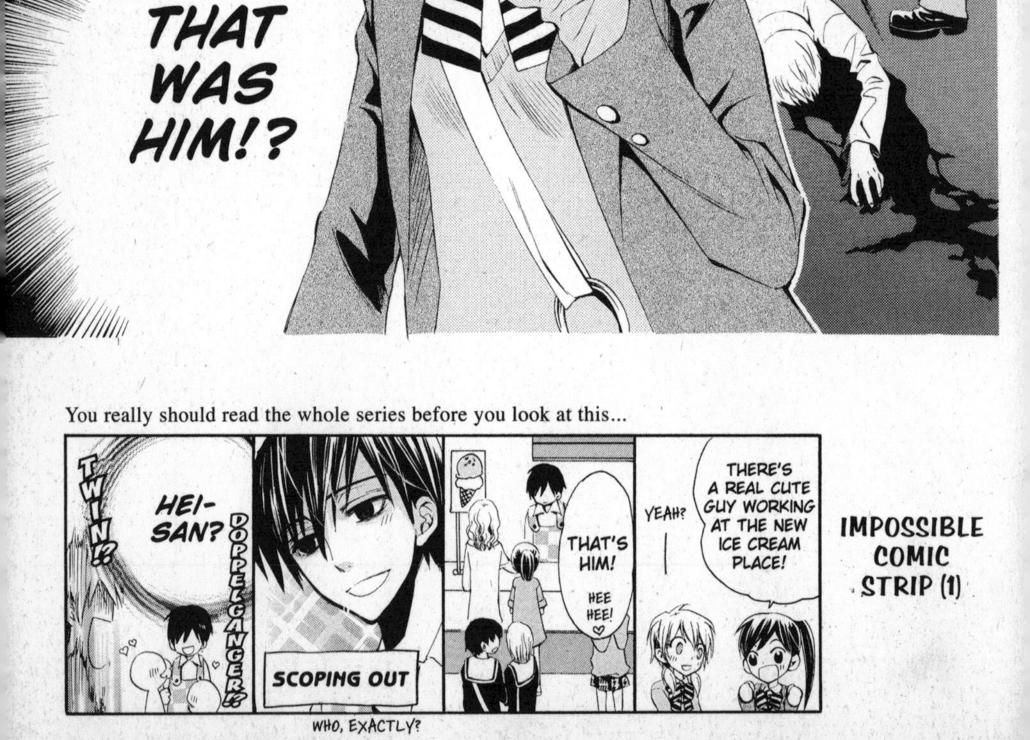
THERE'S A REAL CUTE GUY WORKING AT THE NEW ICE CREAM PLACE!
YEAH?
THAT'S HIM!
HEE HEE!
SCOPING OUT
HEI-SAN?
DOPPELGANGER!?
TWIN!?

WHO, EXACTLY?

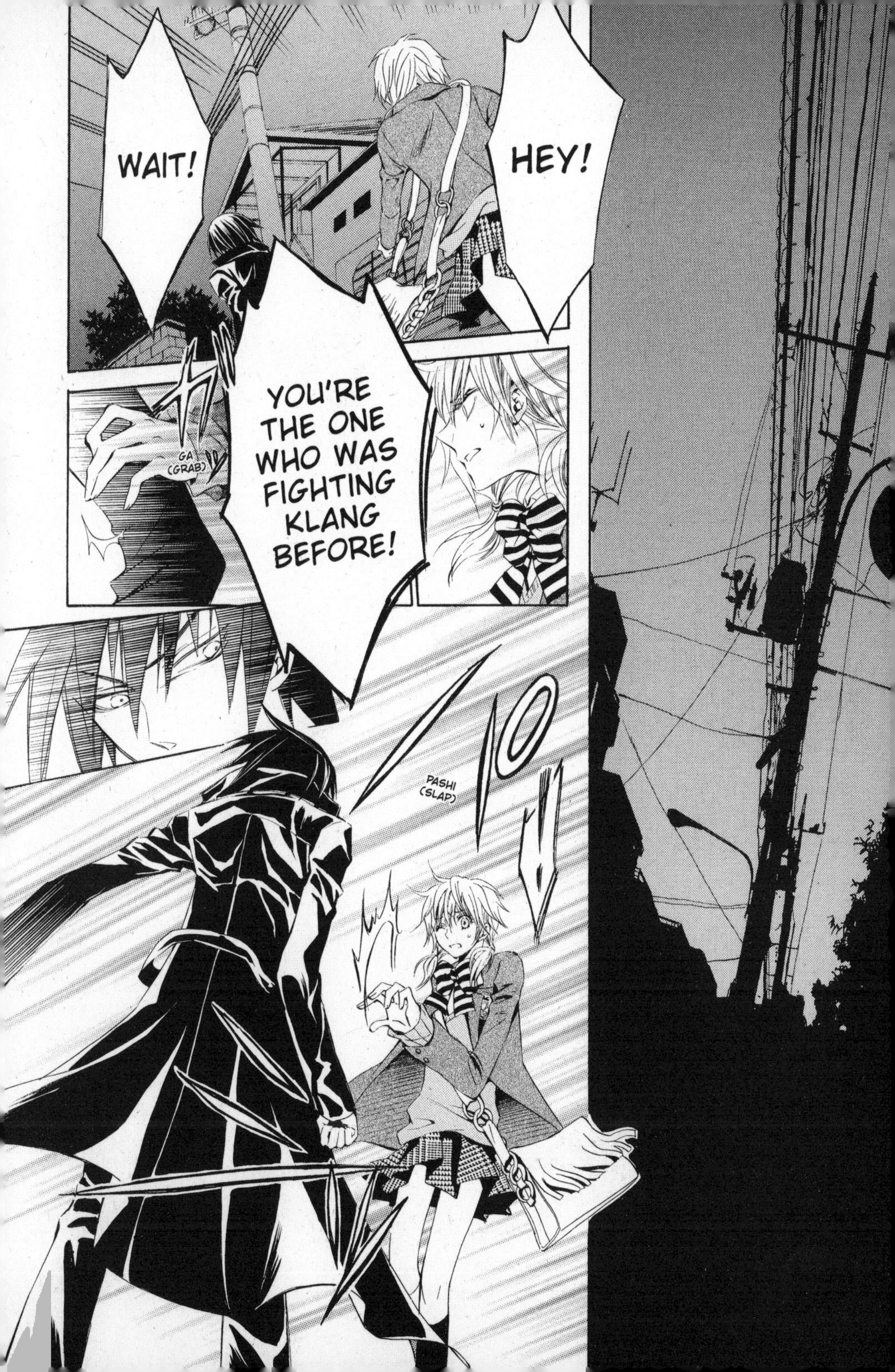
HEY!
WAIT!
YOU'RE THE ONE WHO WAS FIGHTING KLANG BEFORE!
GA (GRAB)
PASHI (SLAP)

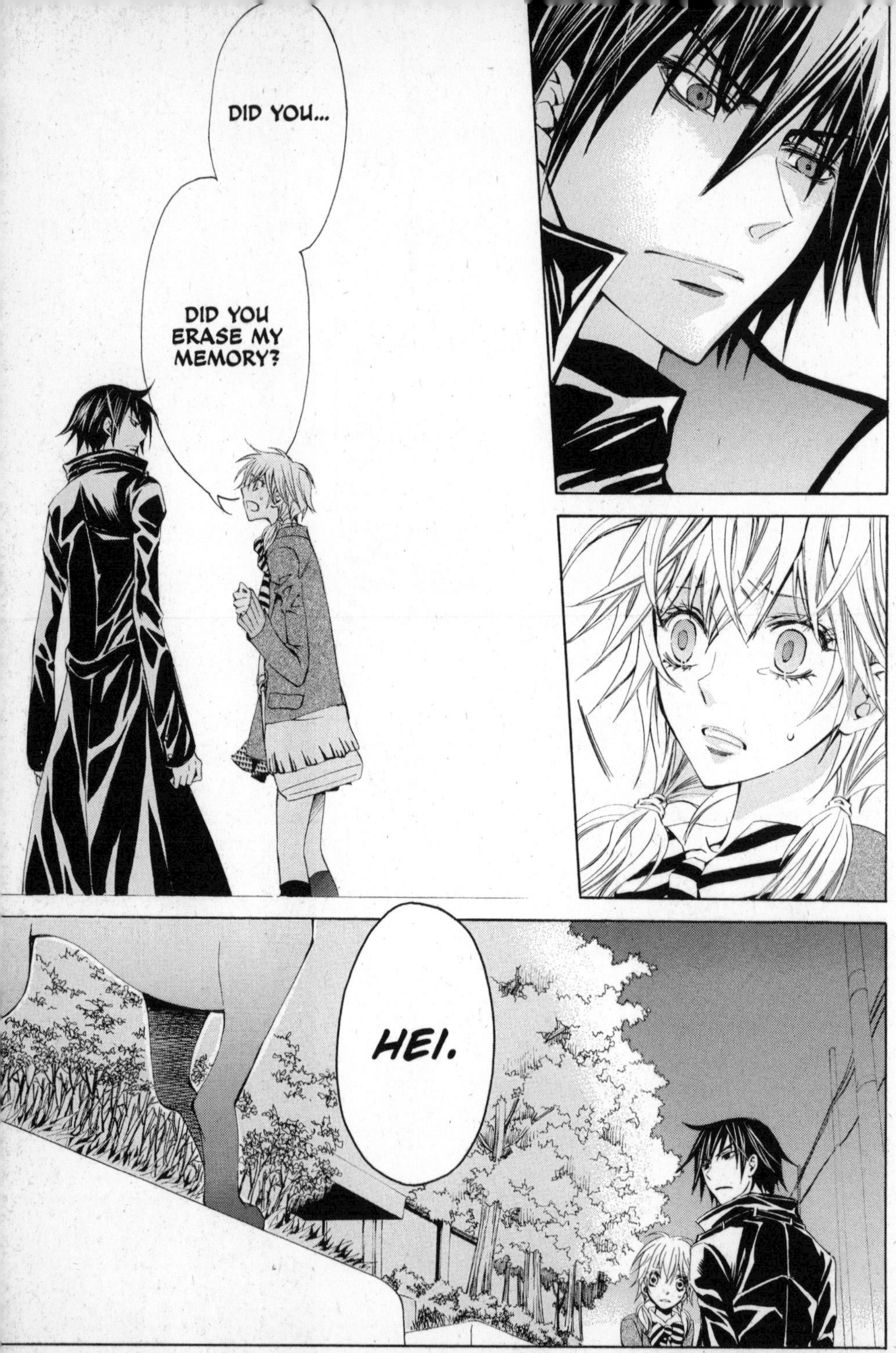
DID YOU...
DID YOU ERASE MY MEMORY?
HEI.

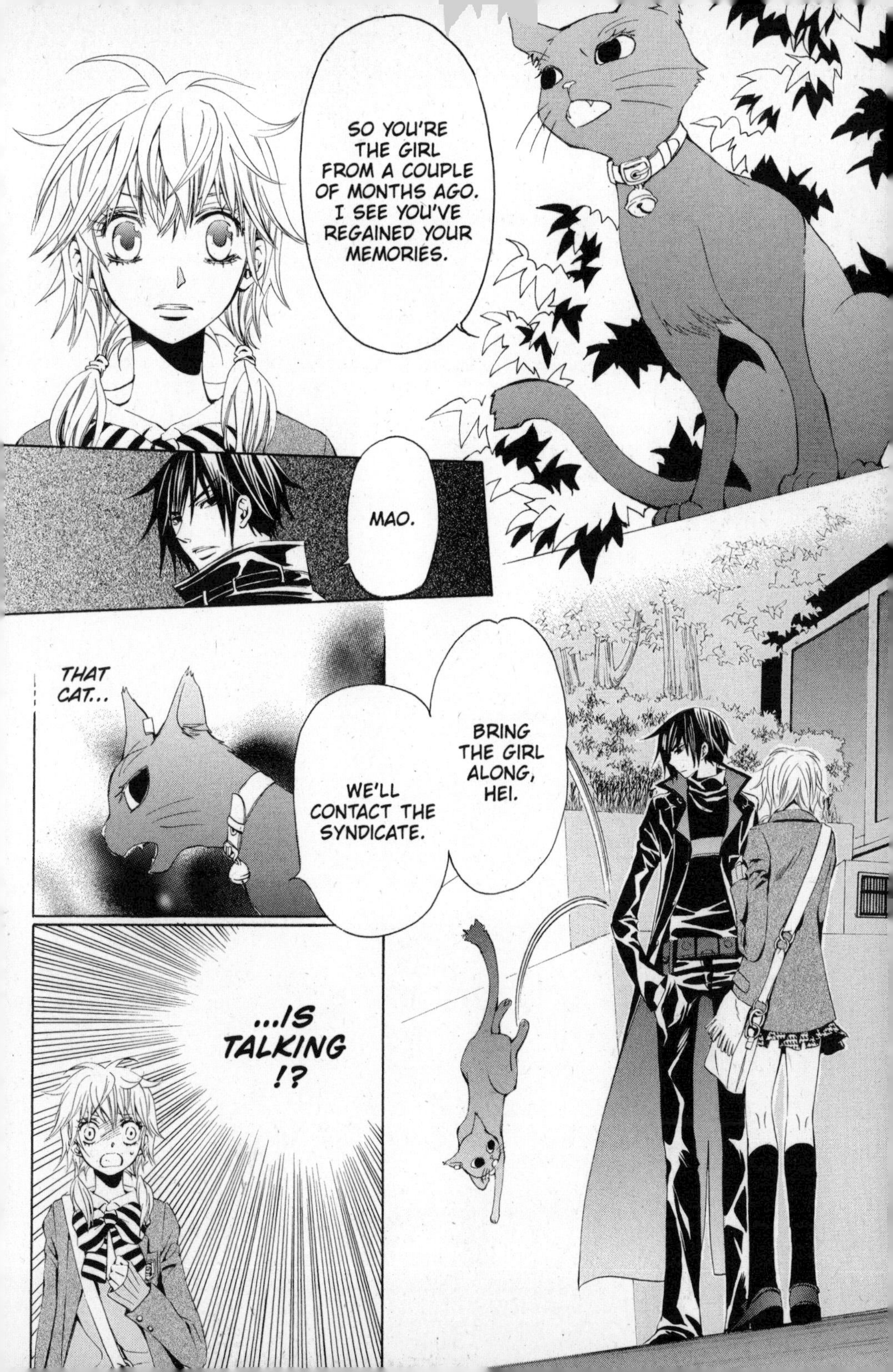
SO YOU'RE THE GIRL FROM A COUPLE OF MONTHS AGO. I SEE YOU'VE REGAINED YOUR MEMORIES.
MAO.
BRING THE GIRL ALONG, HEI.
WE'LL CONTACT THE SYNDICATE.
THAT CAT...
...IS TALKING !?

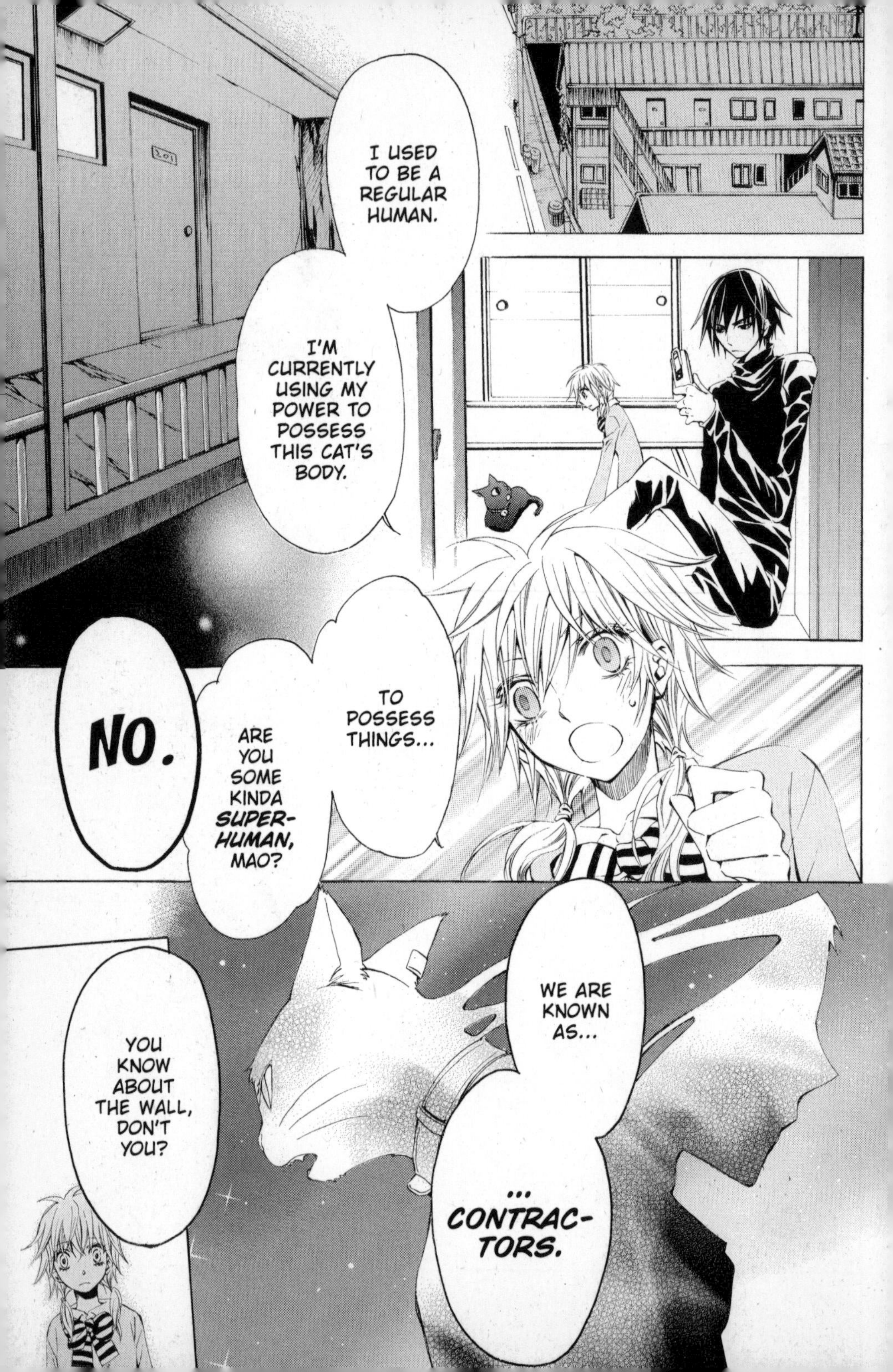
I USED TO BE A REGULAR HUMAN.
I'M CURRENTLY USING MY POWER TO POSSESS THIS CAT'S BODY.
TO POSSESS THINGS...
ARE YOU SOME KINDA *SUPER-HUMAN*, MAO?
NO.
WE ARE KNOWN AS...
...CONTRAC-TORS.
YOU KNOW ABOUT THE WALL, DON'T YOU?

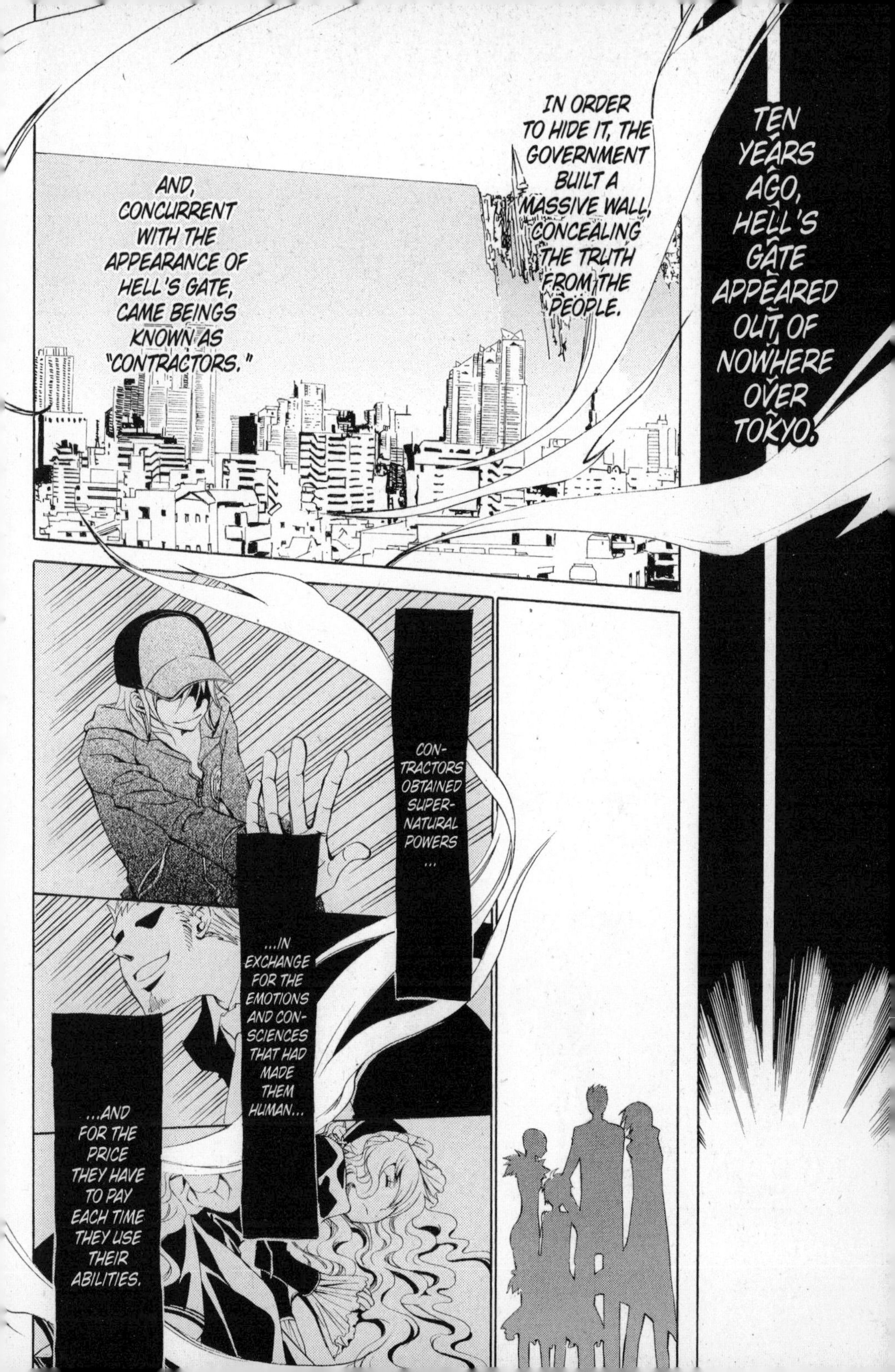
TEN YEARS AGO, HELL'S GATE APPEARED OUT OF NOWHERE OVER TOKYO.
IN ORDER TO HIDE IT, THE GOVERNMENT BUILT A MASSIVE WALL, CONCEALING THE TRUTH FROM THE PEOPLE.
AND, CONCURRENT WITH THE APPEARANCE OF HELL'S GATE, CAME BEINGS KNOWN AS "CONTRACTORS."
CON-TRACTORS OBTAINED SUPER-NATURAL POWERS ...
...IN EXCHANGE FOR THE EMOTIONS AND CON-SCIENCES THAT HAD MADE THEM HUMAN...
...AND FOR THE PRICE THEY HAVE TO PAY EACH TIME THEY USE THEIR ABILITIES.

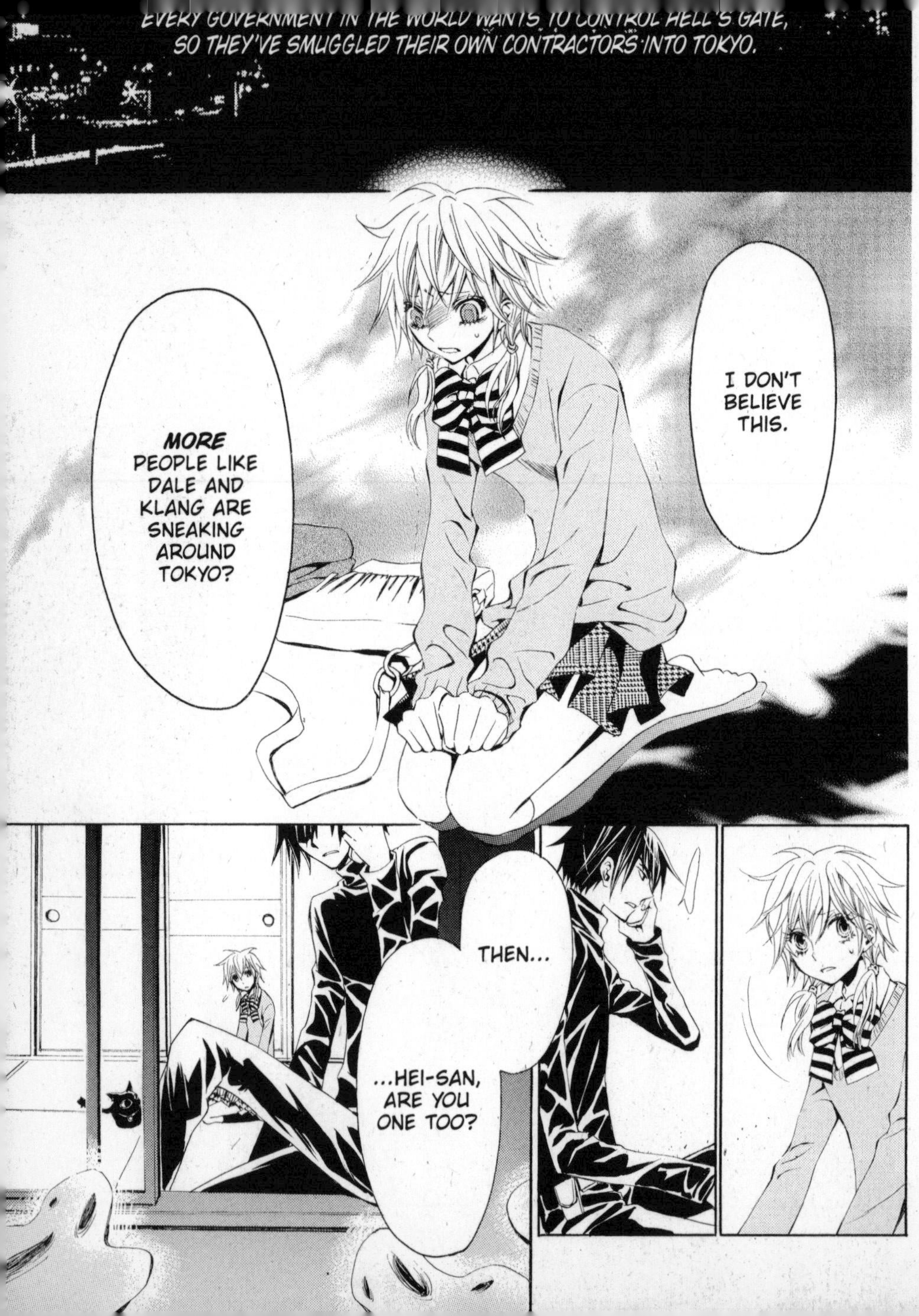
EVERY GOVERNMENT IN THE WORLD WANTS TO CONTROL HELL'S GATE, SO THEY'VE SMUGGLED THEIR OWN CONTRACTORS INTO TOKYO.
I DON'T BELIEVE THIS.
MORE PEOPLE LIKE DALE AND KLANG ARE SNEAKING AROUND TOKYO?
THEN...
...HEI-SAN, ARE YOU ONE TOO?

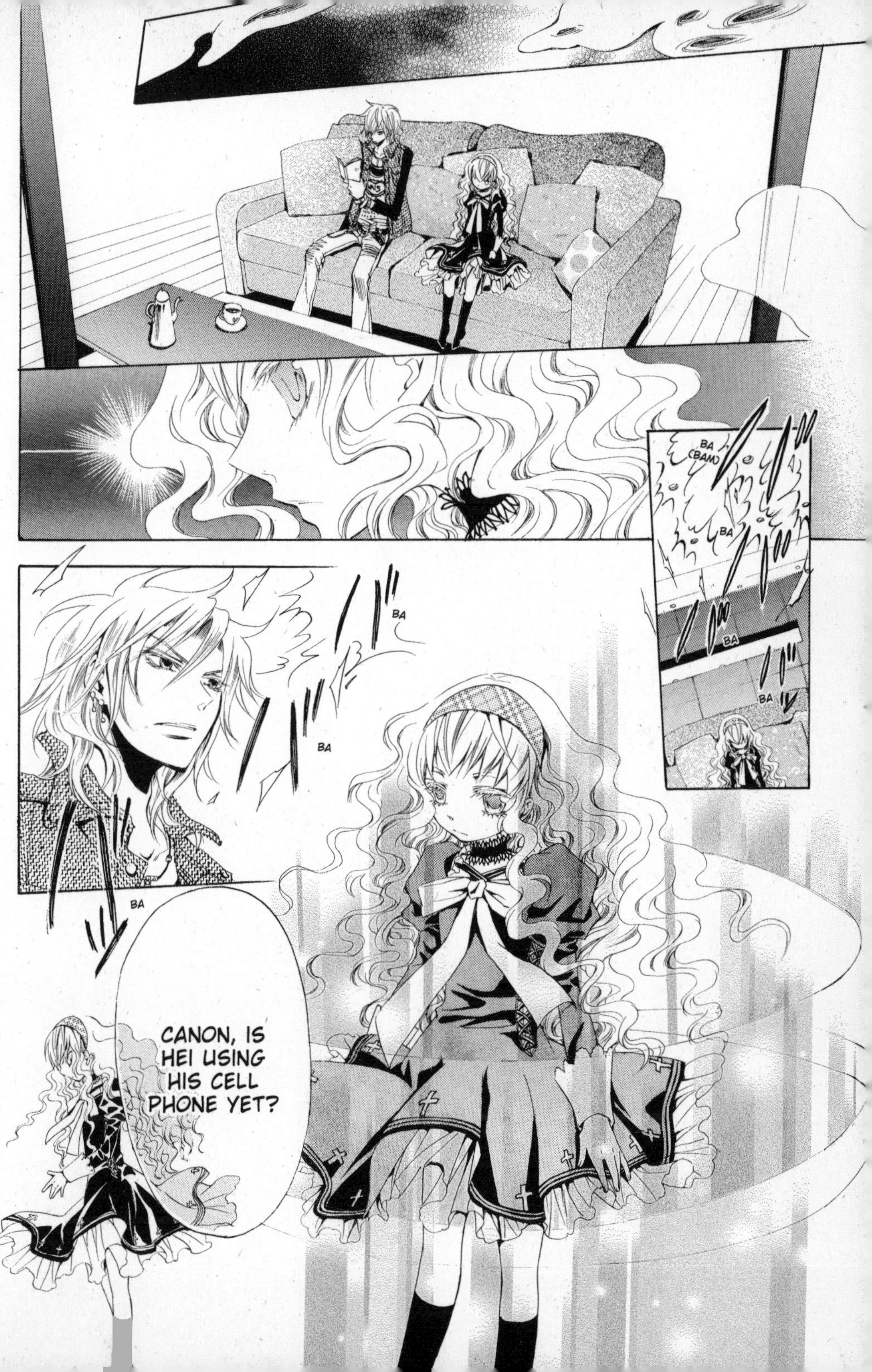
BA
(BAM)
BA
BA
BA
BA
BA
BA
CANON, IS HEI USING HIS CELL PHONE YET?

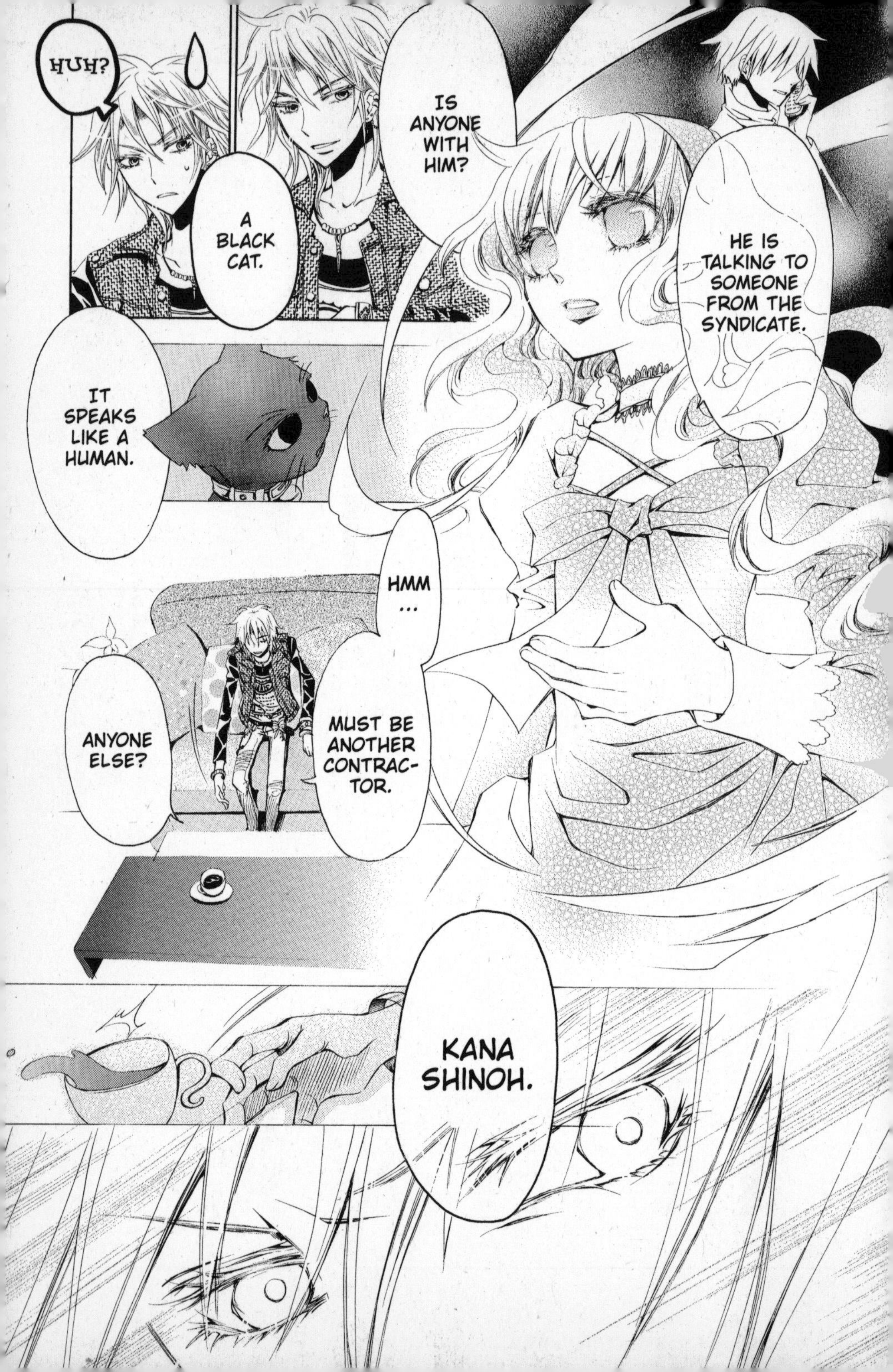
HE IS TALKING TO SOMEONE FROM THE SYNDICATE.
IS ANYONE WITH HIM?
A BLACK CAT.
HUH?
IT SPEAKS LIKE A HUMAN.
HMM...
MUST BE ANOTHER CONTRACTOR.
ANYONE ELSE?
KANA SHINOH.

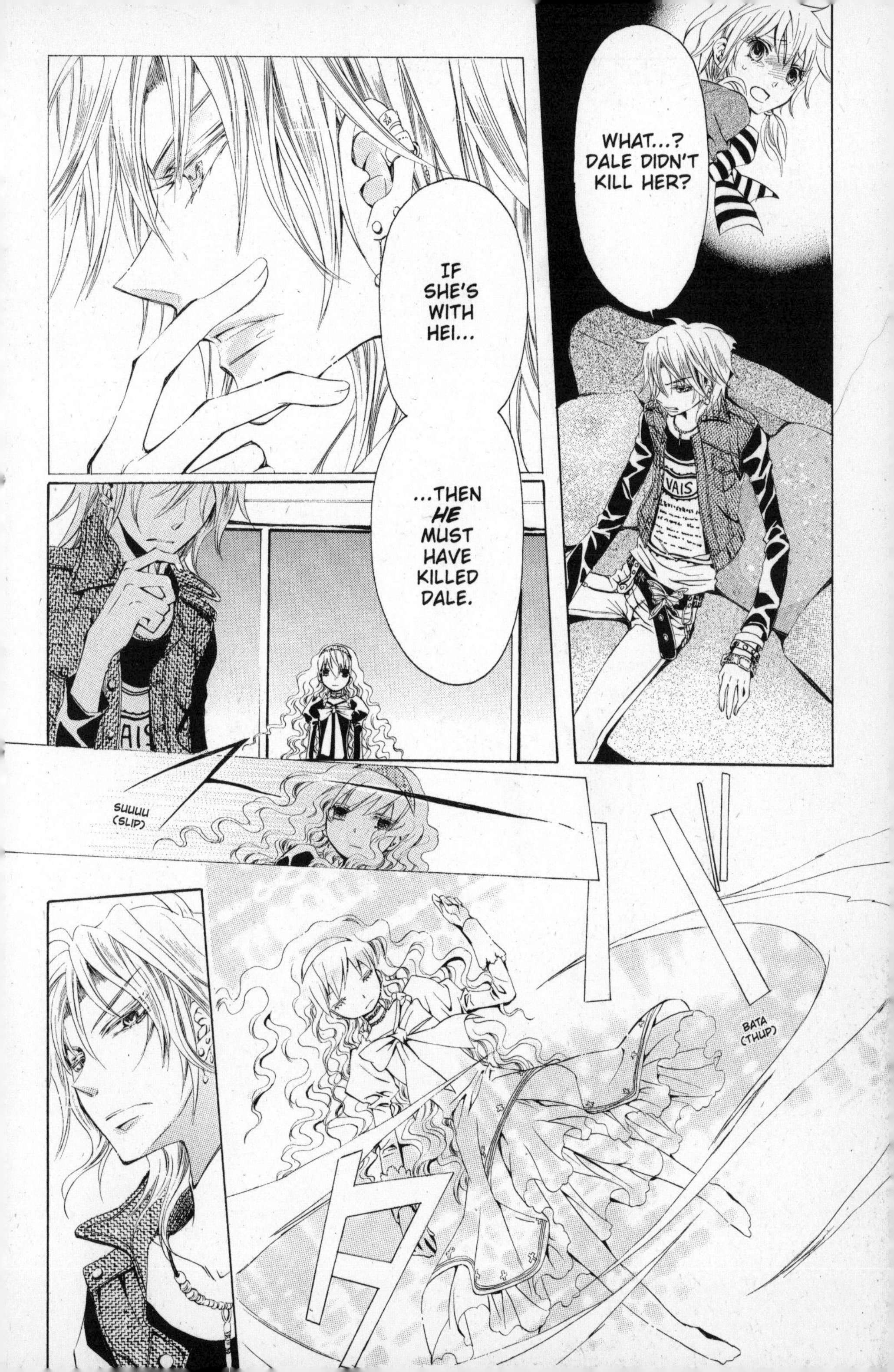
WHAT...? DALE DIDN'T KILL HER?
IF SHE'S WITH HEI...
...THEN *HE* MUST HAVE KILLED DALE.
SUUUU (SLIP)
BATA (THUP)

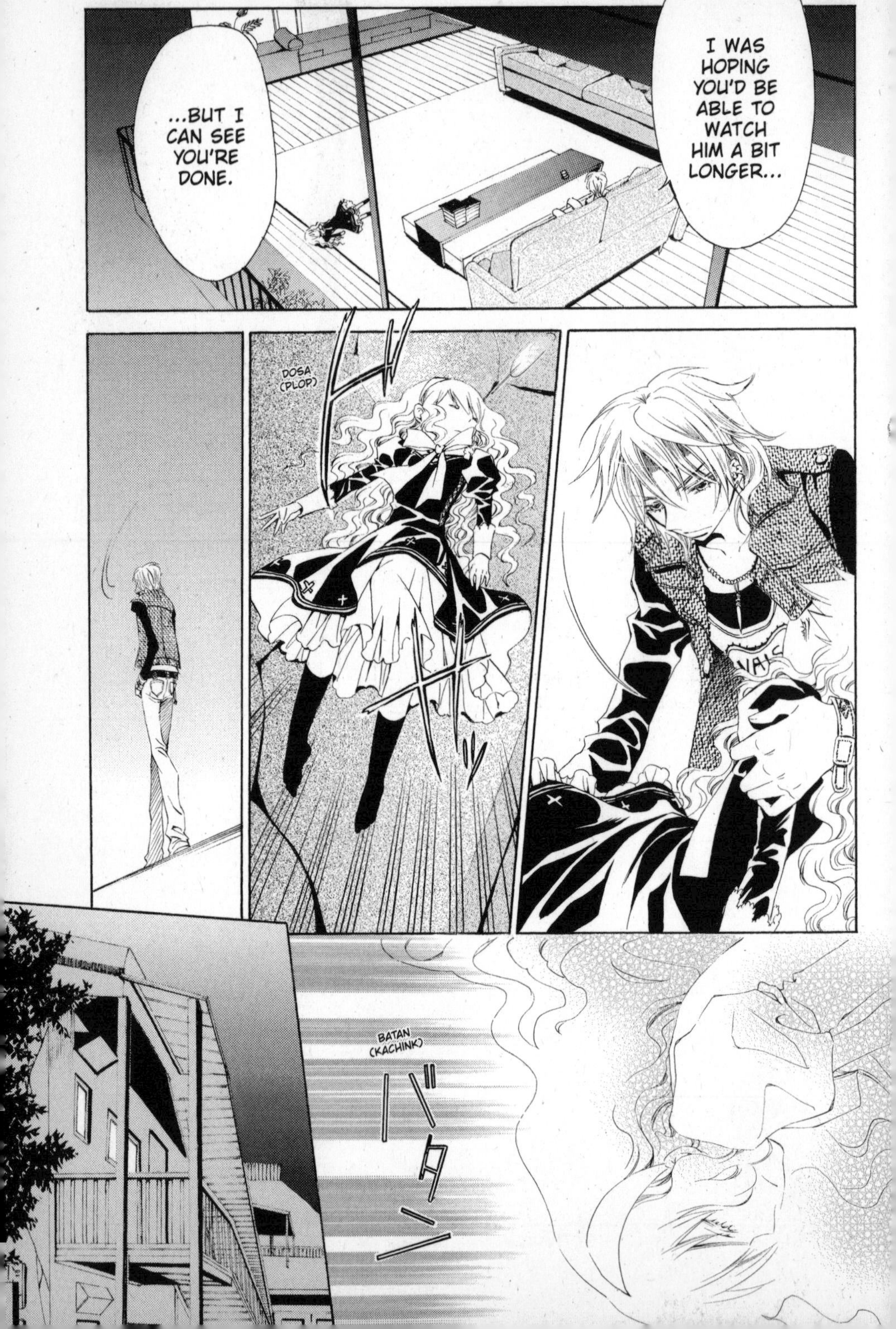
I WAS HOPING YOU'D BE ABLE TO WATCH HIM A BIT LONGER...
...BUT I CAN SEE YOU'RE DONE.
DOSA (PLOP)
BATAN (KACHINK)

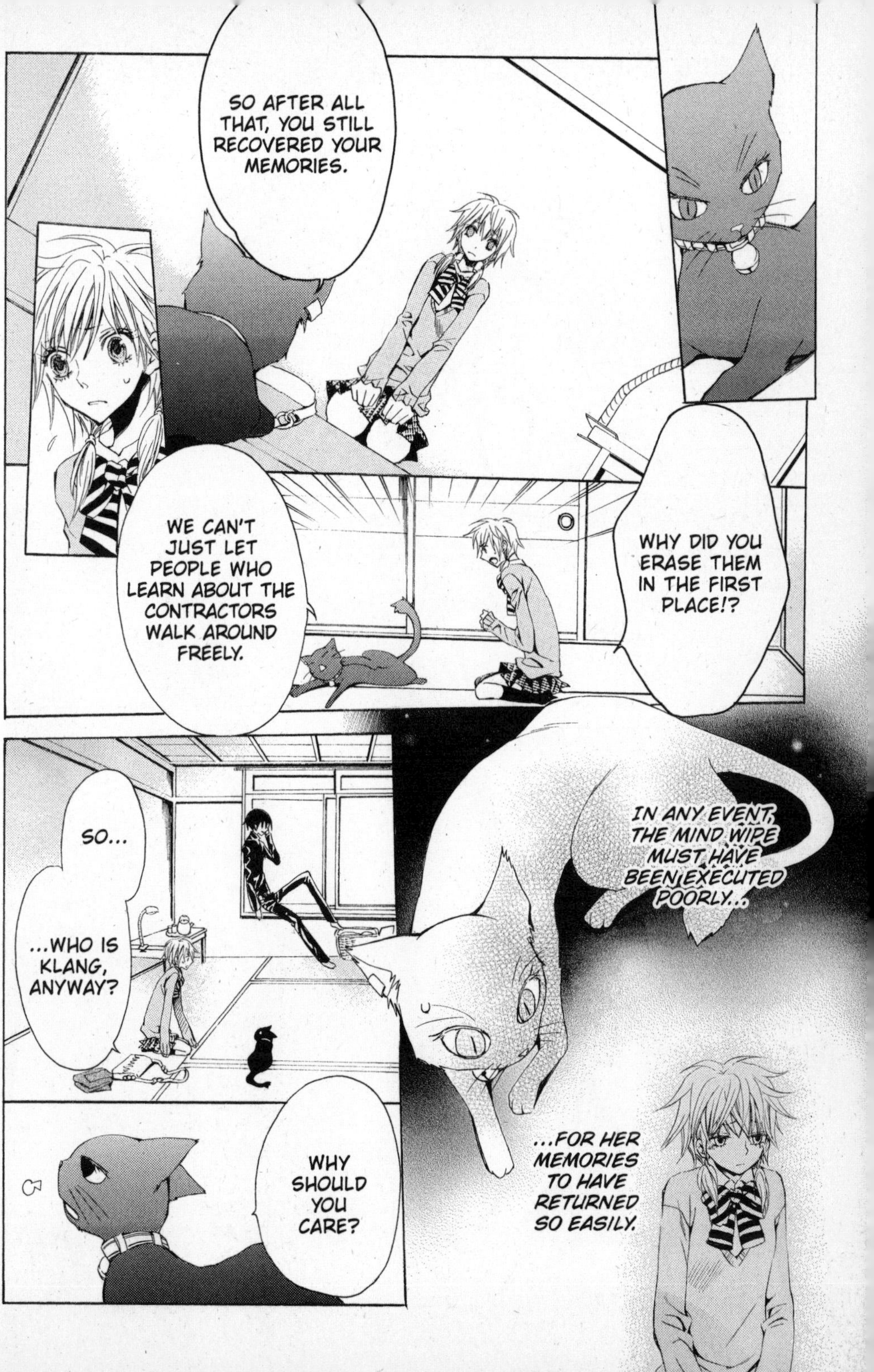
SO AFTER ALL THAT, YOU STILL RECOVERED YOUR MEMORIES.
WHY DID YOU ERASE THEM IN THE FIRST PLACE!?
WE CAN'T JUST LET PEOPLE WHO LEARN ABOUT THE CONTRACTORS WALK AROUND FREELY.
IN ANY EVENT, THE MIND WIPE MUST HAVE BEEN EXECUTED POORLY...
...FOR HER MEMORIES TO HAVE RETURNED SO EASILY.
SO...
...WHO IS KLANG, ANYWAY?
WHY SHOULD YOU CARE?

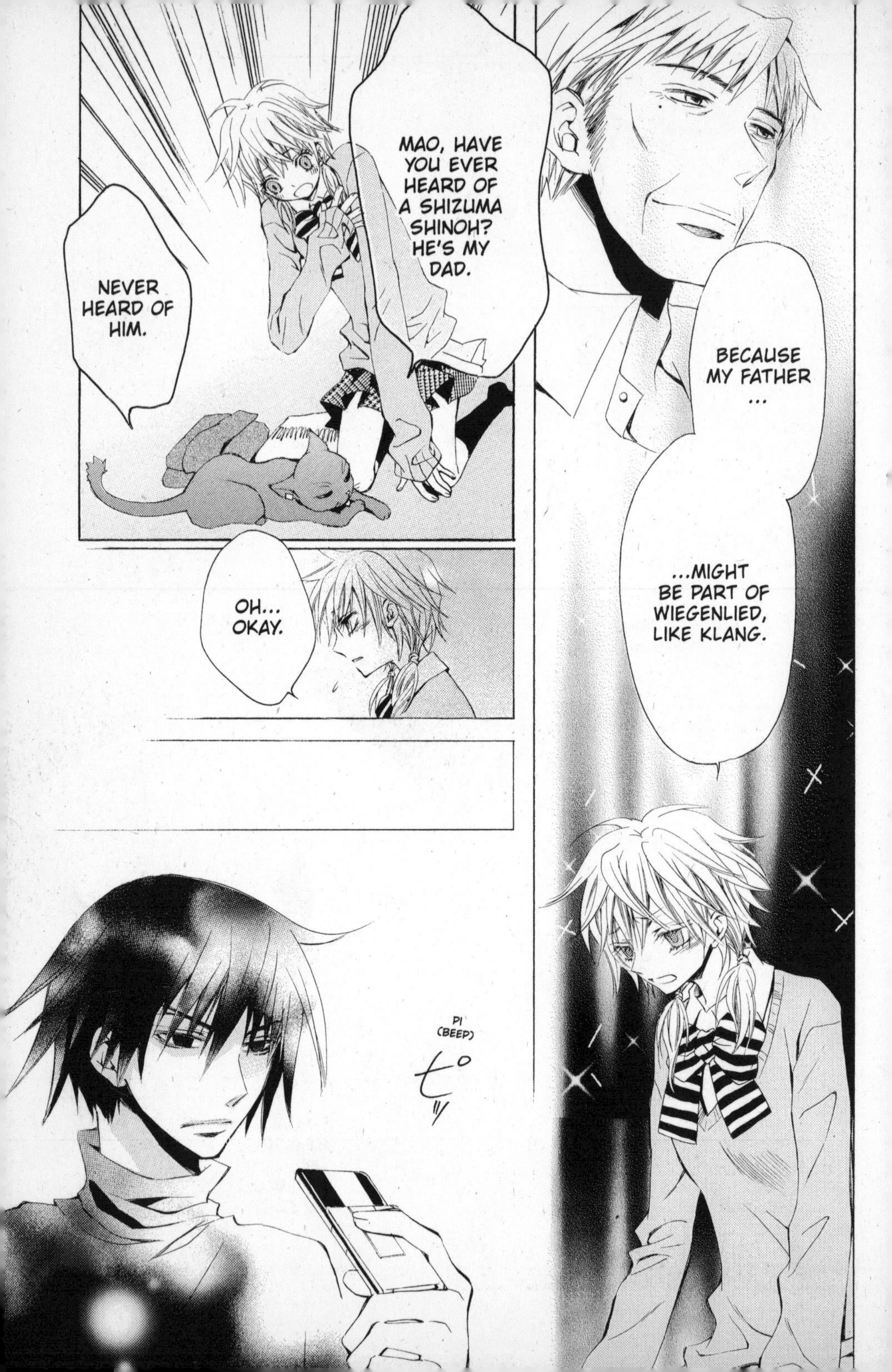
MAO, HAVE YOU EVER HEARD OF A SHIZUMA SHINOH? HE'S MY DAD.
NEVER HEARD OF HIM.
OH... OKAY.
BECAUSE MY FATHER ...
...MIGHT BE PART OF WIEGENLIED, LIKE KLANG.
PI (BEEP)

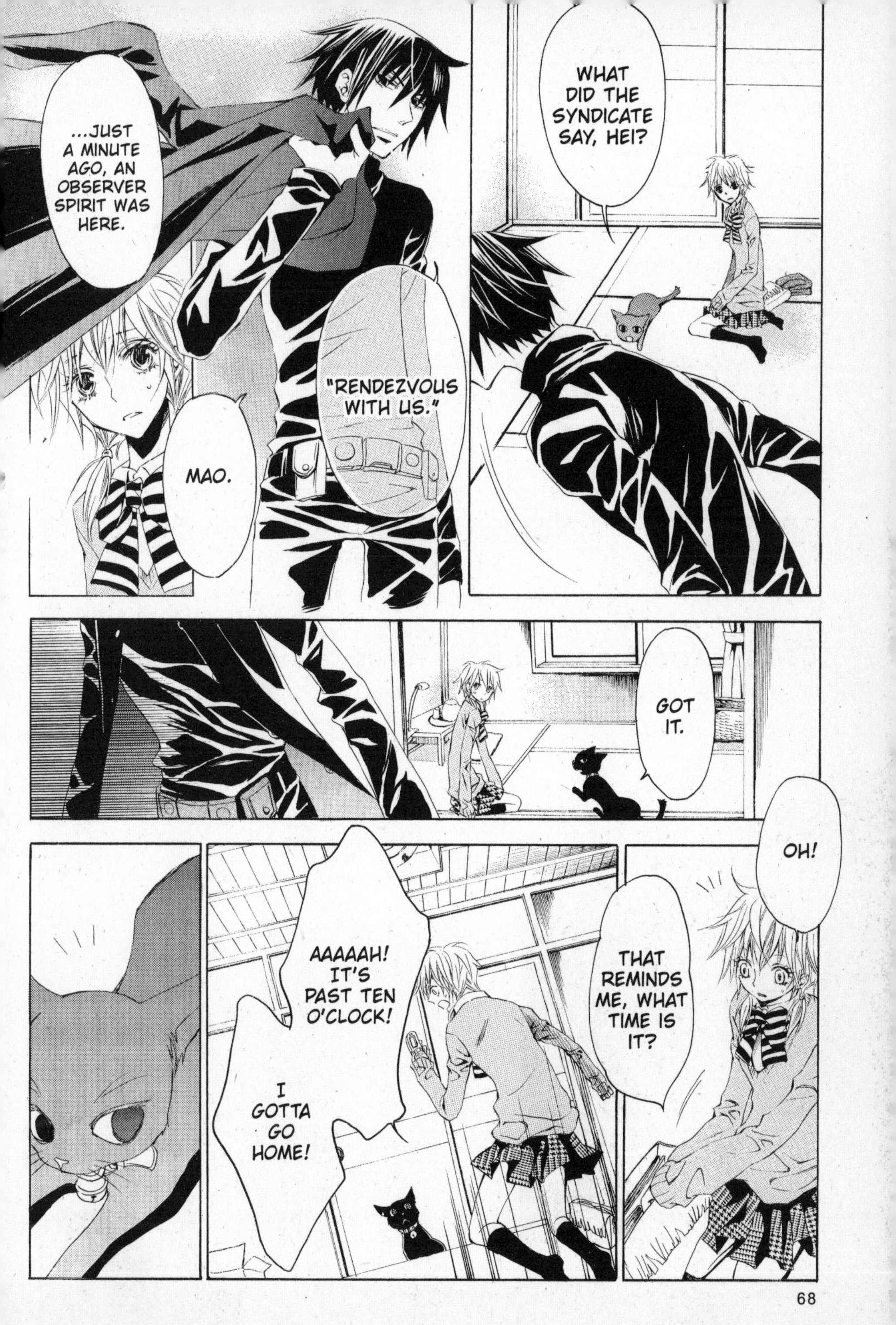
WHAT DID THE SYNDICATE SAY, HEI?
...JUST A MINUTE AGO, AN OBSERVER SPIRIT WAS HERE.
"RENDEZVOUS WITH US."
MAO.
GOT IT.
OH!
THAT REMINDS ME, WHAT TIME IS IT?
AAAAAH! IT'S PAST TEN O'CLOCK!
I GOTTA GO HOME!

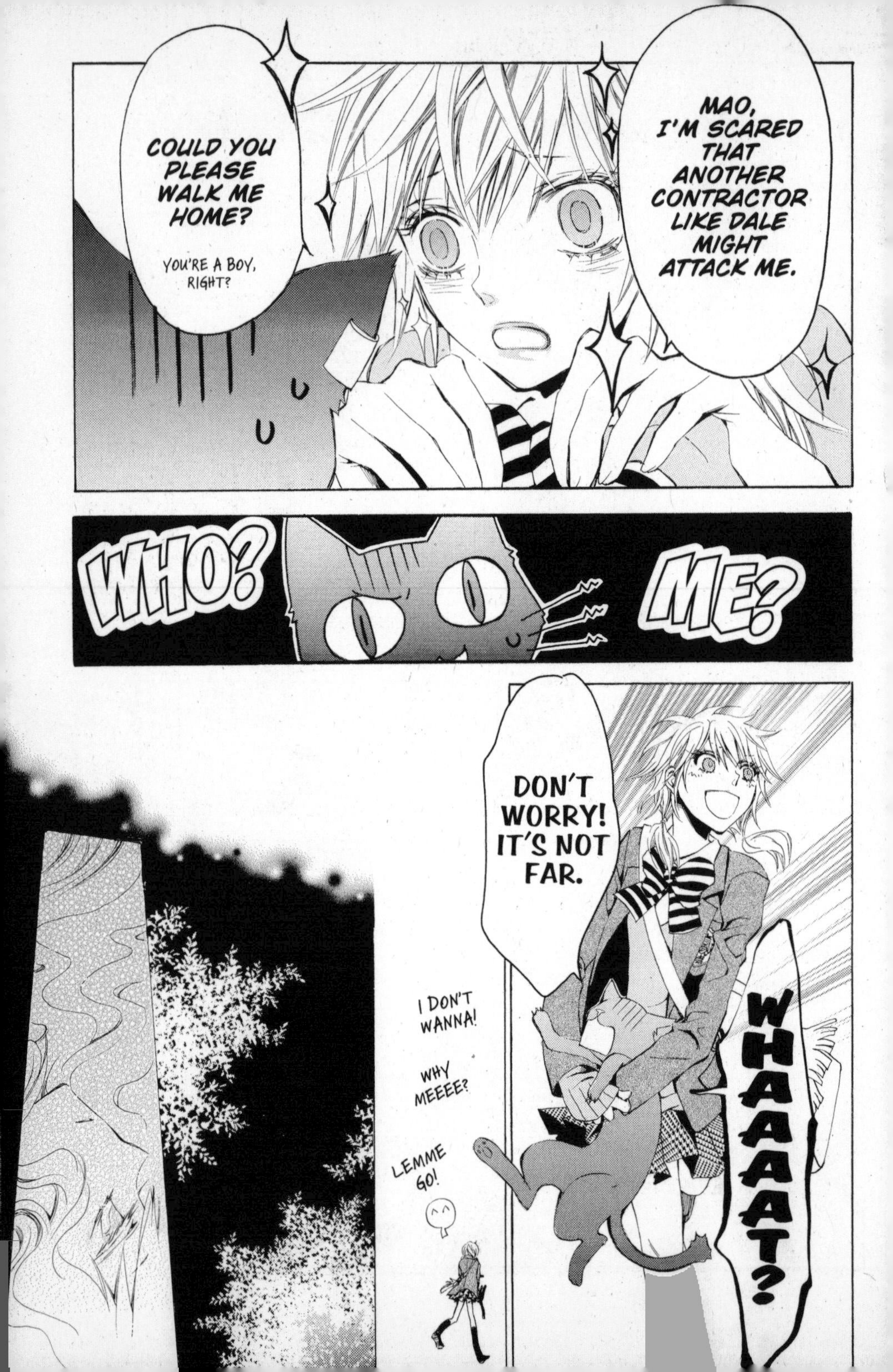
MAO, I'M SCARED THAT ANOTHER CONTRACTOR LIKE DALE MIGHT ATTACK ME.
COULD YOU PLEASE WALK ME HOME?
YOU'RE A BOY, RIGHT?
WHO? ME?
DON'T WORRY! IT'S NOT FAR.
WHAAAAT?
I DON'T WANNA!
WHY MEEEE?
LEMME GO!

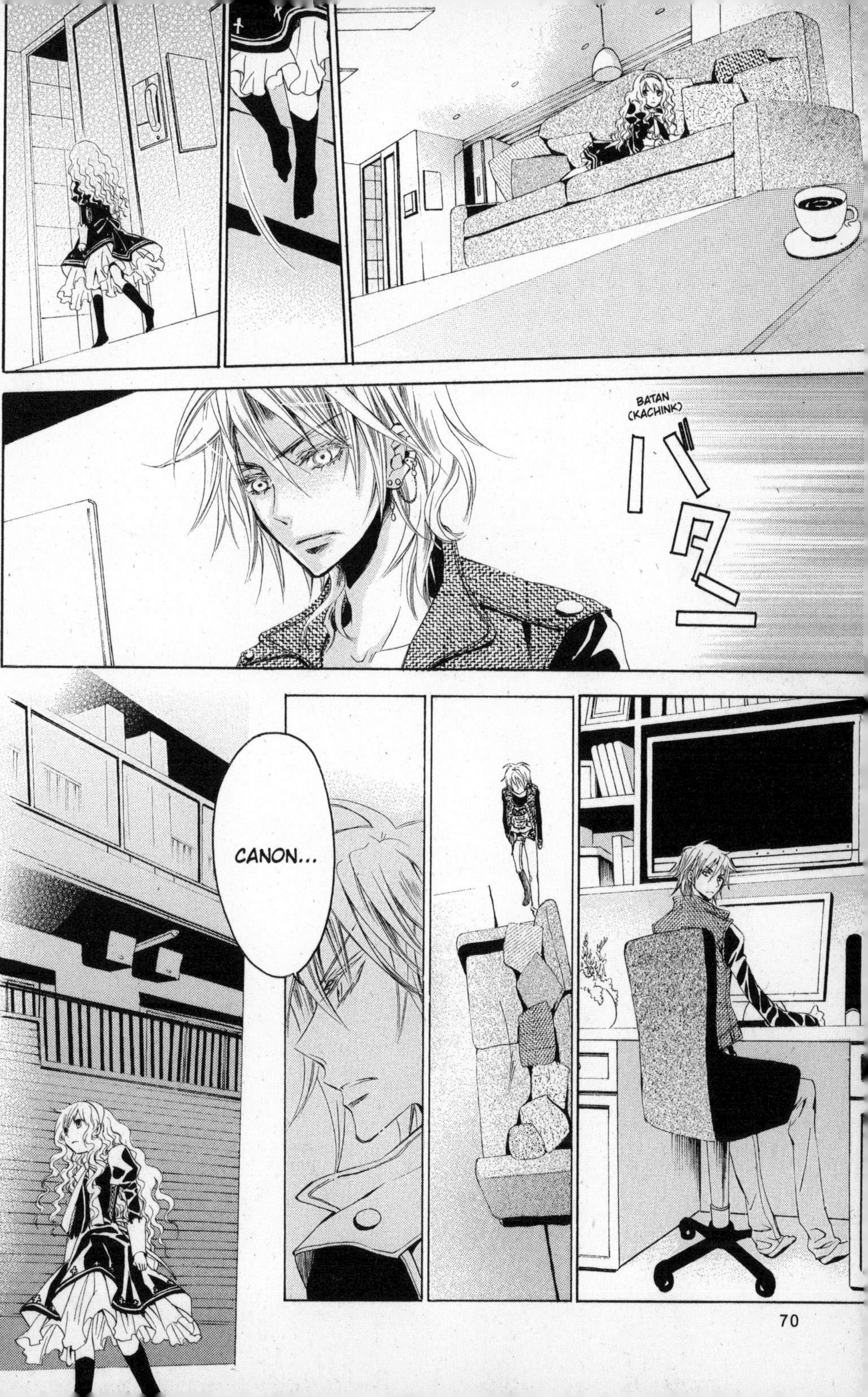
BATAN
(KACHINK)
バタン
CANON...

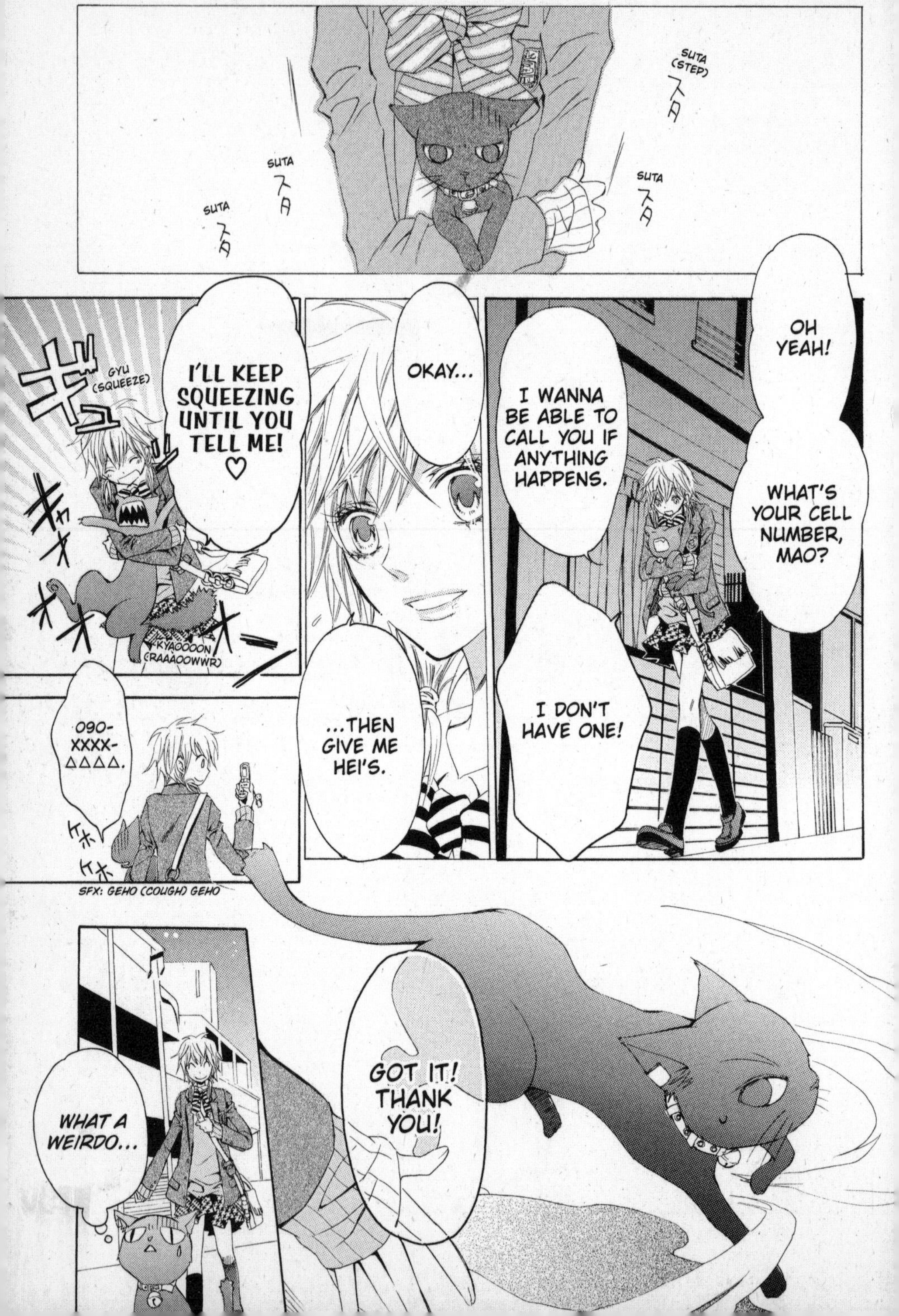
SUTA (STEP)
SUTA
SUTA
SUTA
OH YEAH!
WHAT'S YOUR CELL NUMBER, MAO?
I WANNA BE ABLE TO CALL YOU IF ANYTHING HAPPENS.
I DON'T HAVE ONE!
OKAY...
...THEN GIVE ME HEI'S.
I'LL KEEP SQUEEZING UNTIL YOU TELL ME! ♡
GYU (SQUEEZE)
KYAOOOON (RAAAOOWWR)
090-XXXX-△△△△.
SFX: GEHO (COUGH) GEHO
GOT IT! THANK YOU!
WHAT A WEIRDO...

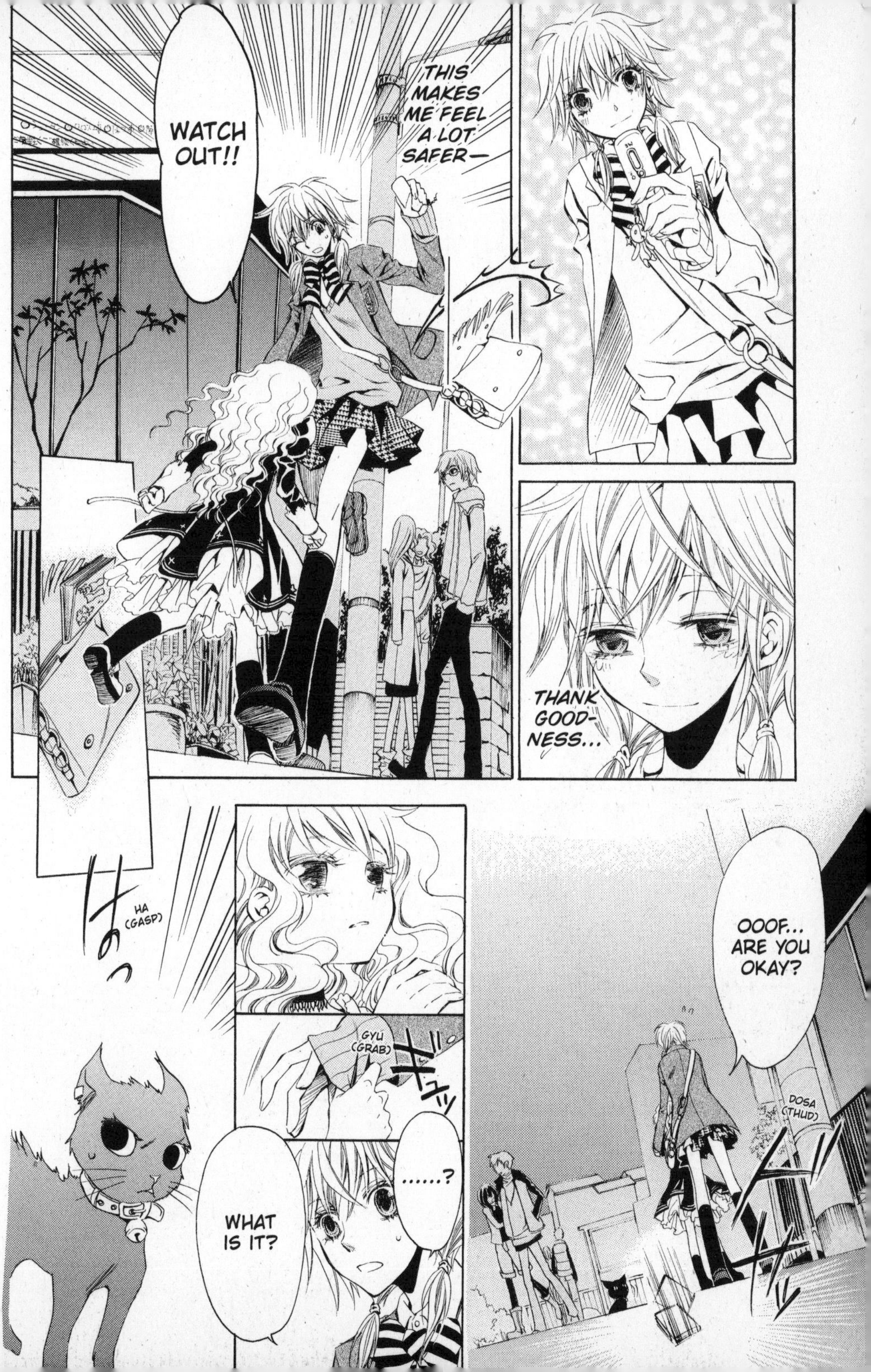
THANK GOODNESS...
THIS MAKES ME FEEL A LOT SAFER—
WATCH OUT!!
OOOF... ARE YOU OKAY?
DOSA (THUD)
GYU (GRAB)
......?
WHAT IS IT?
HA (GASP)

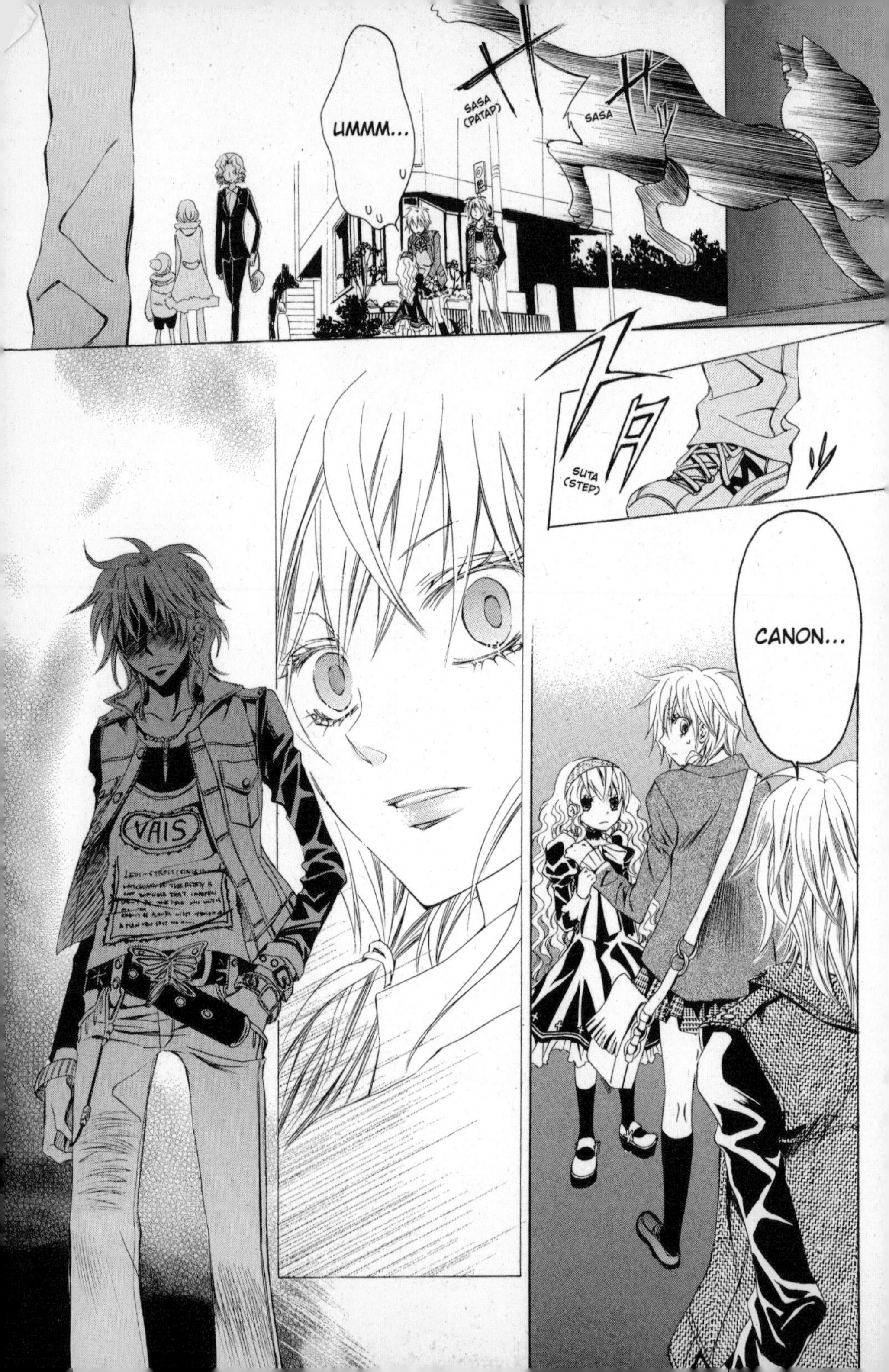
SASA
SASA
(PATAP)
UMMM...
SUTA
(STEP)
CANON...
VAIS

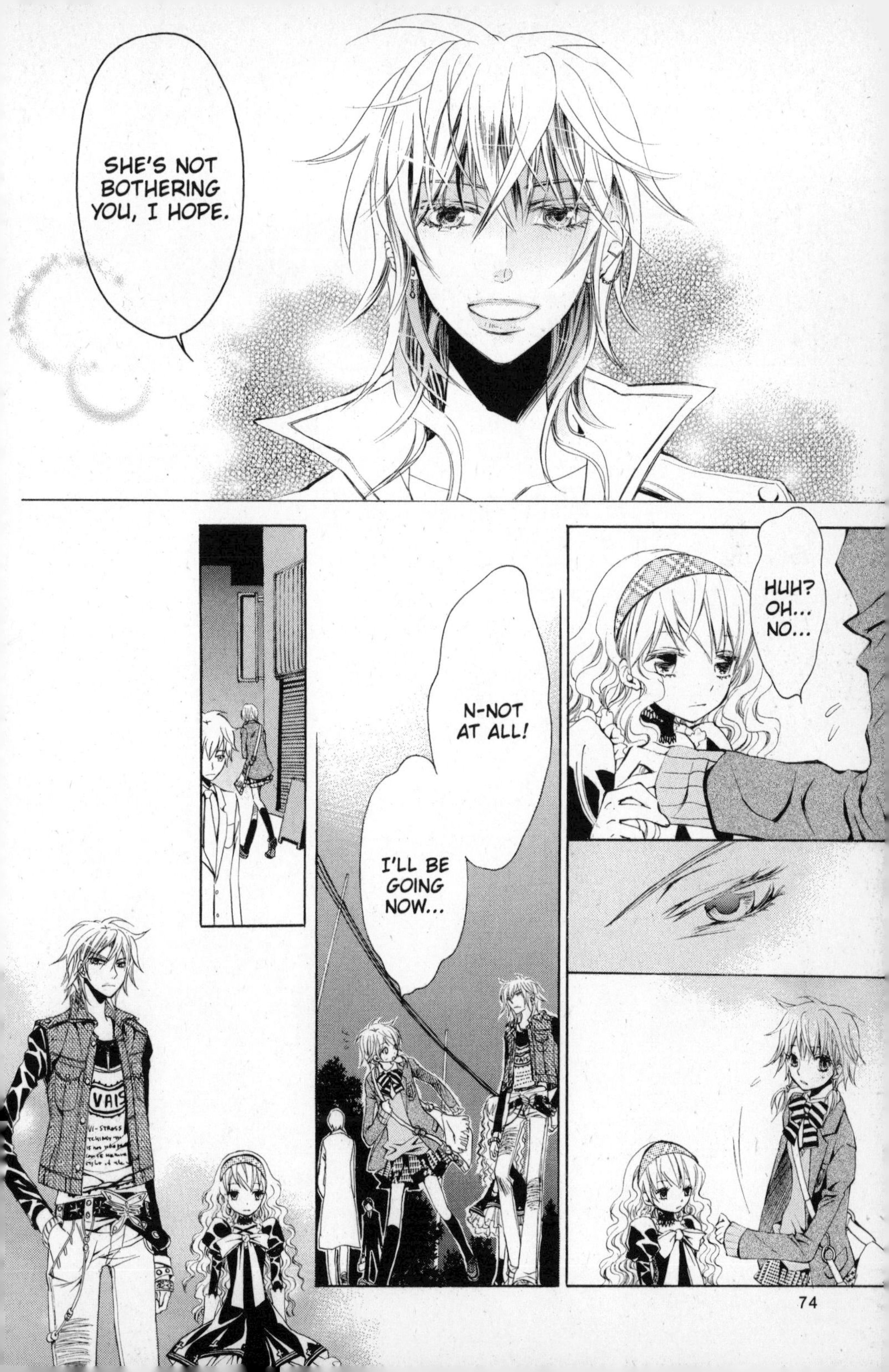
SHE'S NOT BOTHERING YOU, I HOPE.
HUH? OH... NO...
N-NOT AT ALL!
I'LL BE GOING NOW...

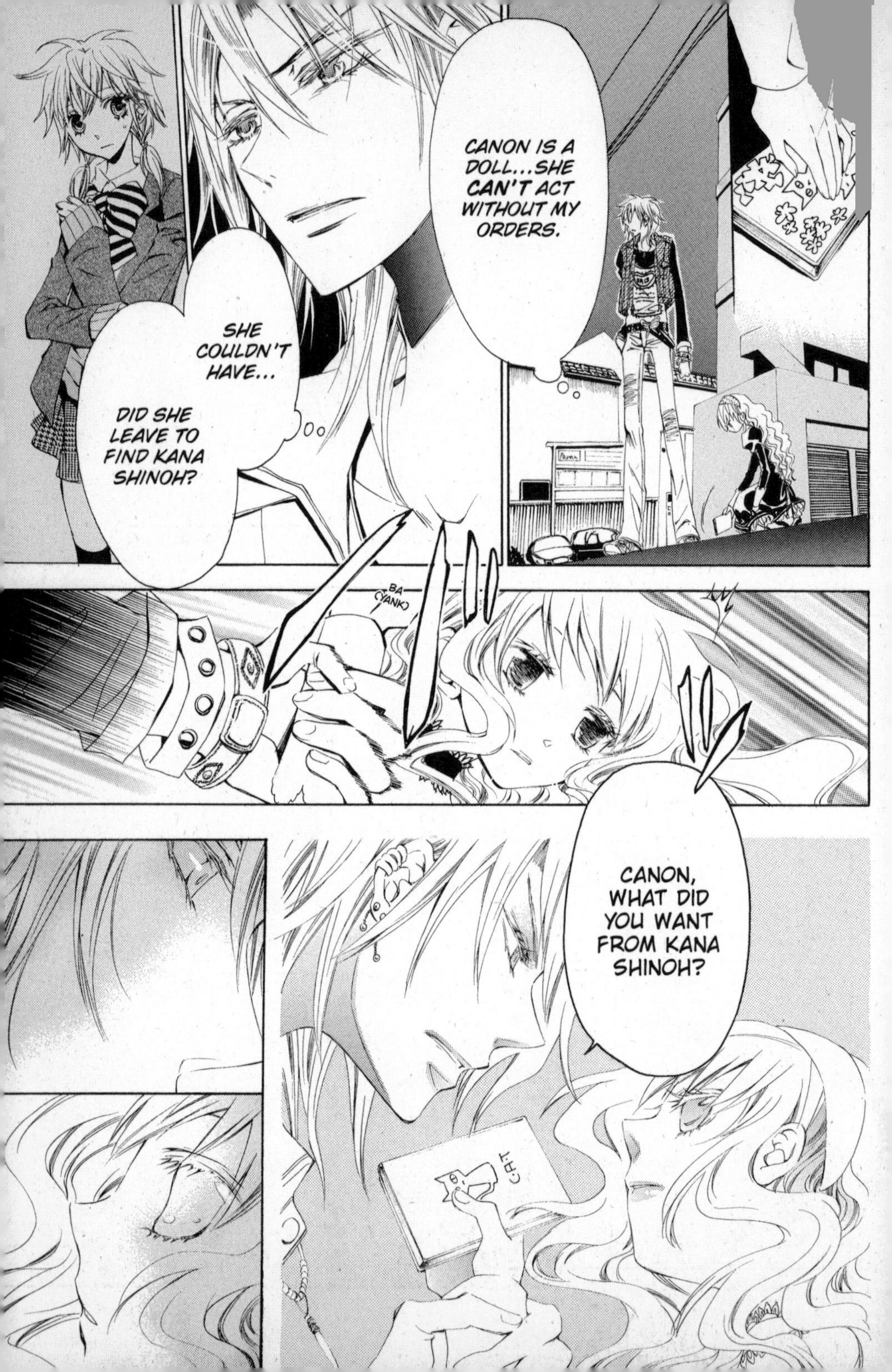
CANON IS A DOLL...SHE CAN'T ACT WITHOUT MY ORDERS.
SHE COULDN'T HAVE...
DID SHE LEAVE TO FIND KANA SHINOH?
BA (YANK)
CANON, WHAT DID YOU WANT FROM KANA SHINOH?
C.A.T

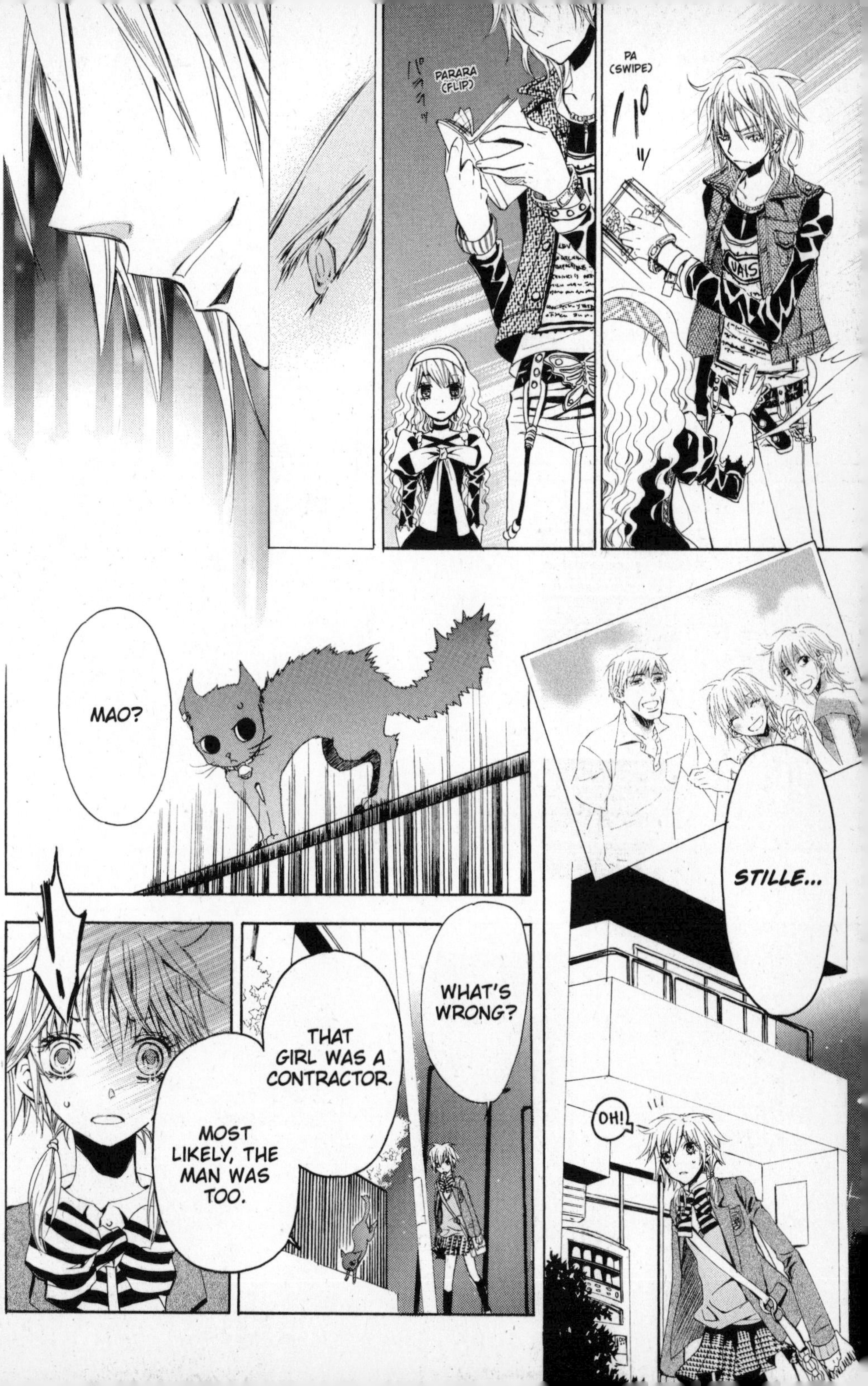
PA (SWIPE)
PARARA (FLIP)
STILLE...
MAO?
OH!
WHAT'S WRONG?
THAT GIRL WAS A CONTRACTOR.
MOST LIKELY, THE MAN WAS TOO.

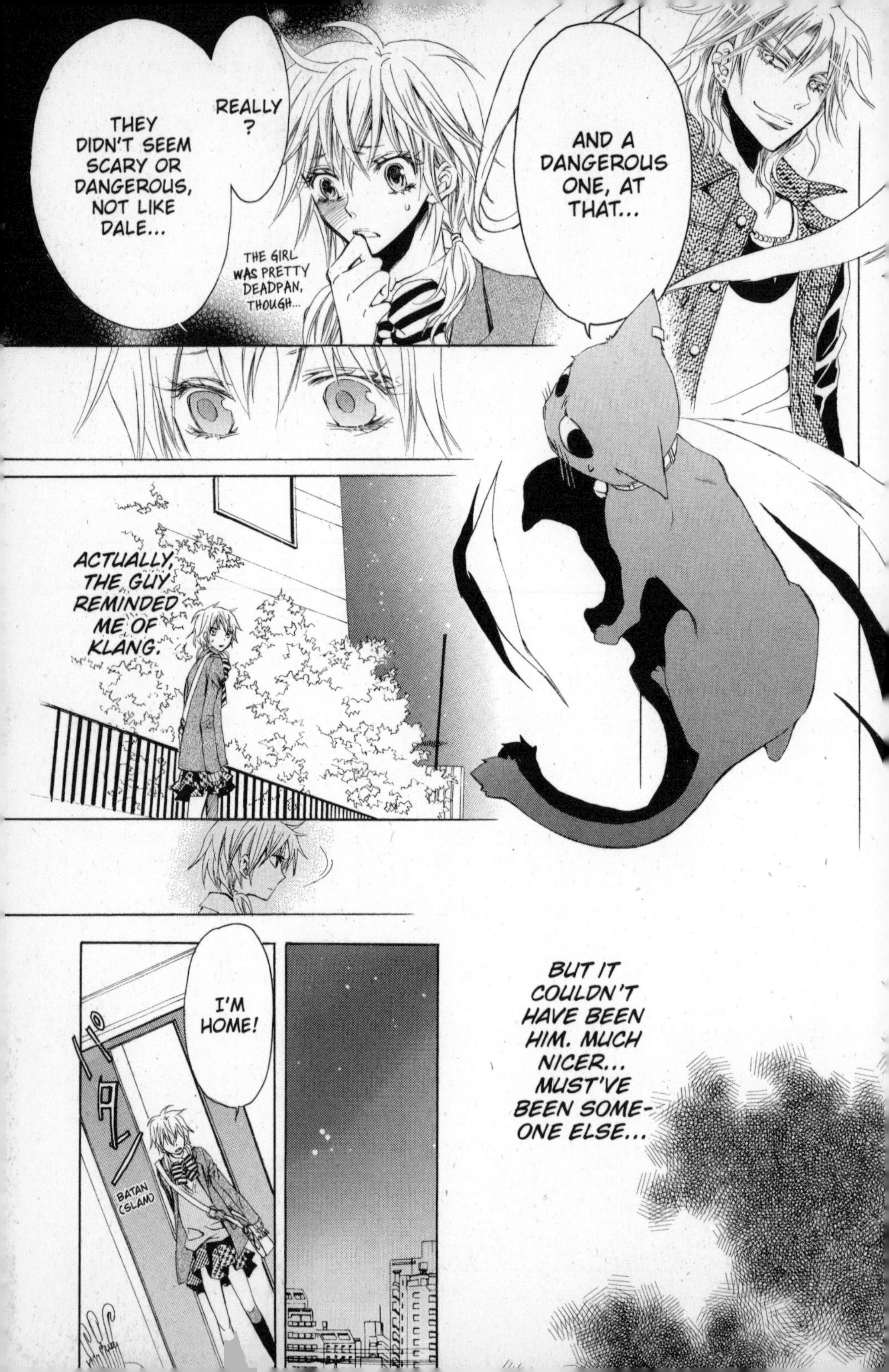
AND A DANGEROUS ONE, AT THAT...
REALLY?
THEY DIDN'T SEEM SCARY OR DANGEROUS, NOT LIKE DALE...
THE GIRL WAS PRETTY DEADPAN, THOUGH...
ACTUALLY THE GUY REMINDED ME OF KLANG.
BUT IT COULDN'T HAVE BEEN HIM. MUCH NICER... MUST'VE BEEN SOMEONE ELSE...
I'M HOME!
BATAN (SLAM)

SORRY...

YOU'RE HOME LATE, KANA.

HURRY UP AND EAT YOUR DINNER...

...WHILE YOUR DADDY'S STILL AT THE TABLE.

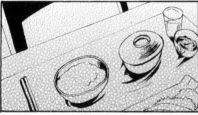

HONEY, DADDY THINKS YOU'VE BEEN ACTING STRANGE LATELY TOO.

ALL THAT TALK ABOUT SEARCHING FOR HIM...

MOM...

...DAD'S NOT HERE.

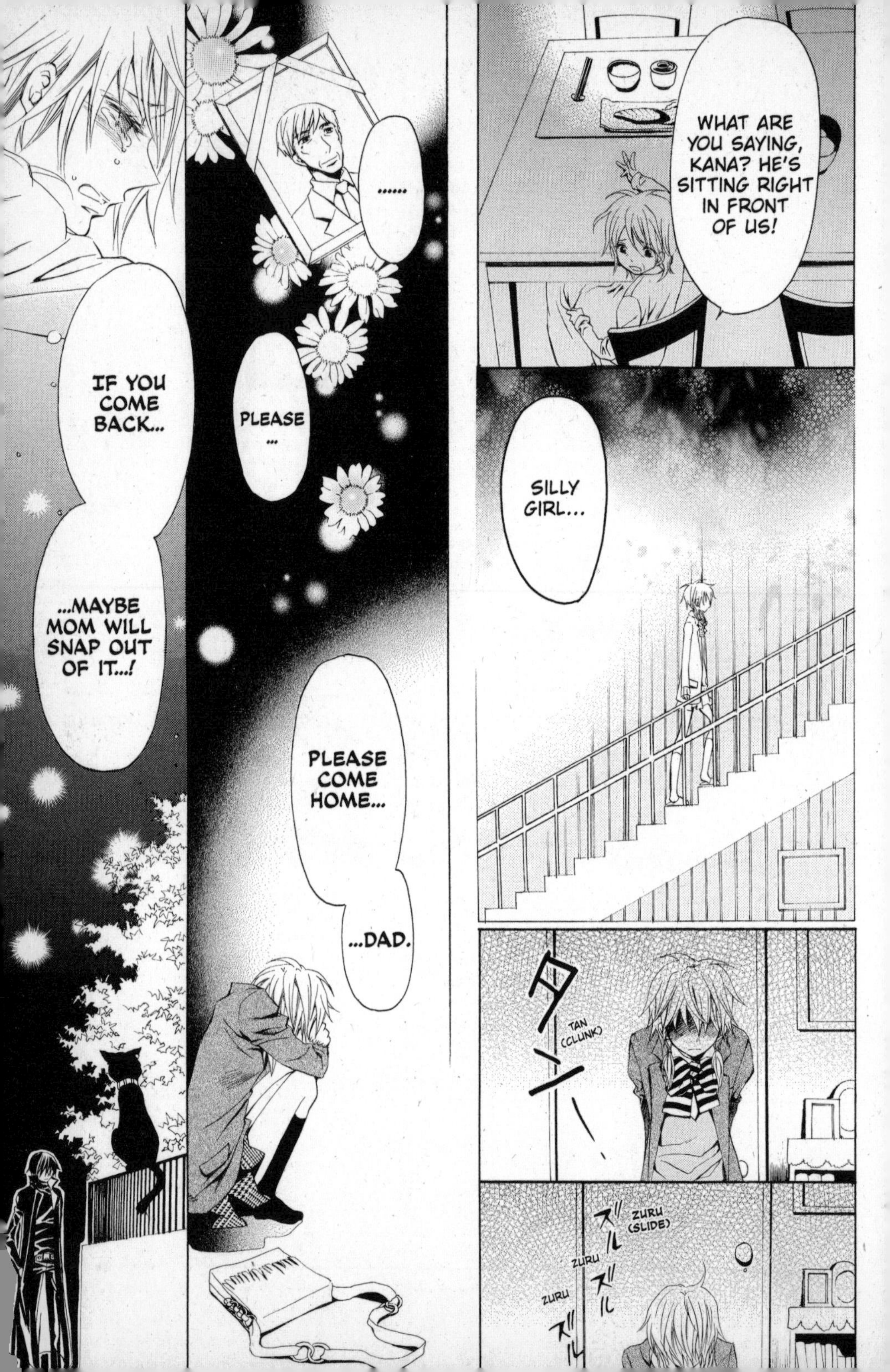
WHAT ARE YOU SAYING, KANA? HE'S SITTING RIGHT IN FRONT OF US!
SILLY GIRL...
タン
TAN (CLUNK)
ズル
ZURU (SLIDE)
ズル
ZURU
ズル
ZURU
......
PLEASE ...
PLEASE COME HOME...
...DAD.
IF YOU COME BACK...
...MAYBE MOM WILL SNAP OUT OF IT...!

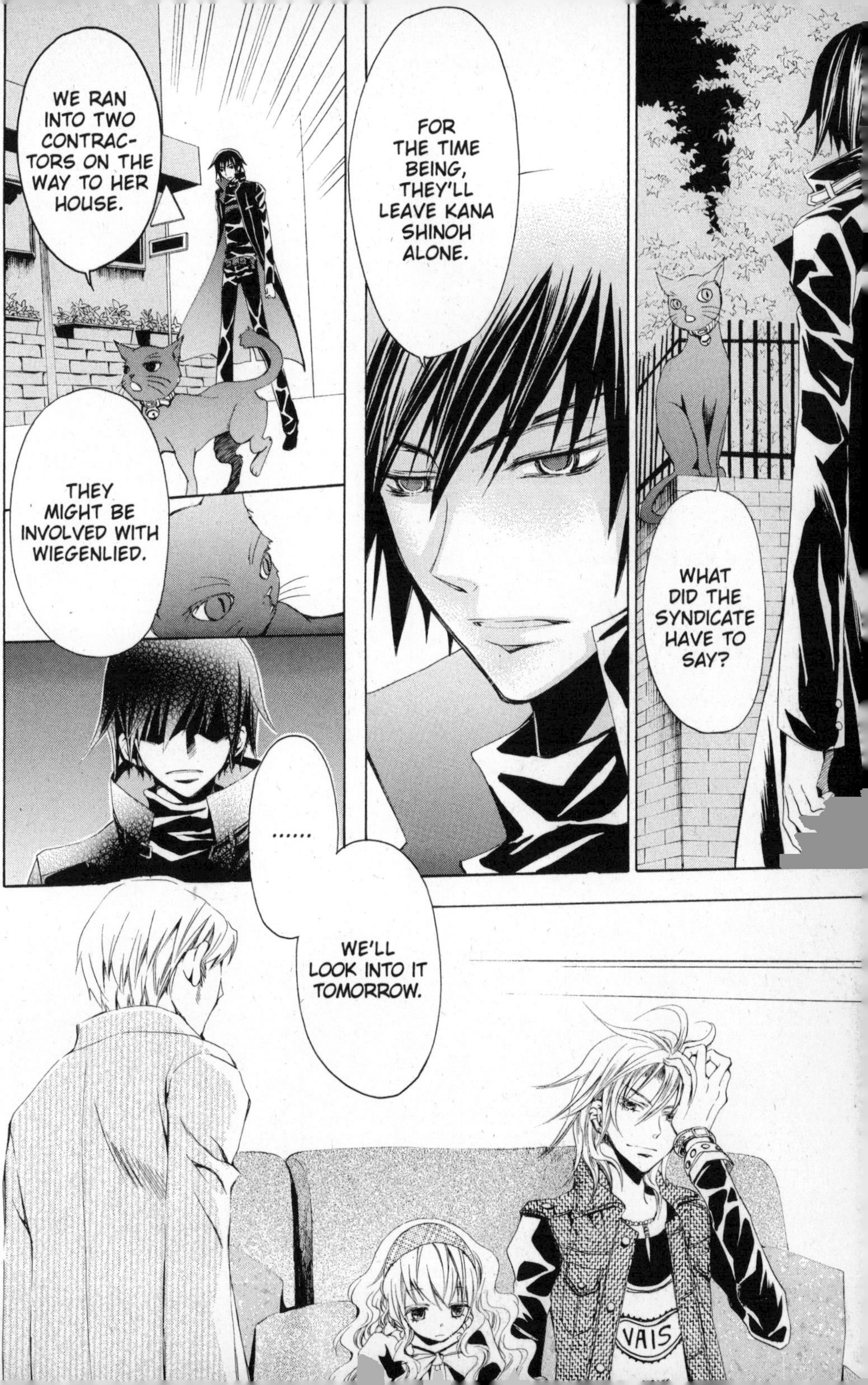
WHAT DID THE SYNDICATE HAVE TO SAY?
FOR THE TIME BEING, THEY'LL LEAVE KANA SHINOH ALONE.
WE RAN INTO TWO CONTRAC-TORS ON THE WAY TO HER HOUSE.
THEY MIGHT BE INVOLVED WITH WIEGENLIED.
......
WE'LL LOOK INTO IT TOMORROW.
VAIS

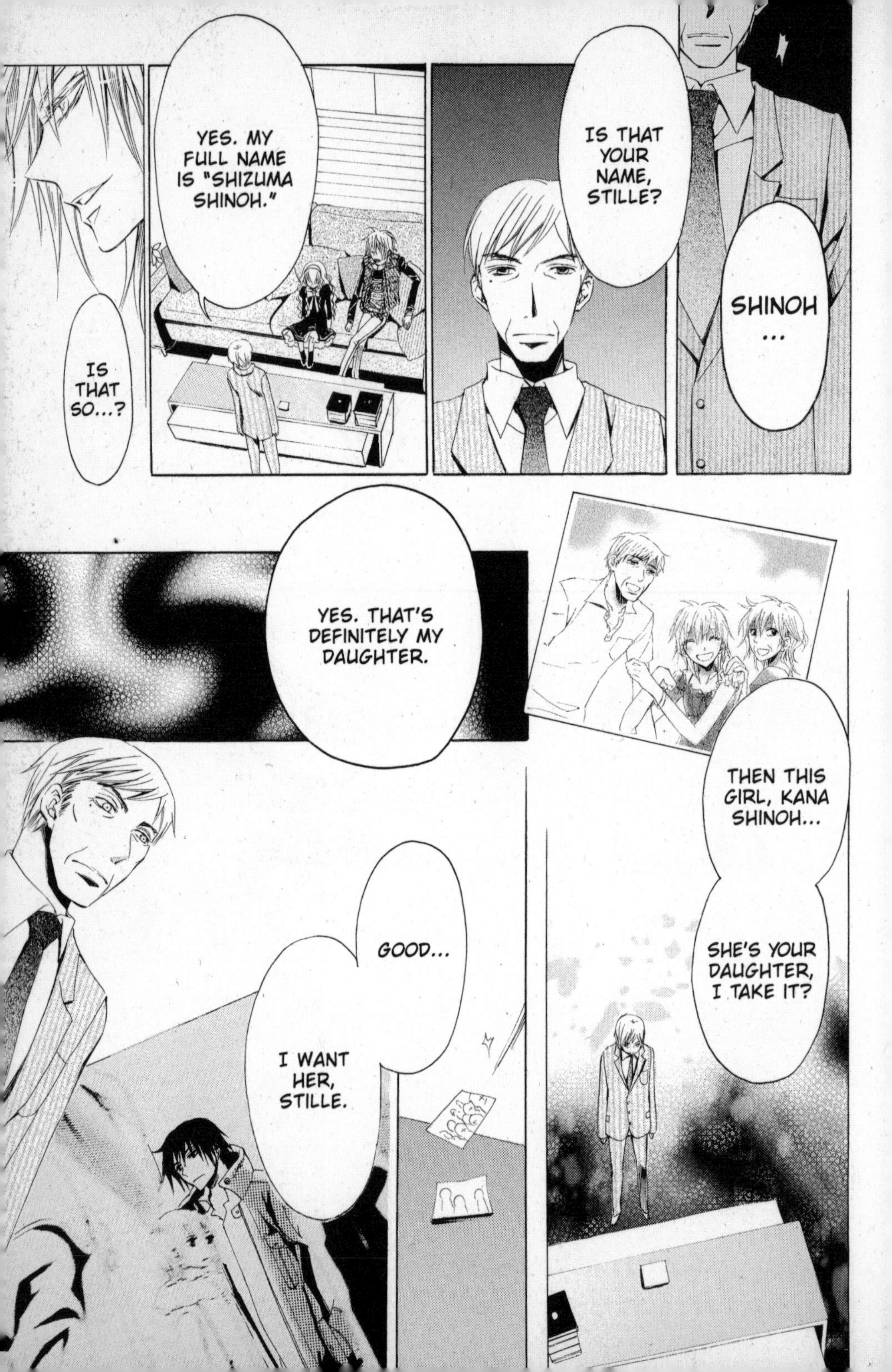

IS THAT YOUR NAME, STILLE?
SHINOH...
YES. MY FULL NAME IS "SHIZUMA SHINOH."
IS THAT SO...?
THEN THIS GIRL, KANA SHINOH...
SHE'S YOUR DAUGHTER, I TAKE IT?
YES. THAT'S DEFINITELY MY DAUGHTER.
GOOD...
I WANT HER, STILLE.

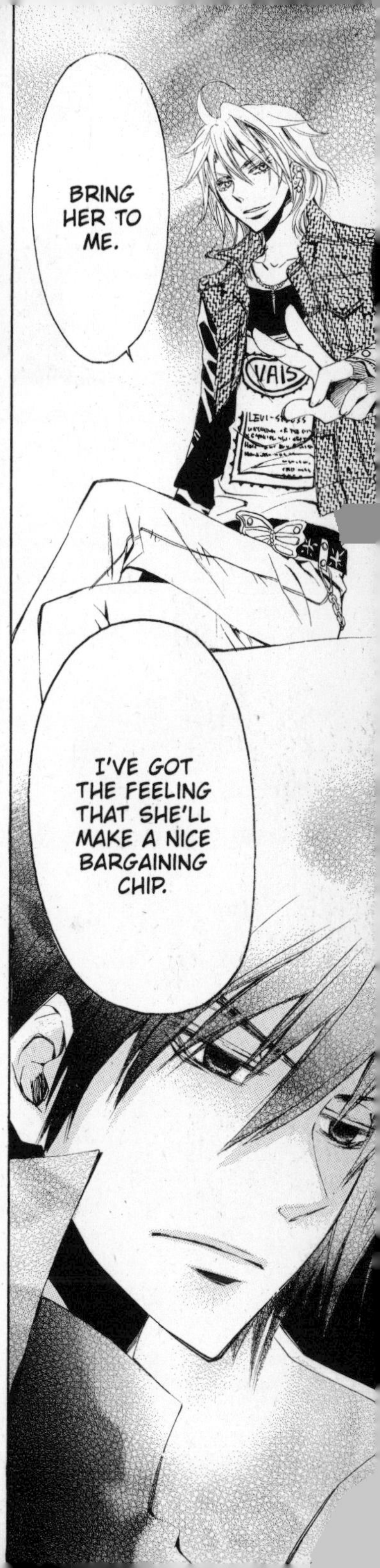
BRING HER TO ME.
I'VE GOT THE FEELING THAT SHE'LL MAKE A NICE BARGAINING CHIP.

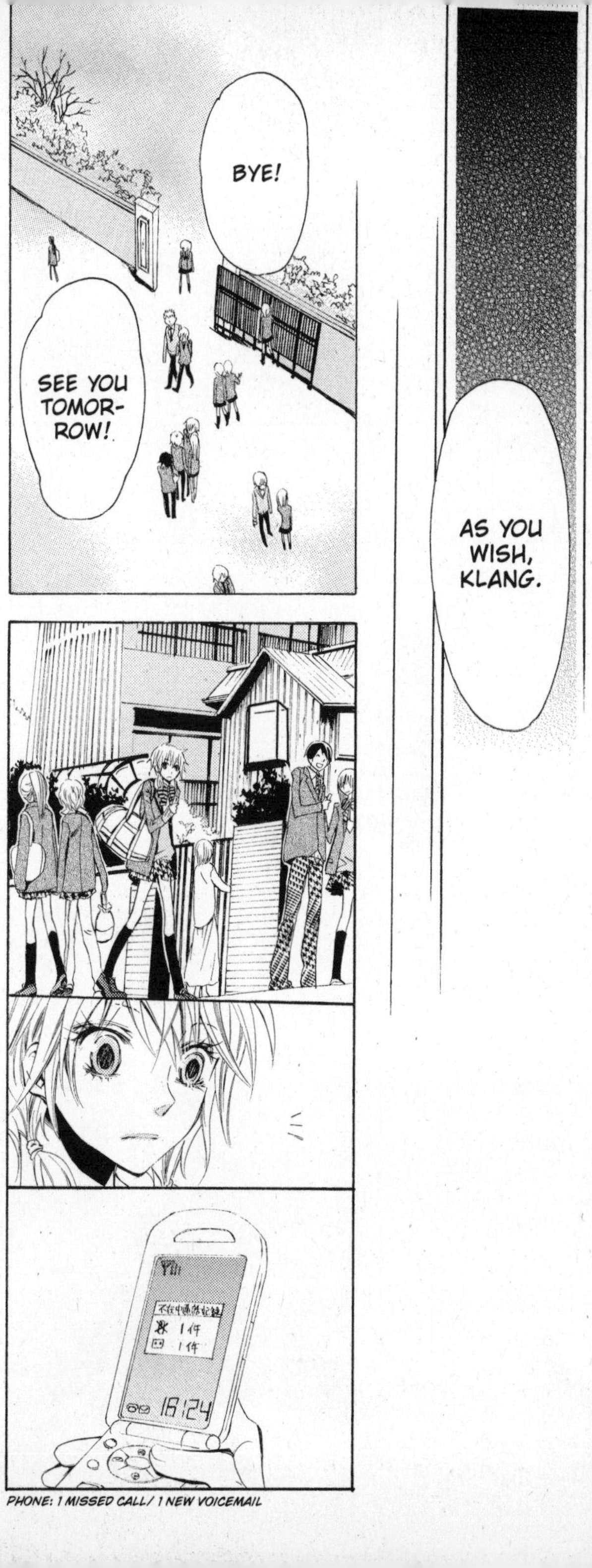
AS YOU WISH, KLANG.
BYE!
SEE YOU TOMOR-ROW!

PHONE: 1 MISSED CALL/ 1 NEW VOICEMAIL

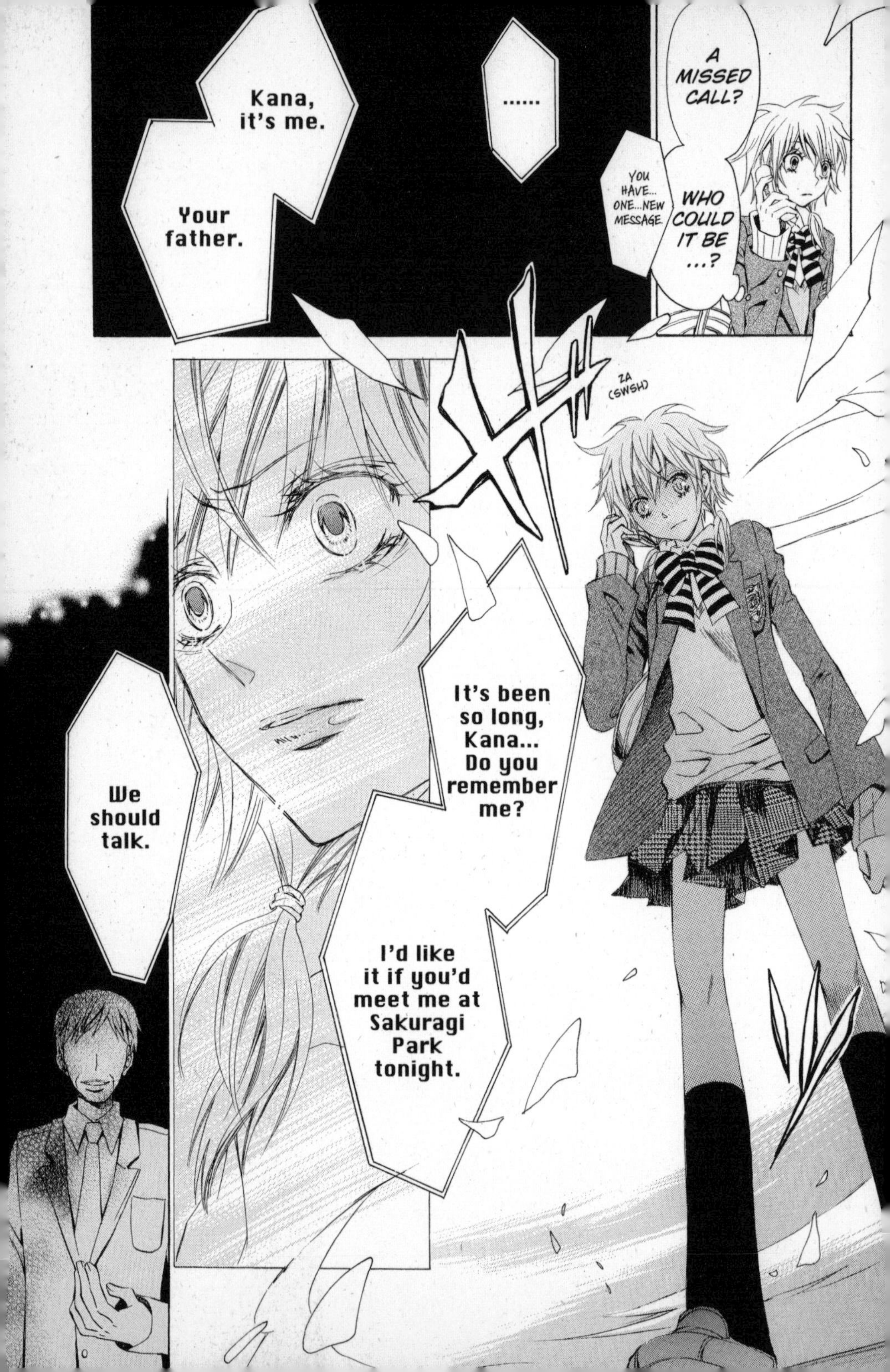
A MISSED CALL?
WHO COULD IT BE ...?
YOU HAVE... ONE...NEW MESSAGE.
......
Kana, it's me.
Your father.
ZA (SWSH)
It's been so long, Kana... Do you remember me?
I'd like it if you'd meet me at Sakuragi Park tonight.
We should talk.

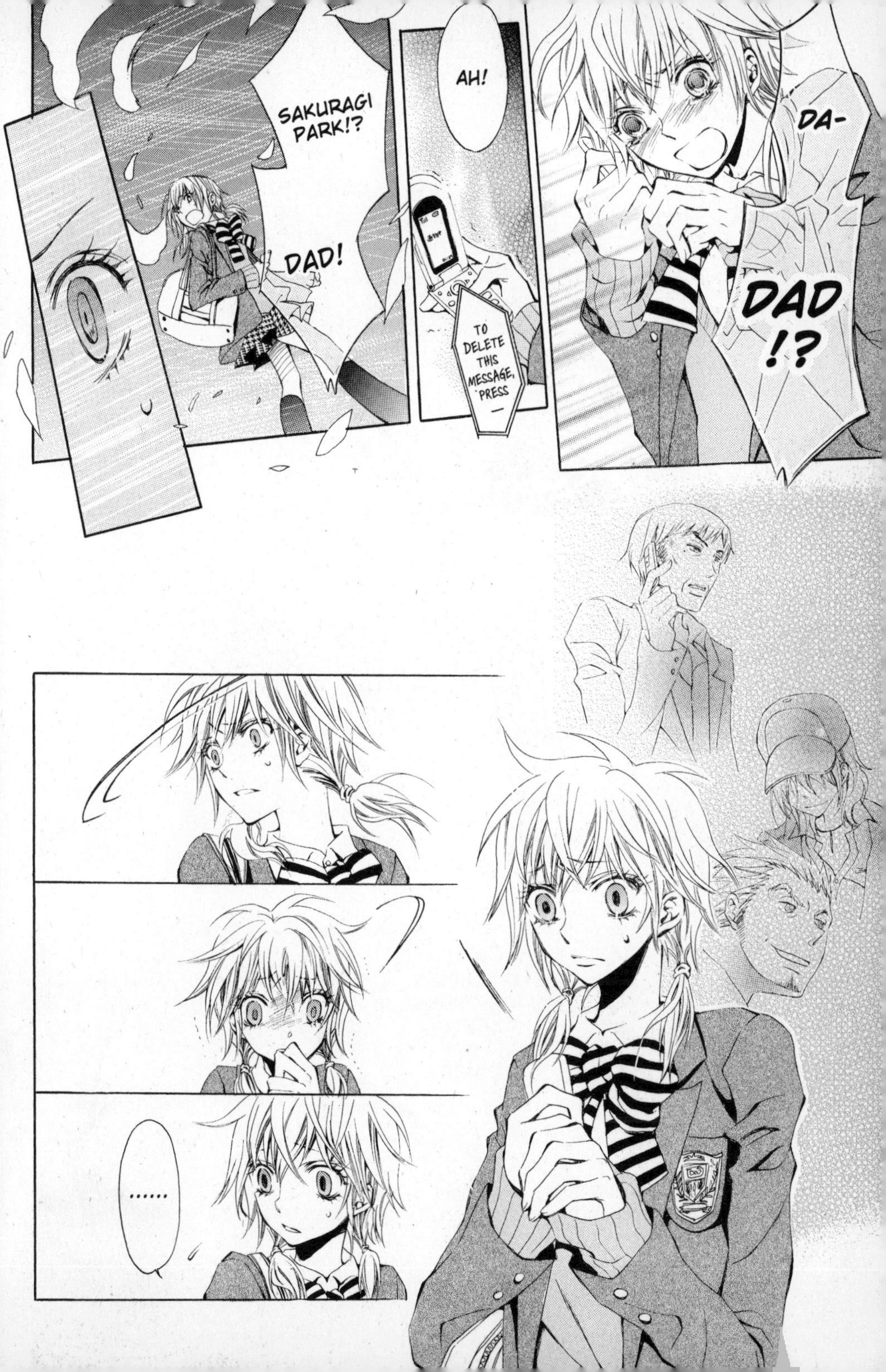
DA-
DAD!?
AH!
TO DELETE THIS MESSAGE, PRESS —
SAKURAGI PARK!?
DAD!
……

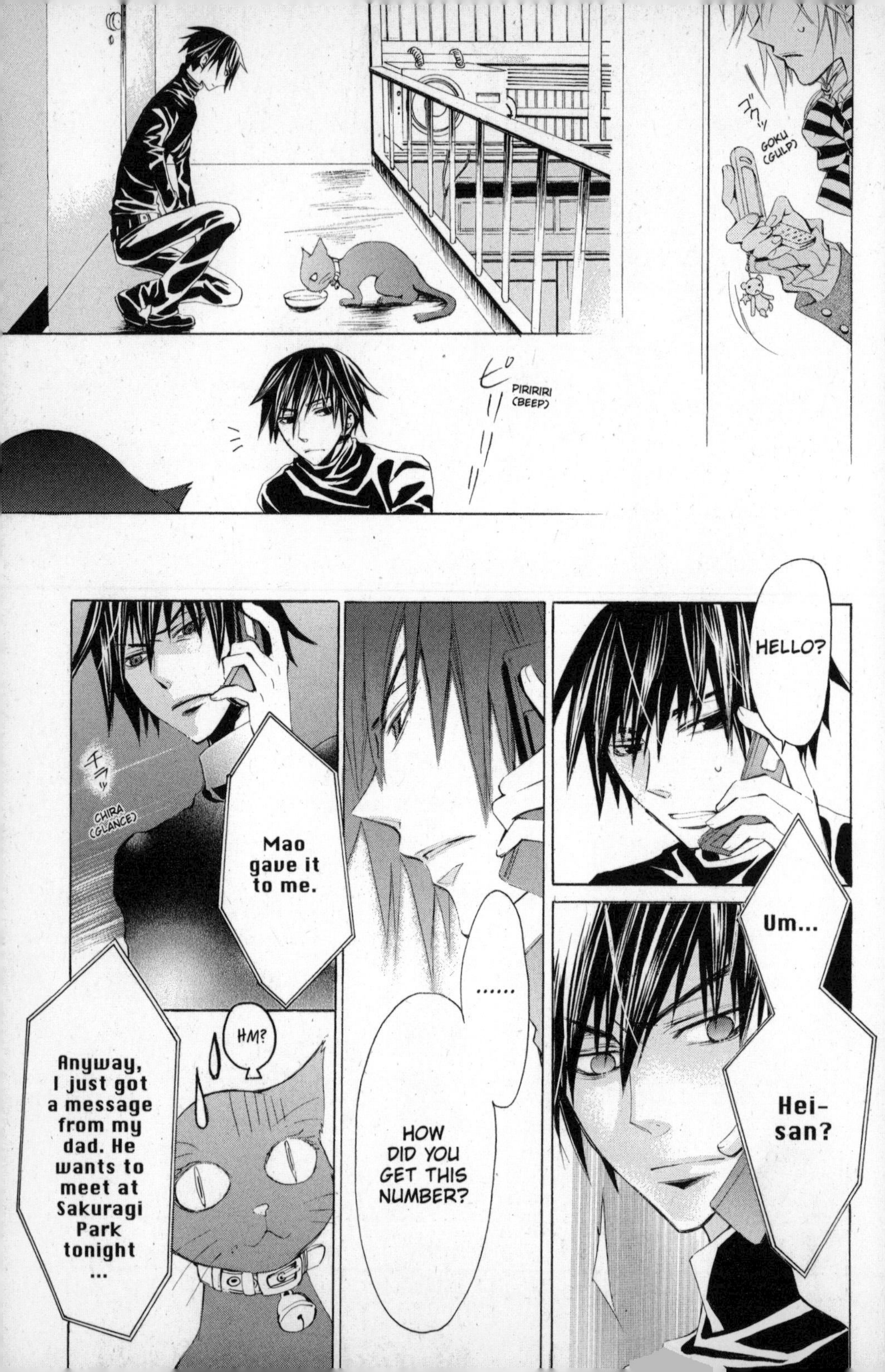

ゴクッ
GOKU (GULP)
PIRIRIRI (BEEP)
HELLO?
Um...
Hei-san?
......
HOW DID YOU GET THIS NUMBER?
チラッ
CHIRA (GLANCE)
Mao gave it to me.
HM?
Anyway, I just got a message from my dad. He wants to meet at Sakuragi Park tonight ...

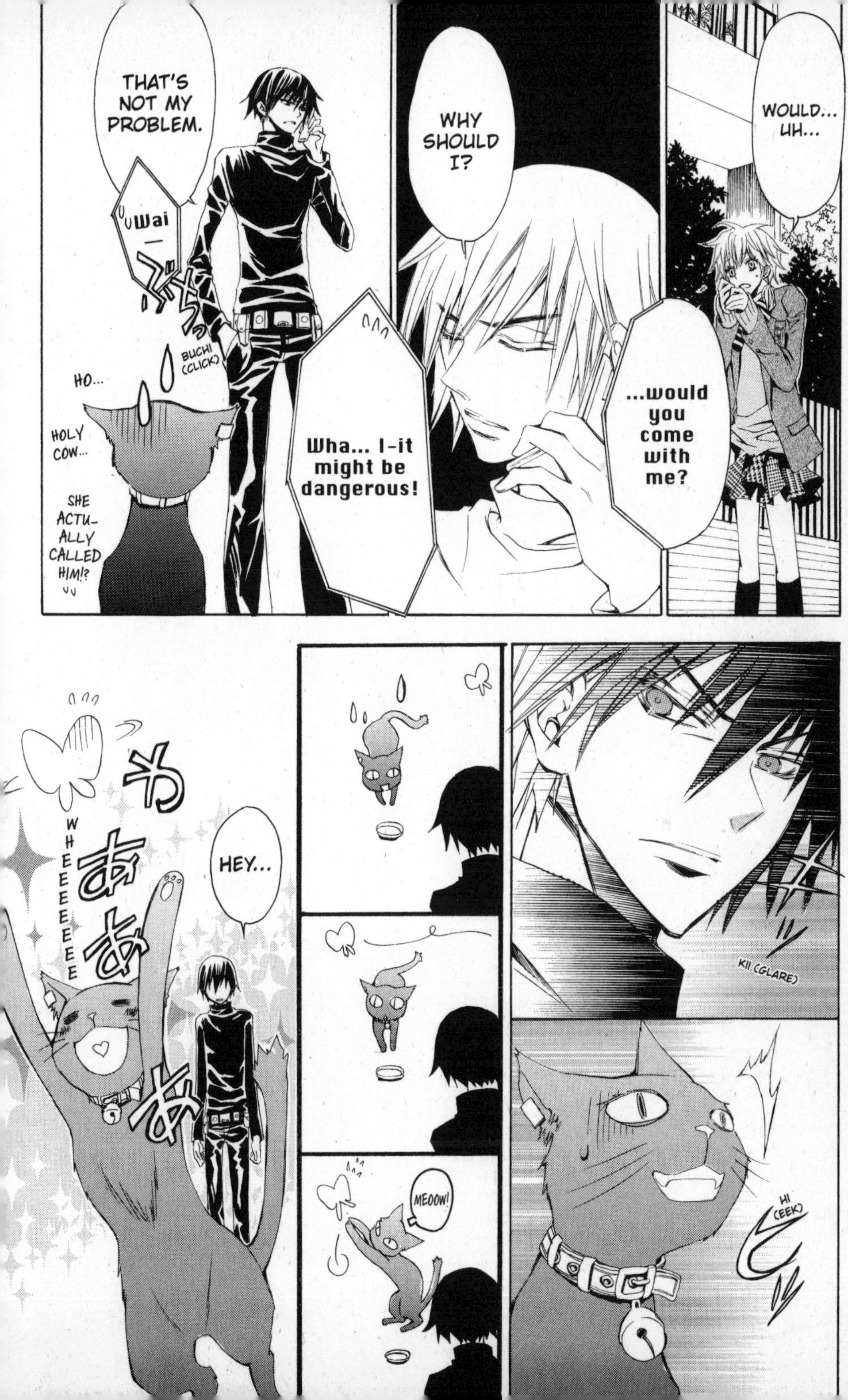
WOULD... UH...
...would you come with me?
WHY SHOULD I?
Wha... I-it might be dangerous!
THAT'S NOT MY PROBLEM.
Wai—
ぶちっ
BUCHI (CLICK)
HO...
HOLY COW...
SHE ACTU-ALLY CALLED HIM!?
KII (GLARE)
HI (EEK)
MEOOW!
HEY...
わあああ
WHEEEEEEEE

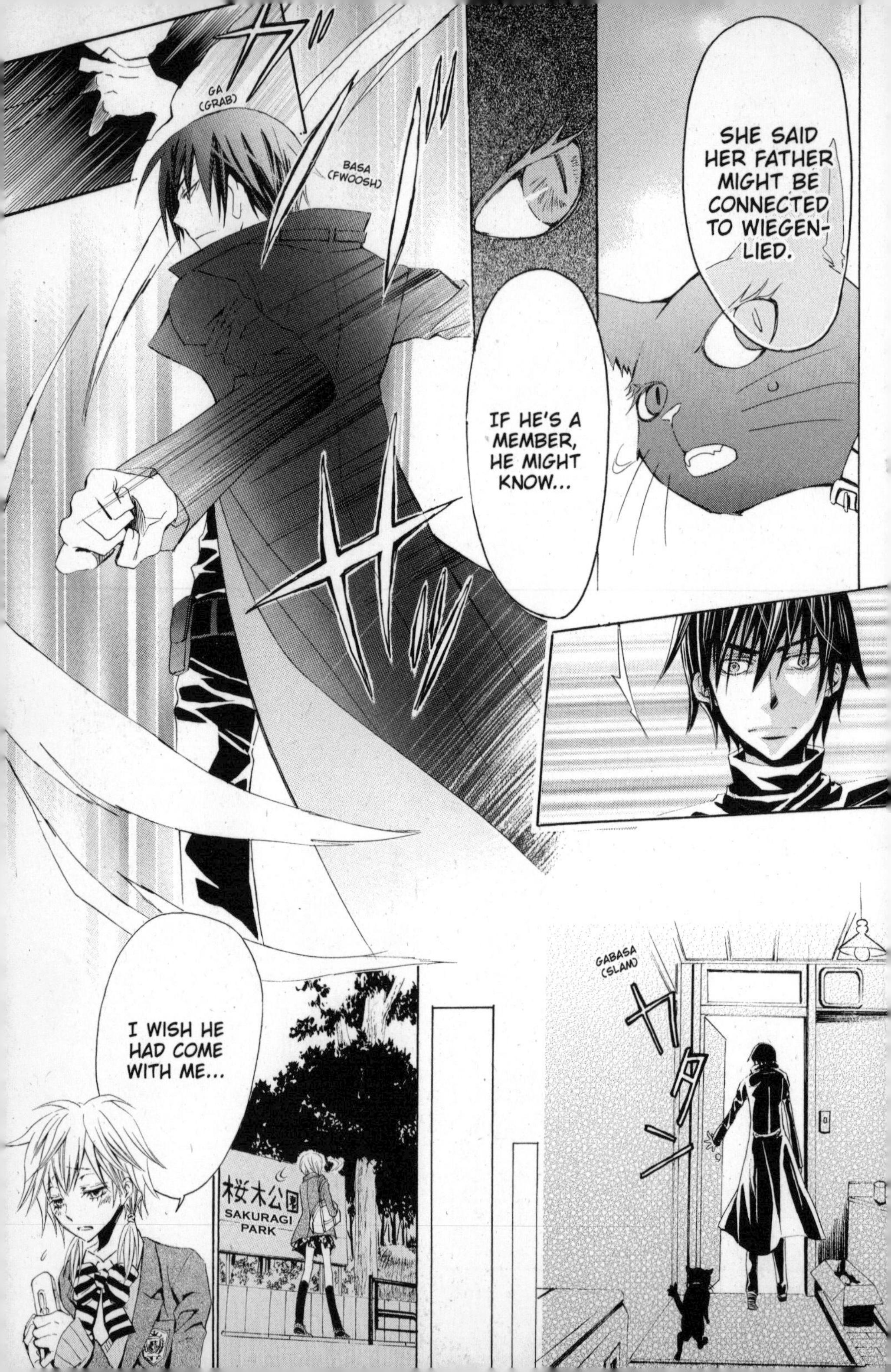
SHE SAID HER FATHER MIGHT BE CONNECTED TO WIEGEN-LIED.
IF HE'S A MEMBER, HE MIGHT KNOW...
GA (GRAB)
BASA (FWOOSH)
GABASA (SLAM)
I WISH HE HAD COME WITH ME...
桜木公園
SAKURAGI PARK

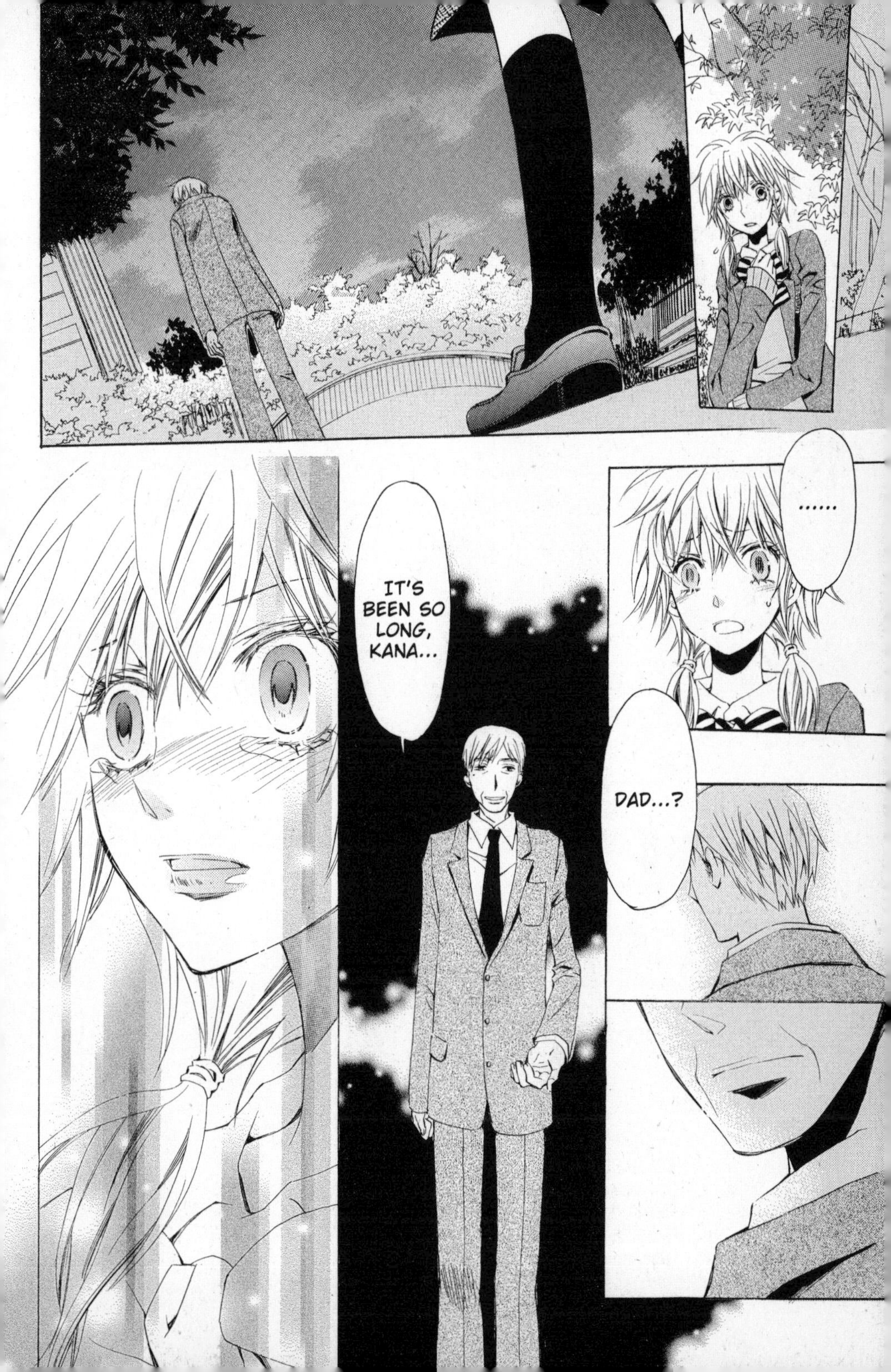
......
DAD...?
IT'S BEEN SO LONG, KANA...

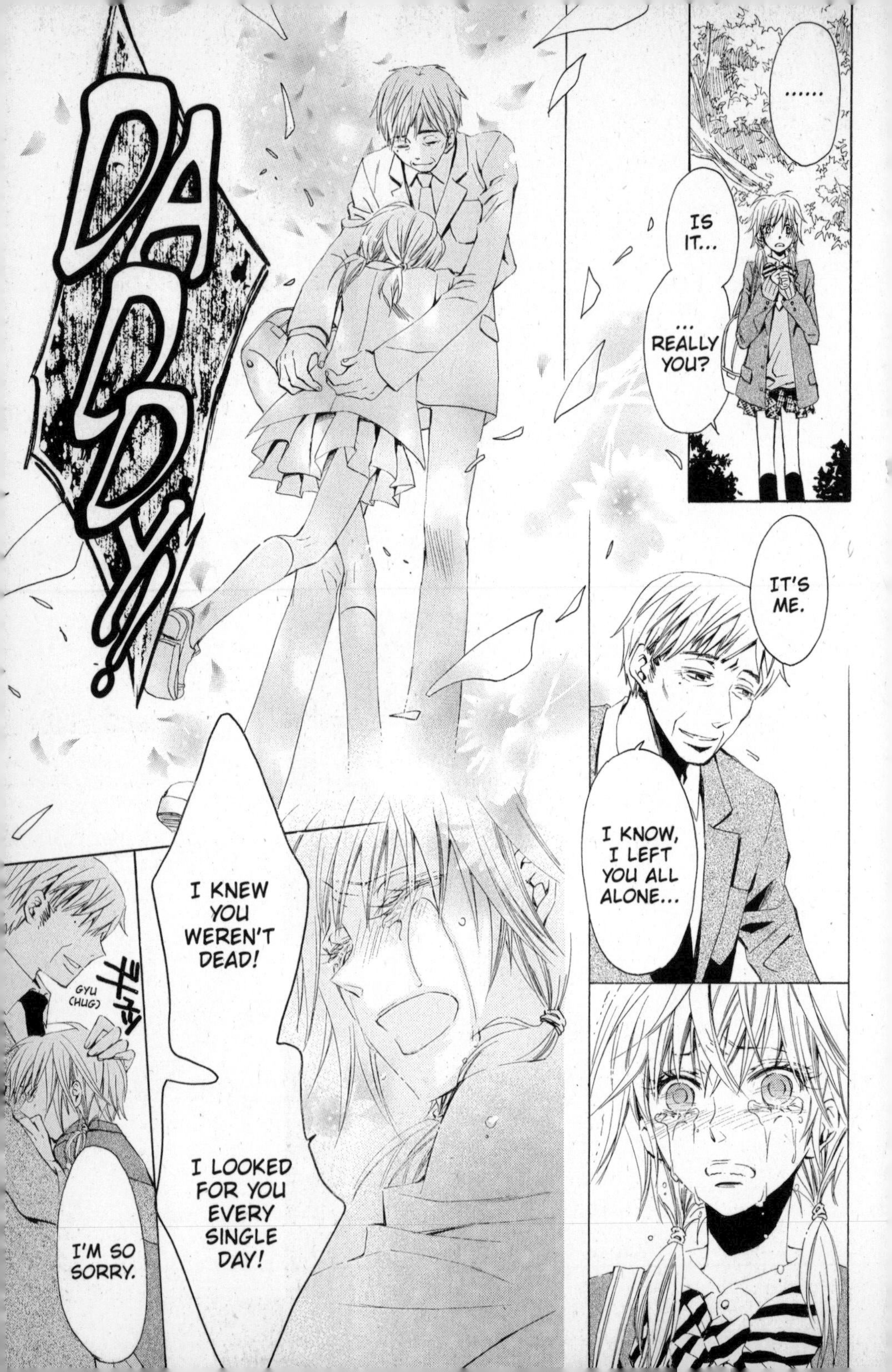
......
IS IT...
...REALLY YOU?
IT'S ME.
I KNOW, I LEFT YOU ALL ALONE...
DADDY!!
I KNEW YOU WEREN'T DEAD!
I LOOKED FOR YOU EVERY SINGLE DAY!
GYU (HUG)
I'M SO SORRY.

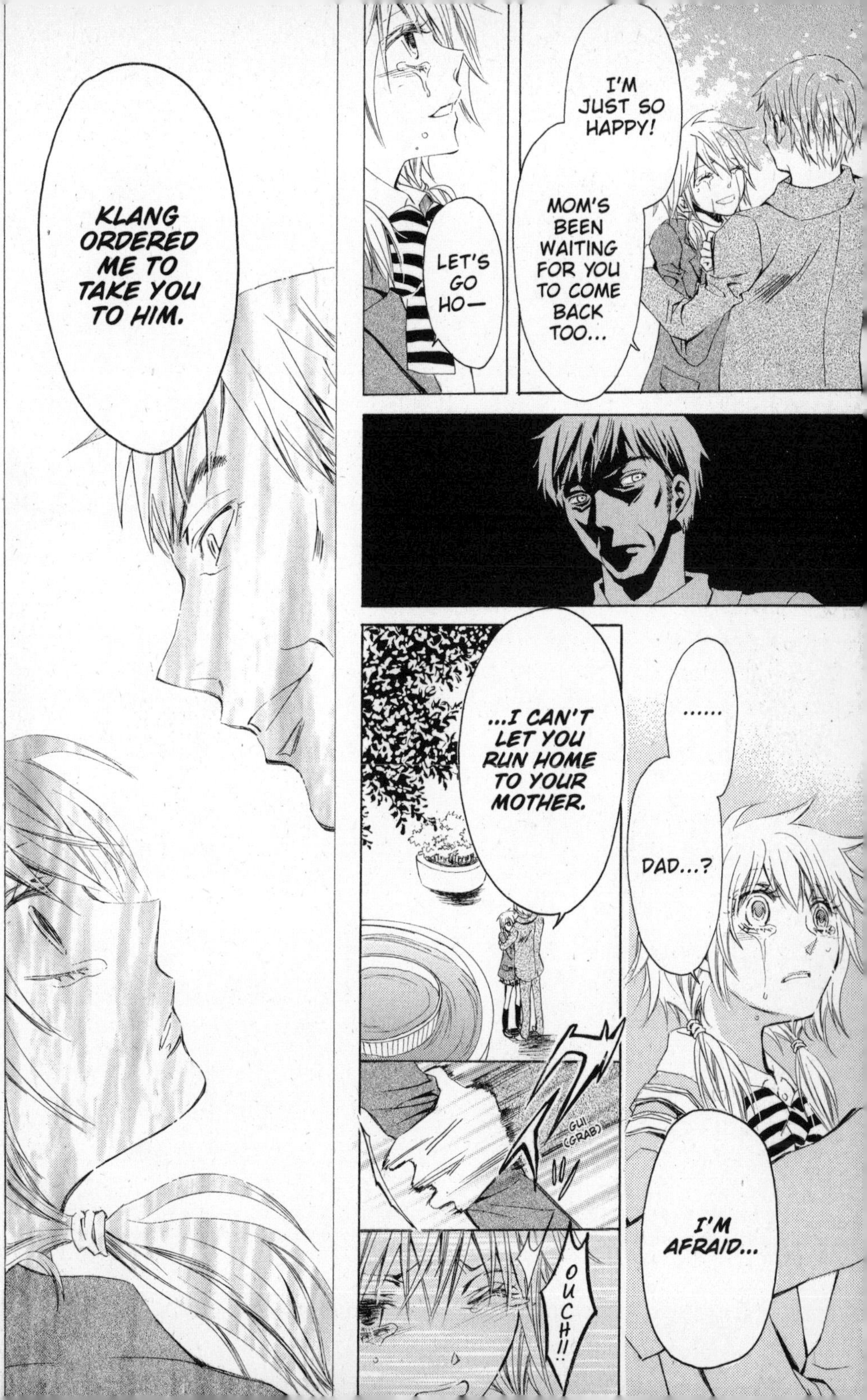
I'M JUST SO HAPPY!
MOM'S BEEN WAITING FOR YOU TO COME BACK TOO...
LET'S GO HO—
......
DAD...?
I'M AFRAID...
...I CAN'T LET YOU RUN HOME TO YOUR MOTHER.
GUI (GRAB)
OUCH!!
KLANG ORDERED ME TO TAKE YOU TO HIM.

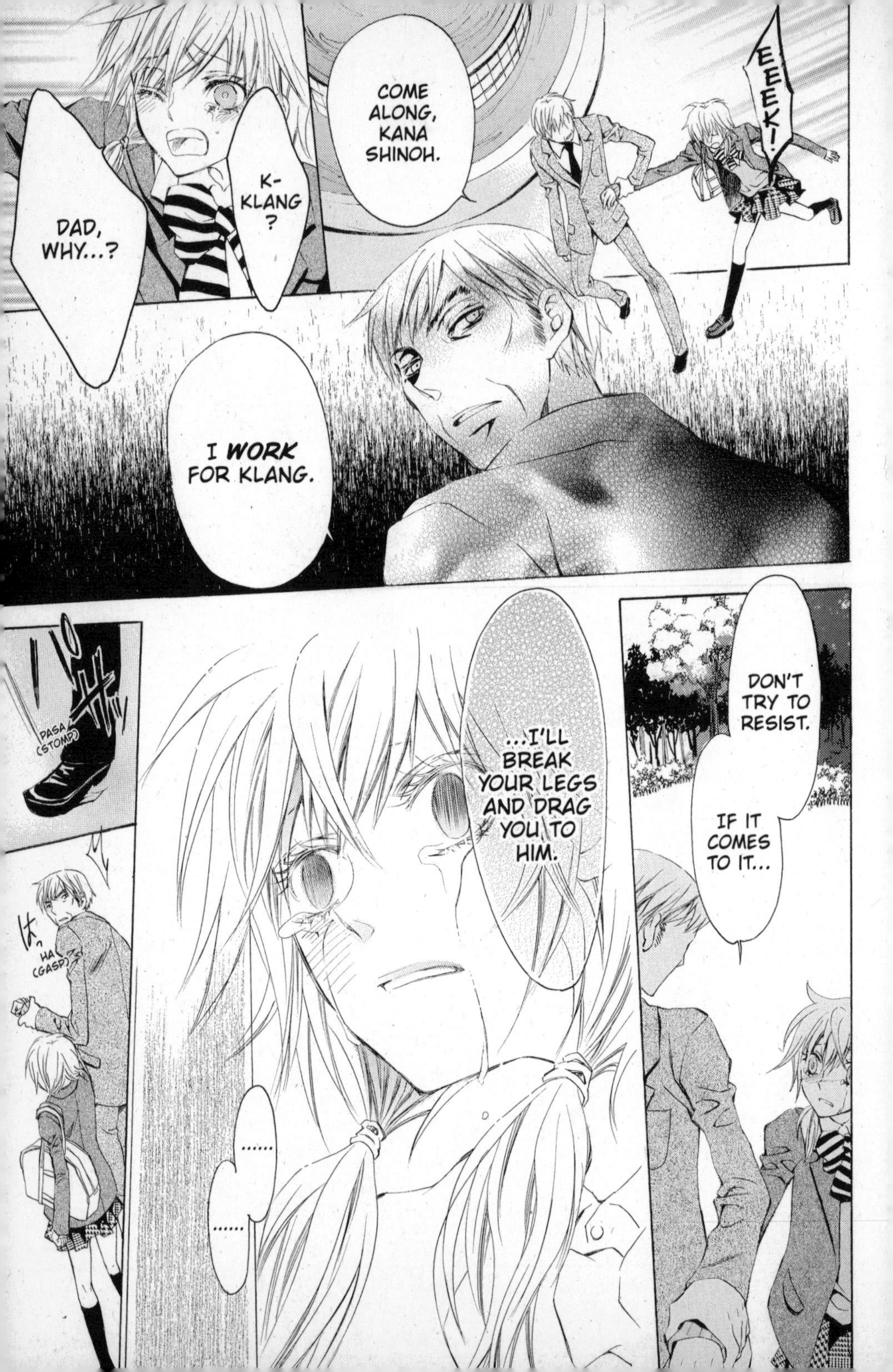
EEEK!
COME ALONG, KANA SHINOH.
K-KLANG?
DAD, WHY...?
I WORK FOR KLANG.
DON'T TRY TO RESIST.
IF IT COMES TO IT...
...I'LL BREAK YOUR LEGS AND DRAG YOU TO HIM.
......
......
PASA (STOMP)
は
HA (GASP)

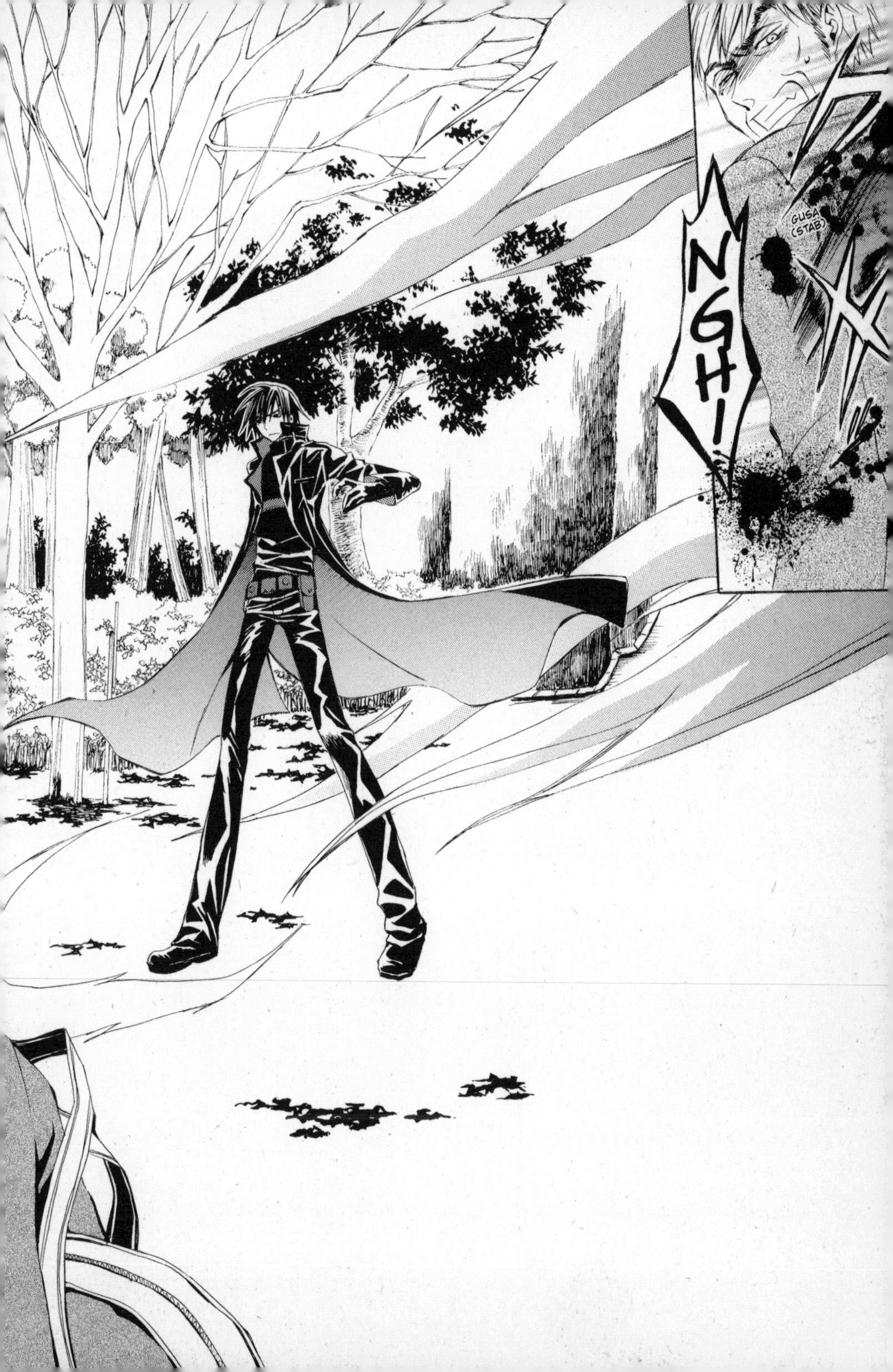
NSHI!
GUSA (STAB)

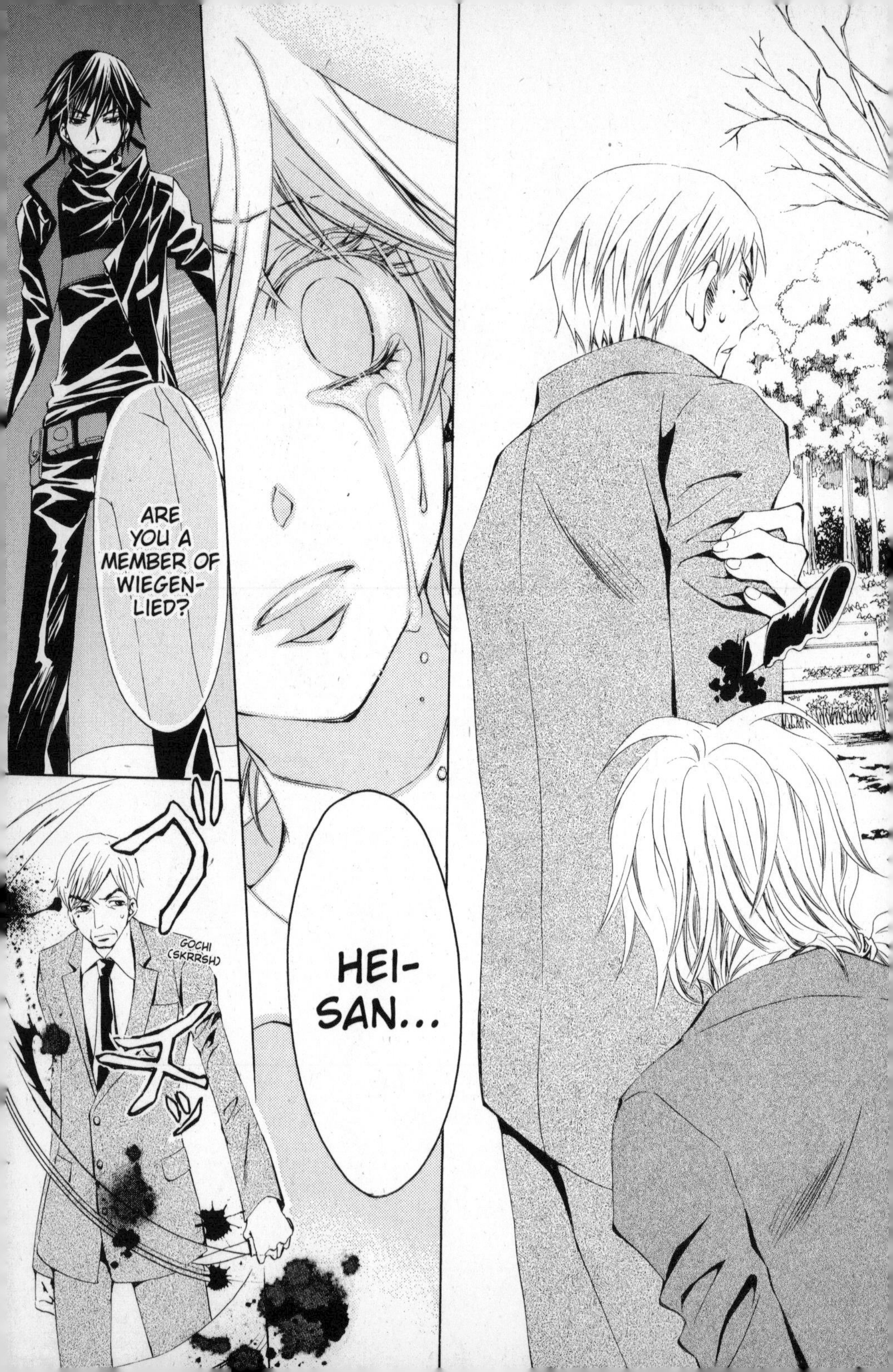
HEI-SAN...
ARE YOU A MEMBER OF WIEGEN-LIED?
GOCHI (SKRRSH)

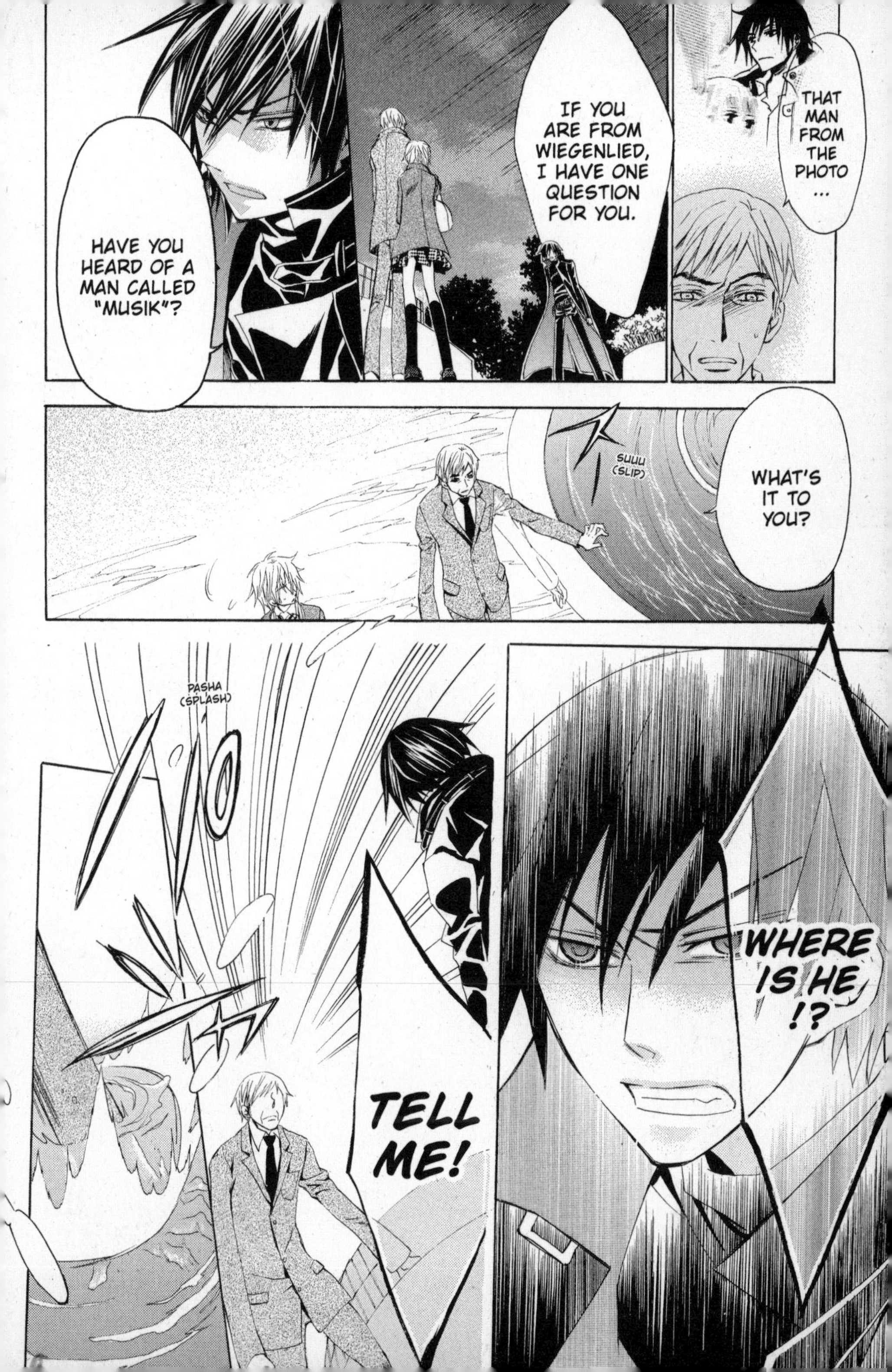
THAT MAN FROM THE PHOTO ...
IF YOU ARE FROM WIEGENLIED, I HAVE ONE QUESTION FOR YOU.
HAVE YOU HEARD OF A MAN CALLED "MUSIK"?
WHAT'S IT TO YOU?
SUUU (SLIP)
WHERE IS HE !?
PASHA (SPLASH)
TELL ME!

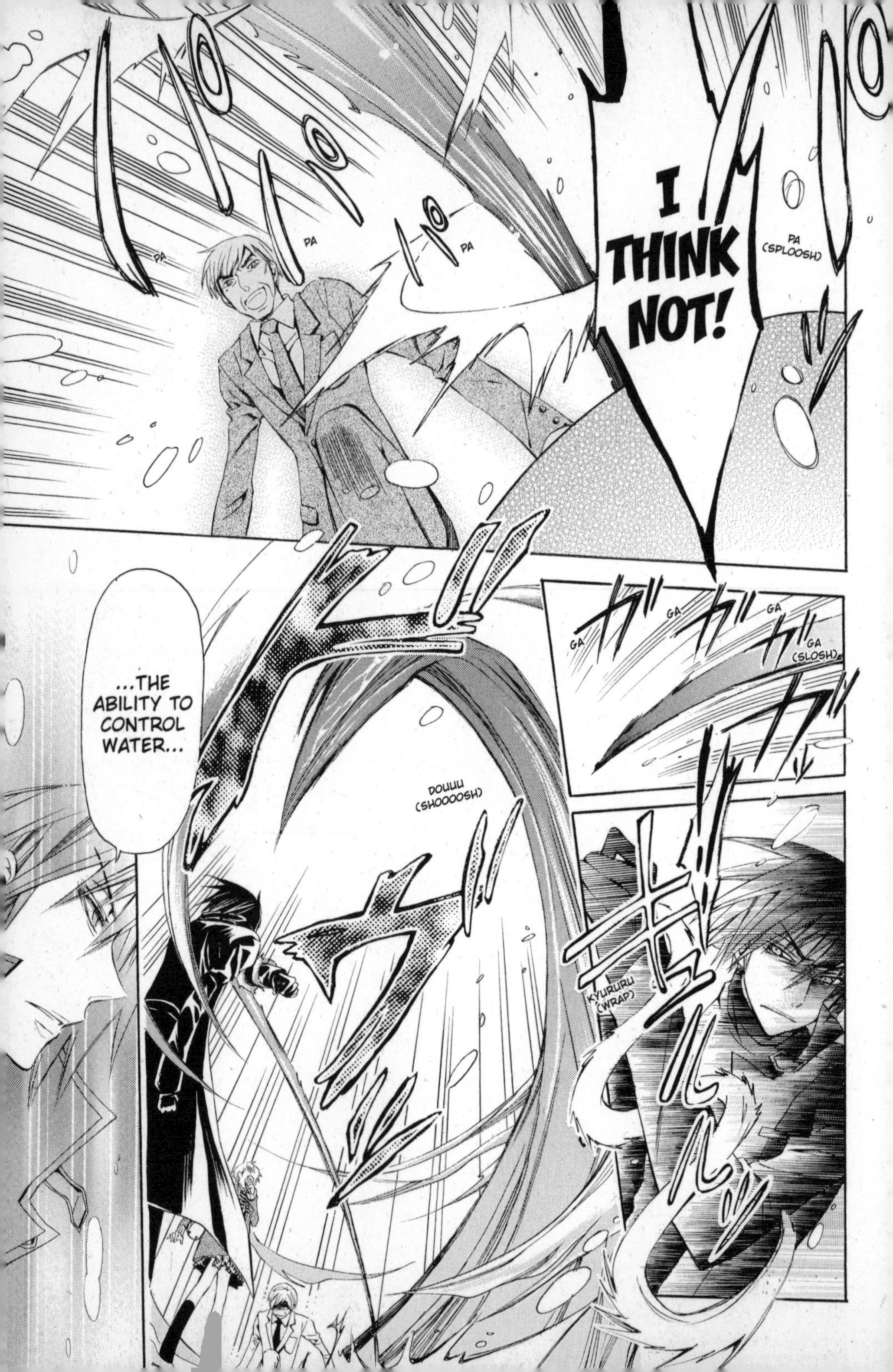
PA (SPLOOSH)
I THINK NOT!
PA
PA
PA
GA
GA
GA (SLOSH)
KYURURU (WRAP)
DOUUU (SHOOOOSH)
...THE ABILITY TO CONTROL WATER...

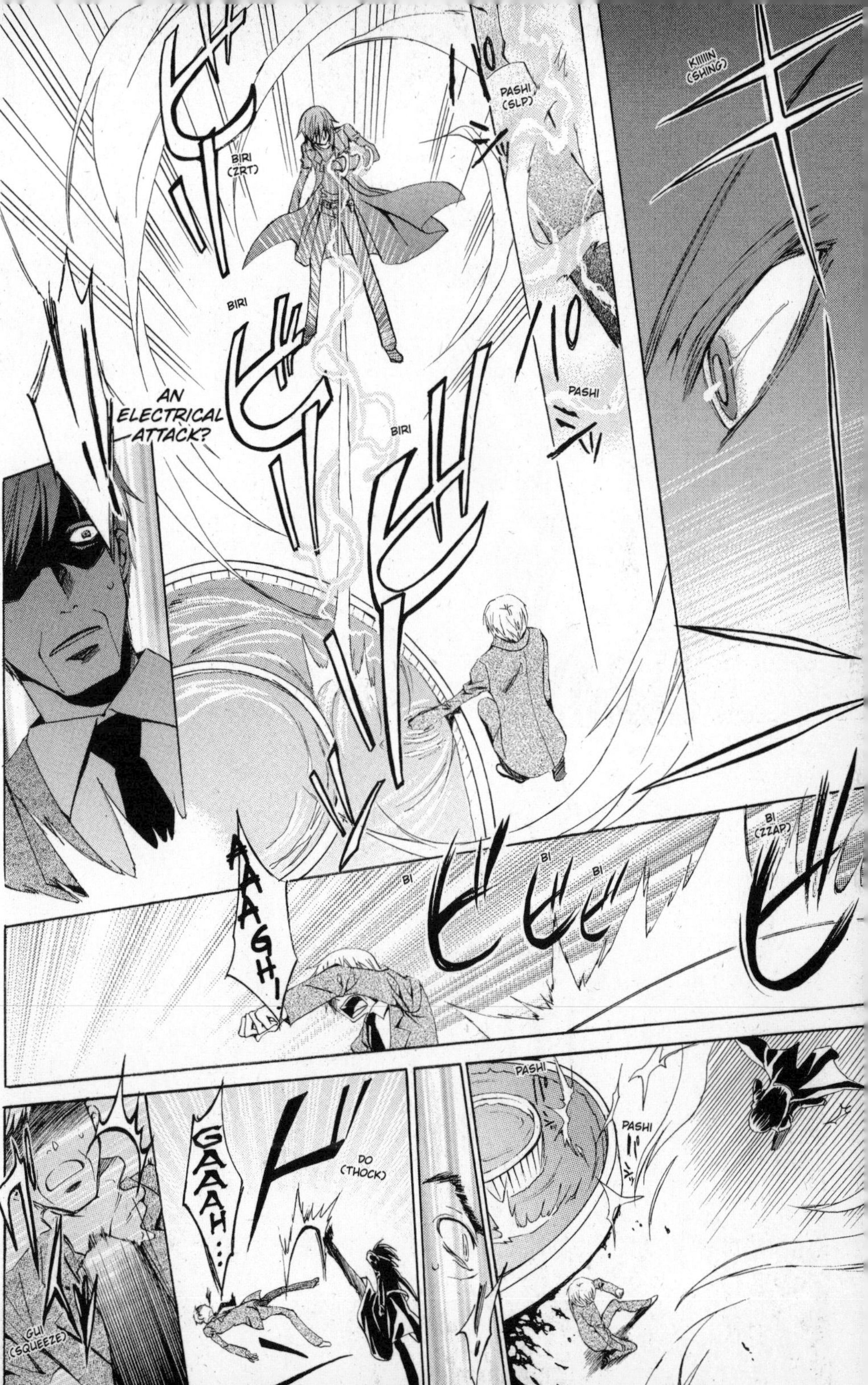
KIIIIN
(SHING)
PASHI
(SLP)
BIRI
(ZRT)
BIRI
PASHI
BIRI
AN ELECTRICAL ATTACK?
BI
(ZZAP)
BI
BI
BI
AAAGH!
PASHI
PASHI
DO
(THOCK)
GAAAH...
GUI
(SQUEEZE)

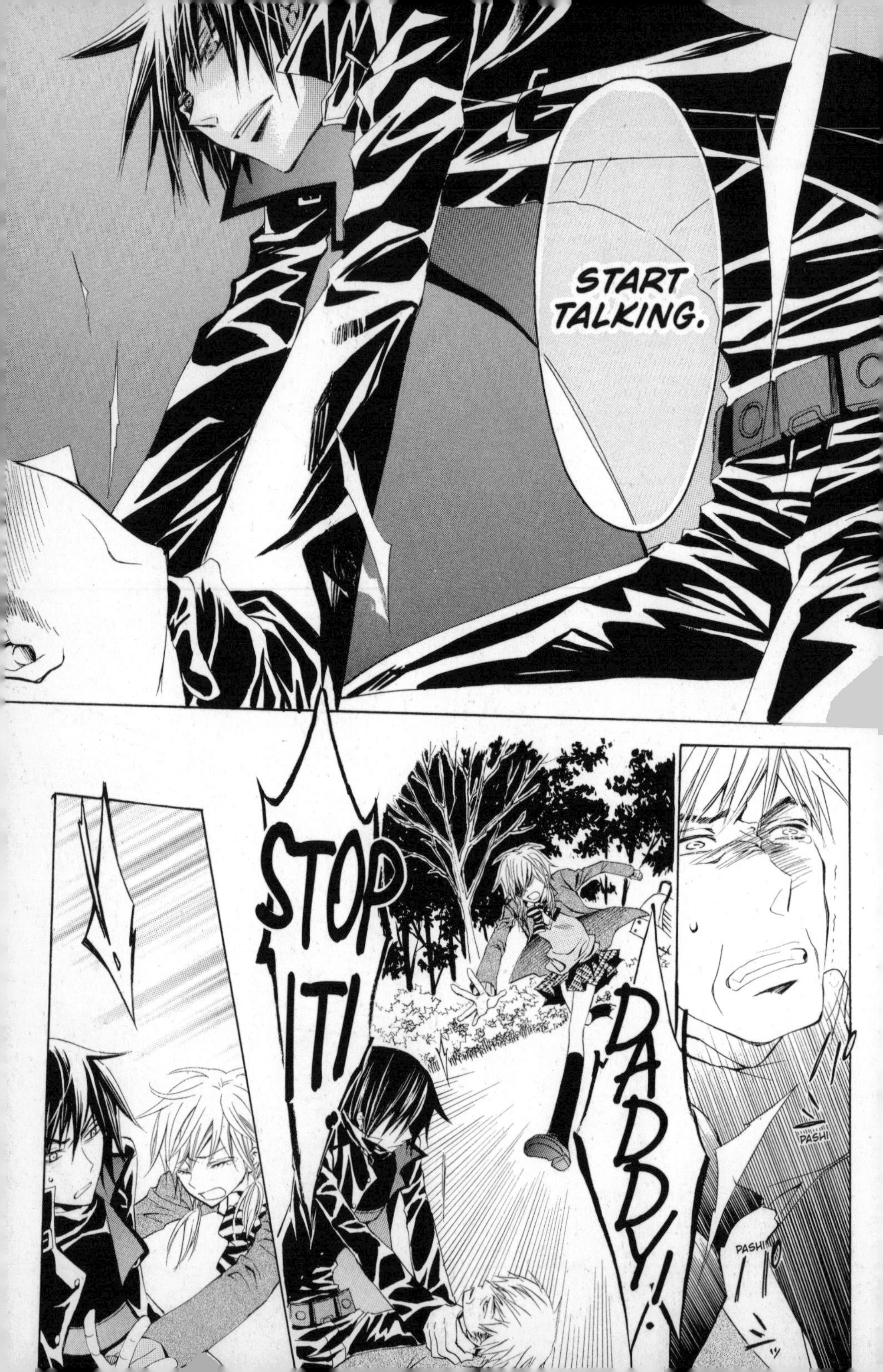
START TALKING.
PASHI
PASHI
STOP IT!
DADDY!

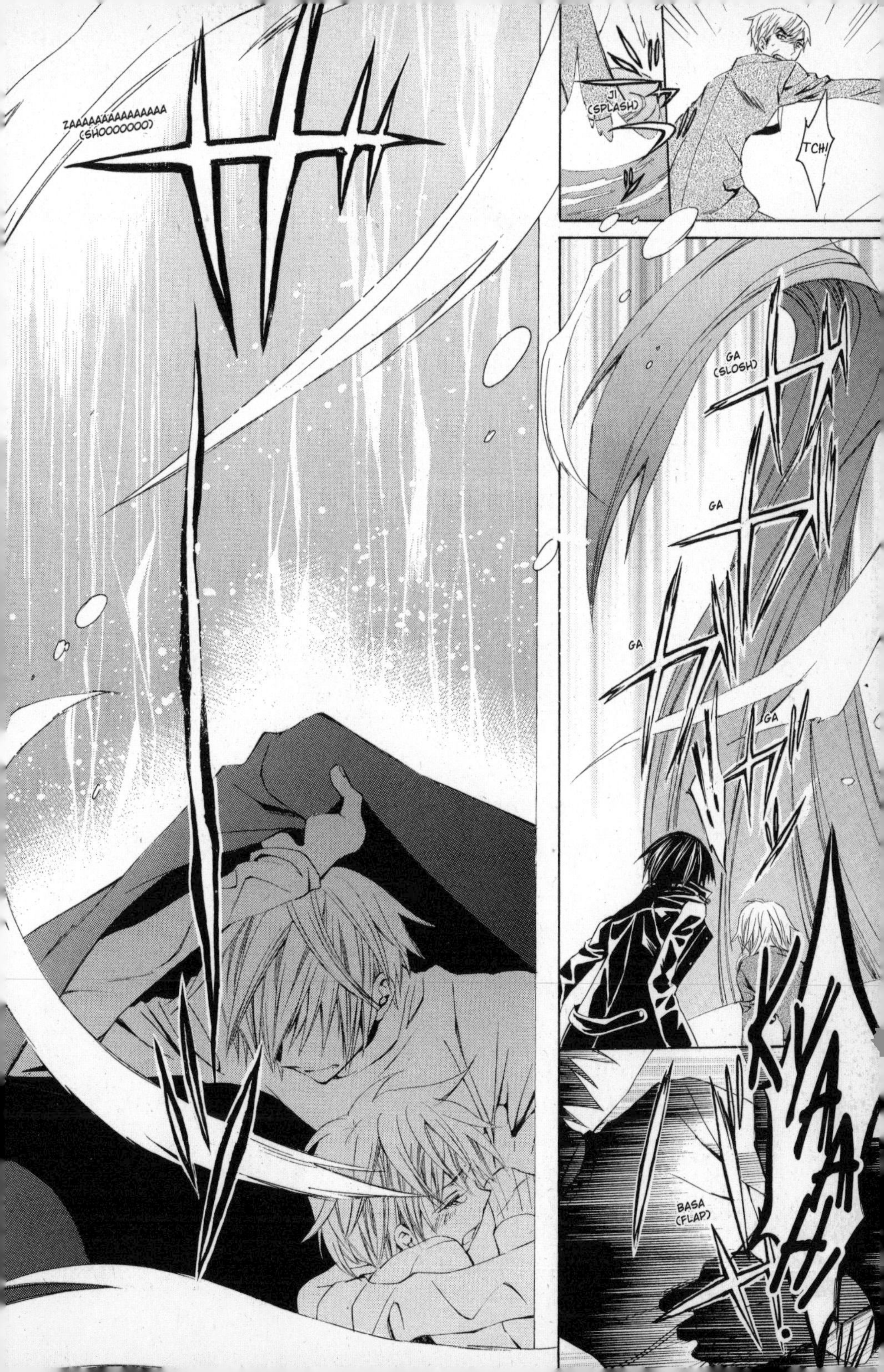
TCHI!
JI (SPLASH)
GA (SLOSH)
GA
GA
GA
BASA (FLAP)
KYAAH!
ZAAAAAAAAAAAAAAA (SHOOOOOOO)

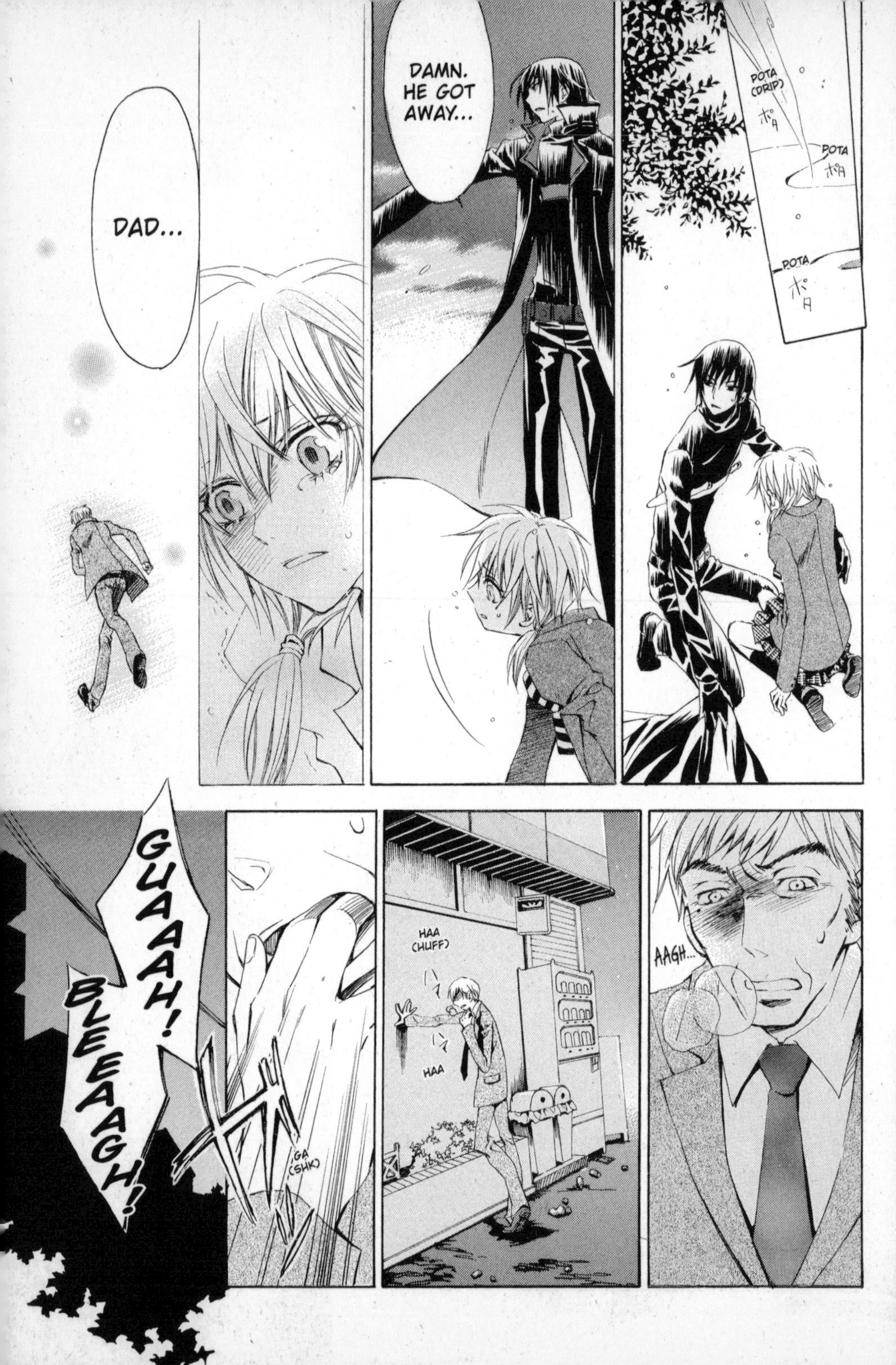
POTA (DRIP)
ポタ
POTA
ポタ
POTA
ポタ
DAMN. HE GOT AWAY...
DAD...
AAGH...
HAA (HUFF)
ハァ
ハァ
HAA
GA (SHK)
GUAAAH!
BLEEAAGH!

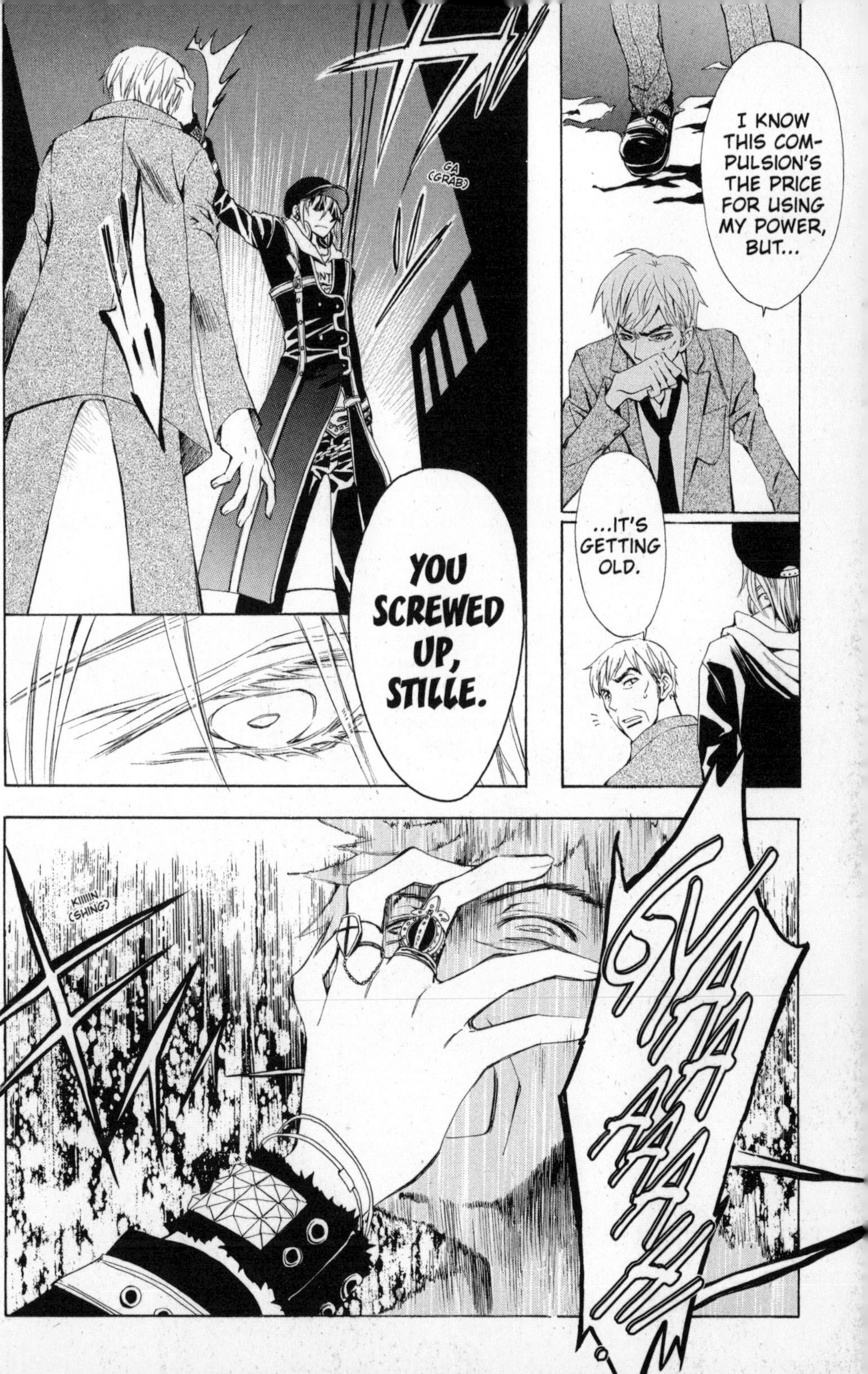
I KNOW THIS COMPULSION'S THE PRICE FOR USING MY POWER, BUT...
...IT'S GETTING OLD.
GA (GRAB)
YOU SCREWED UP, STILLE.
GYAAAAAAH
KIIIIN (SHING)

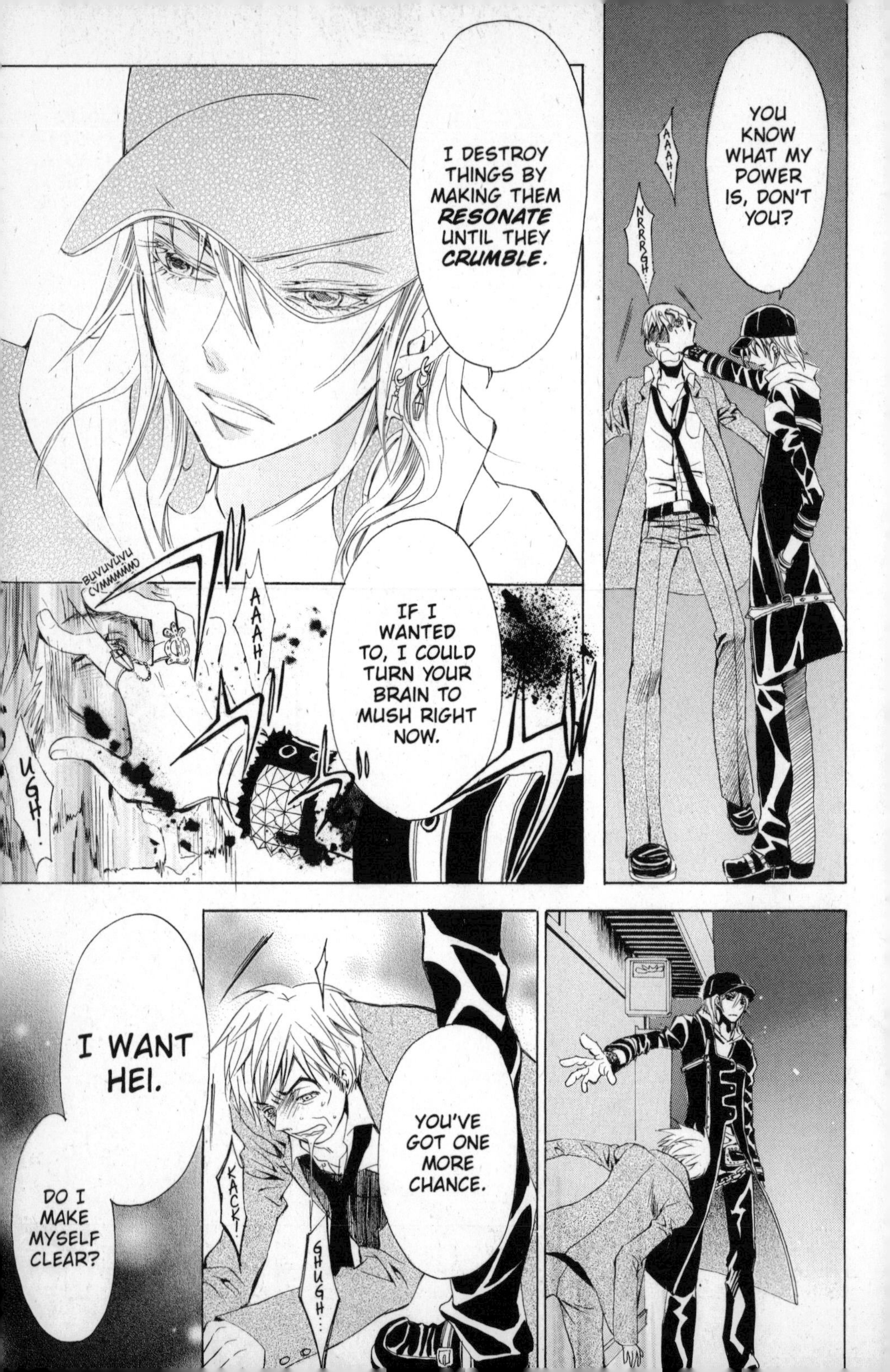
YOU KNOW WHAT MY POWER IS, DON'T YOU?
AAAH!
NRRRGH...
I DESTROY THINGS BY MAKING THEM RESONATE UNTIL THEY CRUMBLE.
IF I WANTED TO, I COULD TURN YOUR BRAIN TO MUSH RIGHT NOW.
AAAAH!
UGH!
YOU'VE GOT ONE MORE CHANCE.
KACK!
GHUGH...
I WANT HEI.
DO I MAKE MYSELF CLEAR?

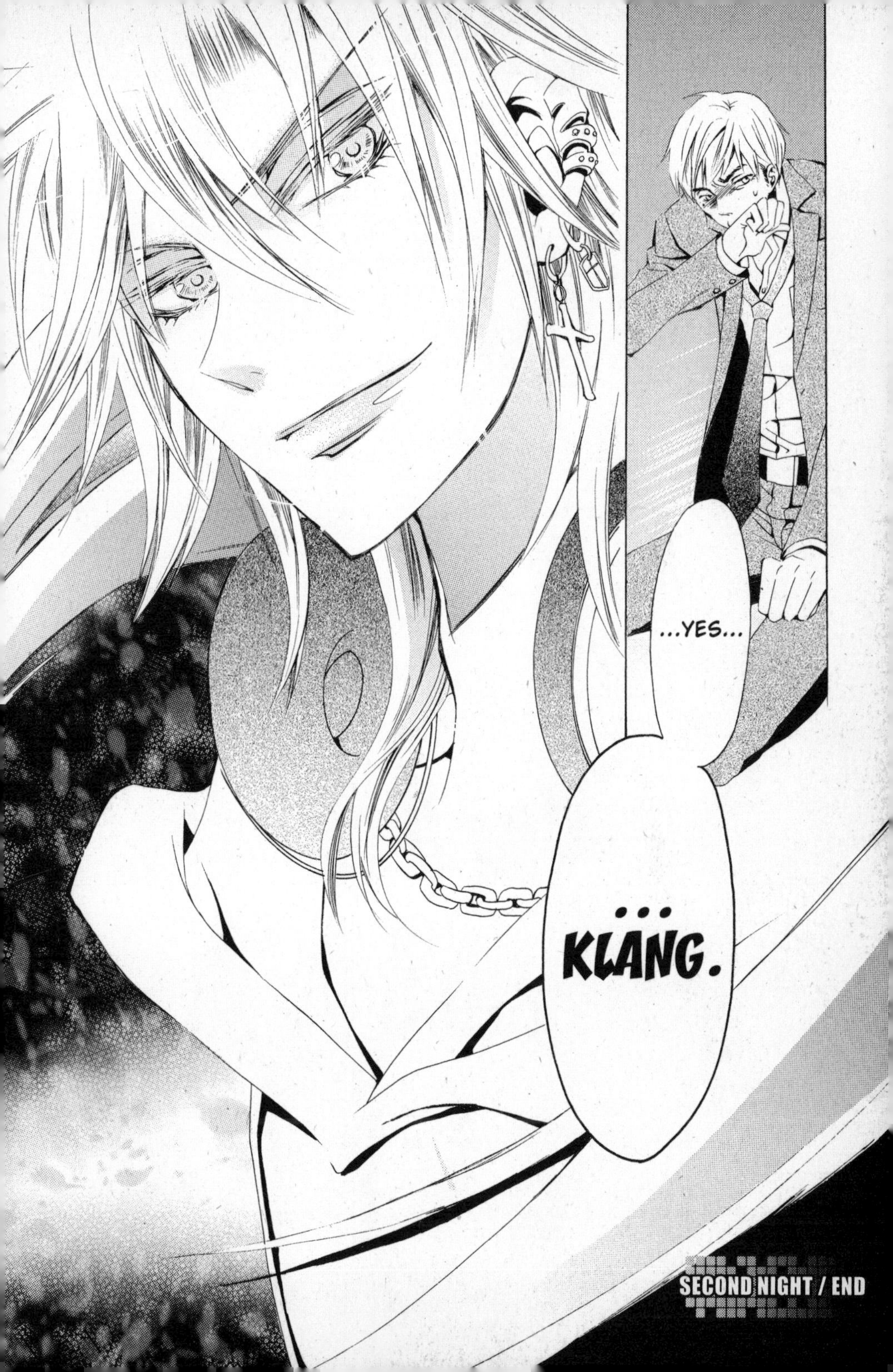
...YES...
... KLÄNG.
SECOND NIGHT / END

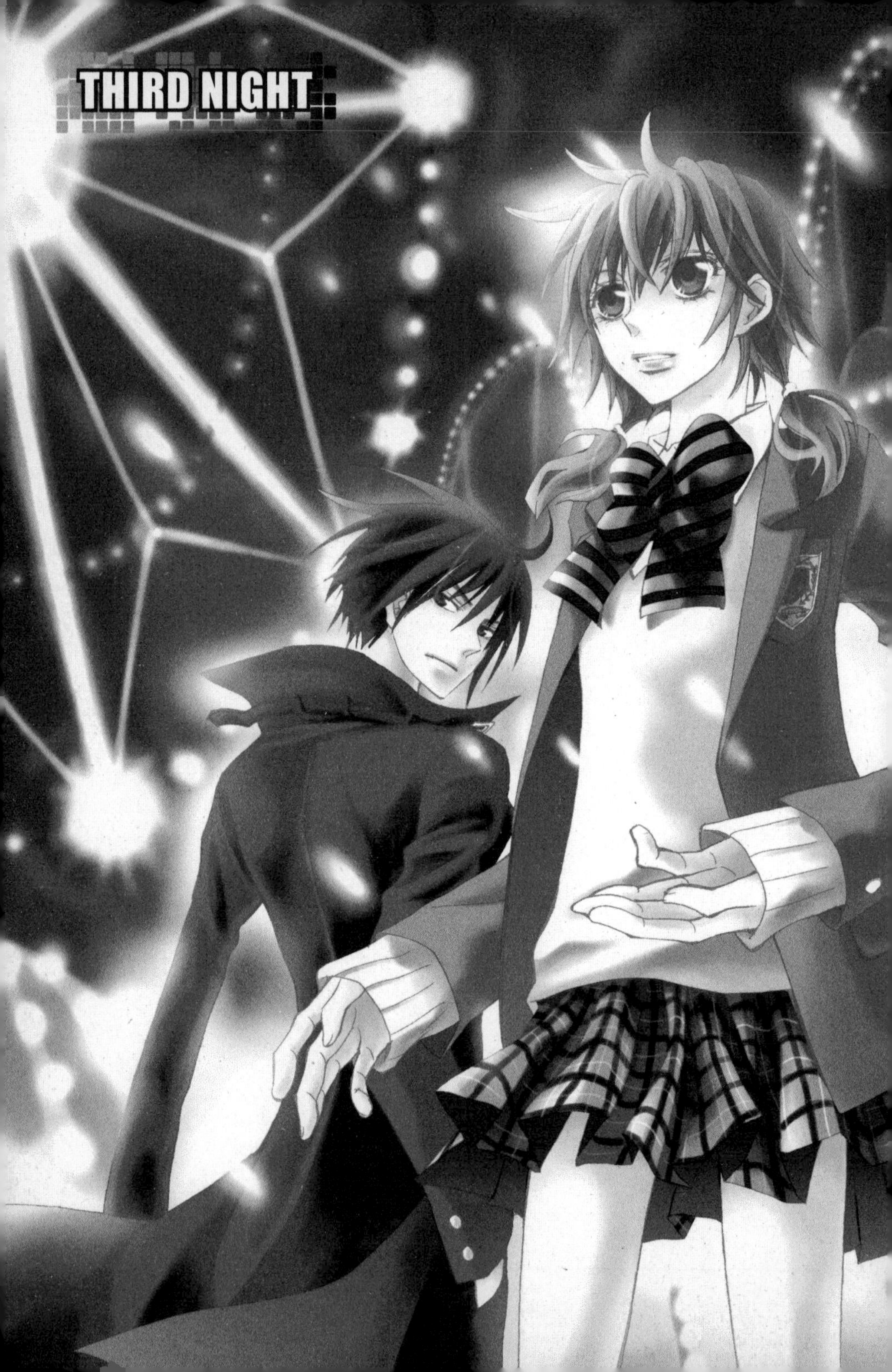
THIRD NIGHT

DARKER THAN
BLACK
THE BLACK CONTRACTOR

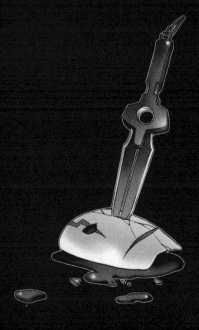

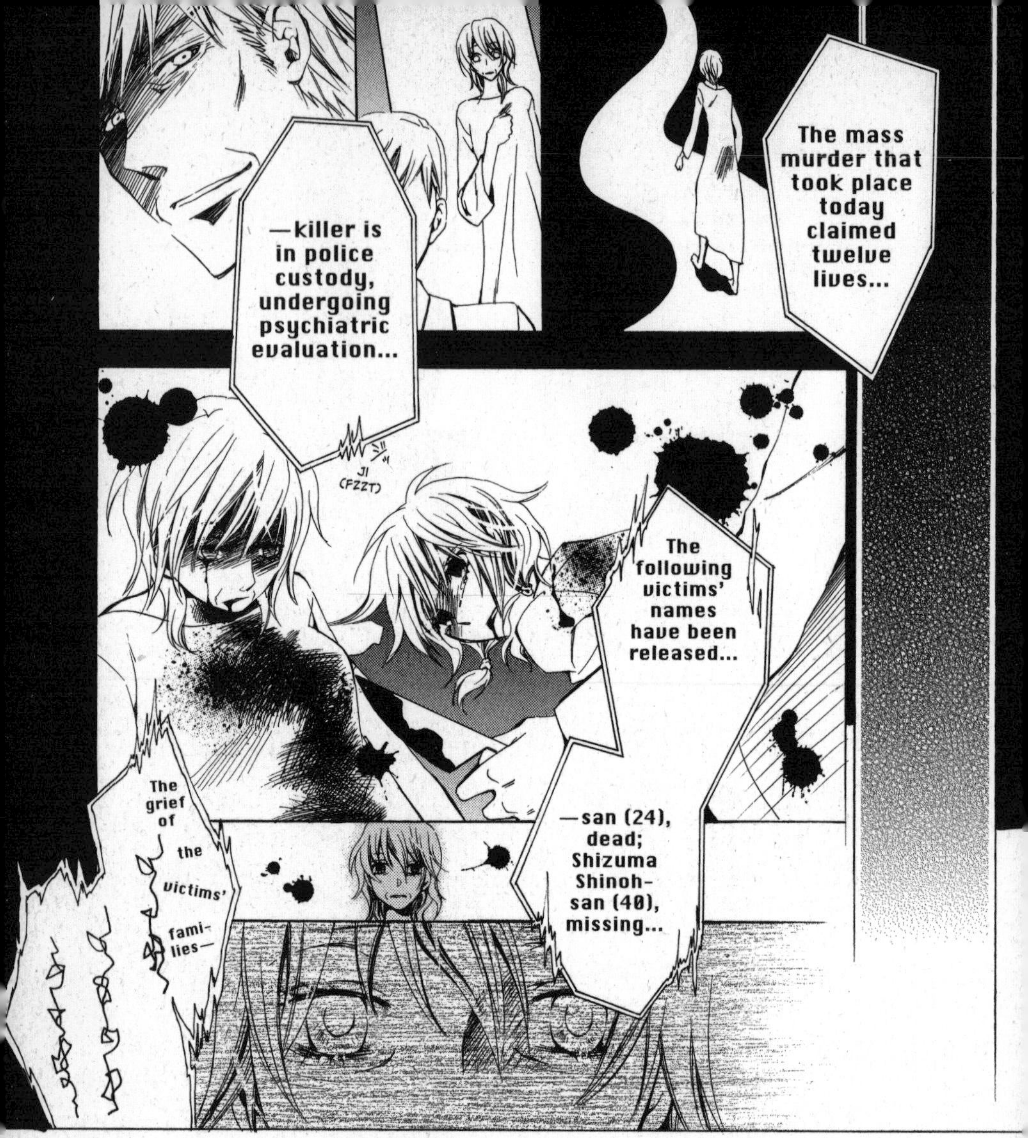
The mass murder that took place today claimed twelve lives...
—killer is in police custody, undergoing psychiatric evaluation...
JI (FZZT)
The following victims' names have been released...
—san (24), dead; Shizuma Shinoh-san (40), missing...
The grief of the victims' families—

IMPOSSIBLE COMIC STRIP (2)

You really should read the whole series before you look at this...

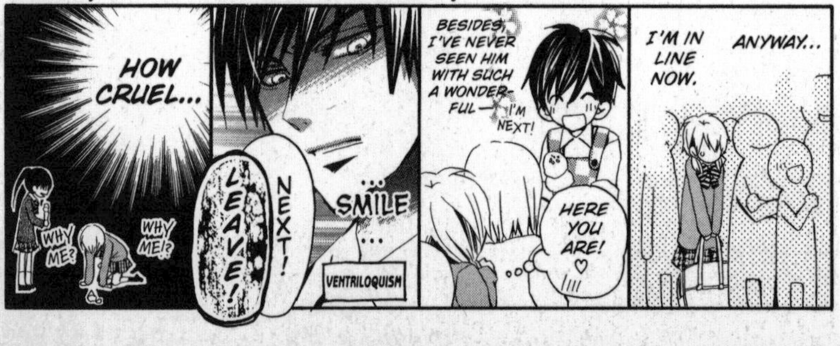
I'M IN LINE NOW.
ANYWAY...
BESIDES, I'VE NEVER SEEN HIM WITH SUCH A WONDER-FUL—
I'M NEXT!
HERE YOU ARE! ♡
...SMILE...
NEXT!
LEAVE!
VENTRILOQUISM
HOW CRUEL...
WHY ME?
WHY ME!?

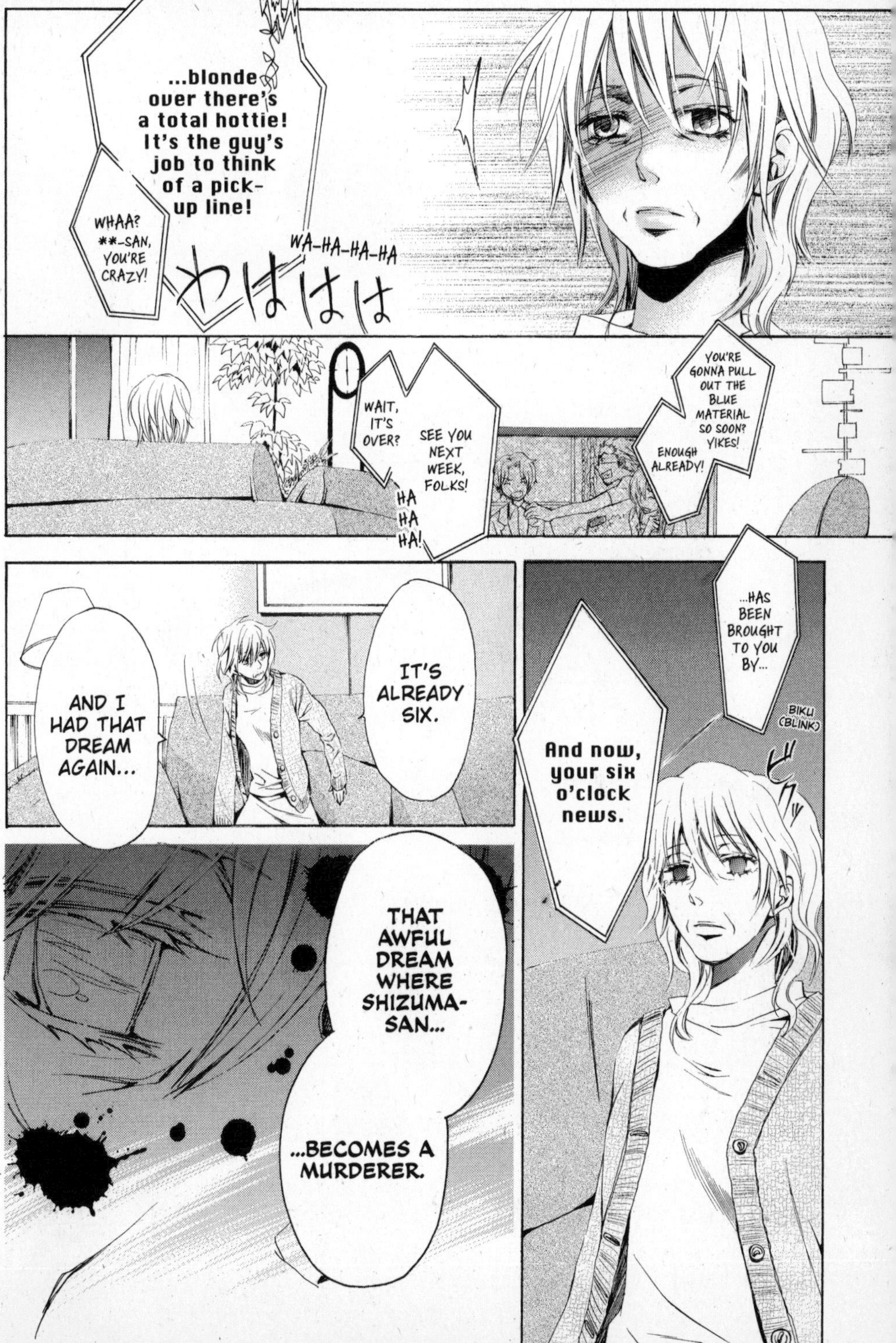
...blonde over there's a total hottie! It's the guy's job to think of a pick-up line!
WHAA? **-SAN, YOU'RE CRAZY!
WA-HA-HA-HA
やははは
YOU'RE GONNA PULL OUT THE BLUE MATERIAL SO SOON? YIKES!
ENOUGH ALREADY!
SEE YOU NEXT WEEK, FOLKS!
WAIT, IT'S OVER?
HA HA HA!
...HAS BEEN BROUGHT TO YOU BY...
BIKU (BLINK)
And now, your six o'clock news.
IT'S ALREADY SIX.
AND I HAD THAT DREAM AGAIN...
THAT AWFUL DREAM WHERE SHIZUMA-SAN...
...BECOMES A MURDERER.

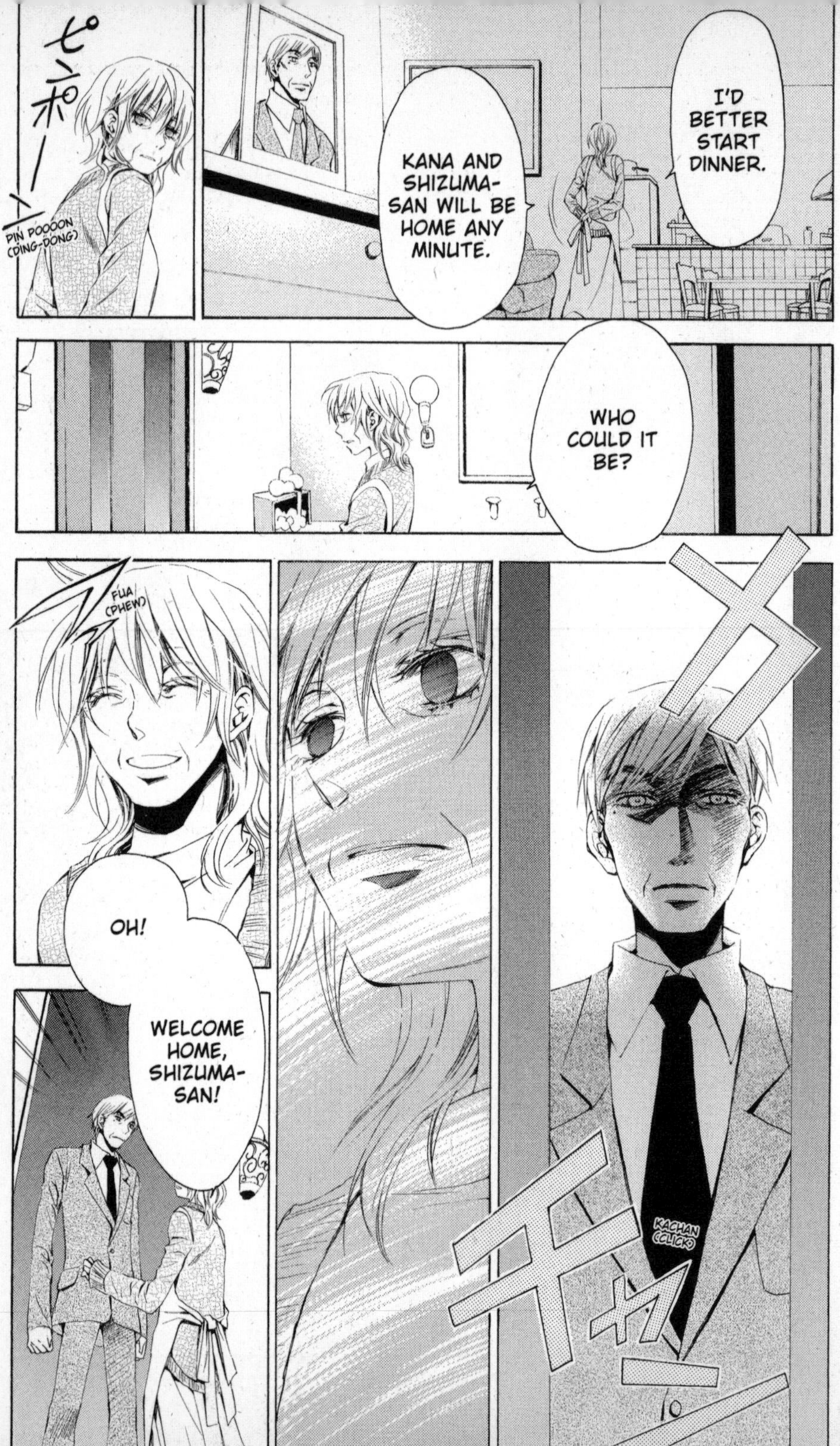
I'D BETTER START DINNER.
KANA AND SHIZUMA-SAN WILL BE HOME ANY MINUTE.
ピンポーン
PIN POOOON (DING-DONG)
WHO COULD IT BE?
カチャ
KACHAN (CLICK)
FUA (PHEW)
OH!
WELCOME HOME, SHIZUMA-SAN!

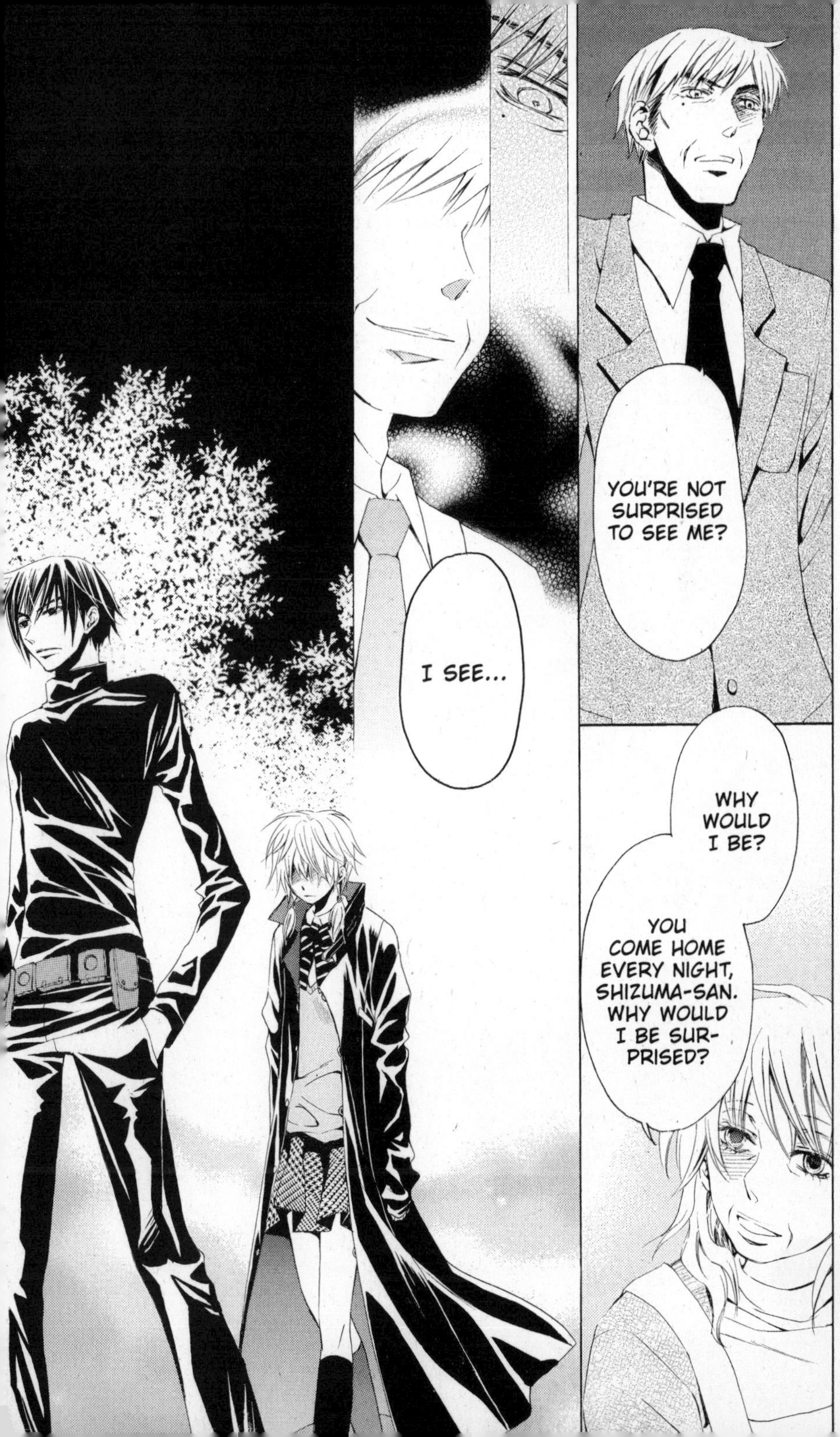

YOU'RE NOT SURPRISED TO SEE ME?
I SEE...
WHY WOULD I BE?
YOU COME HOME EVERY NIGHT, SHIZUMA-SAN. WHY WOULD I BE SUR-PRISED?

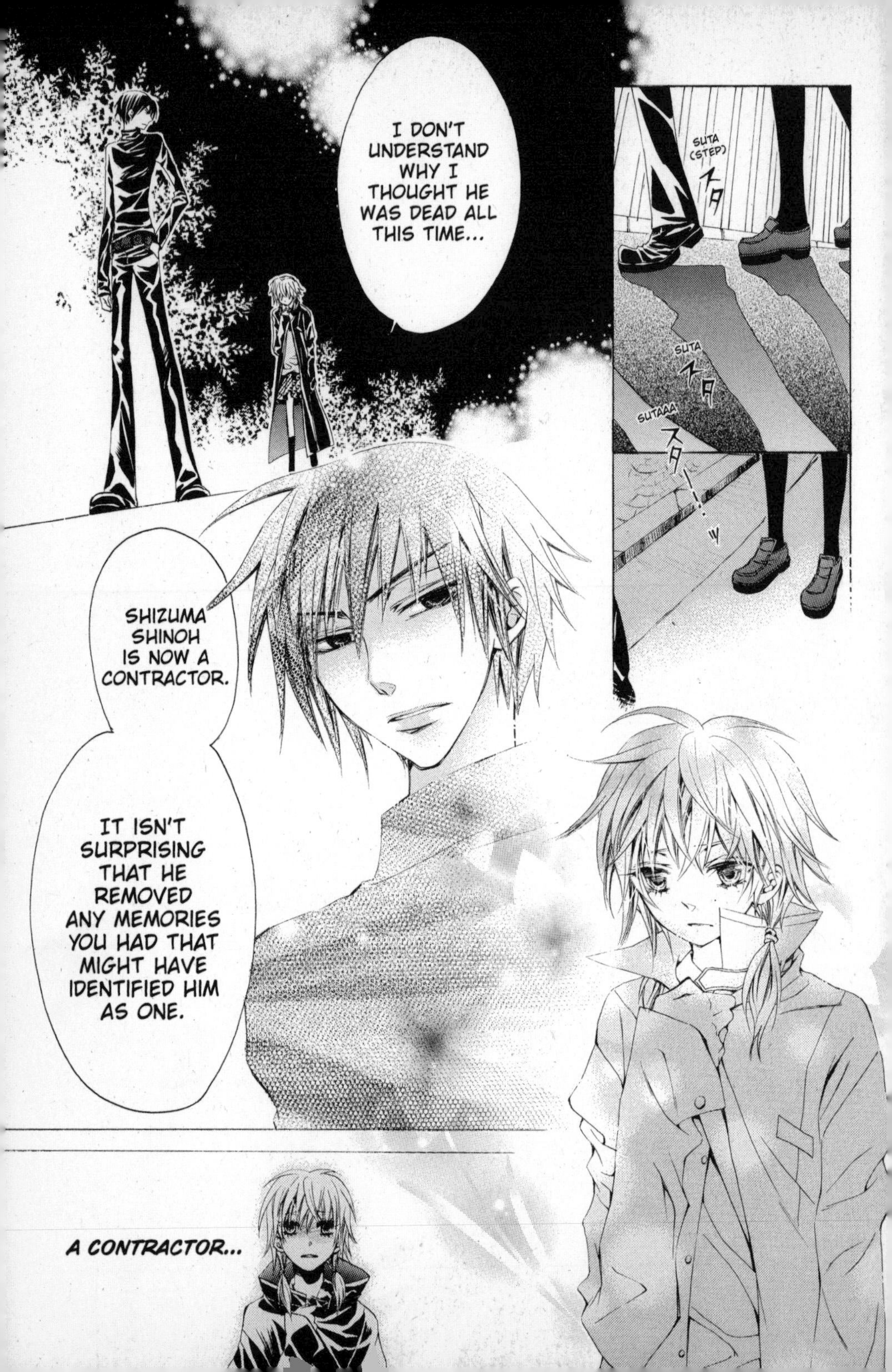

SUTA (STEP)
スタ
SUTA
スタ
SUTAAA
スター!!
I DON'T UNDERSTAND WHY I THOUGHT HE WAS DEAD ALL THIS TIME...
SHIZUMA SHINOH IS NOW A CONTRACTOR.
IT ISN'T SURPRISING THAT HE REMOVED ANY MEMORIES YOU HAD THAT MIGHT HAVE IDENTIFIED HIM AS ONE.
A CONTRACTOR...

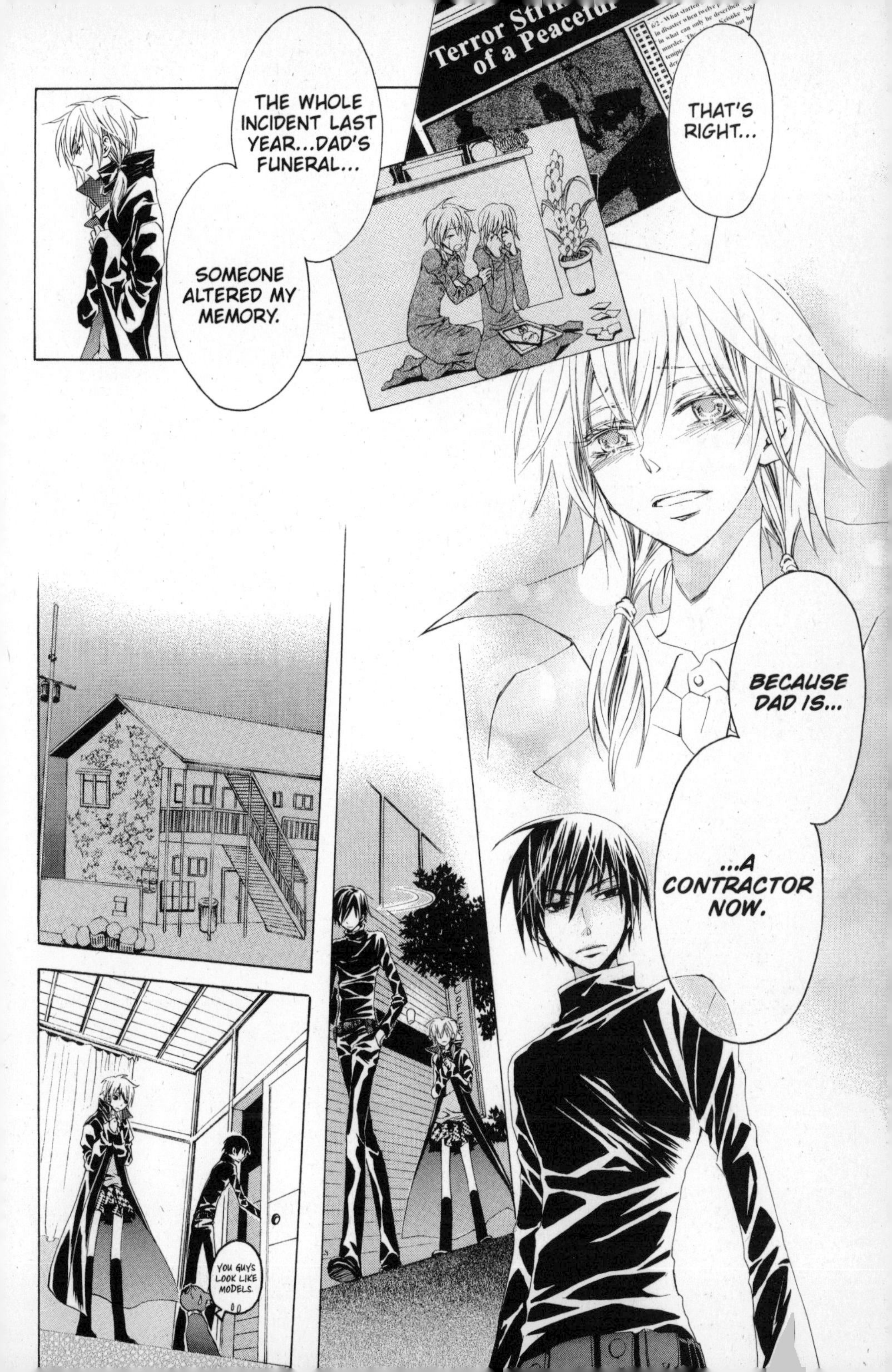
THAT'S RIGHT...
THE WHOLE INCIDENT LAST YEAR...DAD'S FUNERAL...
SOMEONE ALTERED MY MEMORY.
BECAUSE DAD IS...
...A CONTRACTOR NOW.
YOU GUYS LOOK LIKE MODELS.

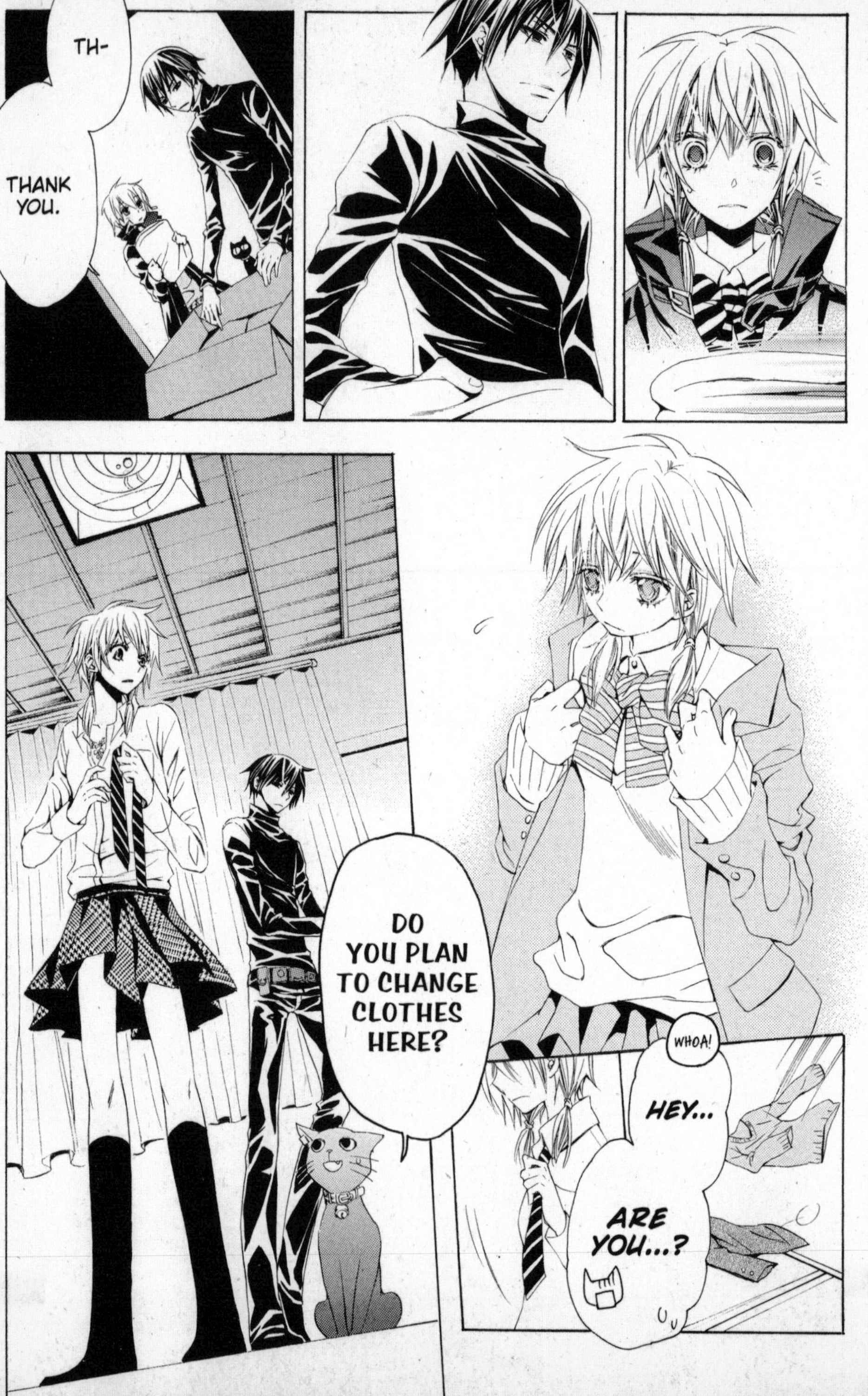
TH-
THANK YOU.
WHOA!
HEY... ARE YOU...?
DO YOU PLAN TO CHANGE CLOTHES HERE?

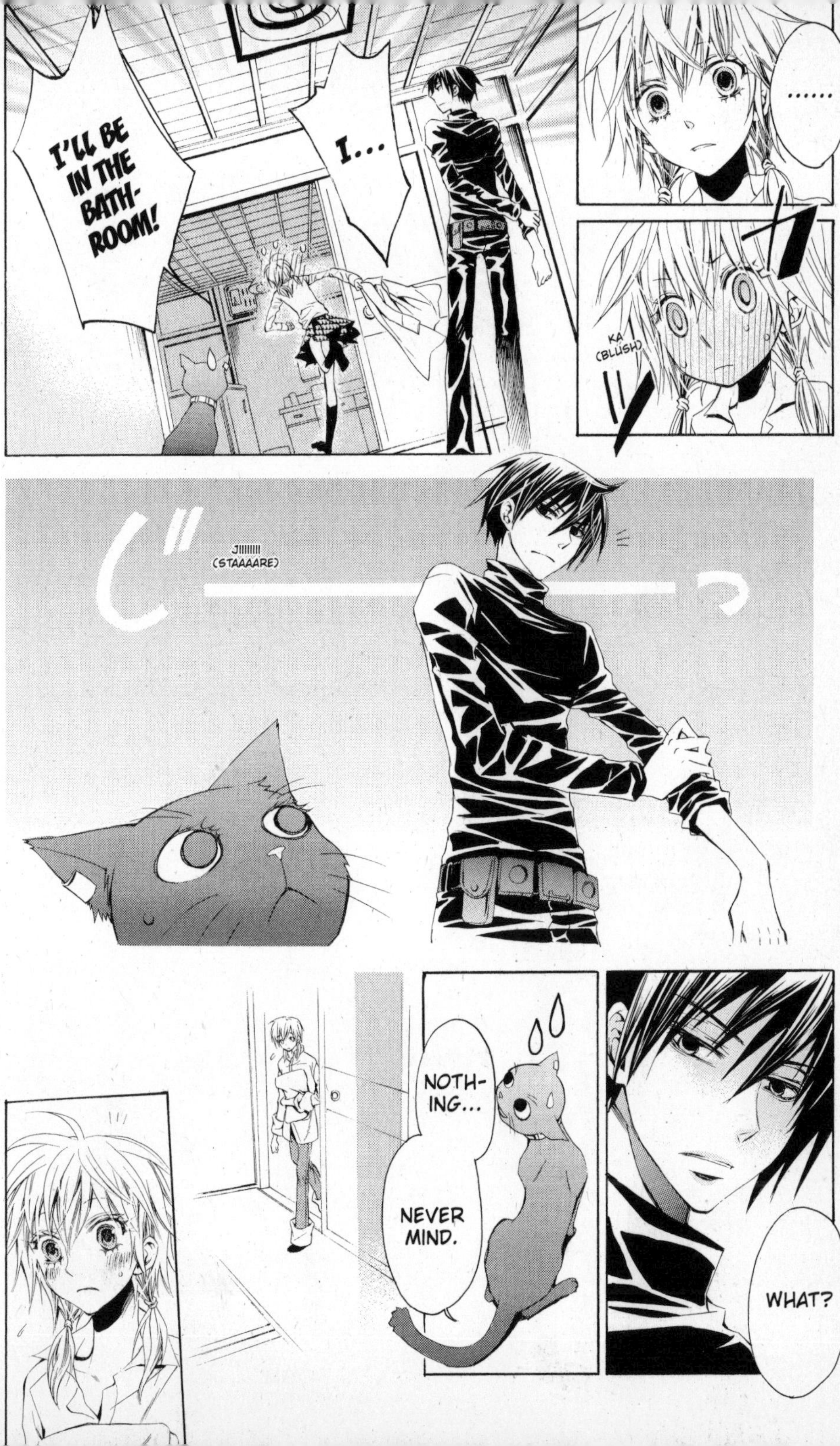
......
KA
(BLUSH)
I...
I'LL BE IN THE BATH-ROOM!
JIIIIIII
(STAAAARE)
WHAT?
NOTH-ING...
NEVER MIND.

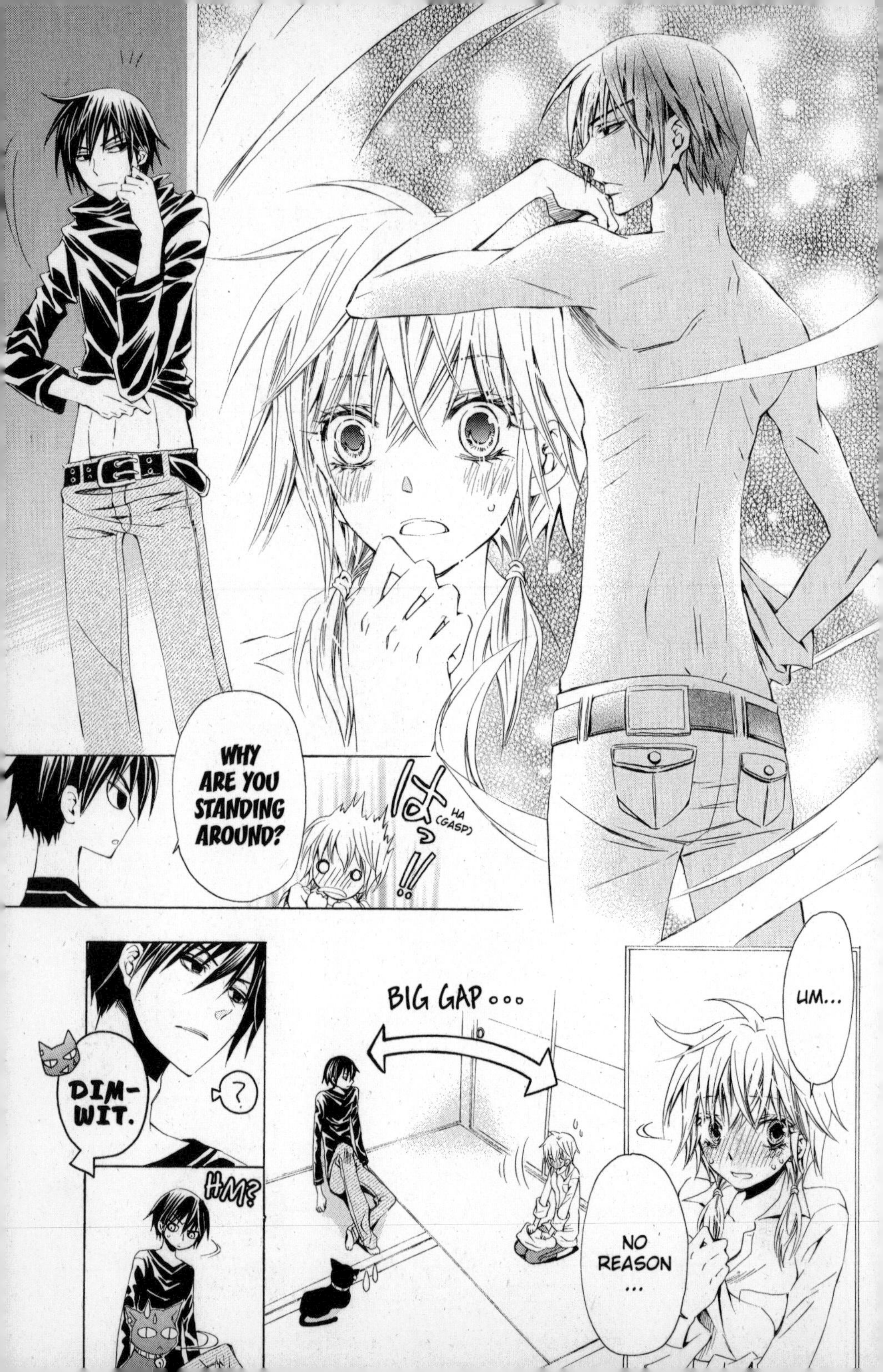
WHY ARE YOU STANDING AROUND?
は
HA (GASP)
!!
UM...
NO REASON ...
BIG GAP...
DIM-WIT.
?
HM?

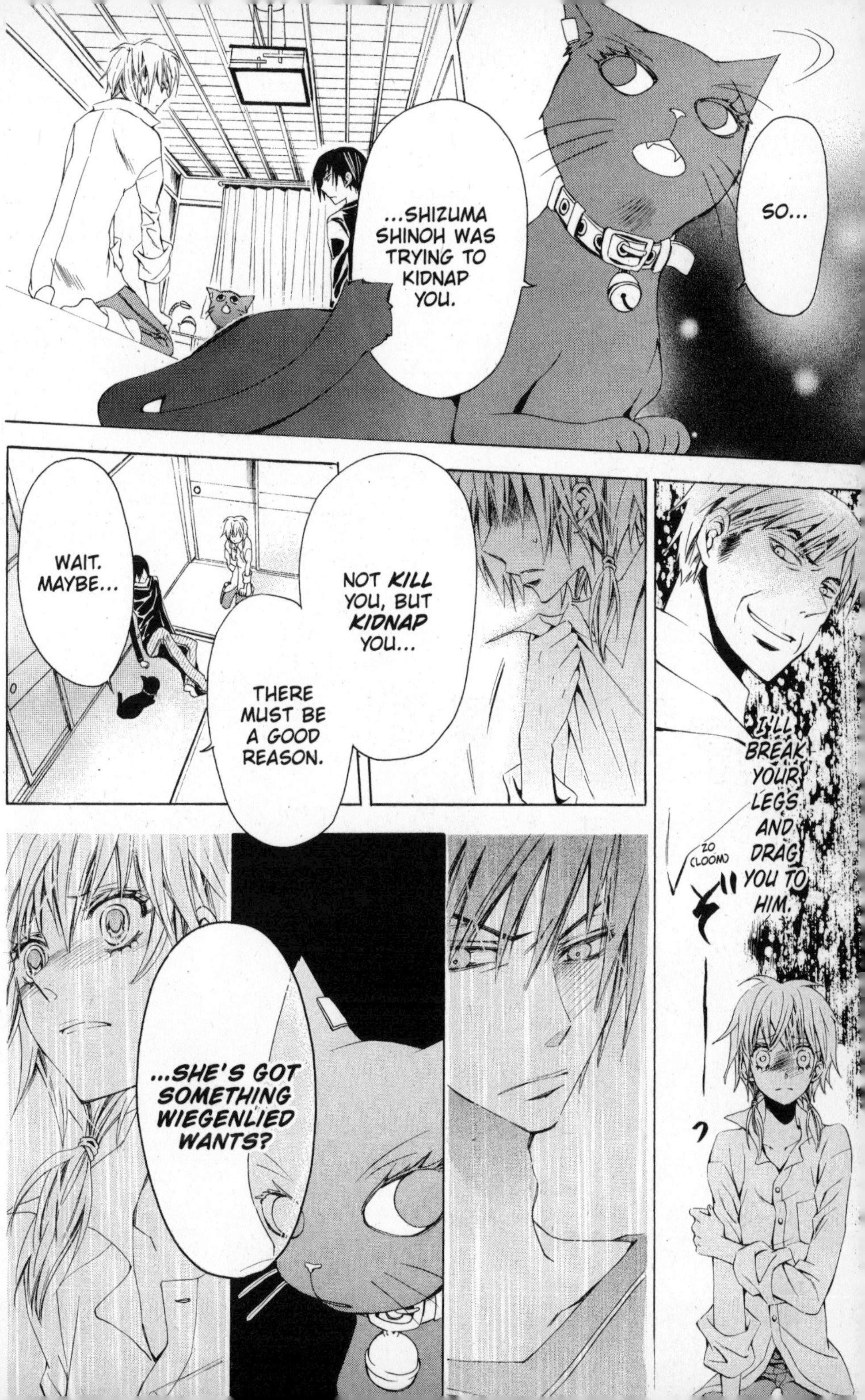
SO...
...SHIZUMA SHINOH WAS TRYING TO KIDNAP YOU.
I'LL BREAK YOUR LEGS AND DRAG YOU TO HIM.
ZO (CLOOM)
NOT *KILL* YOU, BUT *KIDNAP* YOU...
THERE MUST BE A GOOD REASON.
WAIT. MAYBE...
...SHE'S GOT SOMETHING WIEGENLIED WANTS?

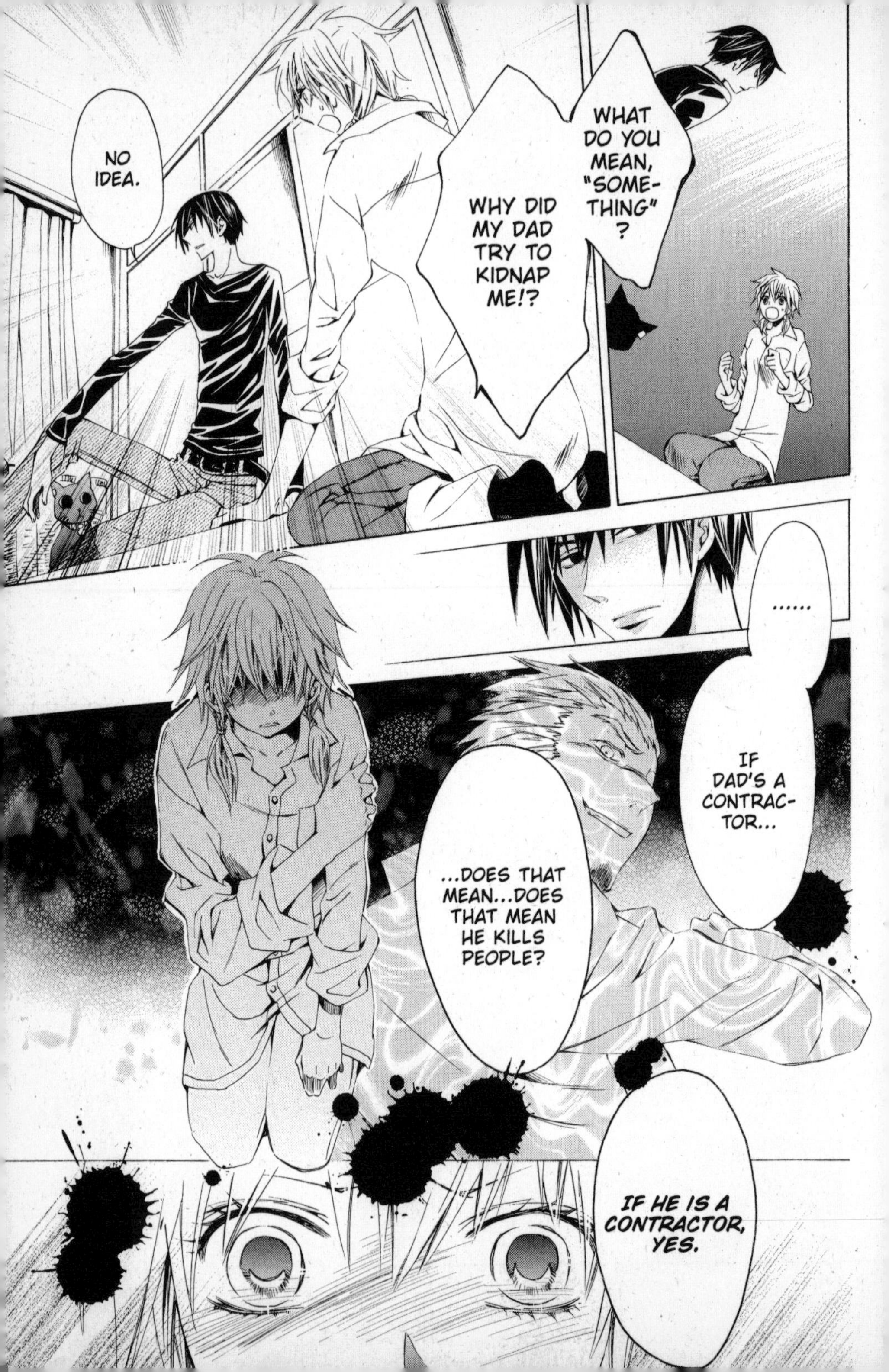
WHAT DO YOU MEAN, "SOME-THING"?
WHY DID MY DAD TRY TO KIDNAP ME!?
NO IDEA.
......
IF DAD'S A CONTRAC-TOR...
...DOES THAT MEAN...DOES THAT MEAN HE KILLS PEOPLE?
IF HE IS A CONTRACTOR, YES.

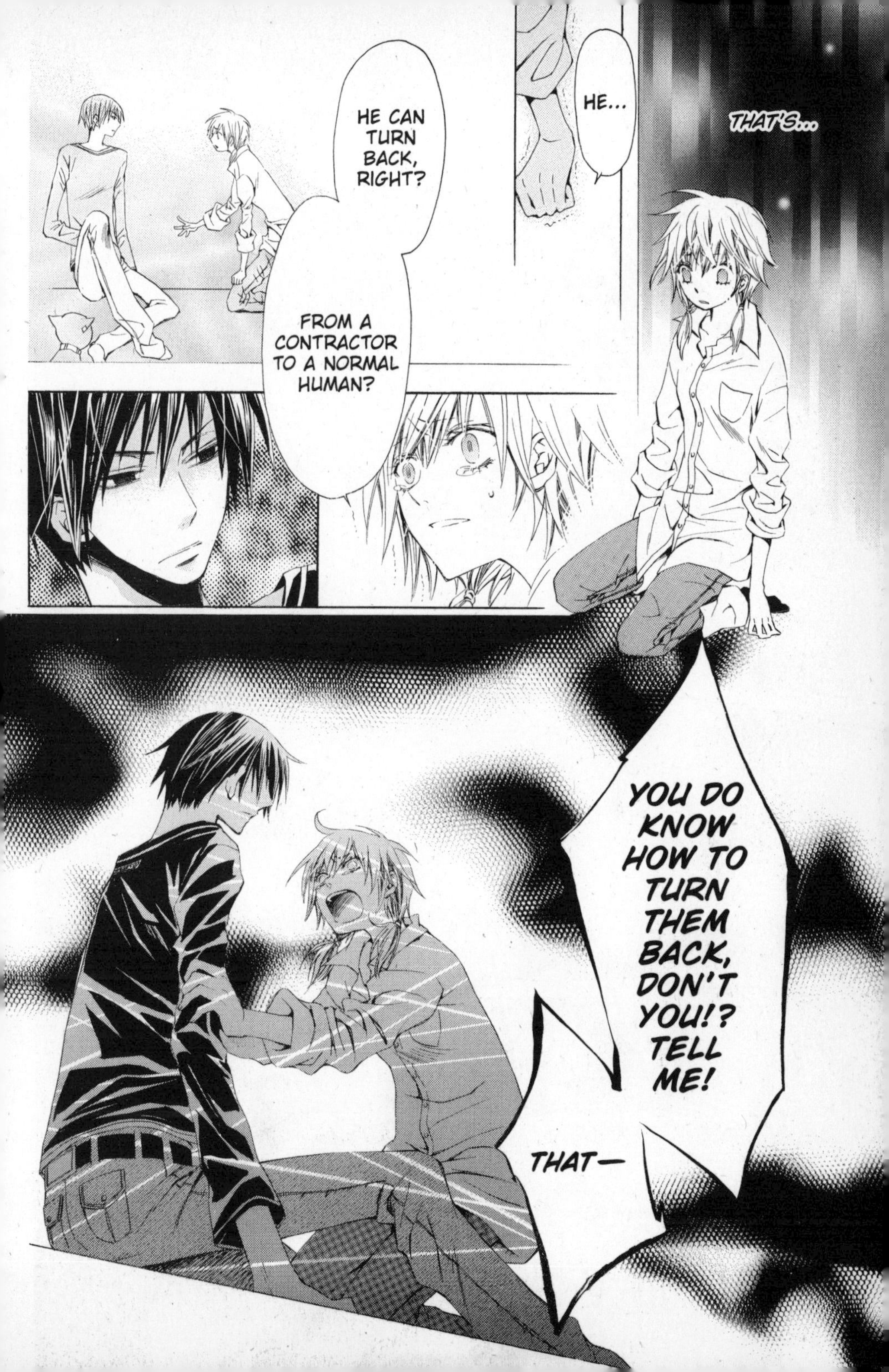
THAT'S...
HE...
HE CAN TURN BACK, RIGHT?
FROM A CONTRACTOR TO A NORMAL HUMAN?
YOU DO KNOW HOW TO TURN THEM BACK, DON'T YOU!? TELL ME!
THAT—

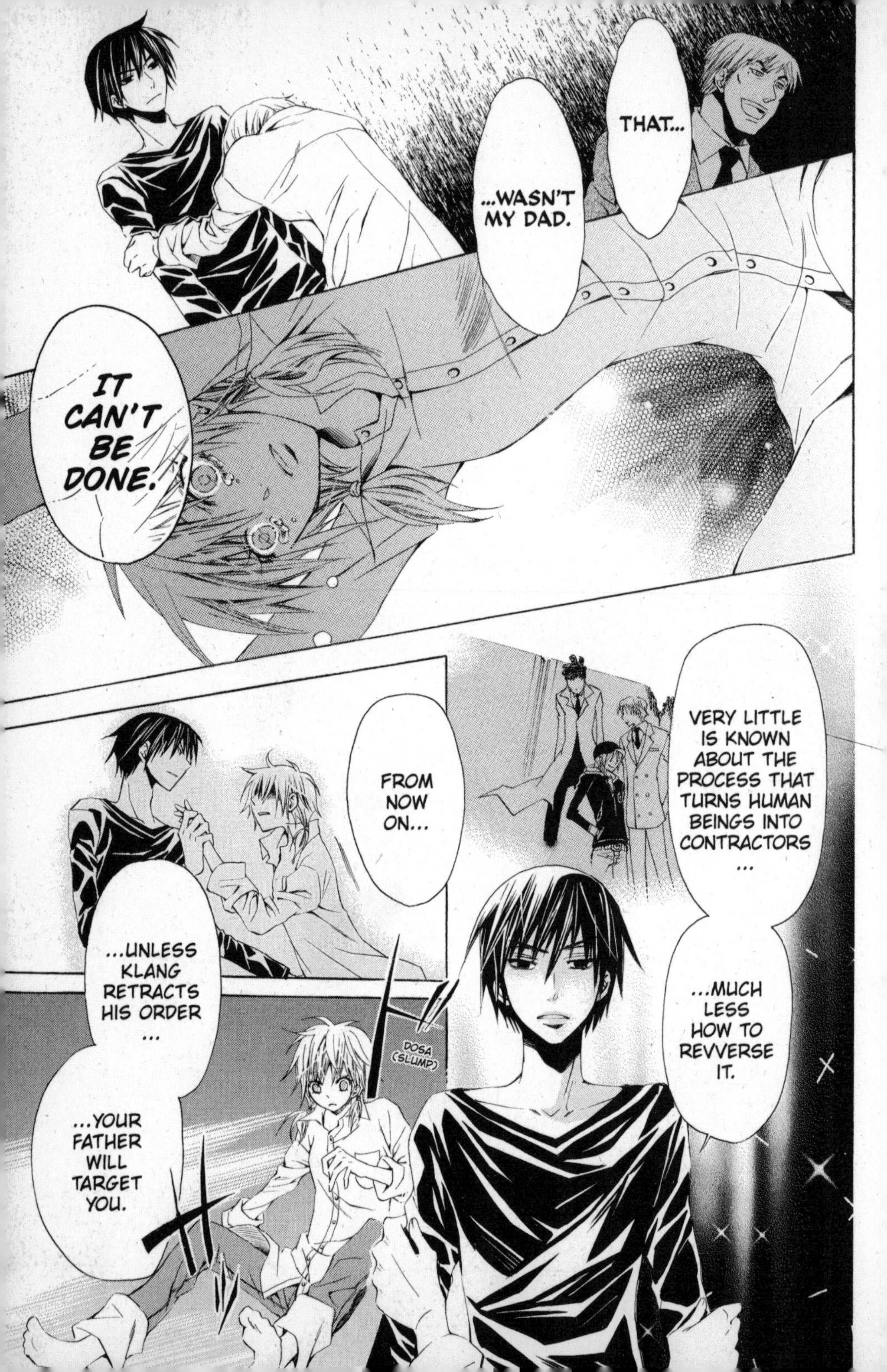
THAT...
...WASN'T MY DAD.
IT CAN'T BE DONE.
VERY LITTLE IS KNOWN ABOUT THE PROCESS THAT TURNS HUMAN BEINGS INTO CONTRACTORS ...
...MUCH LESS HOW TO REVVERSE IT.
FROM NOW ON...
...UNLESS KLANG RETRACTS HIS ORDER ...
DOSA (SLUMP)
...YOUR FATHER WILL TARGET YOU.

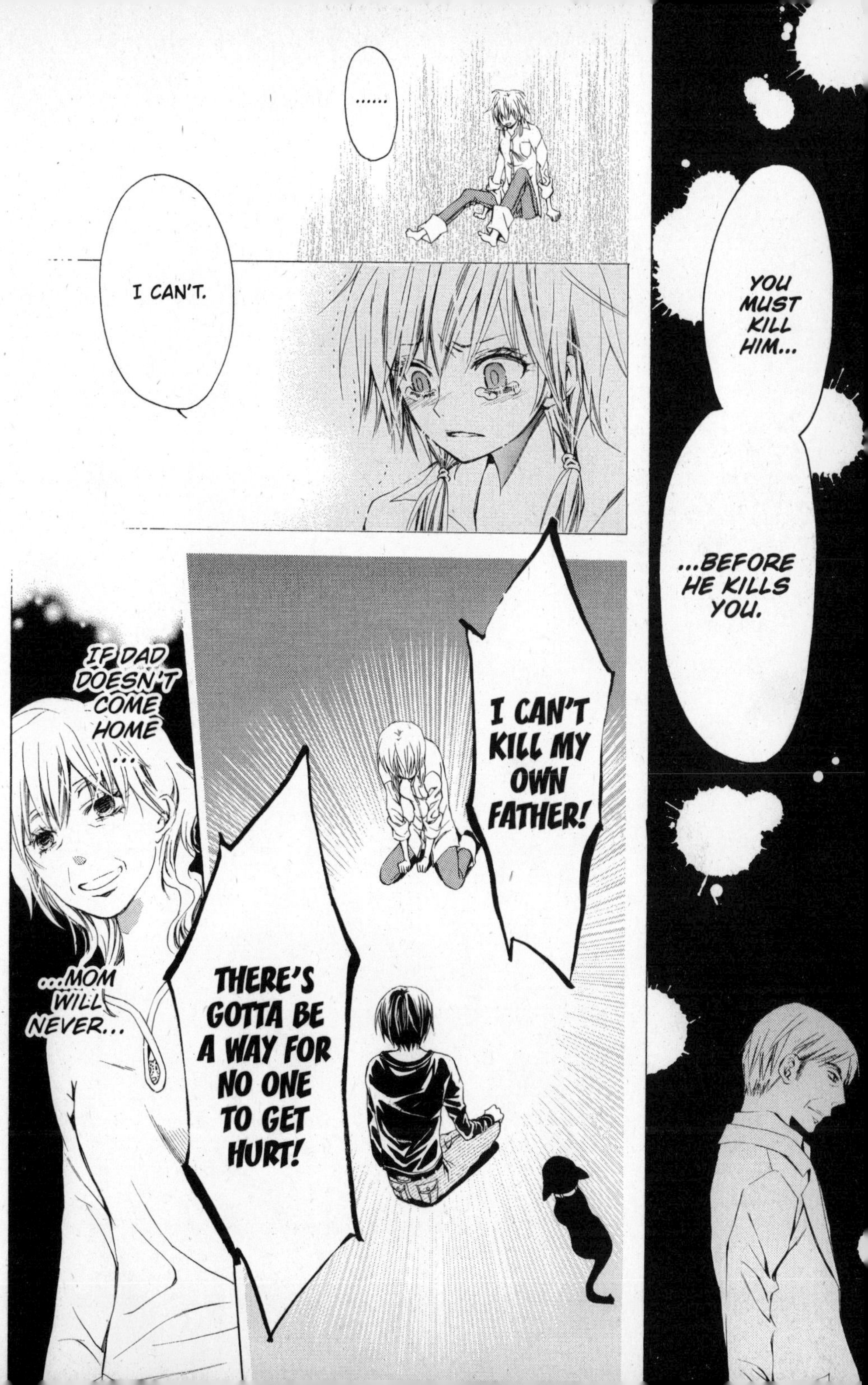
YOU MUST KILL HIM...
...BEFORE HE KILLS YOU.
......
I CAN'T.
I CAN'T KILL MY OWN FATHER!
THERE'S GOTTA BE A WAY FOR NO ONE TO GET HURT!
IF DAD DOESN'T COME HOME...
...MOM WILL NEVER...

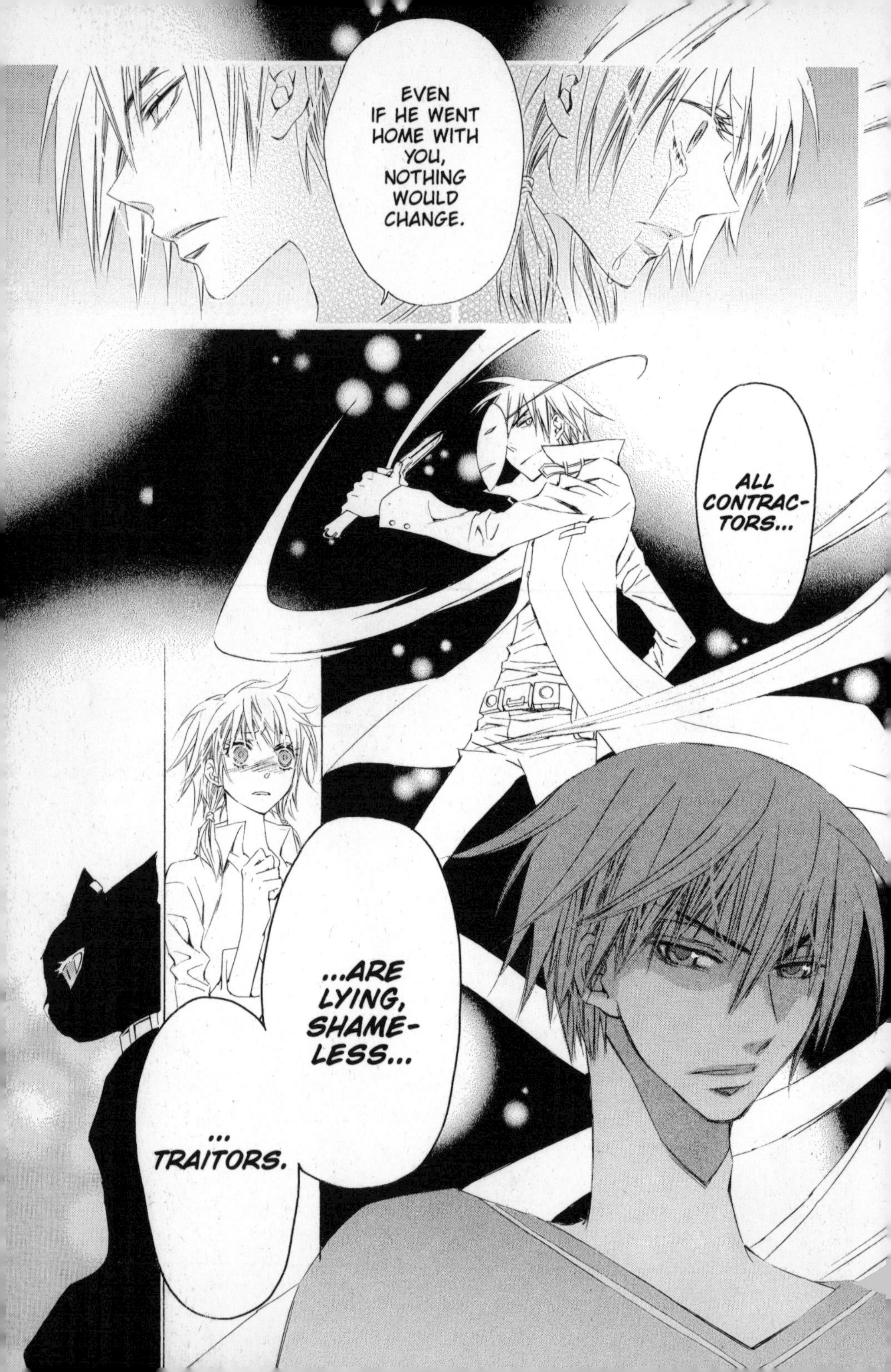
EVEN IF HE WENT HOME WITH YOU, NOTHING WOULD CHANGE.
ALL CONTRACTORS...
...ARE LYING, SHAMELESS...
...TRAITORS.

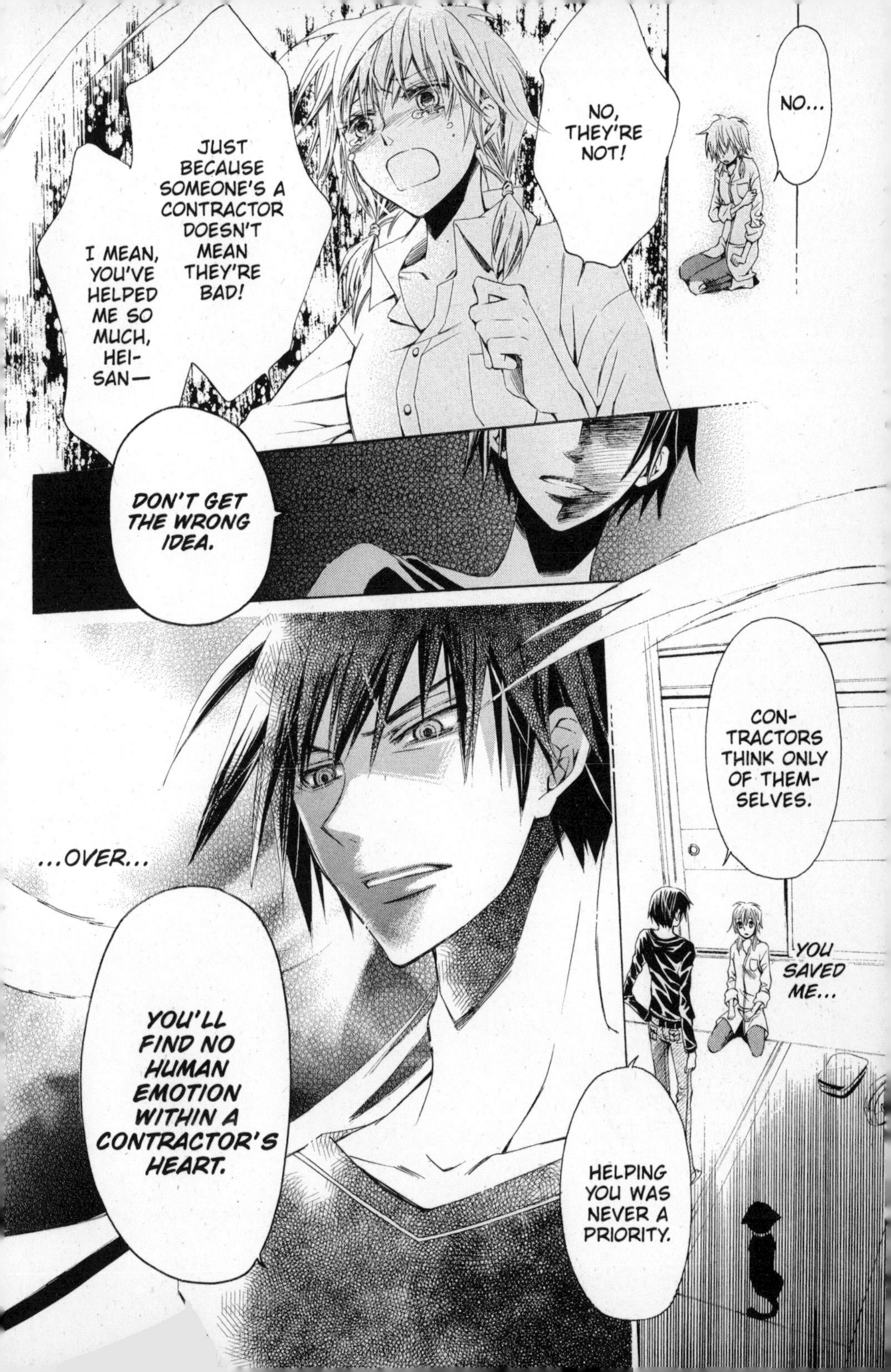
NO...
NO, THEY'RE NOT!
JUST BECAUSE SOMEONE'S A CONTRACTOR DOESN'T MEAN THEY'RE BAD!
I MEAN, YOU'VE HELPED ME SO MUCH, HEI-SAN—
DON'T GET THE WRONG IDEA.
CON-TRACTORS THINK ONLY OF THEM-SELVES.
YOU SAVED ME...
...OVER...
HELPING YOU WAS NEVER A PRIORITY.
YOU'LL FIND NO HUMAN EMOTION WITHIN A CONTRACTOR'S HEART.

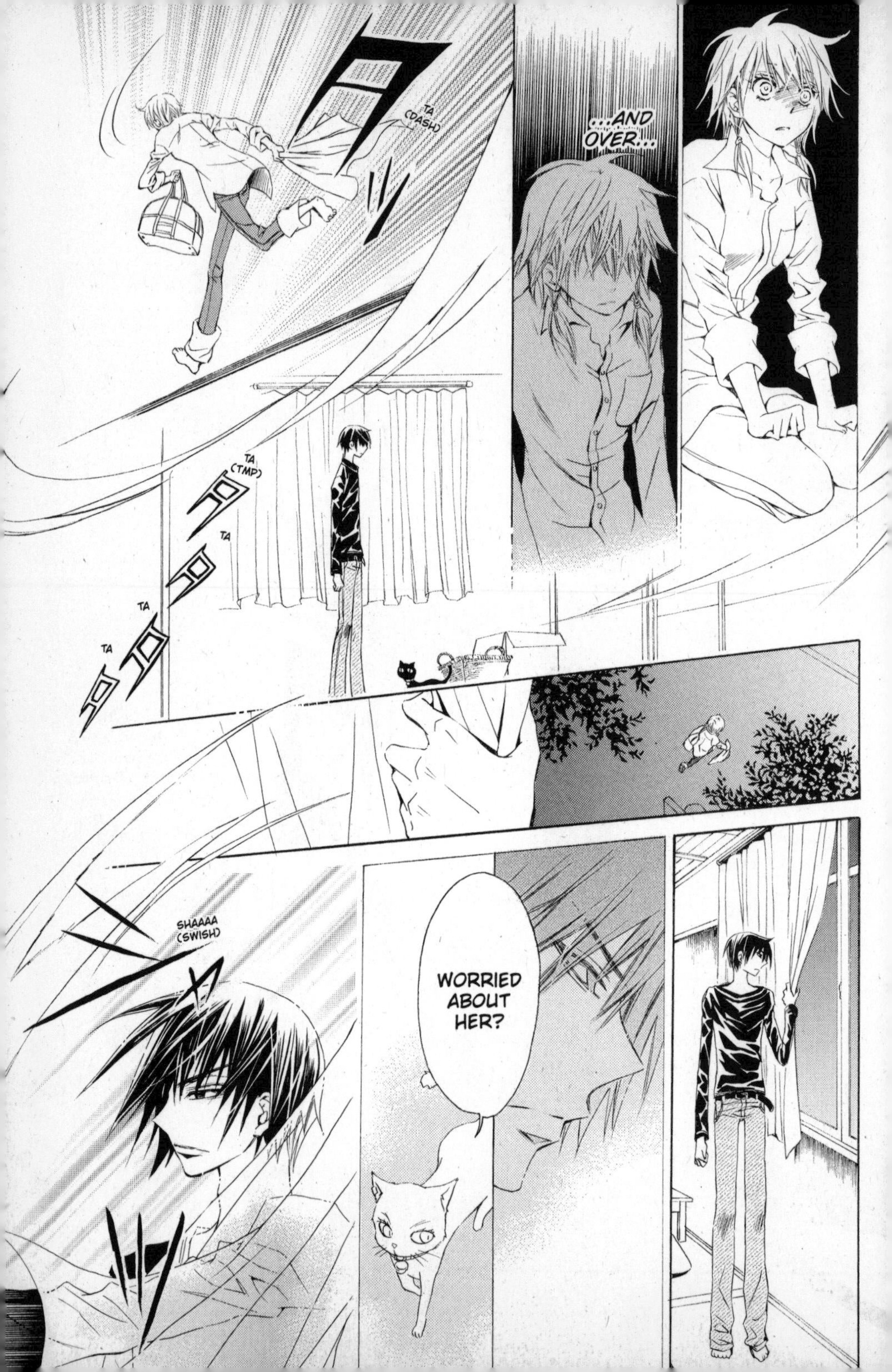
...AND OVER...
TA (DASH)
TA (TMP)
TA
TA
TA
WORRIED ABOUT HER?
SHAAAA (SWISH)

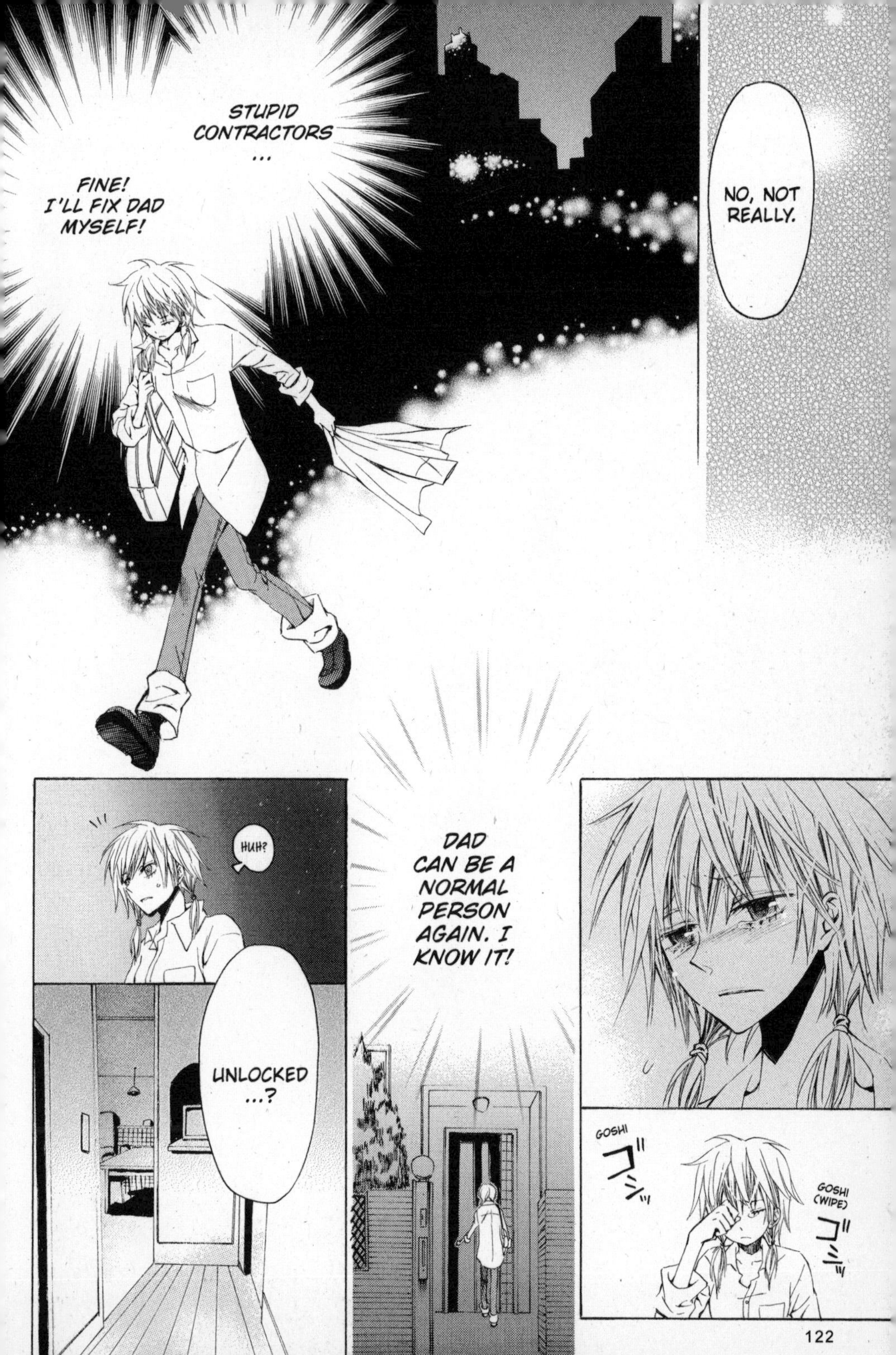
NO, NOT REALLY.
STUPID CONTRACTORS ...
FINE! I'LL FIX DAD MYSELF!
GOSHI
GOSHI (WIPE)
DAD CAN BE A NORMAL PERSON AGAIN. I KNOW IT!
HUH?
UNLOCKED ...?

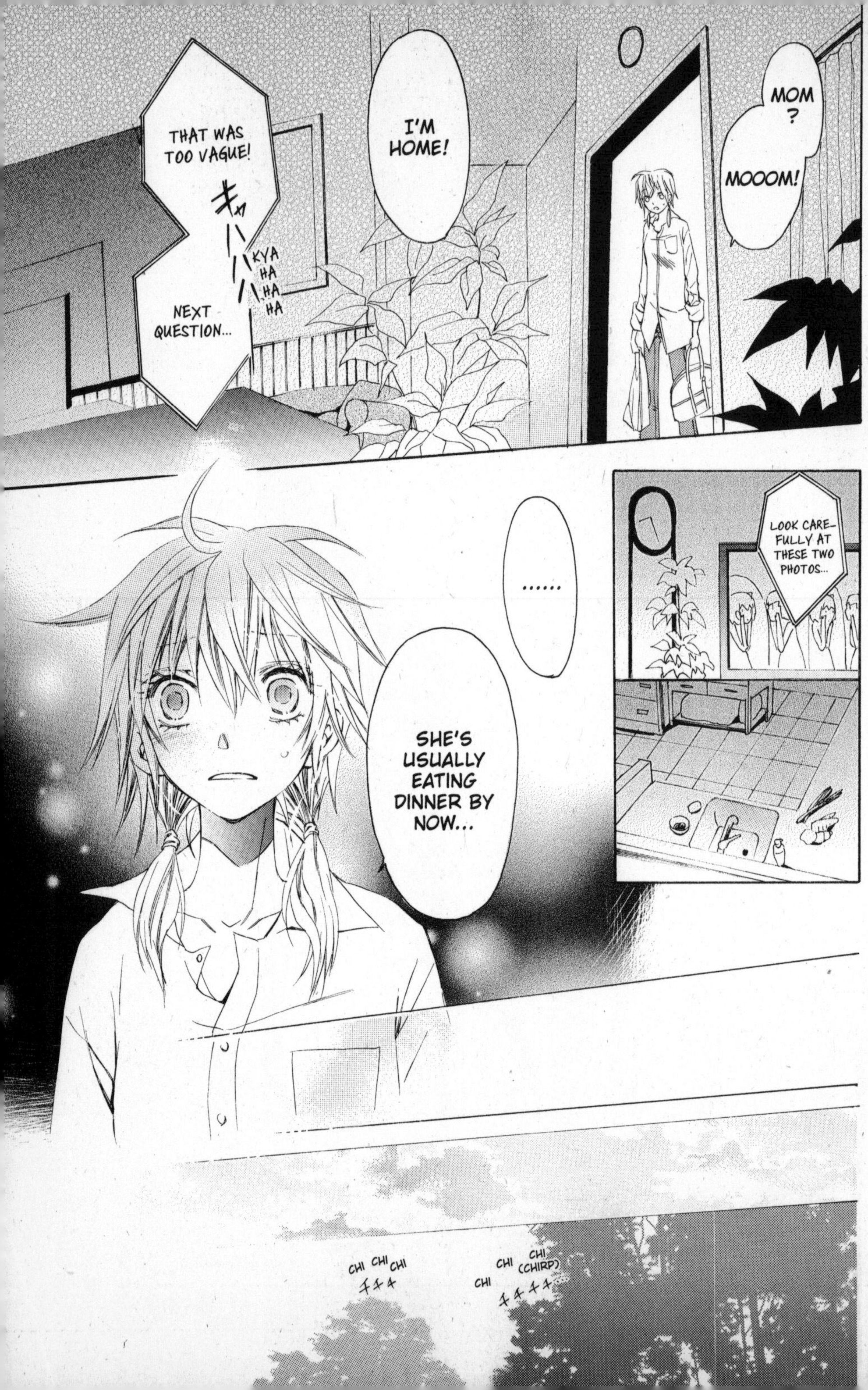
MOM?
MOOOM!
I'M HOME!
THAT WAS TOO VAGUE!
KYA HA HA HA
NEXT QUESTION...
LOOK CAREFULLY AT THESE TWO PHOTOS...
......
SHE'S USUALLY EATING DINNER BY NOW...
CHI CHI CHI (CHIRP)
CHI CHI CHI

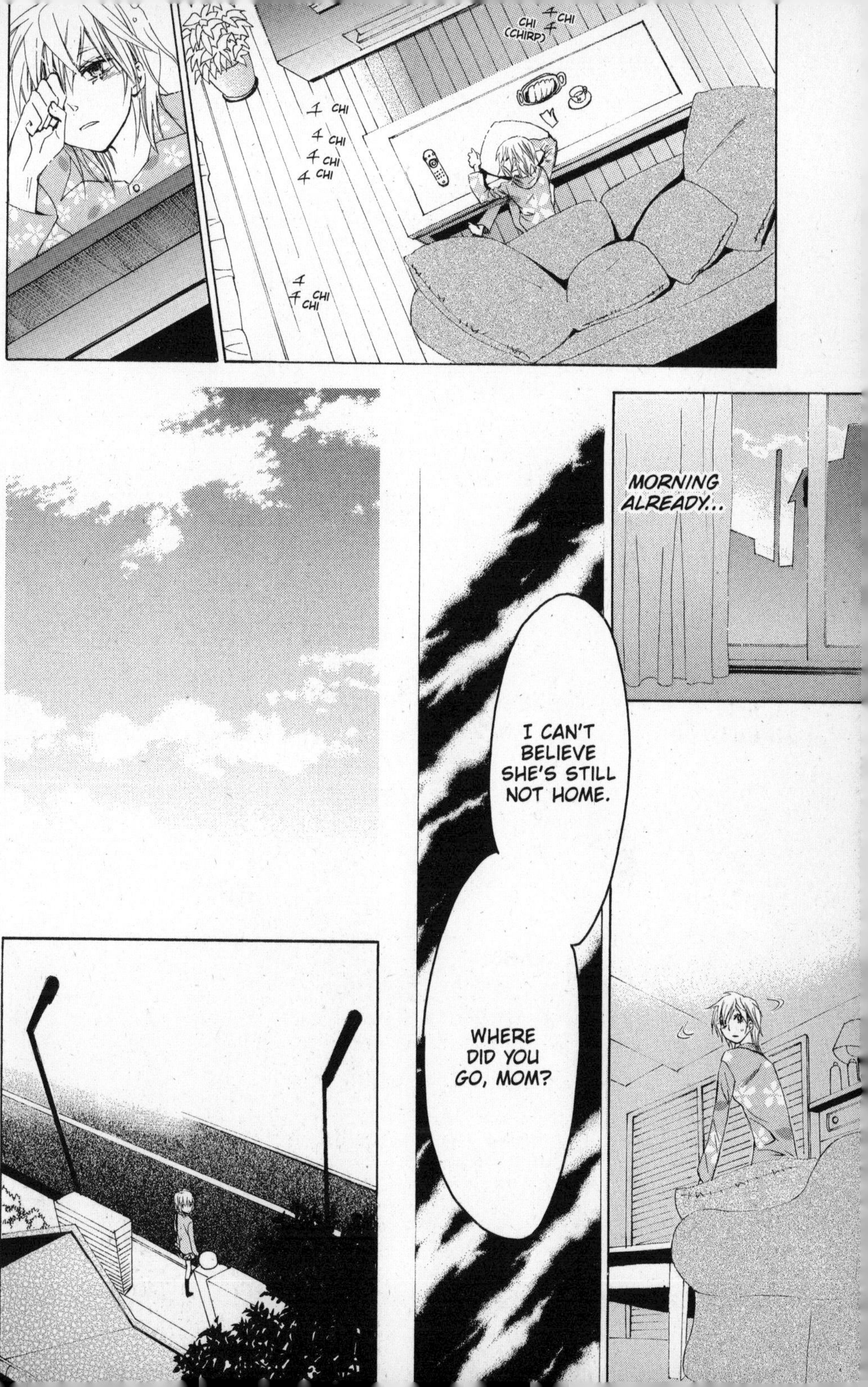
CHI CHI (CHIRP)
CHI CHI CHI CHI
CHI CHI
MORNING ALREADY...
I CAN'T BELIEVE SHE'S STILL NOT HOME.
WHERE DID YOU GO, MOM?

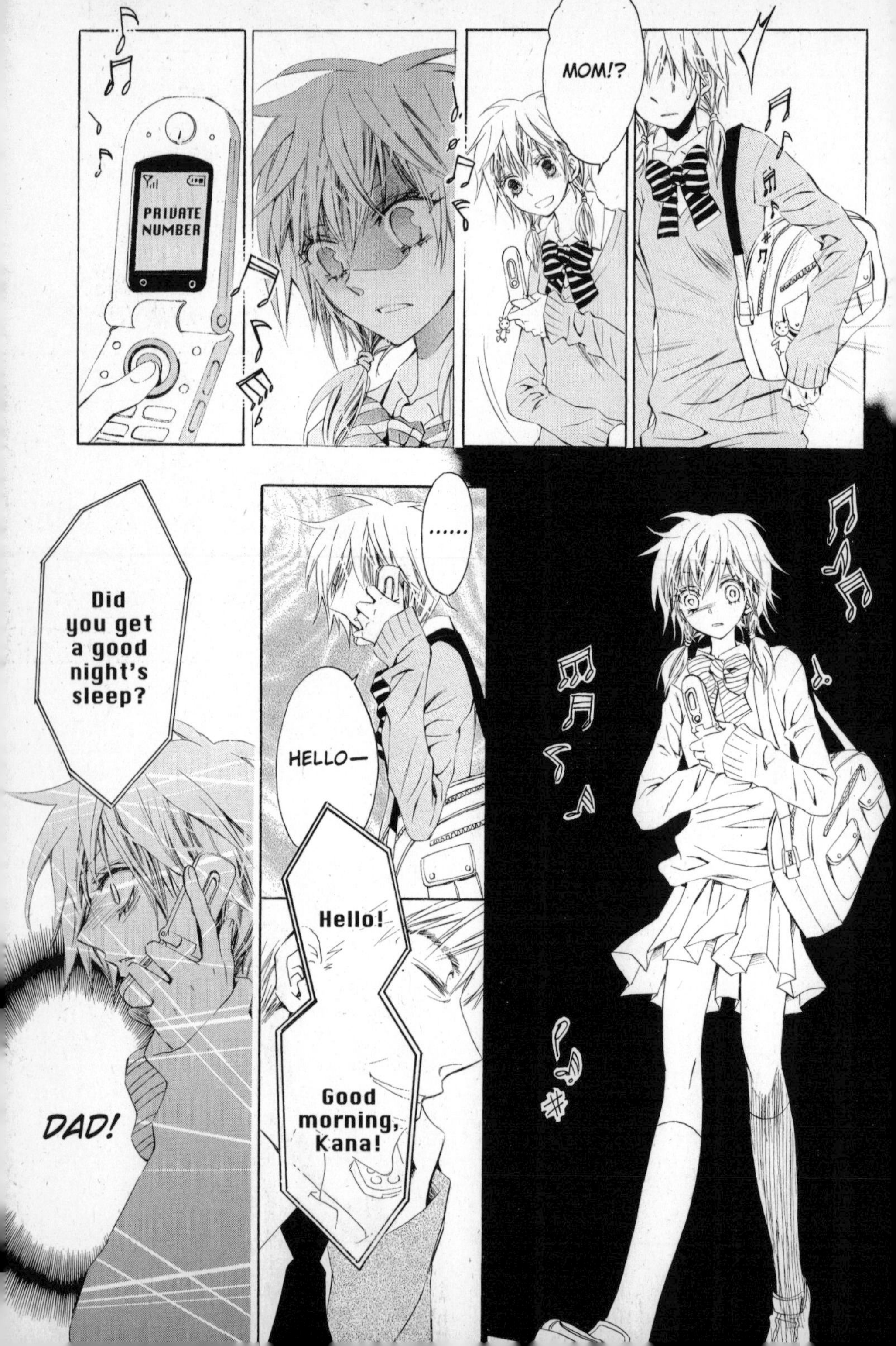
MOM!?
PRIVATE NUMBER
......
HELLO—
Hello!
Good morning, Kana!
Did you get a good night's sleep?
DAD!

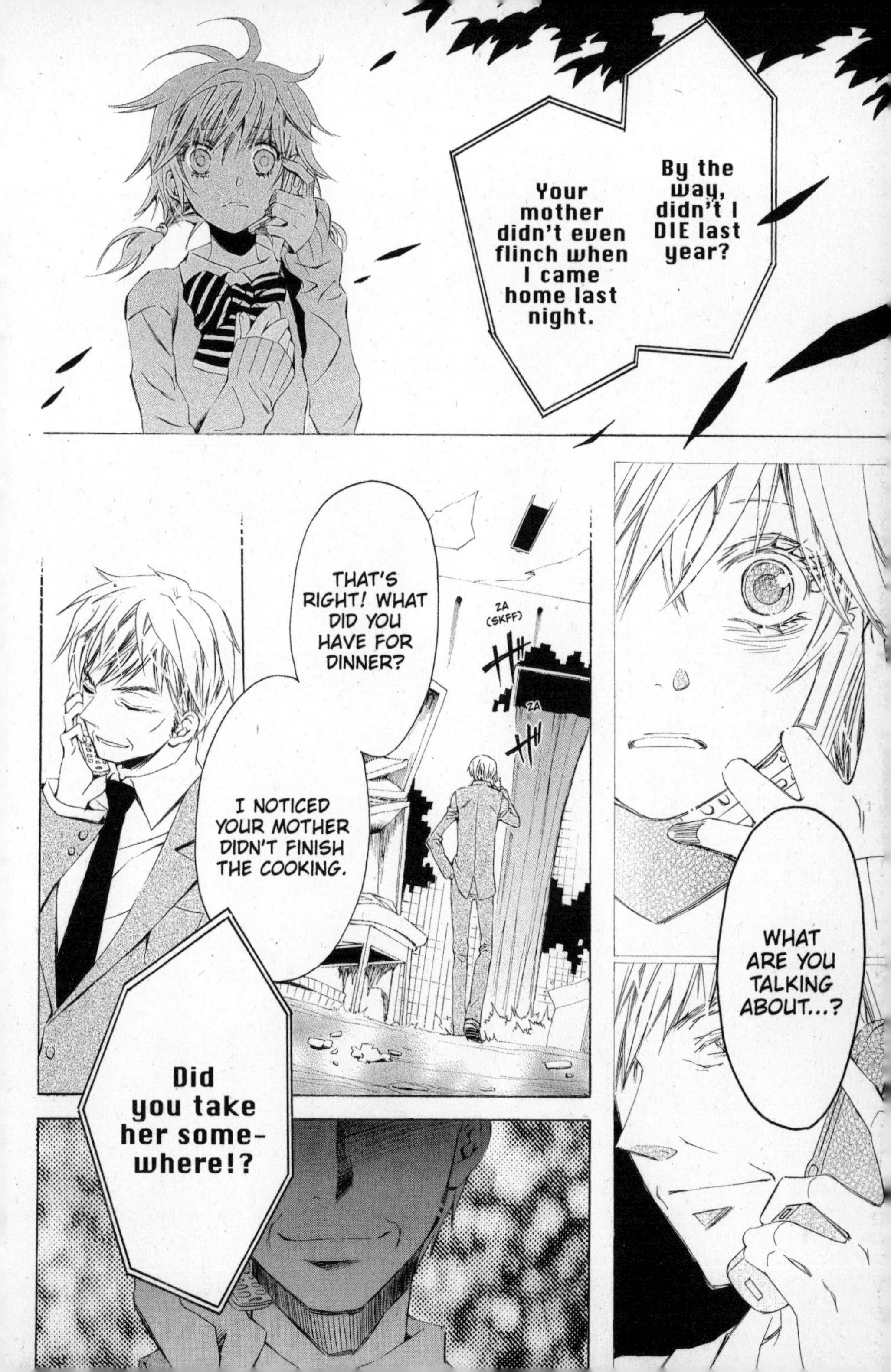
By the way, didn't I DIE last year?
Your mother didn't even flinch when I came home last night.
WHAT ARE YOU TALKING ABOUT...?
THAT'S RIGHT! WHAT DID YOU HAVE FOR DINNER?
ZA (SKFF)
ZA
I NOTICED YOUR MOTHER DIDN'T FINISH THE COOKING.
Did you take her some-where!?

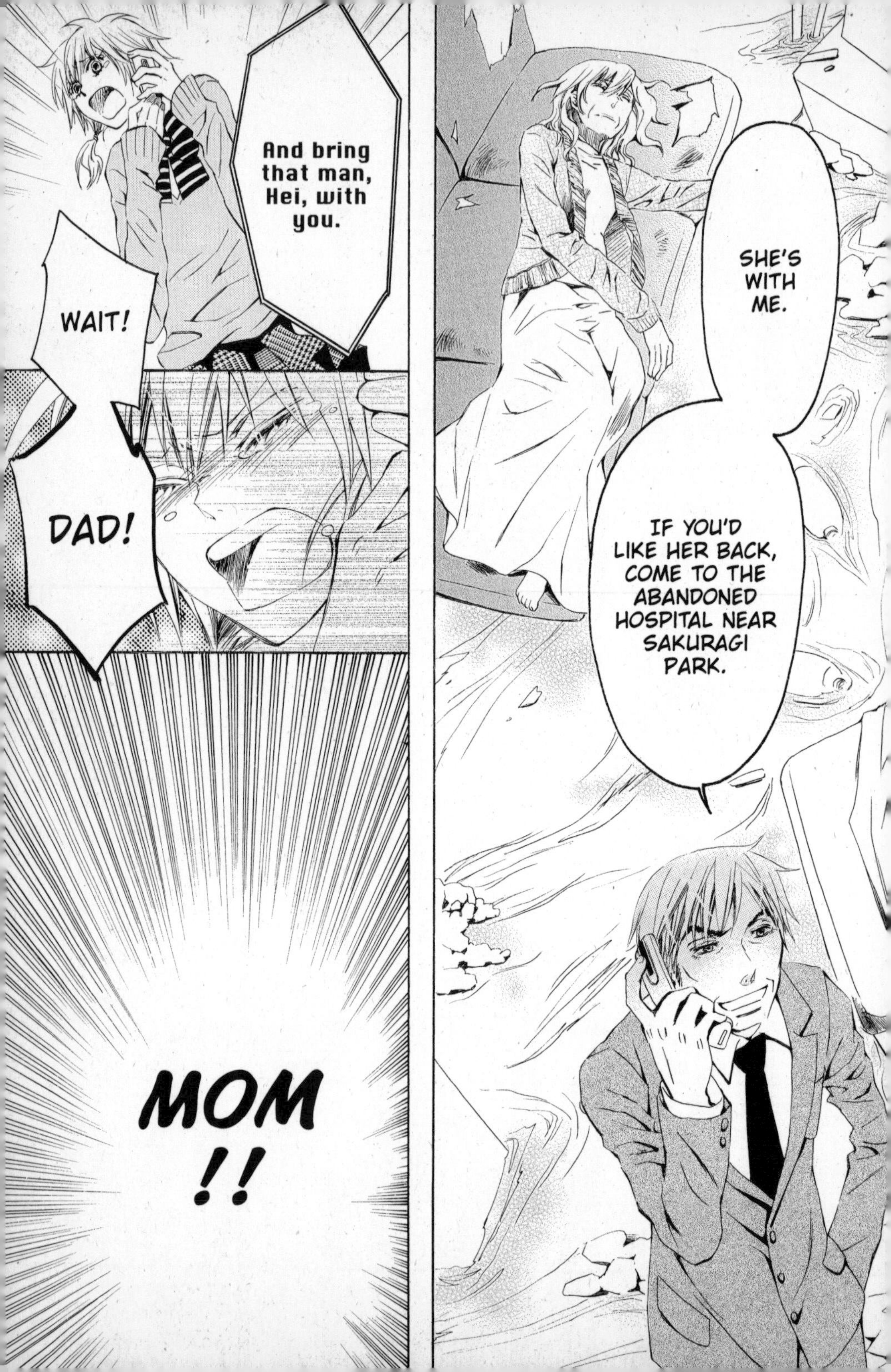
SHE'S WITH ME.
IF YOU'D LIKE HER BACK, COME TO THE ABANDONED HOSPITAL NEAR SAKURAGI PARK.
And bring that man, Hei, with you.
WAIT!
DAD!
MOM !!

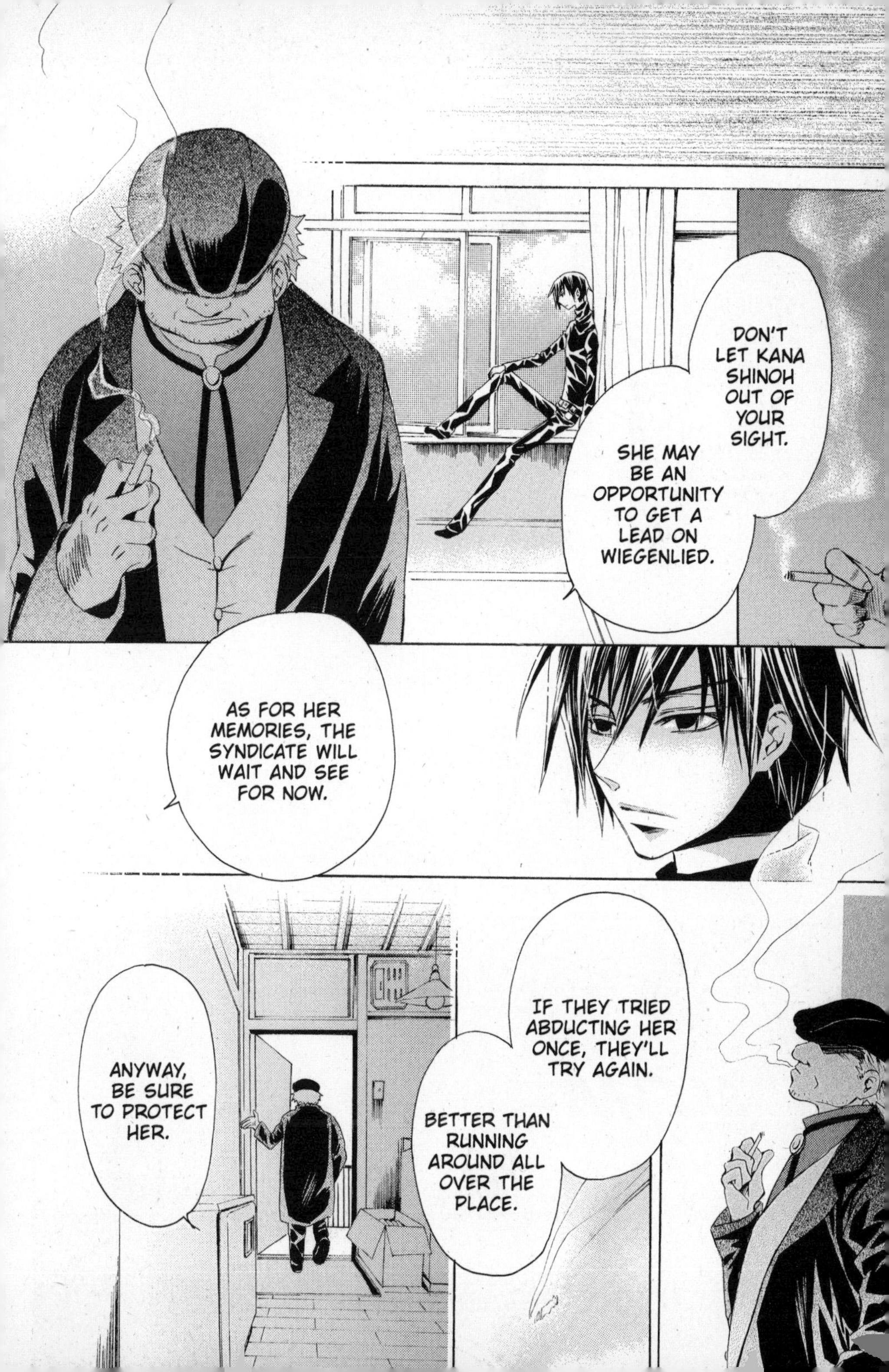
DON'T LET KANA SHINOH OUT OF YOUR SIGHT.
SHE MAY BE AN OPPORTUNITY TO GET A LEAD ON WIEGENLIED.
AS FOR HER MEMORIES, THE SYNDICATE WILL WAIT AND SEE FOR NOW.
IF THEY TRIED ABDUCTING HER ONCE, THEY'LL TRY AGAIN.
BETTER THAN RUNNING AROUND ALL OVER THE PLACE.
ANYWAY, BE SURE TO PROTECT HER.

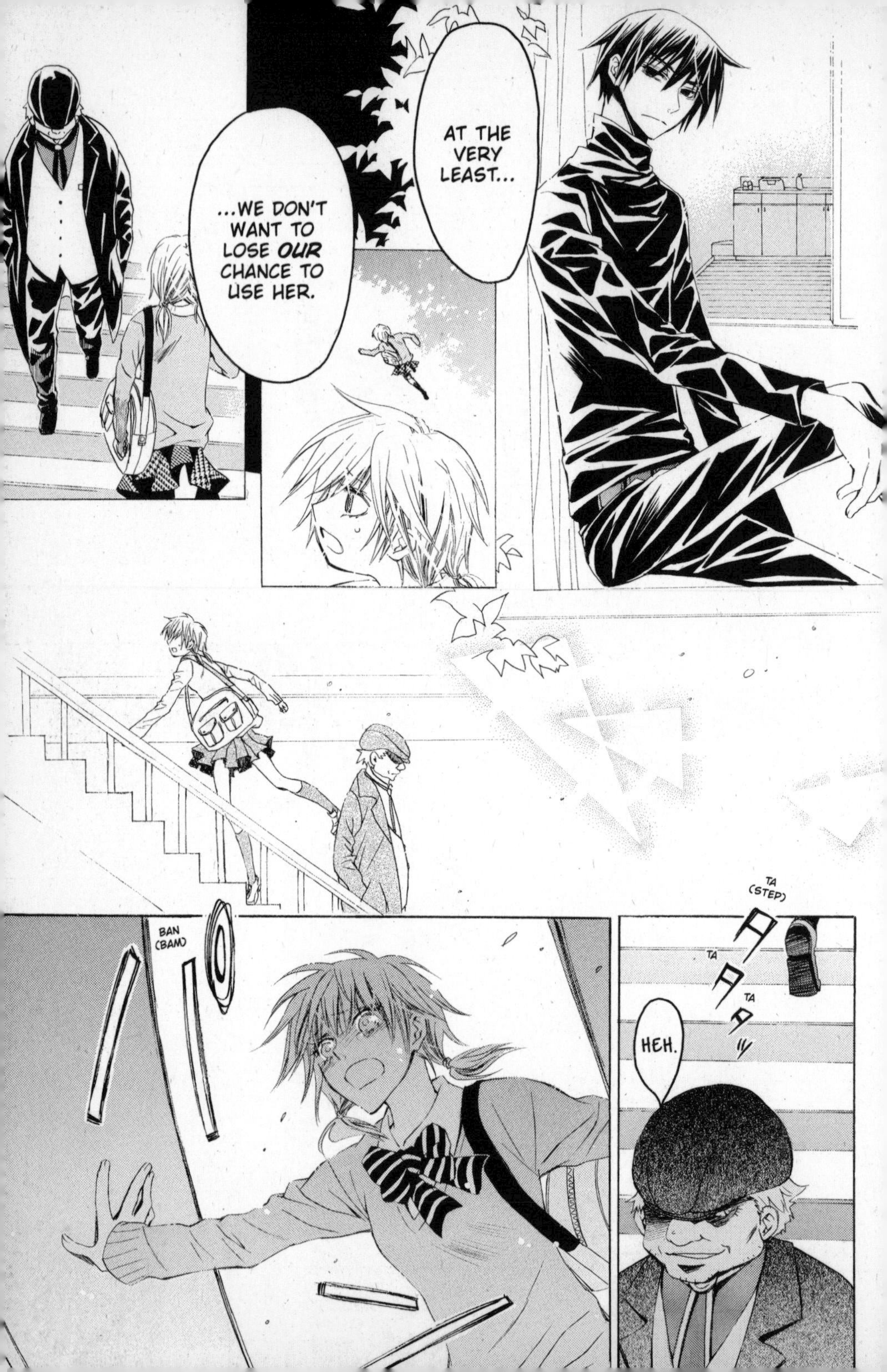
AT THE VERY LEAST...
...WE DON'T WANT TO LOSE OUR CHANCE TO USE HER.
TA (STEP)
TA
TA
HEH.
BAN (BAM)

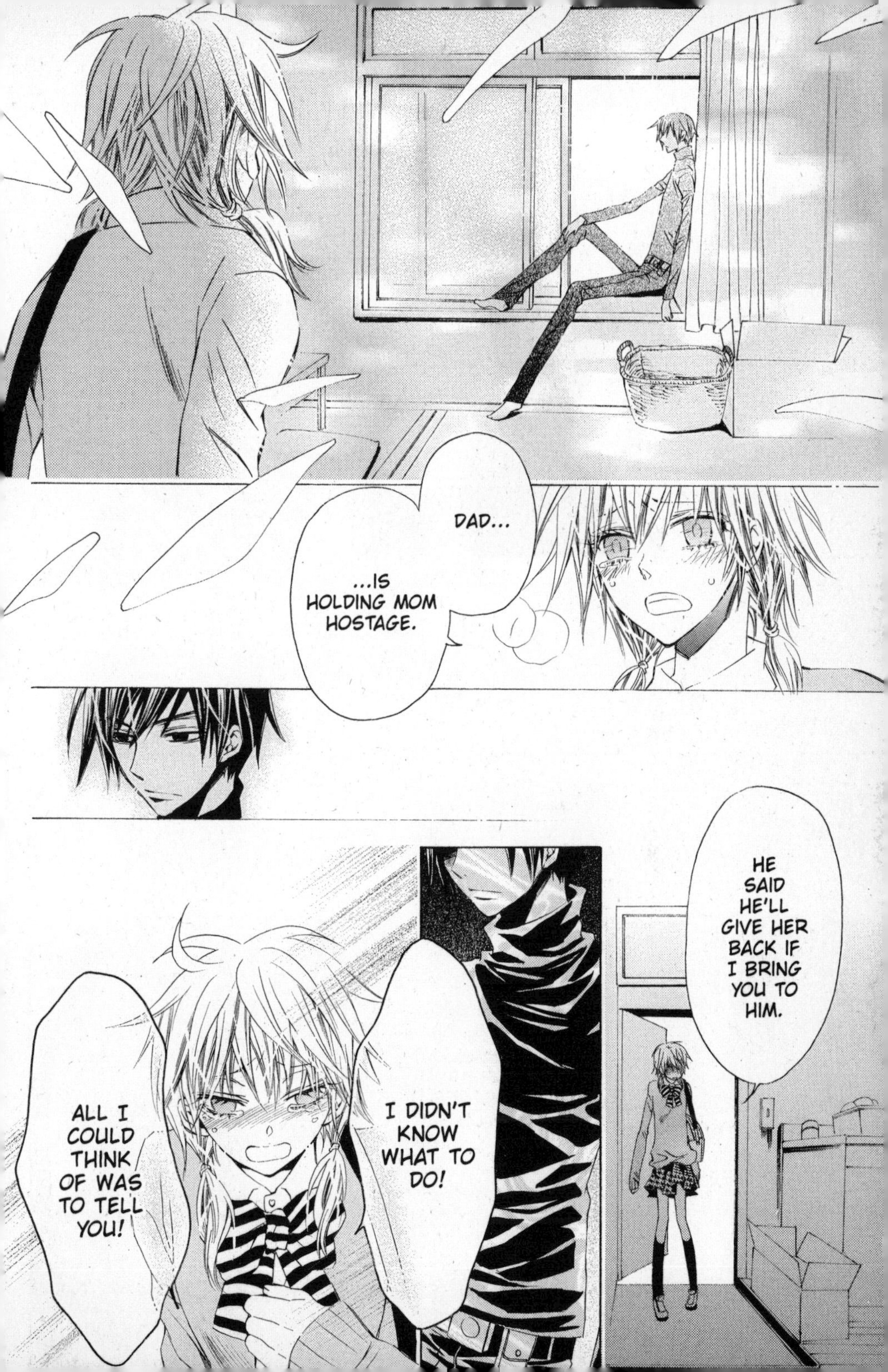
DAD...
...IS HOLDING MOM HOSTAGE.
HE SAID HE'LL GIVE HER BACK IF I BRING YOU TO HIM.
I DIDN'T KNOW WHAT TO DO!
ALL I COULD THINK OF WAS TO TELL YOU!

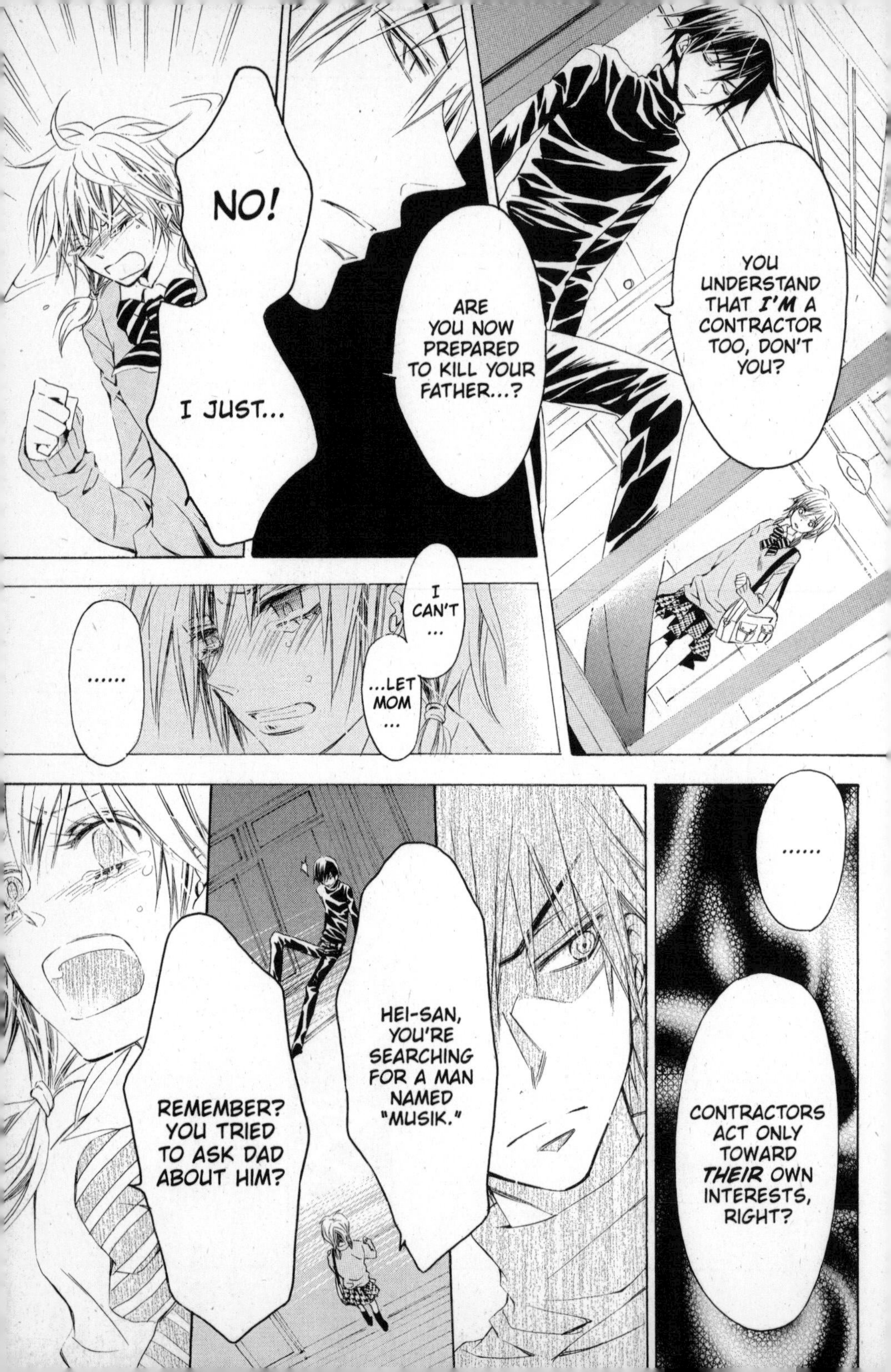
YOU UNDERSTAND THAT I'M A CONTRACTOR TOO, DON'T YOU?
ARE YOU NOW PREPARED TO KILL YOUR FATHER...?
NO!
I JUST...
I CAN'T...
...LET MOM...
......
......
CONTRACTORS ACT ONLY TOWARD THEIR OWN INTERESTS, RIGHT?
HEI-SAN, YOU'RE SEARCHING FOR A MAN NAMED "MUSIK."
REMEMBER? YOU TRIED TO ASK DAD ABOUT HIM?

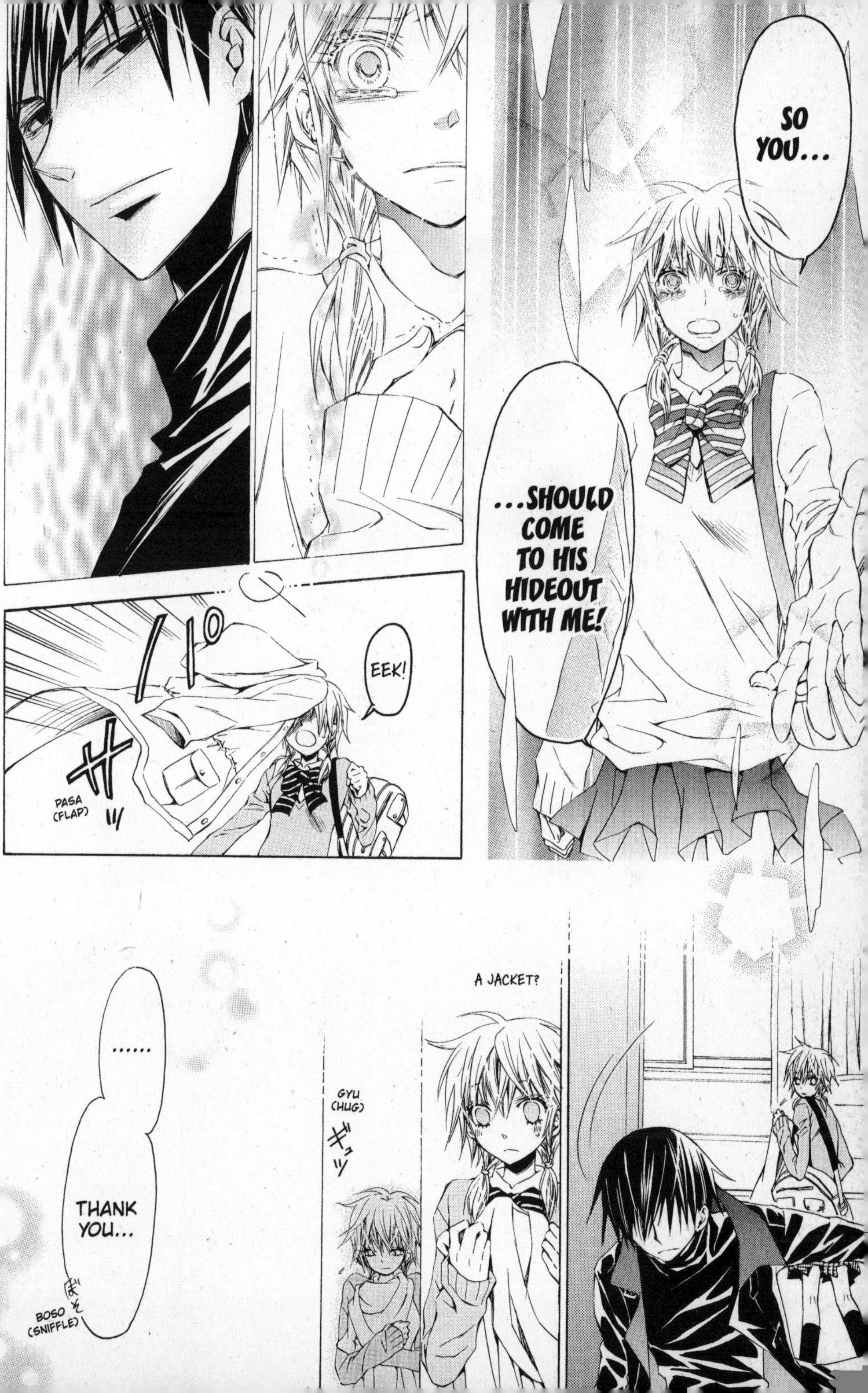
SO YOU...
...SHOULD COME TO HIS HIDEOUT WITH ME!
EEK!
PASA (FLAP)
A JACKET?
ギュッ
GYU (HUG)
......
THANK YOU...
ぼそ
BOSO (SNIFFLE)

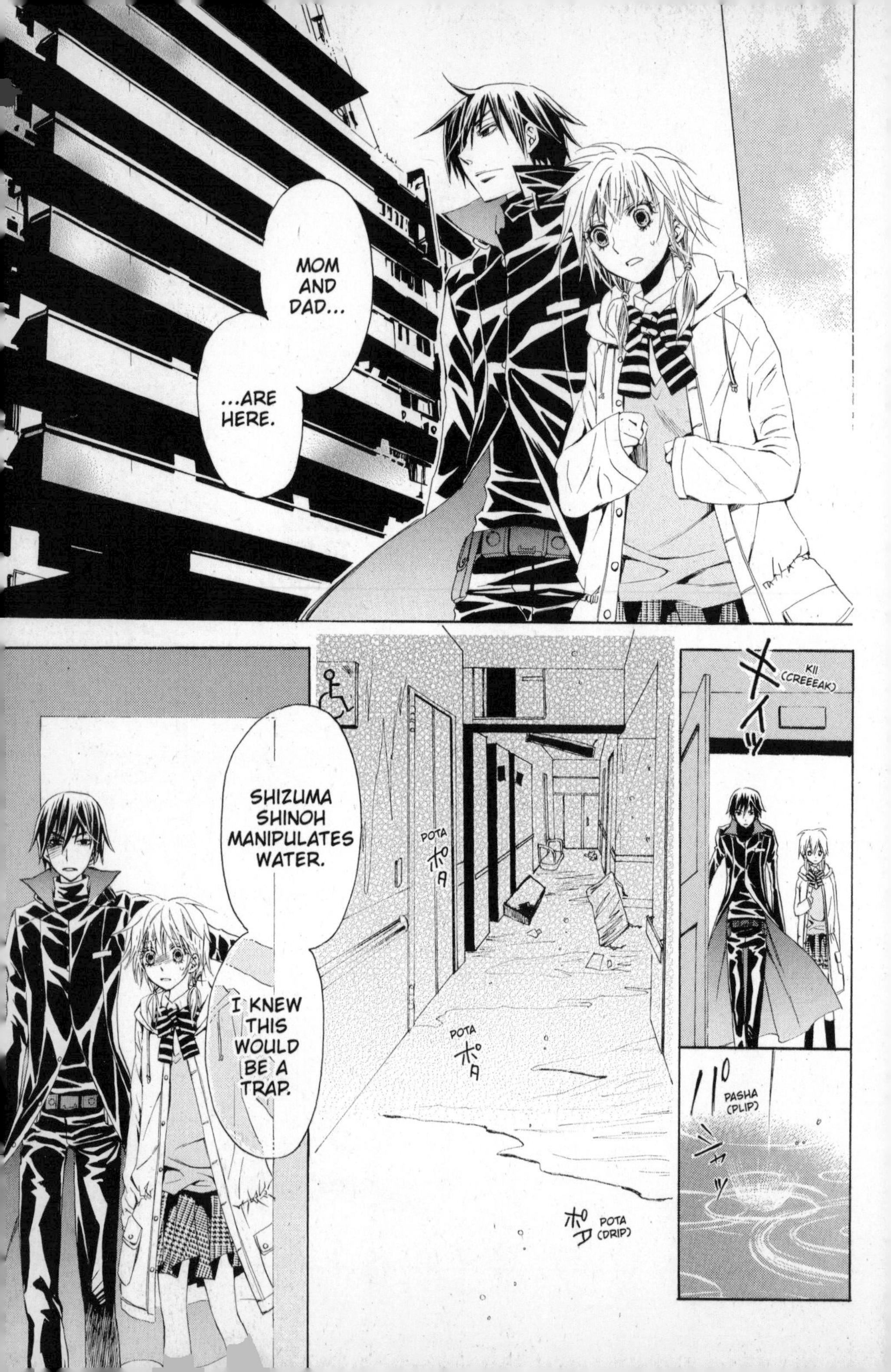
MOM AND DAD...
...ARE HERE.
キイッ
KII (CREEEAK)
パシャッ
PASHA (PLIP)
ポタ
POTA
ポタ
POTA
ポタ
POTA (DRIP)
SHIZUMA SHINOH MANIPULATES WATER.
I KNEW THIS WOULD BE A TRAP.

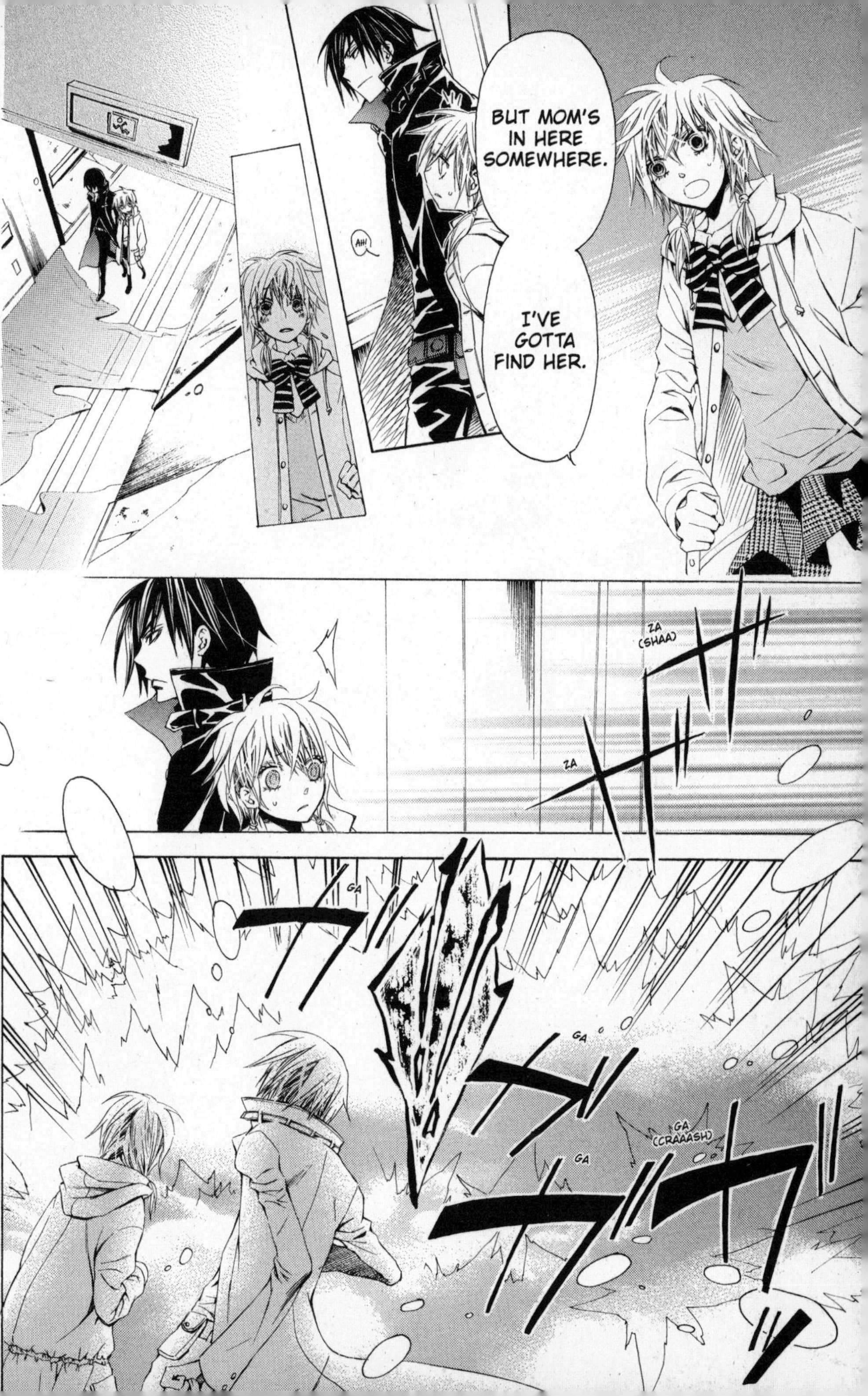
BUT MOM'S IN HERE SOMEWHERE.
I'VE GOTTA FIND HER.
AH!
ZA (SHAA)
ZA
GA
GA
GA (CRAAASH)
GA

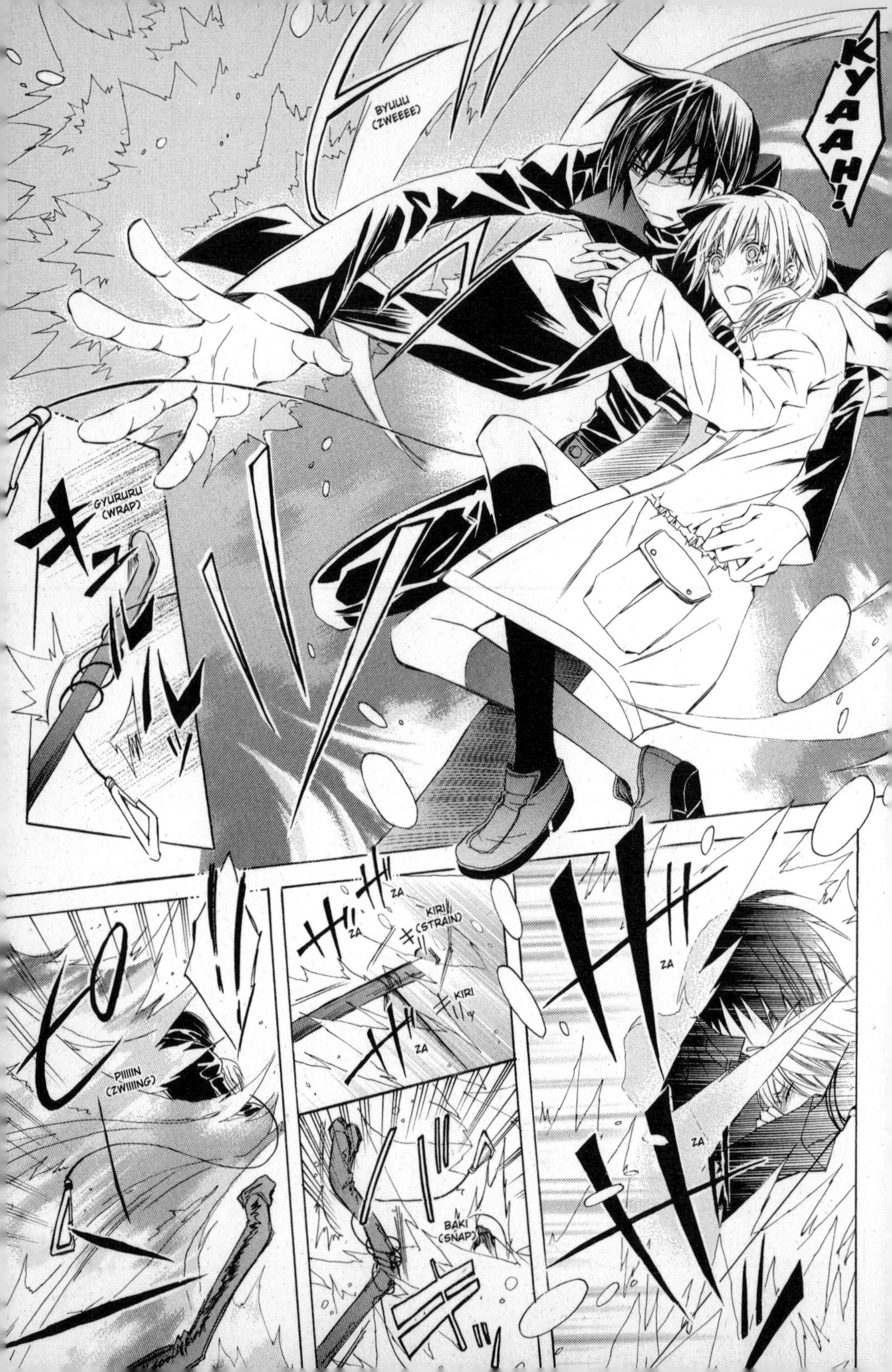
KYAAH!
BYUUU (ZWEEEE)
GYURURU (WRAP)
ZA
ZA
ZA
KIRI (STRAIN)
ZA
KIRI
ZA
BAKI (SNAP)
PIIIIN (ZWIIIING)

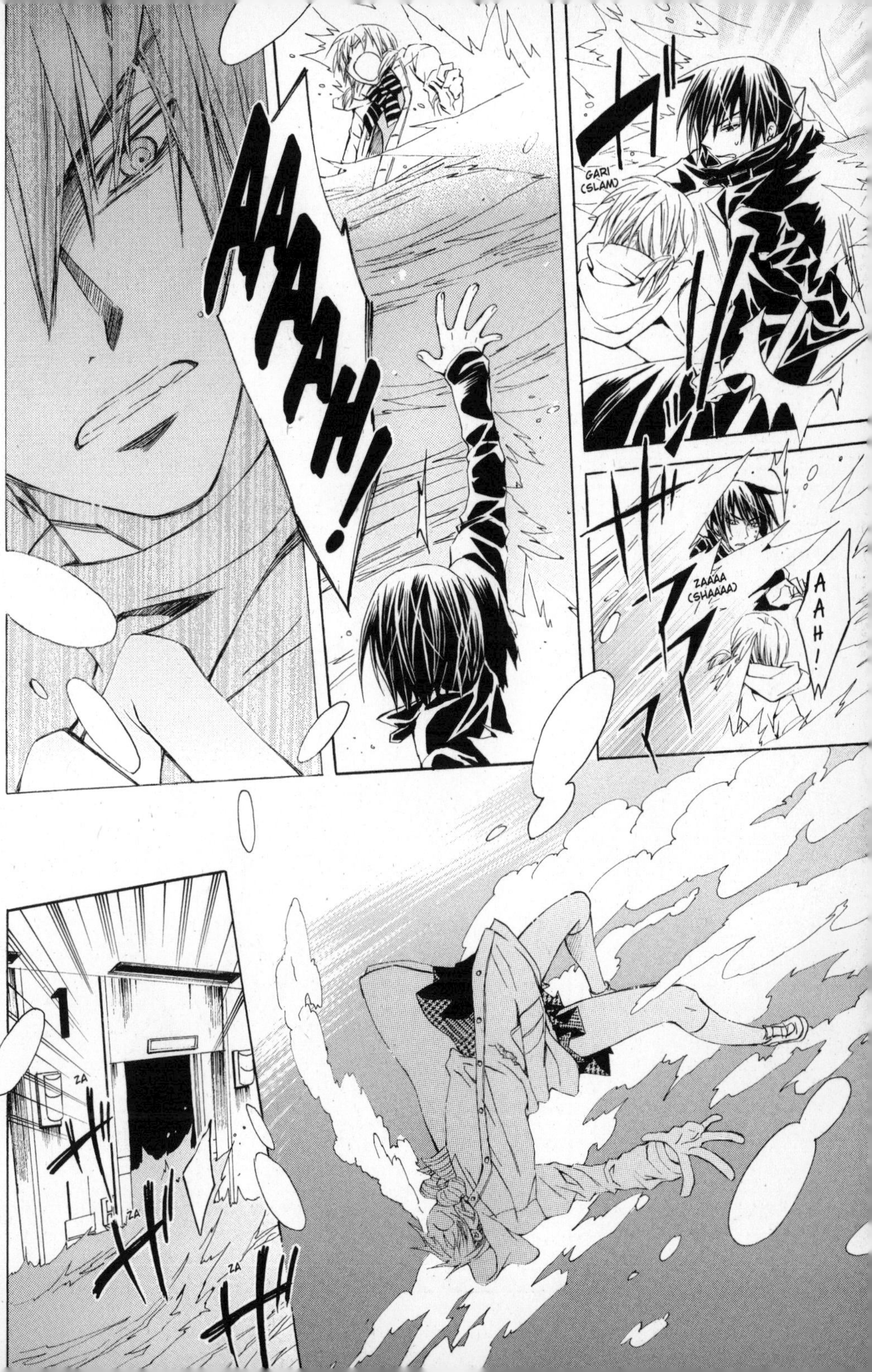
GARI (SLAM)
ZAAAA (SHAAAA)
AAH!
AAAAH!!
ZA
ZA
ZA

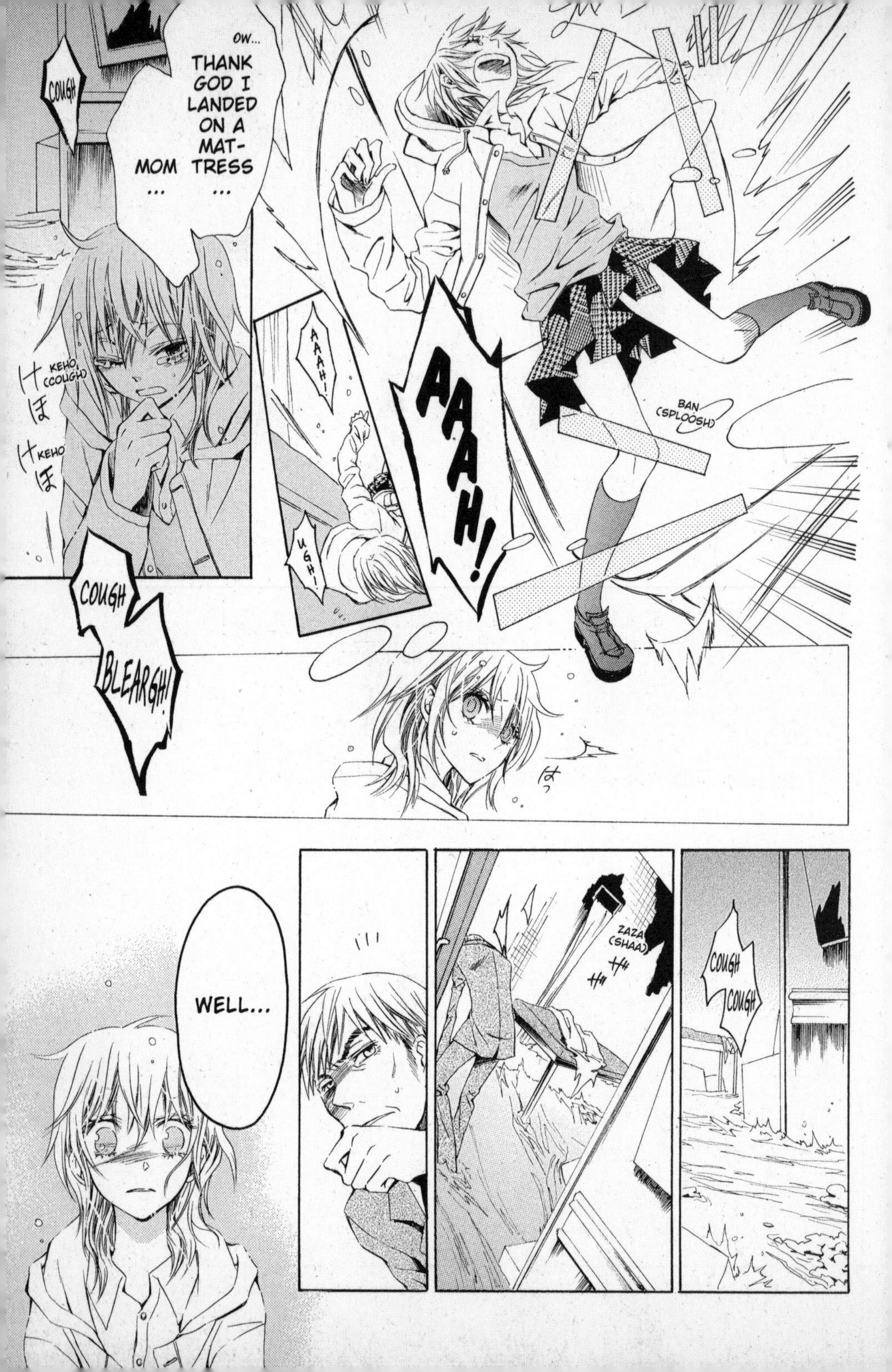
AAAH!
BAN (SPLOOSH)
AAAH!
UGH!
OW... THANK GOD I LANDED ON A MATTRESS...
MOM...
COUGH
けほ KEHO (COUGH)
けほ KEHO
COUGH BLEARGH!
COUGH COUGH
ZAZA (SHAA)
WELL...

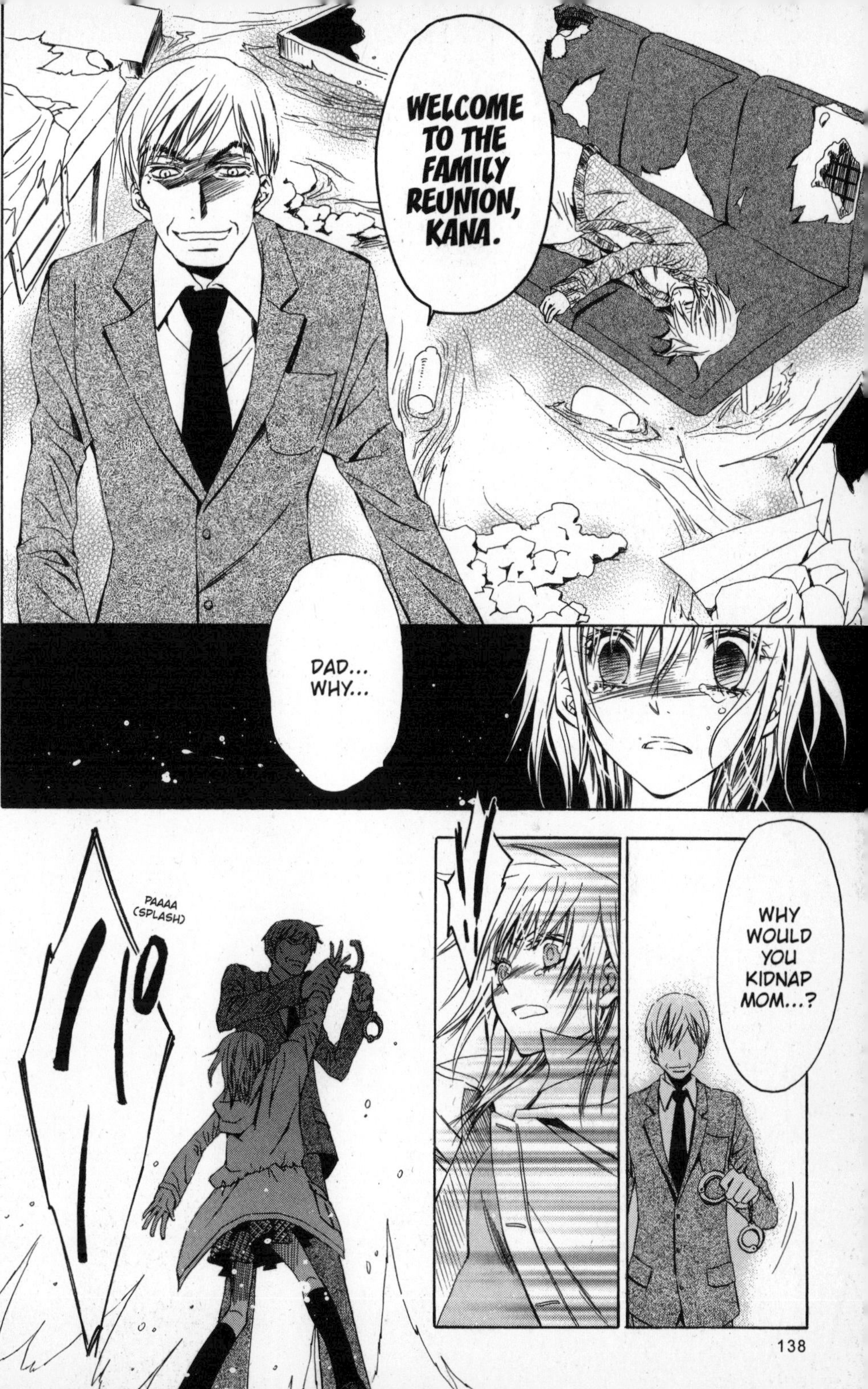
WELCOME TO THE FAMILY REUNION, KANA.
DAD... WHY...
WHY WOULD YOU KIDNAP MOM...?
PAAAA (SPLASH)

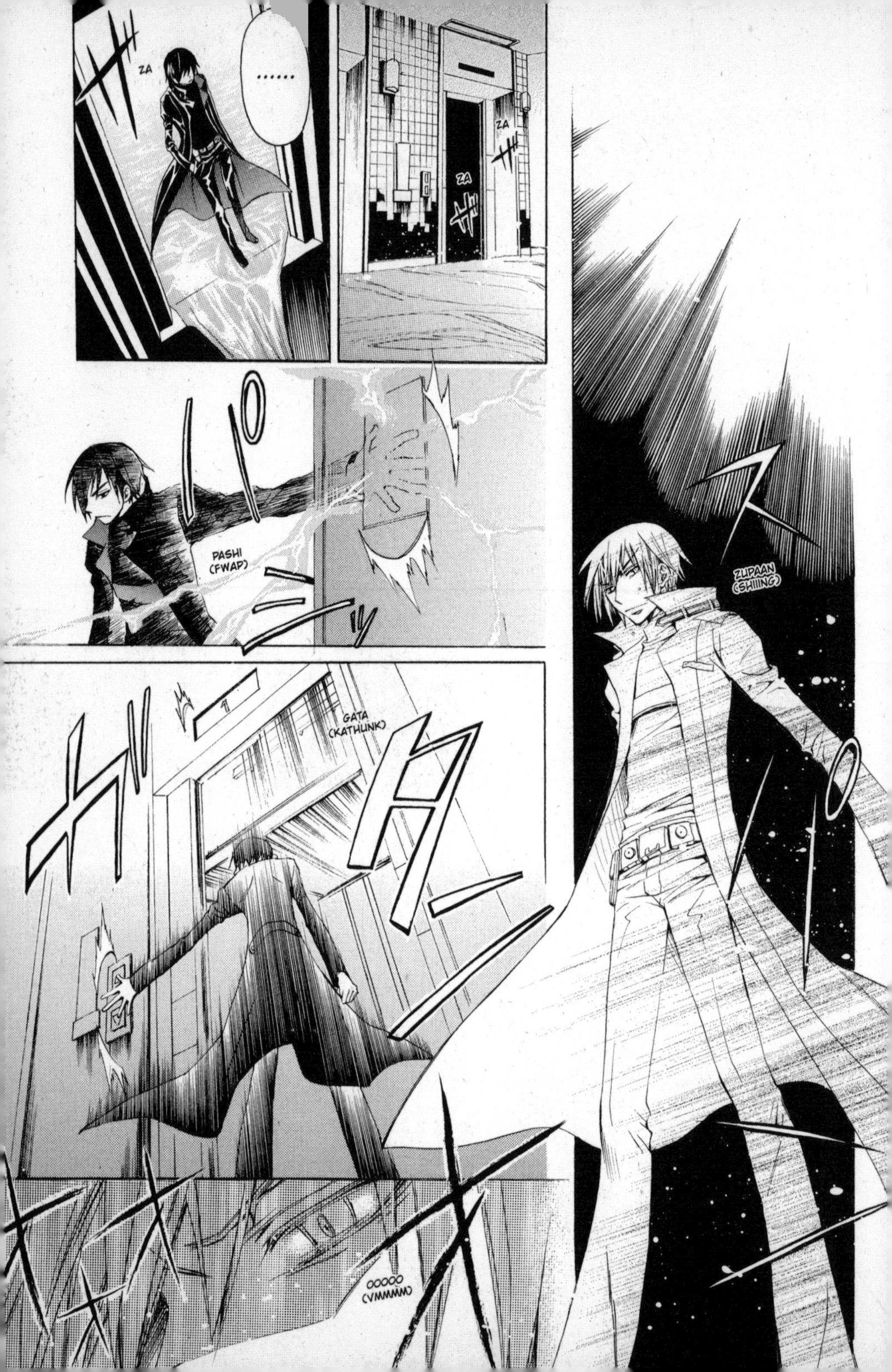
ZUPAAN
(SHIIING)
ZA
ZA
......
ZA
PASHI
(FWAP)
GATA
(KATHUNK)
OOOOO
(VMMMM)

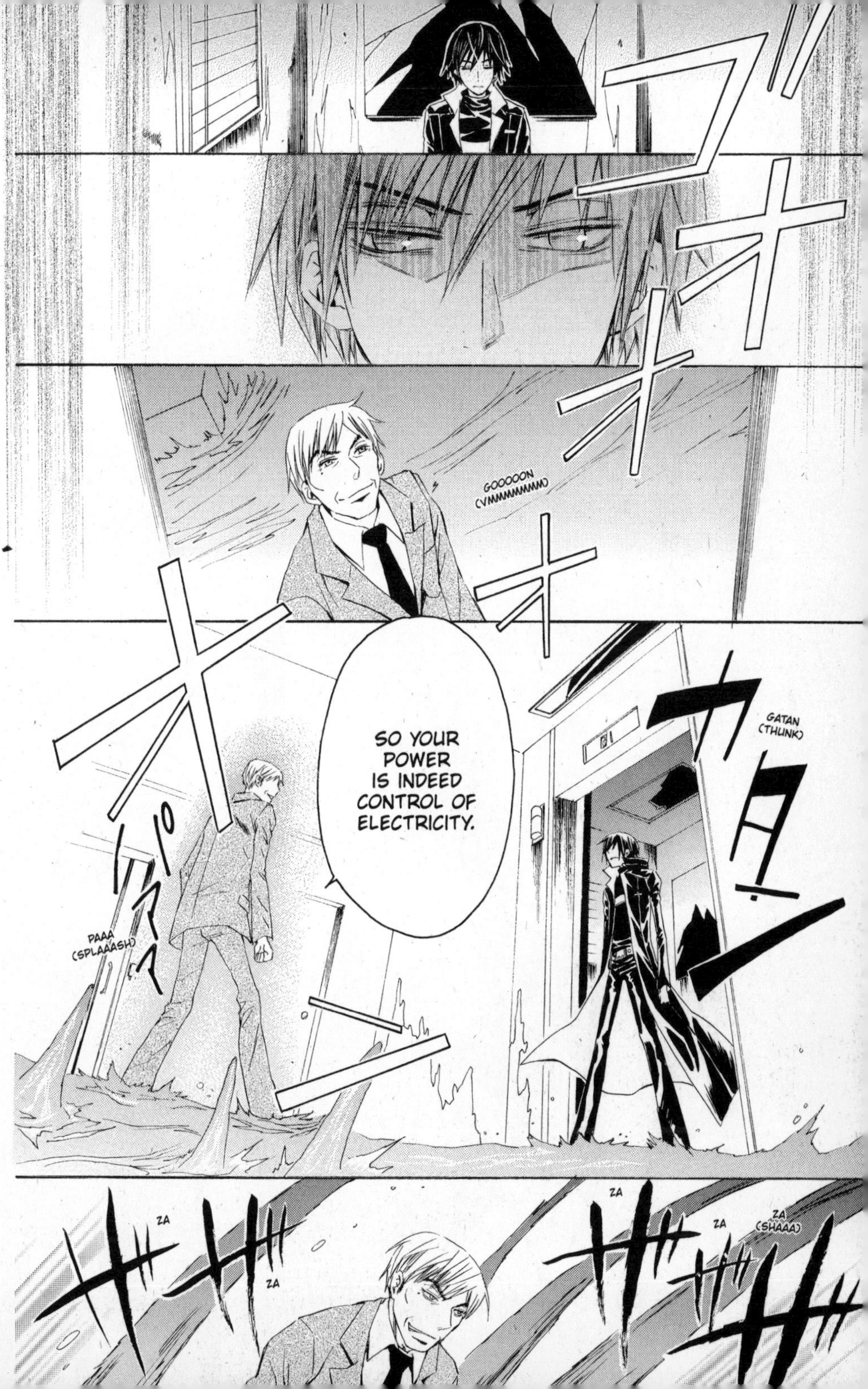
GOOOOON (VMMMMMMM)
GATAN (THUNK)
SO YOUR POWER IS INDEED CONTROL OF ELECTRICITY.
PAAA (SPLAAASH)
ZA (SHAAA)
ZA
ZA
ZA
ZA

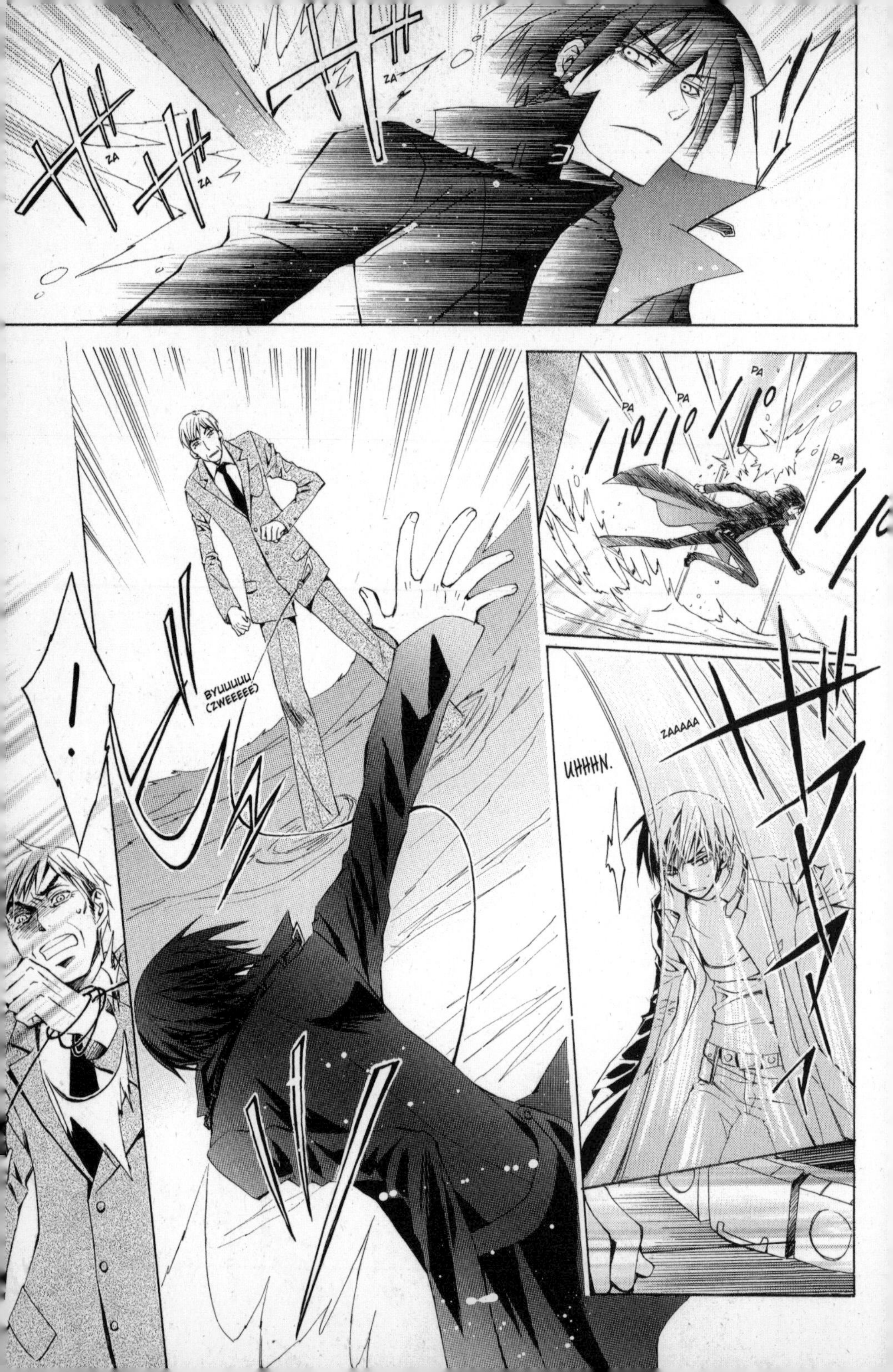

ZA
ZA
ZA
PA
PA
PA
PA
ZAAAAA
UHHHN.
BYUUUUU (ZWEEEEE)

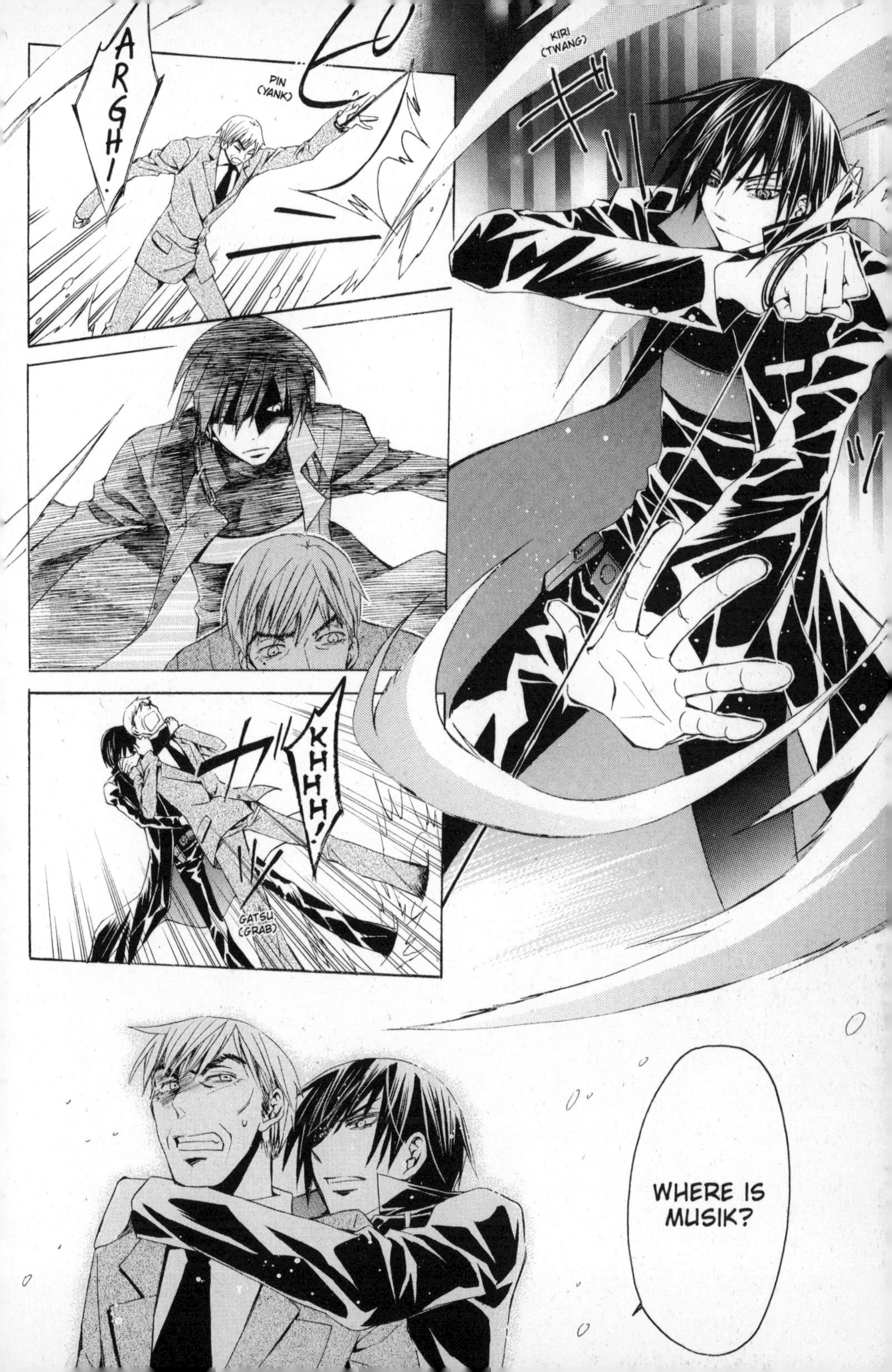
KIRI (TWANG)
PIN (YANK)
ARGH!
KHHH!
GATSU (GRAB)
WHERE IS MUSIK?

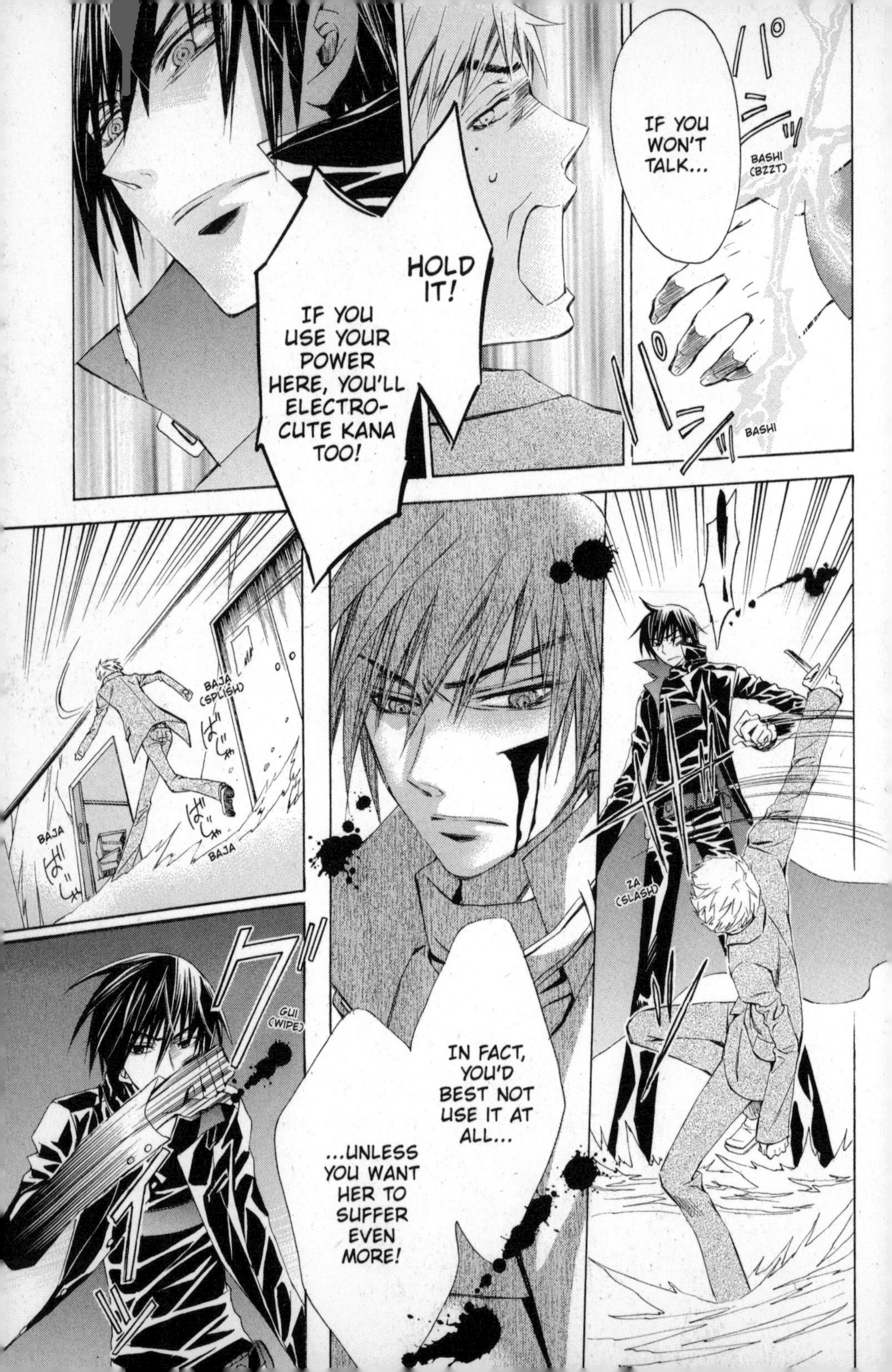
IF YOU WON'T TALK...
BASHI (BZZT)
BASHI
HOLD IT!
IF YOU USE YOUR POWER HERE, YOU'LL ELECTROCUTE KANA TOO!
ZA (SLASH)
IN FACT, YOU'D BEST NOT USE IT AT ALL...
...UNLESS YOU WANT HER TO SUFFER EVEN MORE!
BAJA (SPLISH)
BAJA
BAJA
GUI (WIPE)

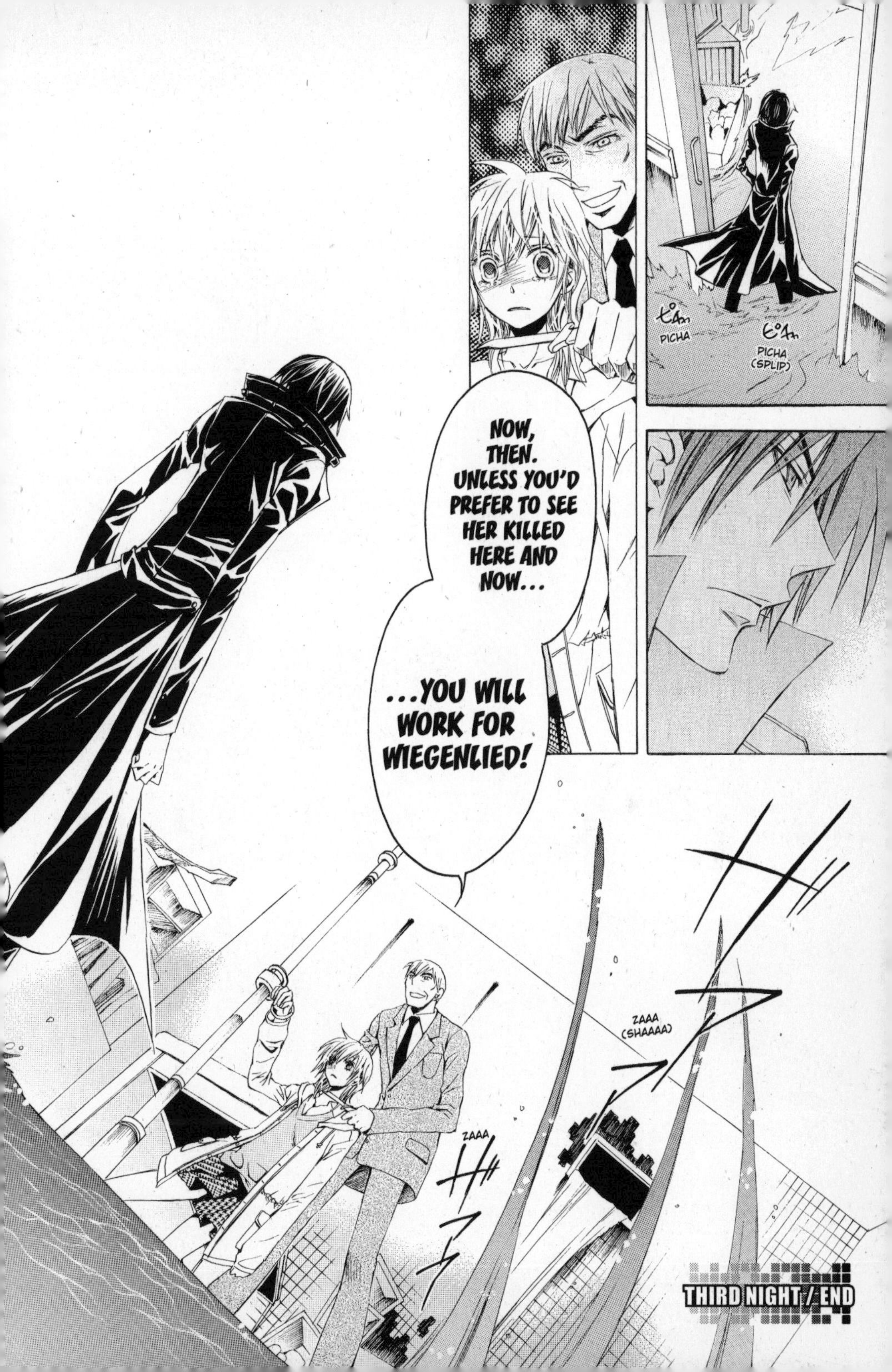
PICHA
PICHA (SPLIP)
NOW, THEN. UNLESS YOU'D PREFER TO SEE HER KILLED HERE AND NOW...
...YOU WILL WORK FOR WIEGENLIED!
ZAAA (SHAAAA)
ZAAA
THIRD NIGHT / END

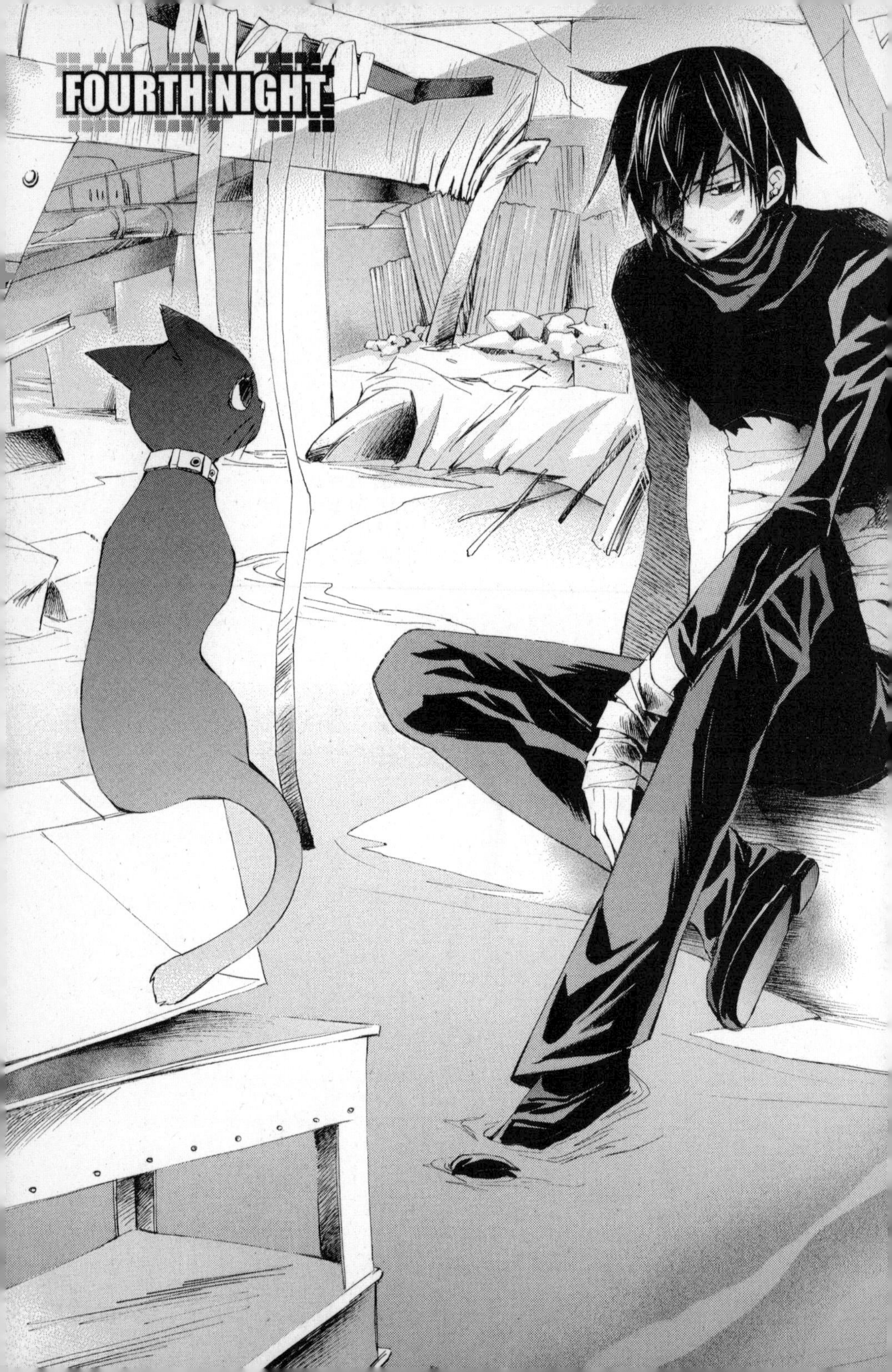
FOURTH NIGHT

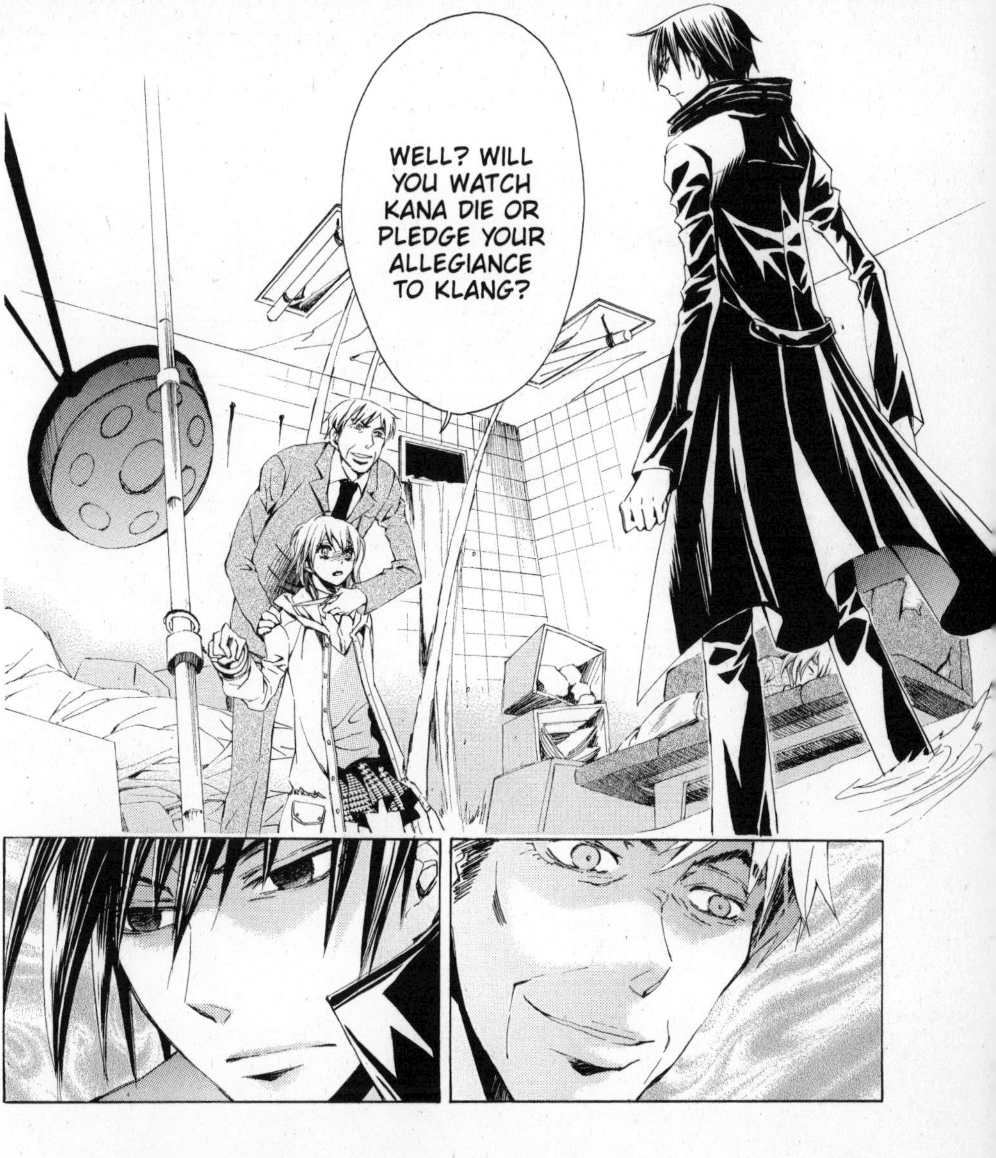
WELL? WILL YOU WATCH KANA DIE OR PLEDGE YOUR ALLEGIANCE TO KLANG?

You really should read the whole series before you look at this...

IMPOSSIBLE COMIC STRIP (3)

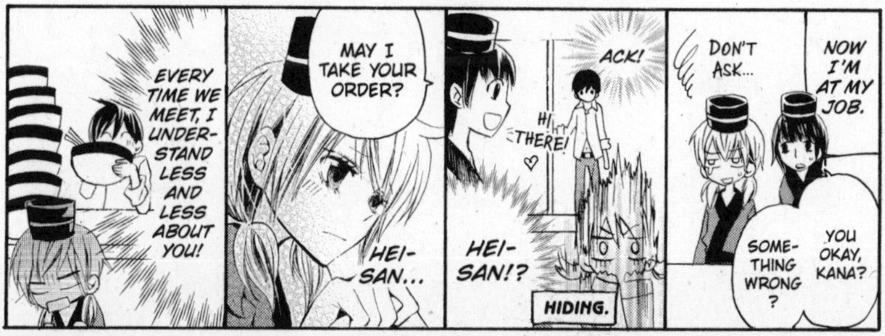
NOW I'M AT MY JOB.
DON'T ASK...
YOU OKAY, KANA?
SOME-THING WRONG?
ACK!
HI THERE!
HEI-SAN!?
HIDING.
MAY I TAKE YOUR ORDER?
HEI-SAN...
EVERY TIME WE MEET, I UNDER-STAND LESS AND LESS ABOUT YOU!

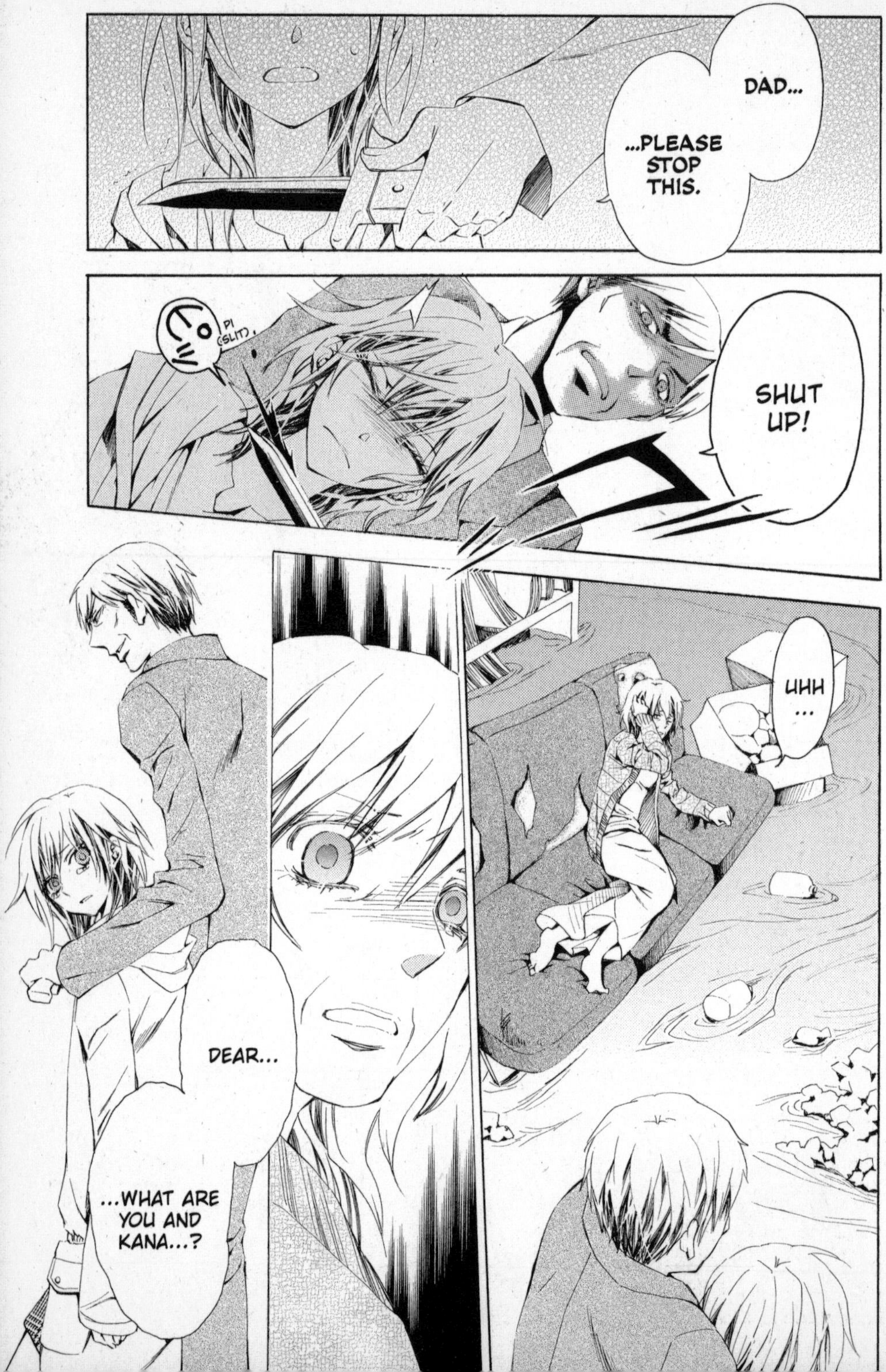
DAD...
...PLEASE STOP THIS.
PI (SLIT)
SHUT UP!
UHH ...
DEAR...
...WHAT ARE YOU AND KANA...?

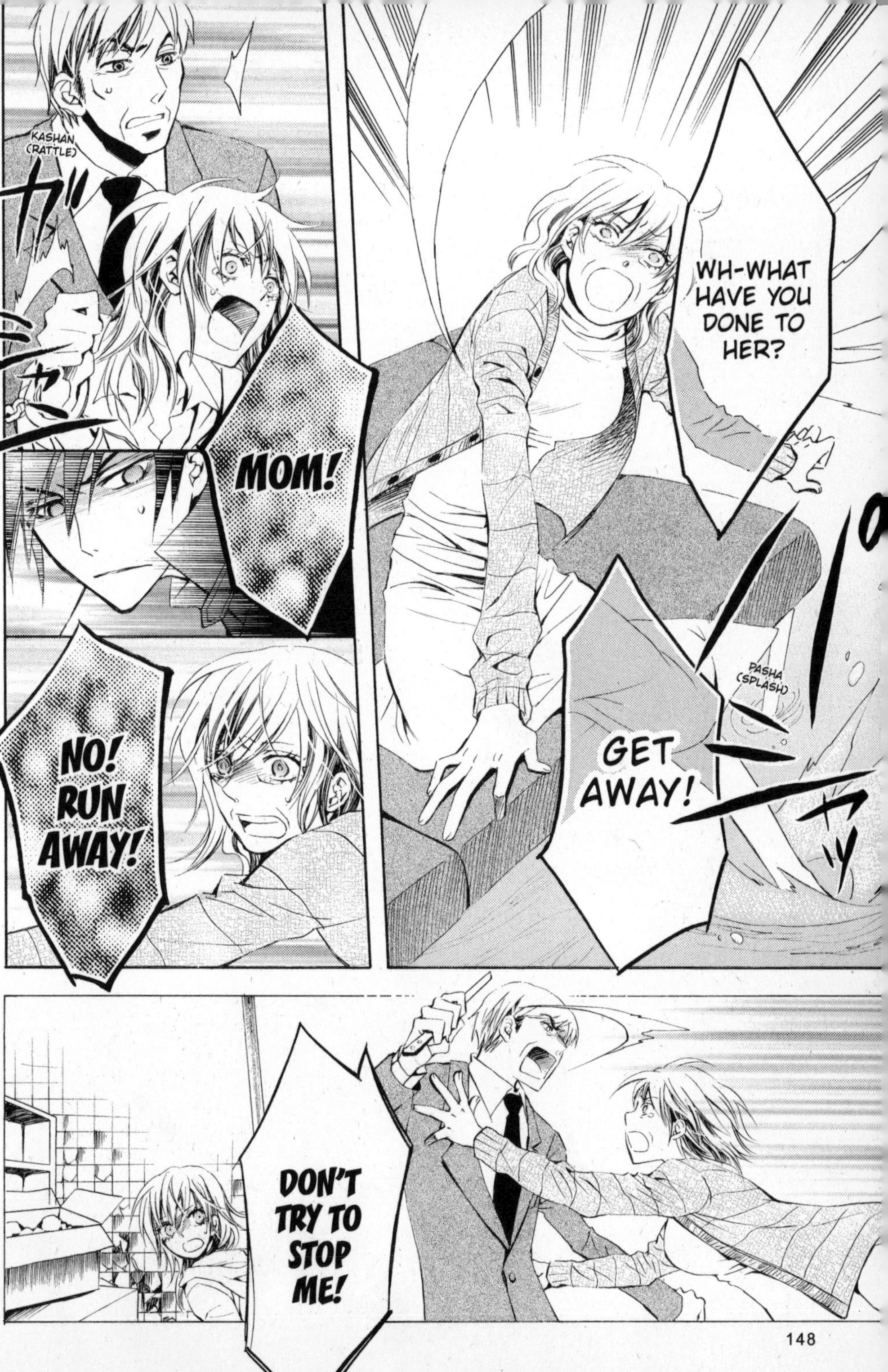
WH-WHAT HAVE YOU DONE TO HER?
PASHA (SPLASH)
GET AWAY!
KASHAN (RATTLE)
MOM!
NO! RUN AWAY!
DON'T TRY TO STOP ME!

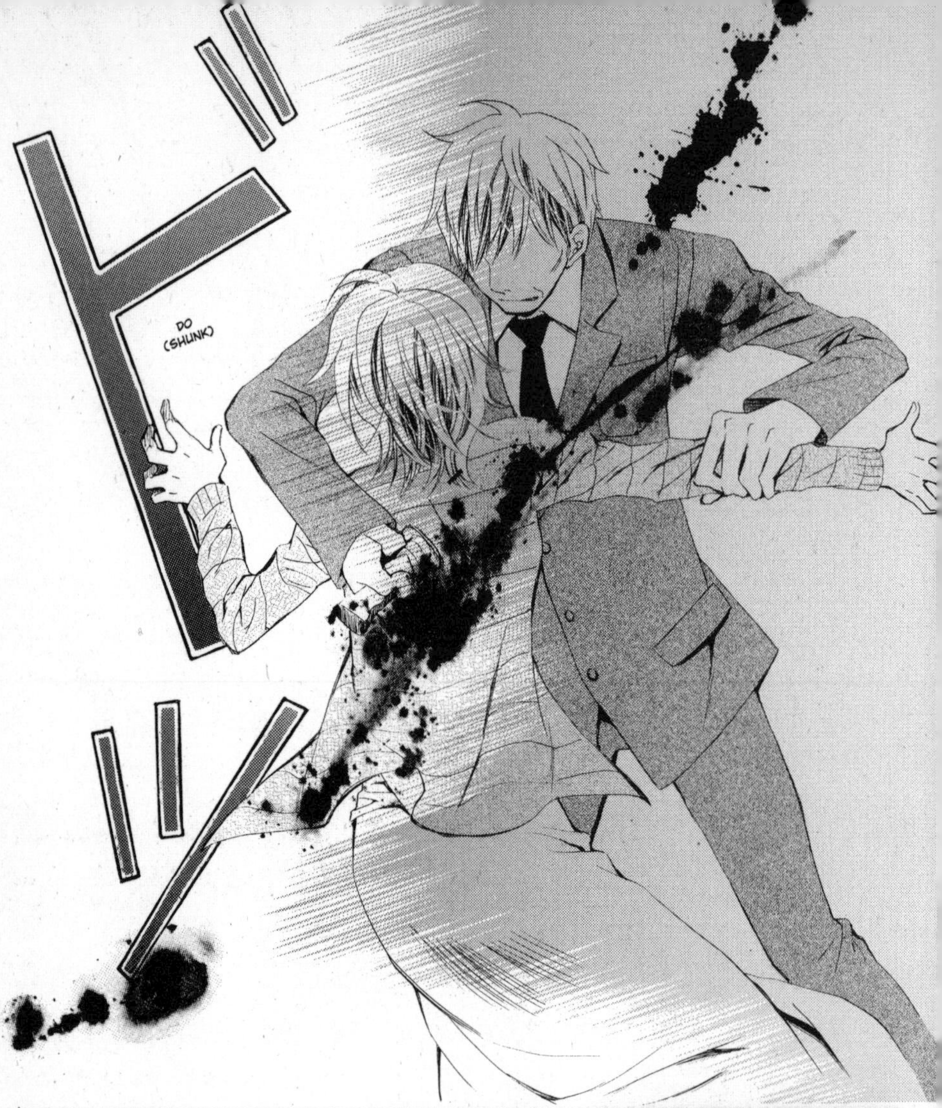
DO
(SHUNK)

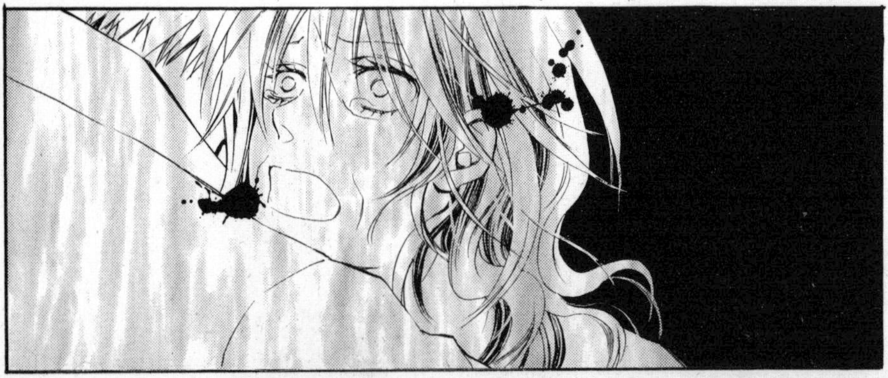

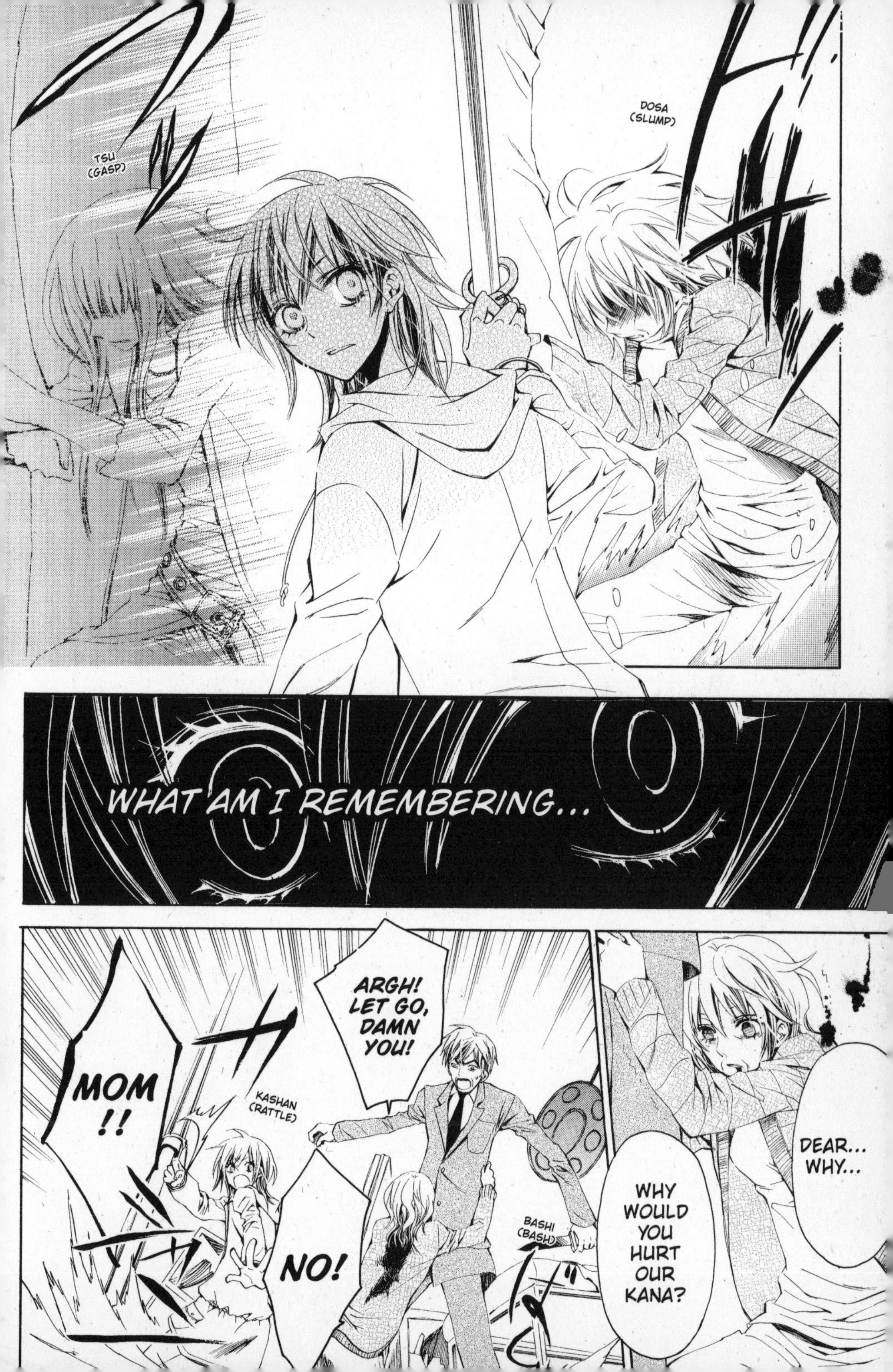
DOSA (SLUMP)
TSU (GASP)
WHAT AM I REMEMBERING...
DEAR... WHY...
WHY WOULD YOU HURT OUR KANA?
BASHI (BASH)
ARGH! LET GO, DAMN YOU!
NO!
KASHAN (RATTLE)
MOM!!

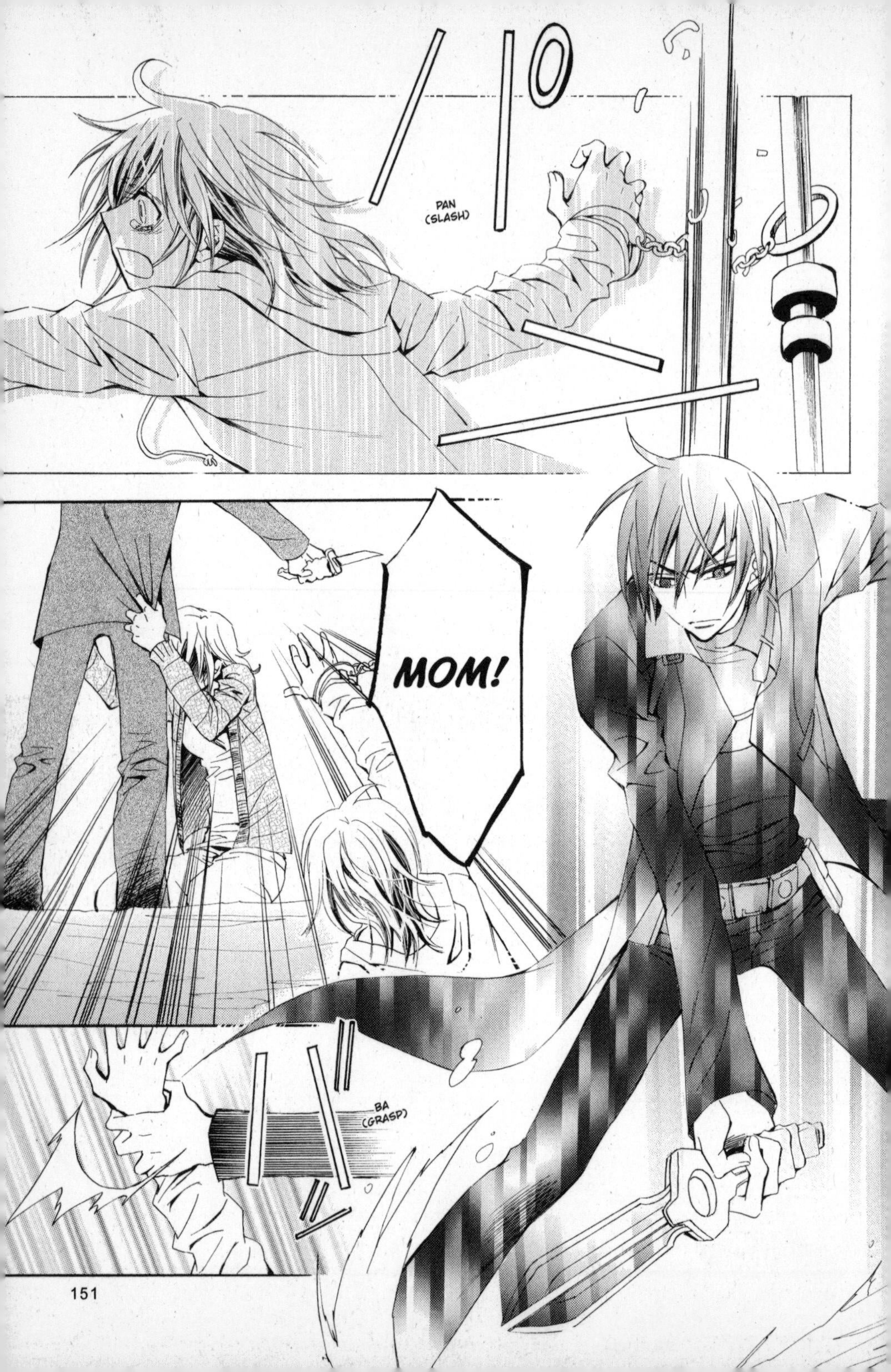
PAN
(SLASH)
MOM!
BA
(GRASP)

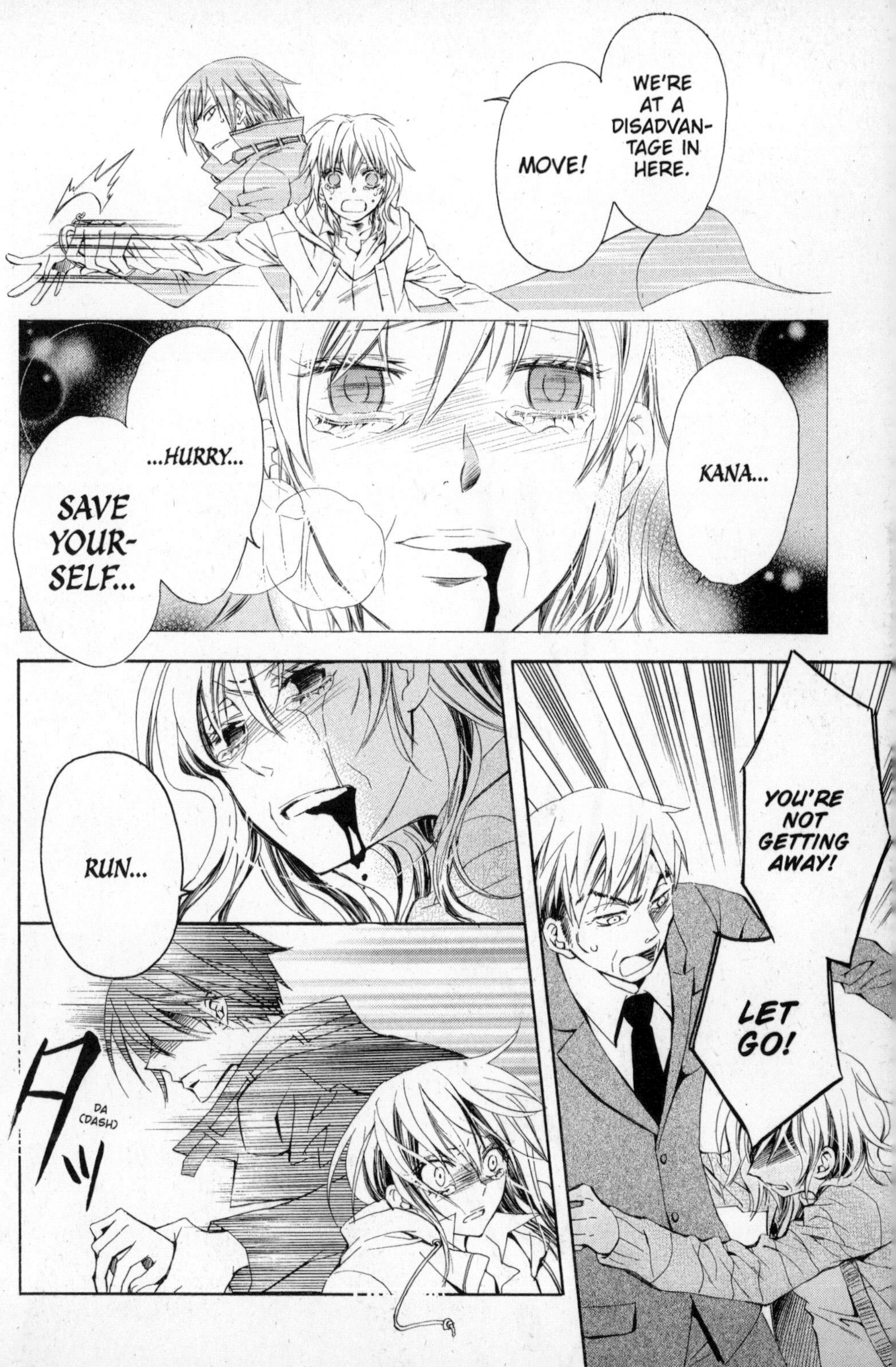
WE'RE AT A DISADVANTAGE IN HERE.
MOVE!
KANA...
...HURRY...
SAVE YOURSELF...
YOU'RE NOT GETTING AWAY!
LET GO!
RUN...
ダッ
DA (DASH)

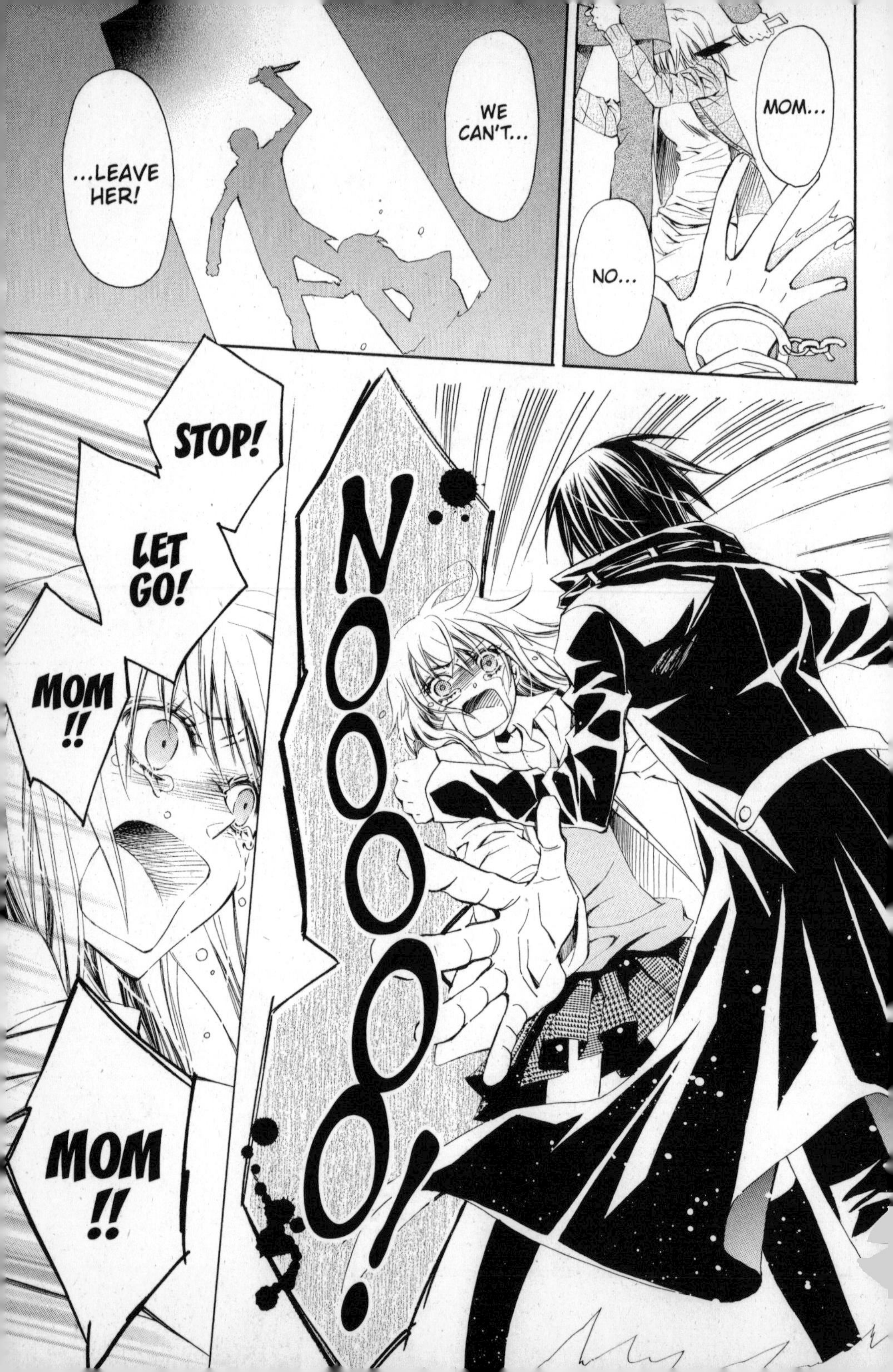
MOM...
NO...
WE CAN'T...
...LEAVE HER!
NOOOOO!
STOP!
LET GO!
MOM!!
MOM!!

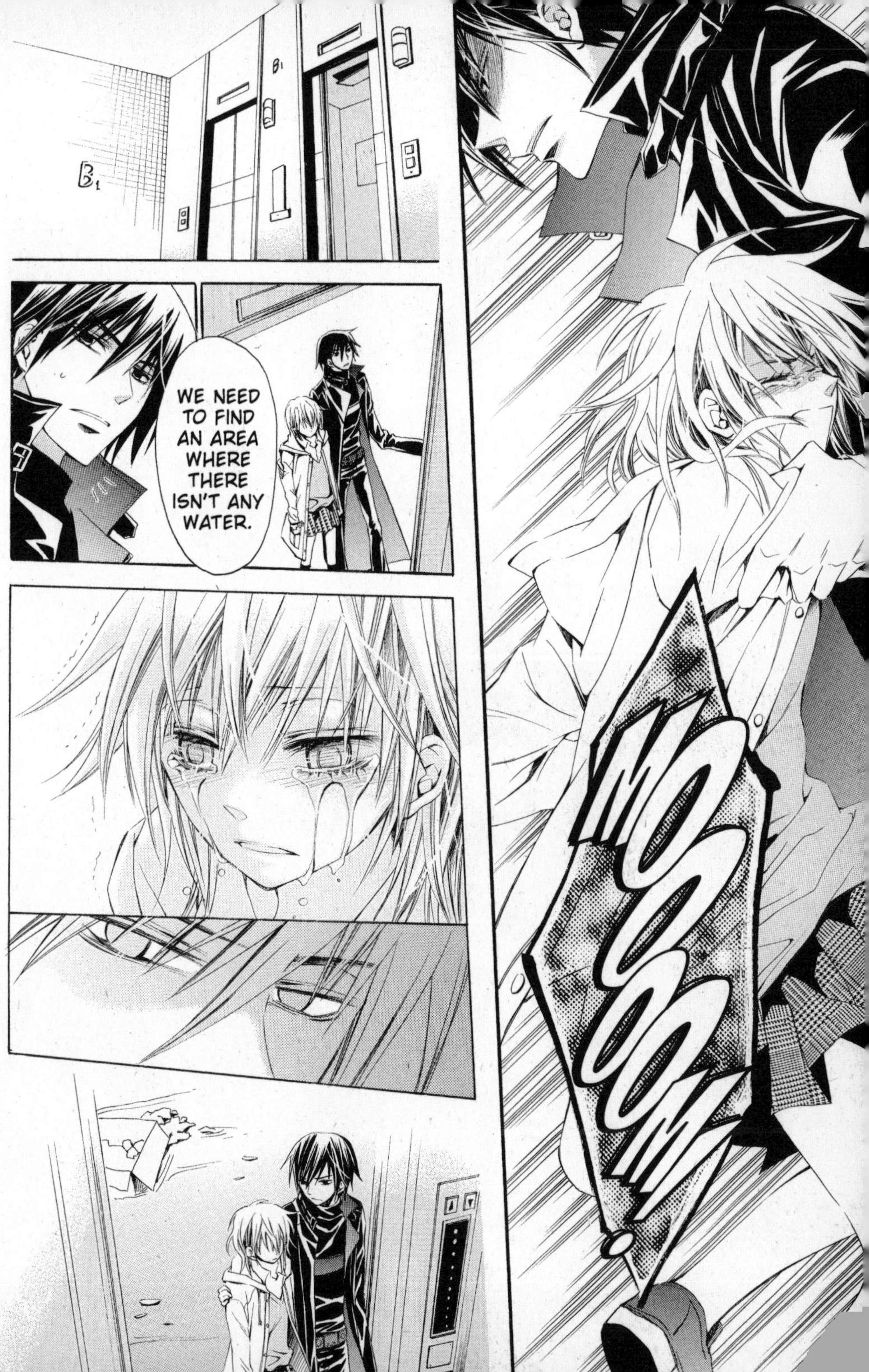
WE NEED TO FIND AN AREA WHERE THERE ISN'T ANY WATER.

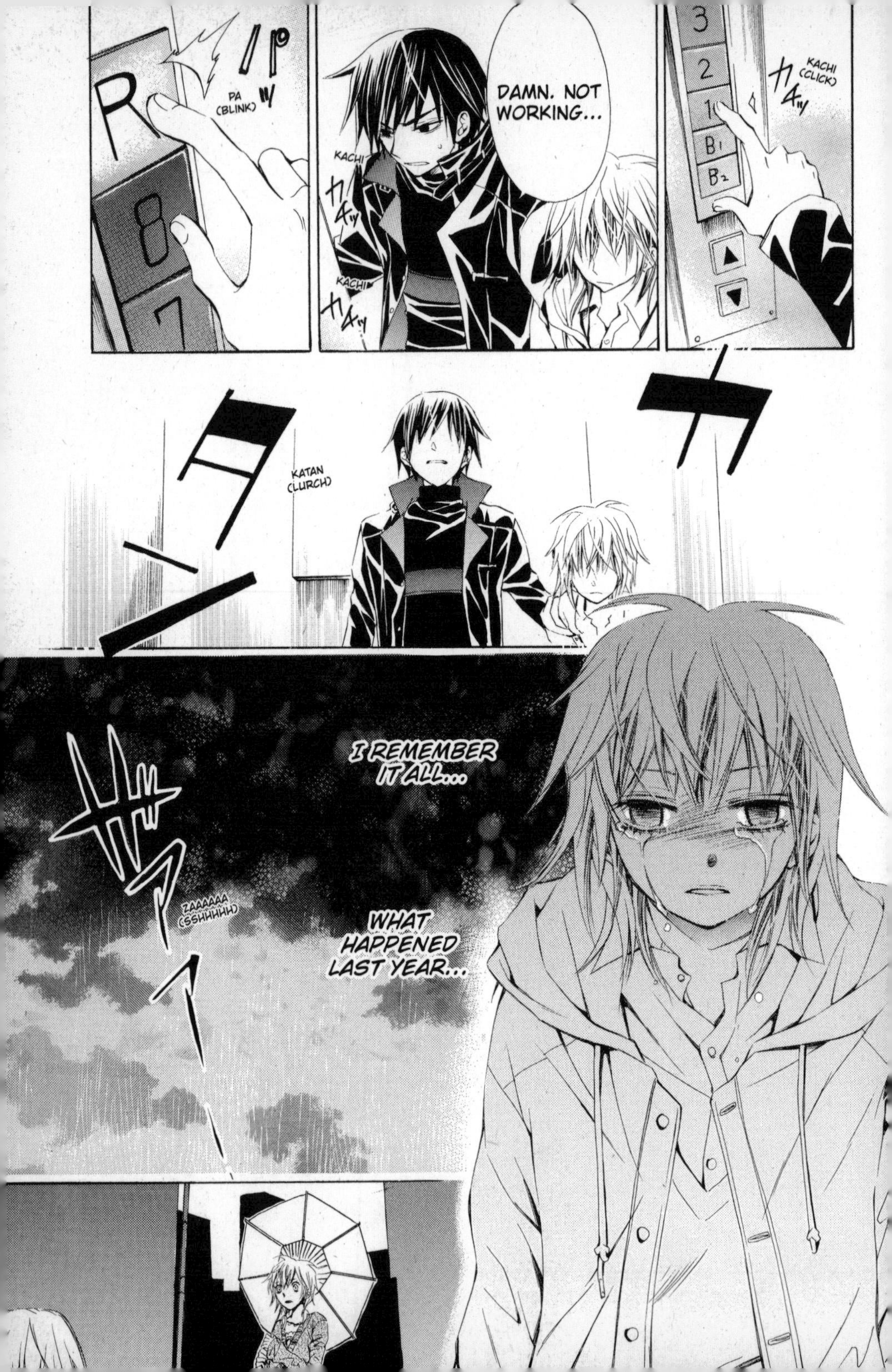
KACHI (CLICK)
DAMN. NOT WORKING...
KACHI
KACHI
PA (BLINK)
KATAN (LURCH)
I REMEMBER IT ALL...
WHAT HAPPENED LAST YEAR...
ZAAAAAA (SSHHHHH)

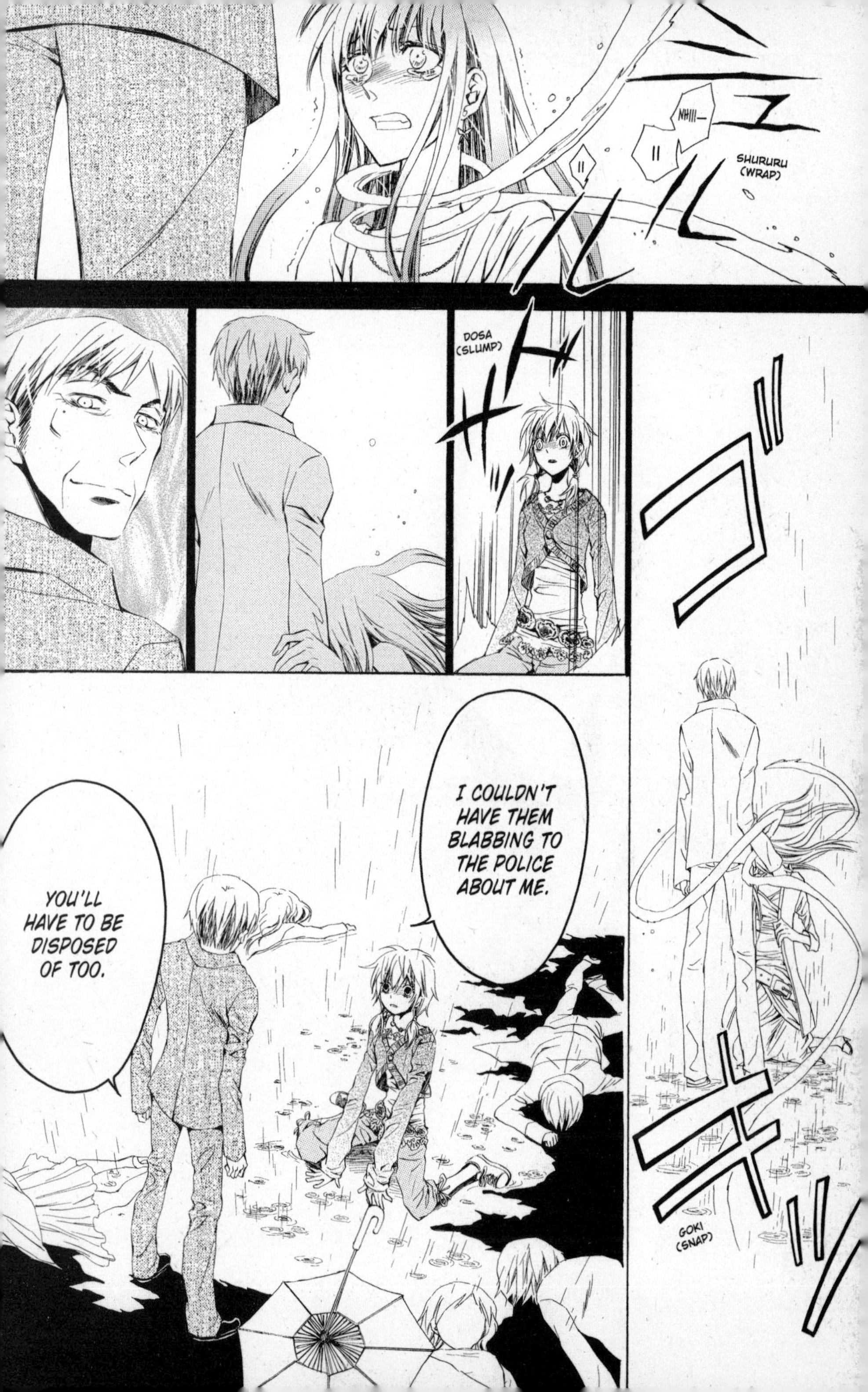
NHIII—
SHURURU (WRAP)
GOKI (SNAP)
DOSA (SLUMP)
I COULDN'T HAVE THEM BLABBING TO THE POLICE ABOUT ME.
YOU'LL HAVE TO BE DISPOSED OF TOO.

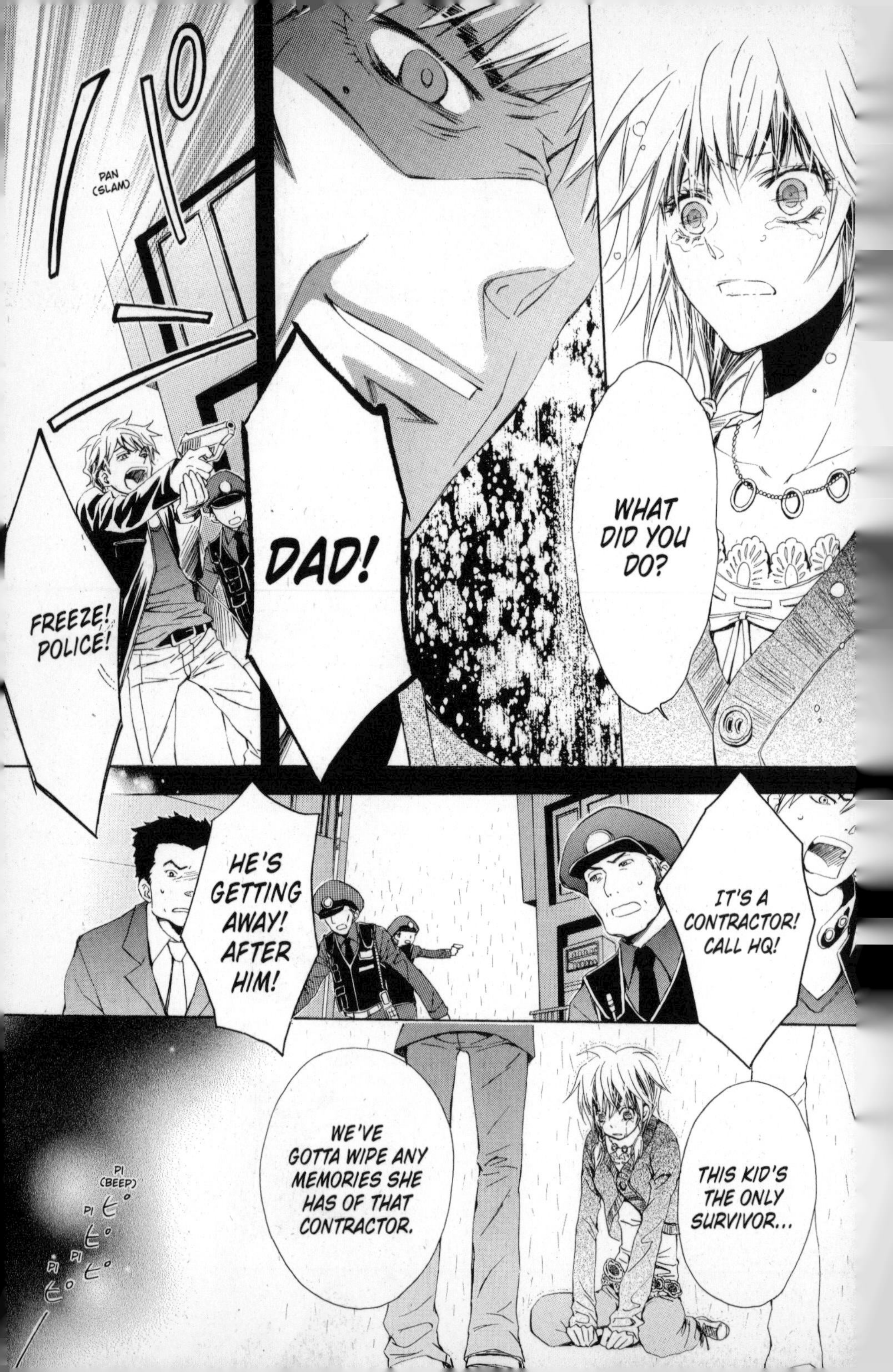
WHAT DID YOU DO?
DAD!
PAN (SLAM)
FREEZE! POLICE!
IT'S A CONTRACTOR! CALL HQ!
HE'S GETTING AWAY! AFTER HIM!
THIS KID'S THE ONLY SURVIVOR...
WE'VE GOTTA WIPE ANY MEMORIES SHE HAS OF THAT CONTRACTOR.
PI (BEEP)
PI
PI
PI

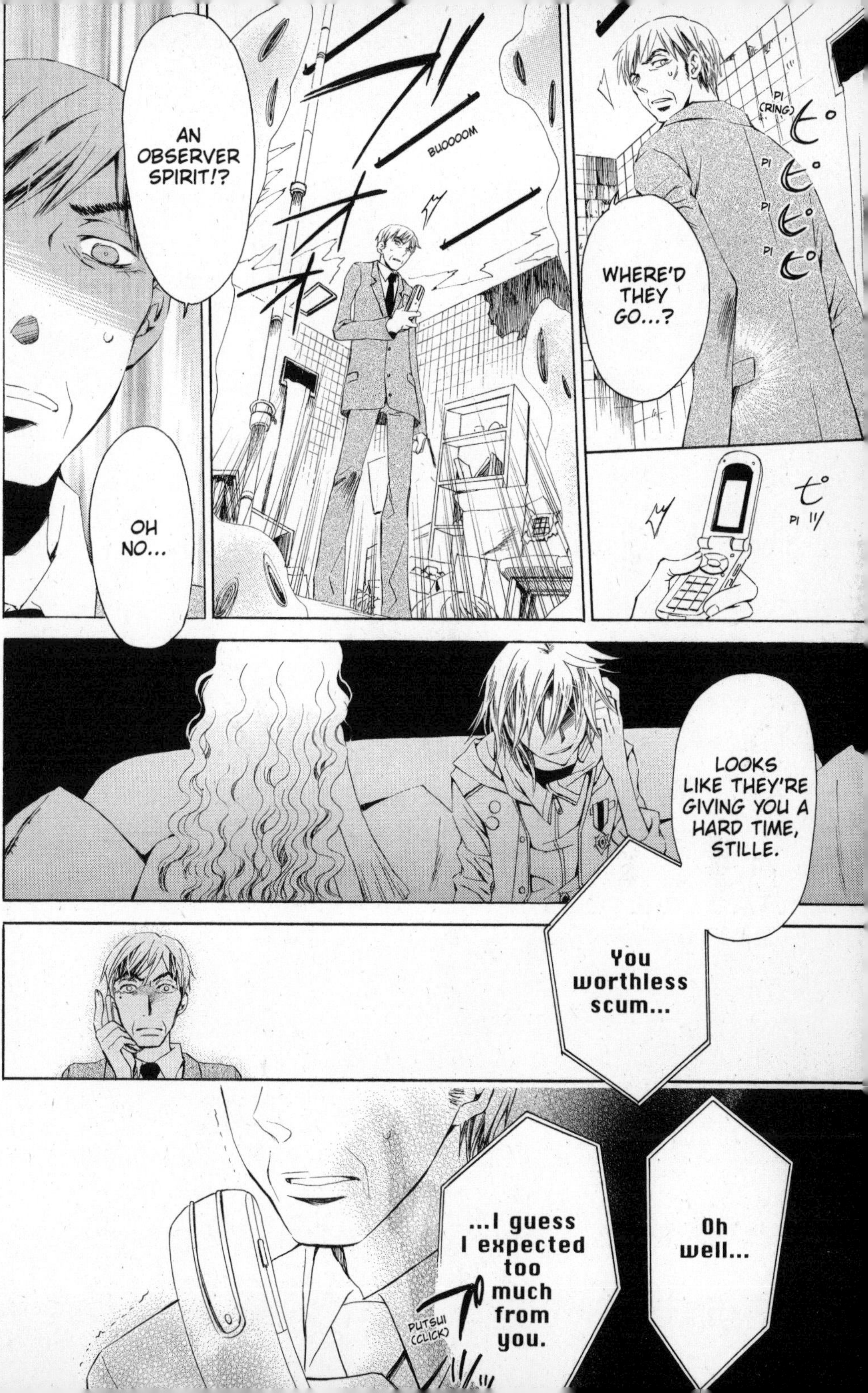
PI (RING)
PI
PI
PI
WHERE'D THEY GO...?
PI
BUOOOOM
AN OBSERVER SPIRIT!?
OH NO...
LOOKS LIKE THEY'RE GIVING YOU A HARD TIME, STILLE.
You worthless scum...
Oh well...
...I guess I expected too much from you.
PUTSU (CLICK)

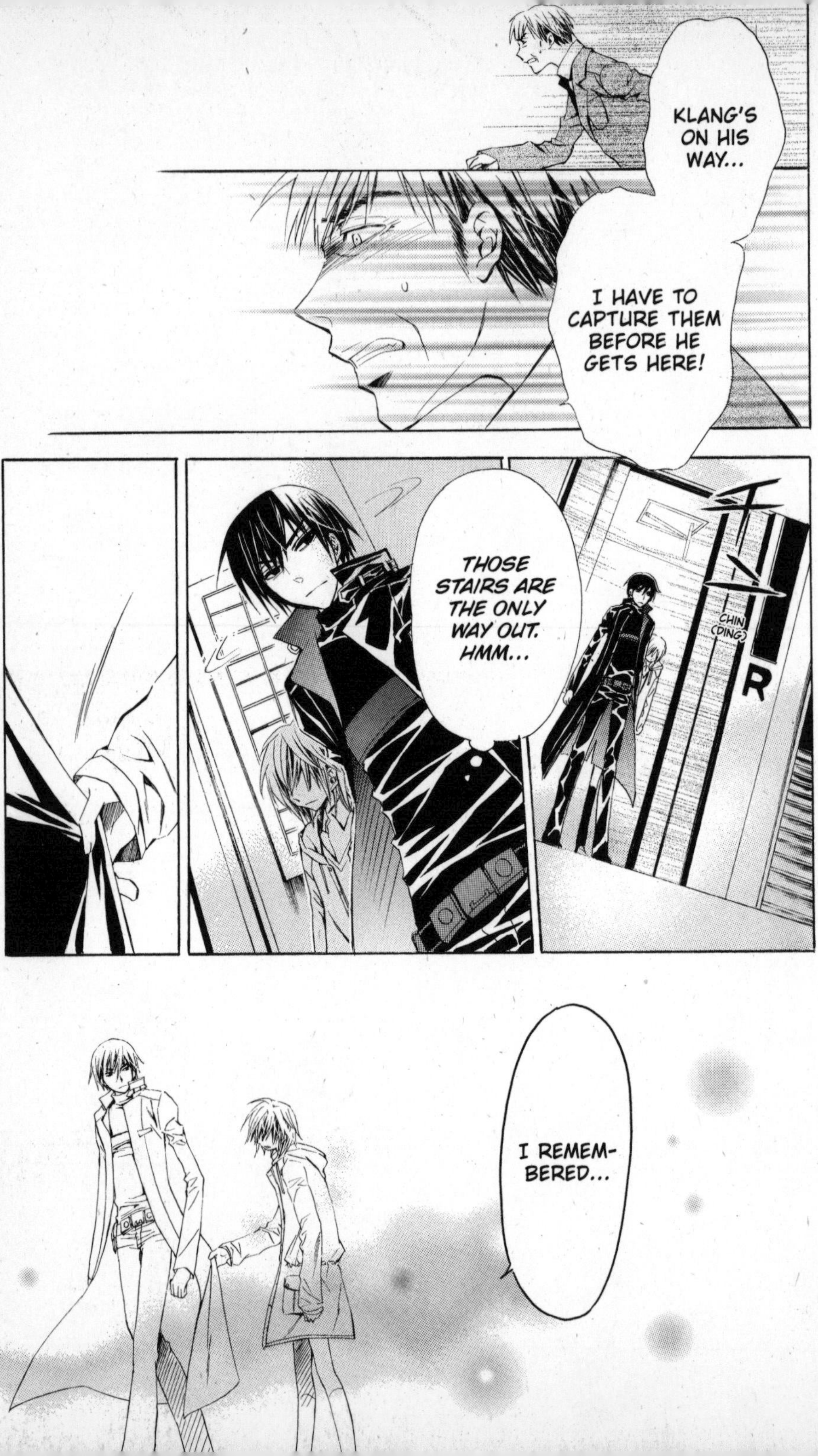
KLANG'S ON HIS WAY...
I HAVE TO CAPTURE THEM BEFORE HE GETS HERE!
CHIN (DING)
R
THOSE STAIRS ARE THE ONLY WAY OUT. HMM...
I REMEMBERED...

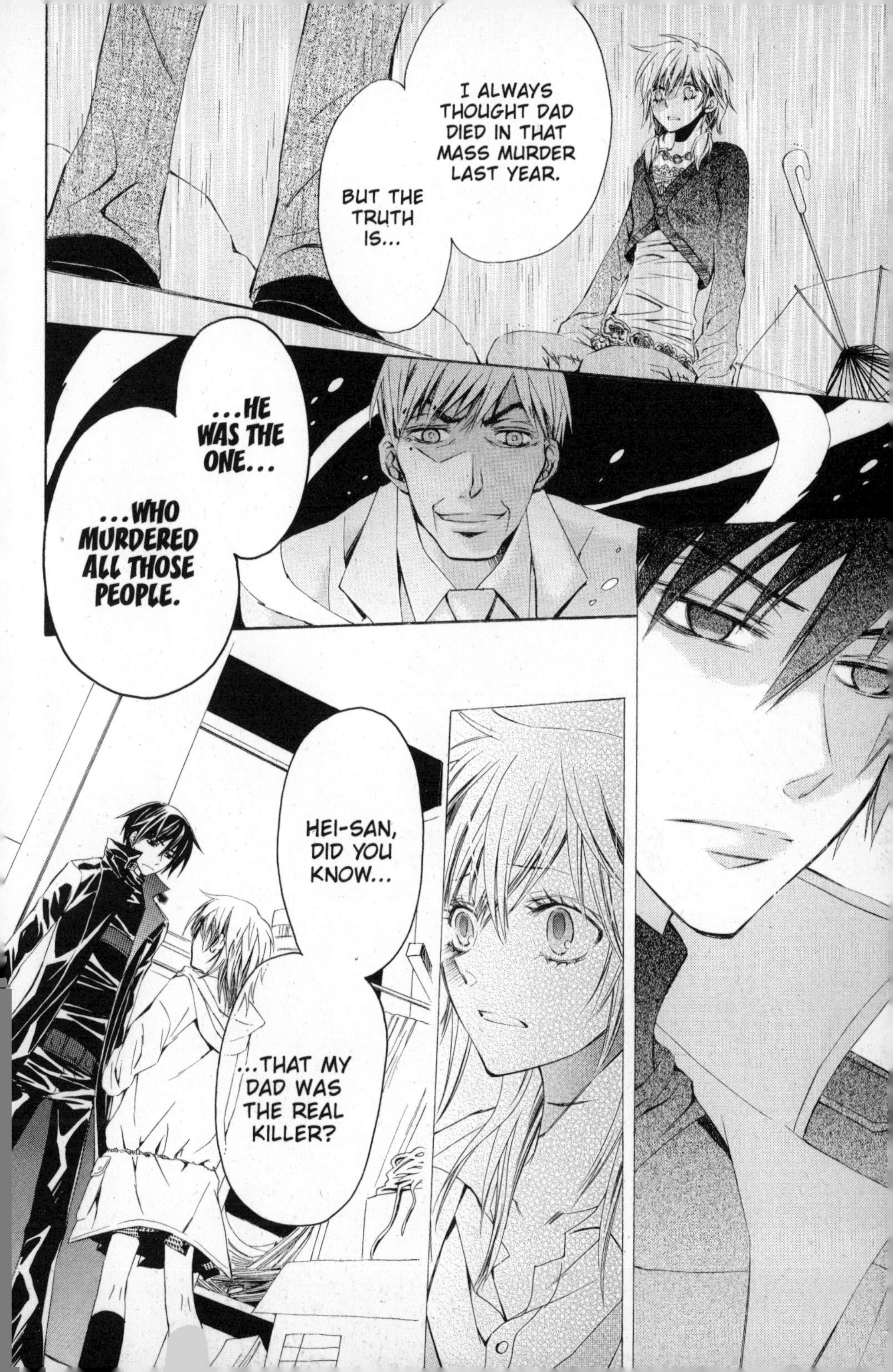
I ALWAYS THOUGHT DAD DIED IN THAT MASS MURDER LAST YEAR.
BUT THE TRUTH IS...
...HE WAS THE ONE...
...WHO MURDERED ALL THOSE PEOPLE.
HEI-SAN, DID YOU KNOW...
...THAT MY DAD WAS THE REAL KILLER?

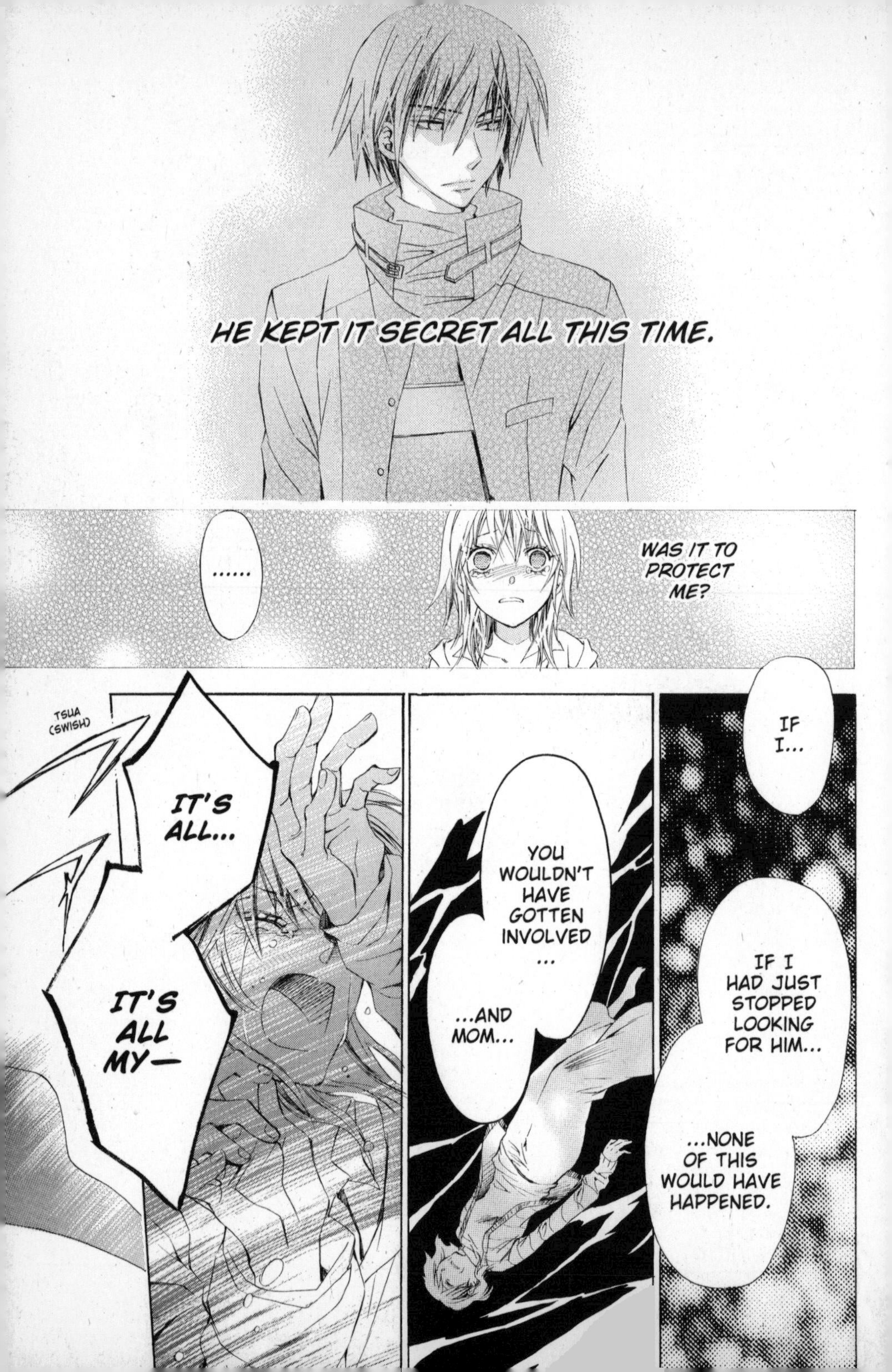
HE KEPT IT SECRET ALL THIS TIME.
WAS IT TO PROTECT ME?
......
IF I...
IF I HAD JUST STOPPED LOOKING FOR HIM...
...NONE OF THIS WOULD HAVE HAPPENED.
YOU WOULDN'T HAVE GOTTEN INVOLVED ...
...AND MOM...
TSUA (SWISH)
IT'S ALL...
IT'S ALL MY—

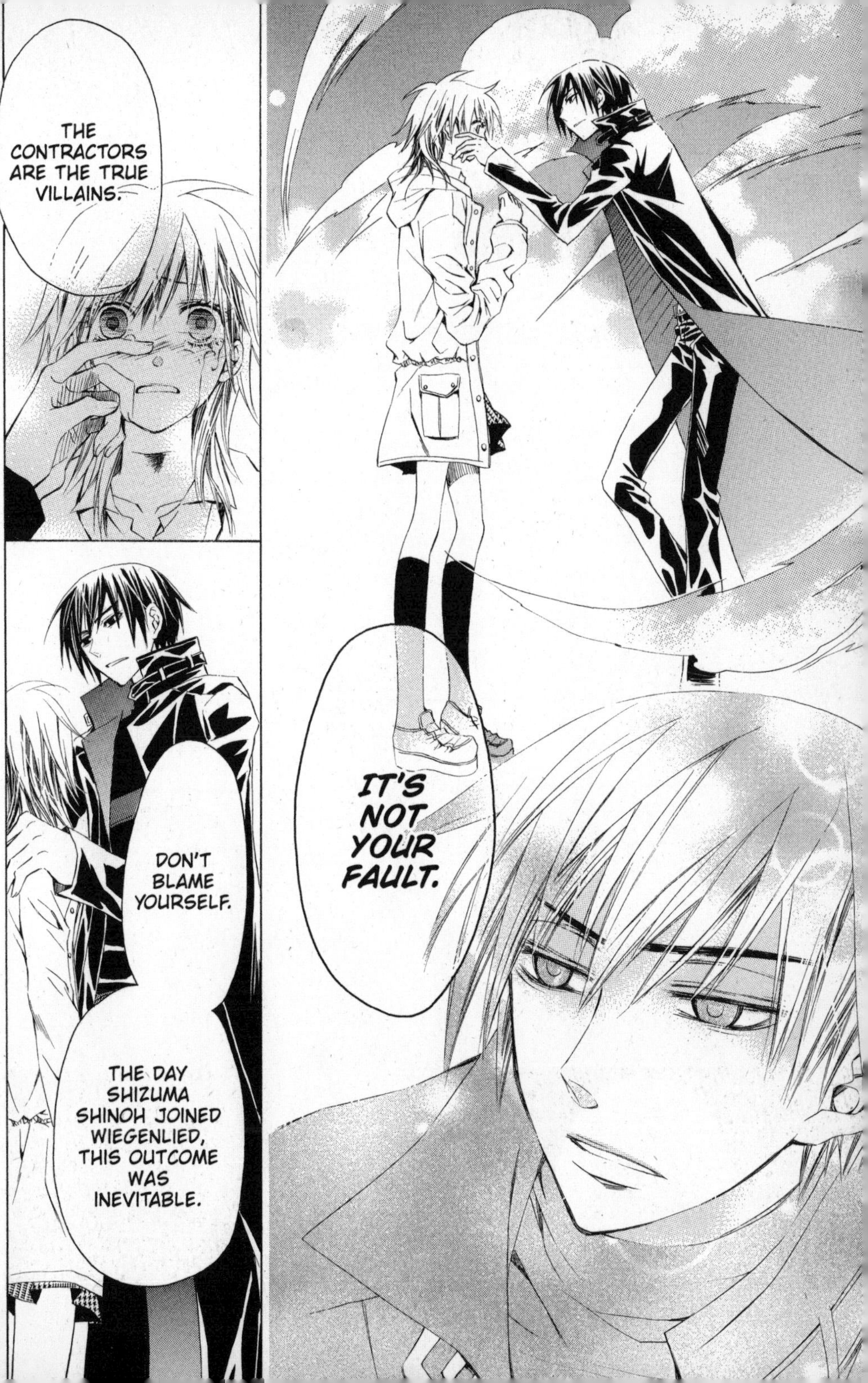
IT'S NOT YOUR FAULT.
THE CONTRACTORS ARE THE TRUE VILLAINS.
DON'T BLAME YOURSELF.
THE DAY SHIZUMA SHINOH JOINED WIEGENLIED, THIS OUTCOME WAS INEVITABLE.

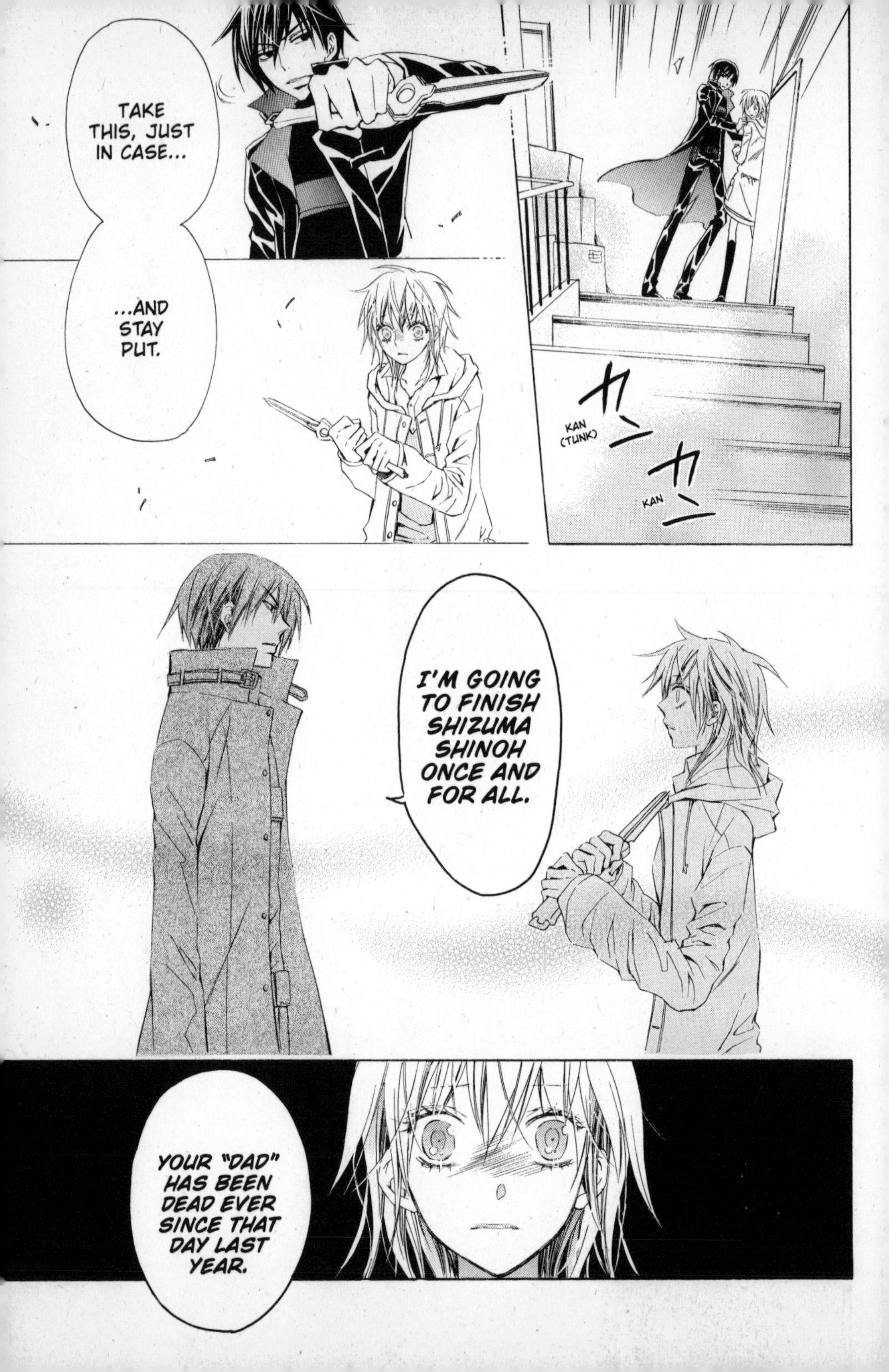
KAN (TUNK)
KAN
TAKE THIS, JUST IN CASE...
...AND STAY PUT.
I'M GOING TO FINISH SHIZUMA SHINOH ONCE AND FOR ALL.
YOUR "DAD" HAS BEEN DEAD EVER SINCE THAT DAY LAST YEAR.

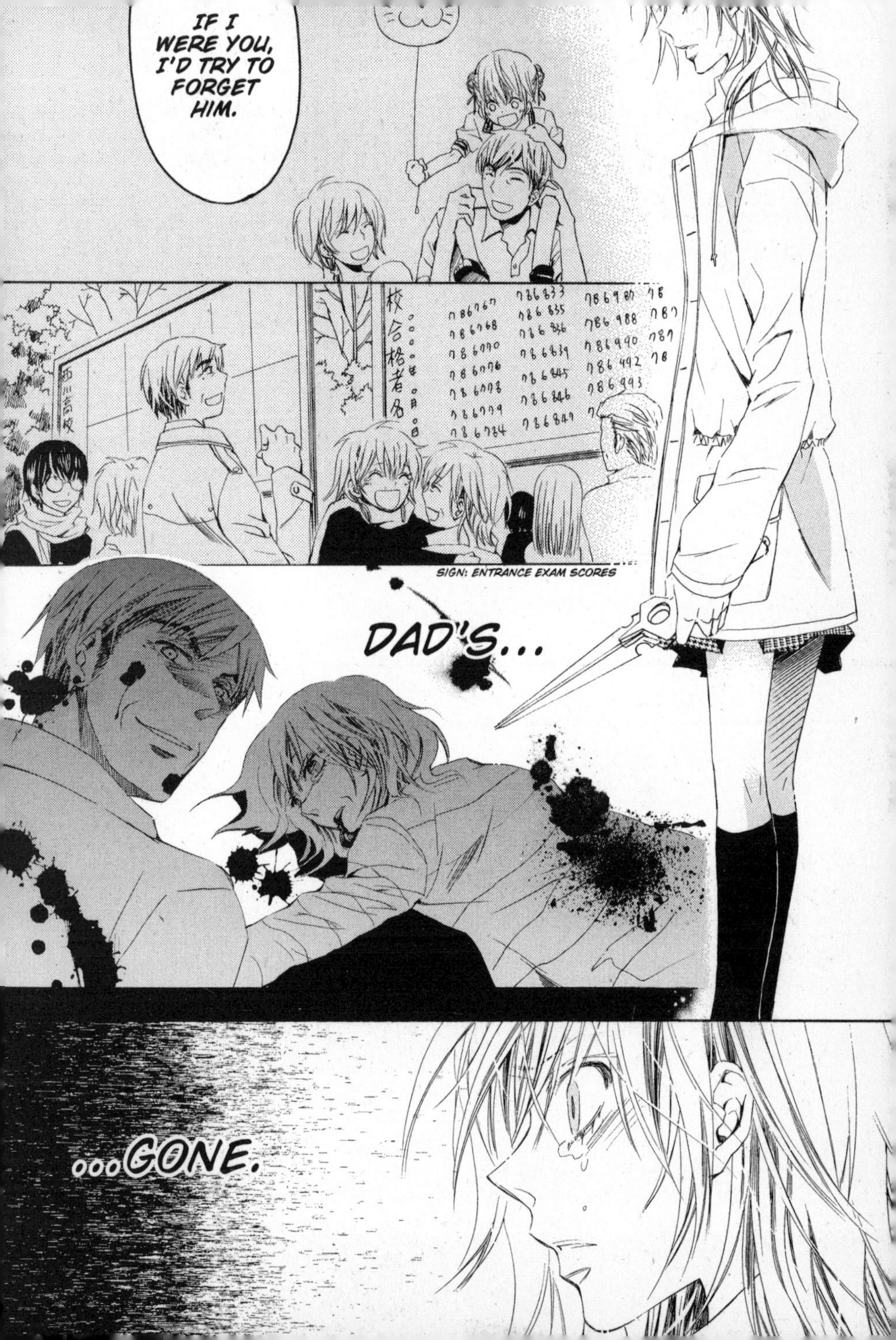
IF I WERE YOU, I'D TRY TO FORGET HIM.
SIGN: ENTRANCE EXAM SCORES
DAD'S...
...GONE.

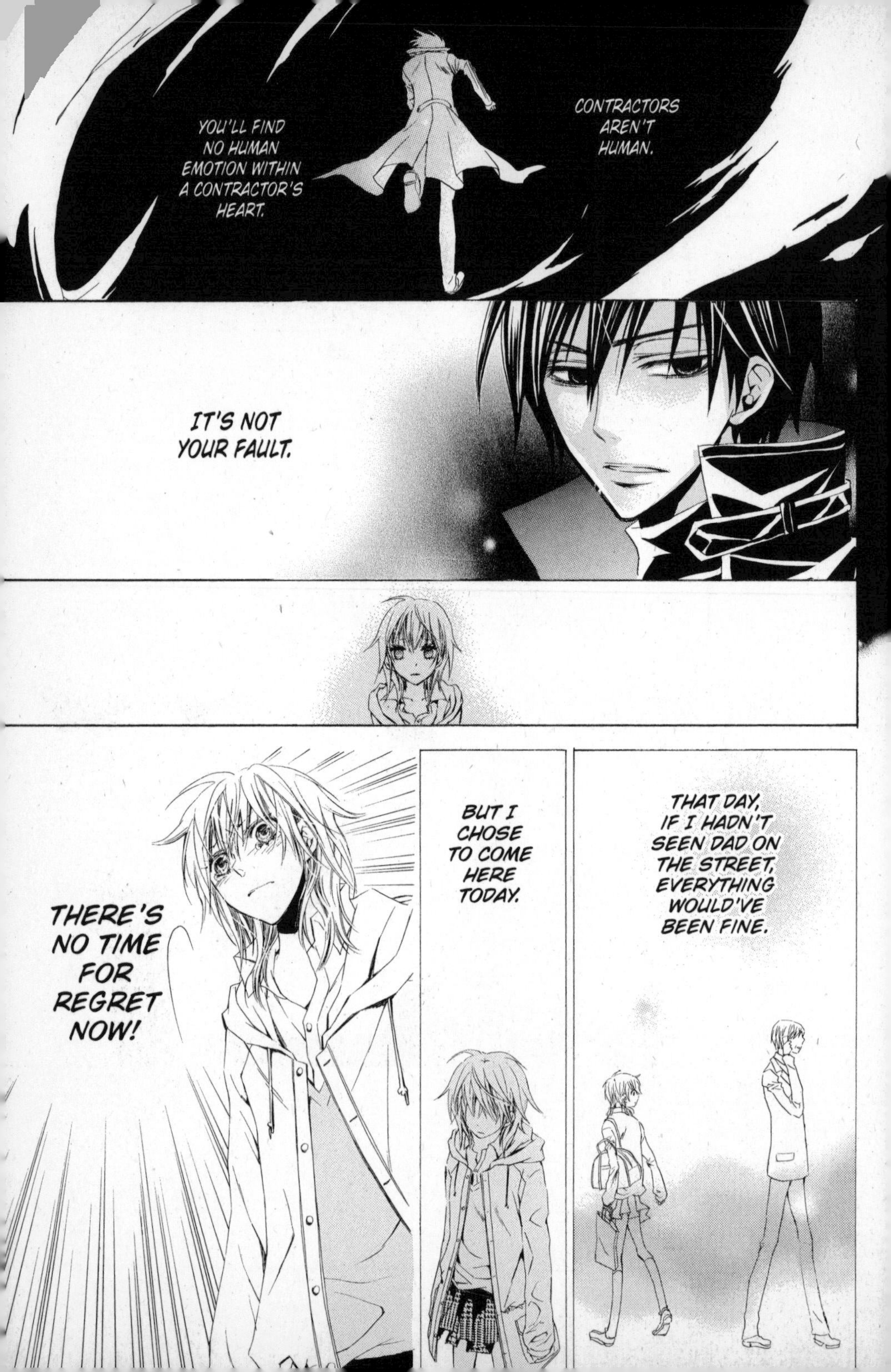
CONTRACTORS AREN'T HUMAN.
YOU'LL FIND NO HUMAN EMOTION WITHIN A CONTRACTOR'S HEART.
IT'S NOT YOUR FAULT.
THAT DAY, IF I HADN'T SEEN DAD ON THE STREET, EVERYTHING WOULD'VE BEEN FINE.
BUT I CHOSE TO COME HERE TODAY.
THERE'S NO TIME FOR REGRET NOW!

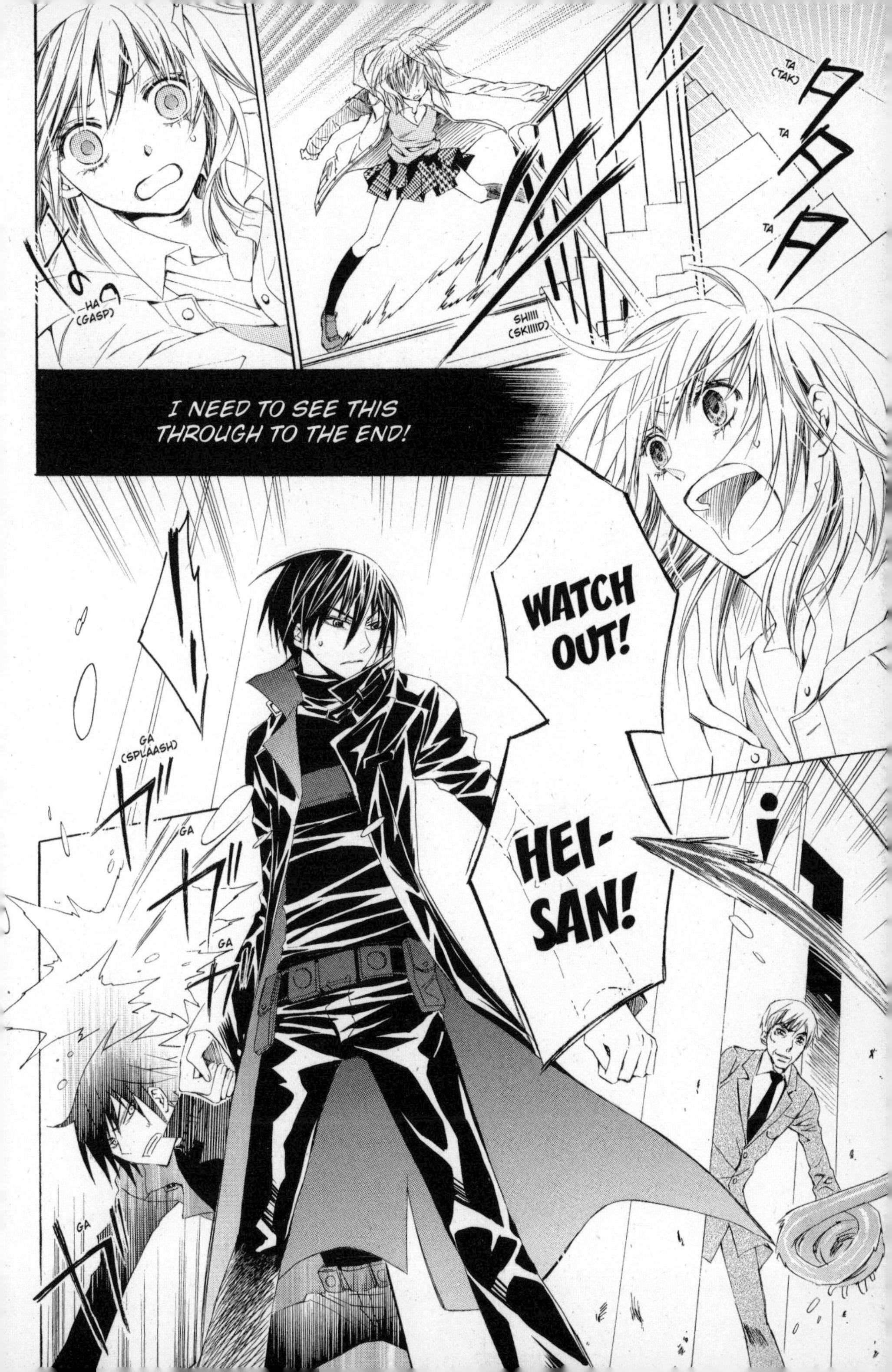

TA (TAK)
TA
TA
SHIII (SKIIIID)
HA (GASP)
I NEED TO SEE THIS THROUGH TO THE END!
WATCH OUT!
HEI-SAN!
GA (SPLAASH)
GA
GA
GA

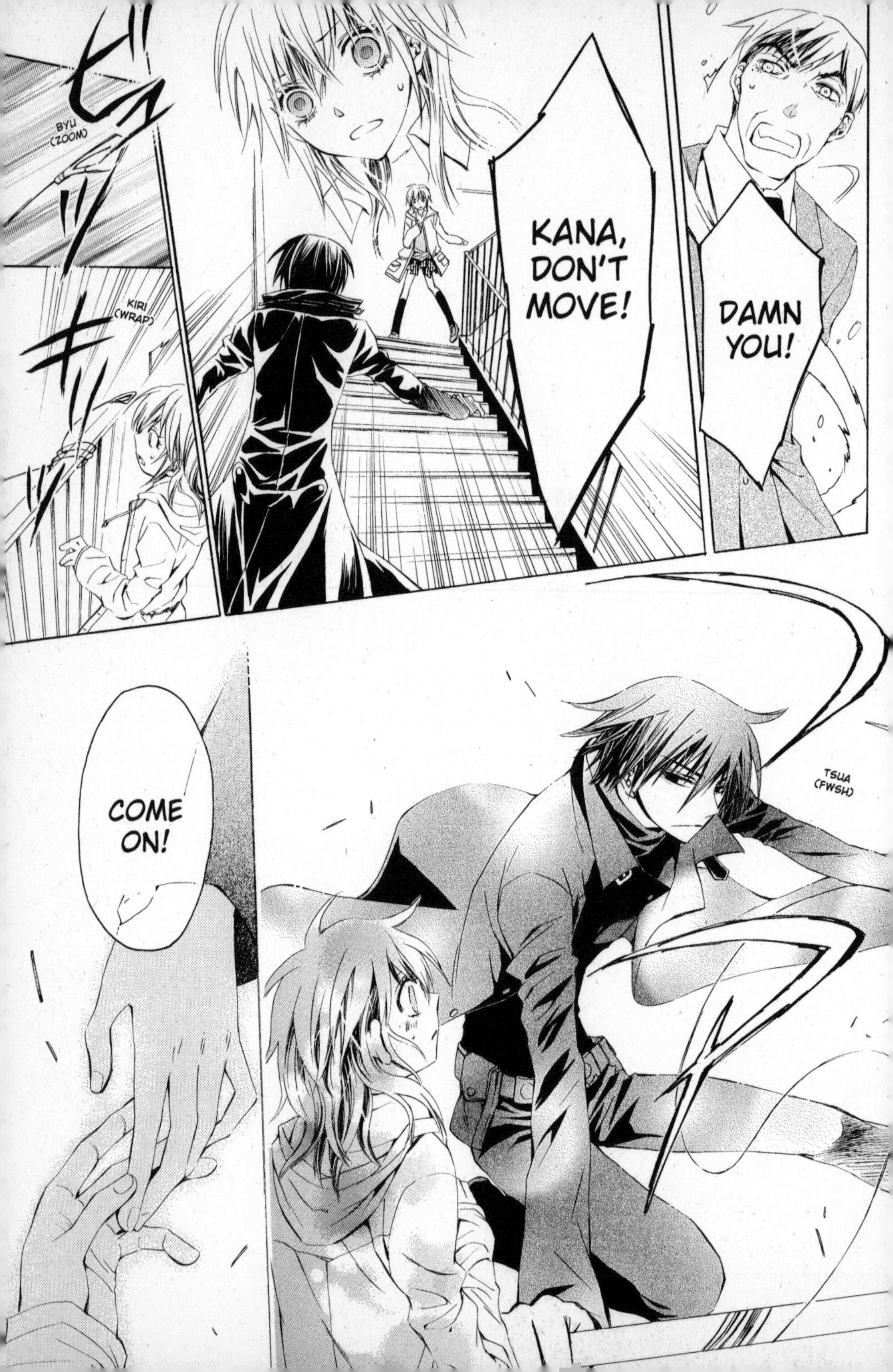
DAMN YOU!
KANA, DON'T MOVE!
BYU (ZOOM)
KIRI (WRAP)
TSUA (FWSH)
COME ON!

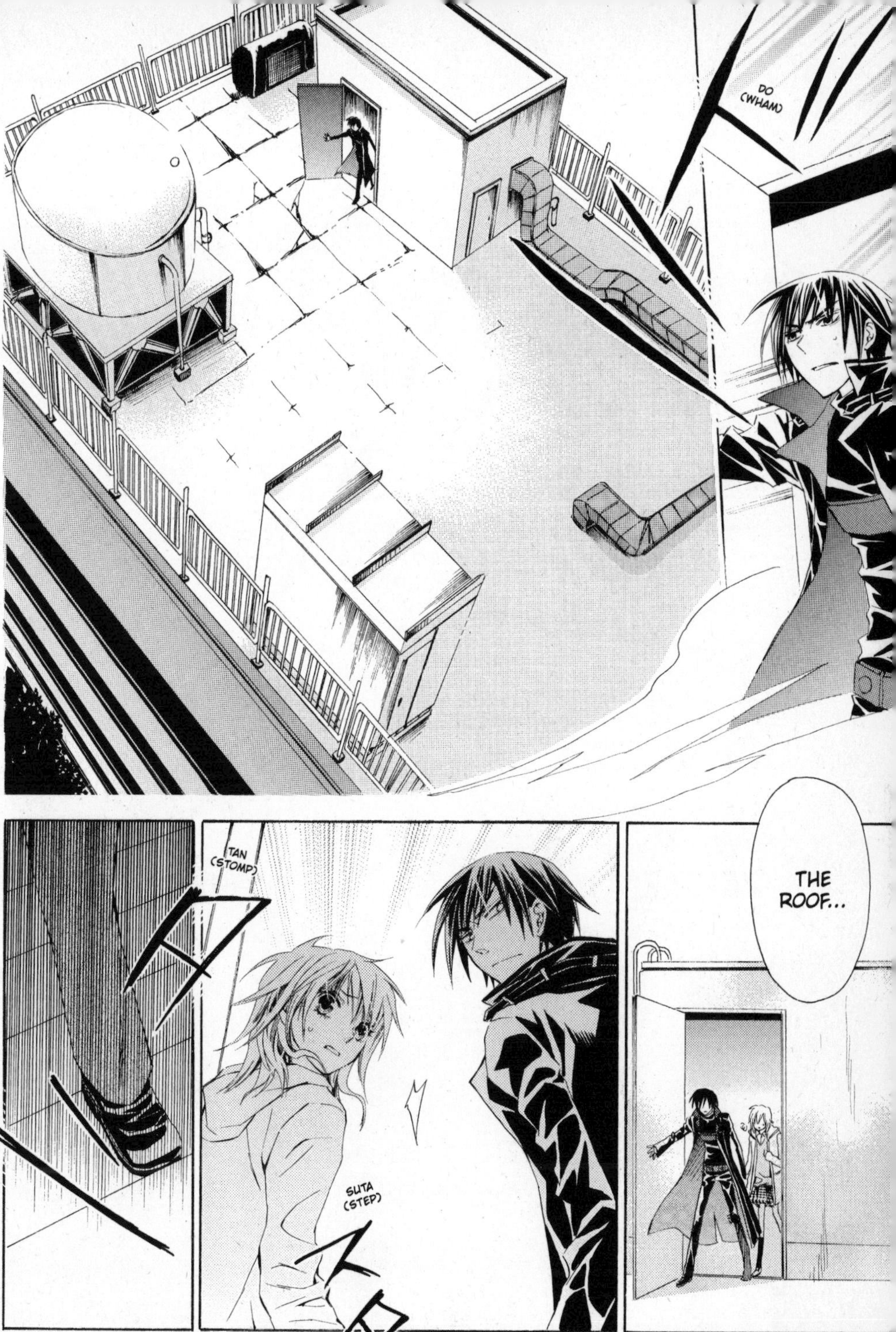
DO (WHAM)
THE ROOF...
TAN (STOMP)
SUTA (STEP)

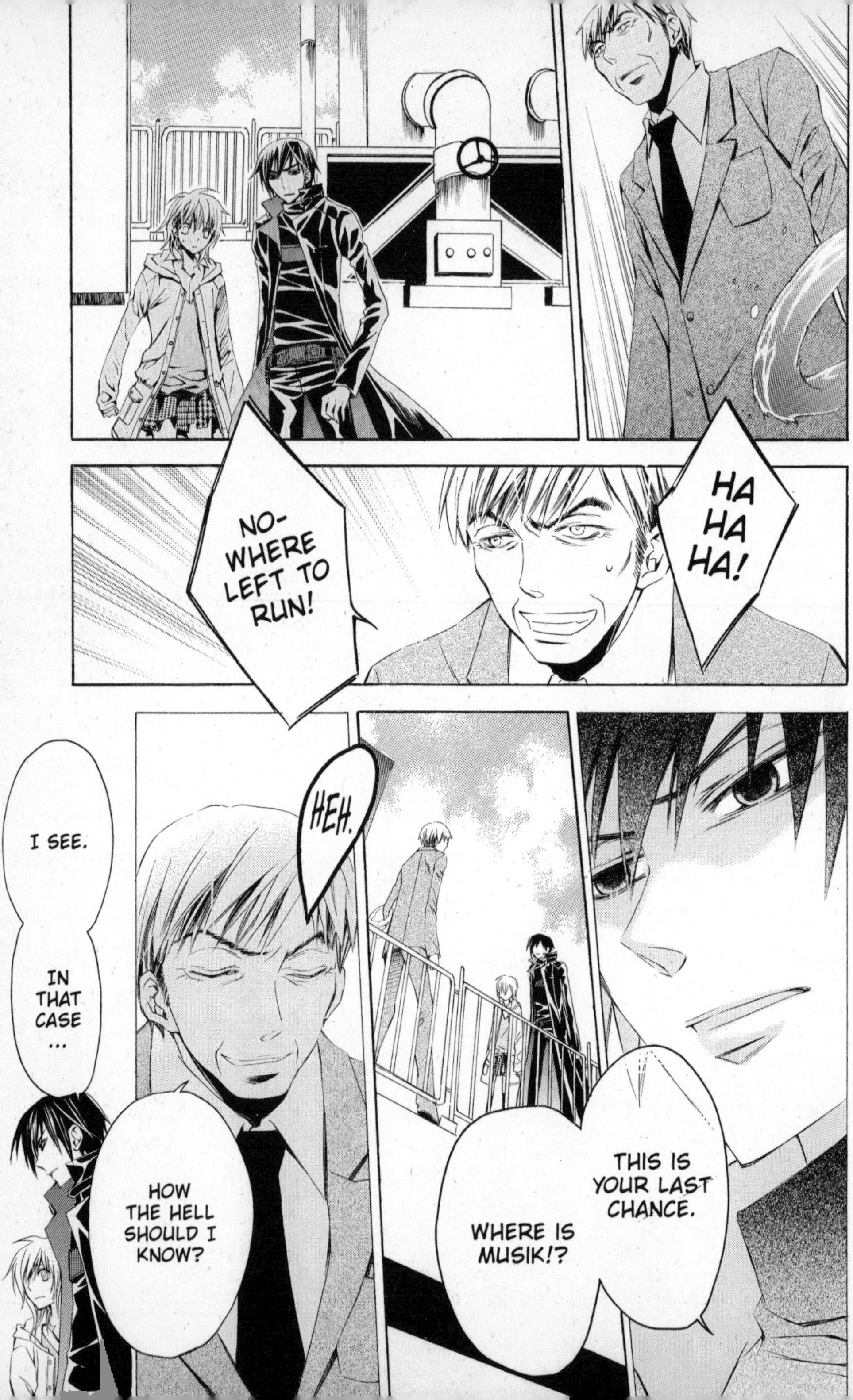
HA HA HA!
NO-WHERE LEFT TO RUN!
THIS IS YOUR LAST CHANCE.
WHERE IS MUSIK!?
HEH.
I SEE.
IN THAT CASE ...
HOW THE HELL SHOULD I KNOW?

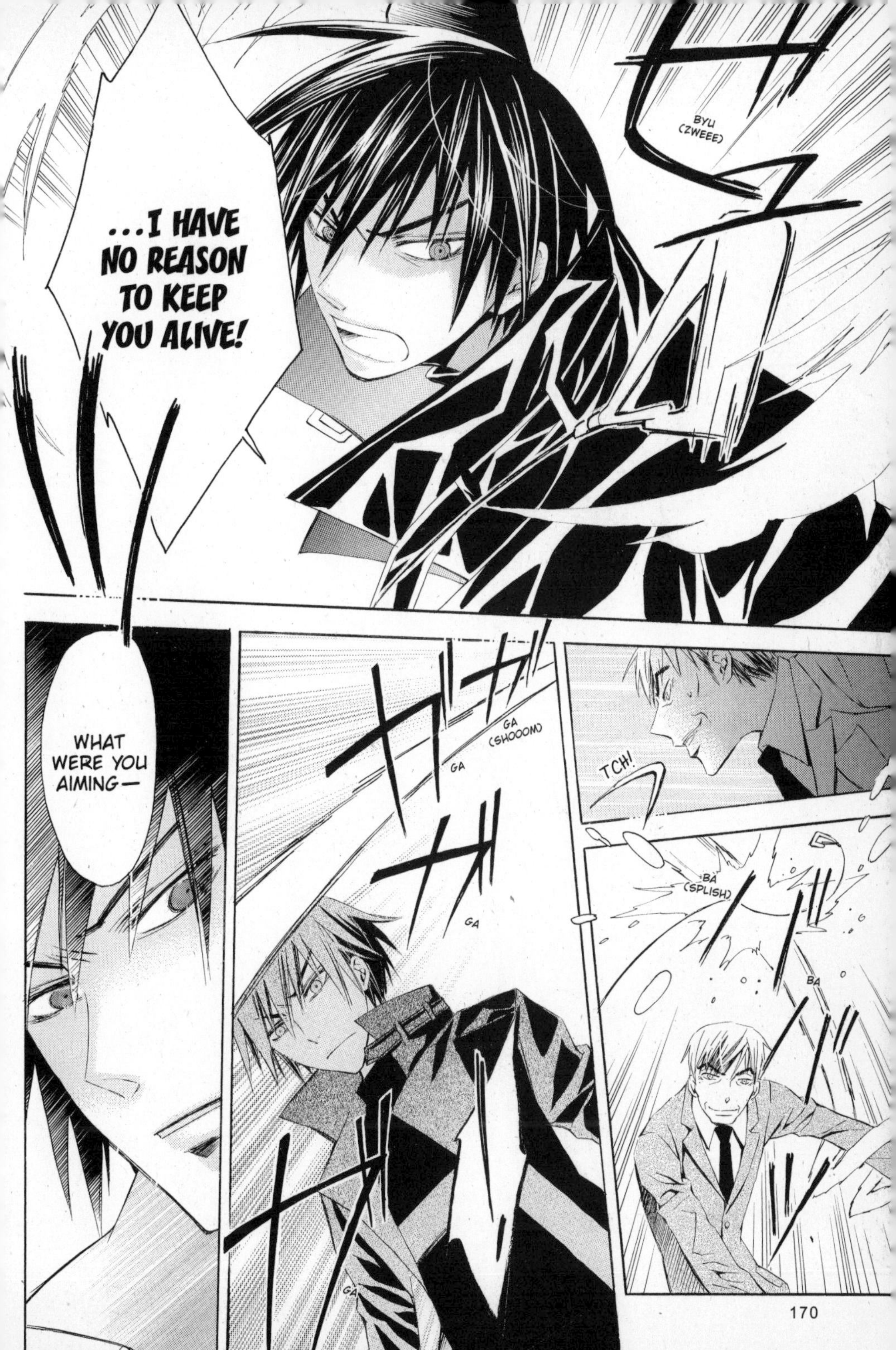
BYU (ZWEEE)
...I HAVE NO REASON TO KEEP YOU ALIVE!
TCH!
BA (SPLISH)
BA
GA (SHOOOM)
GA
GA
GA
WHAT WERE YOU AIMING—

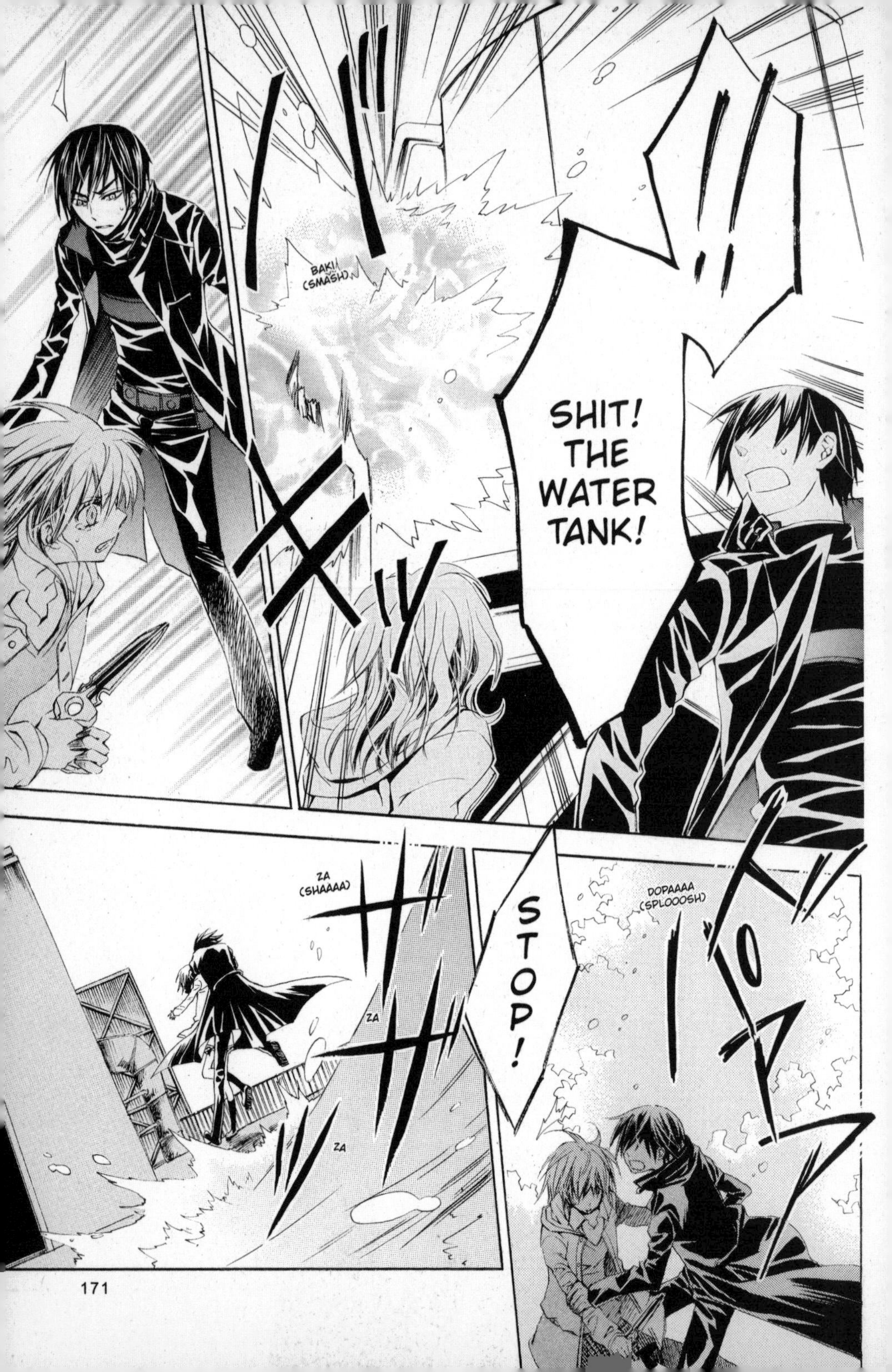
SHIT! THE WATER TANK!
BAKI! (SMASH)
STOP!
DOPAAAA (SPLOOOSH)
ZA (SHAAAA)
ZA
ZA

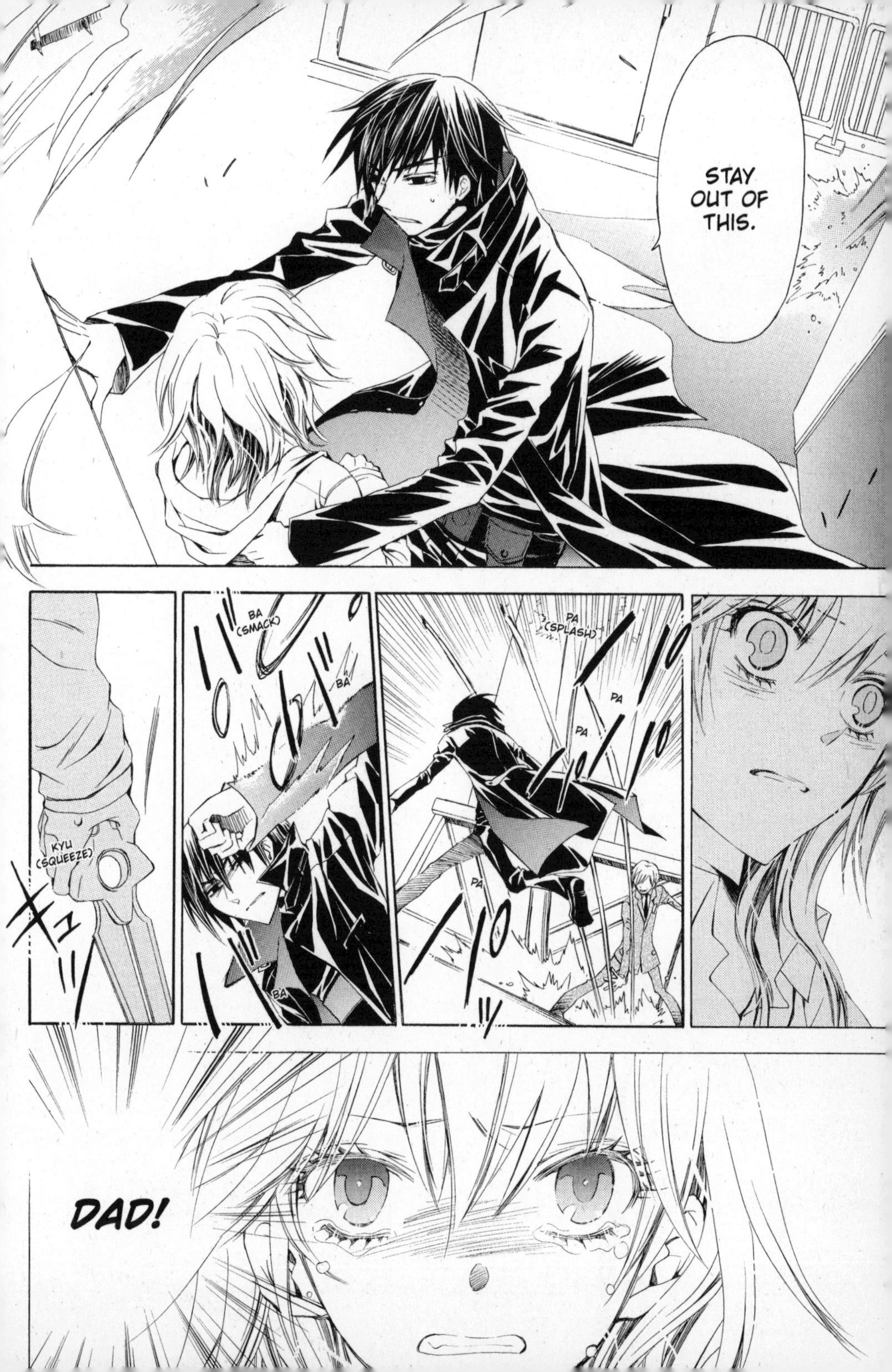
STAY OUT OF THIS.
PA (SPLASH)
PA
PA
PA
BA (SMACK)
BA
BA
KYU (SQUEEZE)
DAD!

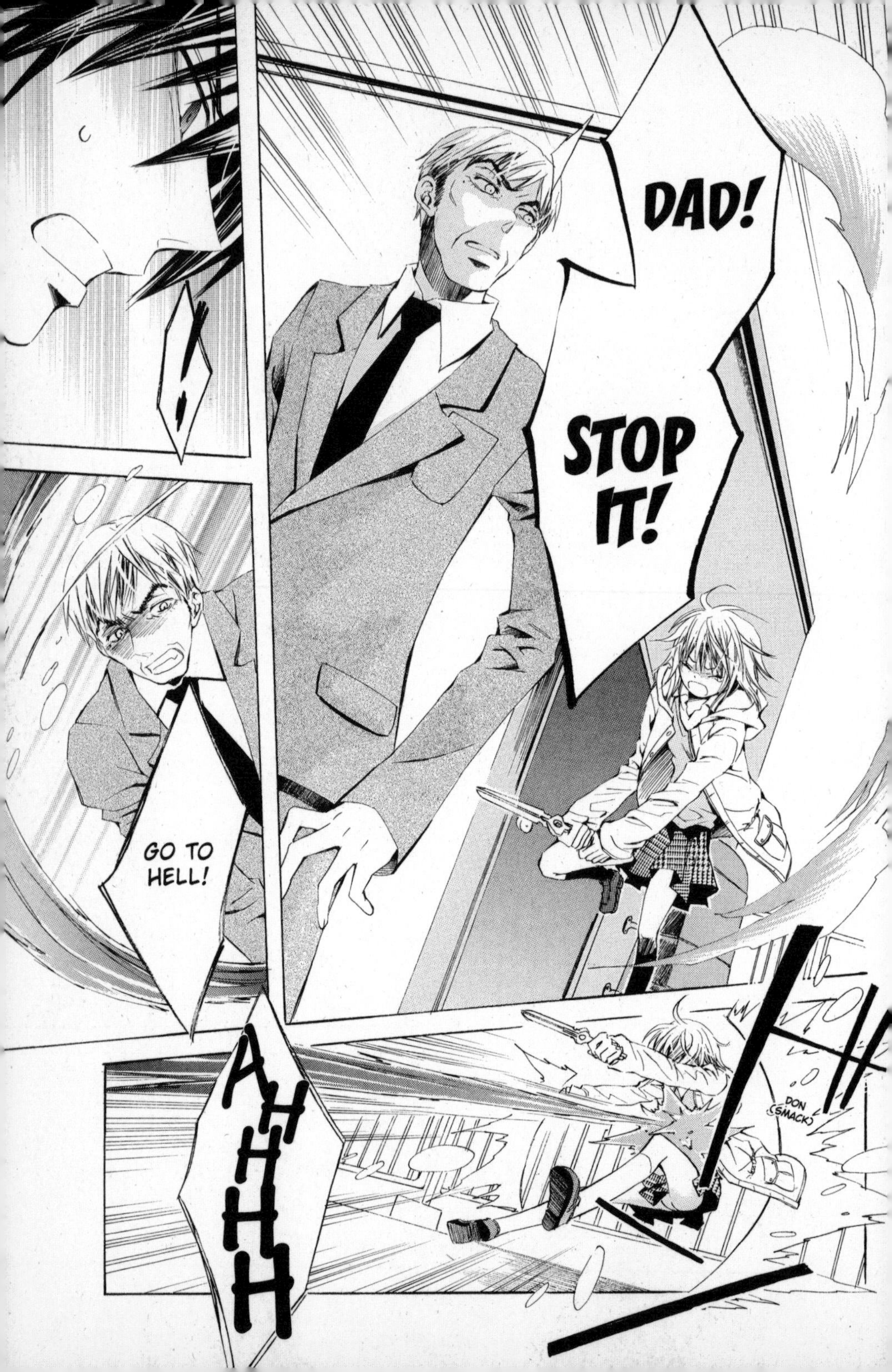
DAD!
STOP IT!
GO TO HELL!
AHHHH
DON (SMACK)

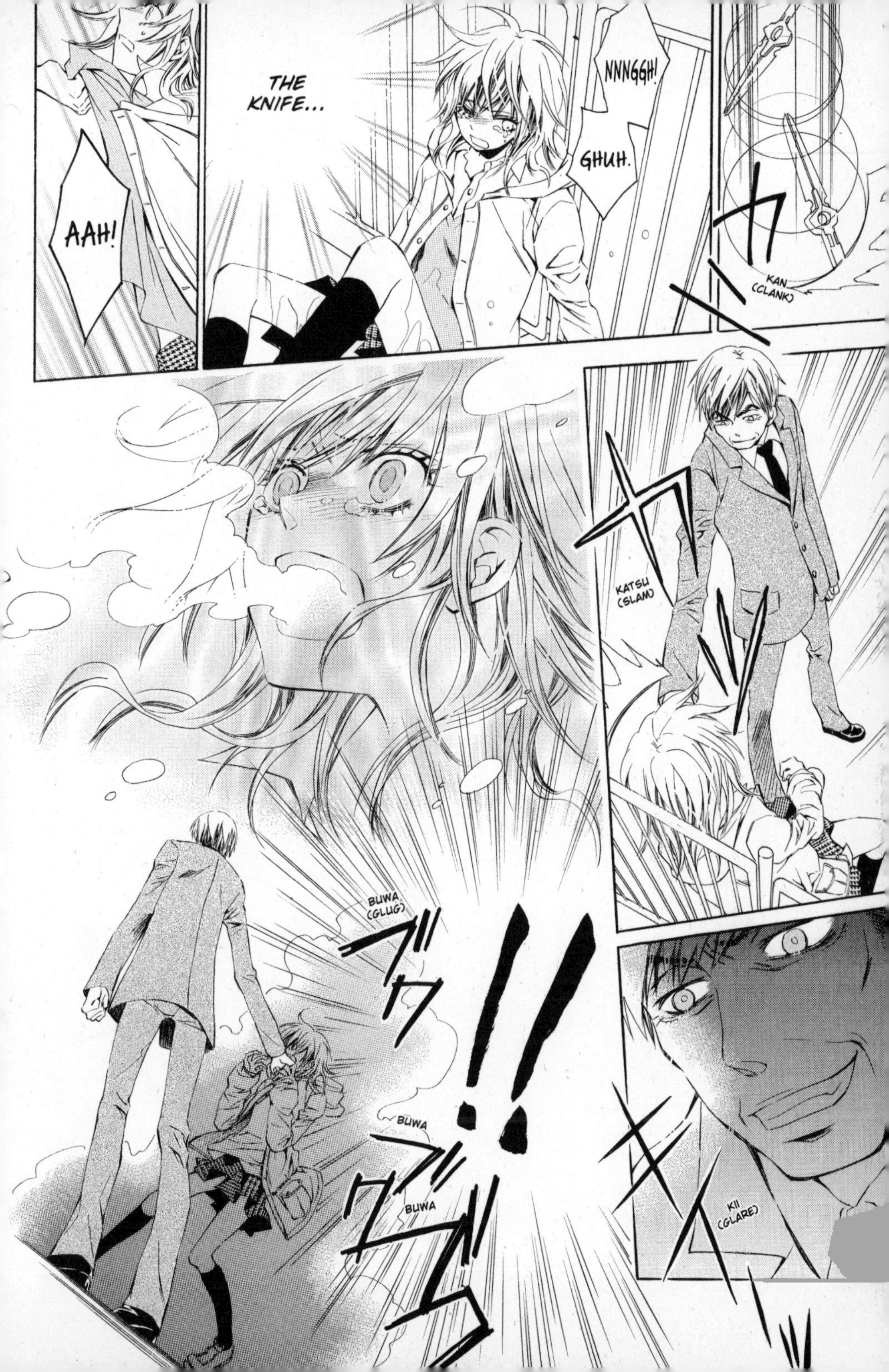
KAN (CLANK)
NNNGGH!
GHUH.
THE KNIFE...
AAH!
KATSU (SLAM)
KII (GLARE)
BUWA (GLUG)
BUWA
BUWA

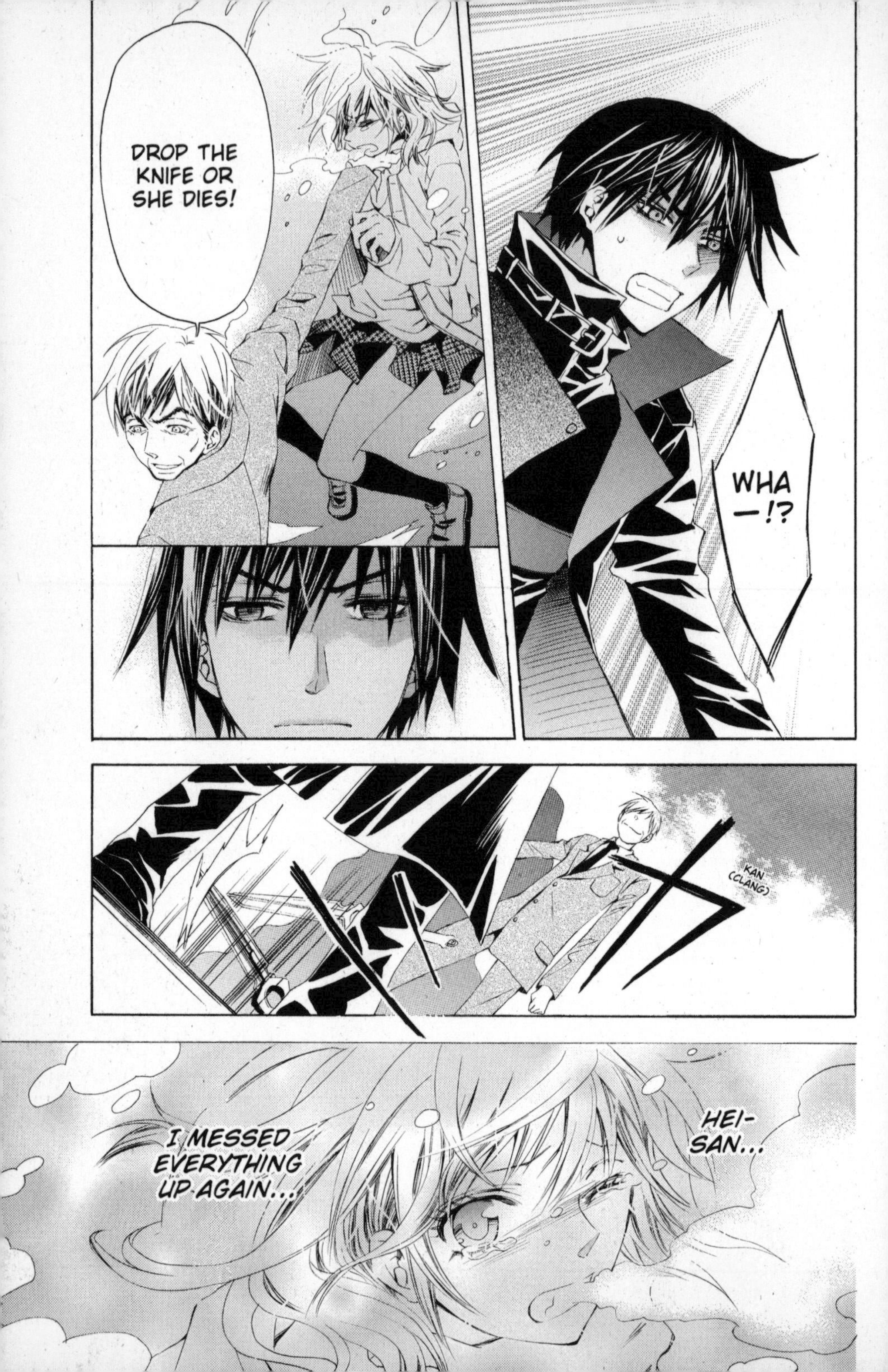
WHA—!?
DROP THE KNIFE OR SHE DIES!
KAN (CLANG)
HEI-SAN...
I MESSED EVERYTHING UP AGAIN...

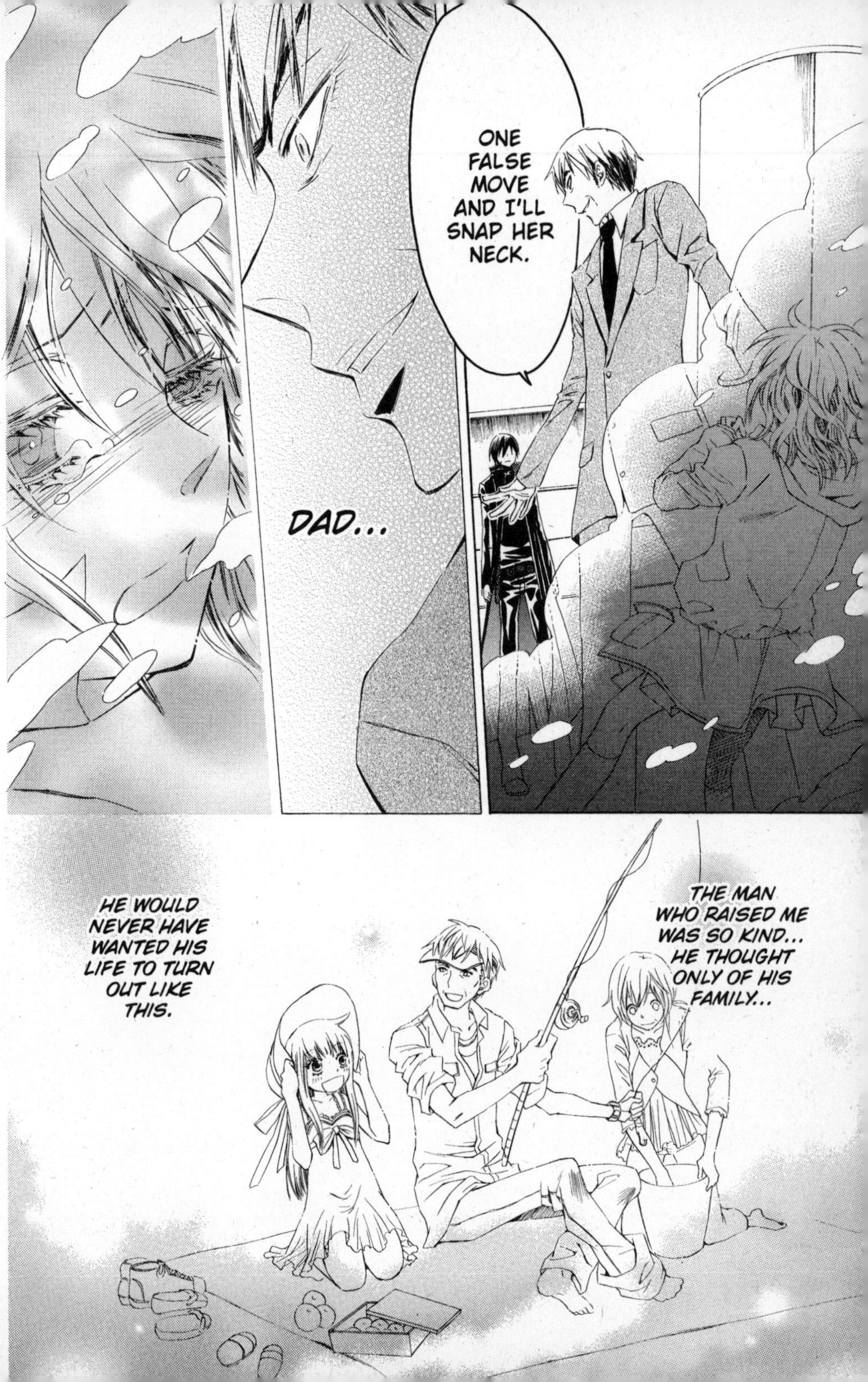
ONE FALSE MOVE AND I'LL SNAP HER NECK.
DAD...
THE MAN WHO RAISED ME WAS SO KIND... HE THOUGHT ONLY OF HIS FAMILY...
HE WOULD NEVER HAVE WANTED HIS LIFE TO TURN OUT LIKE THIS.

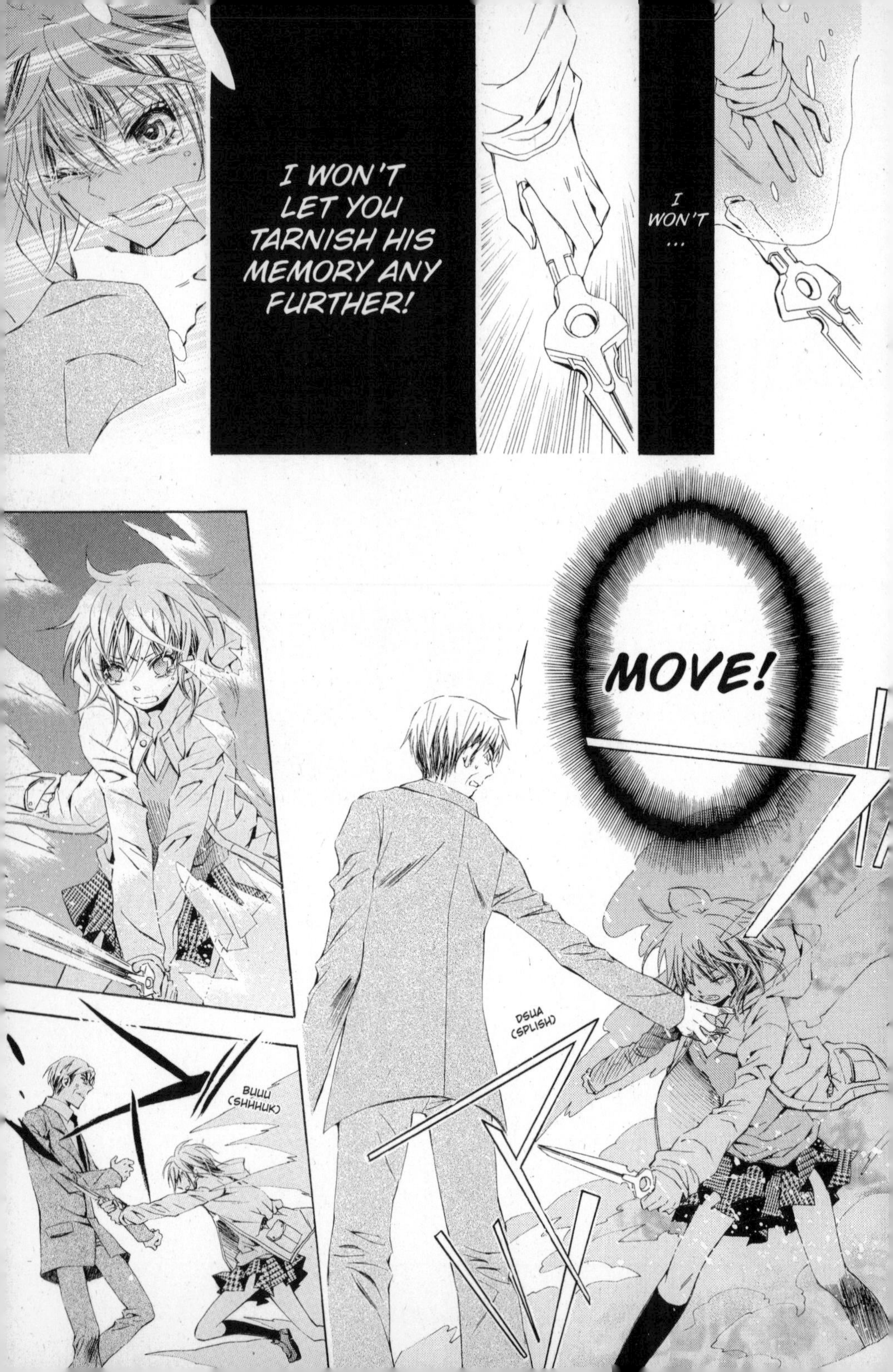
I WON'T ...
I WON'T LET YOU TARNISH HIS MEMORY ANY FURTHER!
MOVE!
DSUA (SPLISH)
BUUU (SHHHUK)

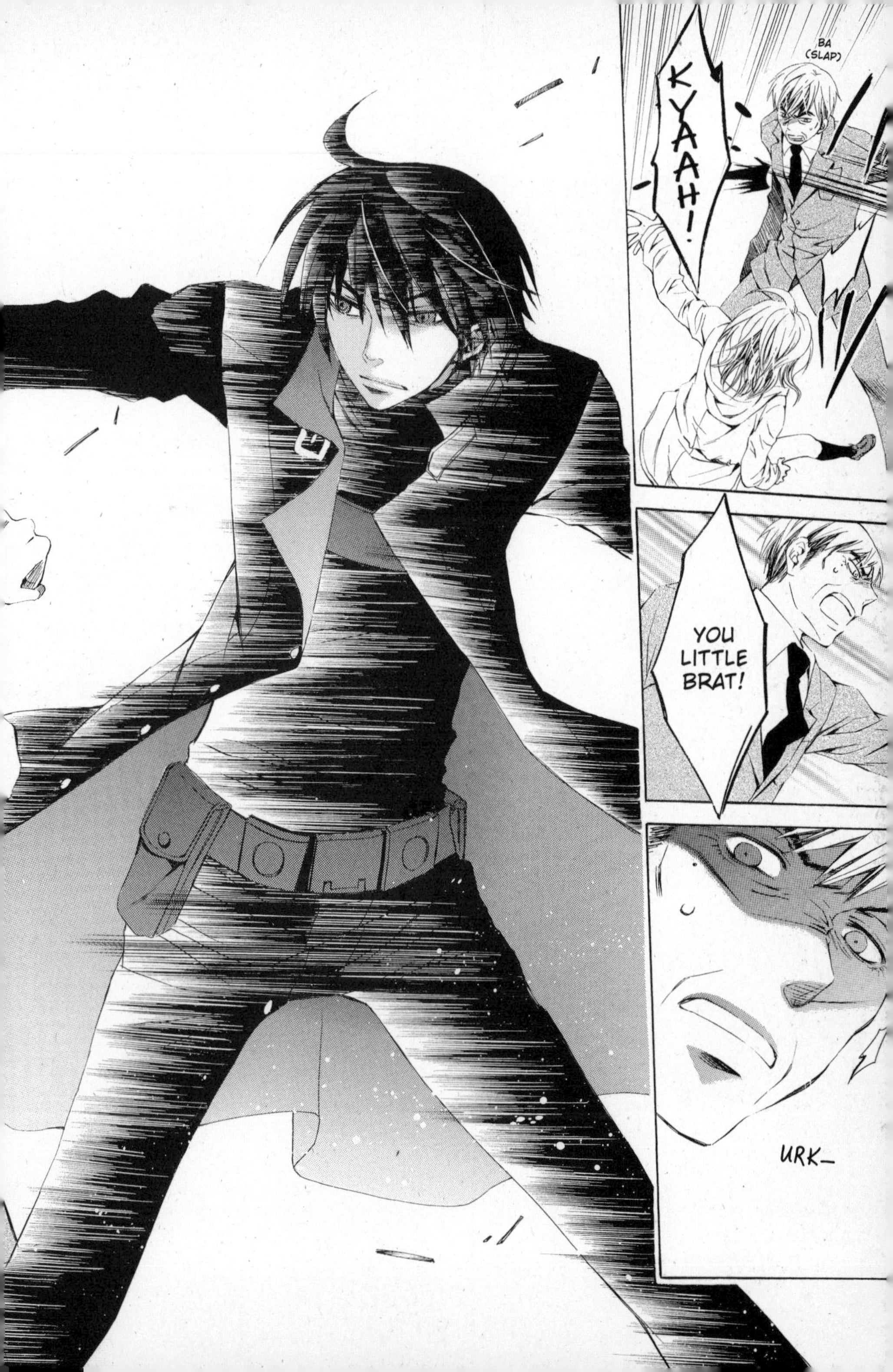
BA (SLAP)
KYAAH!
YOU LITTLE BRAT!
URK—

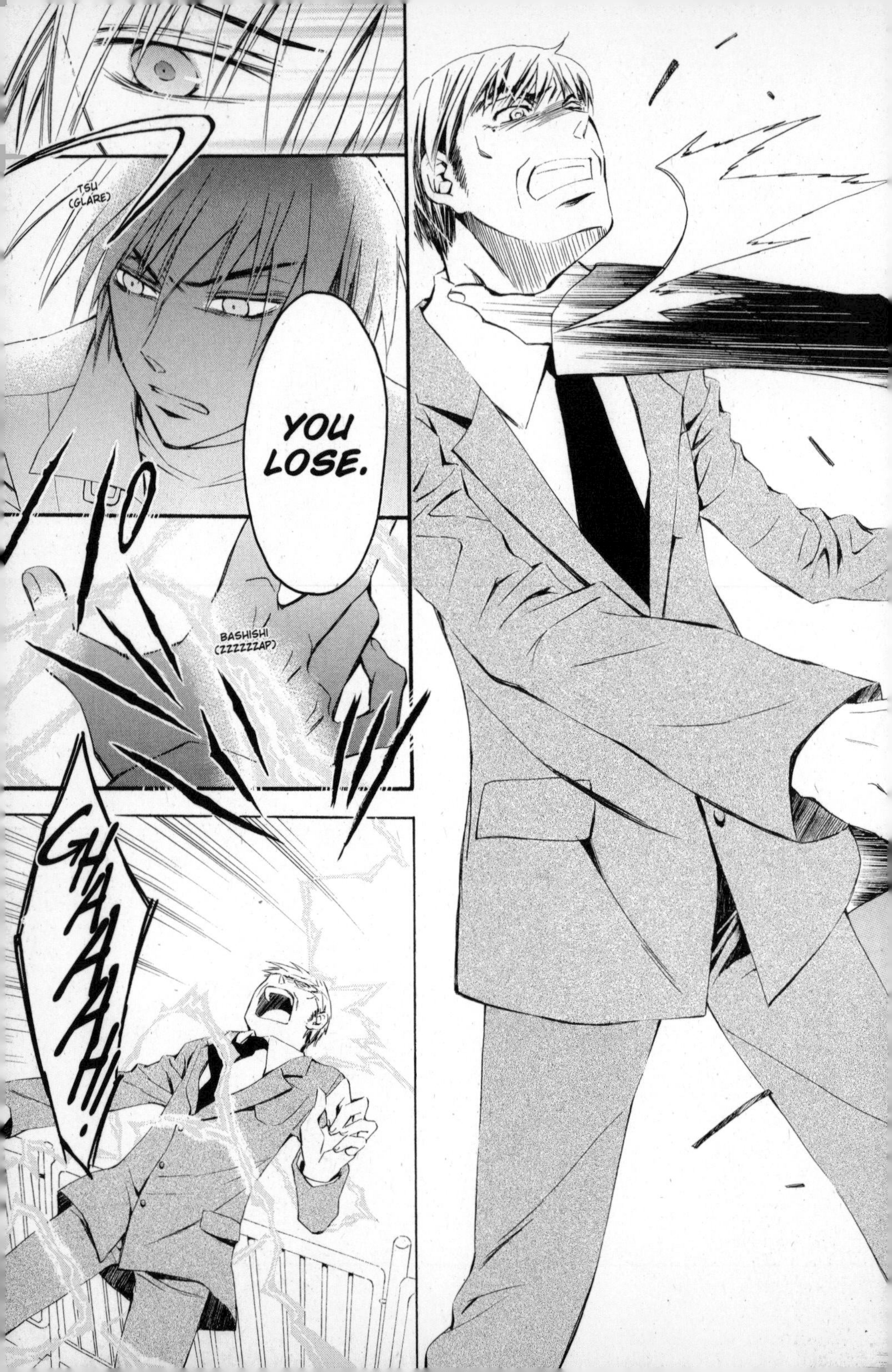
TSU (GLARE)
YOU LOSE.
BASHISHI (ZZZZZZAP)
GHAAAH!!!

I'M SORRY.

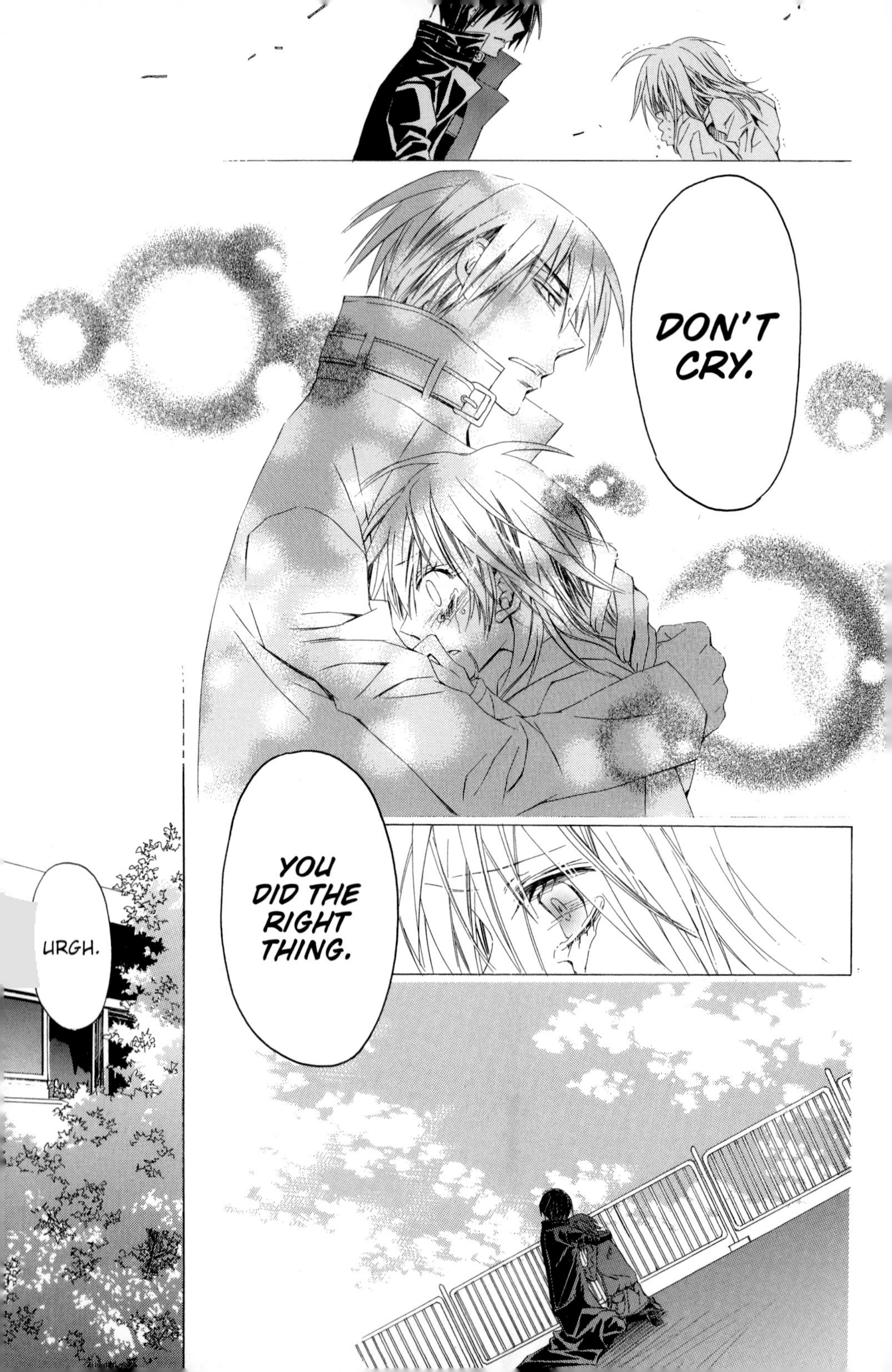
DON'T CRY.
YOU DID THE RIGHT THING.
URGH.

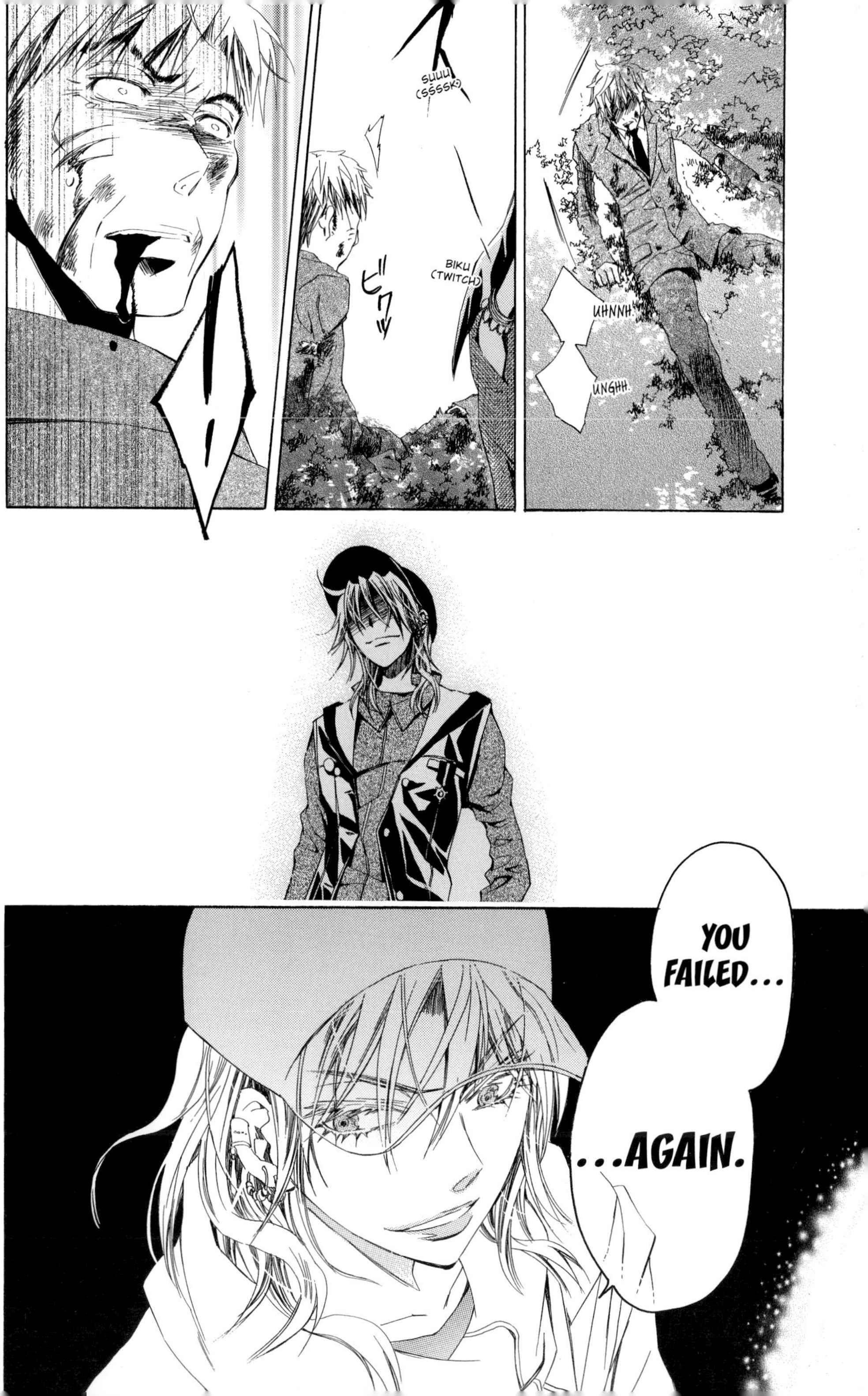
UHNNH.
UNGHH.
SUUU (SSSSK)
ビクッ
BIKU (TWITCH)
YOU FAILED...
...AGAIN.

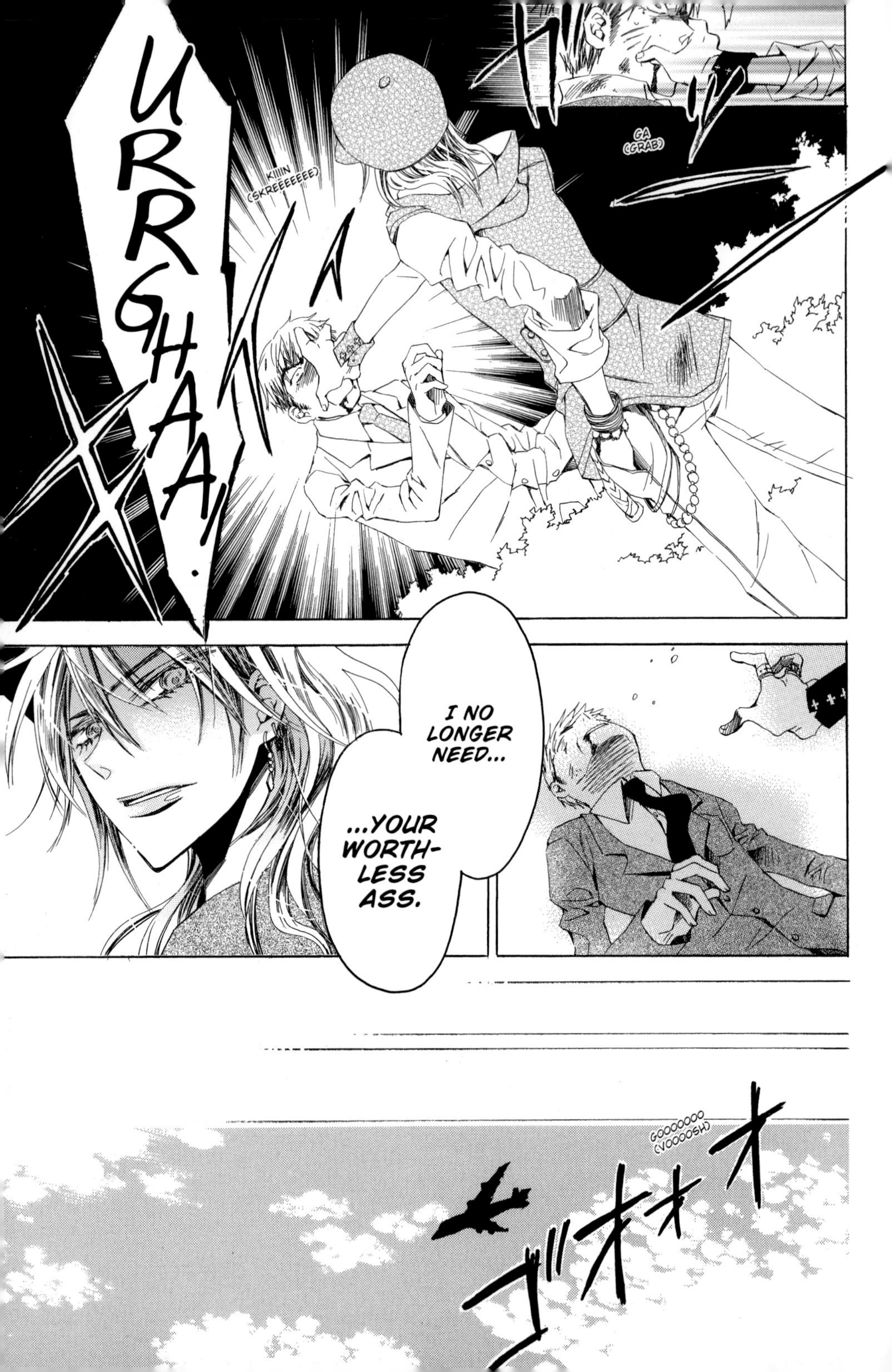
GA (GRAB)
KIIIN (SKREEEEEEE)
URRGHAAA!
I NO LONGER NEED...
...YOUR WORTH-LESS ASS.
GOOOOOOO (VOOOOSH)

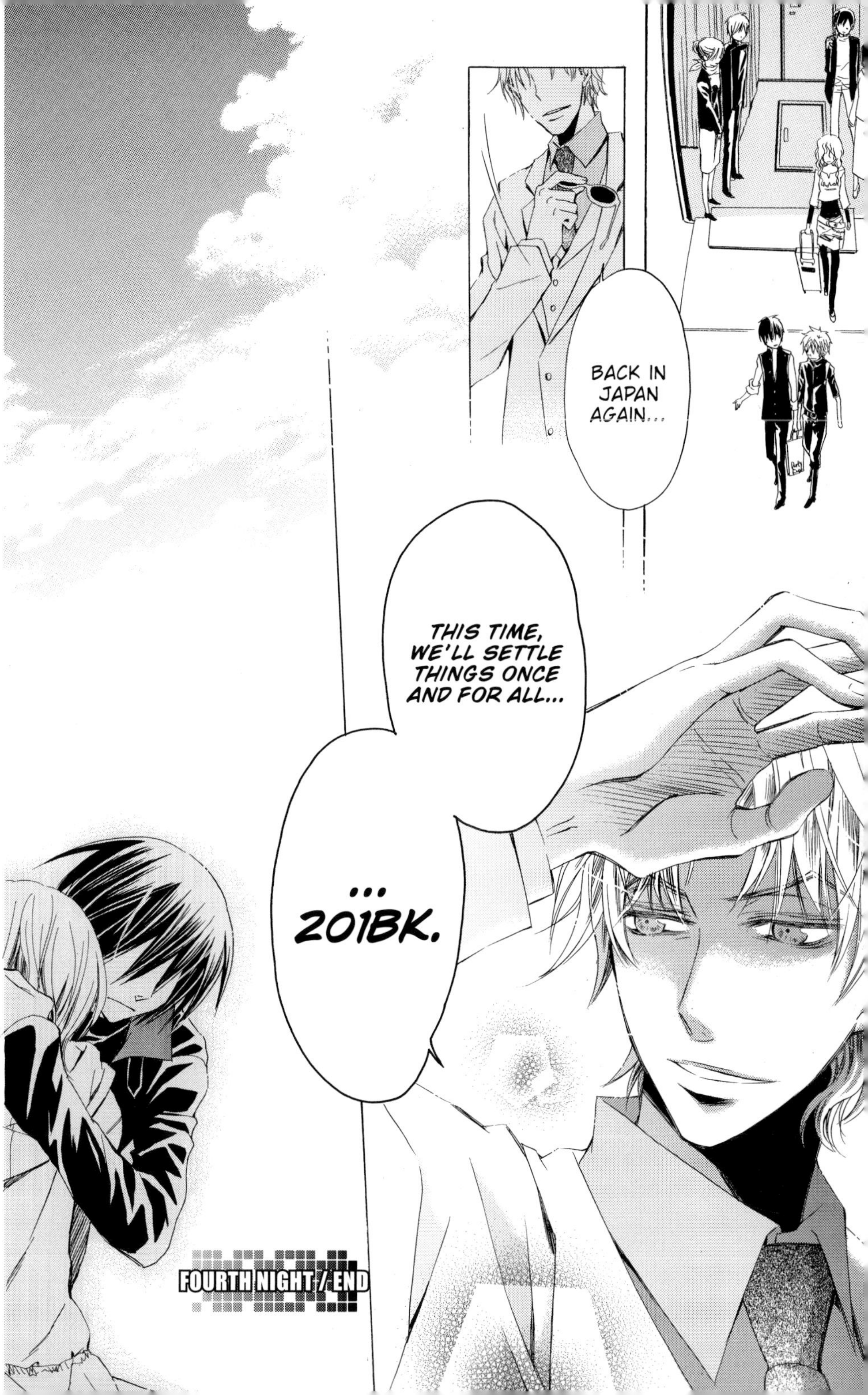
BACK IN JAPAN AGAIN...
THIS TIME, WE'LL SETTLE THINGS ONCE AND FOR ALL...
... 201BK.
FOURTH NIGHT / END

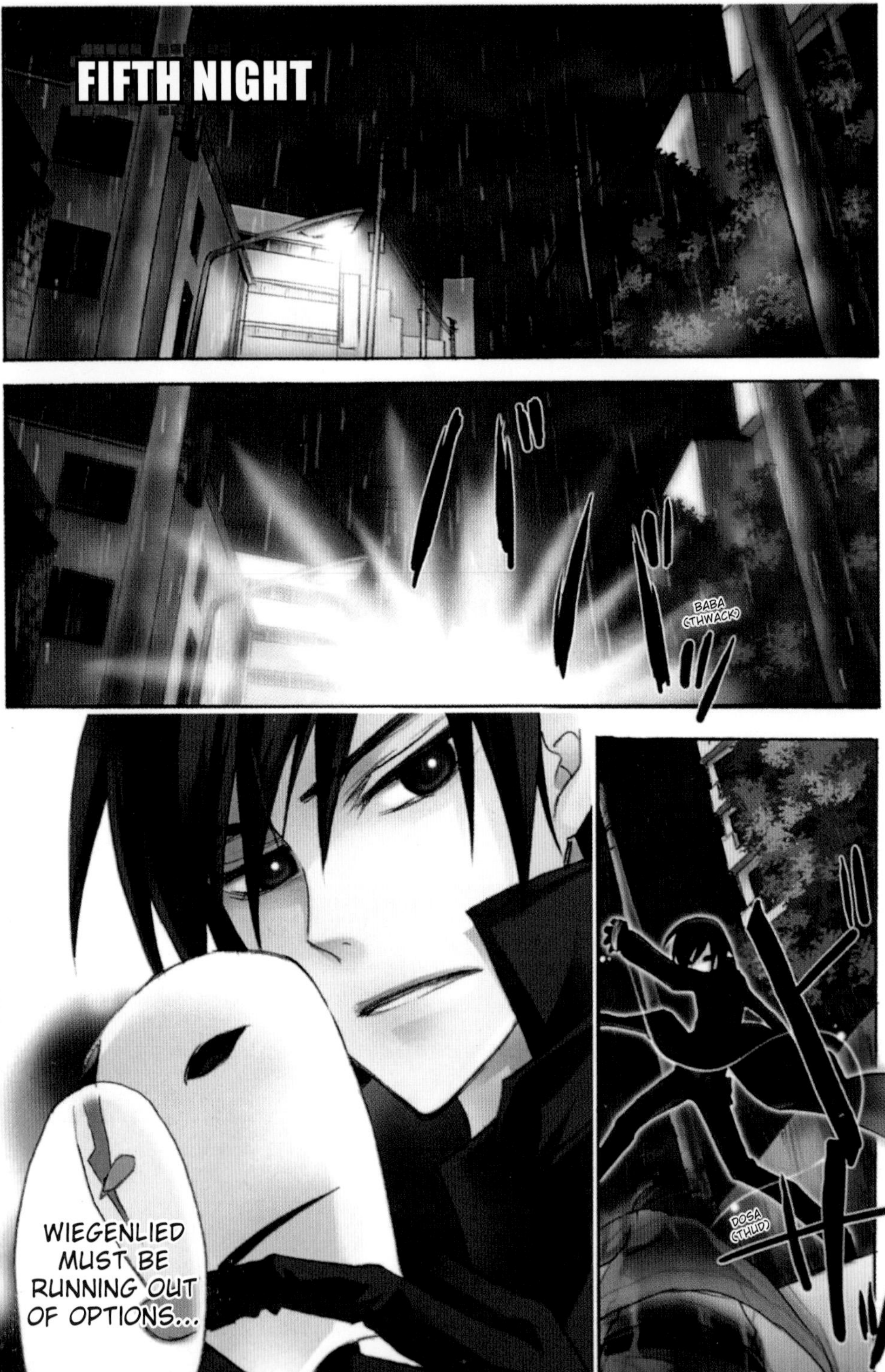
FIFTH NIGHT
BABA (THWACK)
DOSA (THUD)
WIEGENLIED MUST BE RUNNING OUT OF OPTIONS...

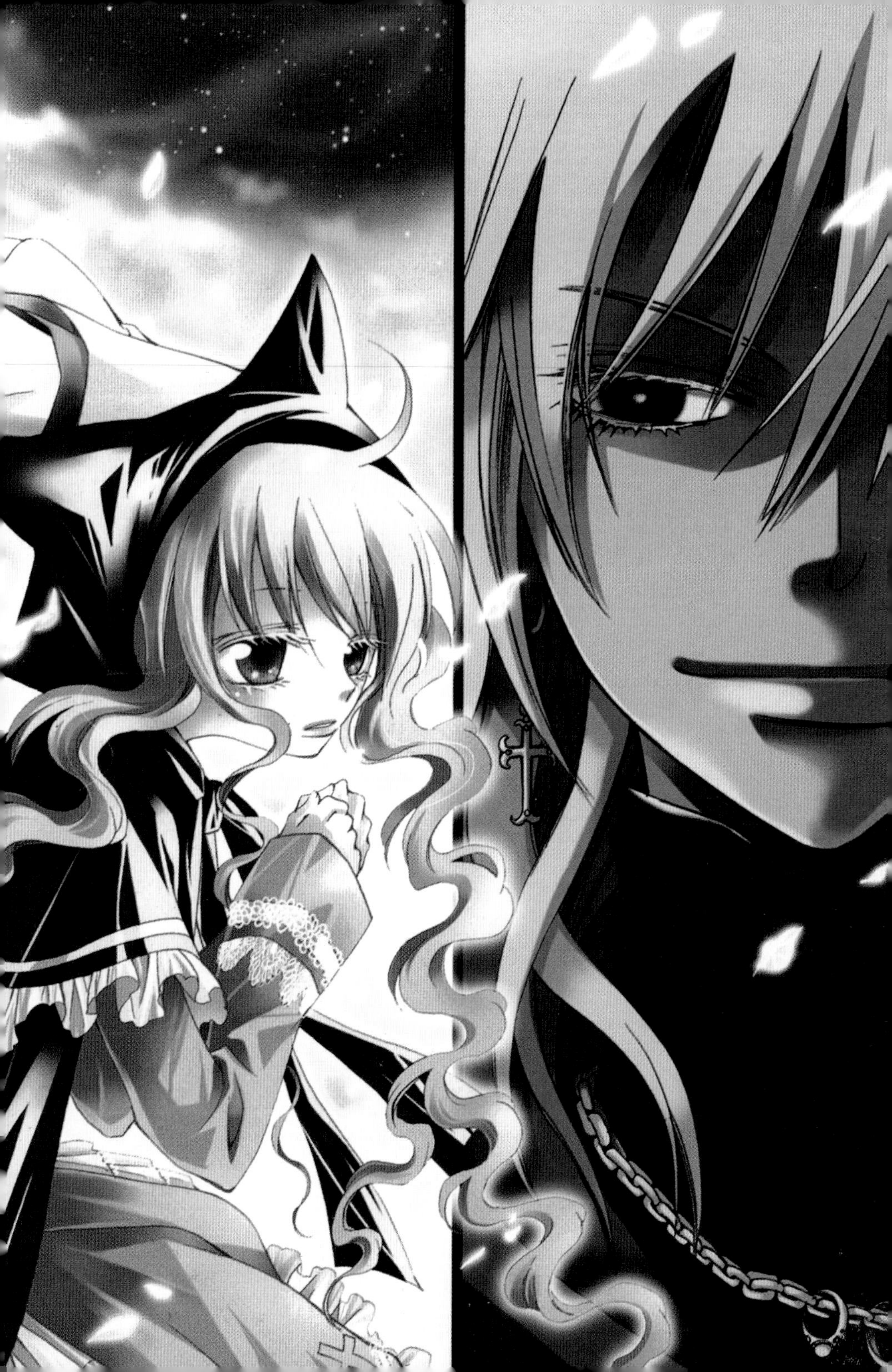

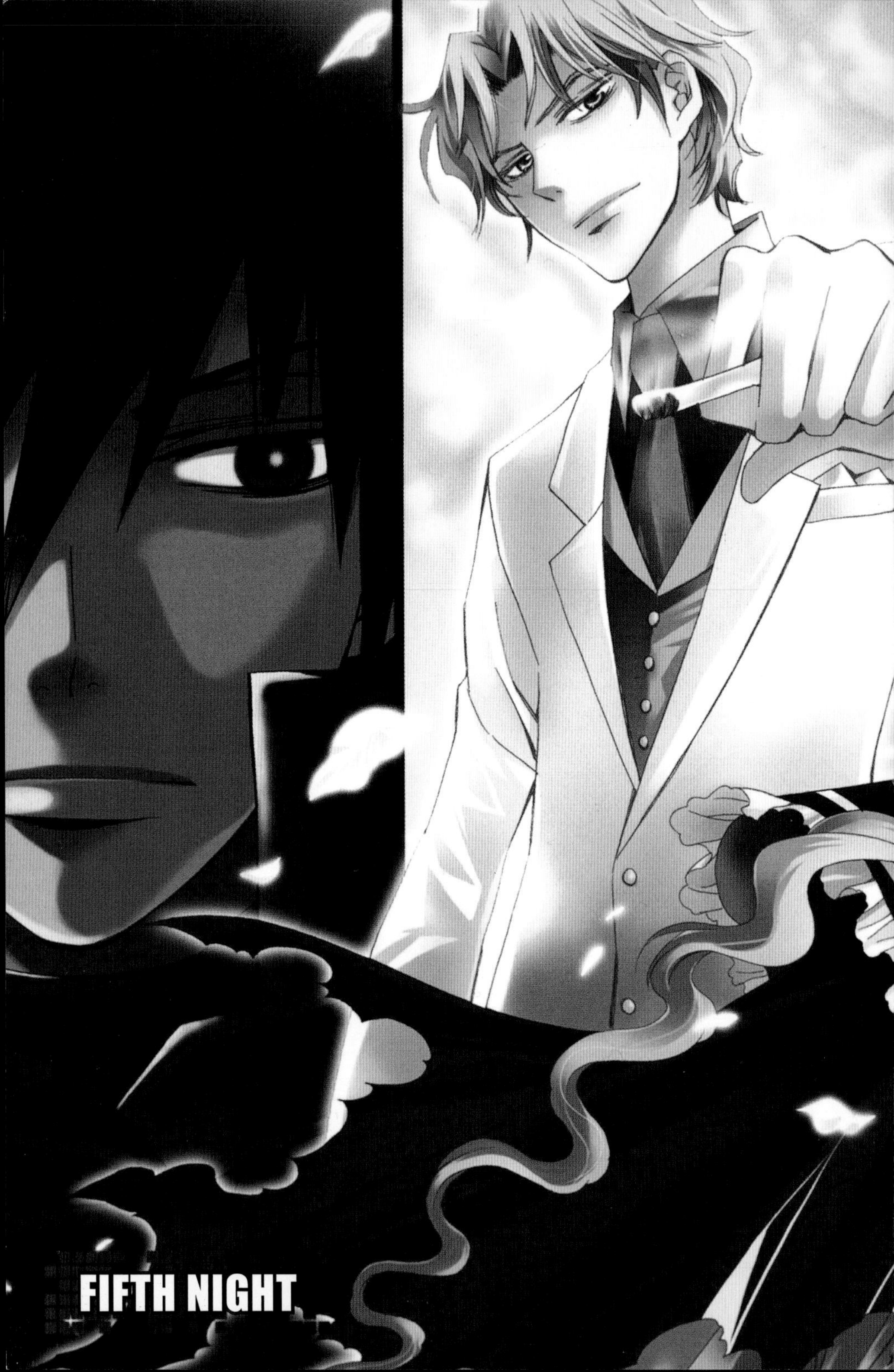
FIFTH NIGHT

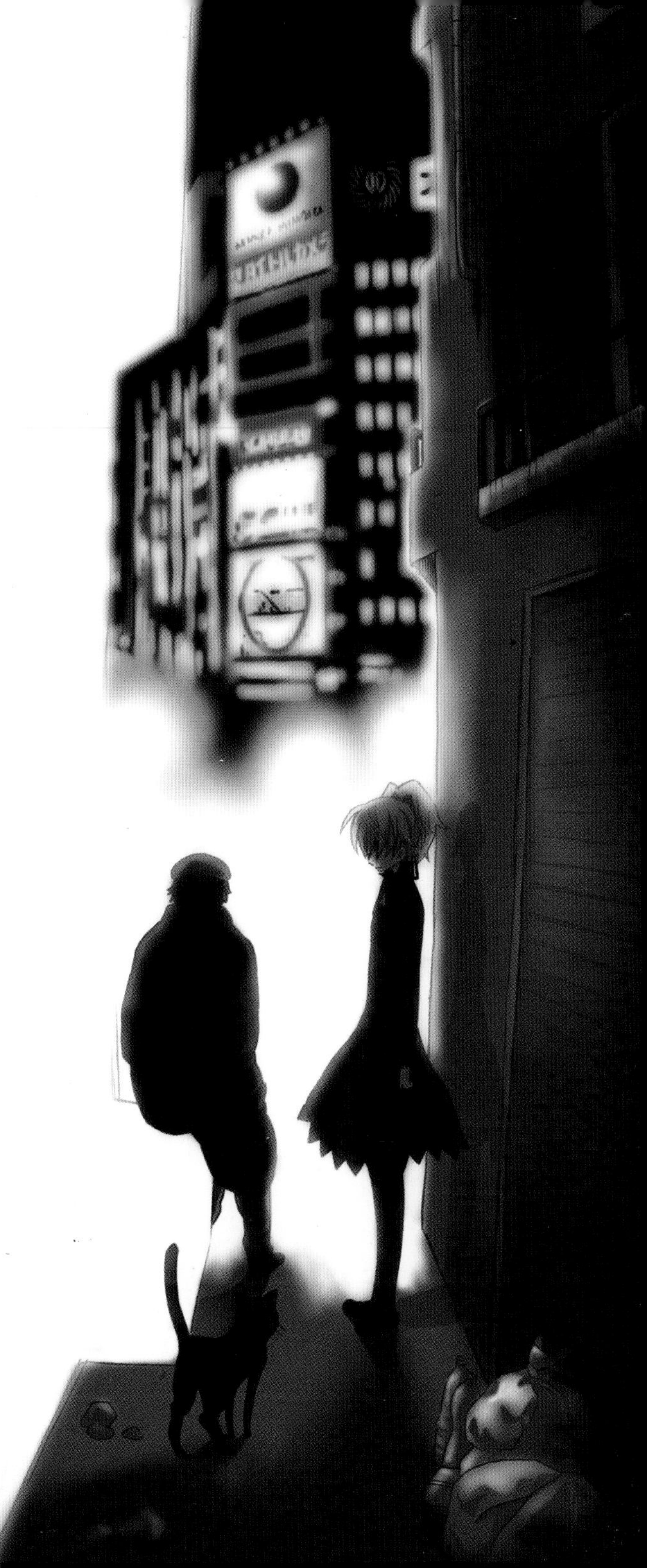

DARKER THAN BLACK

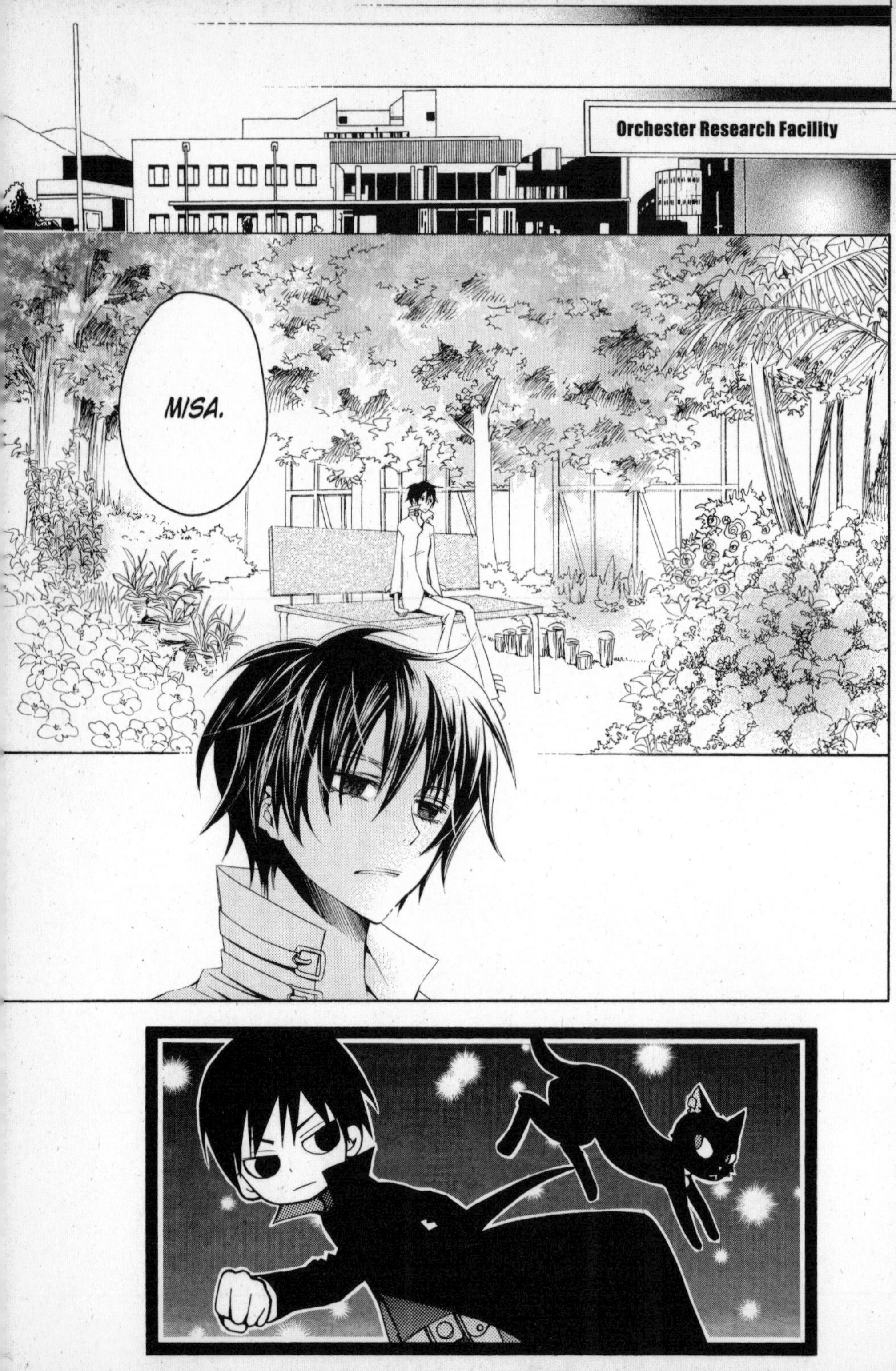
Orchester Research Facility
MISA.

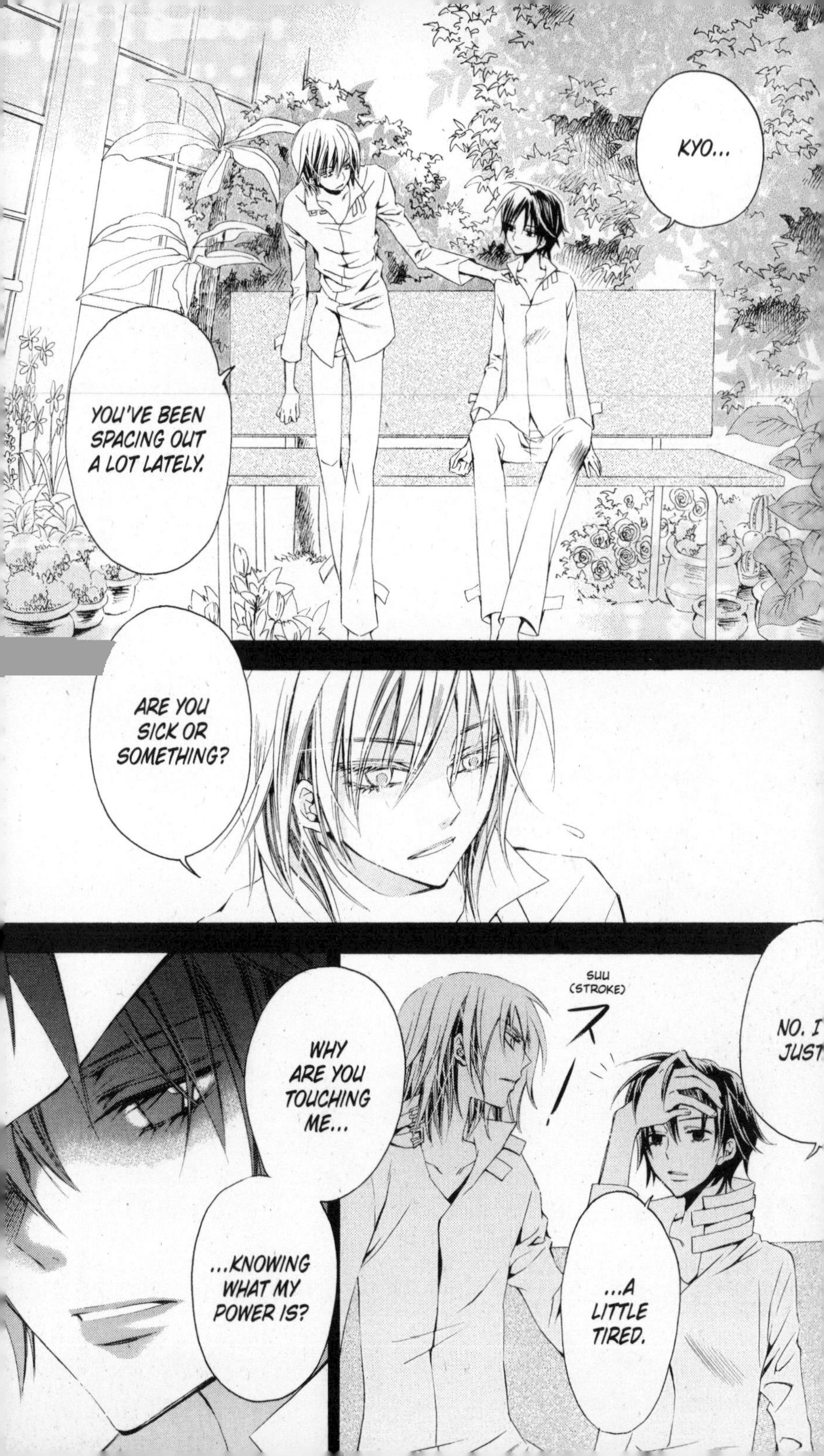
KYO...
YOU'VE BEEN SPACING OUT A LOT LATELY.
ARE YOU SICK OR SOMETHING?
NO. I JUST
...A LITTLE TIRED.
SUU (STROKE)
WHY ARE YOU TOUCHING ME...
...KNOWING WHAT MY POWER IS?

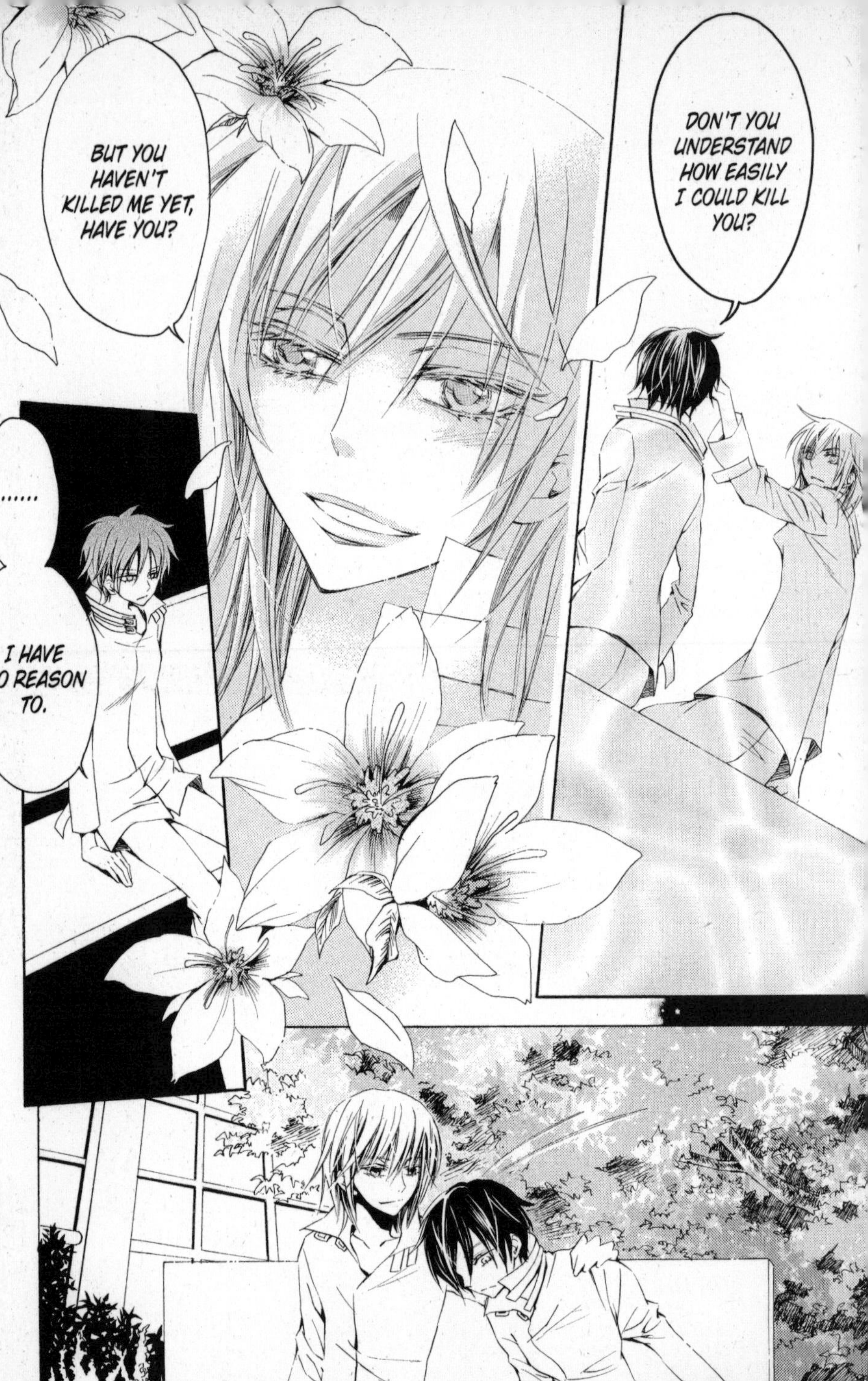
DON'T YOU UNDERSTAND HOW EASILY I COULD KILL YOU?
BUT YOU HAVEN'T KILLED ME YET, HAVE YOU?
......
I HAVE NO REASON TO.

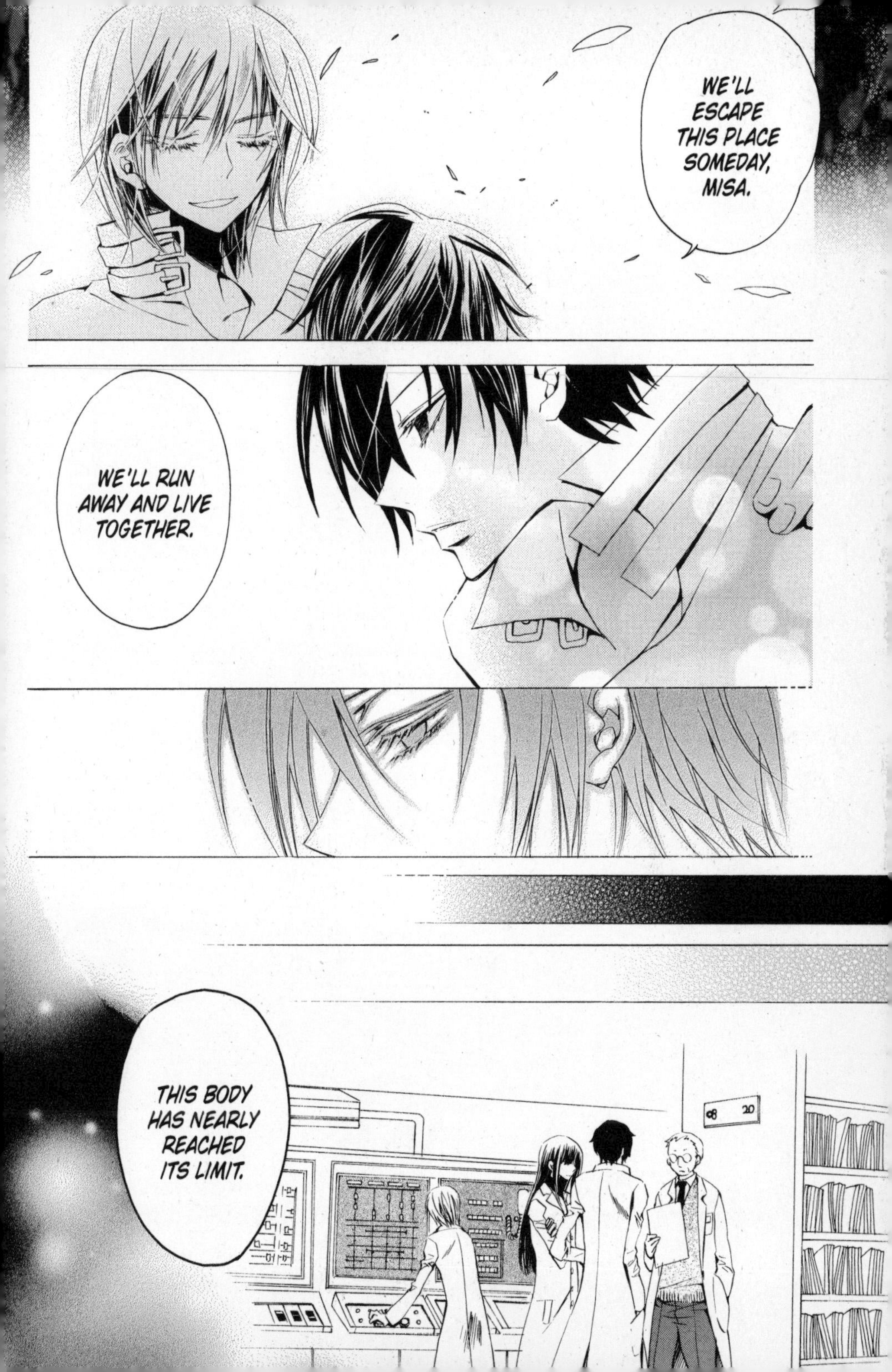
WE'LL ESCAPE THIS PLACE SOMEDAY, MISA.
WE'LL RUN AWAY AND LIVE TOGETHER.
THIS BODY HAS NEARLY REACHED ITS LIMIT.

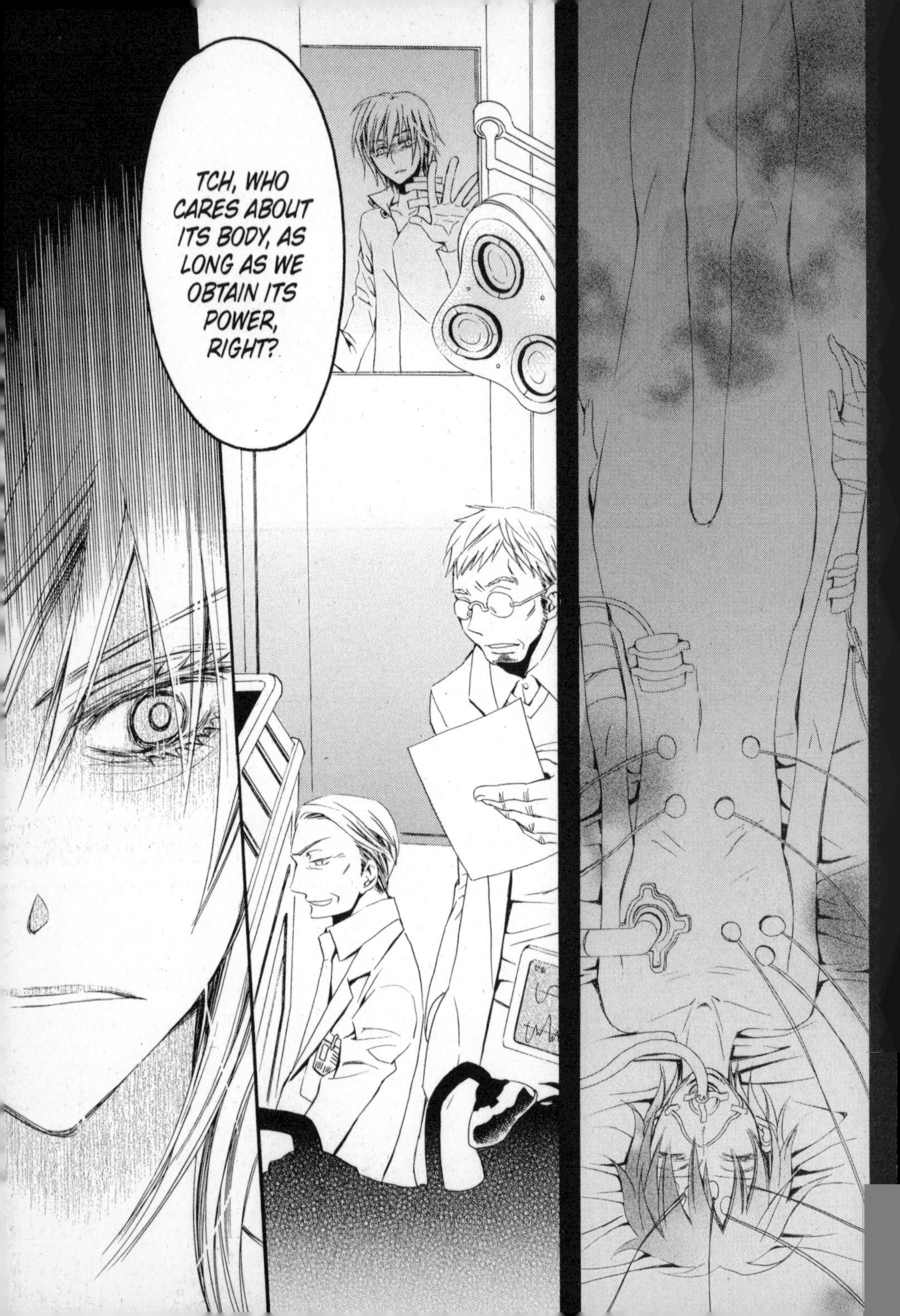
TCH, WHO CARES ABOUT ITS BODY, AS LONG AS WE OBTAIN ITS POWER, RIGHT?

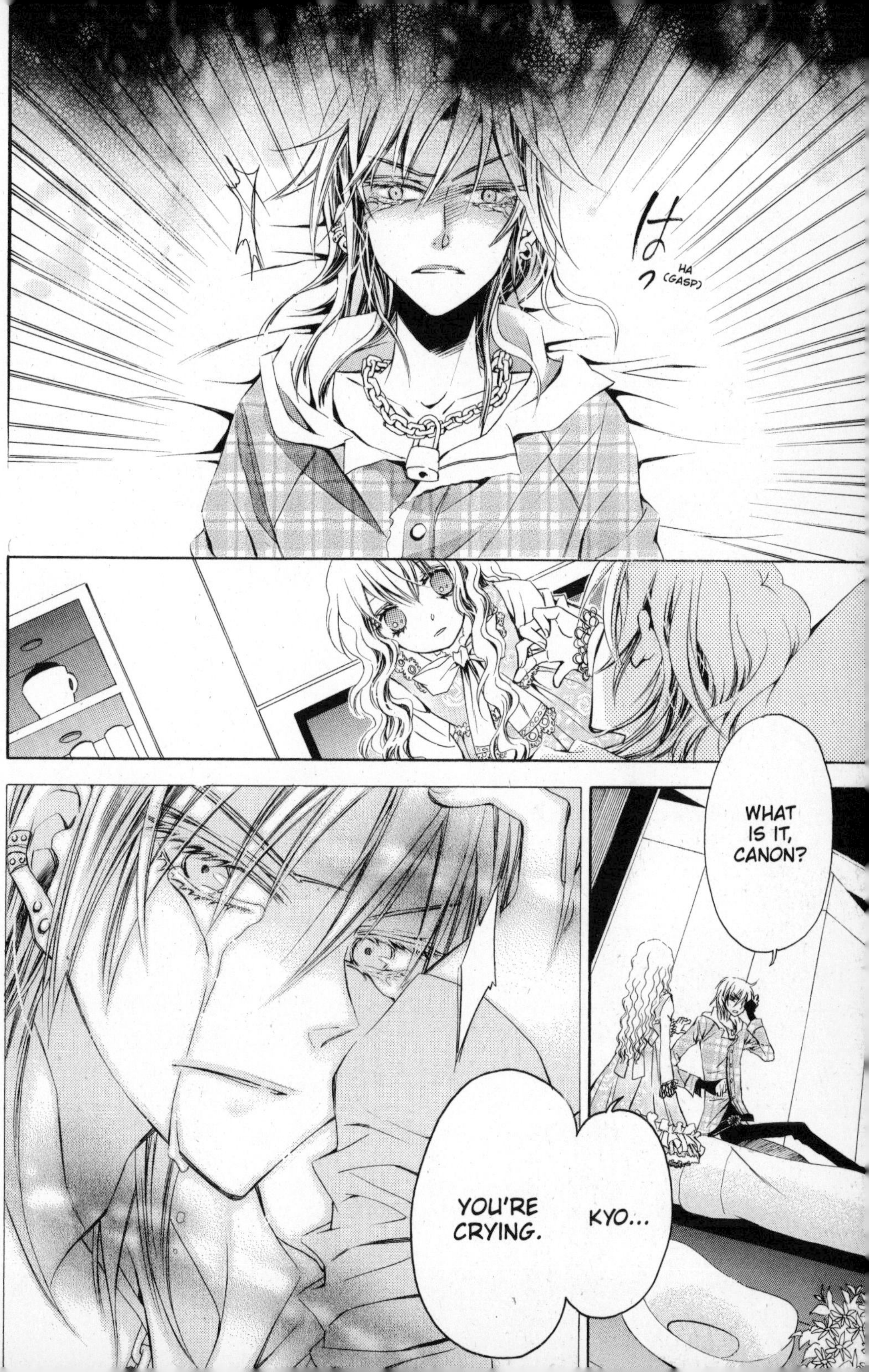
はっ
HA (GASP)
WHAT IS IT, CANON?
KYO...
YOU'RE CRYING.

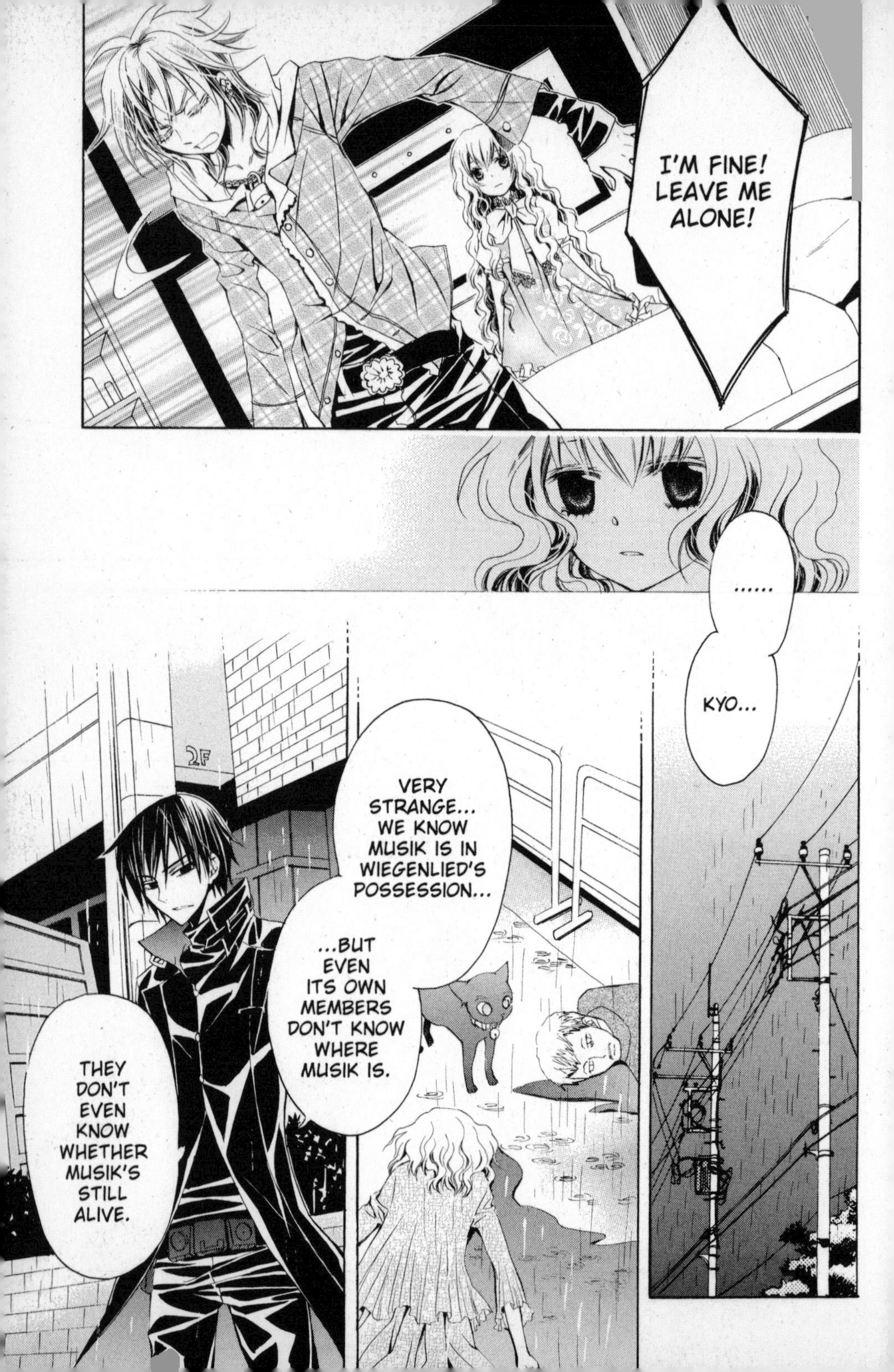
I'M FINE! LEAVE ME ALONE!
......
KYO...
VERY STRANGE... WE KNOW MUSIK IS IN WIEGENLIED'S POSSESSION...
...BUT EVEN ITS OWN MEMBERS DON'T KNOW WHERE MUSIK IS.
THEY DON'T EVEN KNOW WHETHER MUSIK'S STILL ALIVE.
2F

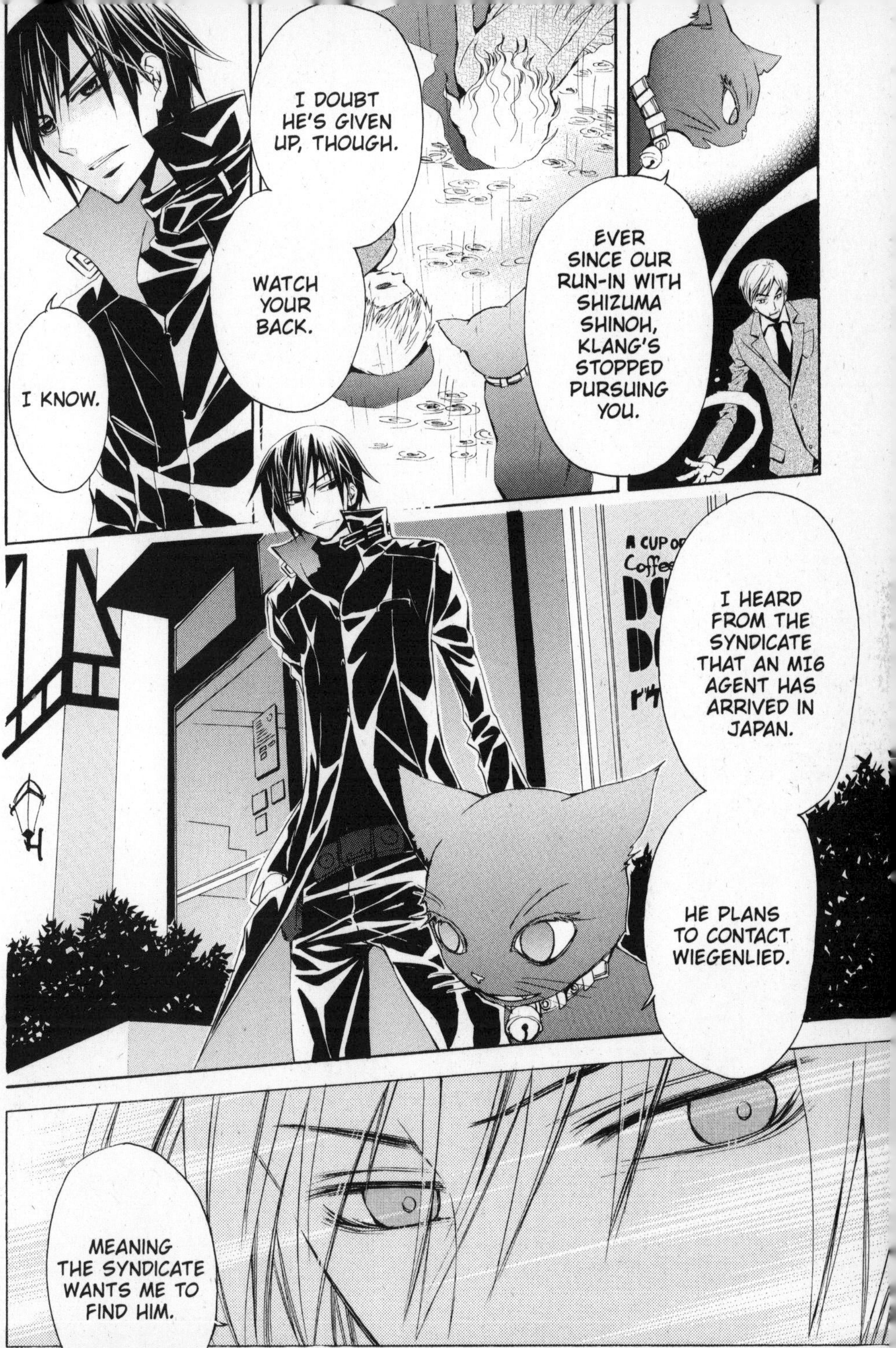
EVER SINCE OUR RUN-IN WITH SHIZUMA SHINOH, KLANG'S STOPPED PURSUING YOU.
I DOUBT HE'S GIVEN UP, THOUGH.
WATCH YOUR BACK.
I KNOW.
I HEARD FROM THE SYNDICATE THAT AN MI6 AGENT HAS ARRIVED IN JAPAN.
HE PLANS TO CONTACT WIEGENLIED.
MEANING THE SYNDICATE WANTS ME TO FIND HIM.

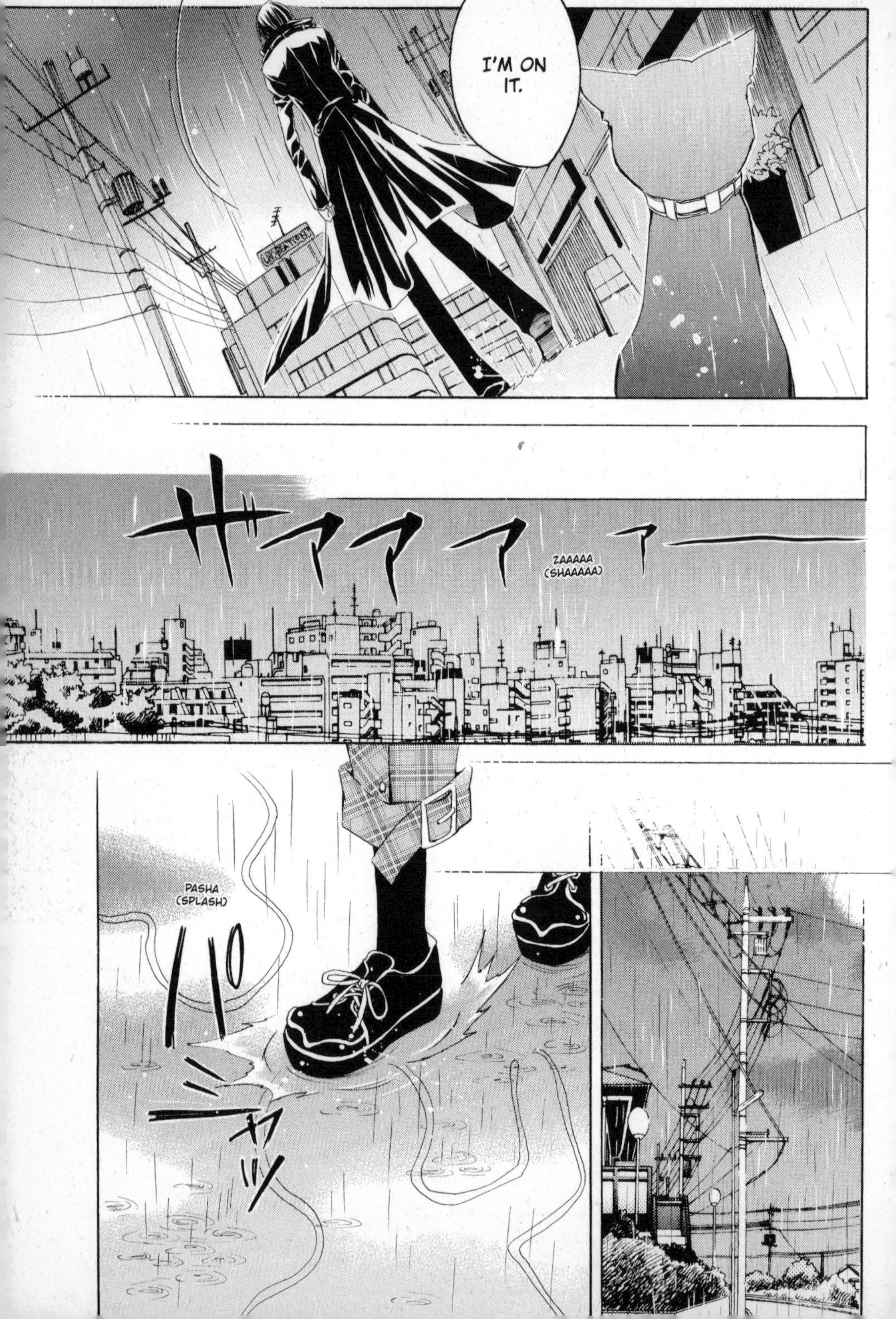
I'M ON IT.
ZAAAAA (SHAAAAA)
PASHA (SPLASH)

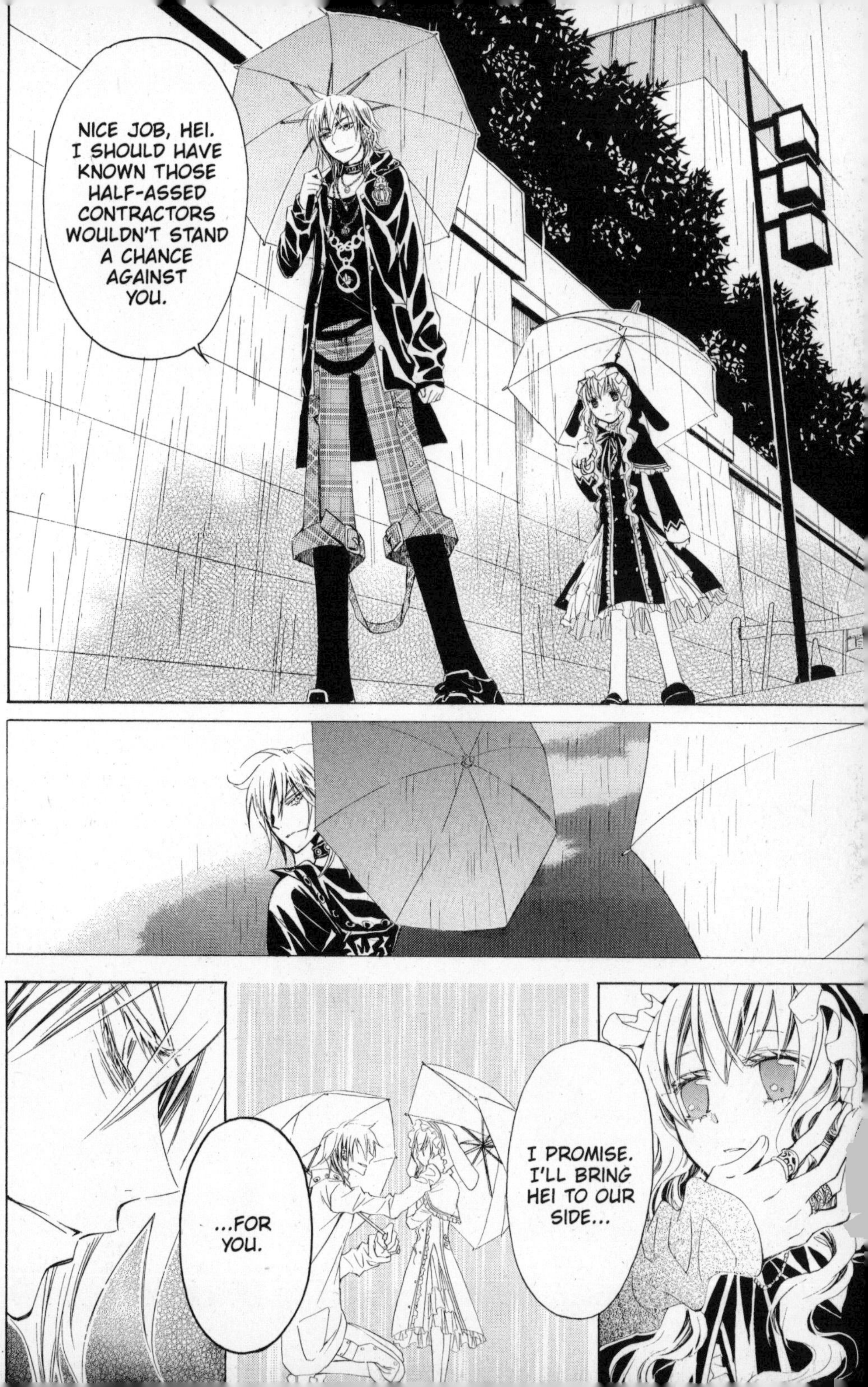
NICE JOB, HEI. I SHOULD HAVE KNOWN THOSE HALF-ASSED CONTRACTORS WOULDN'T STAND A CHANCE AGAINST YOU.
I PROMISE. I'LL BRING HEI TO OUR SIDE...
...FOR YOU.

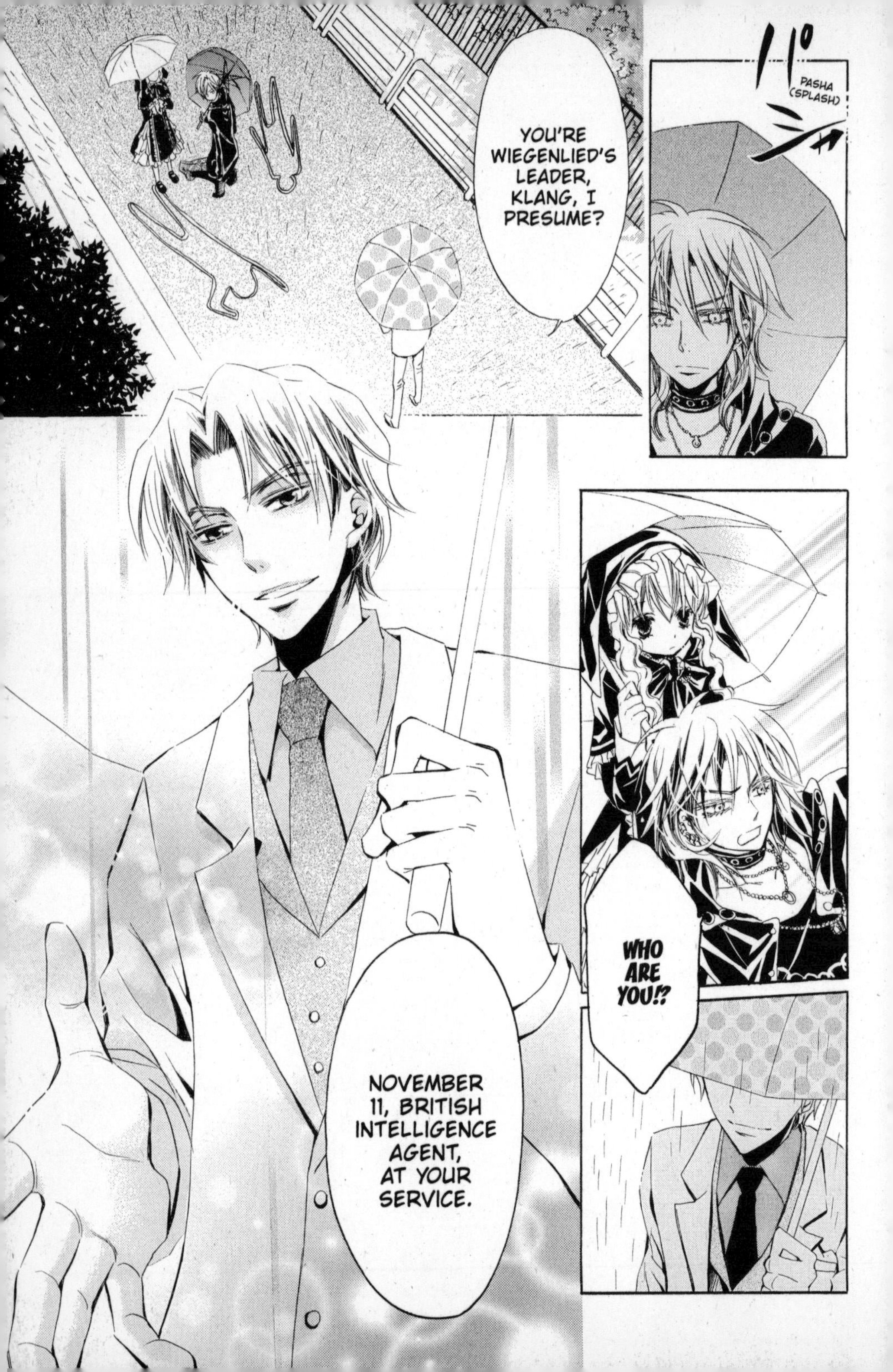
パシャ
PASHA (SPLASH)
YOU'RE WIEGENLIED'S LEADER, KLANG, I PRESUME?
WHO ARE YOU!?
NOVEMBER 11, BRITISH INTELLIGENCE AGENT, AT YOUR SERVICE.

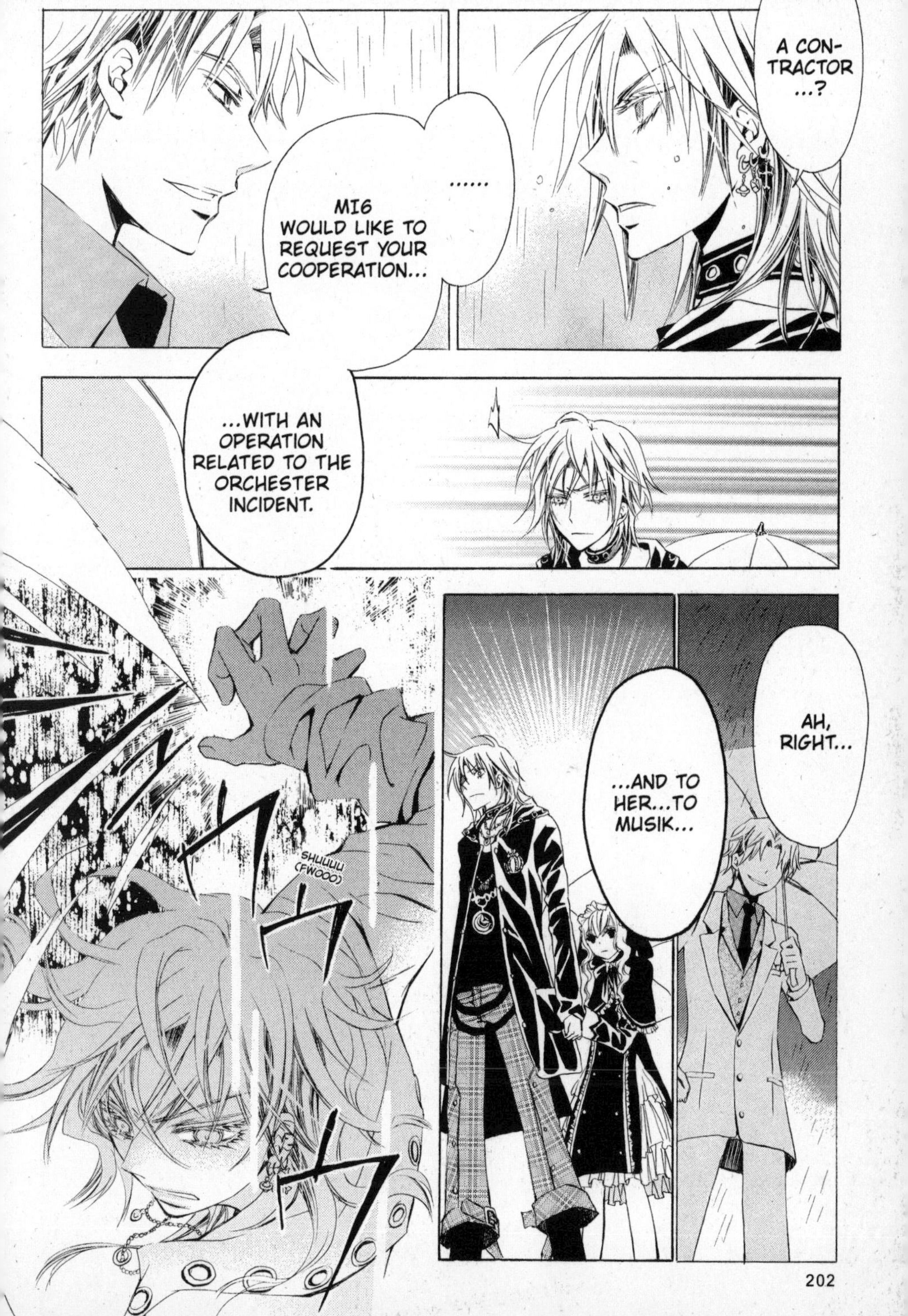
A CON-TRACTOR ...?
......
MI6 WOULD LIKE TO REQUEST YOUR COOPERATION...
...WITH AN OPERATION RELATED TO THE ORCHESTER INCIDENT.
AH, RIGHT...
...AND TO HER...TO MUSIK...
SHUUUU (FWOOO)

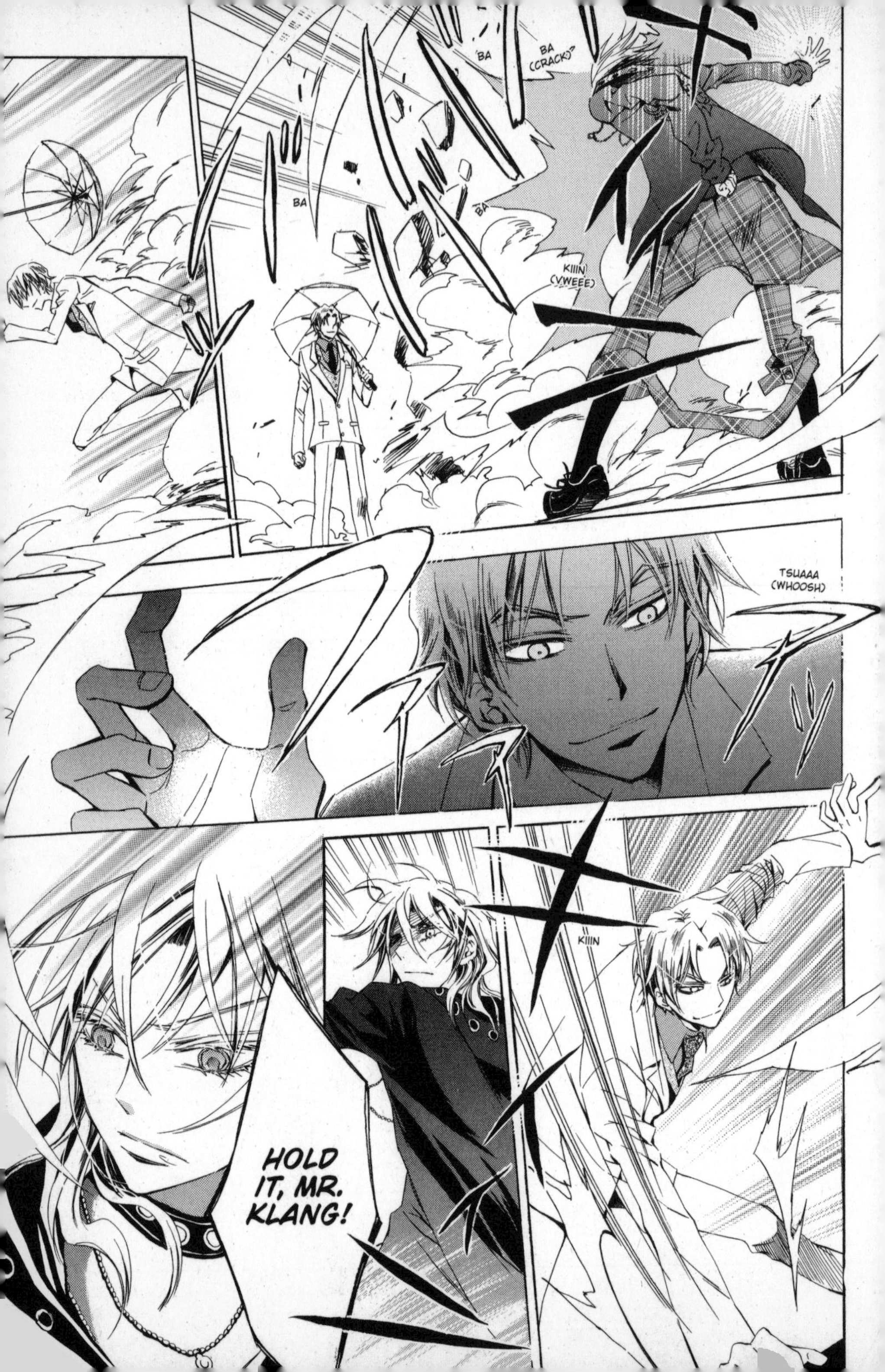
BA
(CRACK)
BA
KIIIN
(VWEEE)
BA
BA
TSUAAA
(WHOOSH)
KIIIN
HOLD IT, MR. KLANG!

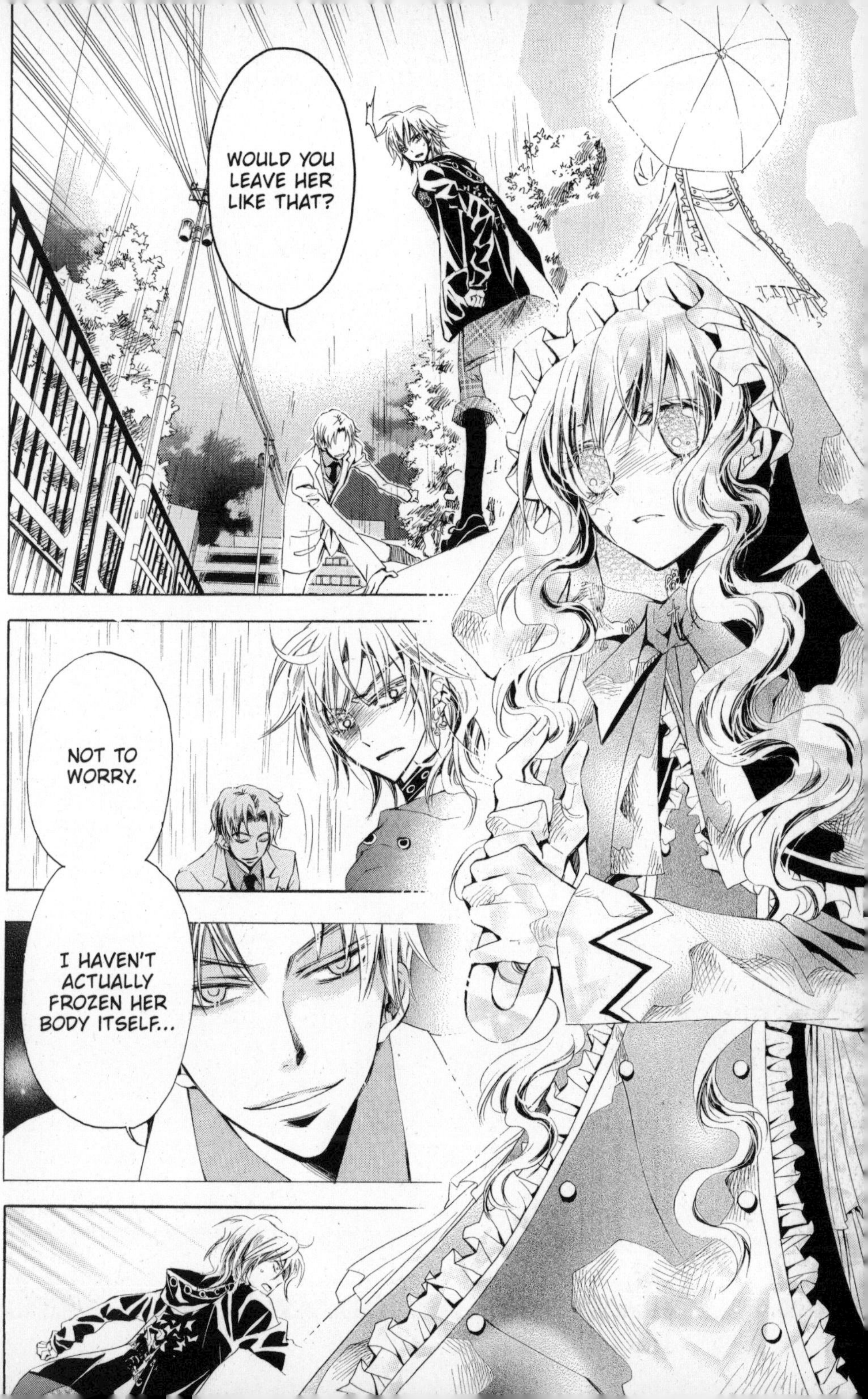
WOULD YOU LEAVE HER LIKE THAT?
NOT TO WORRY.
I HAVEN'T ACTUALLY FROZEN HER BODY ITSELF...

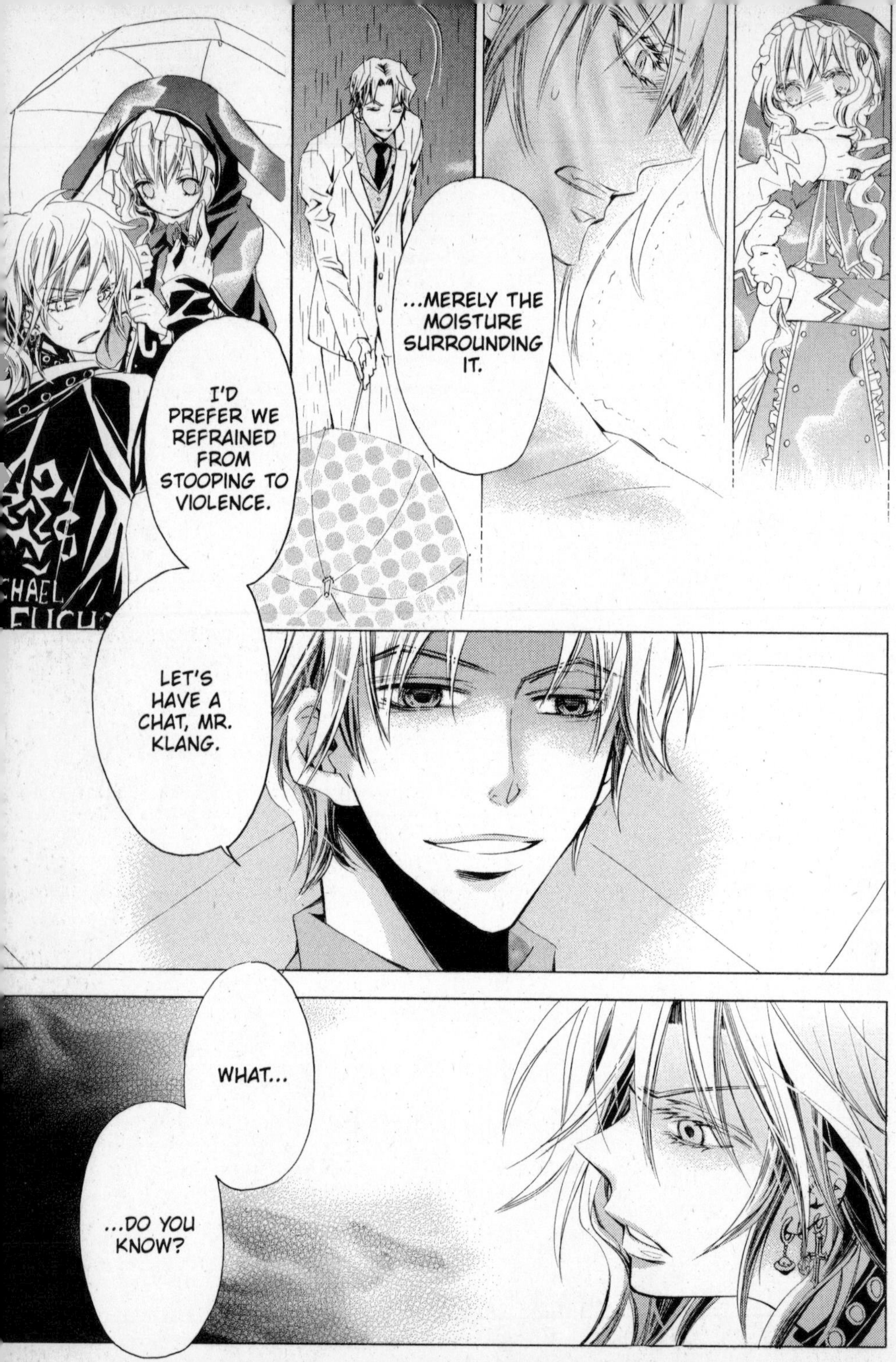
...MERELY THE MOISTURE SURROUNDING IT.
I'D PREFER WE REFRAINED FROM STOOPING TO VIOLENCE.
LET'S HAVE A CHAT, MR. KLANG.
WHAT...
...DO YOU KNOW?

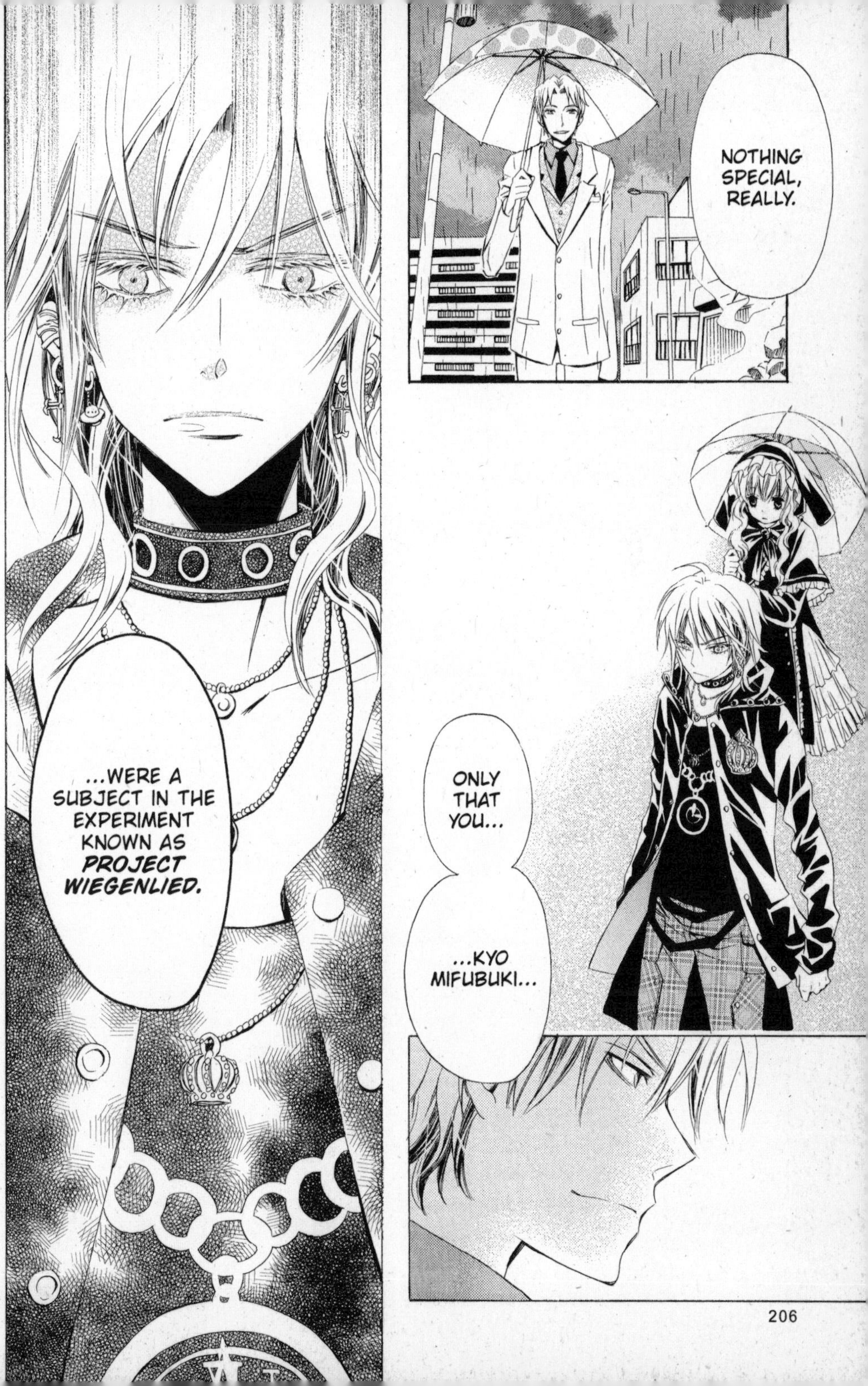
NOTHING SPECIAL, REALLY.
ONLY THAT YOU...
...KYO MIFUBUKI...
...WERE A SUBJECT IN THE EXPERIMENT KNOWN AS PROJECT WIEGENLIED.

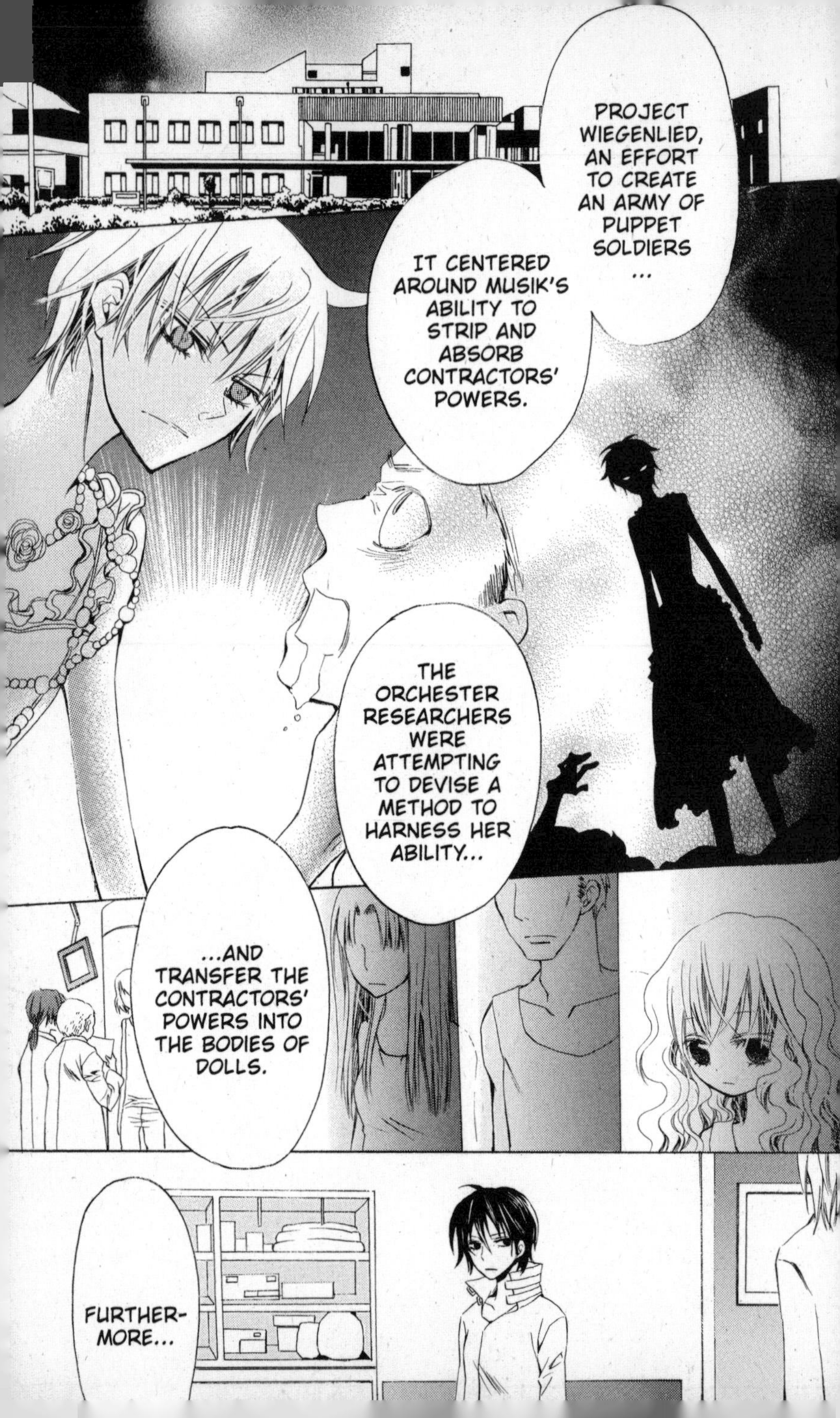
PROJECT WIEGENLIED, AN EFFORT TO CREATE AN ARMY OF PUPPET SOLDIERS ...
IT CENTERED AROUND MUSIK'S ABILITY TO STRIP AND ABSORB CONTRACTORS' POWERS.
THE ORCHESTER RESEARCHERS WERE ATTEMPTING TO DEVISE A METHOD TO HARNESS HER ABILITY...
...AND TRANSFER THE CONTRACTORS' POWERS INTO THE BODIES OF DOLLS.
FURTHER-MORE...

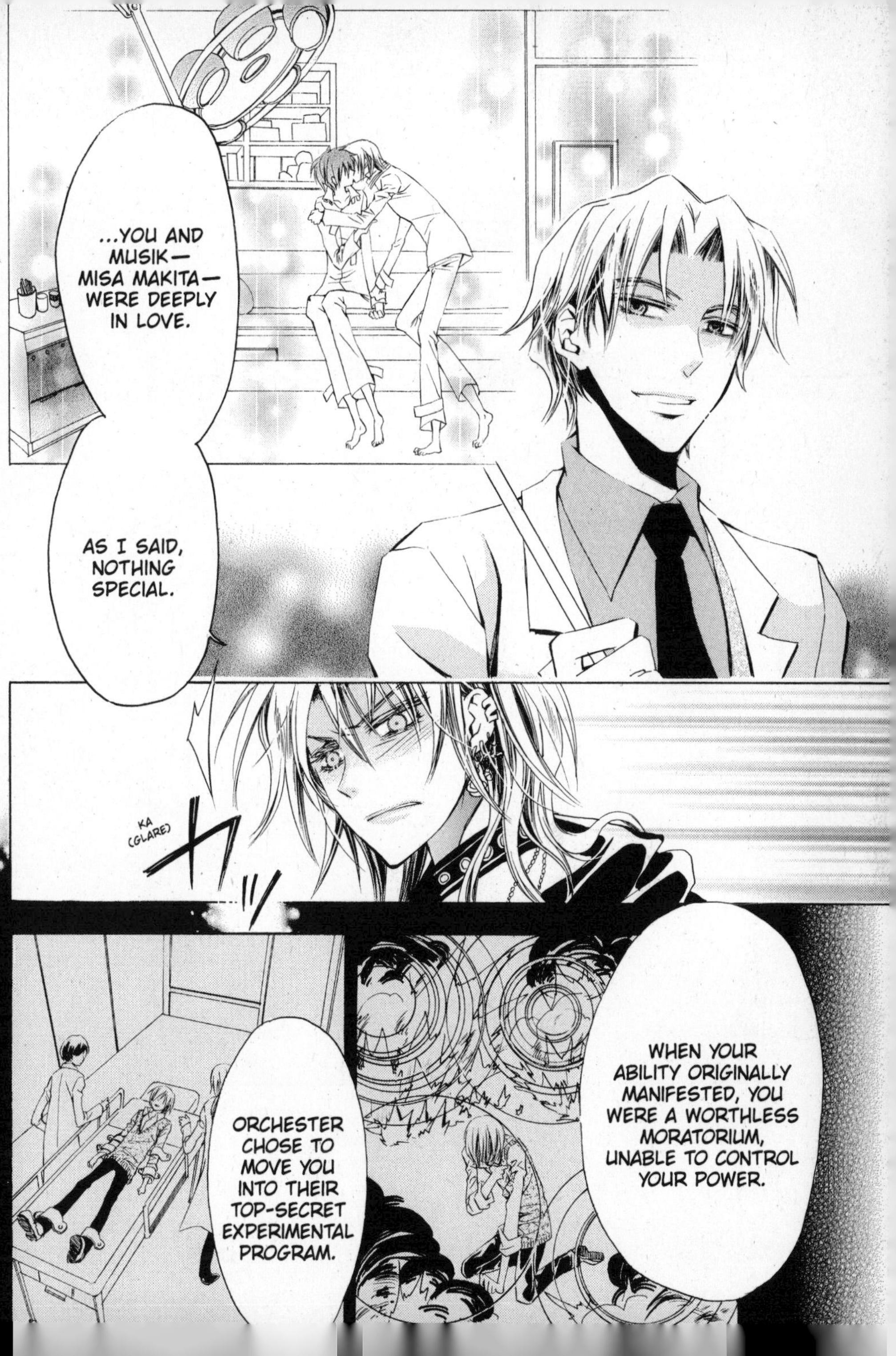
...YOU AND MUSIK—MISA MAKITA—WERE DEEPLY IN LOVE.
AS I SAID, NOTHING SPECIAL.
KA (GLARE)
WHEN YOUR ABILITY ORIGINALLY MANIFESTED, YOU WERE A WORTHLESS MORATORIUM, UNABLE TO CONTROL YOUR POWER.
ORCHESTER CHOSE TO MOVE YOU INTO THEIR TOP-SECRET EXPERIMENTAL PROGRAM.

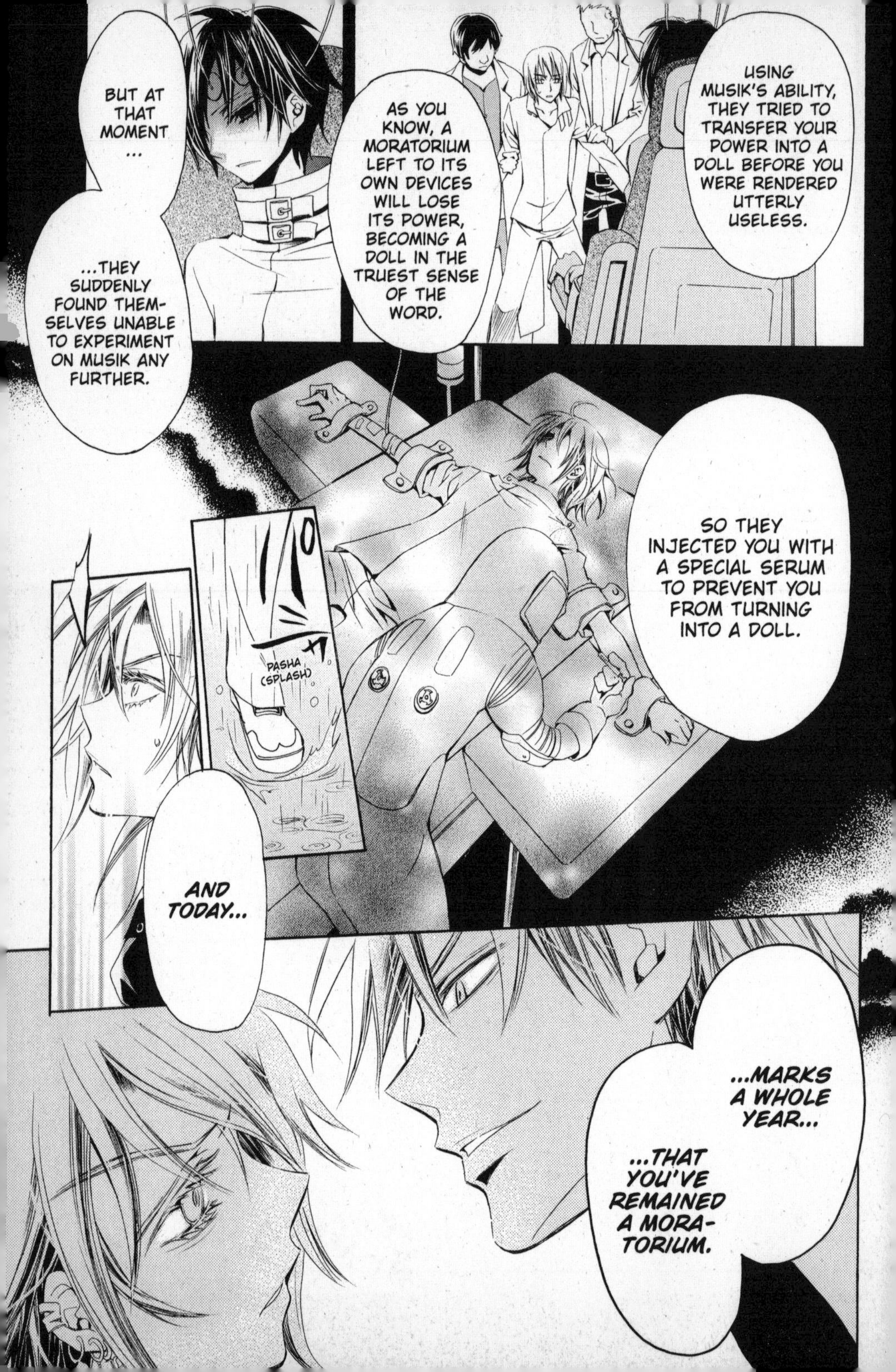
USING MUSIK'S ABILITY, THEY TRIED TO TRANSFER YOUR POWER INTO A DOLL BEFORE YOU WERE RENDERED UTTERLY USELESS.
AS YOU KNOW, A MORATORIUM LEFT TO ITS OWN DEVICES WILL LOSE ITS POWER, BECOMING A DOLL IN THE TRUEST SENSE OF THE WORD.
BUT AT THAT MOMENT...
...THEY SUDDENLY FOUND THEM-SELVES UNABLE TO EXPERIMENT ON MUSIK ANY FURTHER.
SO THEY INJECTED YOU WITH A SPECIAL SERUM TO PREVENT YOU FROM TURNING INTO A DOLL.
PASHA (SPLASH)
AND TODAY...
...MARKS A WHOLE YEAR...
...THAT YOU'VE REMAINED A MORA-TORIUM.

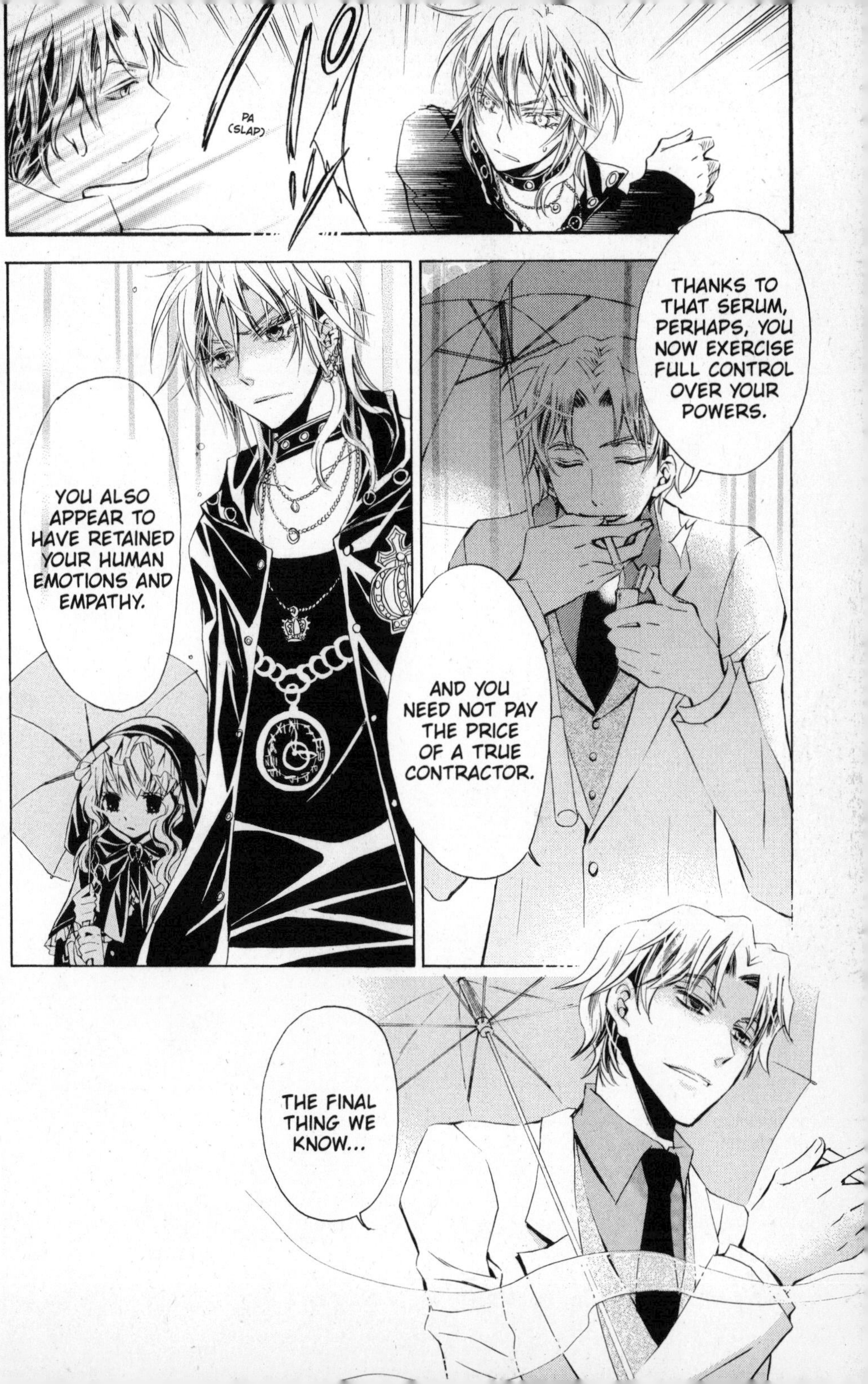
PA (SLAP)
THANKS TO THAT SERUM, PERHAPS, YOU NOW EXERCISE FULL CONTROL OVER YOUR POWERS.
AND YOU NEED NOT PAY THE PRICE OF A TRUE CONTRACTOR.
YOU ALSO APPEAR TO HAVE RETAINED YOUR HUMAN EMOTIONS AND EMPATHY.
THE FINAL THING WE KNOW...

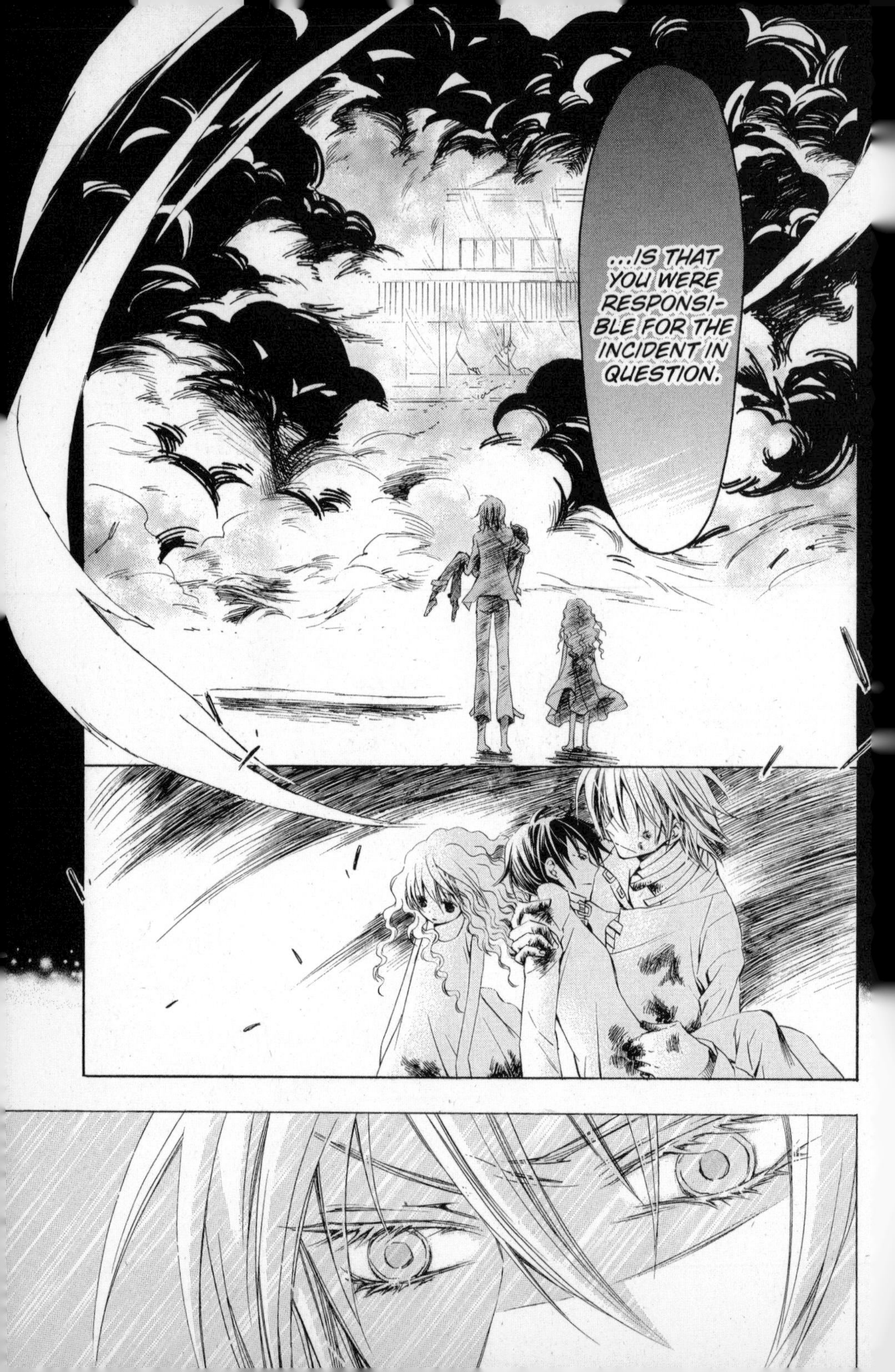
...IS THAT YOU WERE RESPONSI-BLE FOR THE INCIDENT IN QUESTION.

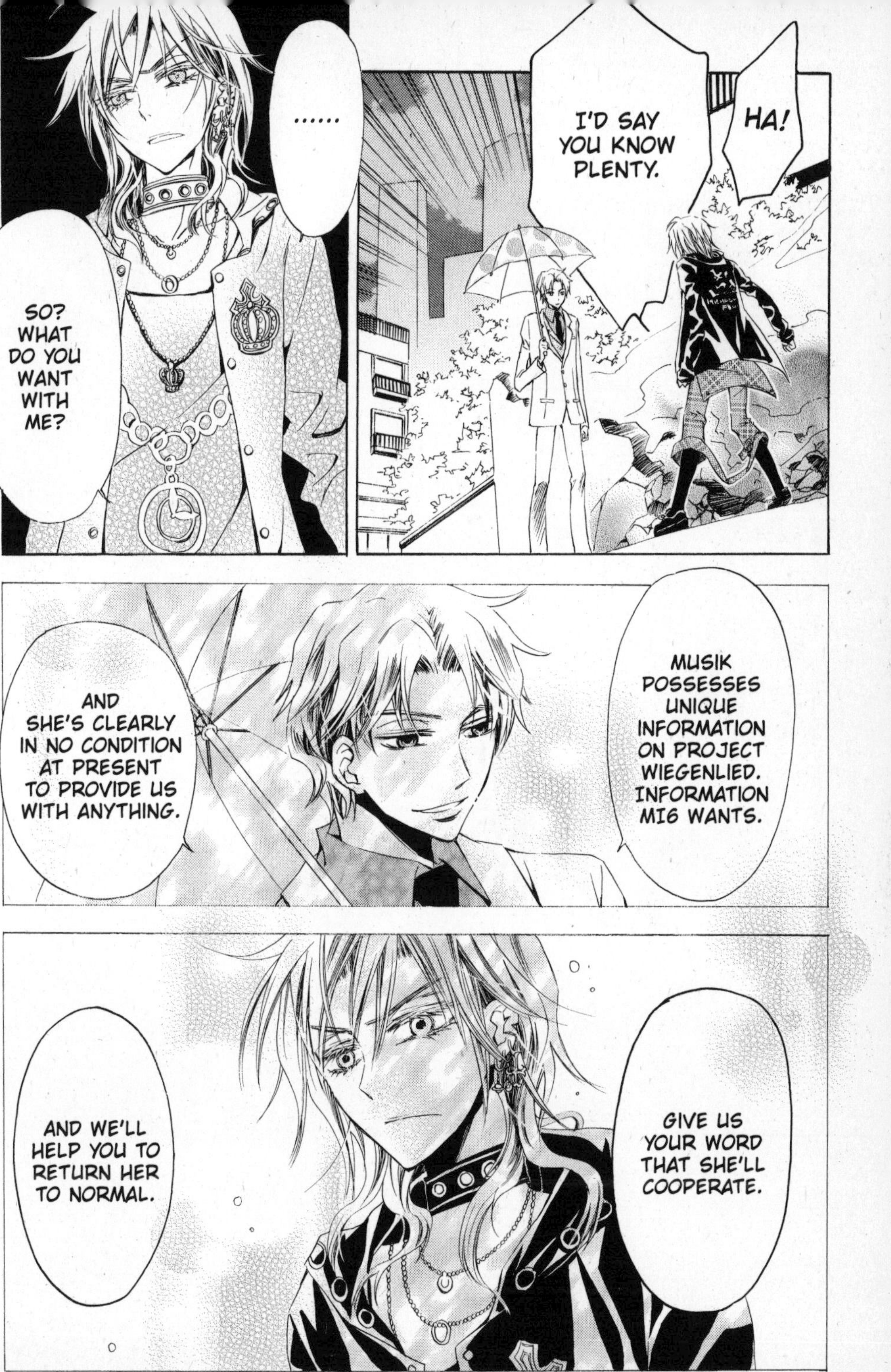
HA!
I'D SAY YOU KNOW PLENTY.
......
SO? WHAT DO YOU WANT WITH ME?
MUSIK POSSESSES UNIQUE INFORMATION ON PROJECT WIEGENLIED. INFORMATION MI6 WANTS.
AND SHE'S CLEARLY IN NO CONDITION AT PRESENT TO PROVIDE US WITH ANYTHING.
GIVE US YOUR WORD THAT SHE'LL COOPERATE.
AND WE'LL HELP YOU TO RETURN HER TO NORMAL.

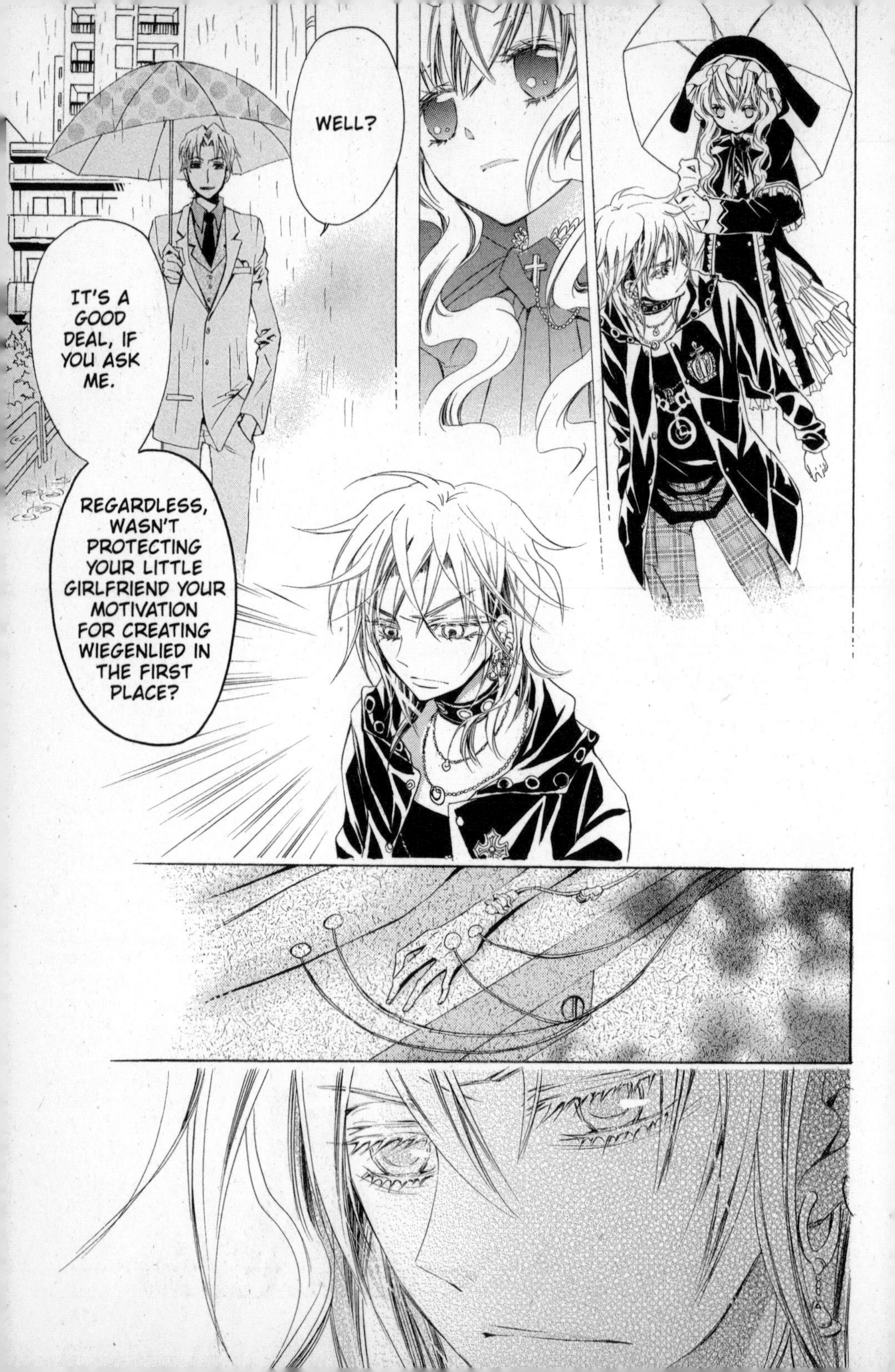
WELL?
IT'S A GOOD DEAL, IF YOU ASK ME.
REGARDLESS, WASN'T PROTECTING YOUR LITTLE GIRLFRIEND YOUR MOTIVATION FOR CREATING WIEGENLIED IN THE FIRST PLACE?

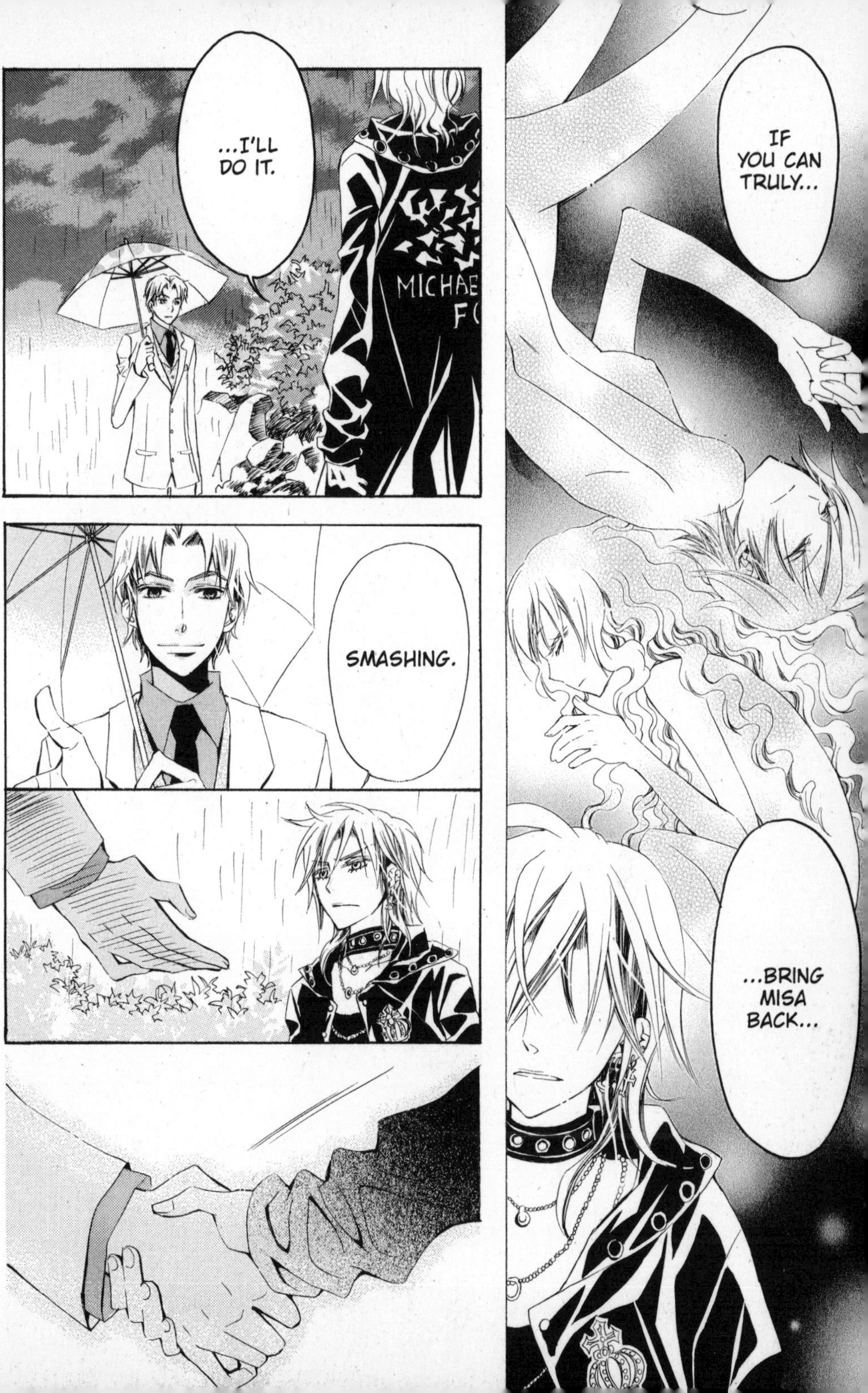
IF YOU CAN TRULY...
...BRING MISA BACK...
...I'LL DO IT.
SMASHING.

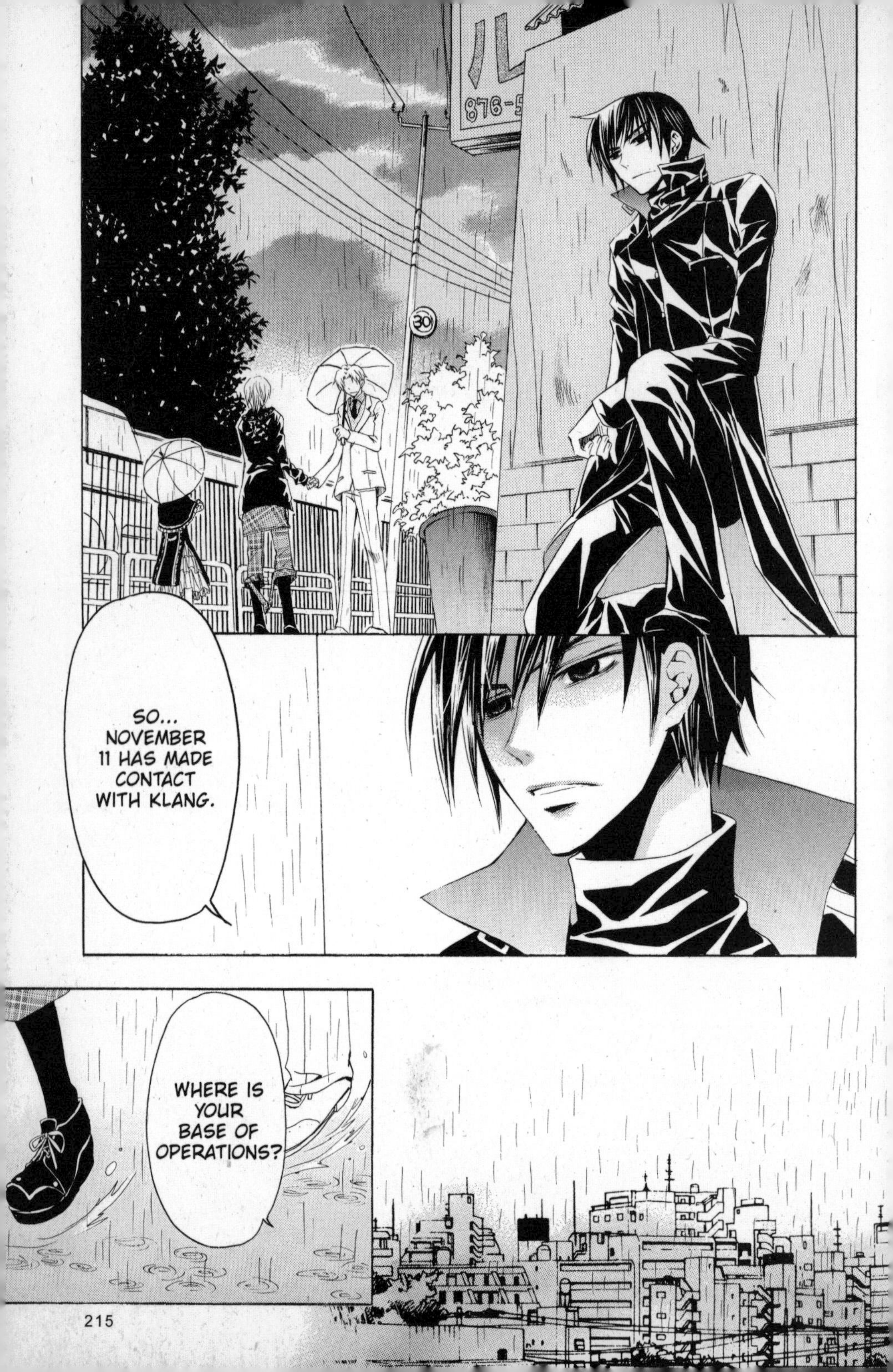
SO... NOVEMBER 11 HAS MADE CONTACT WITH KLANG.
WHERE IS YOUR BASE OF OPERATIONS?

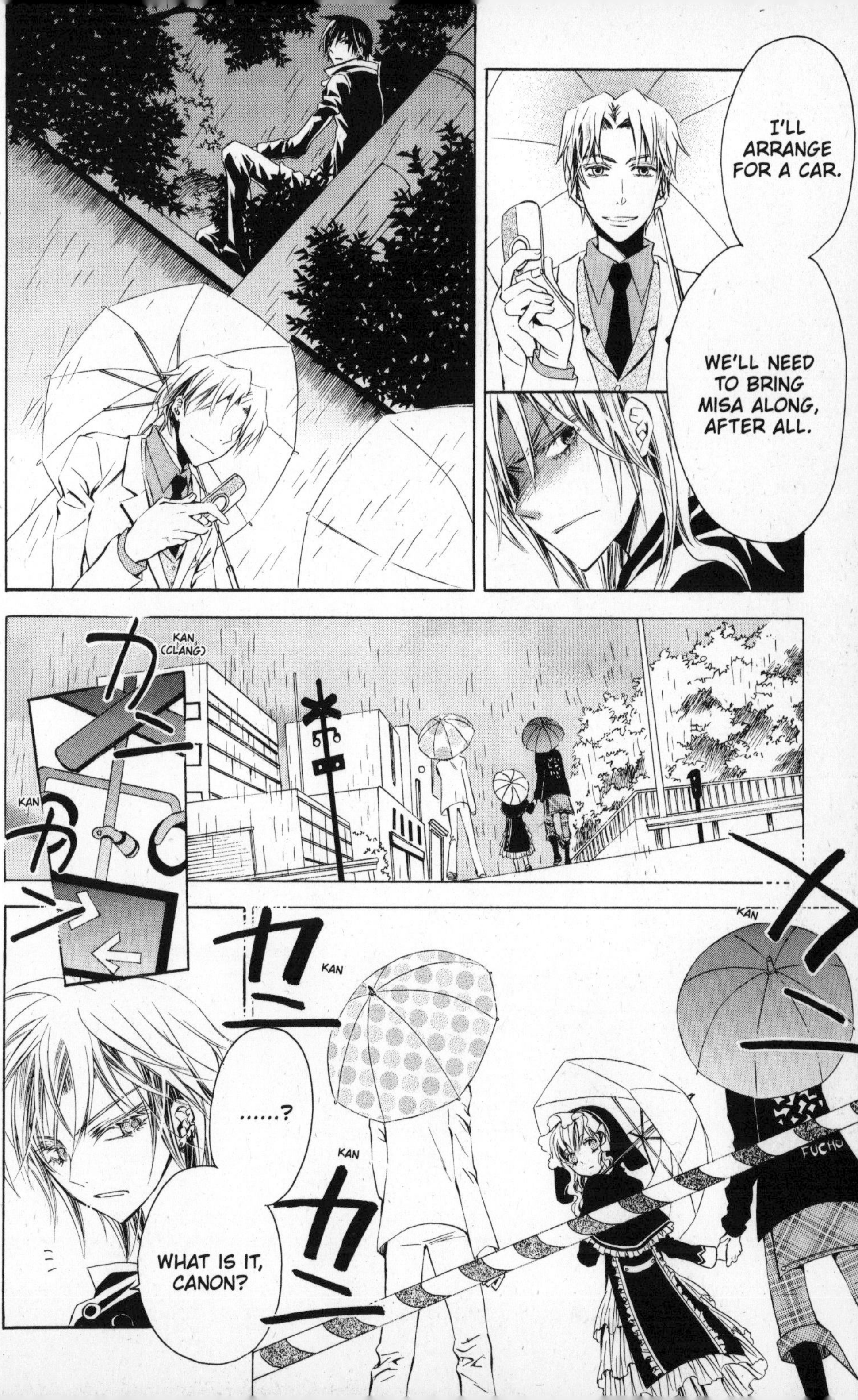
I'LL ARRANGE FOR A CAR.
WE'LL NEED TO BRING MISA ALONG, AFTER ALL.
KAN (CLANG)
KAN
KAN
KAN
......?
KAN
FUCHU
WHAT IS IT, CANON?

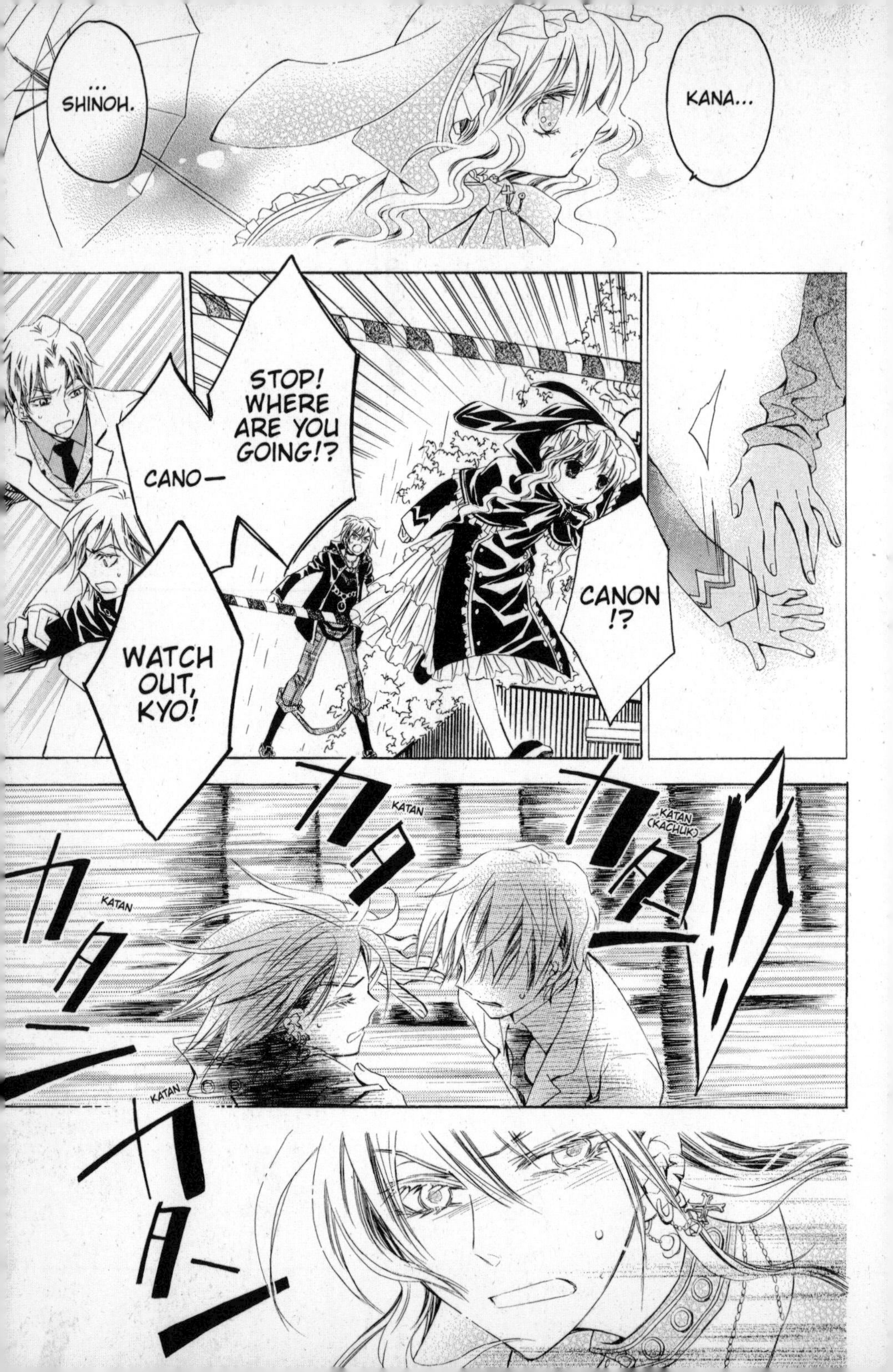
KANA...
... SHINOH.
CANON !?
STOP! WHERE ARE YOU GOING!?
CANO—
WATCH OUT, KYO!
KATAN (KACHUK)
KATAN
KATAN
KATAN

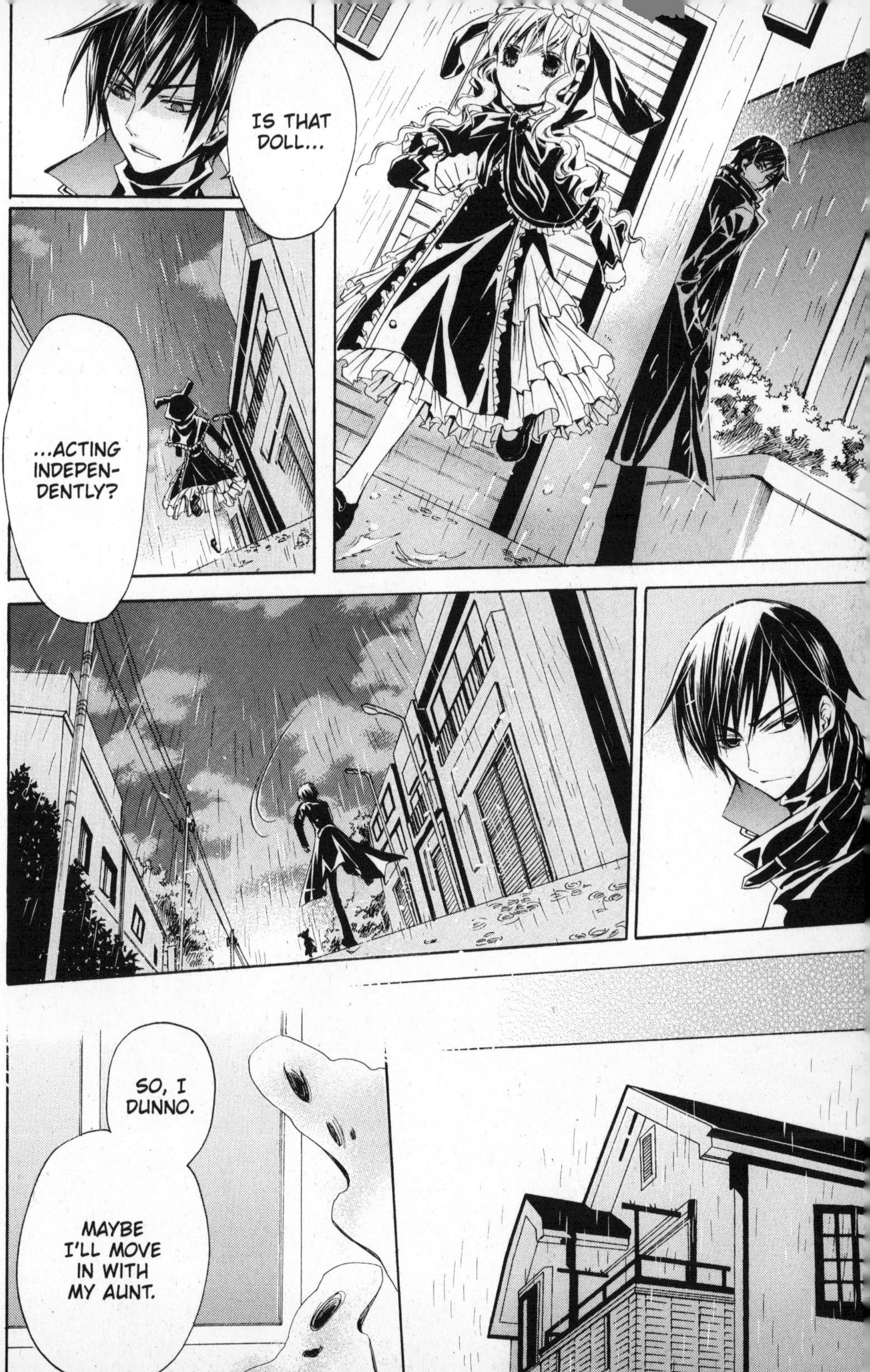
IS THAT DOLL...
...ACTING INDEPEN-DENTLY?
SO, I DUNNO.
MAYBE I'LL MOVE IN WITH MY AUNT.

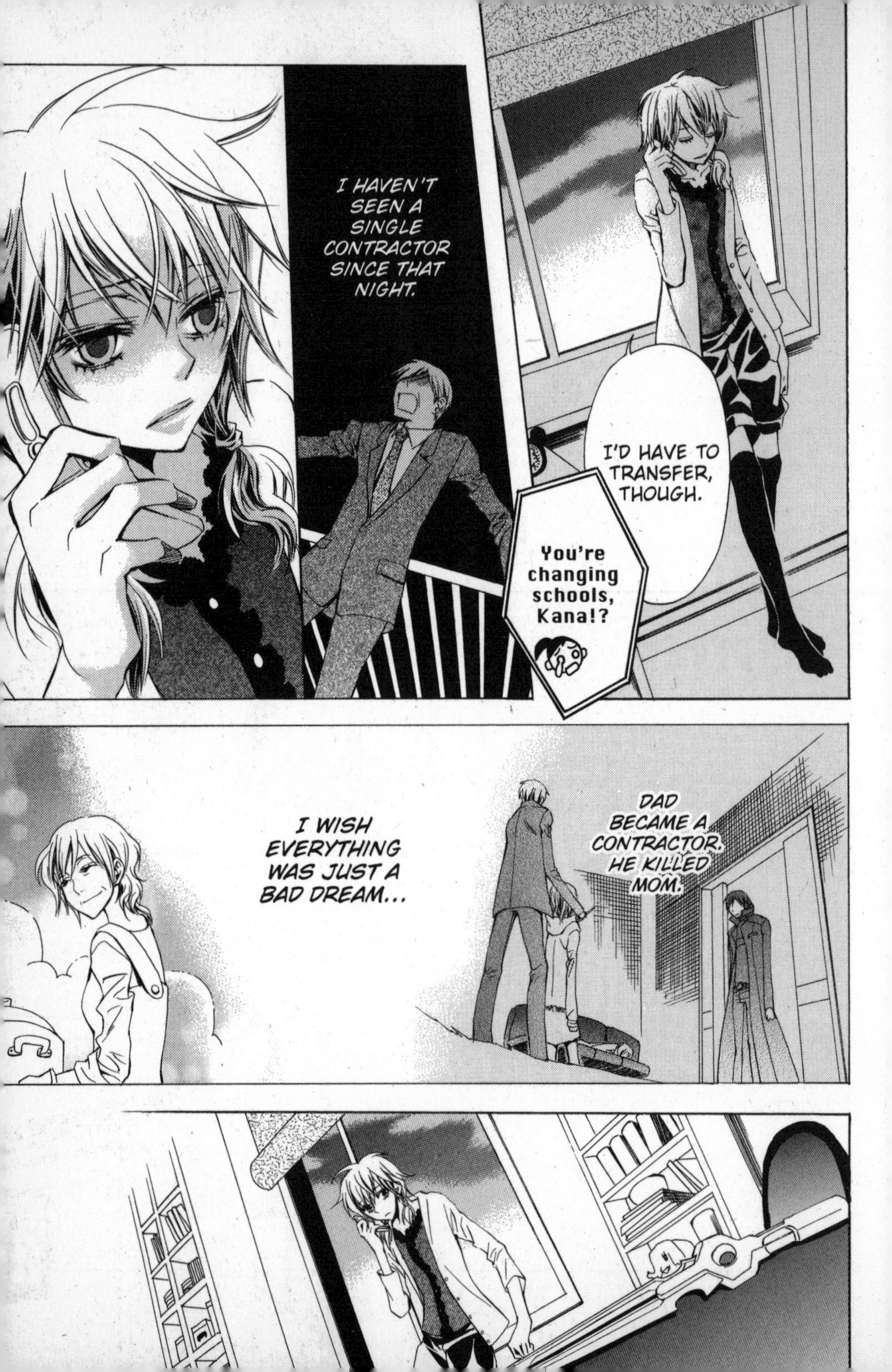

I'D HAVE TO TRANSFER, THOUGH.
You're changing schools, Kana!?
I HAVEN'T SEEN A SINGLE CONTRACTOR SINCE THAT NIGHT.
DAD BECAME A CONTRACTOR. HE KILLED MOM.
I WISH EVERYTHING WAS JUST A BAD DREAM...

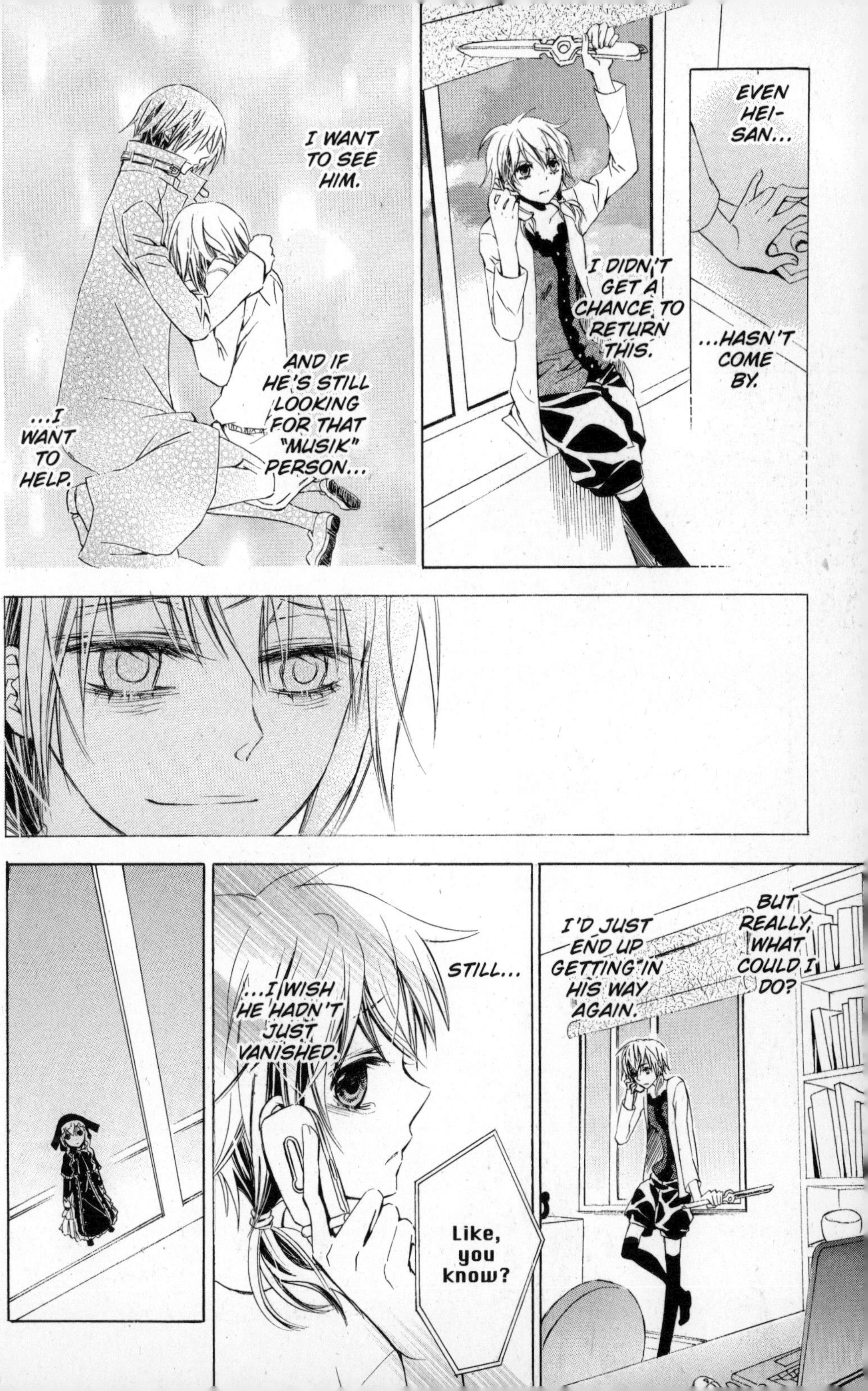
EVEN HEI-SAN...
...HASN'T COME BY.
I DIDN'T GET A CHANCE TO RETURN THIS.
I WANT TO SEE HIM.
AND IF HE'S STILL LOOKING FOR THAT "MUSIK" PERSON...
...I WANT TO HELP.
BUT REALLY, WHAT COULD I DO?
I'D JUST END UP GETTING IN HIS WAY AGAIN.
STILL...
...I WISH HE HADN'T JUST VANISHED.
Like, you know?

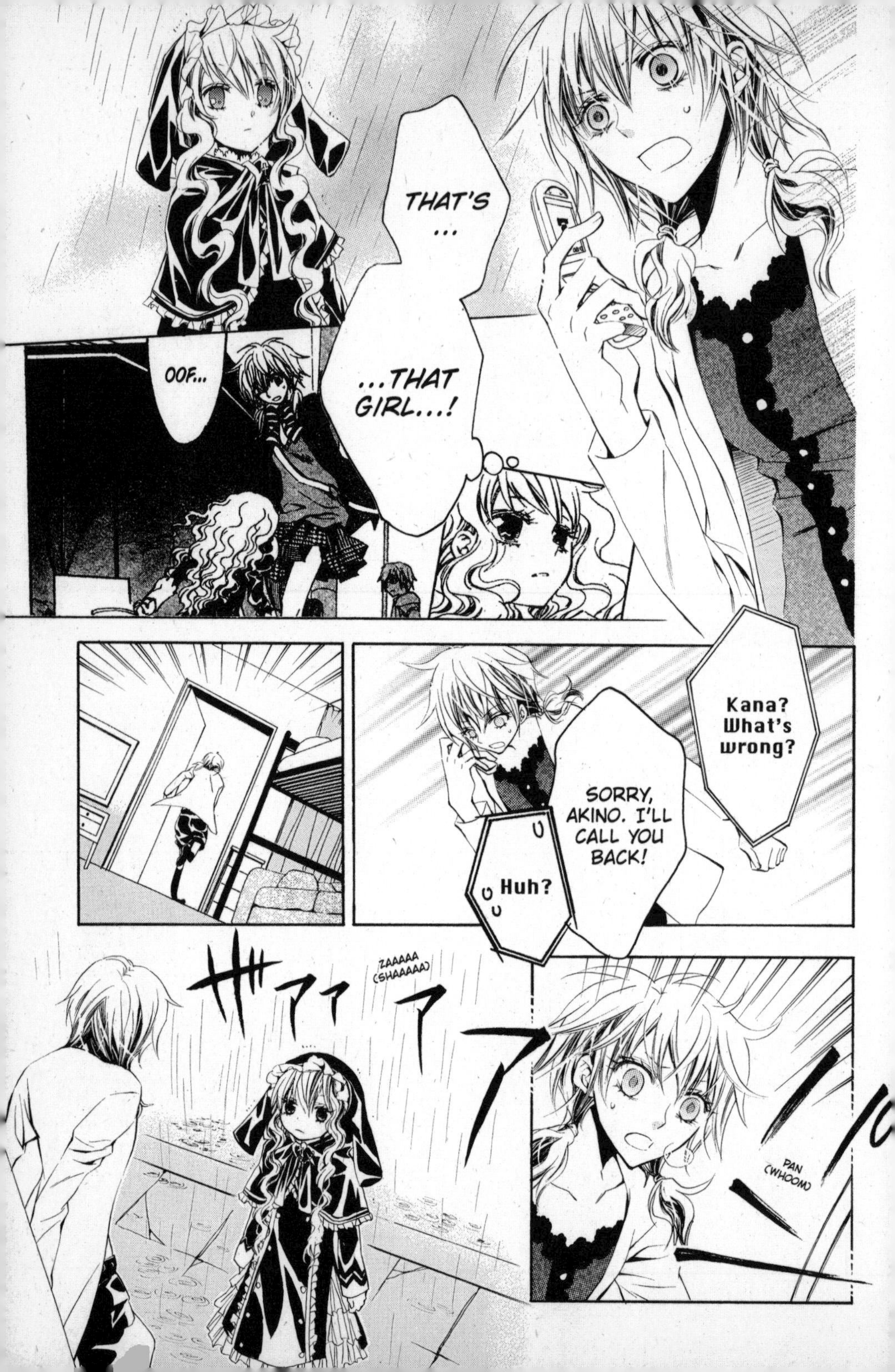
THAT'S ...
...THAT GIRL...!
OOF...
Kana? What's wrong?
SORRY, AKINO. I'LL CALL YOU BACK!
Huh?
PAN (WHOOM)
ZAAAAA (SHAAAAA)

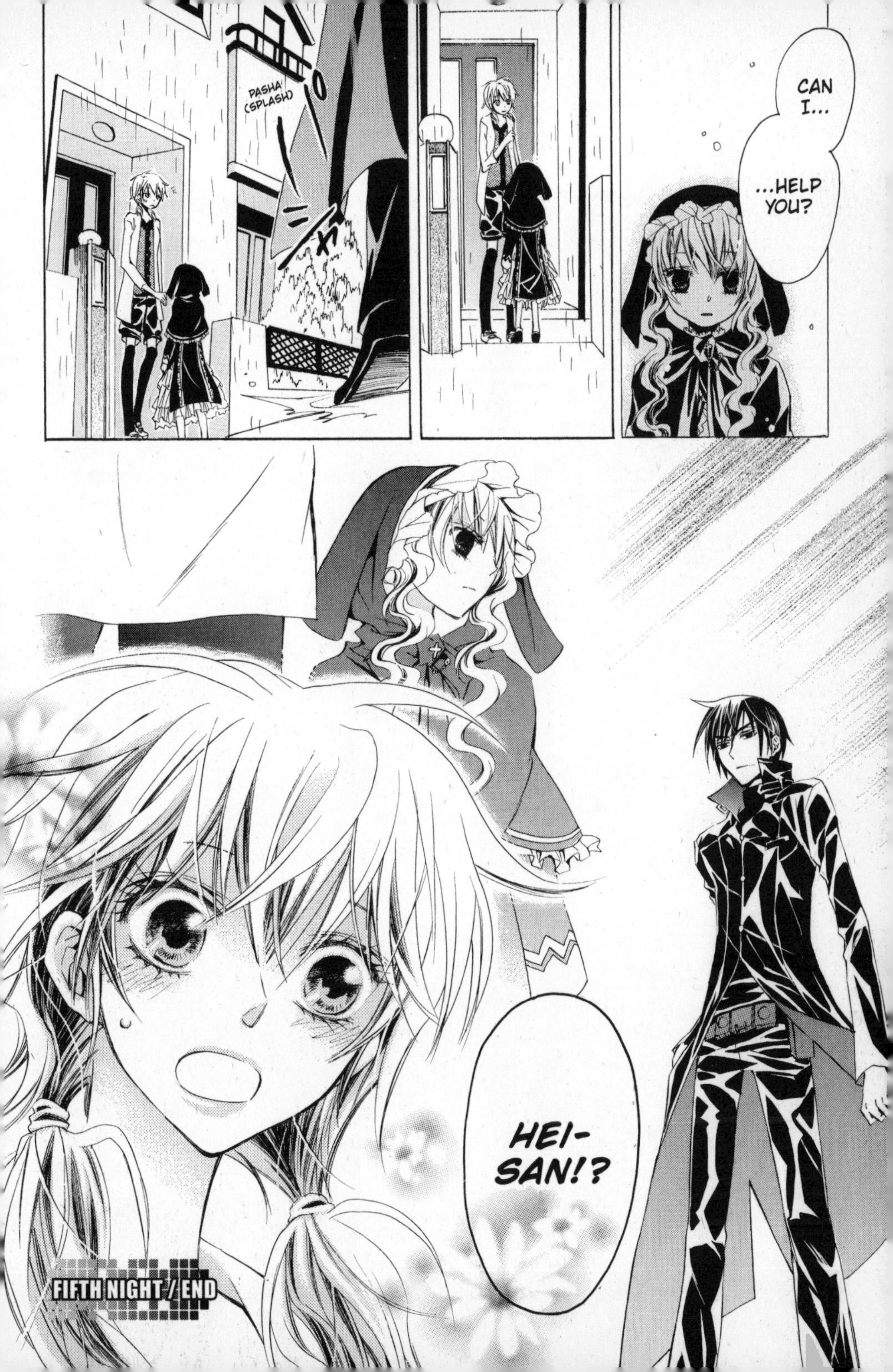
CAN I...
...HELP YOU?
PASHA (SPLASH)
HEI-SAN!?
FIFTH NIGHT / END

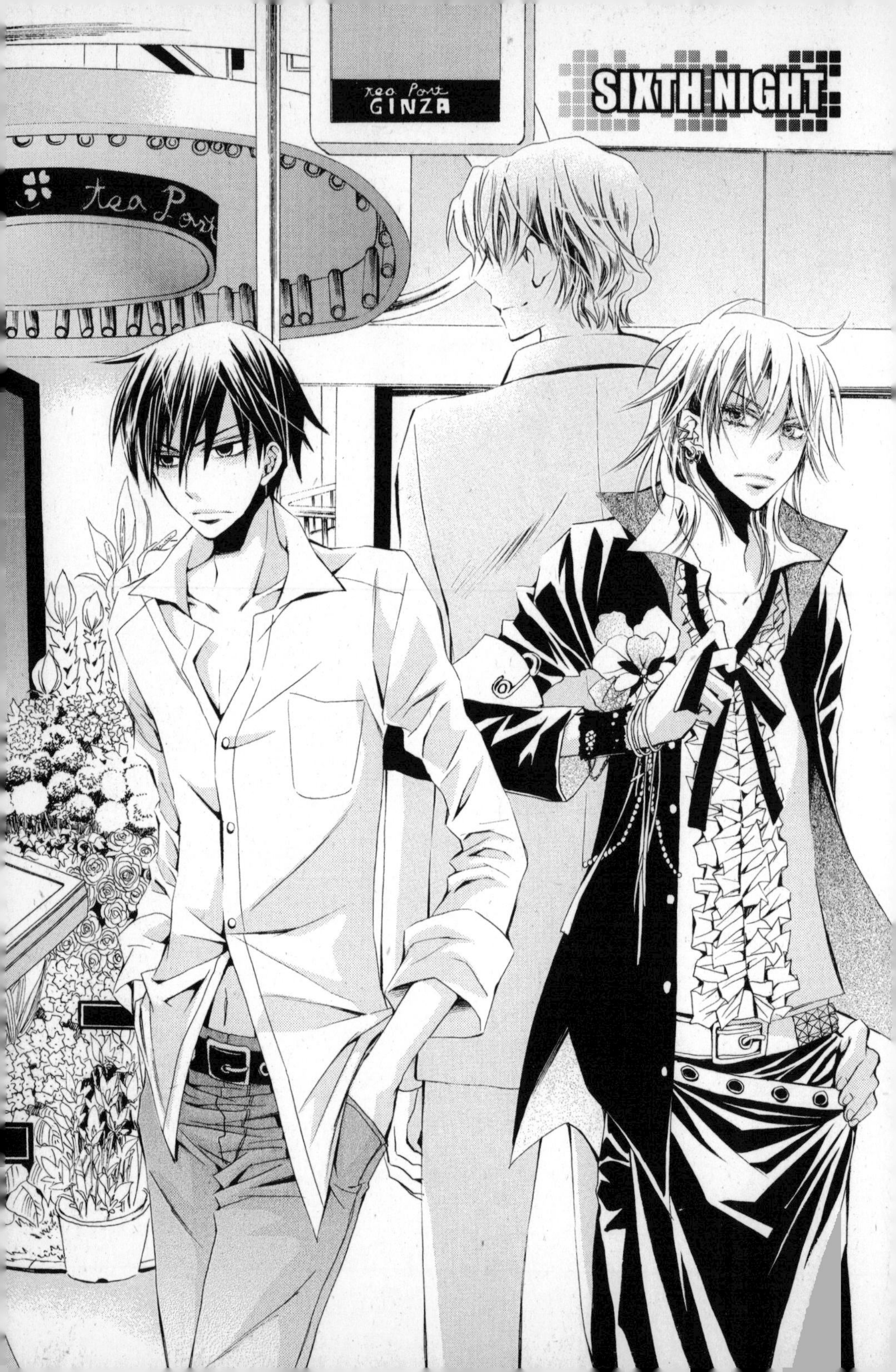
SIXTH NIGHT
tea Port
GINZA
tea Port

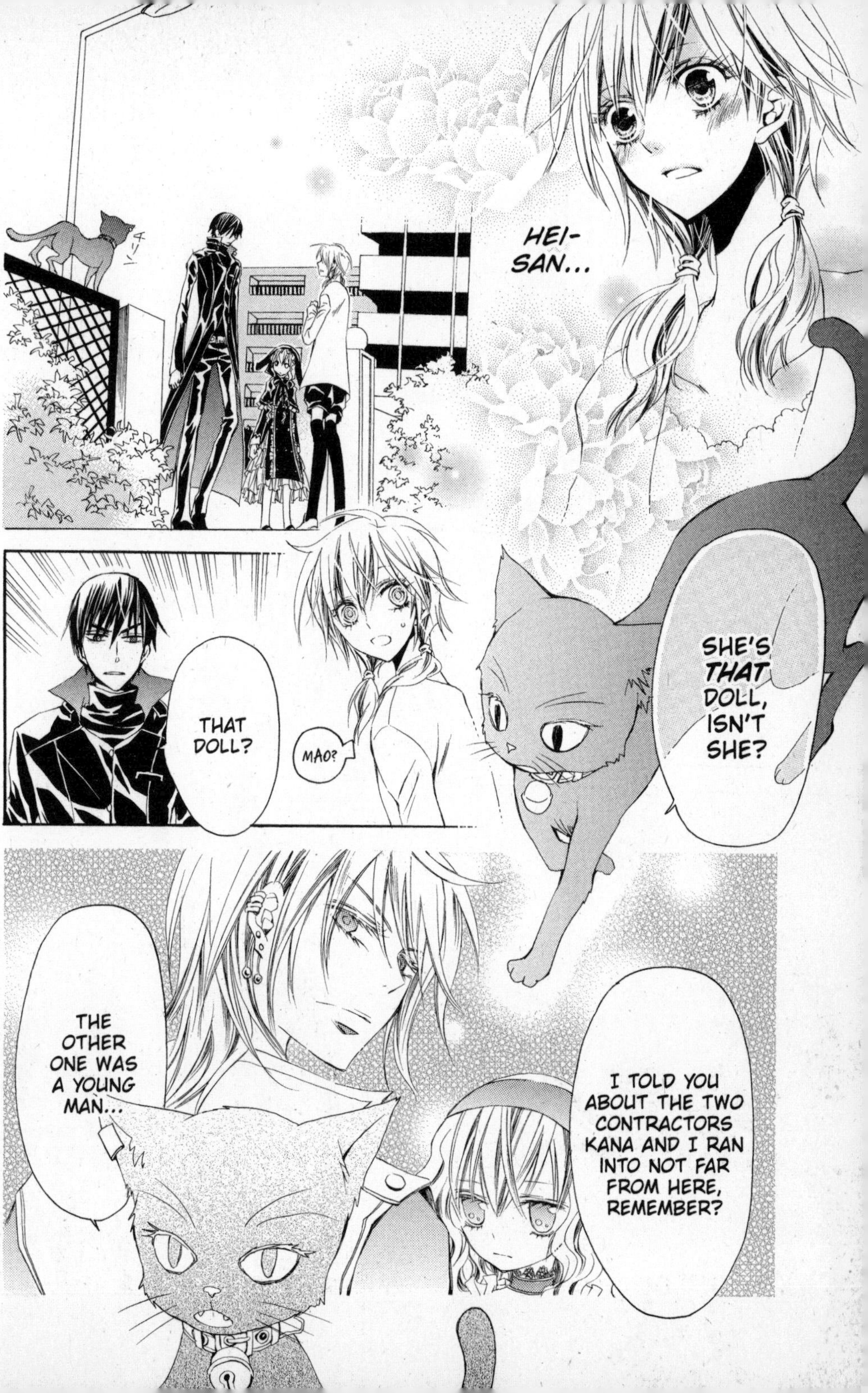
HEI-SAN...
SHE'S *THAT* DOLL, ISN'T SHE?
MAO?
THAT DOLL?
I TOLD YOU ABOUT THE TWO CONTRACTORS KANA AND I RAN INTO NOT FAR FROM HERE, REMEMBER?
THE OTHER ONE WAS A YOUNG MAN...

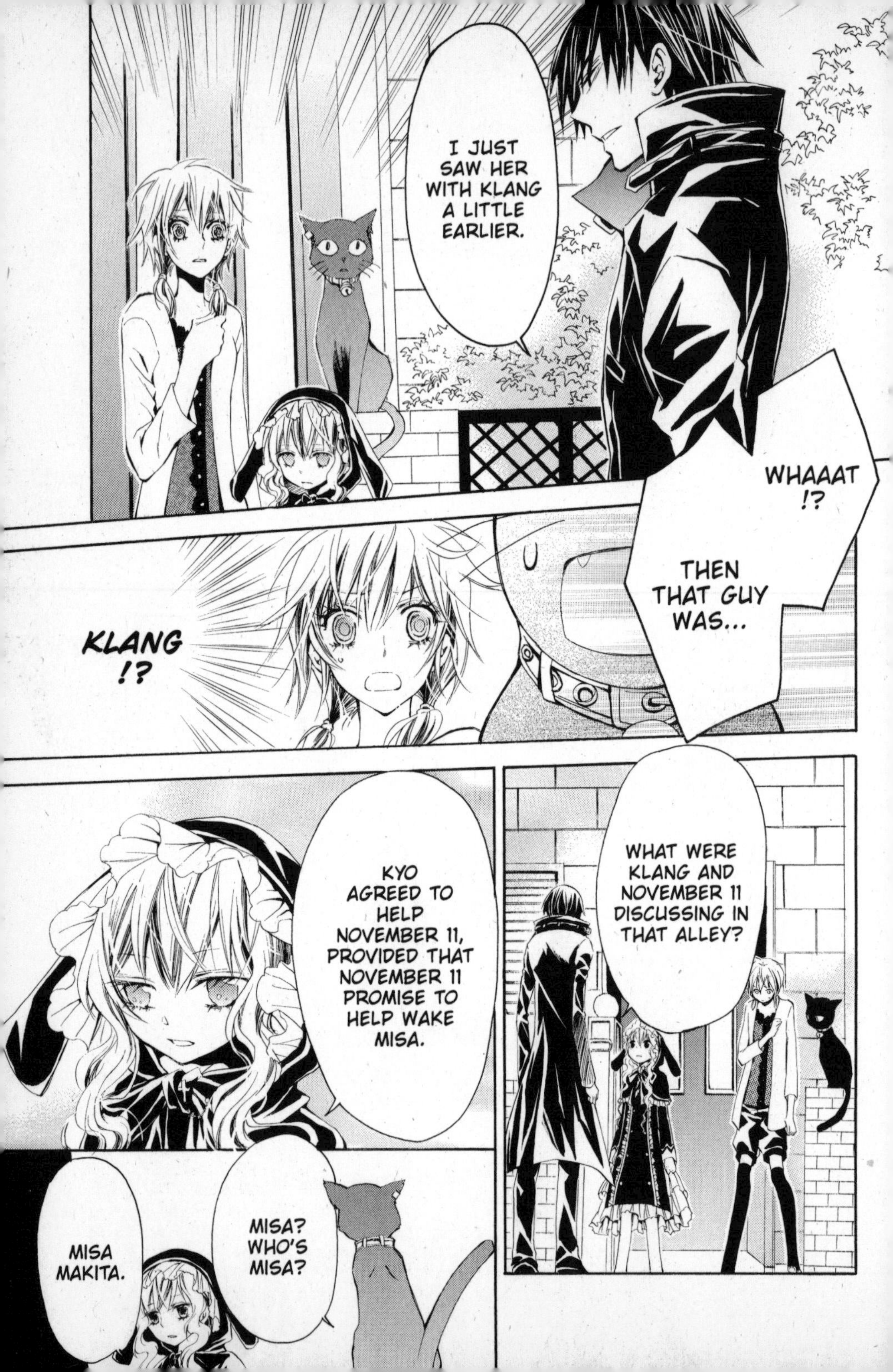
I JUST SAW HER WITH KLANG A LITTLE EARLIER.
WHAAAT !?
THEN THAT GUY WAS...
KLANG !?
WHAT WERE KLANG AND NOVEMBER 11 DISCUSSING IN THAT ALLEY?
KYO AGREED TO HELP NOVEMBER 11, PROVIDED THAT NOVEMBER 11 PROMISE TO HELP WAKE MISA.
MISA? WHO'S MISA?
MISA MAKITA.

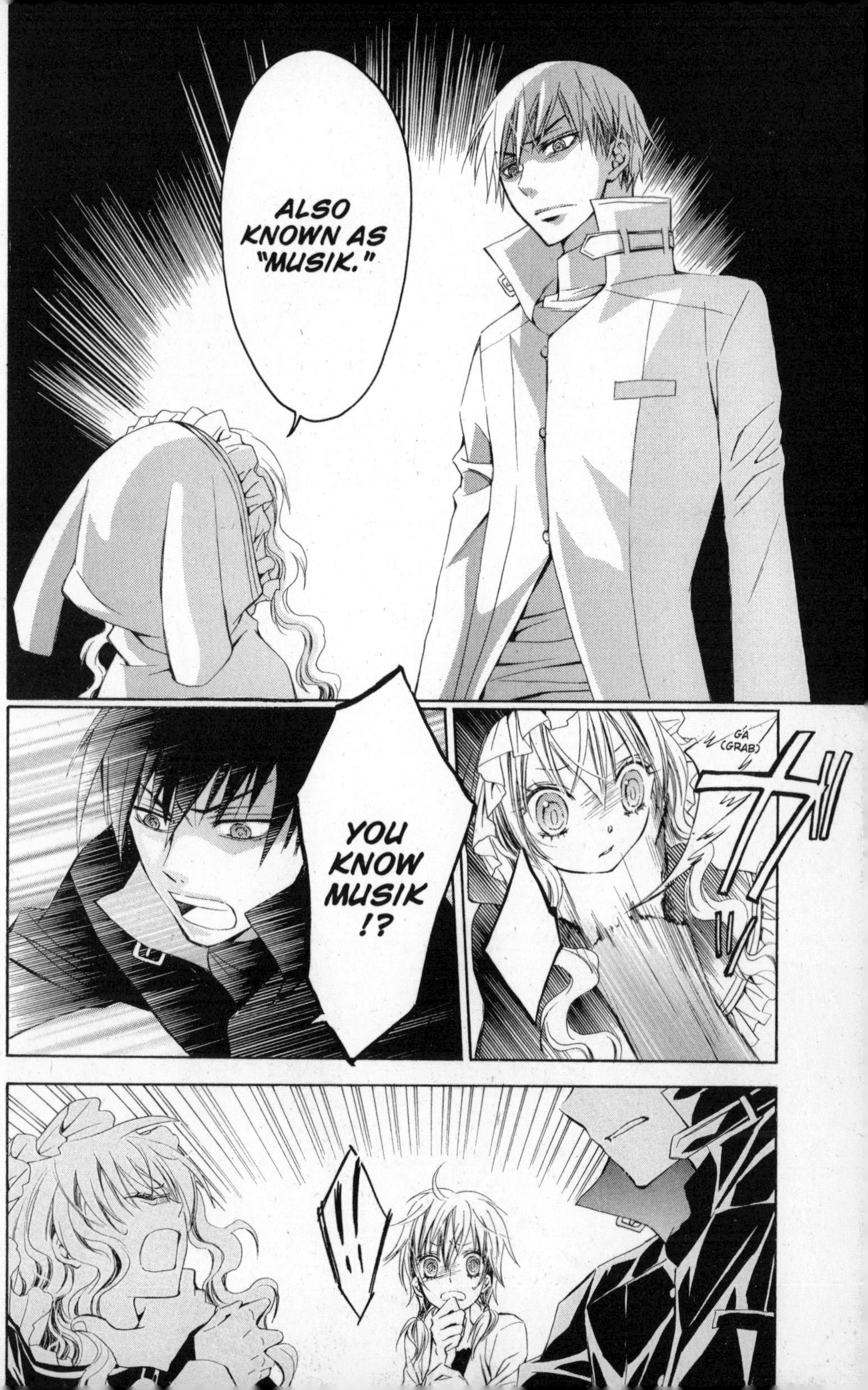
ALSO KNOWN AS "MUSIK."
GA (GRAB)
YOU KNOW MUSIK !?
!

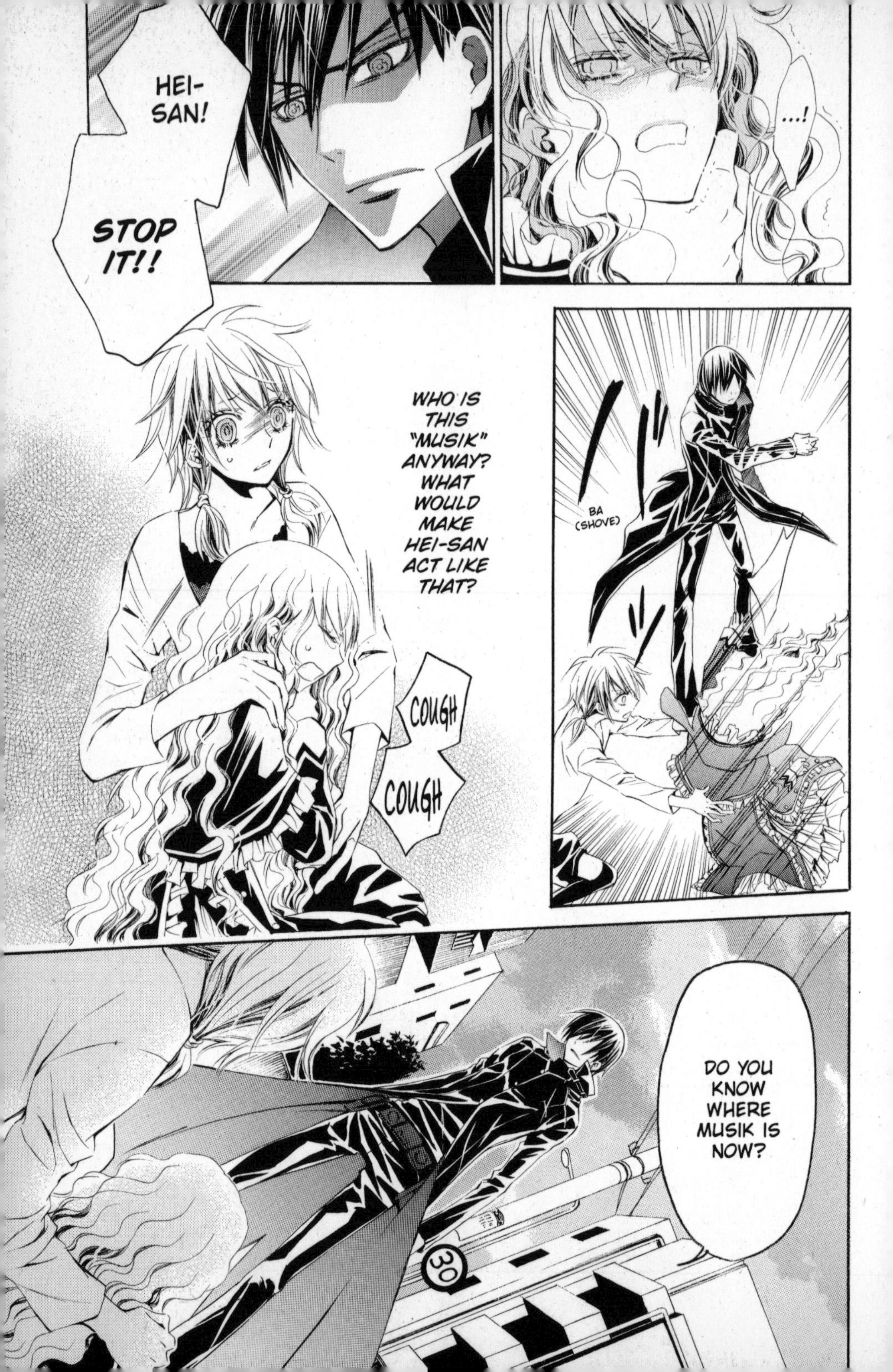
...!
HEI-SAN!
STOP IT!!
BA (SHOVE)
WHO IS THIS "MUSIK" ANYWAY? WHAT WOULD MAKE HEI-SAN ACT LIKE THAT?
COUGH
COUGH
DO YOU KNOW WHERE MUSIK IS NOW?

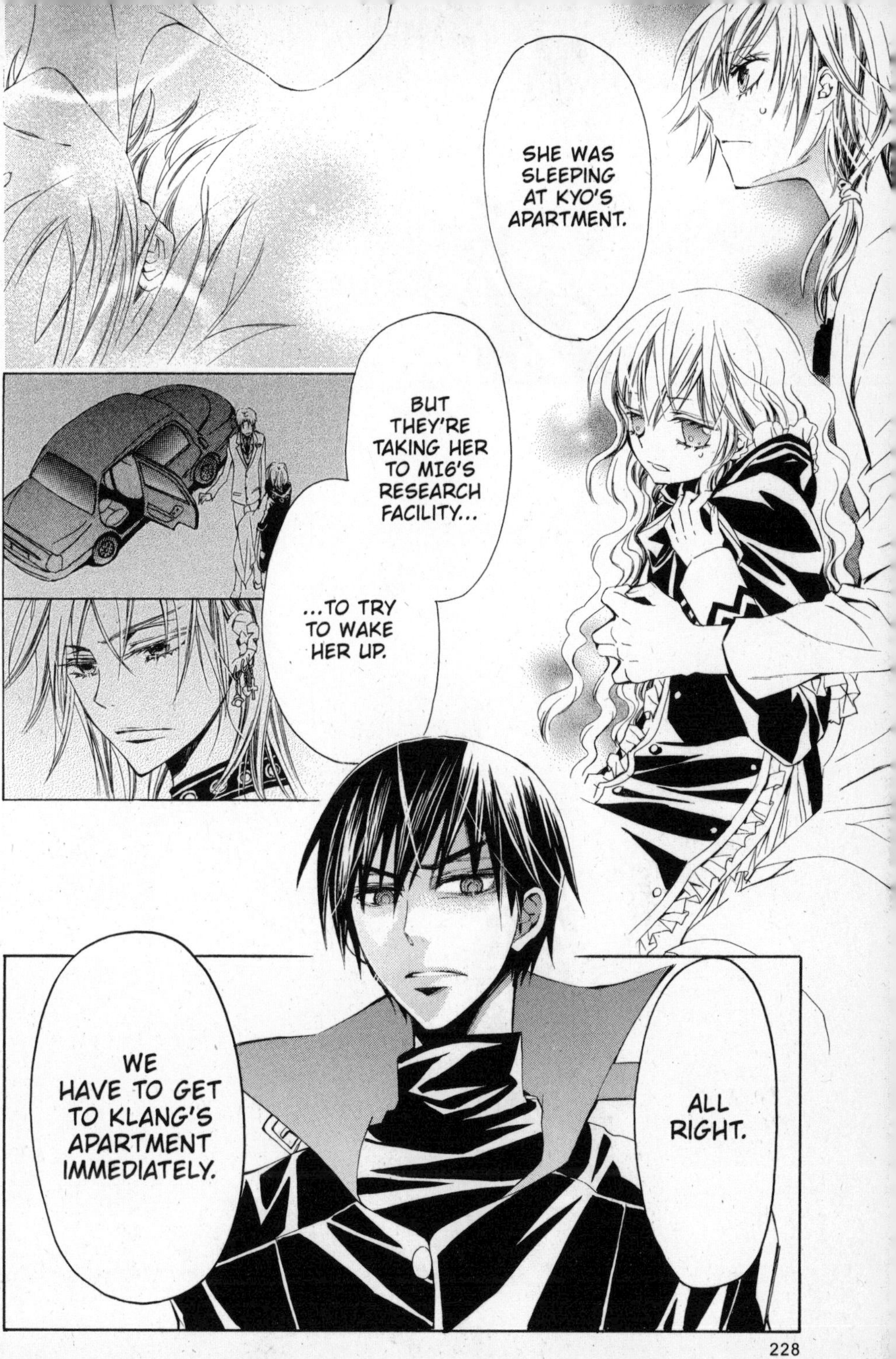
SHE WAS SLEEPING AT KYO'S APARTMENT.
BUT THEY'RE TAKING HER TO MI6'S RESEARCH FACILITY...
...TO TRY TO WAKE HER UP.
WE HAVE TO GET TO KLANG'S APARTMENT IMMEDIATELY.
ALL RIGHT.

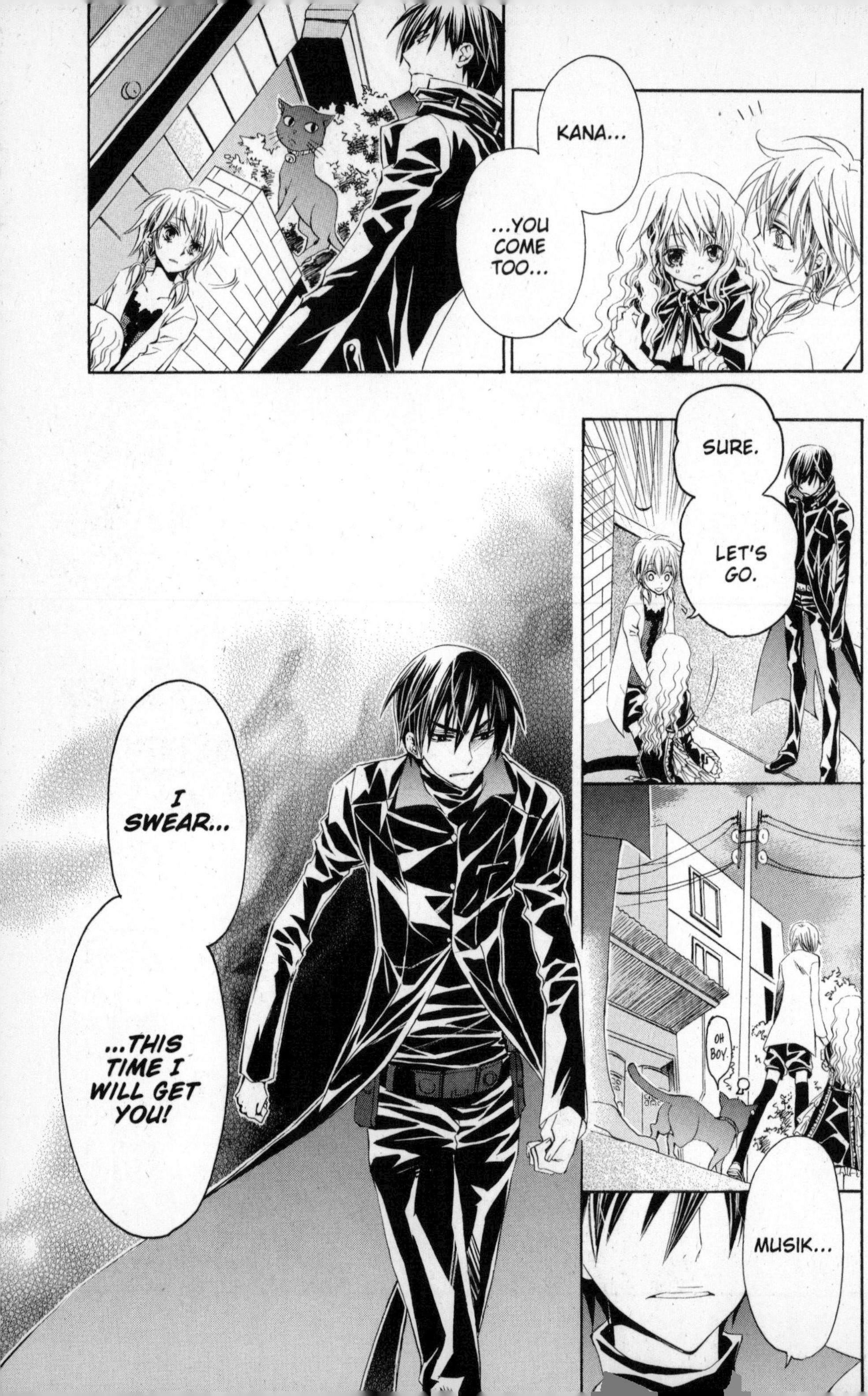
KANA...
...YOU COME TOO...
SURE.
LET'S GO.
OH BOY.
MUSIK...
I SWEAR...
...THIS TIME I WILL GET YOU!

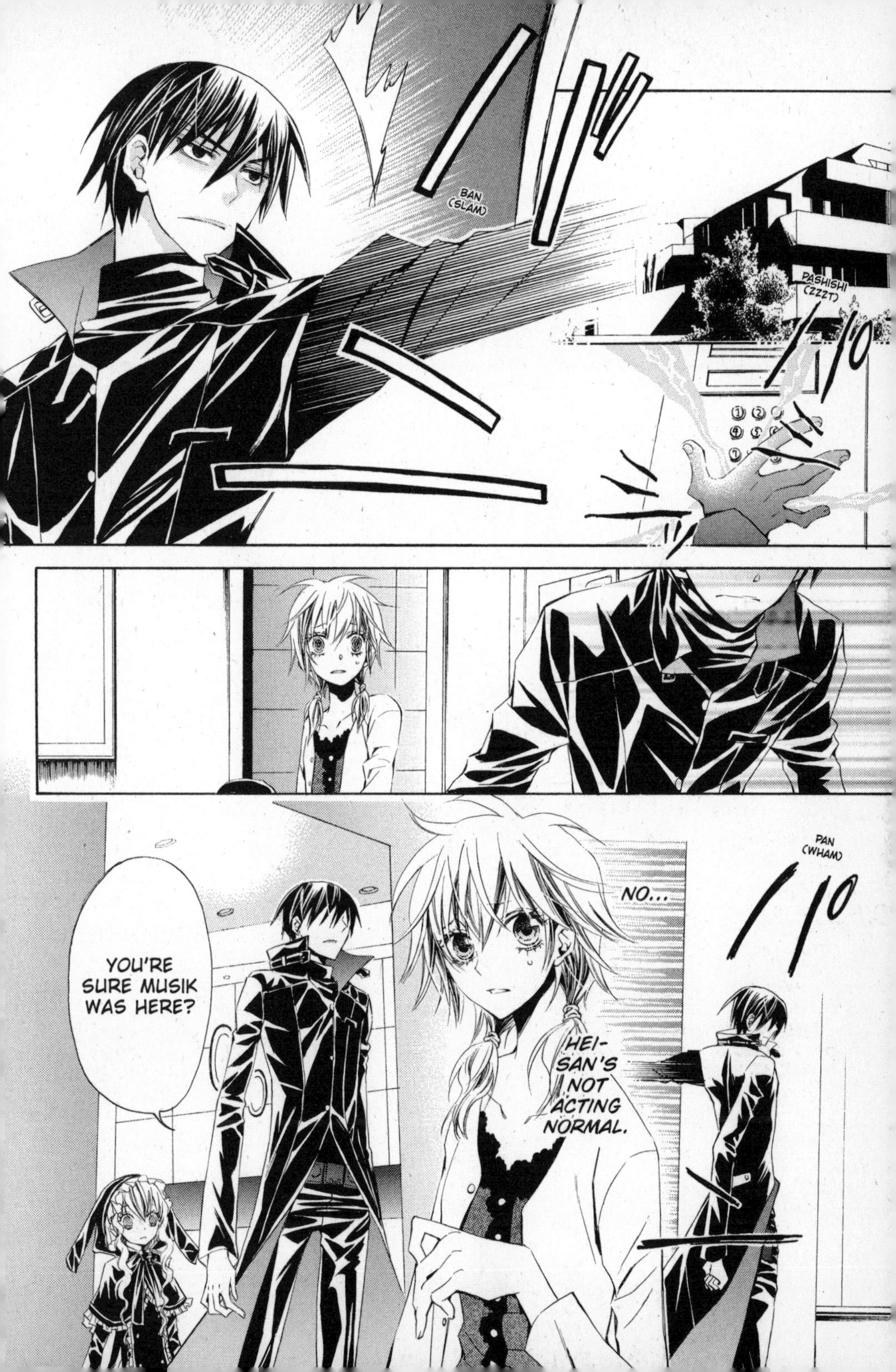
PASHISHI (ZZZT)
BAN (SLAM)
PAN (WHAM)
NO...
HEI-SAN'S NOT ACTING NORMAL.
YOU'RE SURE MUSIK WAS HERE?

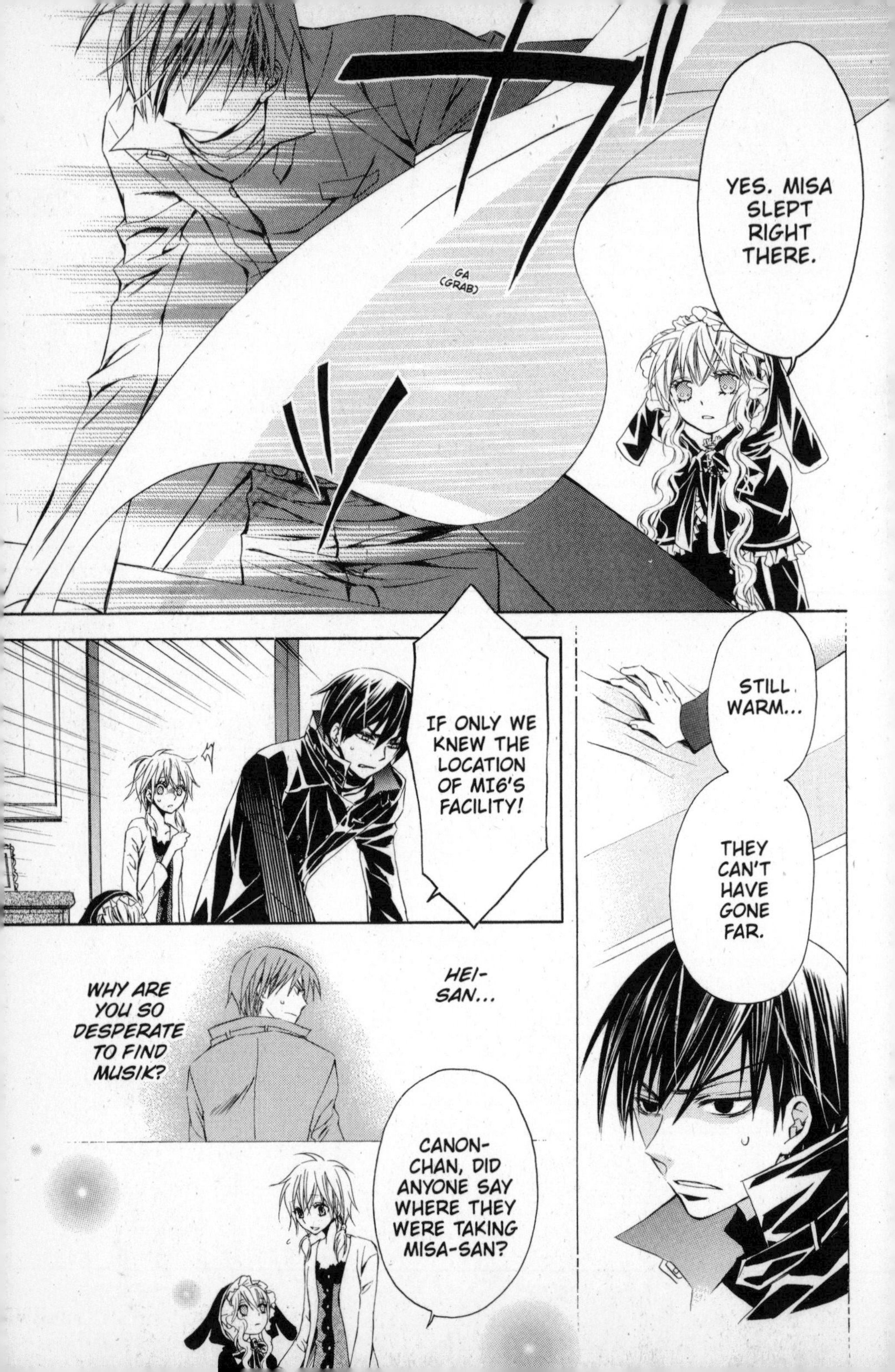
YES. MISA SLEPT RIGHT THERE.
GA (GRAB)
STILL WARM...
THEY CAN'T HAVE GONE FAR.
IF ONLY WE KNEW THE LOCATION OF MI6'S FACILITY!
HEI-SAN...
WHY ARE YOU SO DESPERATE TO FIND MUSIK?
CANON-CHAN, DID ANYONE SAY WHERE THEY WERE TAKING MISA-SAN?

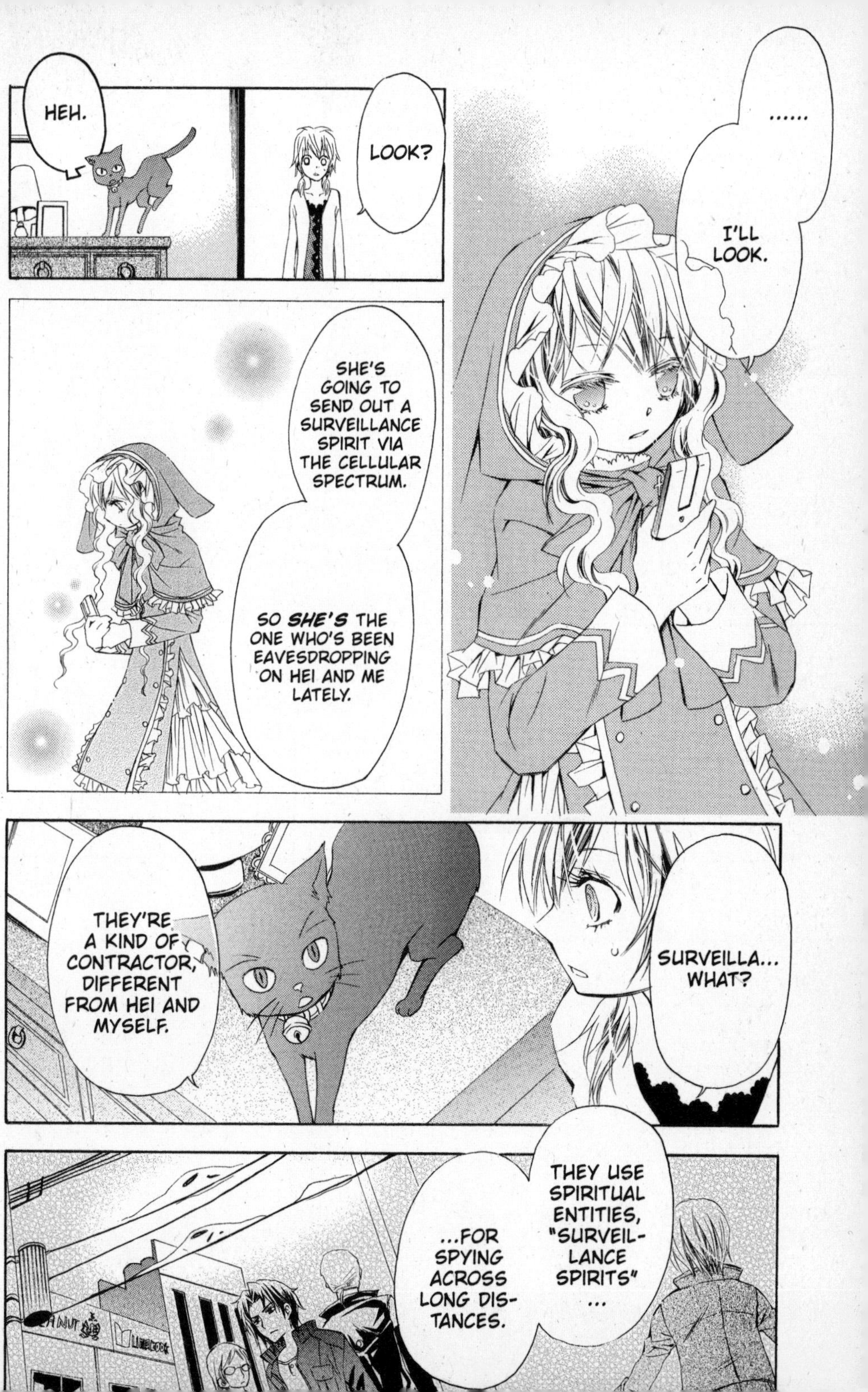
......
I'LL LOOK.
LOOK?
HEH.
SHE'S GOING TO SEND OUT A SURVEILLANCE SPIRIT VIA THE CELLULAR SPECTRUM.
SO SHE'S THE ONE WHO'S BEEN EAVESDROPPING ON HEI AND ME LATELY.
SURVEILLA... WHAT?
THEY'RE A KIND OF CONTRACTOR, DIFFERENT FROM HEI AND MYSELF.
THEY USE SPIRITUAL ENTITIES, "SURVEIL-LANCE SPIRITS" ...
...FOR SPYING ACROSS LONG DIS-TANCES.

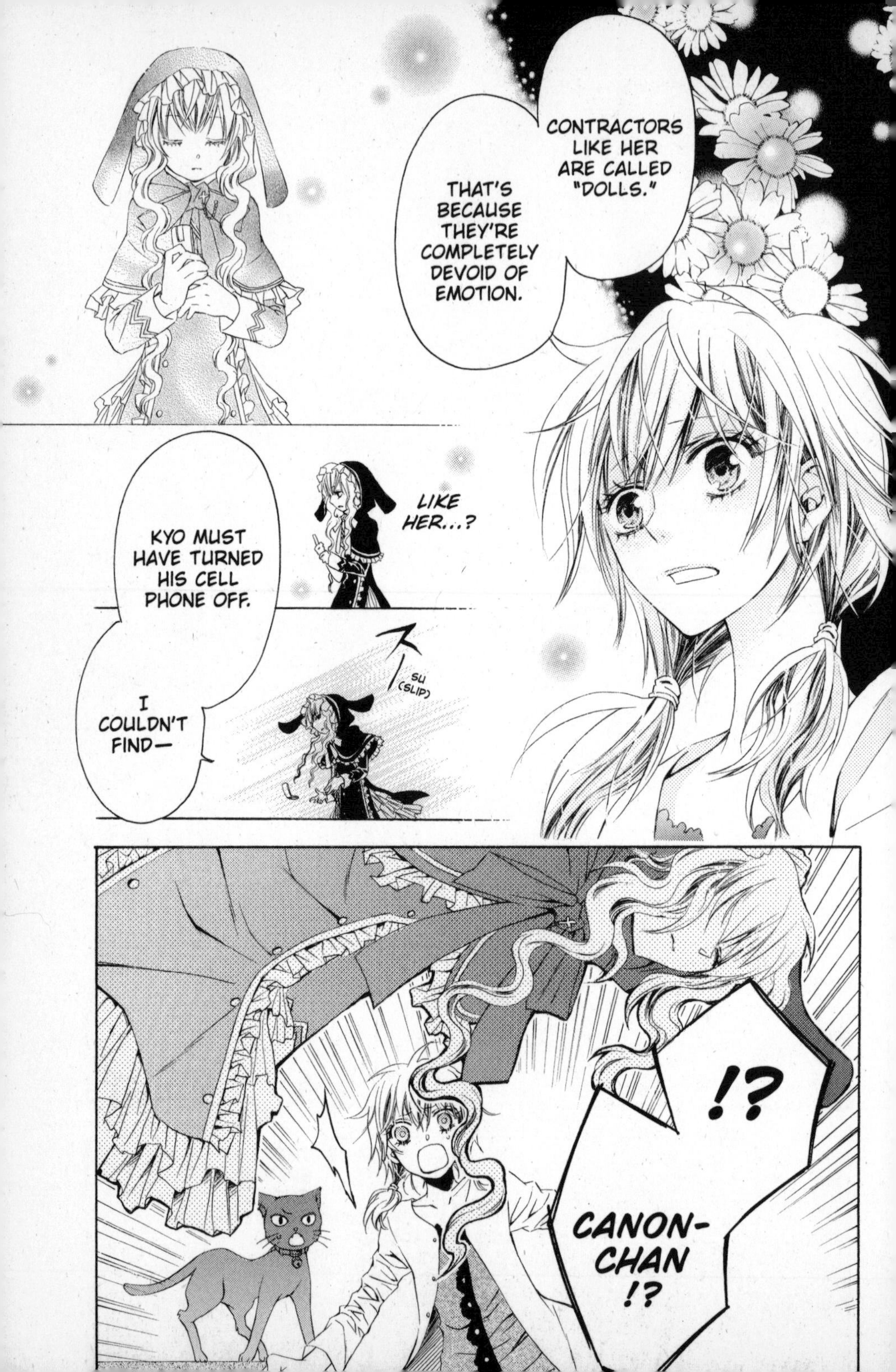
CONTRACTORS LIKE HER ARE CALLED "DOLLS."
THAT'S BECAUSE THEY'RE COMPLETELY DEVOID OF EMOTION.
LIKE HER...?
KYO MUST HAVE TURNED HIS CELL PHONE OFF.
SU (SLIP)
I COULDN'T FIND—
!?
CANON-CHAN!?

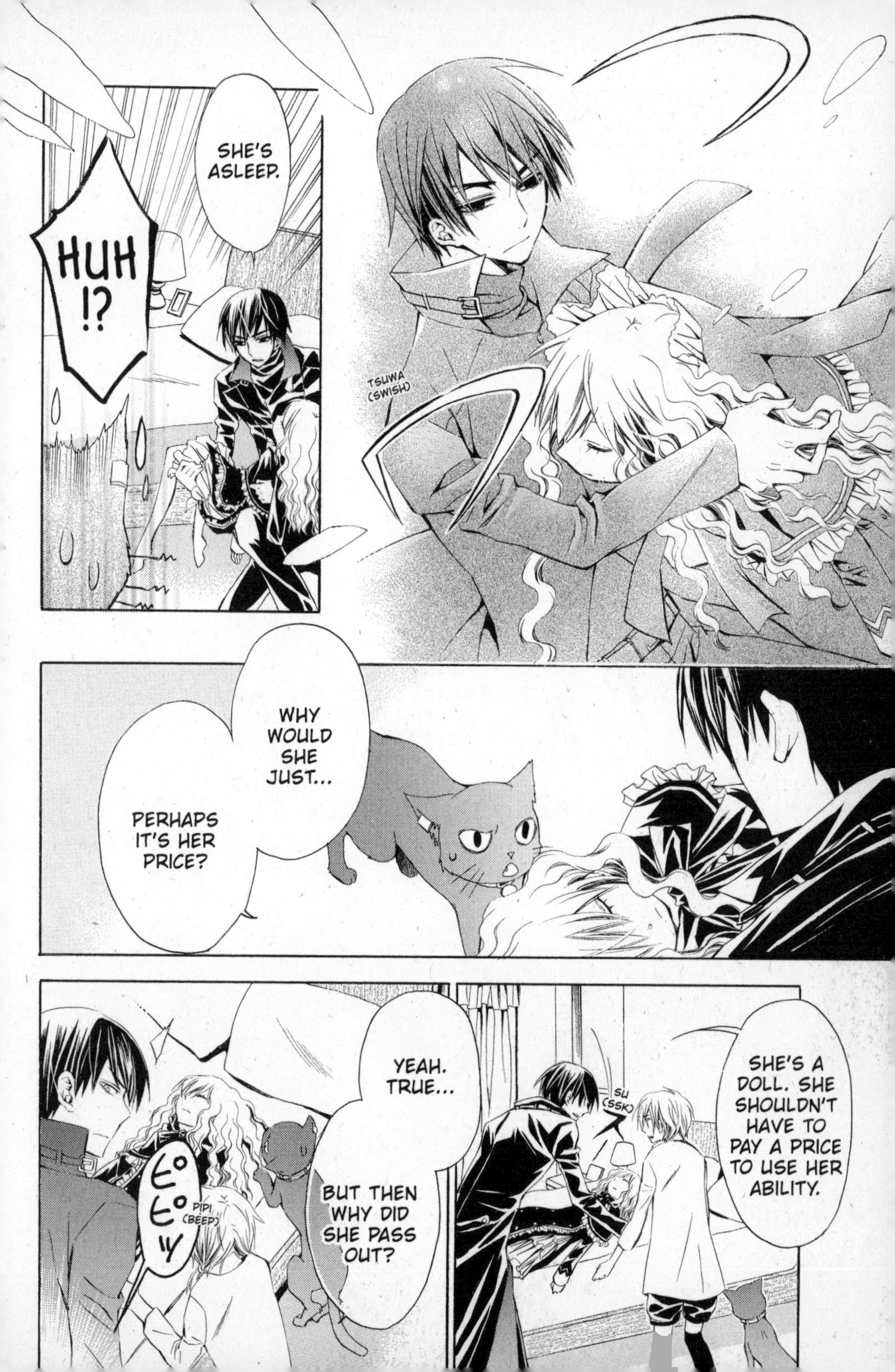
TSUWA (SWISH)
SHE'S ASLEEP.
HUH!?
WHY WOULD SHE JUST...
PERHAPS IT'S HER PRICE?
SHE'S A DOLL. SHE SHOULDN'T HAVE TO PAY A PRICE TO USE HER ABILITY.
SU (SSK)
YEAH. TRUE...
BUT THEN WHY DID SHE PASS OUT?
ピピッ
PIPI (BEEP)

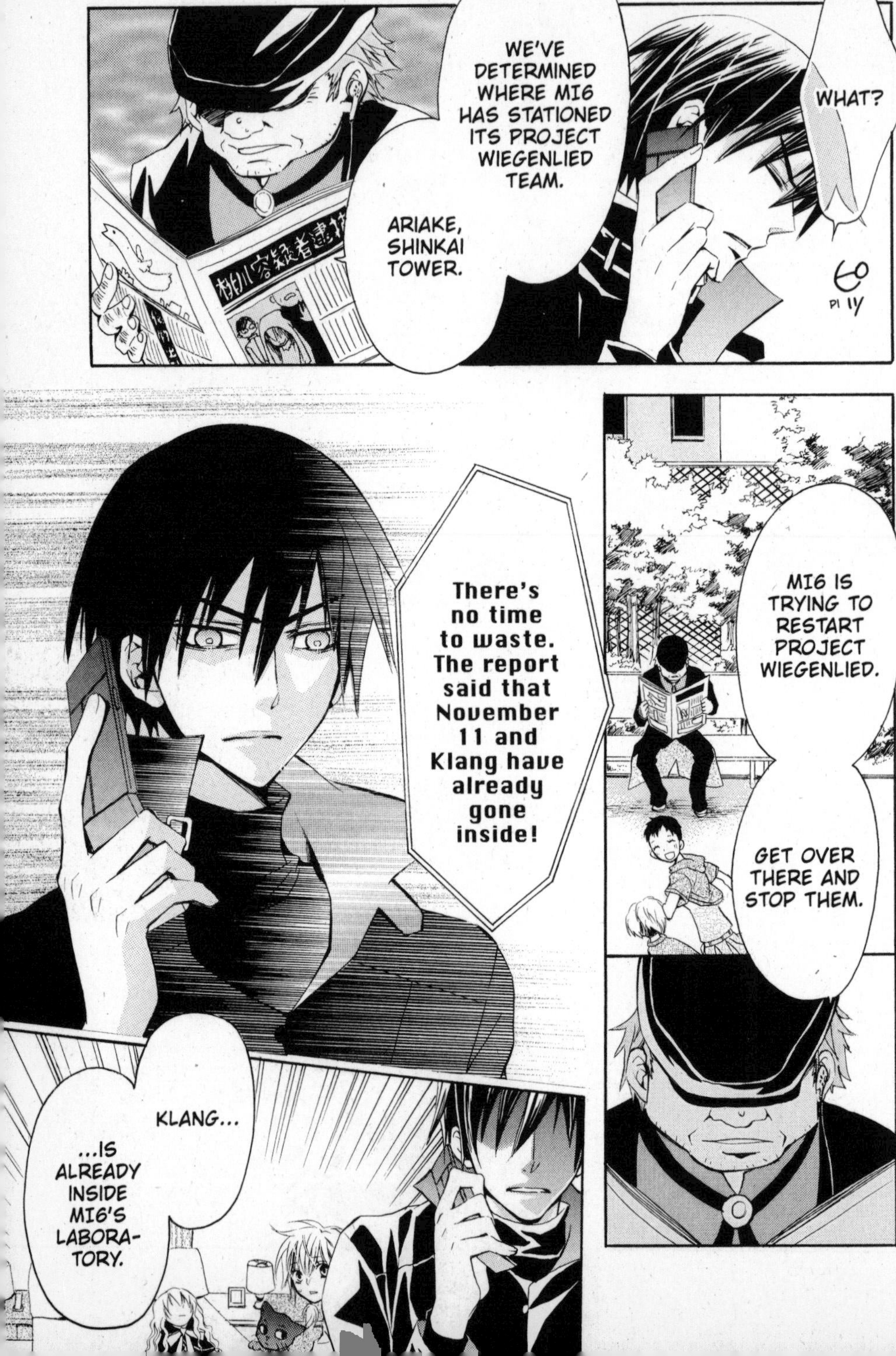
WHAT?
WE'VE DETERMINED WHERE MI6 HAS STATIONED ITS PROJECT WIEGENLIED TEAM.
ARIAKE, SHINKAI TOWER.
MI6 IS TRYING TO RESTART PROJECT WIEGENLIED.
GET OVER THERE AND STOP THEM.
There's no time to waste. The report said that November 11 and Klang have already gone inside!
KLANG...
...IS ALREADY INSIDE MI6'S LABORATORY.

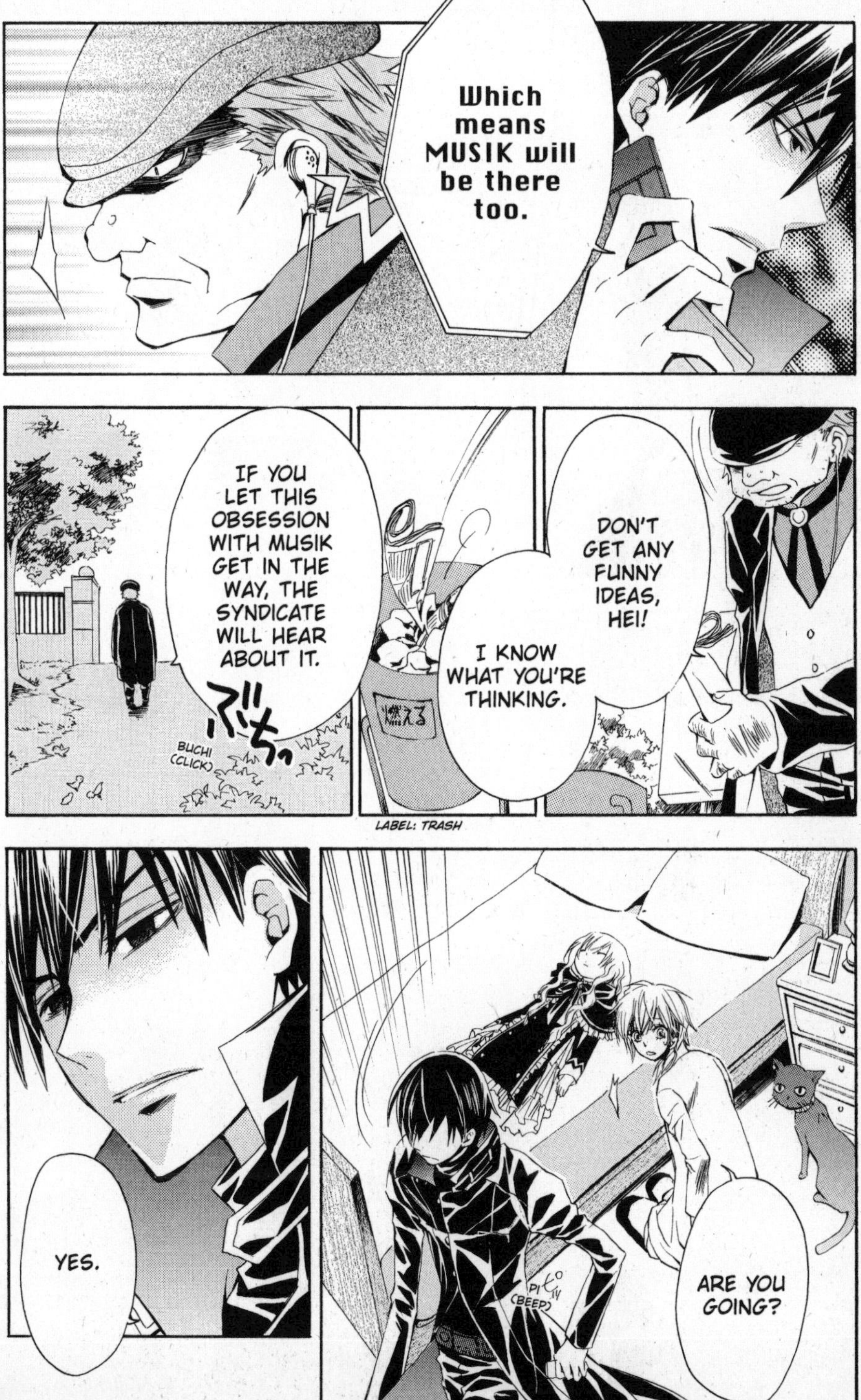
Which means MUSIK will be there too.
DON'T GET ANY FUNNY IDEAS, HEI!
I KNOW WHAT YOU'RE THINKING.
燃える
IF YOU LET THIS OBSESSION WITH MUSIK GET IN THE WAY, THE SYNDICATE WILL HEAR ABOUT IT.
ぶちっ
BUCHI (CLICK)
ARE YOU GOING?
ピッ
PI (BEEP)
YES.

LABEL: TRASH

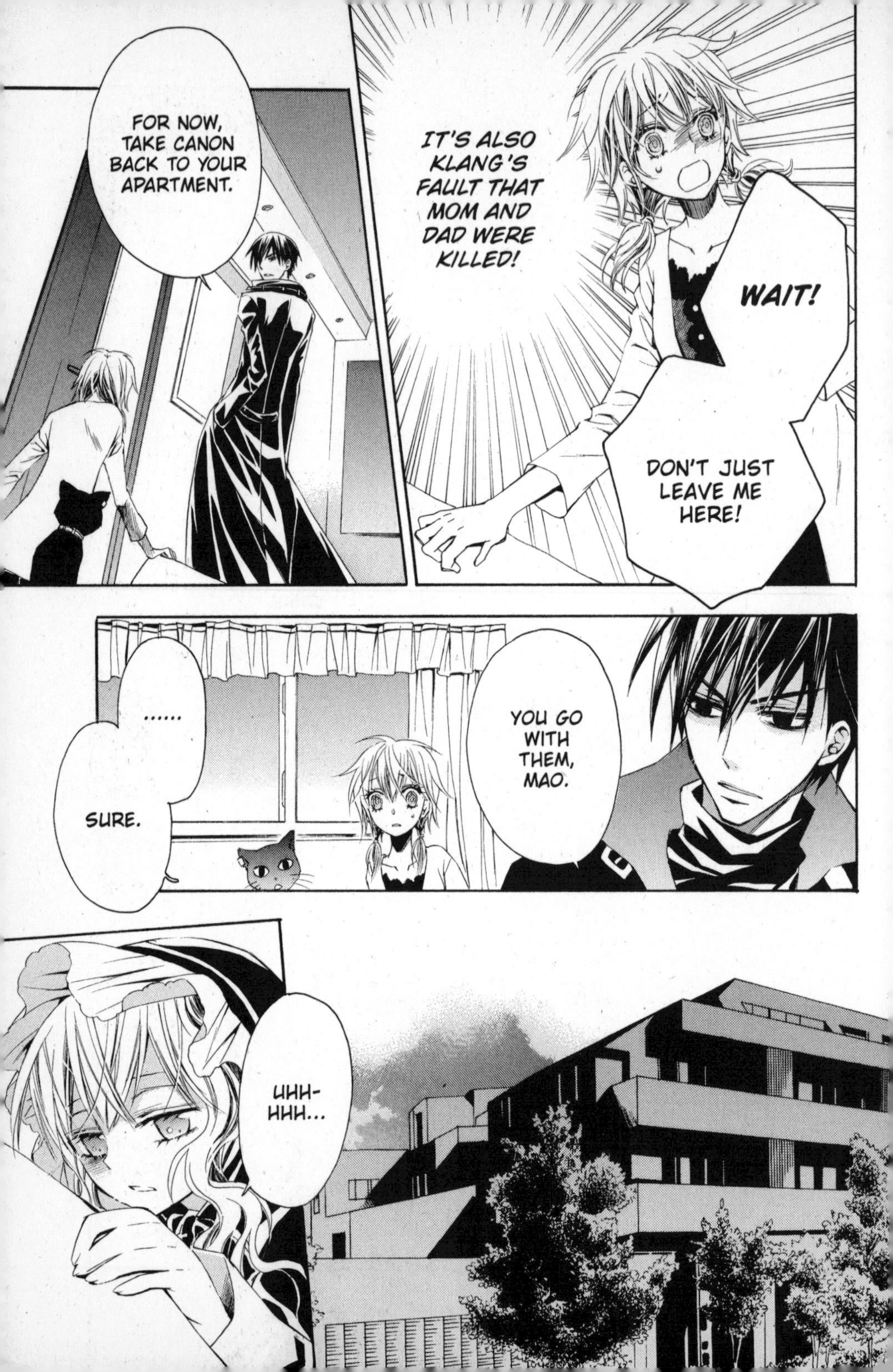
IT'S ALSO KLANG'S FAULT THAT MOM AND DAD WERE KILLED!
WAIT!
DON'T JUST LEAVE ME HERE!
FOR NOW, TAKE CANON BACK TO YOUR APARTMENT.
YOU GO WITH THEM, MAO.
......
SURE.
UHH-HHH...

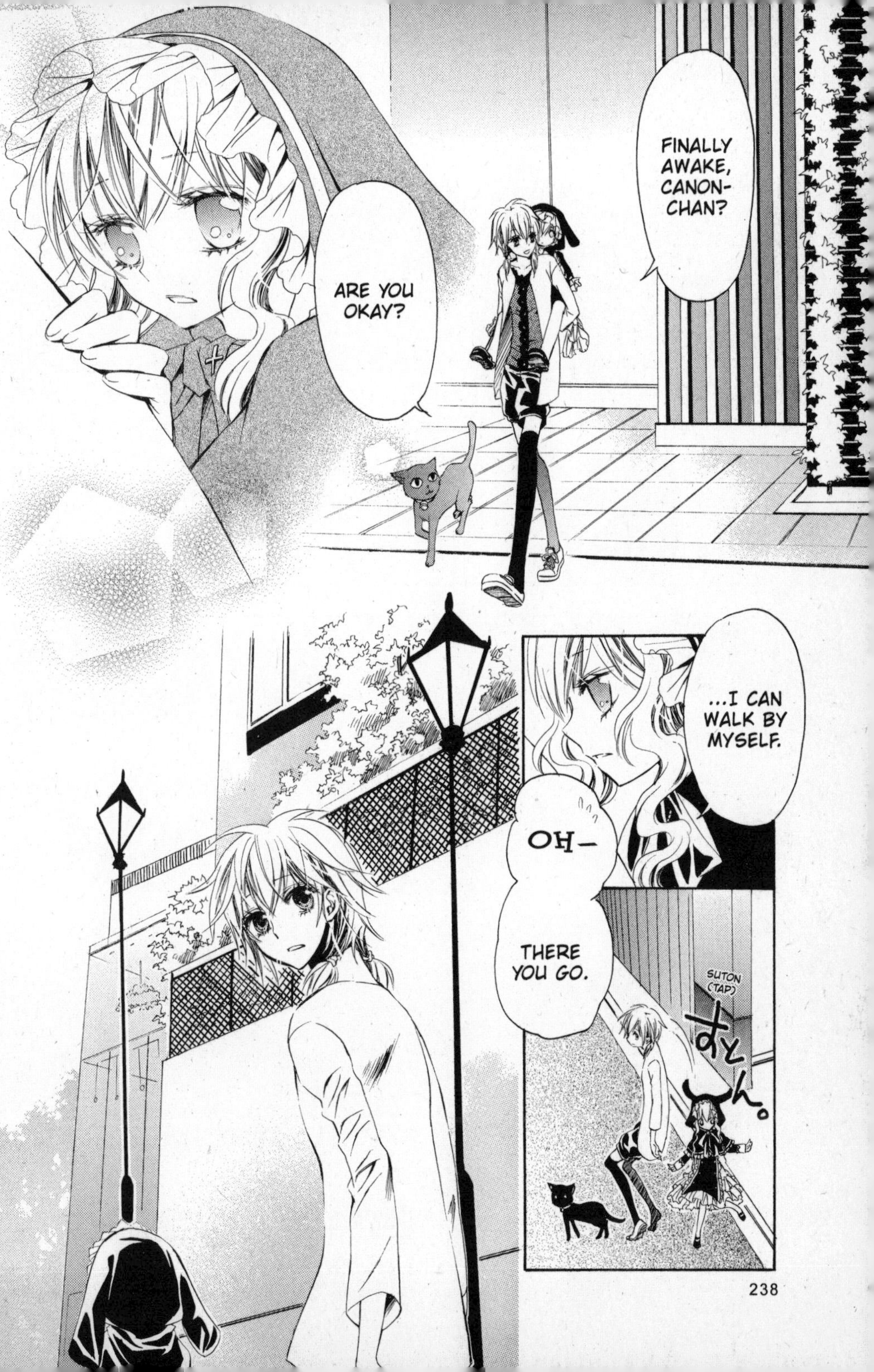
FINALLY AWAKE, CANON-CHAN?
ARE YOU OKAY?
...I CAN WALK BY MYSELF.
OH-
THERE YOU GO.
SUTON (TAP)
すとん。

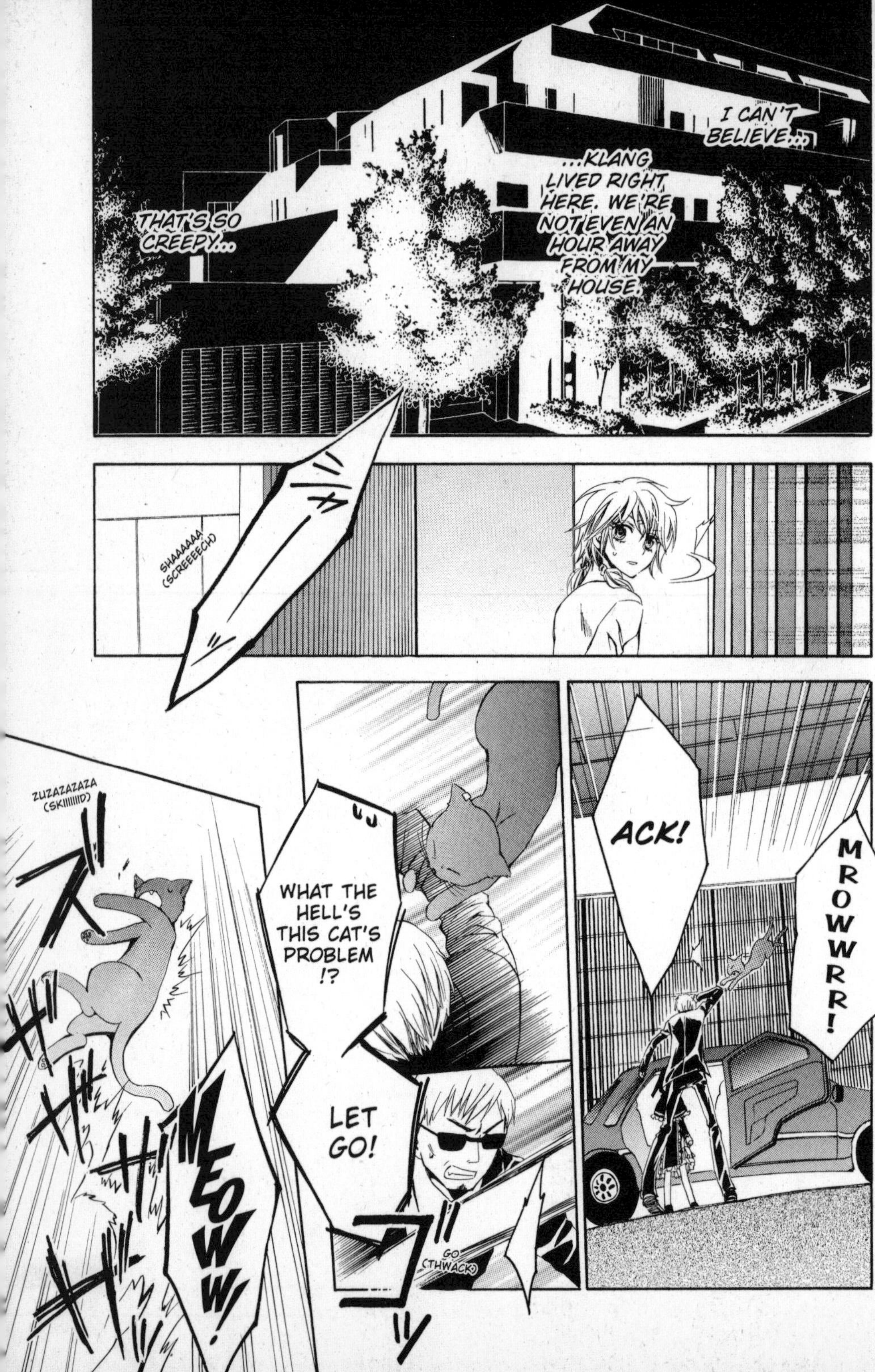
I CAN'T BELIEVE...
...KLANG LIVED RIGHT HERE. WE'RE NOT EVEN AN HOUR AWAY FROM MY HOUSE.
THAT'S SO CREEPY...
SHAAAAAAA (SCREEEECH)
MROWWRR!
ACK!
WHAT THE HELL'S THIS CAT'S PROBLEM !?
LET GO!
GO (THWACK)
ZUZAZAZAZA (SKIIIIIID)
MEOWW!

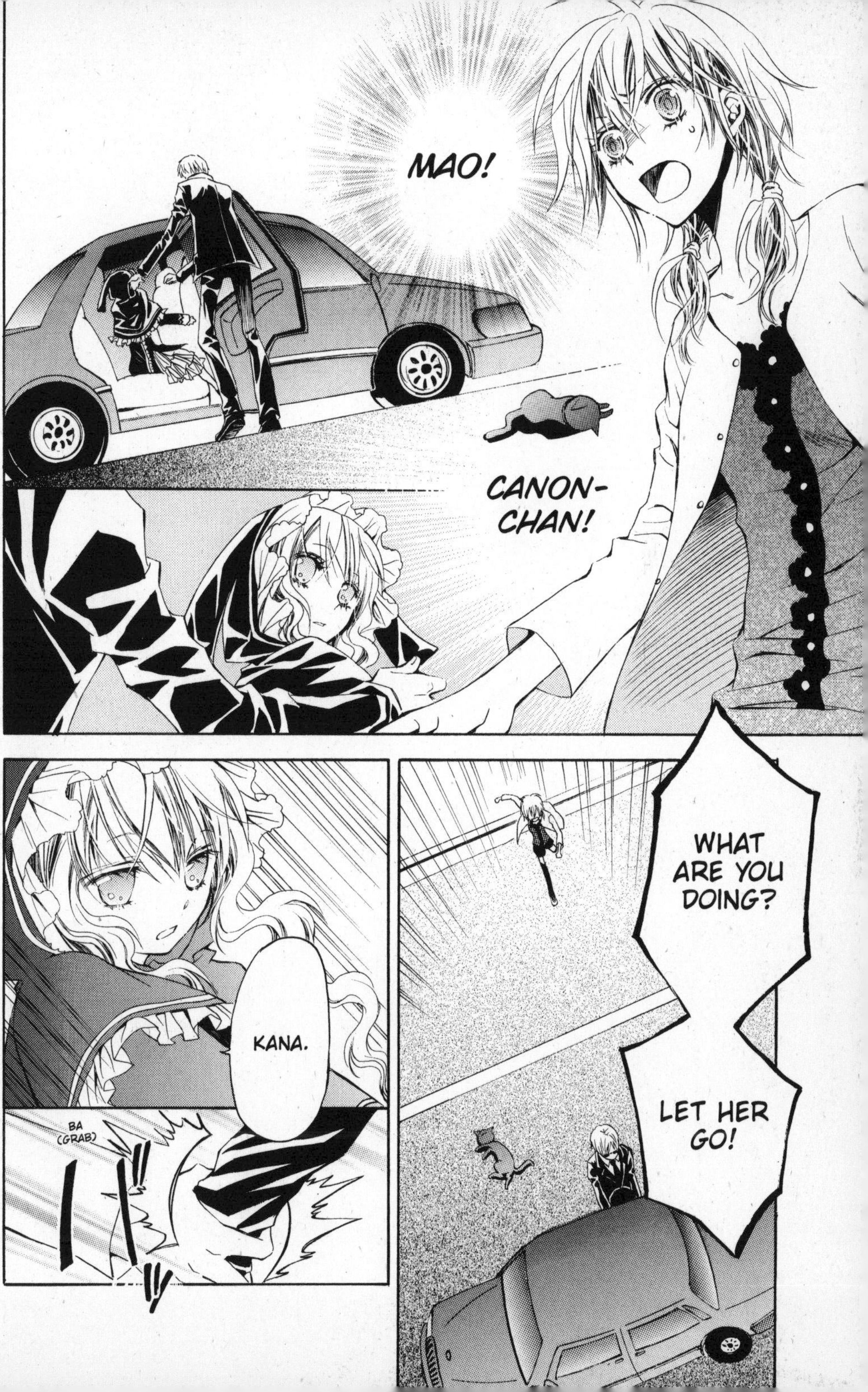
MAO!
CANON-CHAN!
WHAT ARE YOU DOING?
LET HER GO!
KANA.
BA (GRAB)

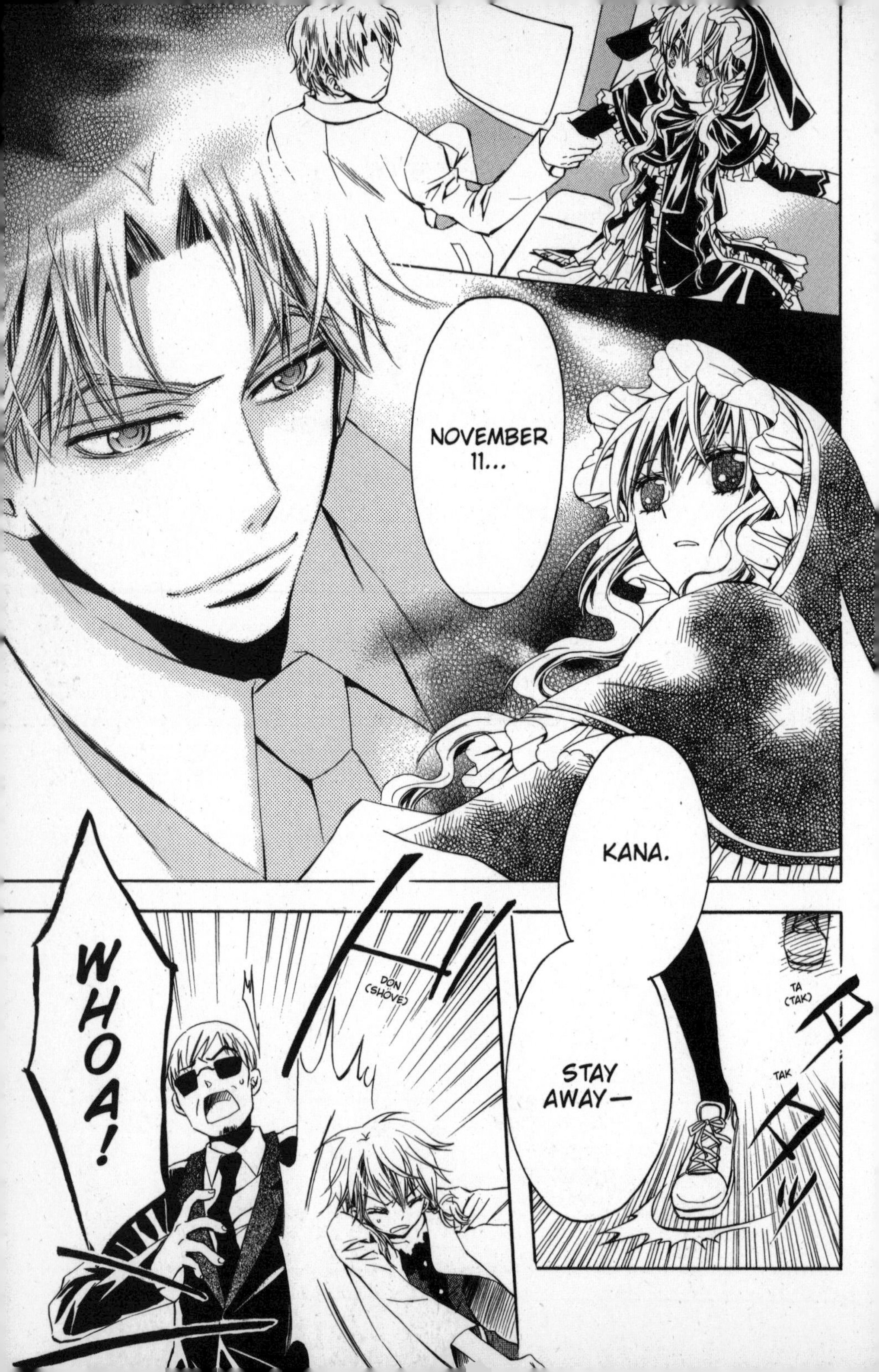
NOVEMBER 11...
KANA.
STAY AWAY—
TA (TAK)
TAK
DON (SHÖVE)
WHOA!

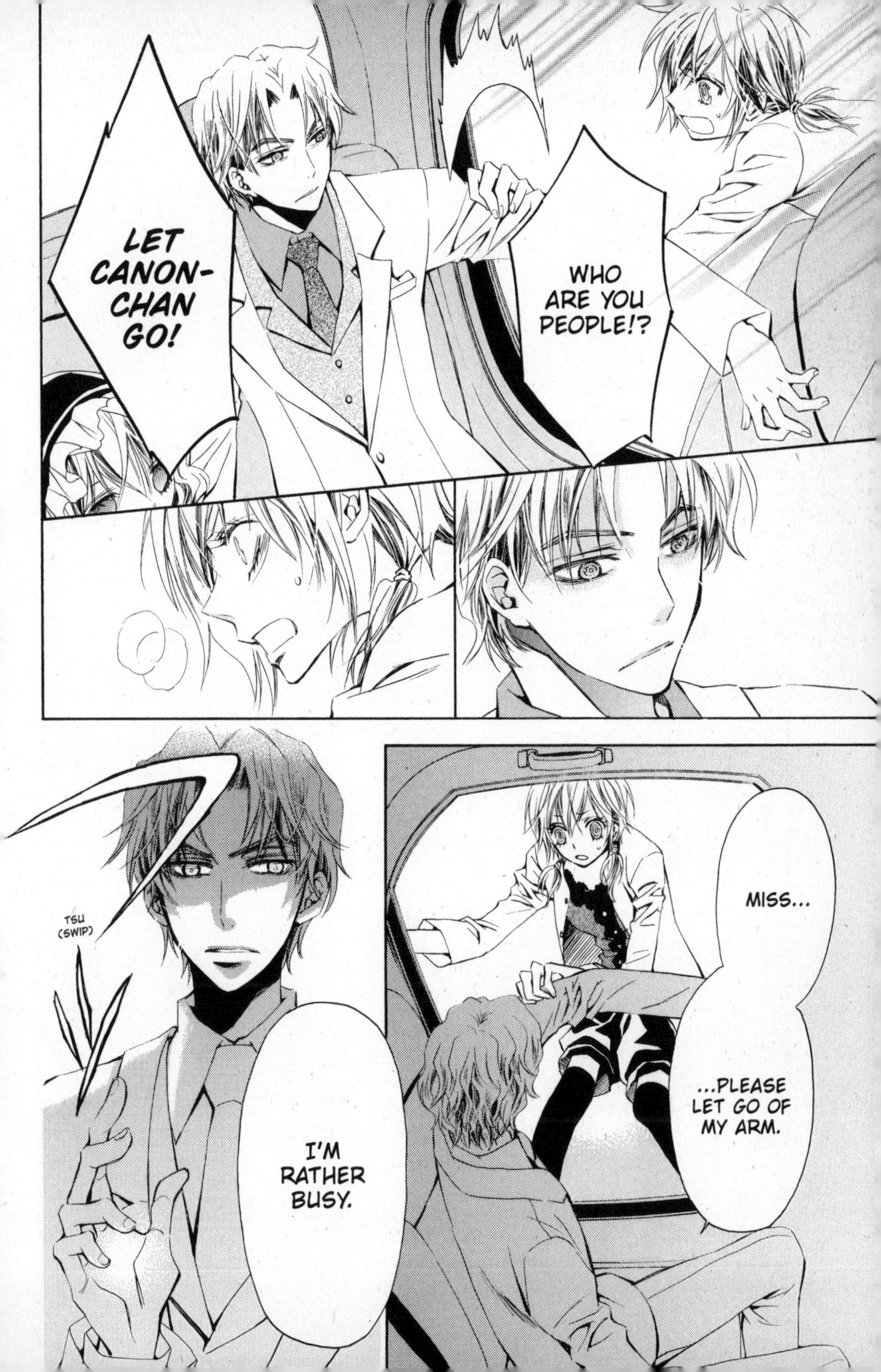
WHO ARE YOU PEOPLE!?
LET CANON-CHAN GO!
MISS...
...PLEASE LET GO OF MY ARM.
TSU (SWIP)
I'M RATHER BUSY.

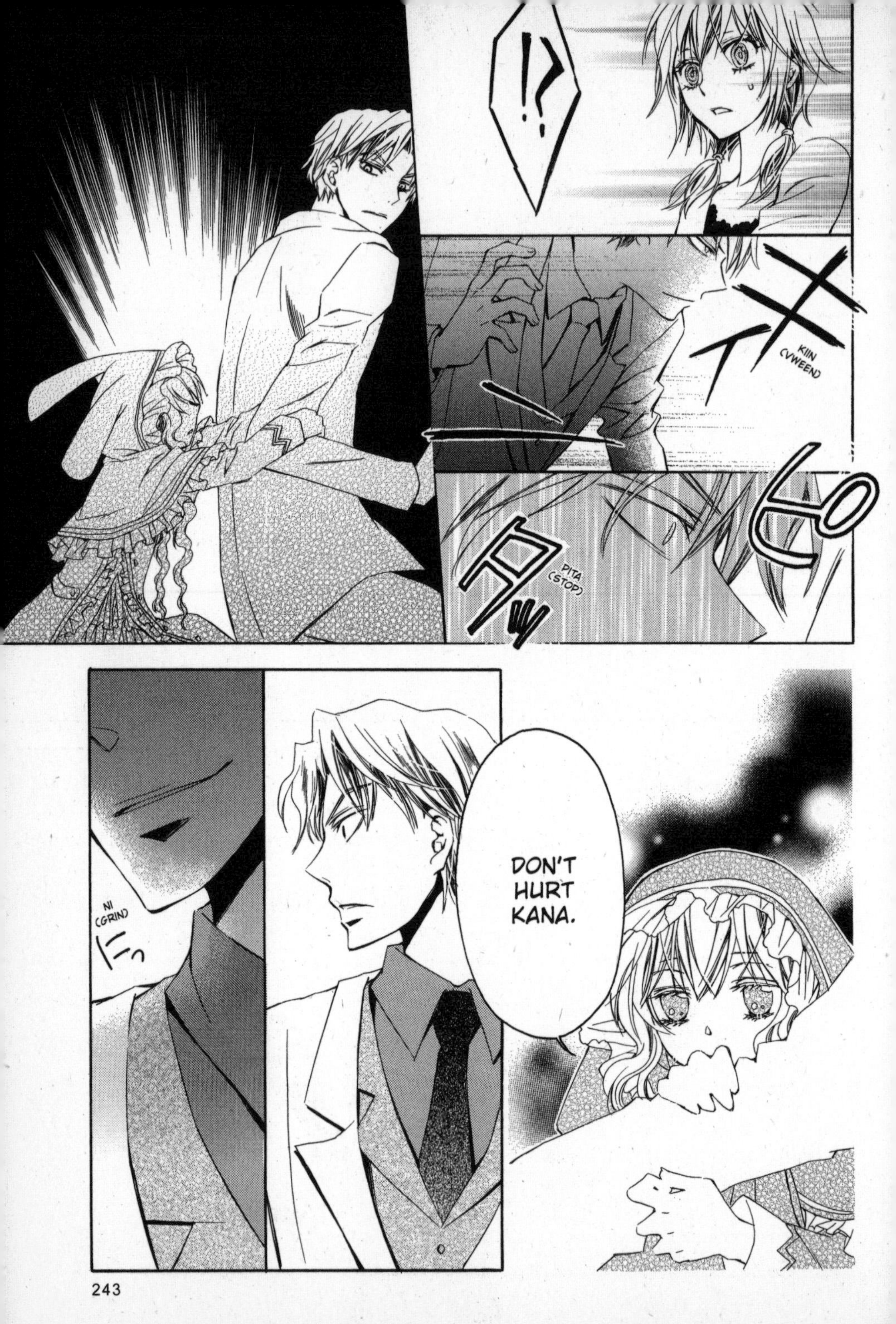
!?
KIIN (VWEEN)
PITA (STOP)
DON'T HURT KANA.
NI (GRIN)

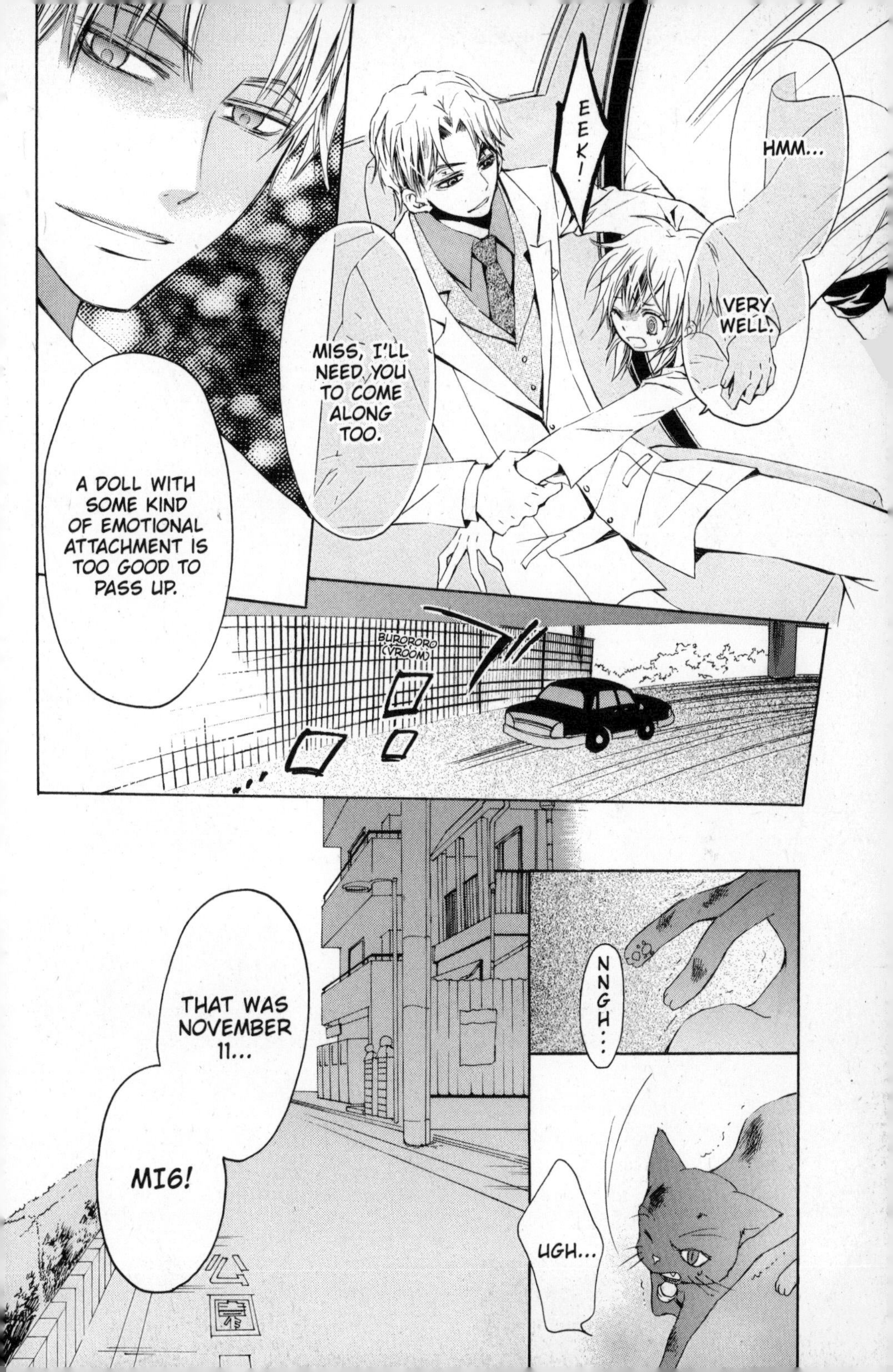
HMM...
VERY WELL.
EEK!
MISS, I'LL NEED YOU TO COME ALONG TOO.
A DOLL WITH SOME KIND OF EMOTIONAL ATTACHMENT IS TOO GOOD TO PASS UP.
BURORORO (VROOM)
NNGH...
UGH...
THAT WAS NOVEMBER 11...
MI6!

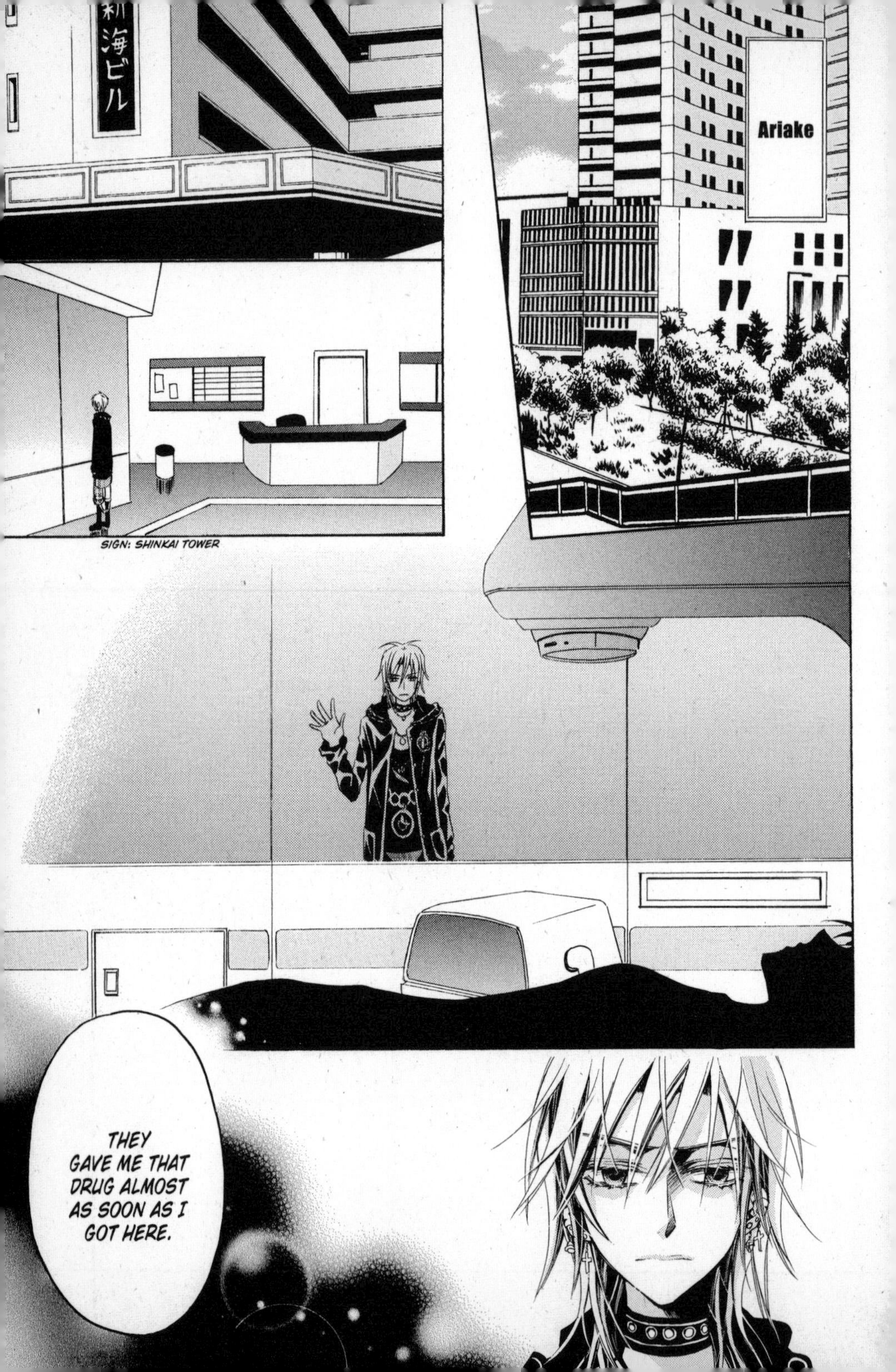
Ariake
新海ビル
SIGN: SHINKAI TOWER
THEY GAVE ME THAT DRUG ALMOST AS SOON AS I GOT HERE.

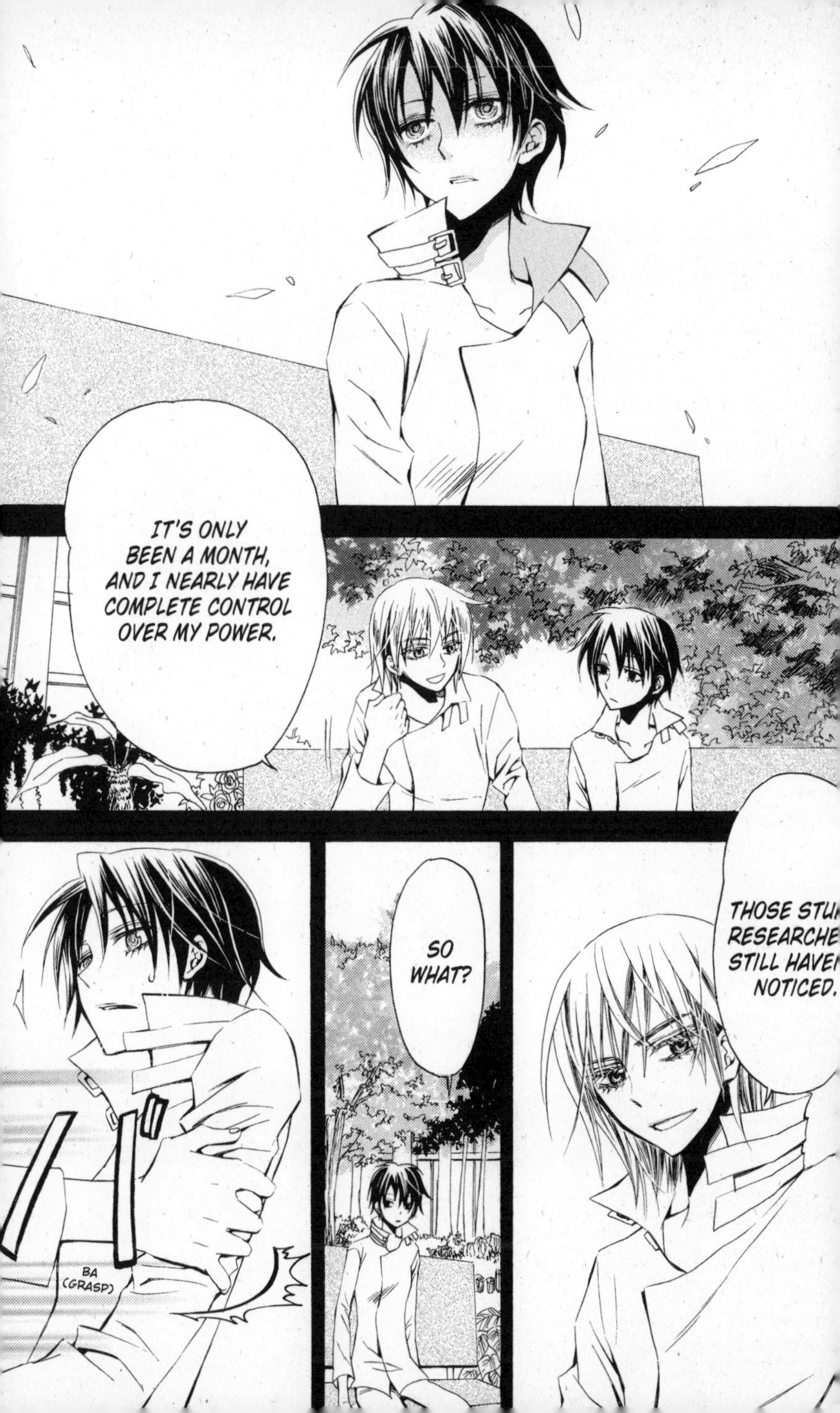
IT'S ONLY BEEN A MONTH, AND I NEARLY HAVE COMPLETE CONTROL OVER MY POWER.
THOSE STU RESEARCHE STILL HAVE NOTICED.
SO WHAT?
BA (GRASP)

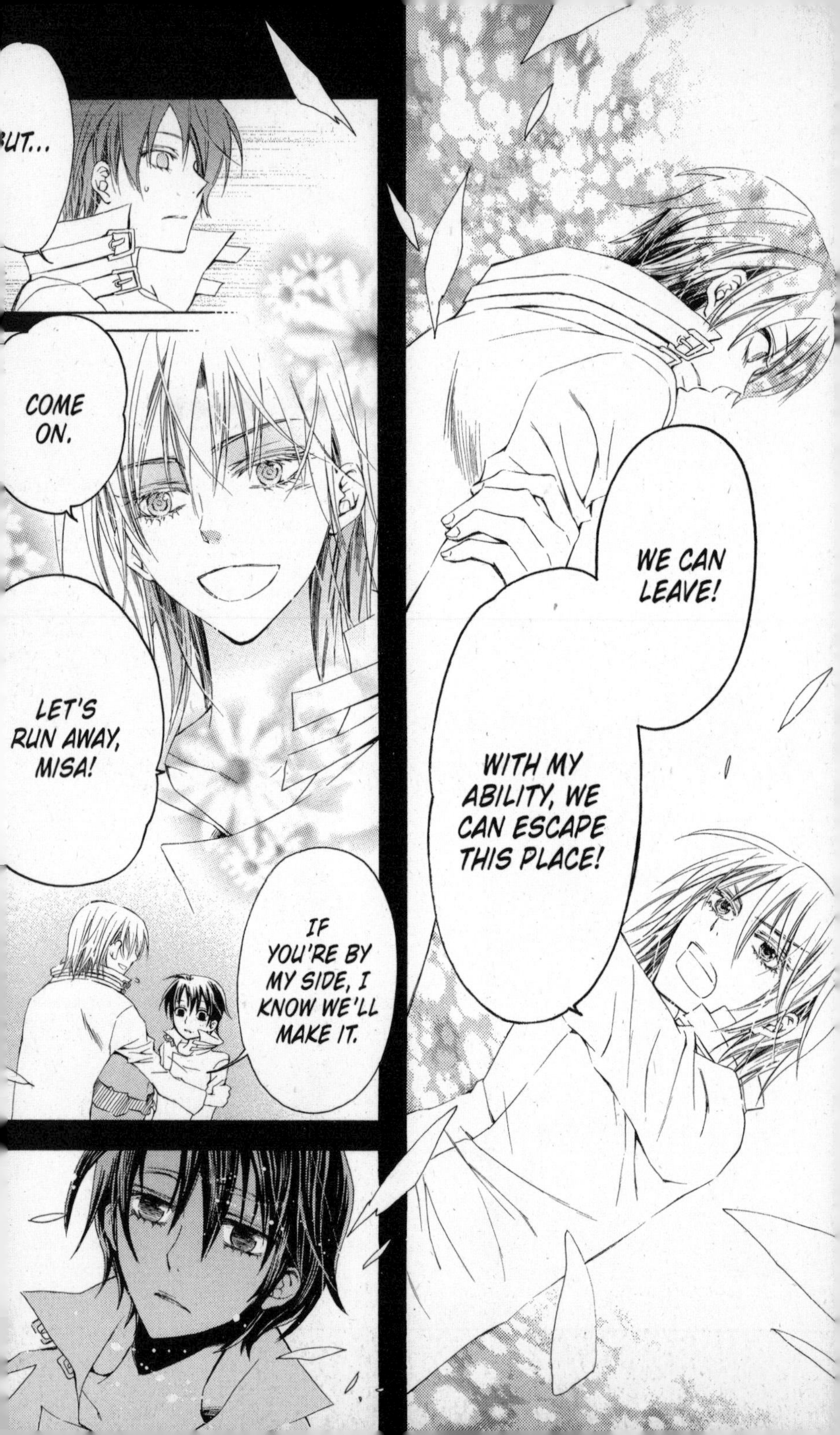
WE CAN LEAVE!
WITH MY ABILITY, WE CAN ESCAPE THIS PLACE!
BUT...
COME ON.
LET'S RUN AWAY, MISA!
IF YOU'RE BY MY SIDE, I KNOW WE'LL MAKE IT.

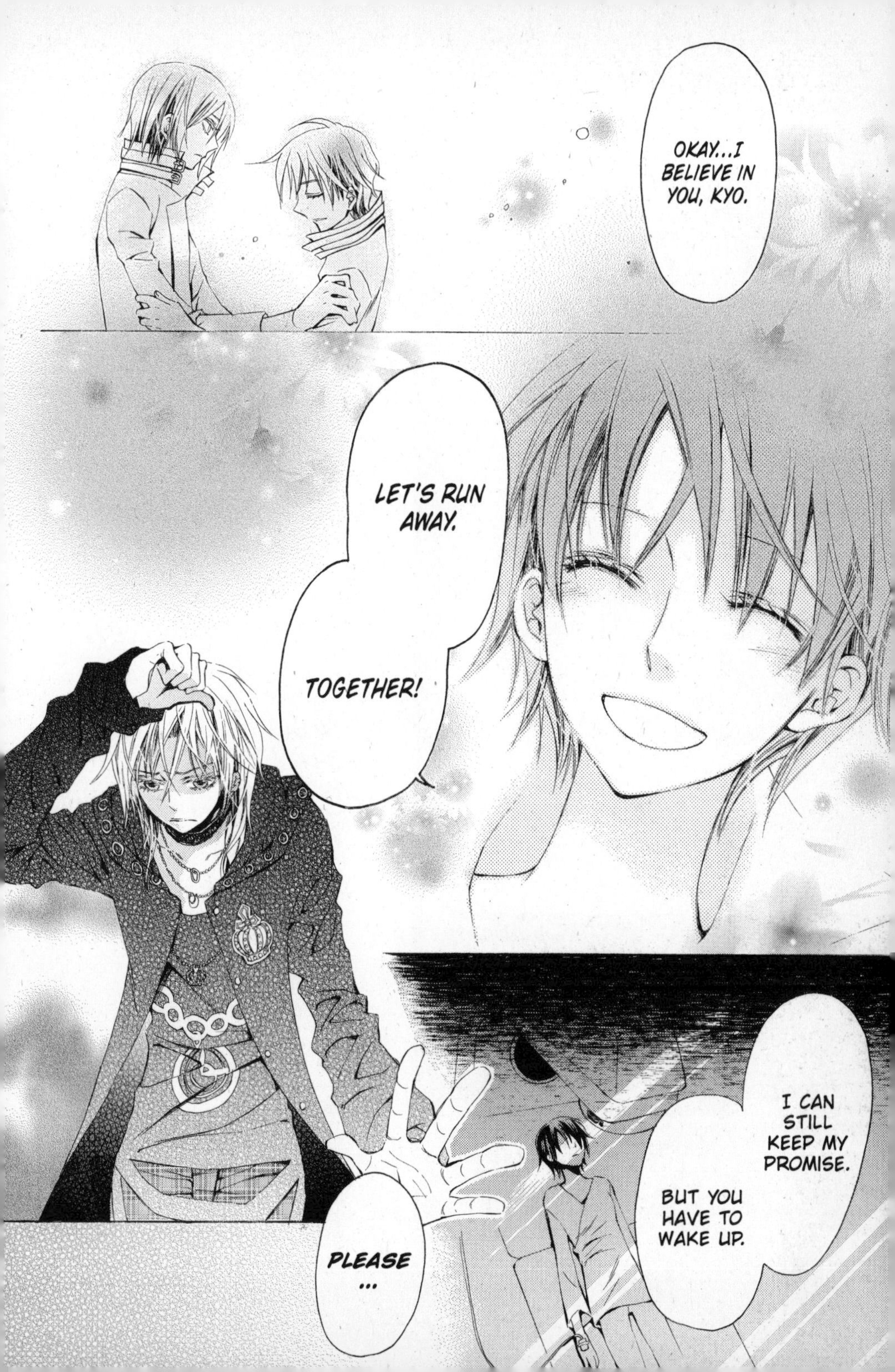
OKAY...I BELIEVE IN YOU, KYO.
LET'S RUN AWAY.
TOGETHER!
I CAN STILL KEEP MY PROMISE.
BUT YOU HAVE TO WAKE UP.
PLEASE ...

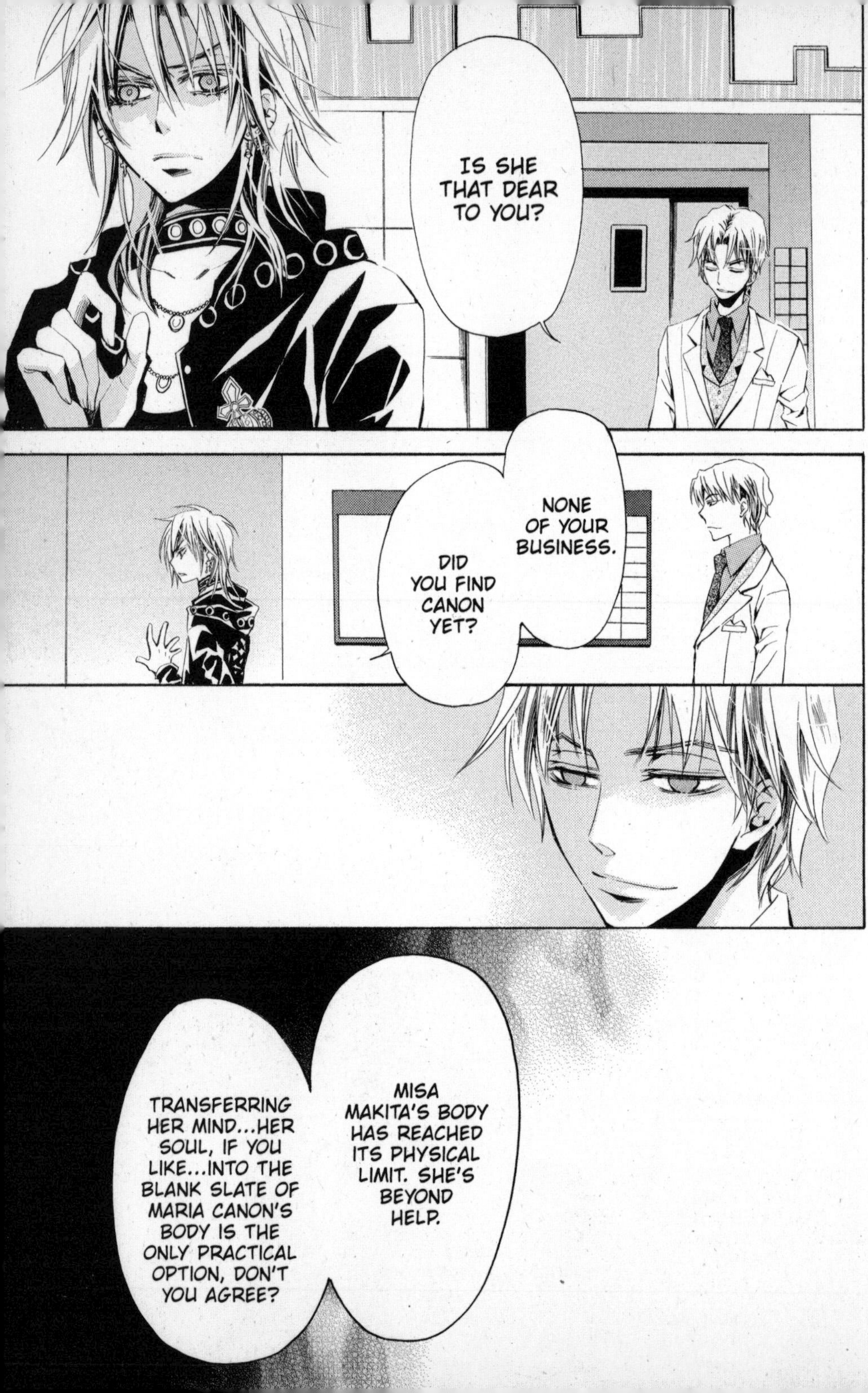
IS SHE THAT DEAR TO YOU?
NONE OF YOUR BUSINESS.
DID YOU FIND CANON YET?
MISA MAKITA'S BODY HAS REACHED ITS PHYSICAL LIMIT. SHE'S BEYOND HELP.
TRANSFERRING HER MIND...HER SOUL, IF YOU LIKE...INTO THE BLANK SLATE OF MARIA CANON'S BODY IS THE ONLY PRACTICAL OPTION, DON'T YOU AGREE?

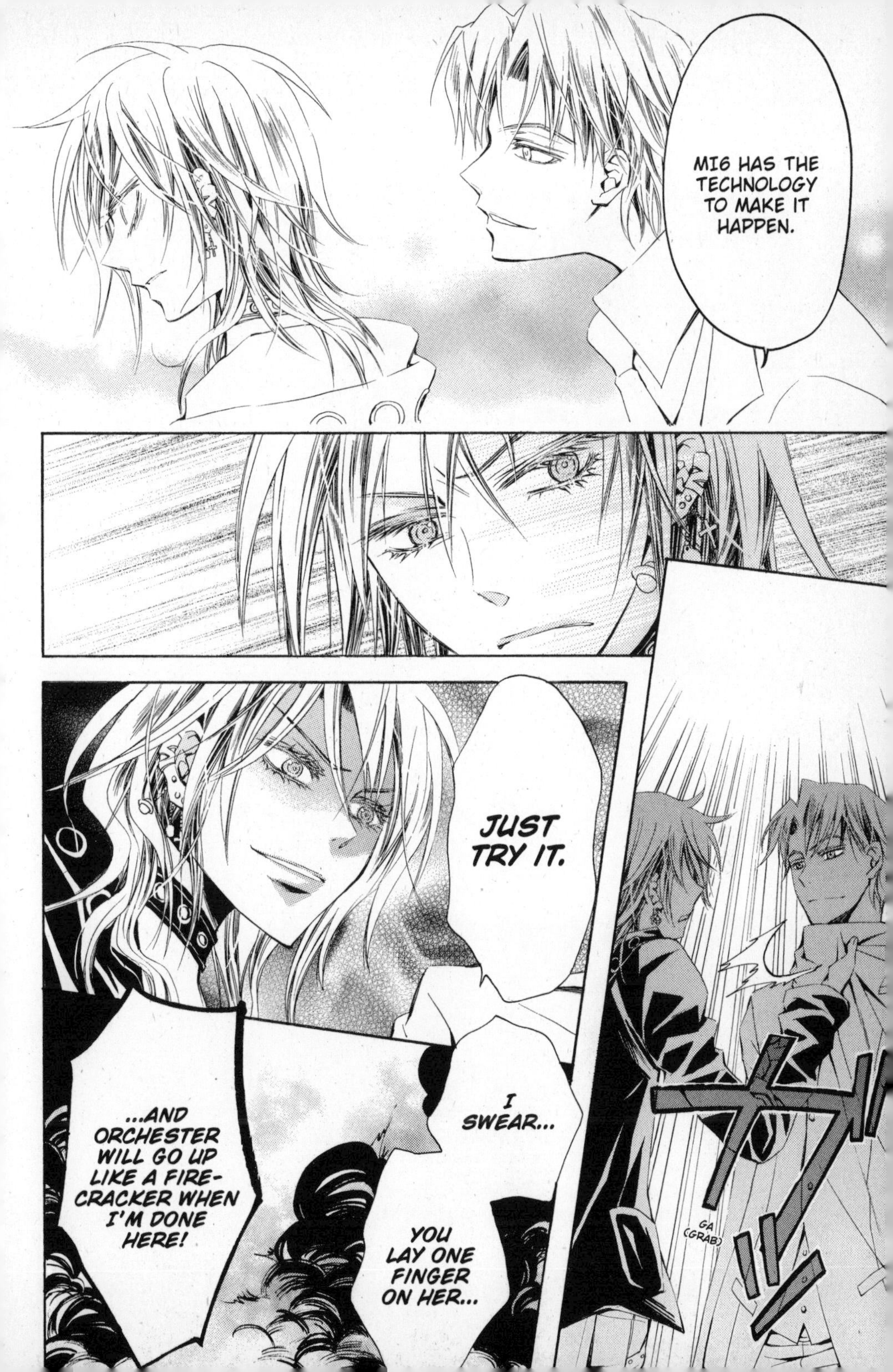
MI6 HAS THE TECHNOLOGY TO MAKE IT HAPPEN.
GA (GRAB)
JUST TRY IT.
I SWEAR...
YOU LAY ONE FINGER ON HER...
...AND ORCHESTER WILL GO UP LIKE A FIRE-CRACKER WHEN I'M DONE HERE!

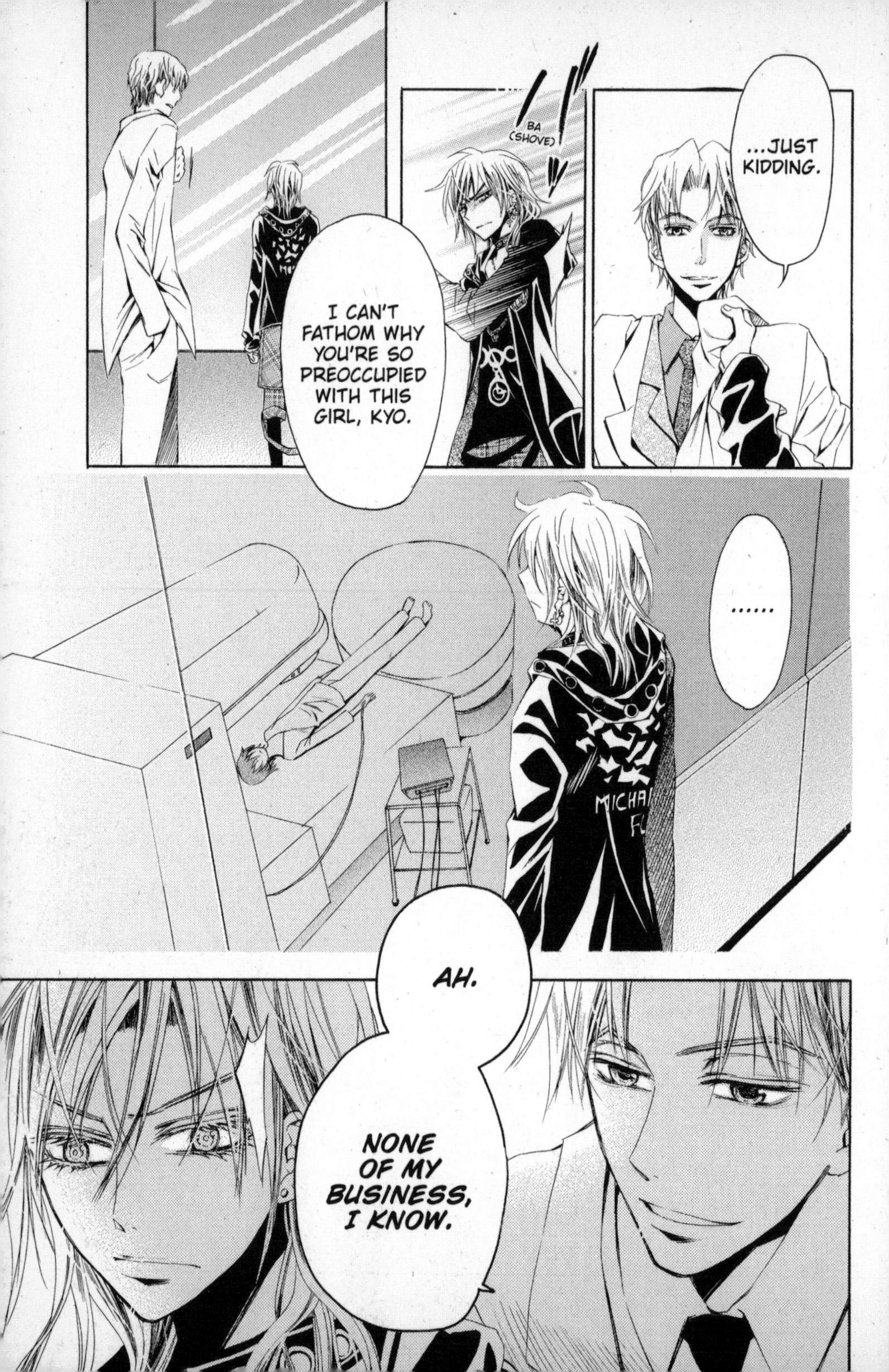
...JUST KIDDING.
BA (SHOVE)
I CAN'T FATHOM WHY YOU'RE SO PREOCCUPIED WITH THIS GIRL, KYO.
......
AH.
NONE OF MY BUSINESS, I KNOW.

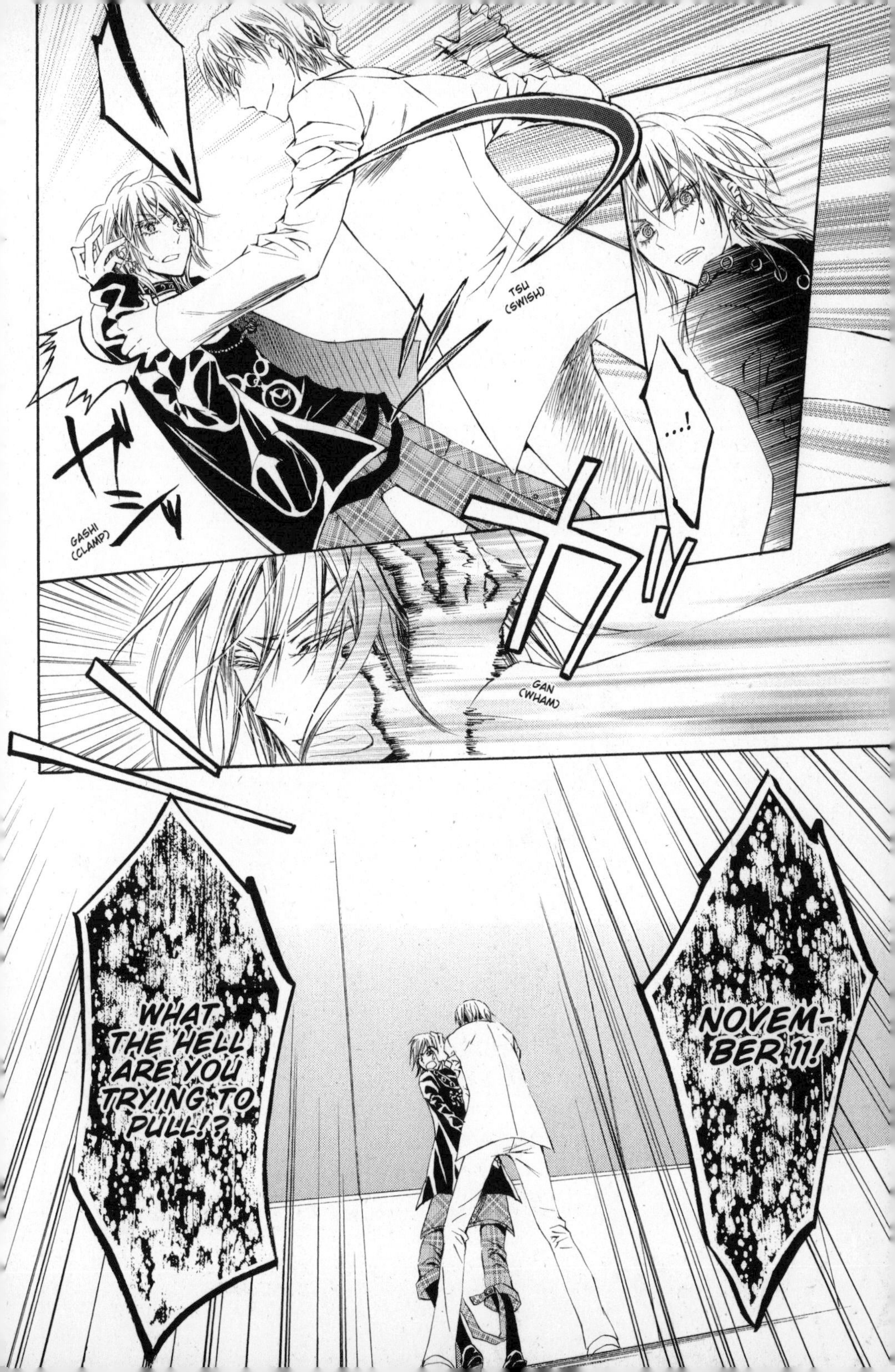
TSU (SWISH)
...!
GASHI (CLAMP)
GAN (WHAM)
NOVEM-BER 11!
WHAT THE HELL ARE YOU TRYING TO PULL!?

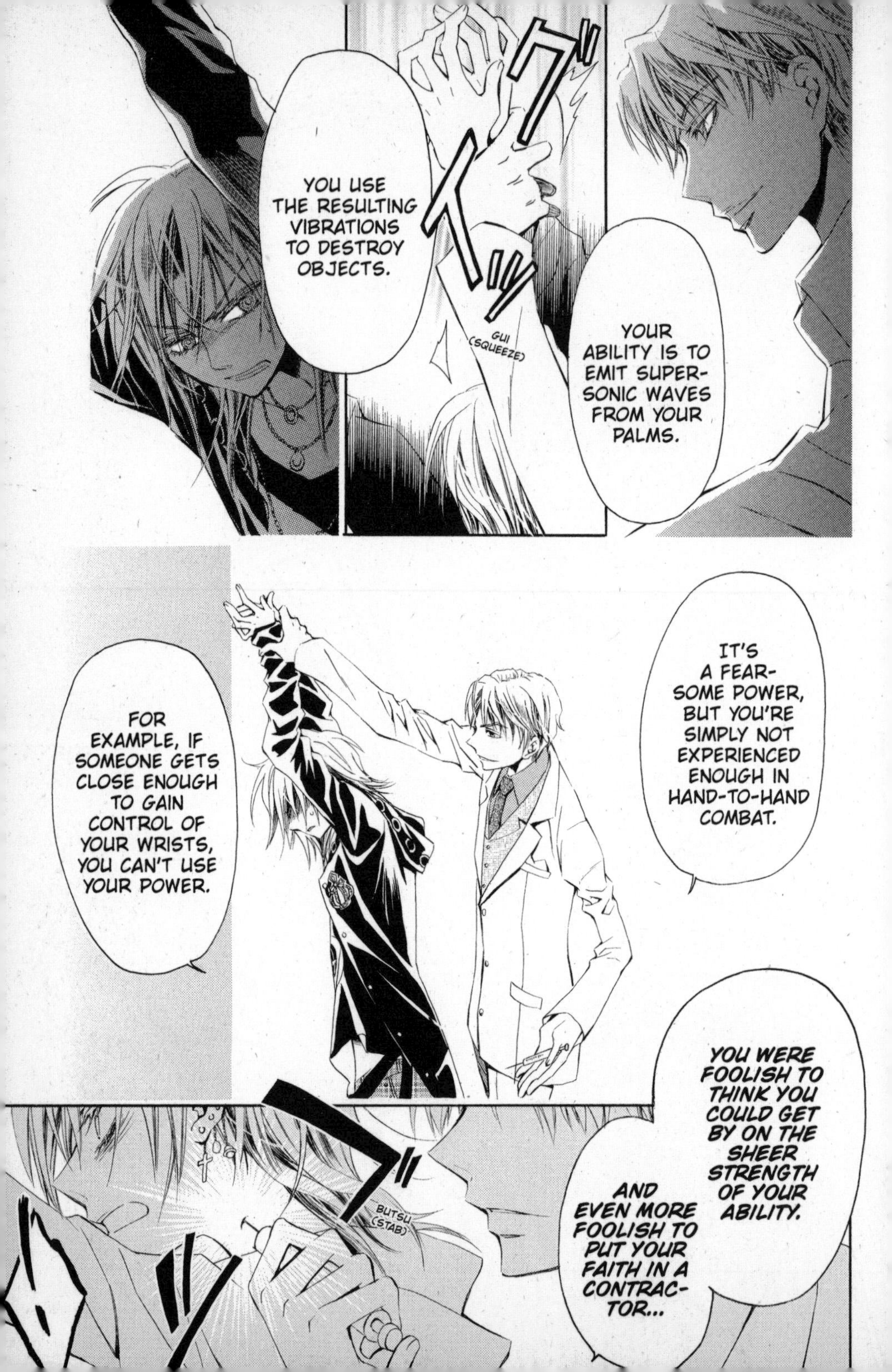
YOUR ABILITY IS TO EMIT SUPER-SONIC WAVES FROM YOUR PALMS.
GUI (SQUEEZE)
YOU USE THE RESULTING VIBRATIONS TO DESTROY OBJECTS.
IT'S A FEAR-SOME POWER, BUT YOU'RE SIMPLY NOT EXPERIENCED ENOUGH IN HAND-TO-HAND COMBAT.
FOR EXAMPLE, IF SOMEONE GETS CLOSE ENOUGH TO GAIN CONTROL OF YOUR WRISTS, YOU CAN'T USE YOUR POWER.
YOU WERE FOOLISH TO THINK YOU COULD GET BY ON THE SHEER STRENGTH OF YOUR ABILITY.
AND EVEN MORE FOOLISH TO PUT YOUR FAITH IN A CONTRAC-TOR...
BUTSU (STAB)

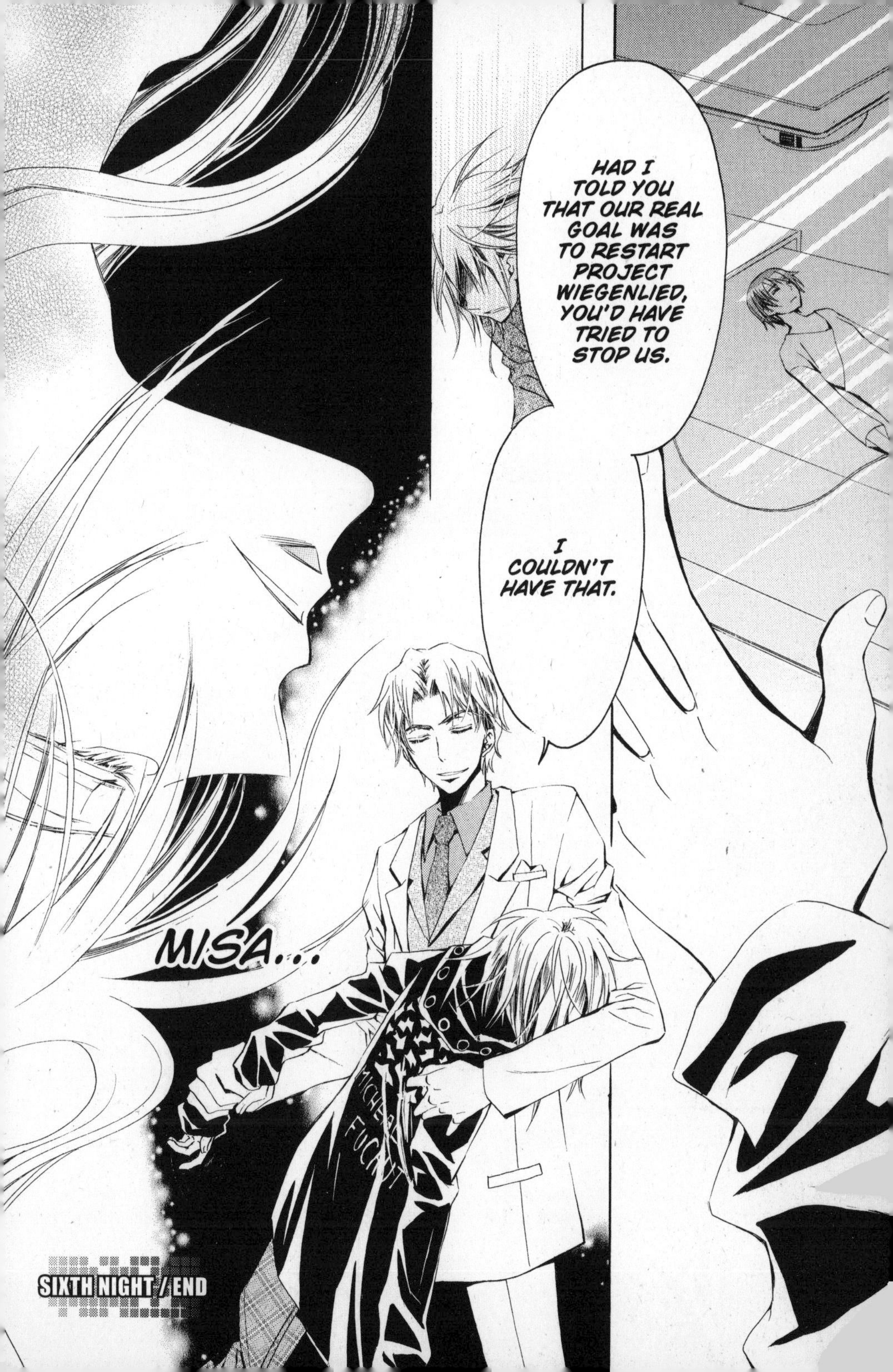
HAD I TOLD YOU THAT OUR REAL GOAL WAS TO RESTART PROJECT WIEGENLIED, YOU'D HAVE TRIED TO STOP US.
I COULDN'T HAVE THAT.
MISA...
SIXTH NIGHT / END

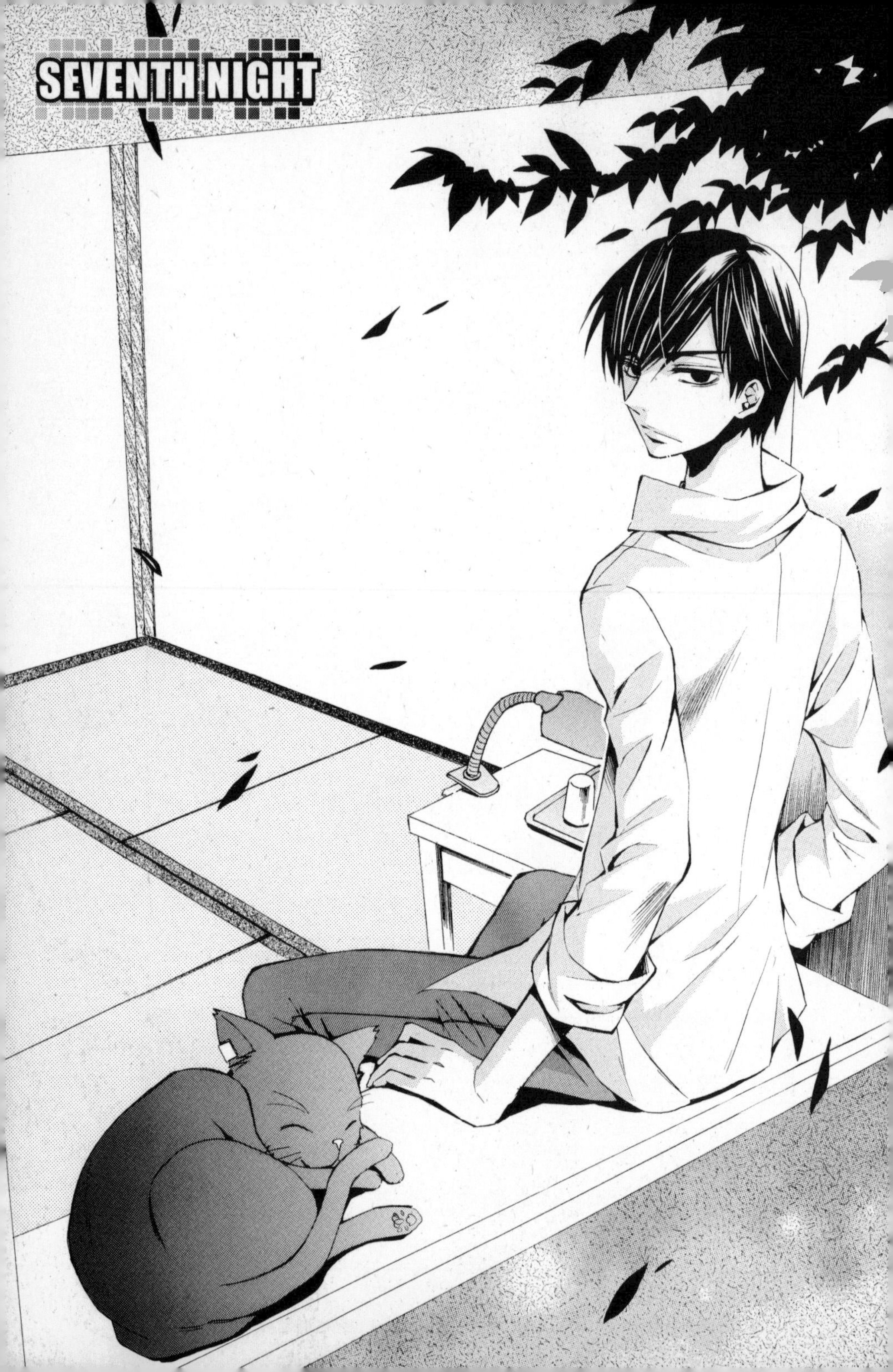
SEVENTH NIGHT

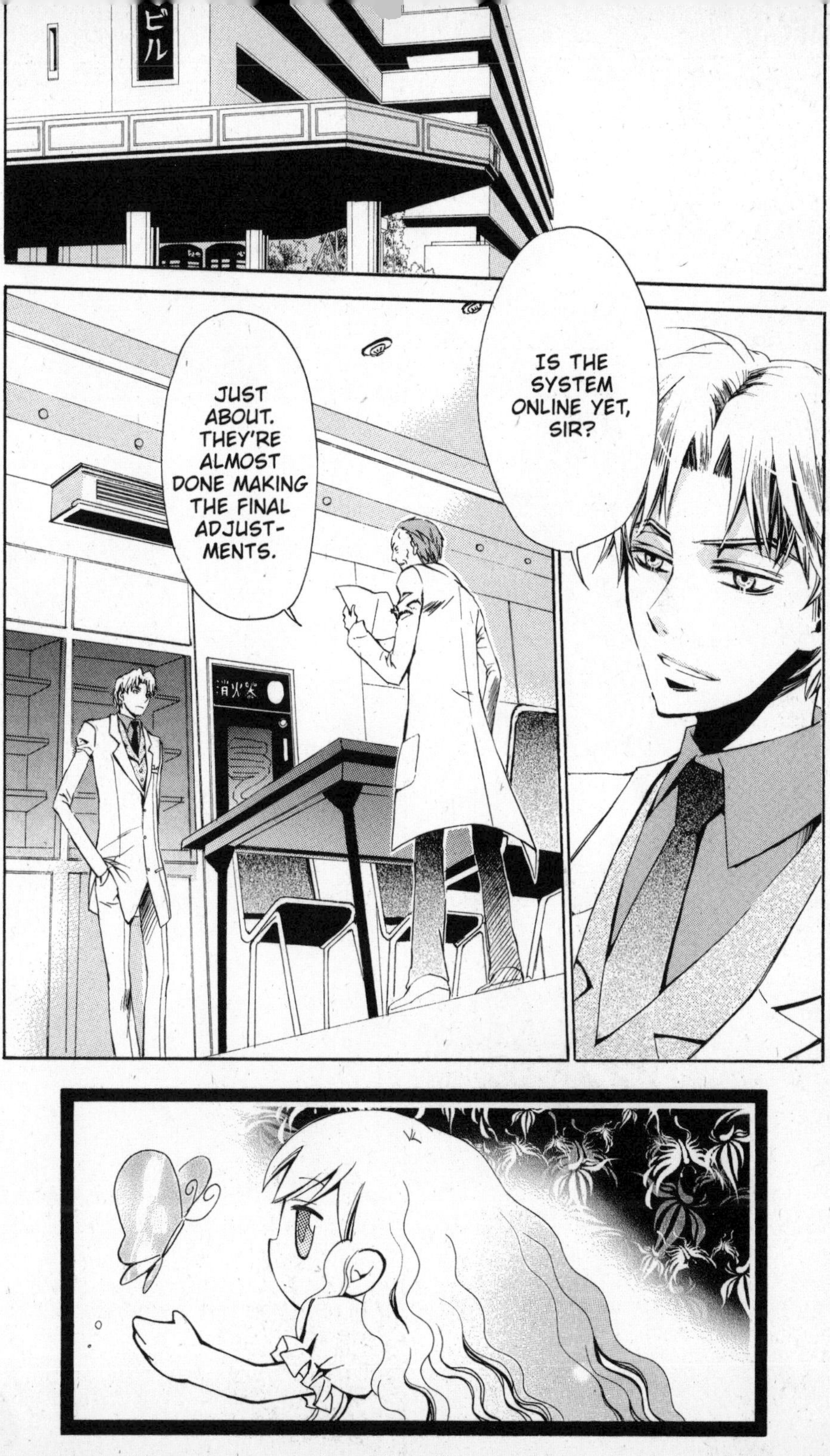
ビル
IS THE SYSTEM ONLINE YET, SIR?
JUST ABOUT. THEY'RE ALMOST DONE MAKING THE FINAL ADJUST-MENTS.

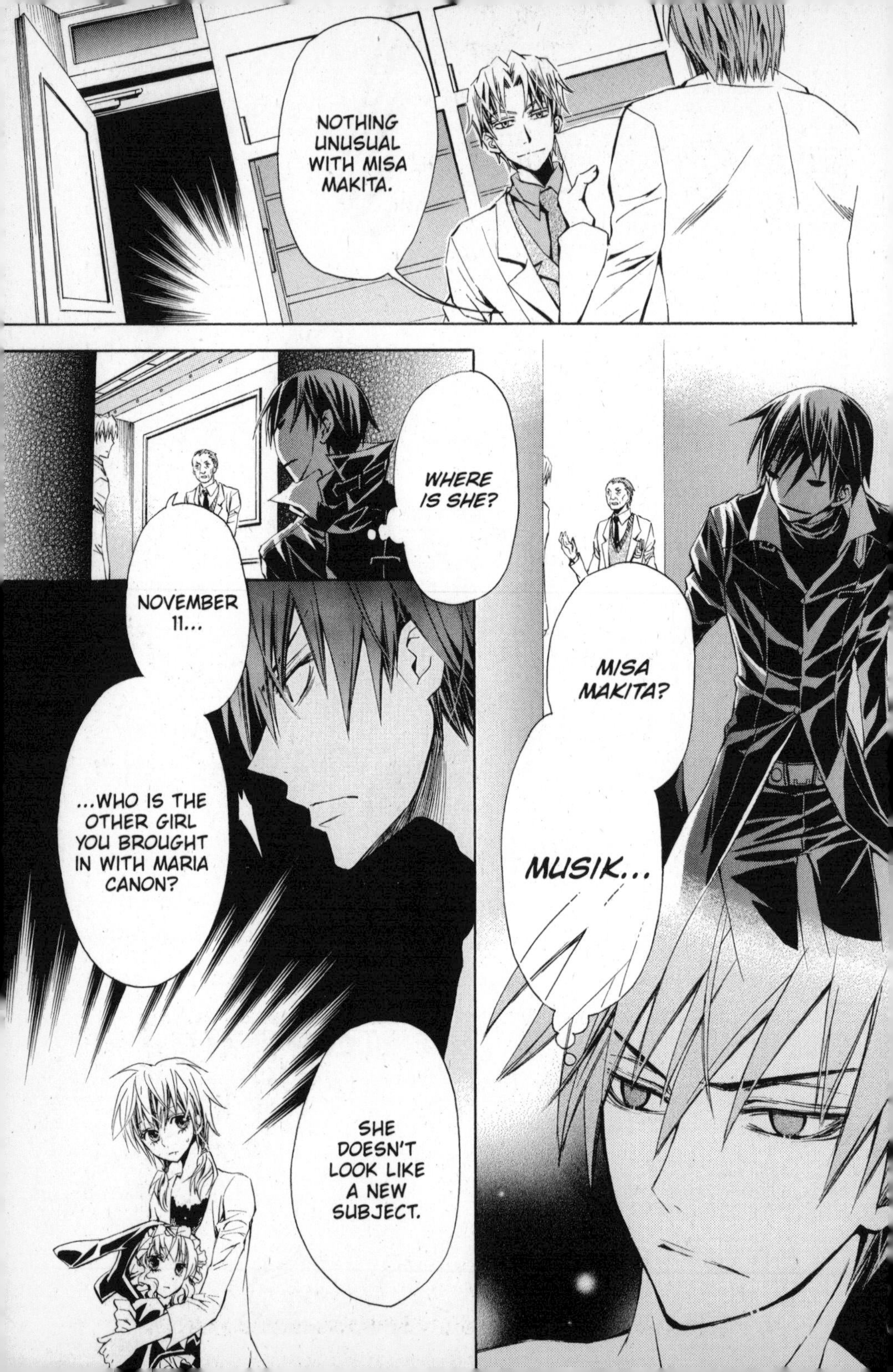
NOTHING UNUSUAL WITH MISA MAKITA.
MISA MAKITA?
MUSIK...
WHERE IS SHE?
NOVEMBER 11...
...WHO IS THE OTHER GIRL YOU BROUGHT IN WITH MARIA CANON?
SHE DOESN'T LOOK LIKE A NEW SUBJECT.

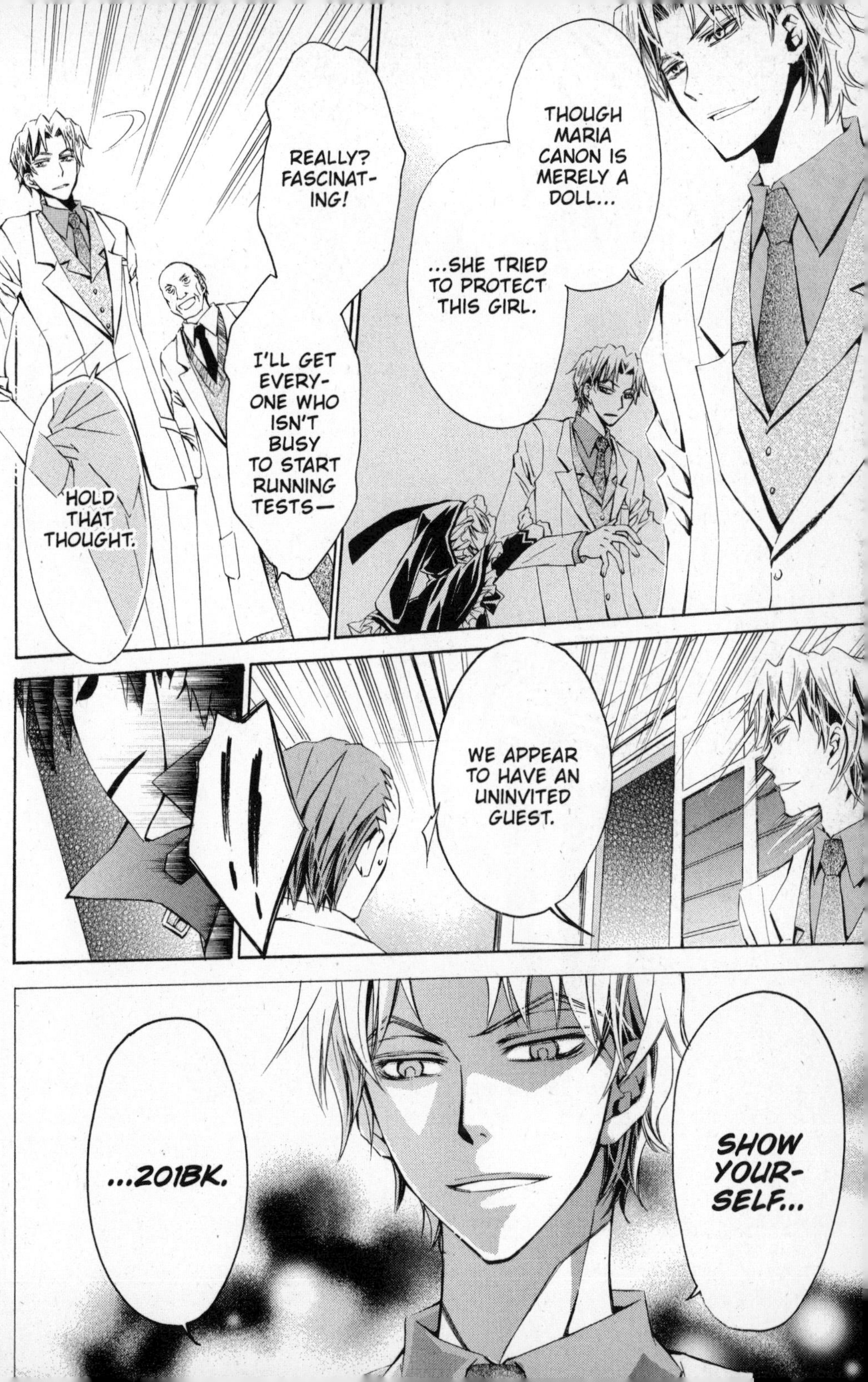
THOUGH MARIA CANON IS MERELY A DOLL...
...SHE TRIED TO PROTECT THIS GIRL.
REALLY? FASCINATING!
I'LL GET EVERYONE WHO ISN'T BUSY TO START RUNNING TESTS—
HOLD THAT THOUGHT.
WE APPEAR TO HAVE AN UNINVITED GUEST.
SHOW YOURSELF...
...201BK.

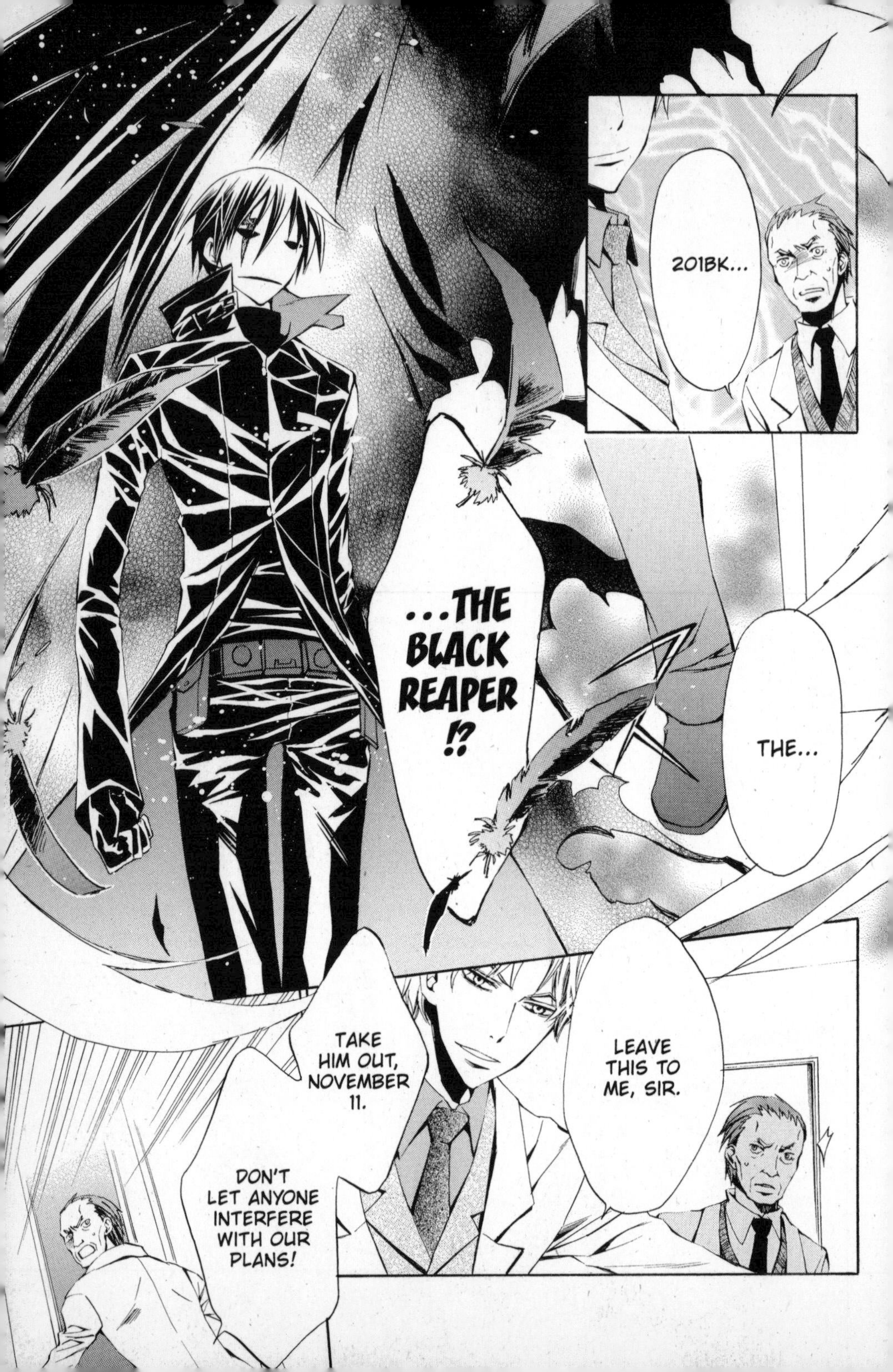
201BK...
THE...
...THE BLACK REAPER!?
TAKE HIM OUT, NOVEMBER 11.
DON'T LET ANYONE INTERFERE WITH OUR PLANS!
LEAVE THIS TO ME, SIR.

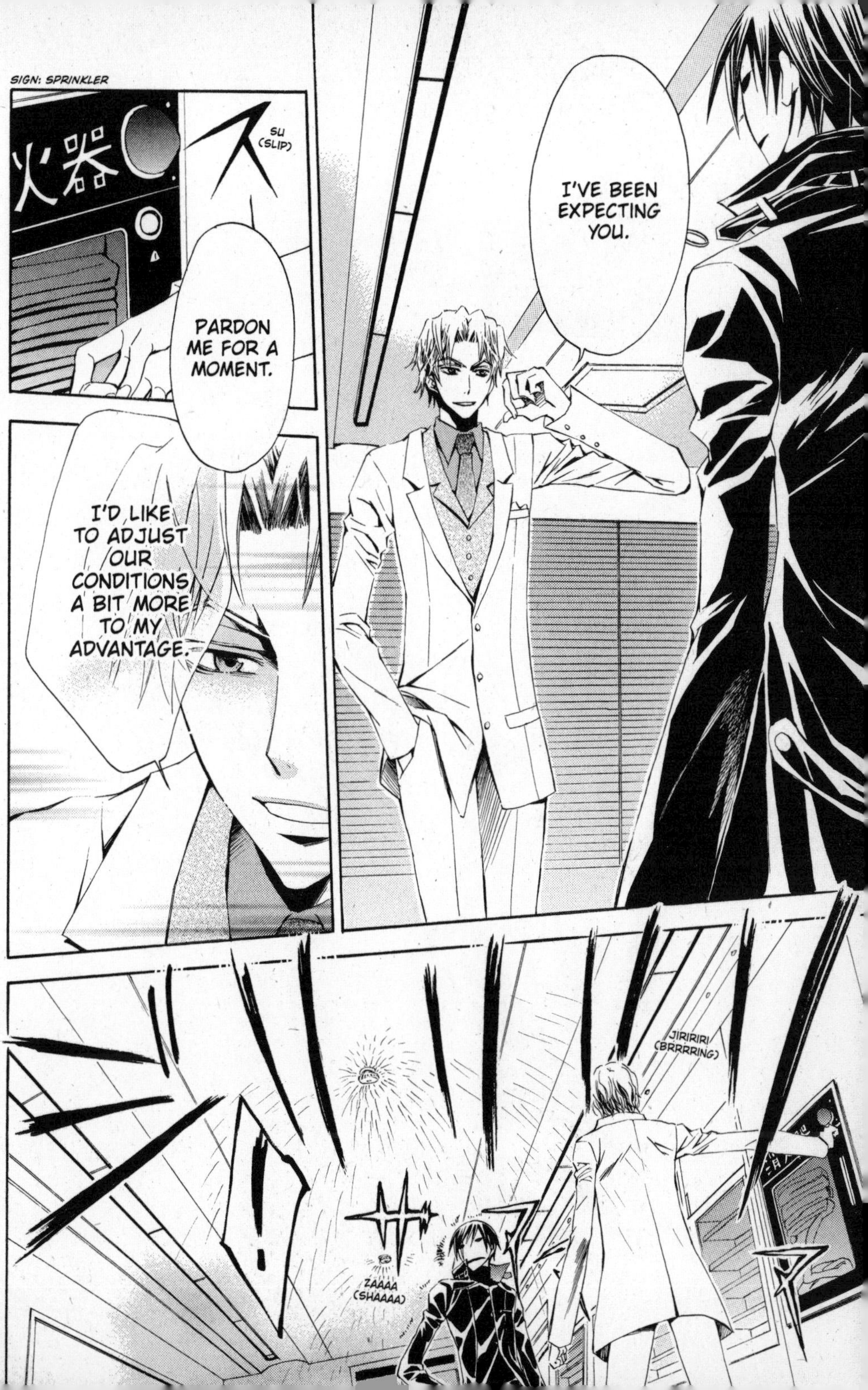
I'VE BEEN EXPECTING YOU.
SIGN: SPRINKLER
SU (SLIP)
PARDON ME FOR A MOMENT.
I'D LIKE TO ADJUST OUR CONDITIONS A BIT MORE TO MY ADVANTAGE.
JIRIRIRI (BRRRRING)
ZAAAA (SHAAAA)

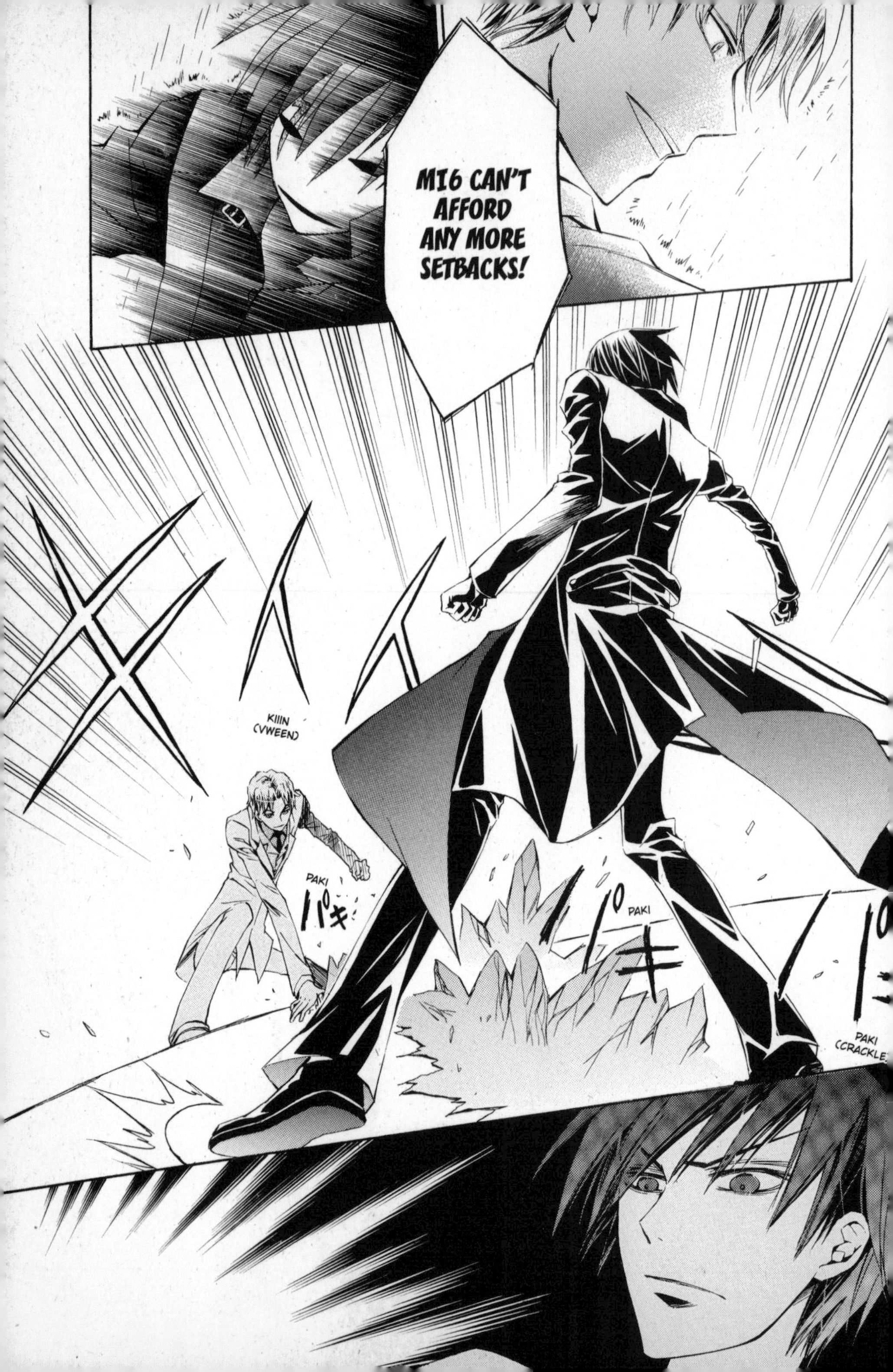
MI6 CAN'T AFFORD ANY MORE SETBACKS!
KIIIN (VWEEN)
PAKI
パキ
PAKI
パキ
PAKI (CRACKLE)

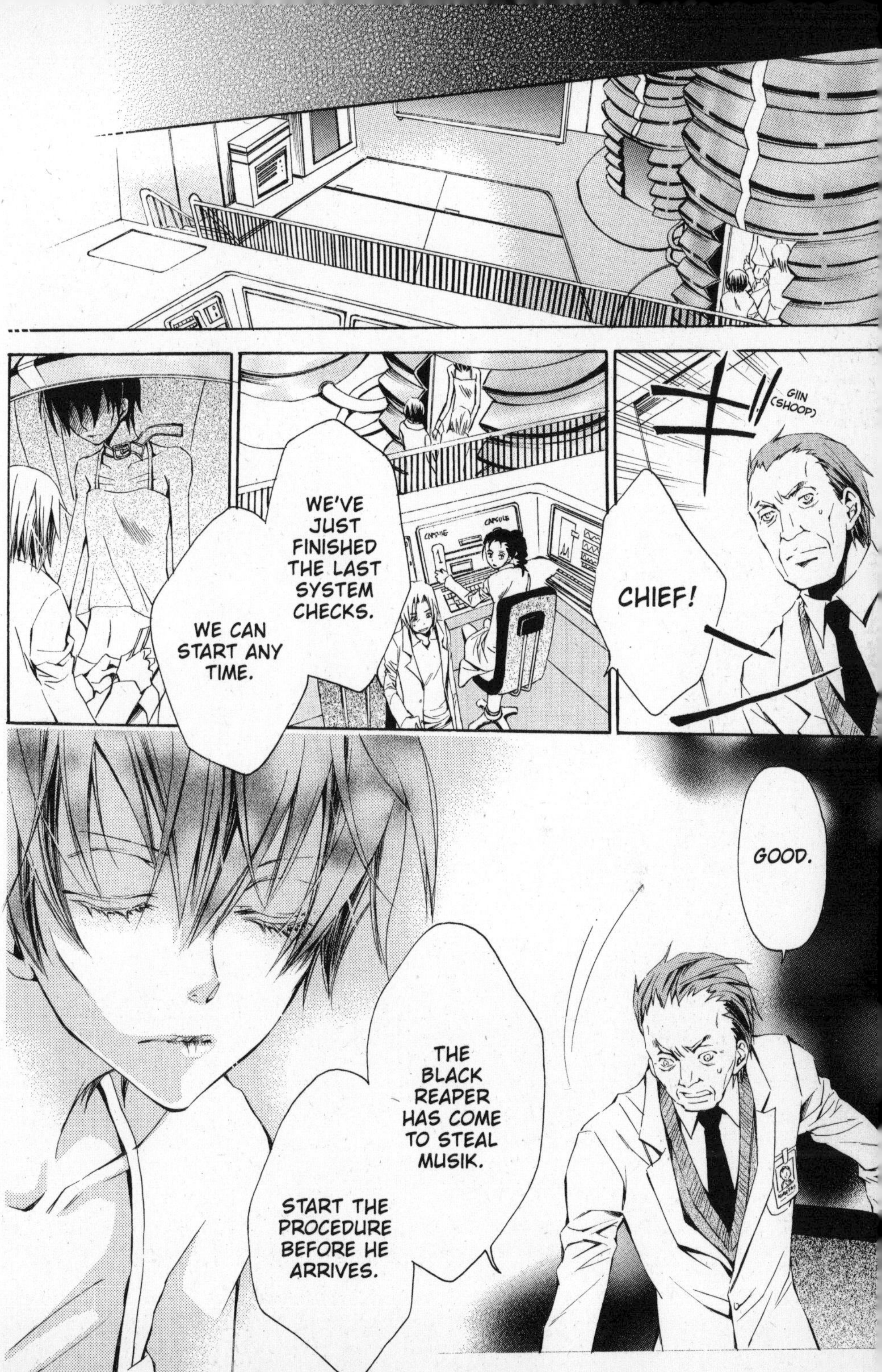
GIIN (SHOOP)
CHIEF!
WE'VE JUST FINISHED THE LAST SYSTEM CHECKS.
WE CAN START ANY TIME.
GOOD.
THE BLACK REAPER HAS COME TO STEAL MUSIK.
START THE PROCEDURE BEFORE HE ARRIVES.

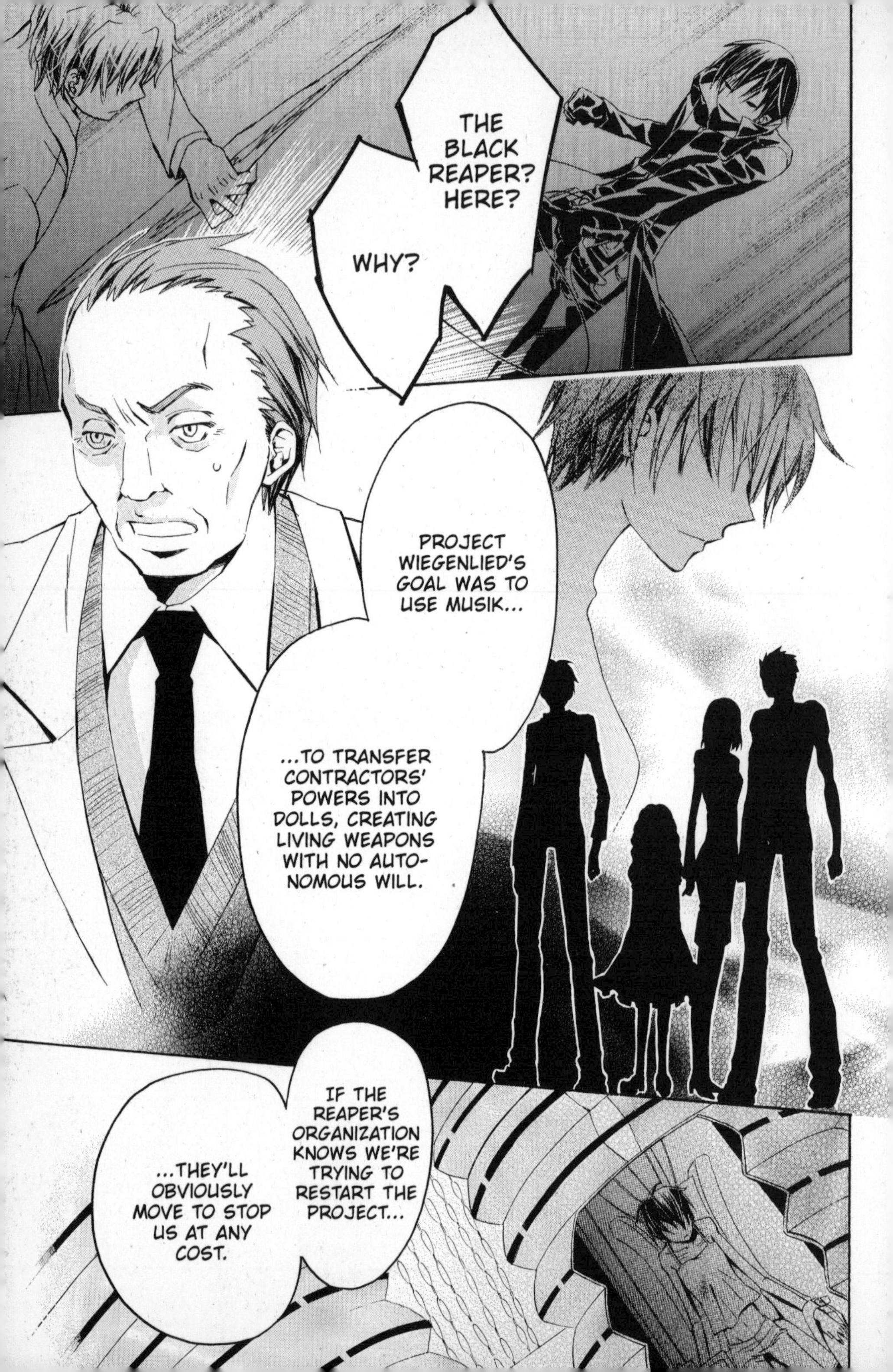
THE BLACK REAPER? HERE?
WHY?
PROJECT WIEGENLIED'S GOAL WAS TO USE MUSIK...
...TO TRANSFER CONTRACTORS' POWERS INTO DOLLS, CREATING LIVING WEAPONS WITH NO AUTO-NOMOUS WILL.
IF THE REAPER'S ORGANIZATION KNOWS WE'RE TRYING TO RESTART THE PROJECT...
...THEY'LL OBVIOUSLY MOVE TO STOP US AT ANY COST.

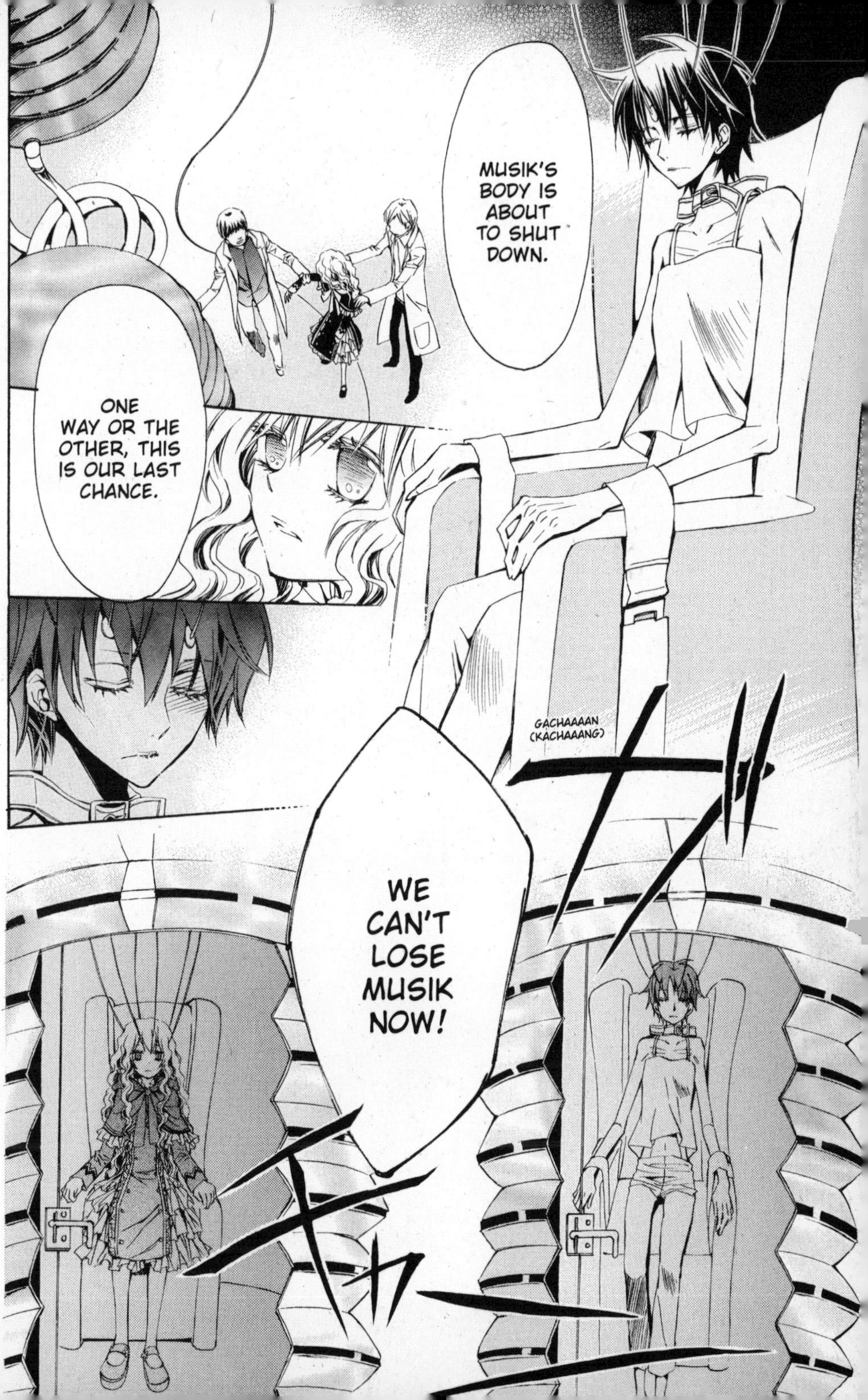
MUSIK'S BODY IS ABOUT TO SHUT DOWN.
ONE WAY OR THE OTHER, THIS IS OUR LAST CHANCE.
GACHAAAAN (KACHAAANG)
WE CAN'T LOSE MUSIK NOW!

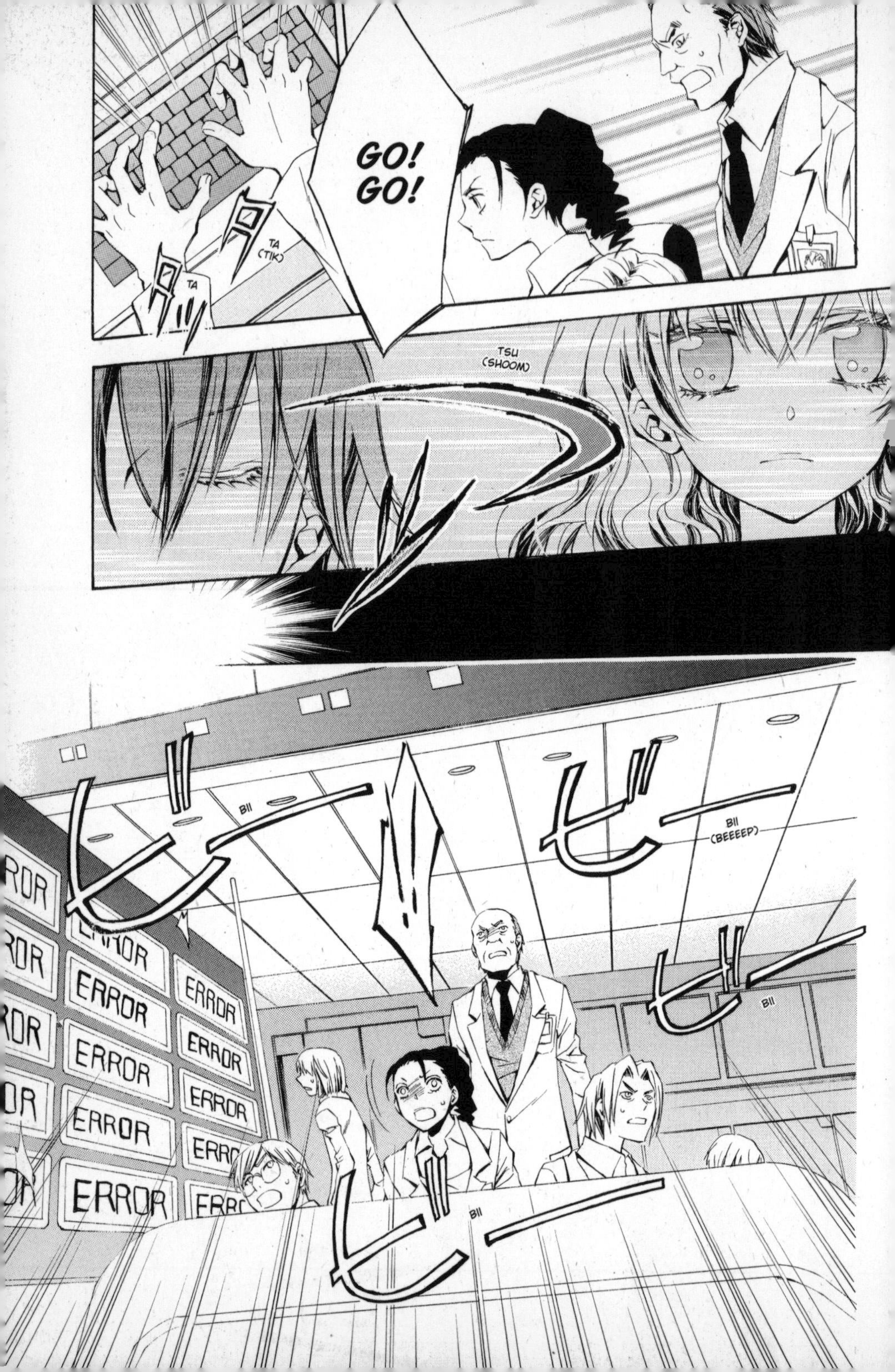
GO! GO!
TA (TIK)
TA
TSU (SHOOM)
BII (BEEEEP)
BII
BII
ERROR
ERROR
ERROR
ERROR
ERROR
ERROR
ERROR
ERROR
ERROR
BII

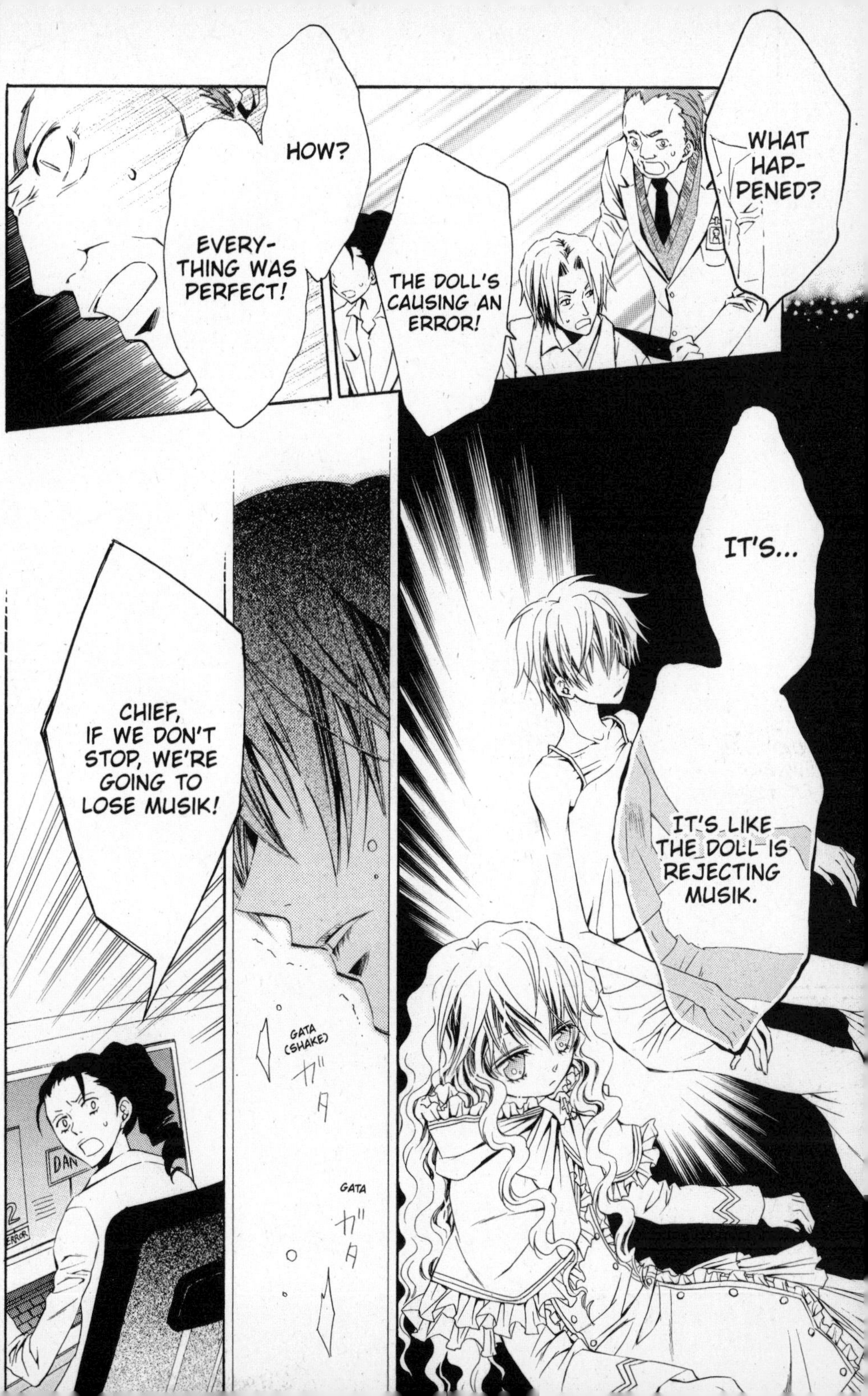
WHAT HAP-PENED?
THE DOLL'S CAUSING AN ERROR!
HOW?
EVERY-THING WAS PERFECT!
IT'S...
IT'S LIKE THE DOLL IS REJECTING MUSIK.
GATA (SHAKE)
ガタ
GATA
ガタ
CHIEF, IF WE DON'T STOP, WE'RE GOING TO LOSE MUSIK!

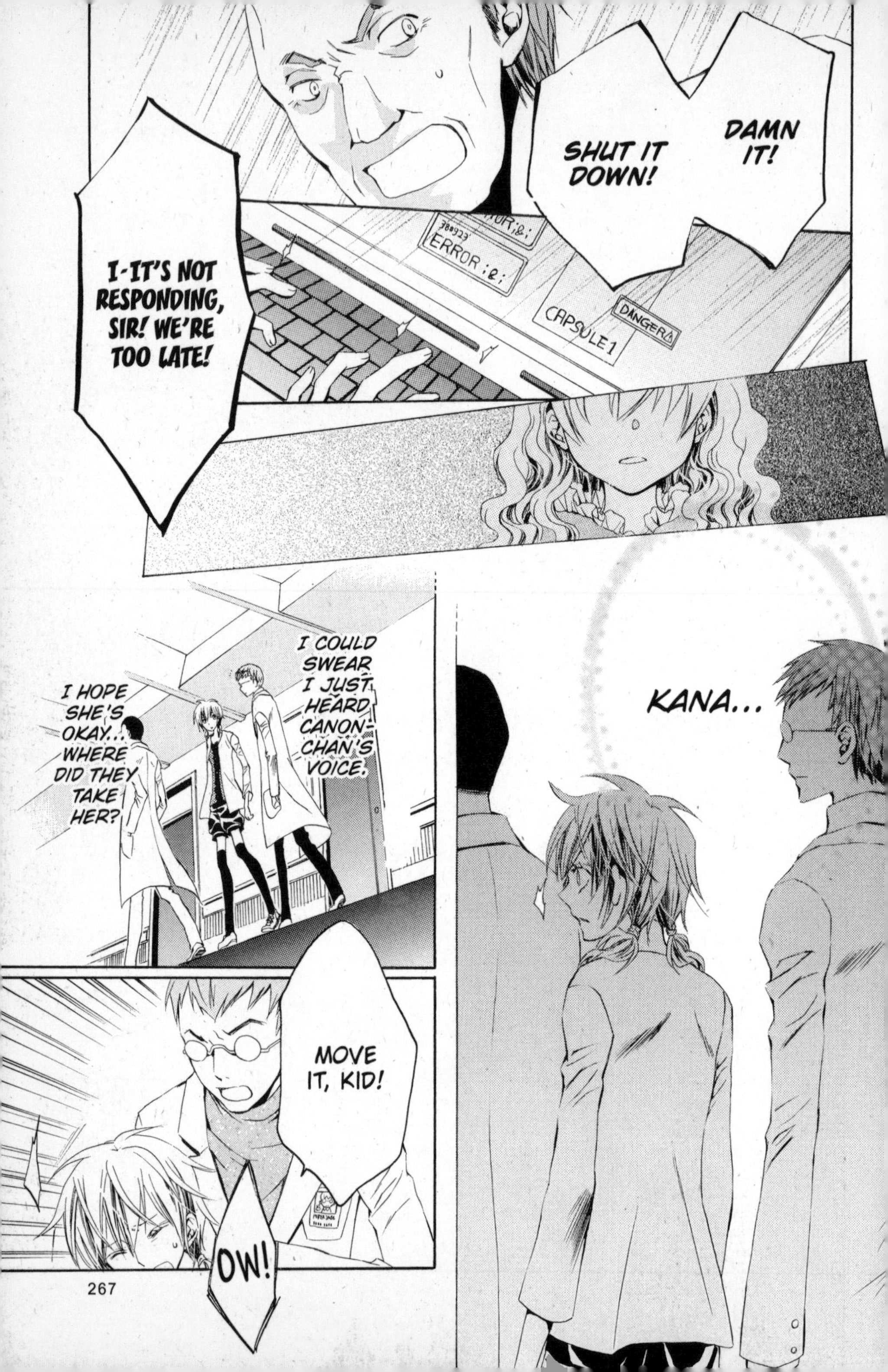
SHUT IT DOWN! DAMN IT!
ERROR
CAPSULE 1
DANGER
I-IT'S NOT RESPONDING, SIR! WE'RE TOO LATE!
KANA...
I COULD SWEAR I JUST HEARD CANON-CHAN'S VOICE.
I HOPE SHE'S OKAY... WHERE DID THEY TAKE HER?
MOVE IT, KID!
OW!

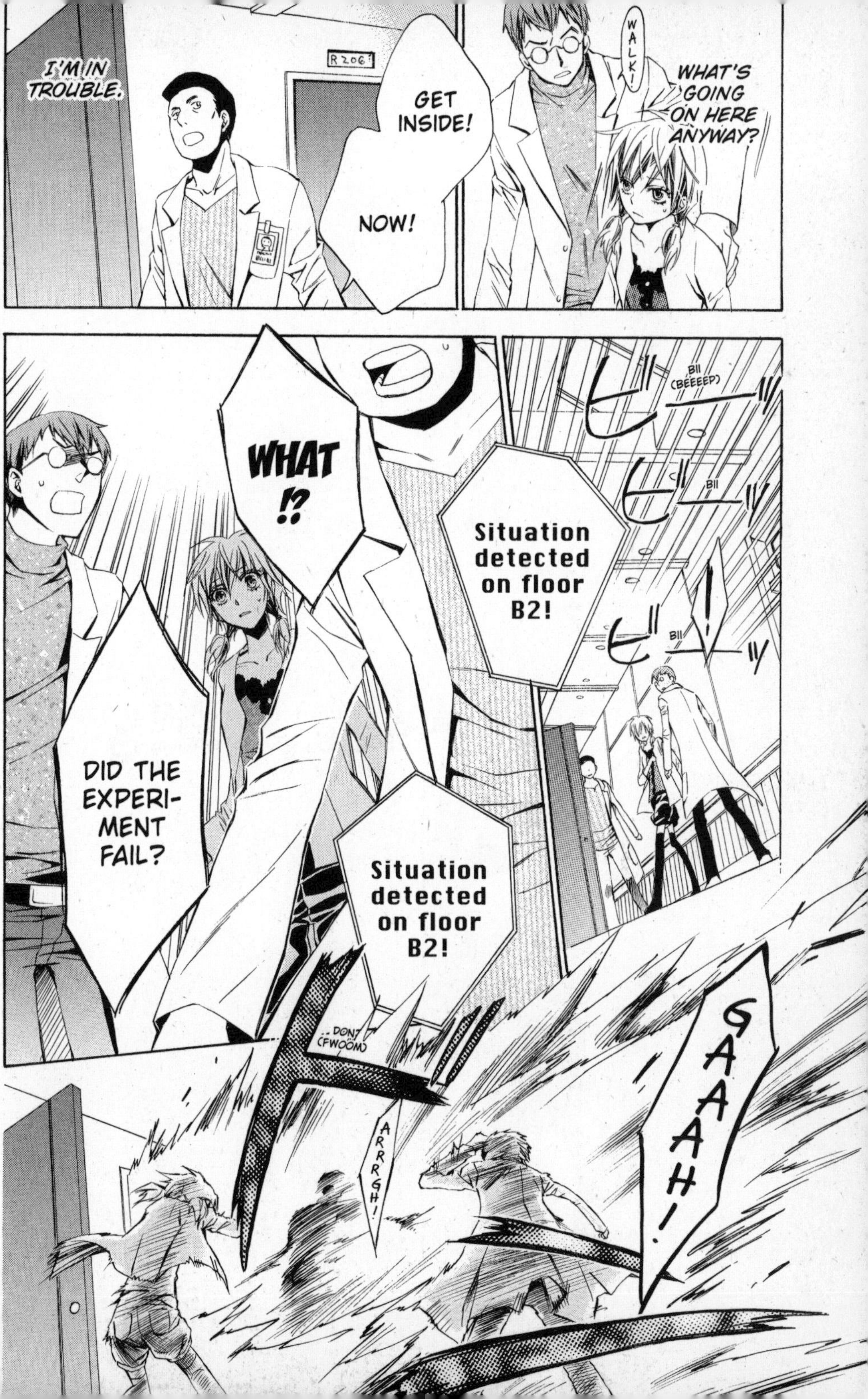
WALK!
WHAT'S GOING ON HERE ANYWAY?
GET INSIDE!
NOW!
R206
I'M IN TROUBLE.
BII (BEEEEP)
WHAT!?
Situation detected on floor B2!
BII
BII
Situation detected on floor B2!
DID THE EXPERIMENT FAIL?
.. DON (FWOOM)
GAAAH!
ARRRGH!

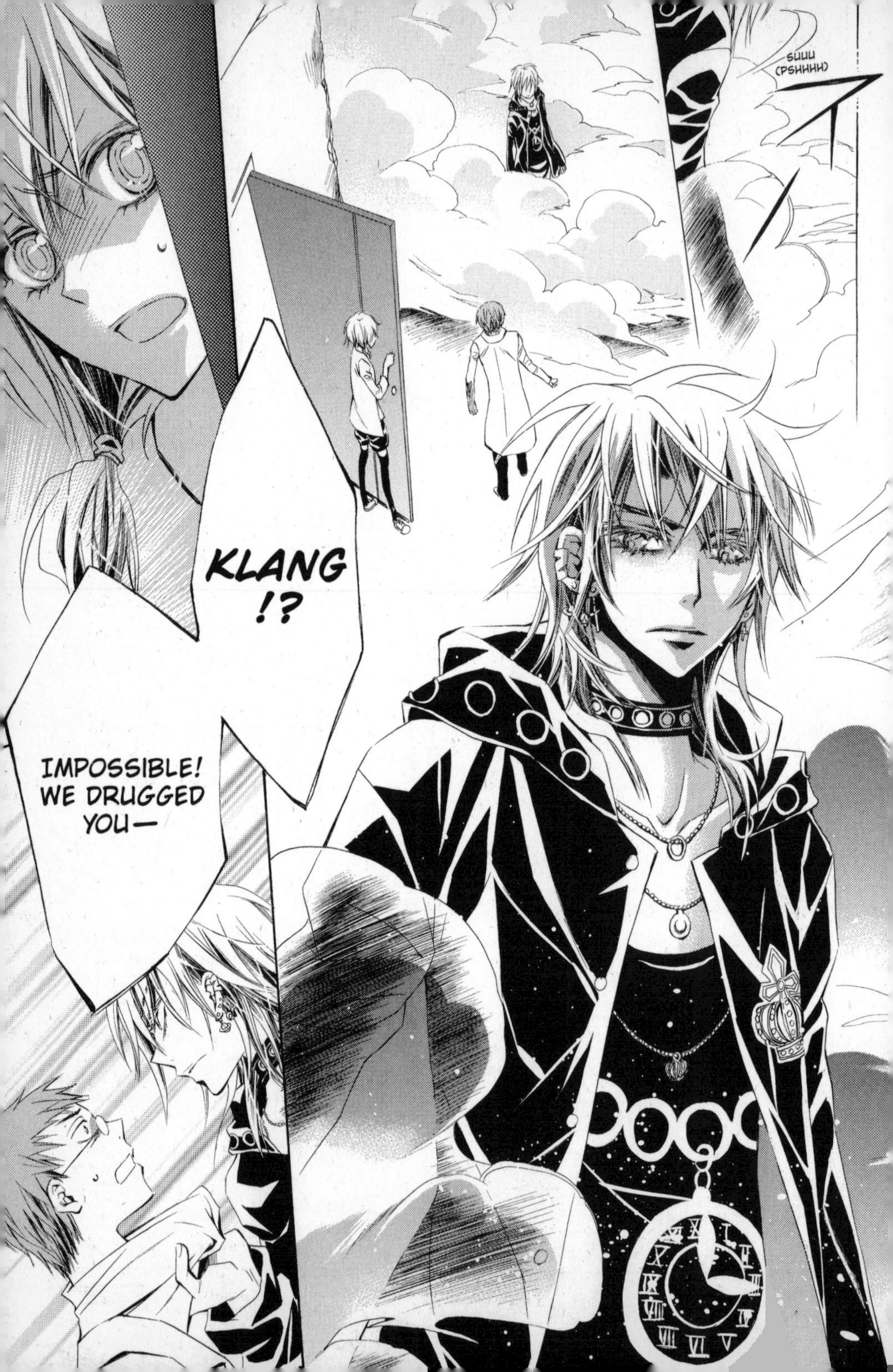
SUUU (PSHHHH)
KLANG !?
IMPOSSIBLE! WE DRUGGED YOU—

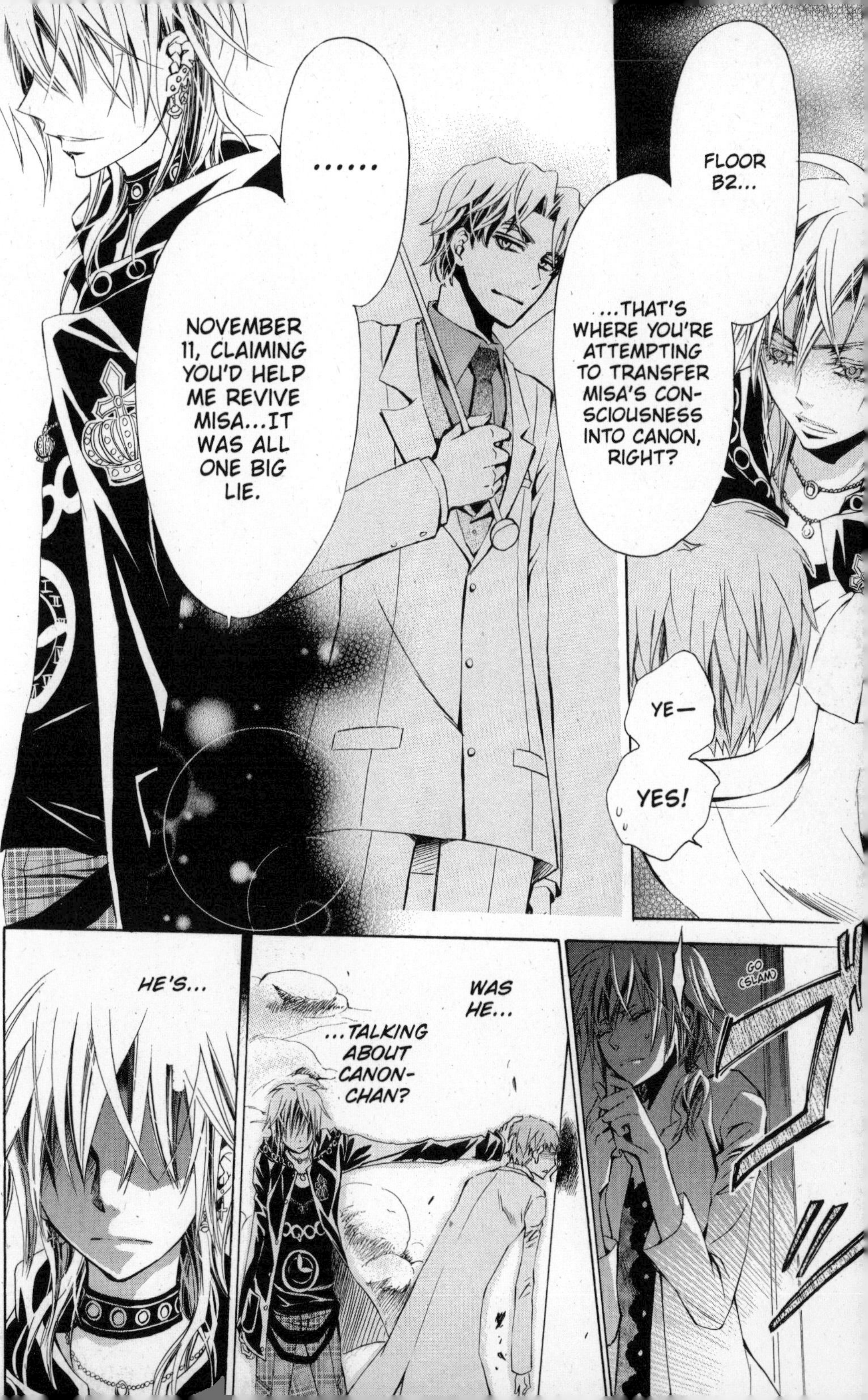
FLOOR B2...
...THAT'S WHERE YOU'RE ATTEMPTING TO TRANSFER MISA'S CONSCIOUSNESS INTO CANON, RIGHT?
YE—
YES!
......
NOVEMBER 11, CLAIMING YOU'D HELP ME REVIVE MISA...IT WAS ALL ONE BIG LIE.
GO (SLAM)
WAS HE...
...TALKING ABOUT CANON-CHAN?
HE'S...

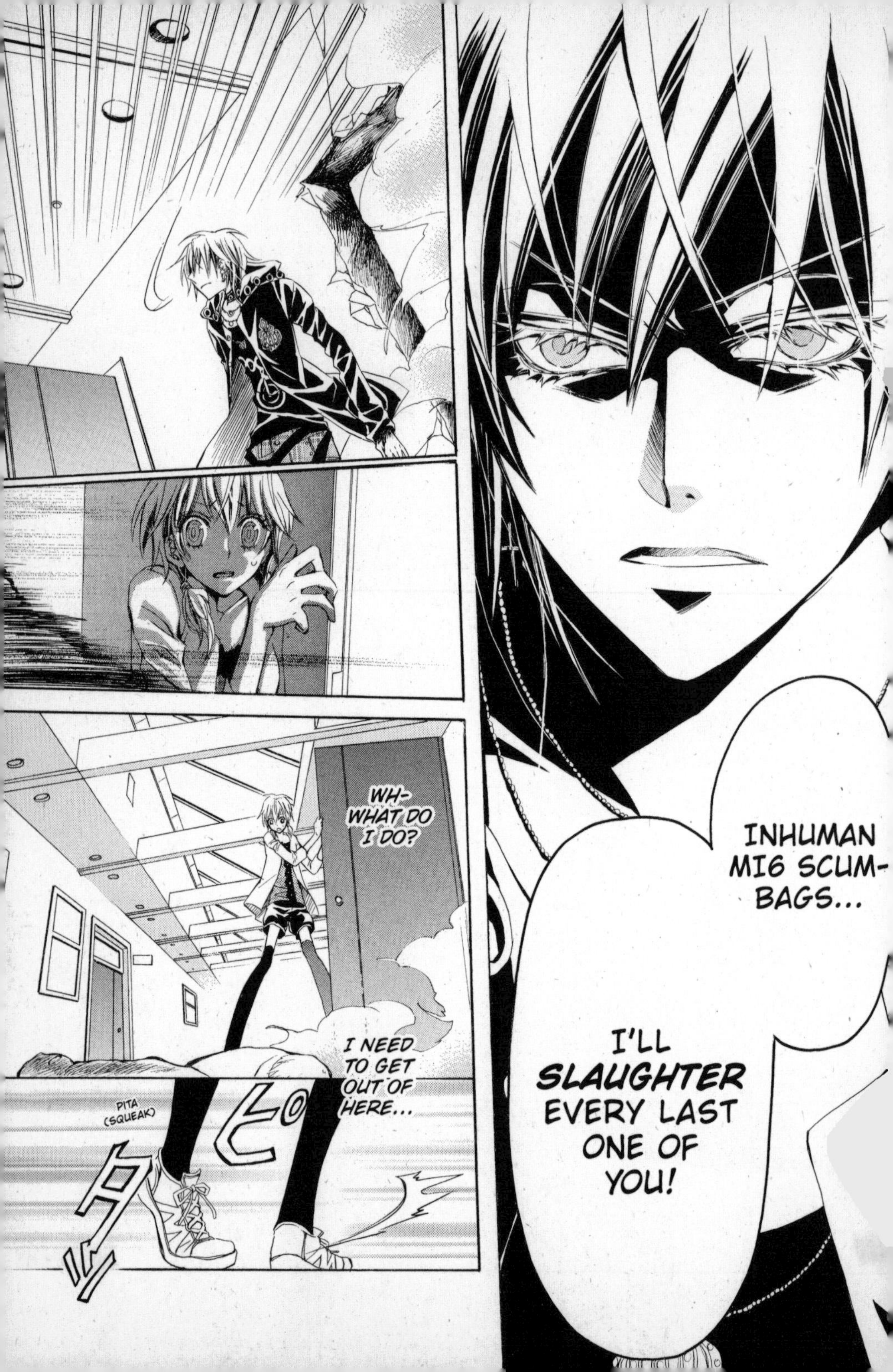
INHUMAN MI6 SCUM-BAGS...
I'LL *SLAUGHTER* EVERY LAST ONE OF YOU!
WH- WHAT DO I DO?
I NEED TO GET OUT OF HERE...
PITA (SQUEAK)

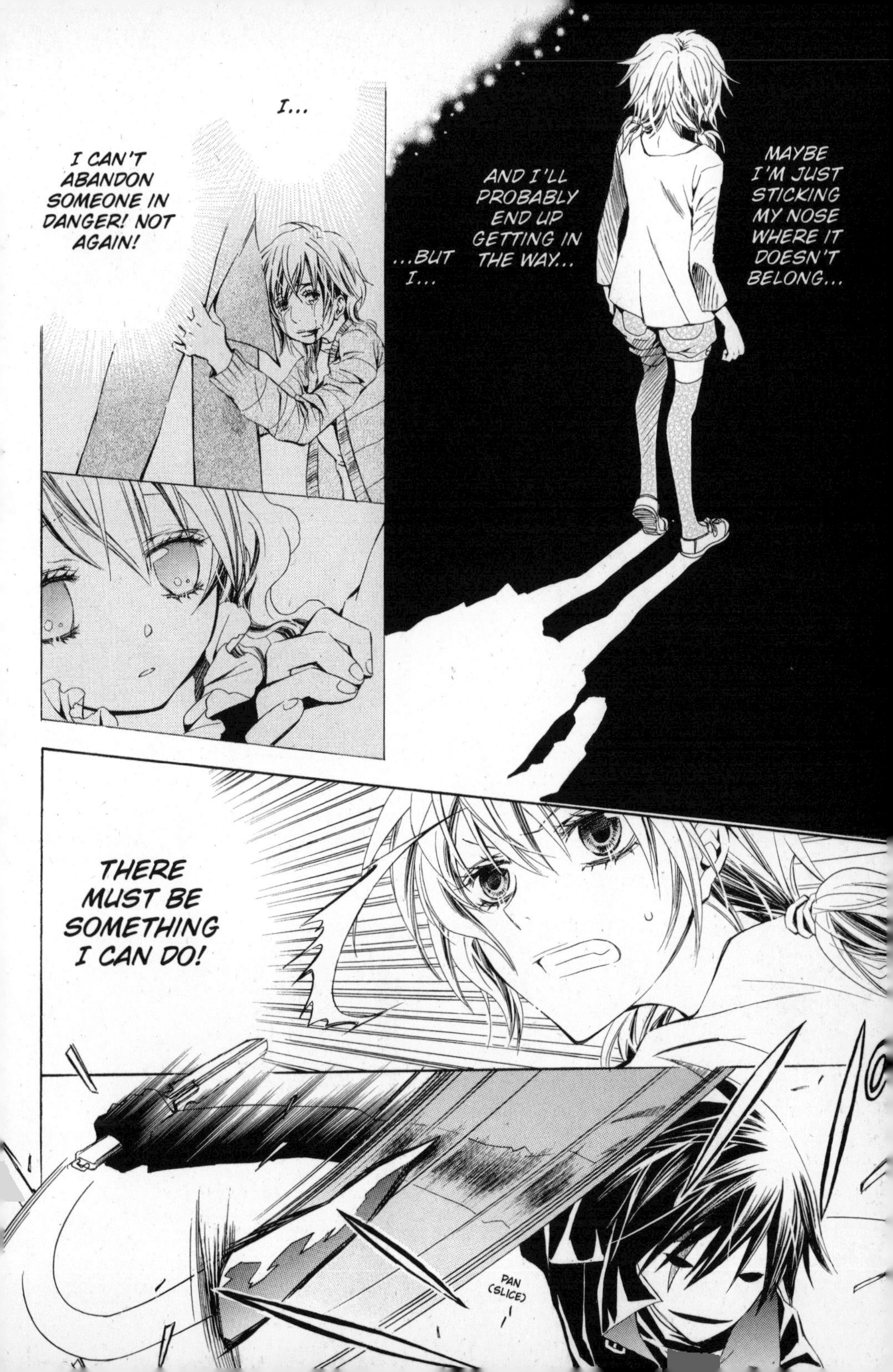
MAYBE I'M JUST STICKING MY NOSE WHERE IT DOESN'T BELONG...
AND I'LL PROBABLY END UP GETTING IN THE WAY...
...BUT I...
I...
I CAN'T ABANDON SOMEONE IN DANGER! NOT AGAIN!
THERE MUST BE SOMETHING I CAN DO!
PAN (SLICE)

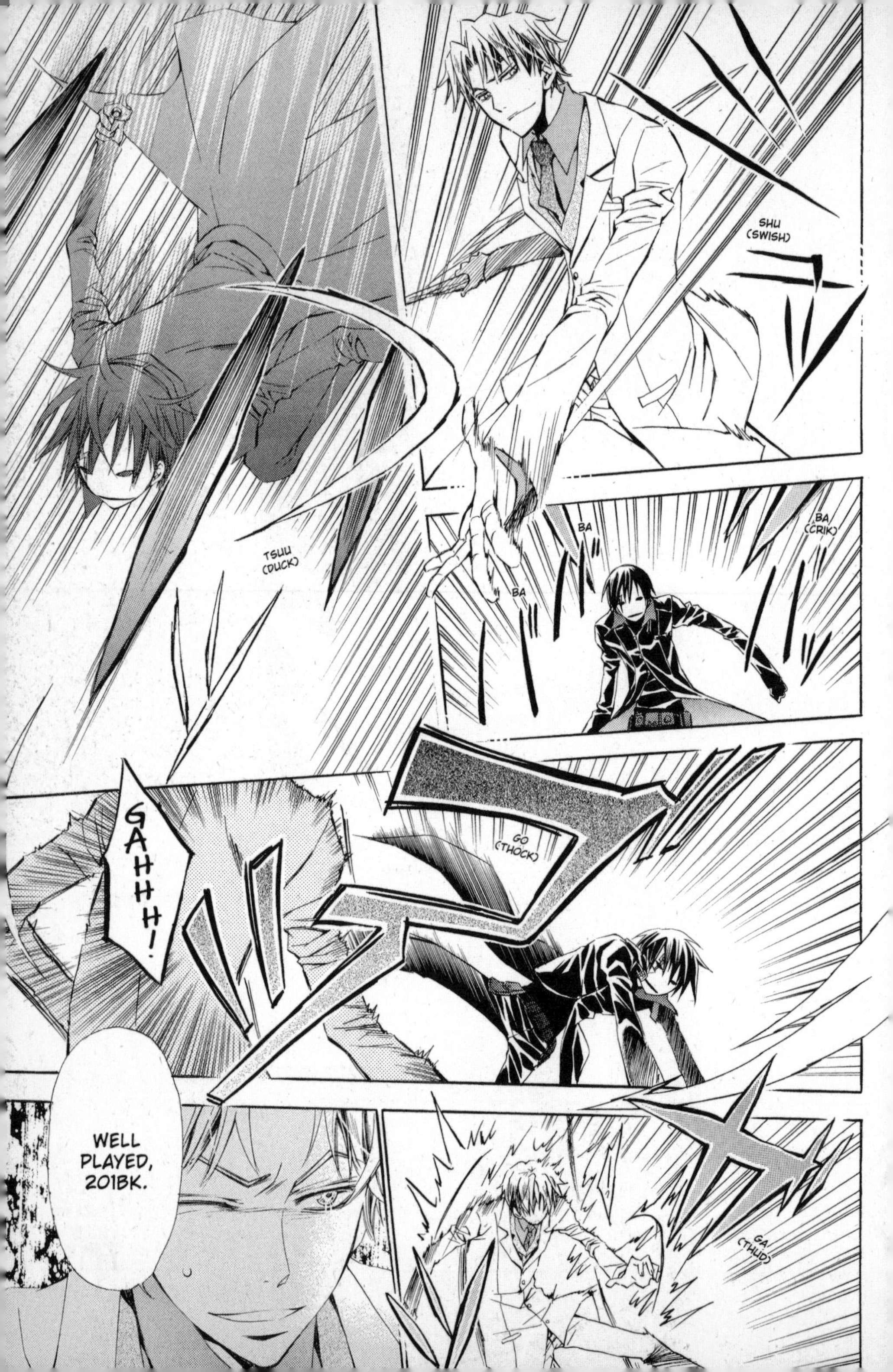
SHU (SWISH)
BA (CRIK)
BA
BA
TSUU (DUCK)
GO (THOCK)
GAHHH!
GA (THUD)
WELL PLAYED, 201BK.

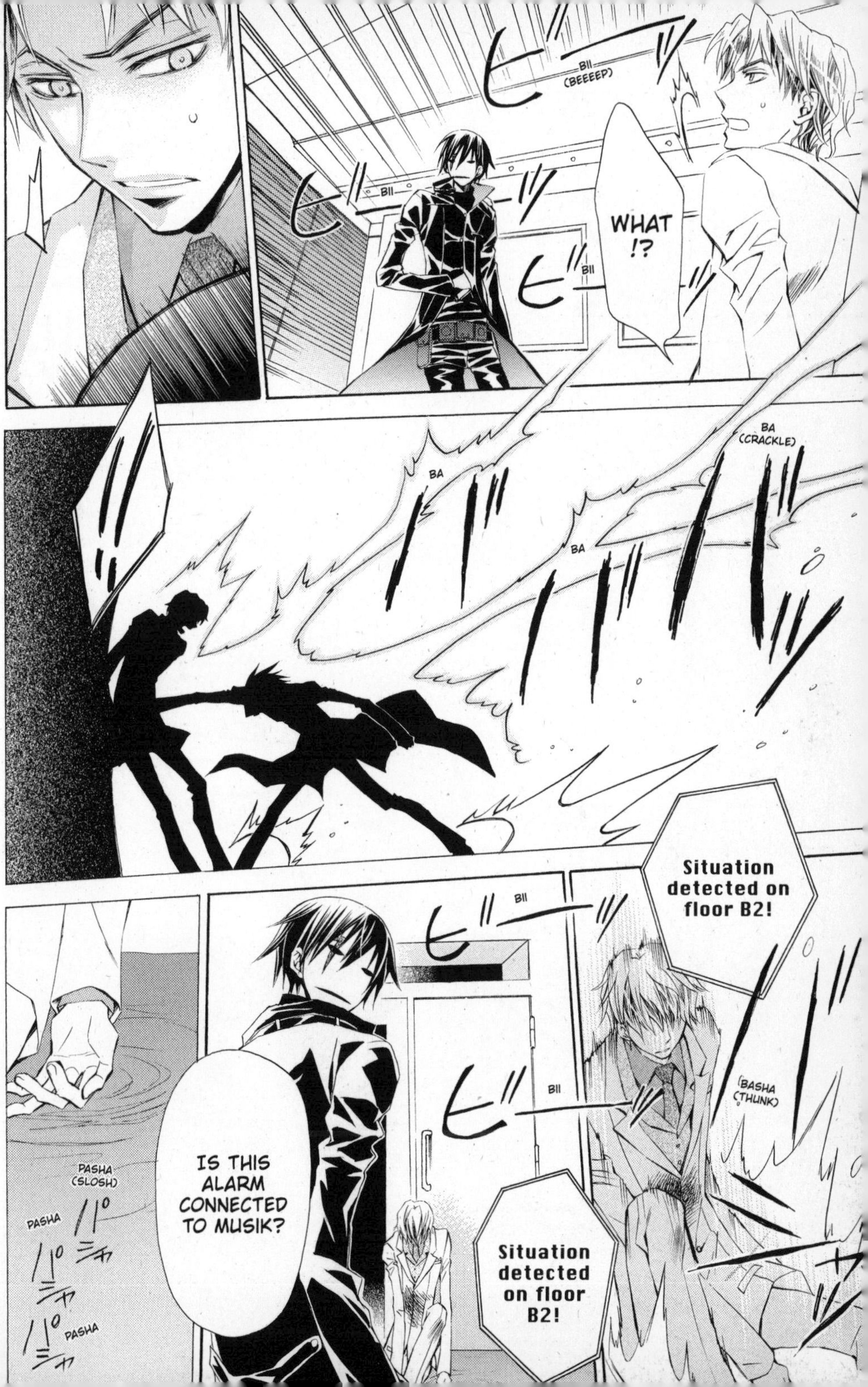
BII (BEEEEP)
WHAT !?
BII
BII
BA (CRACKLE)
BA
BA
Situation detected on floor B2!
BASHA (THUNK)
BII
BII
IS THIS ALARM CONNECTED TO MUSIK?
Situation detected on floor B2!
PASHA (SLOSH)
PASHA
PASHA

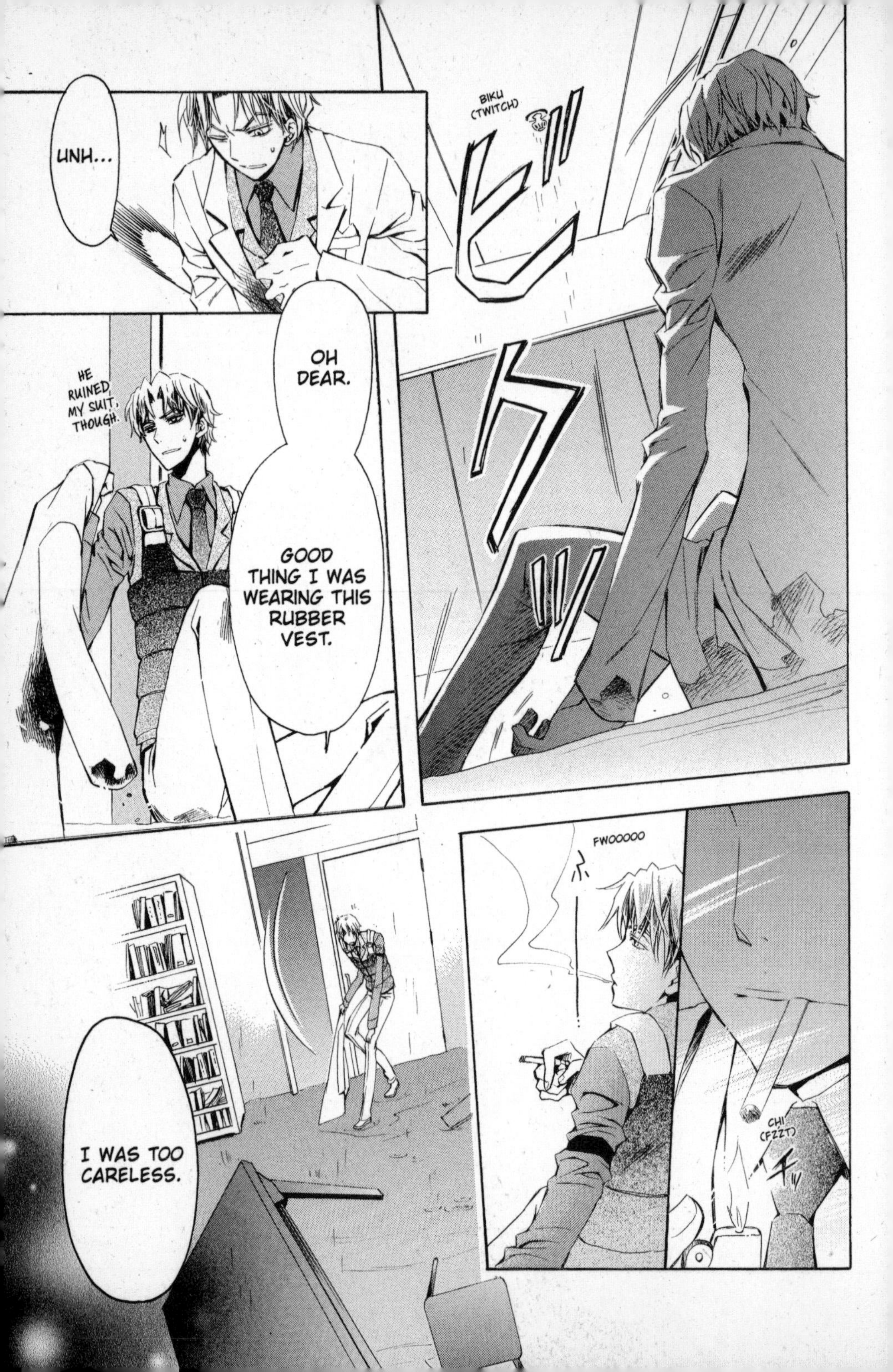
BIKU
(TWITCH)
ビクッ
UNH...
OH DEAR.
GOOD THING I WAS WEARING THIS RUBBER VEST.
HE RUINED MY SUIT, THOUGH.
FWOOOOO
ふー
CHI
(FZZT)
チッ
I WAS TOO CARELESS.

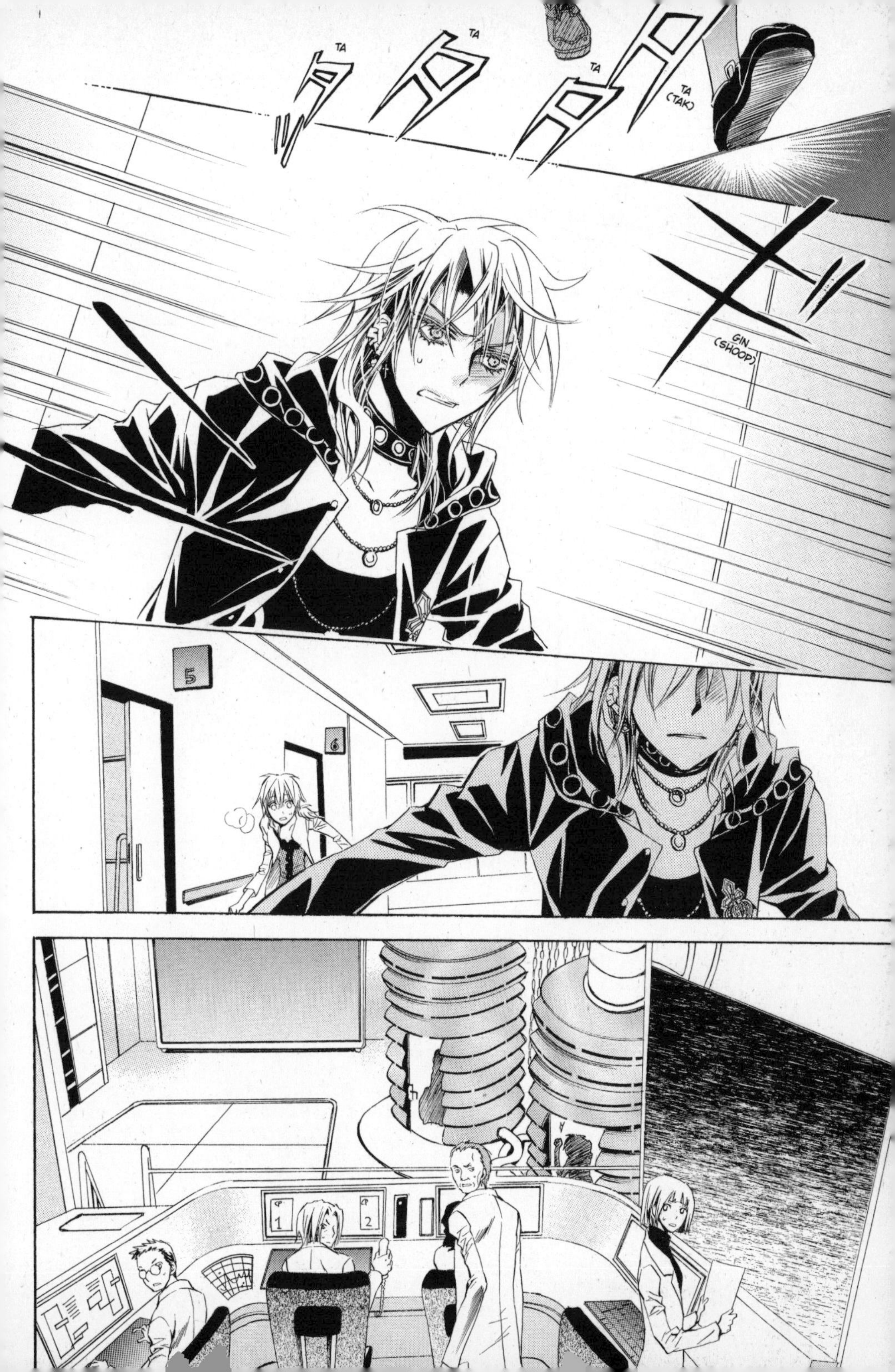

TA TA TA TA (TAK)
GIN (SHOOP)

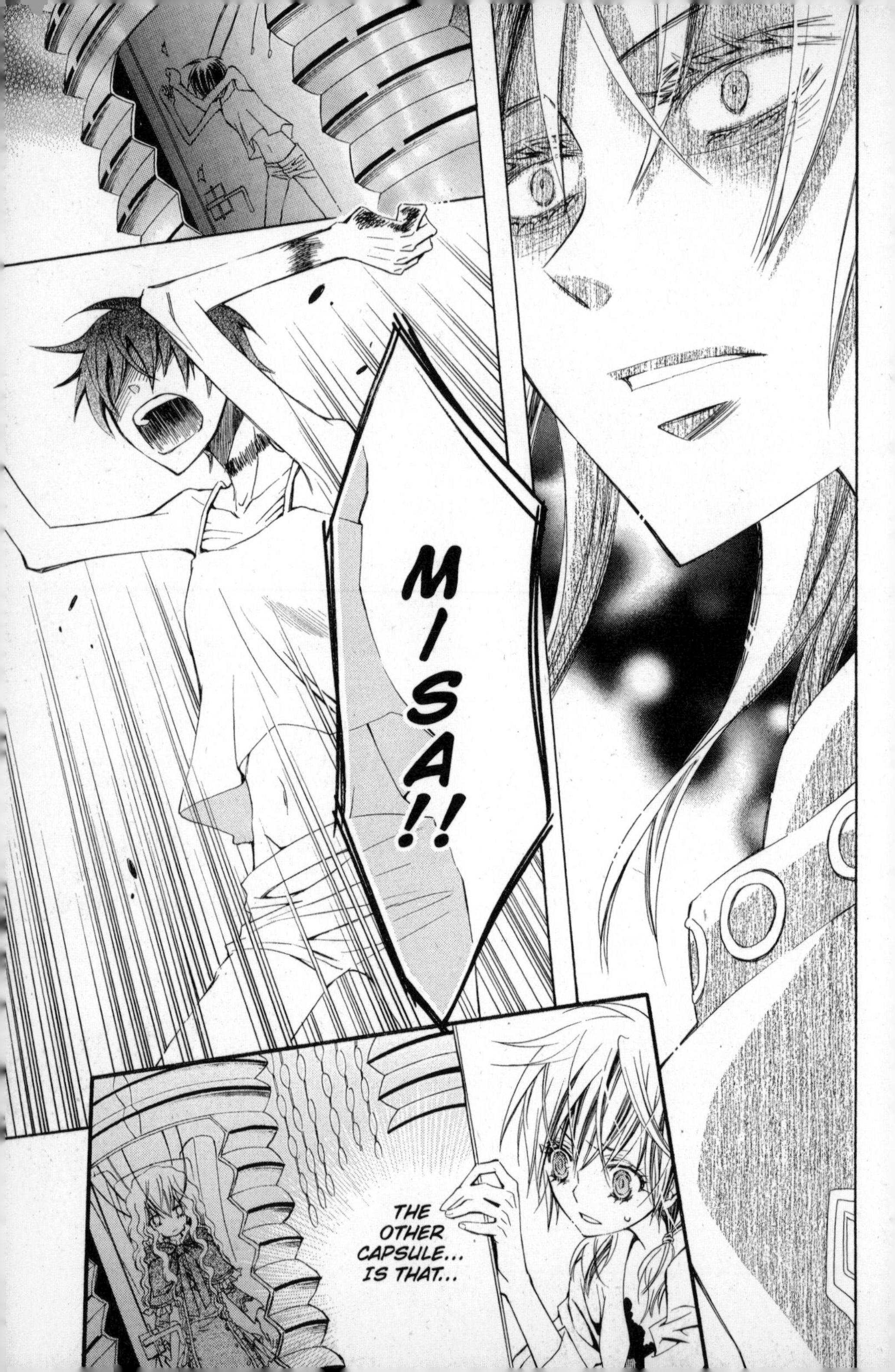
MISA!!
THE OTHER CAPSULE... IS THAT...

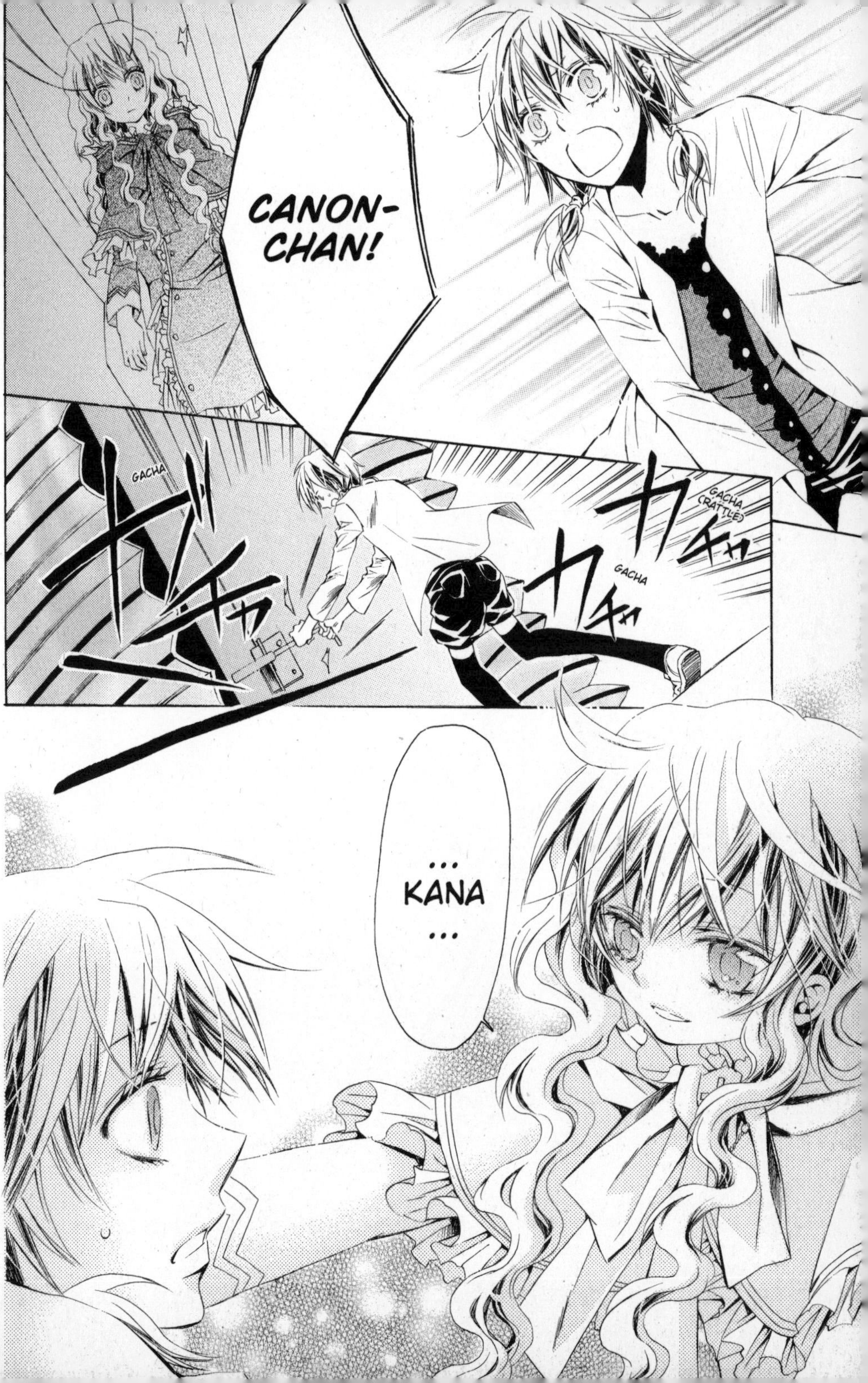

CANON-CHAN!
GACHA (RATTLE)
GACHA
GACHA
...KANA...

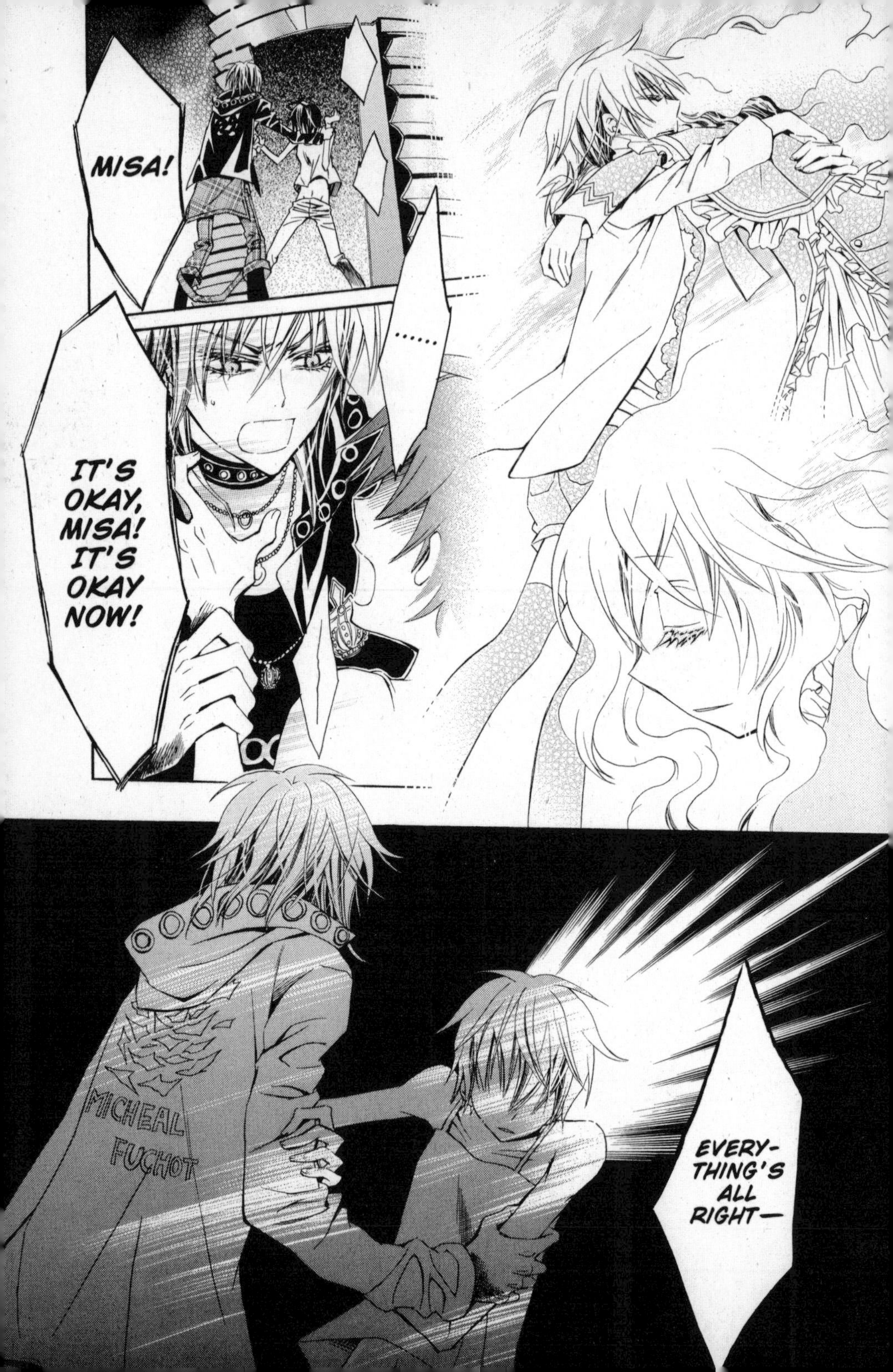
MISA!
......
IT'S OKAY, MISA! IT'S OKAY NOW!
EVERY-THING'S ALL RIGHT—
MICHEAL FUCHOT

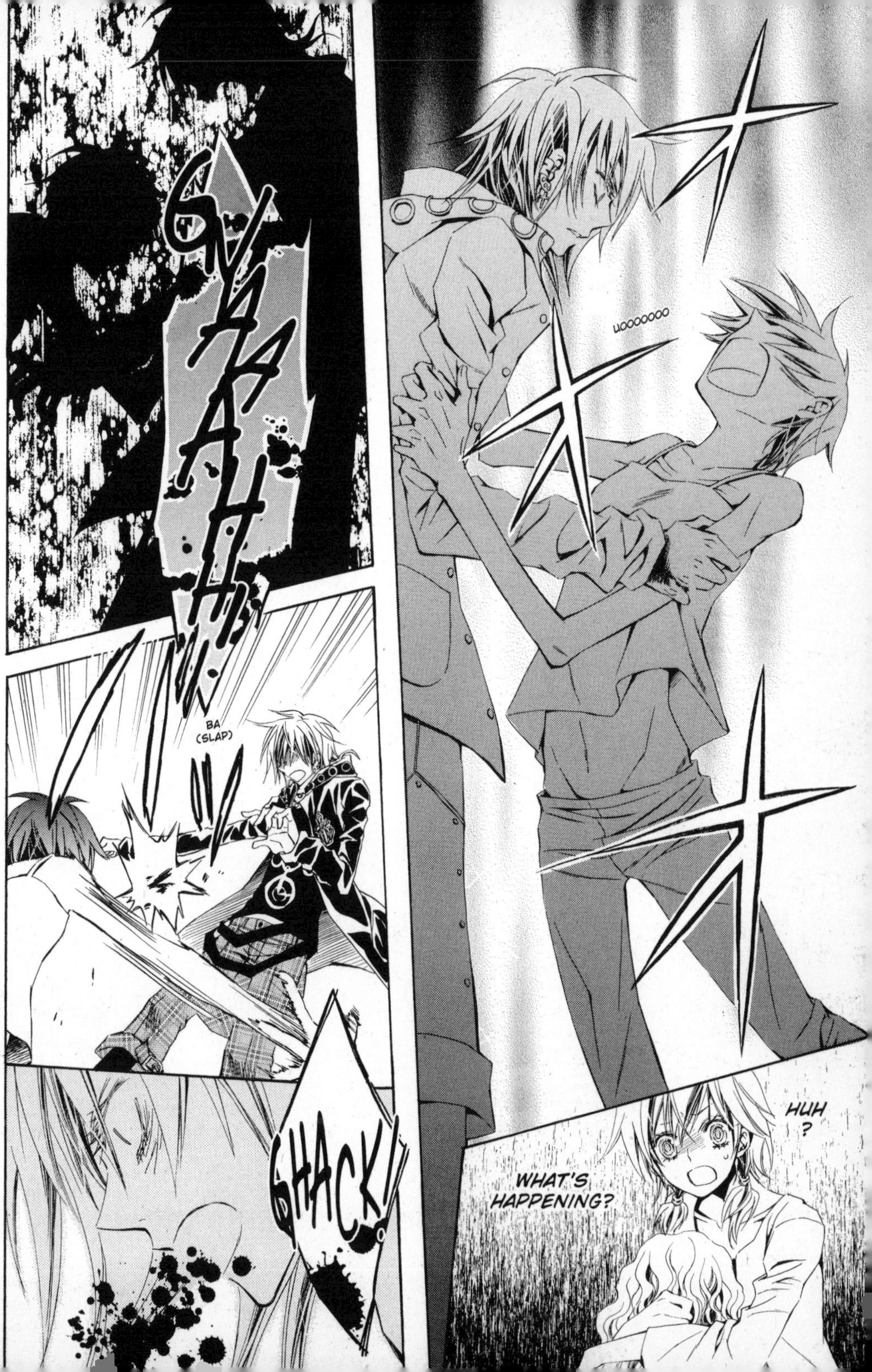
uoooooo
GYAAAHHH!!
BA
(SLAP)
SHACK!!
HUH?
WHAT'S HAPPENING?

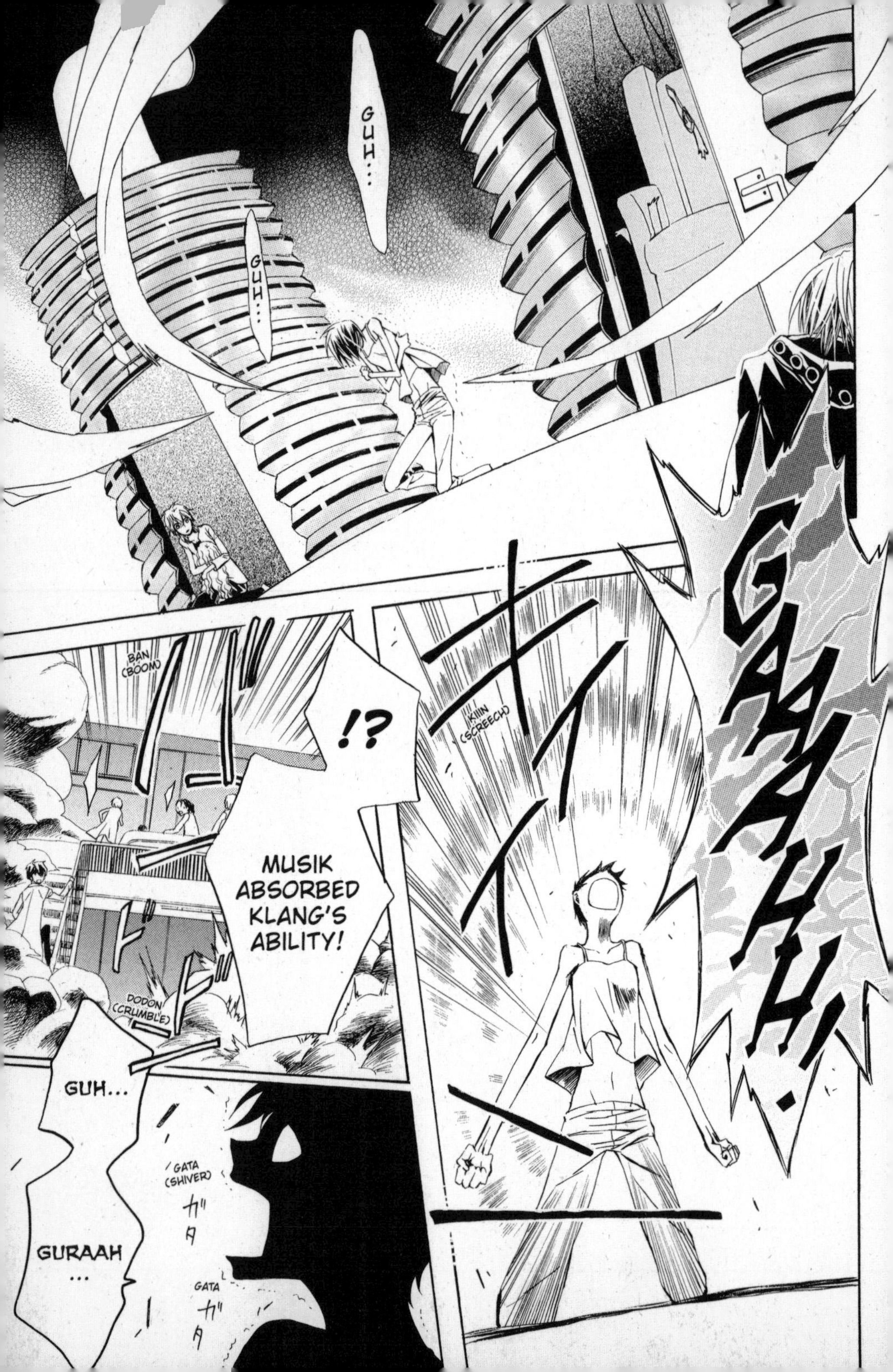

GUH...
GUH...
GAAAHH!
KIIN (SCREECH)
BAN (BOOM)
!?
MUSIK ABSORBED KLANG'S ABILITY!
DODON (CRUMBLE)
GUH...
GATA (SHIVER)
GURAAH...
GATA

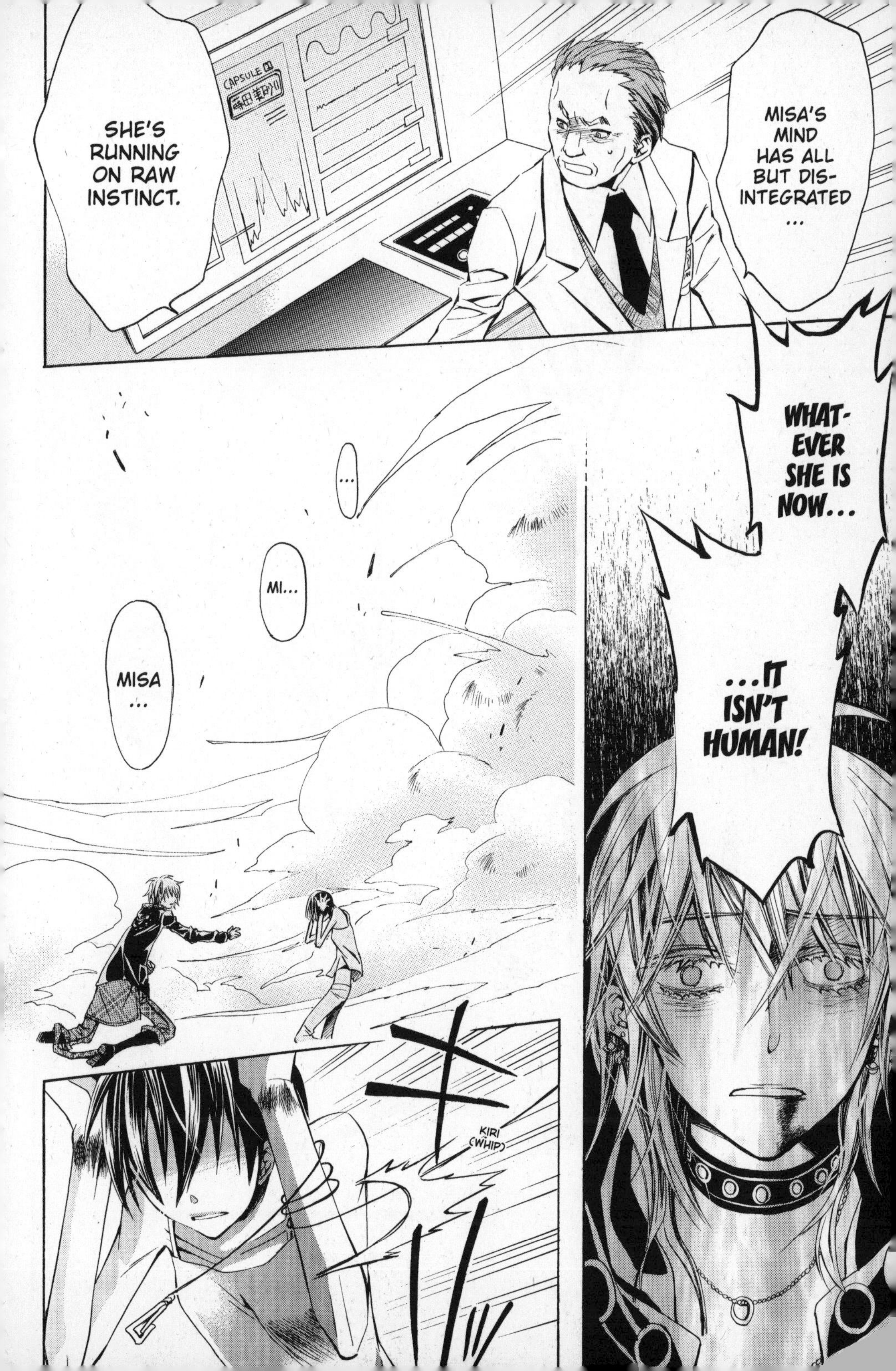
MISA'S MIND HAS ALL BUT DIS-INTEGRATED ...
SHE'S RUNNING ON RAW INSTINCT.
WHAT-EVER SHE IS NOW...
...IT ISN'T HUMAN!
...
MI...
MISA ...
KIRI (WHIP)

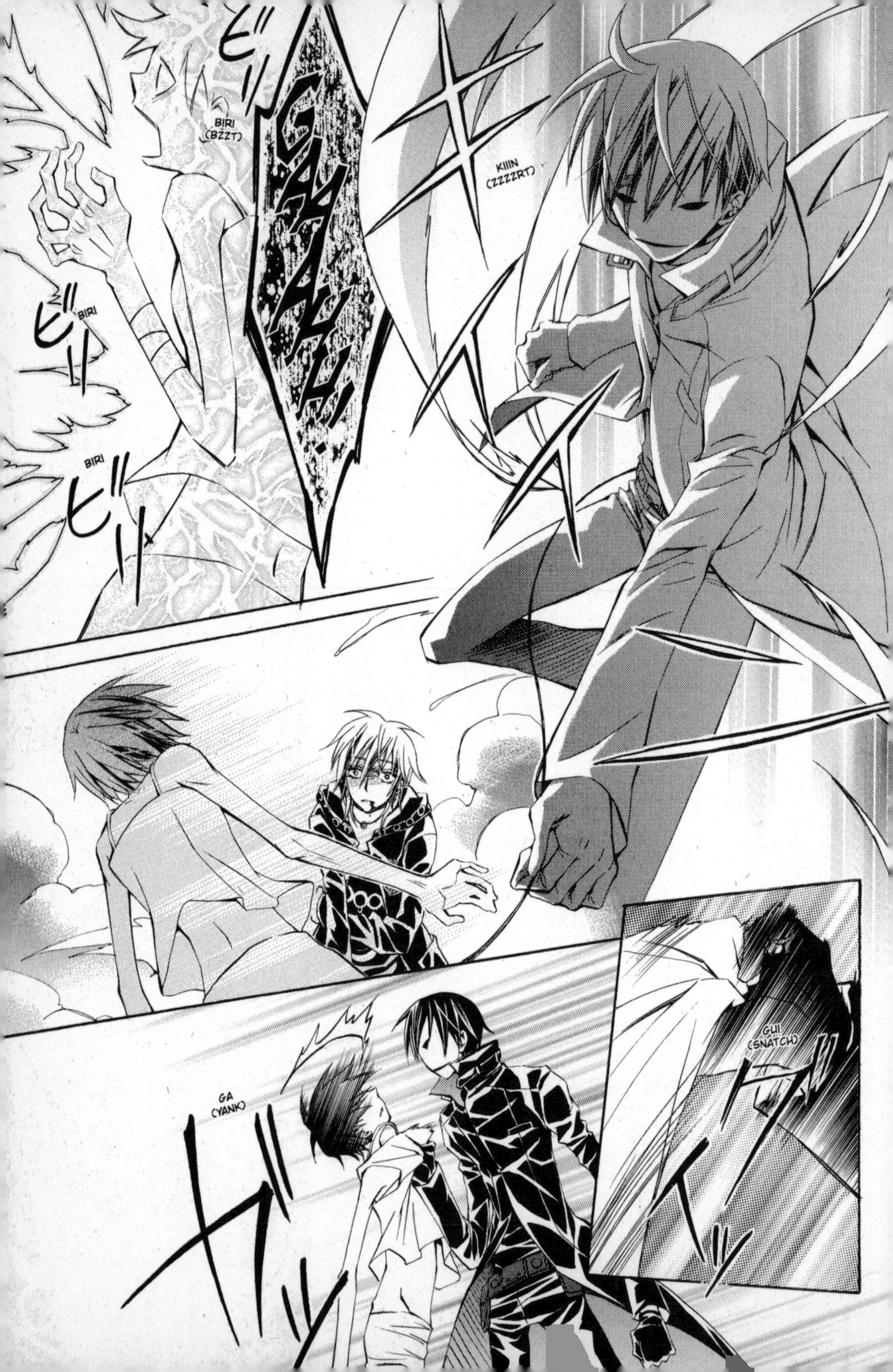
KIIN
(ZZZZRT)
BIRI
(BZZT)
BIRI
BIRI
GUI
(SNATCH)
GA
(YANK)

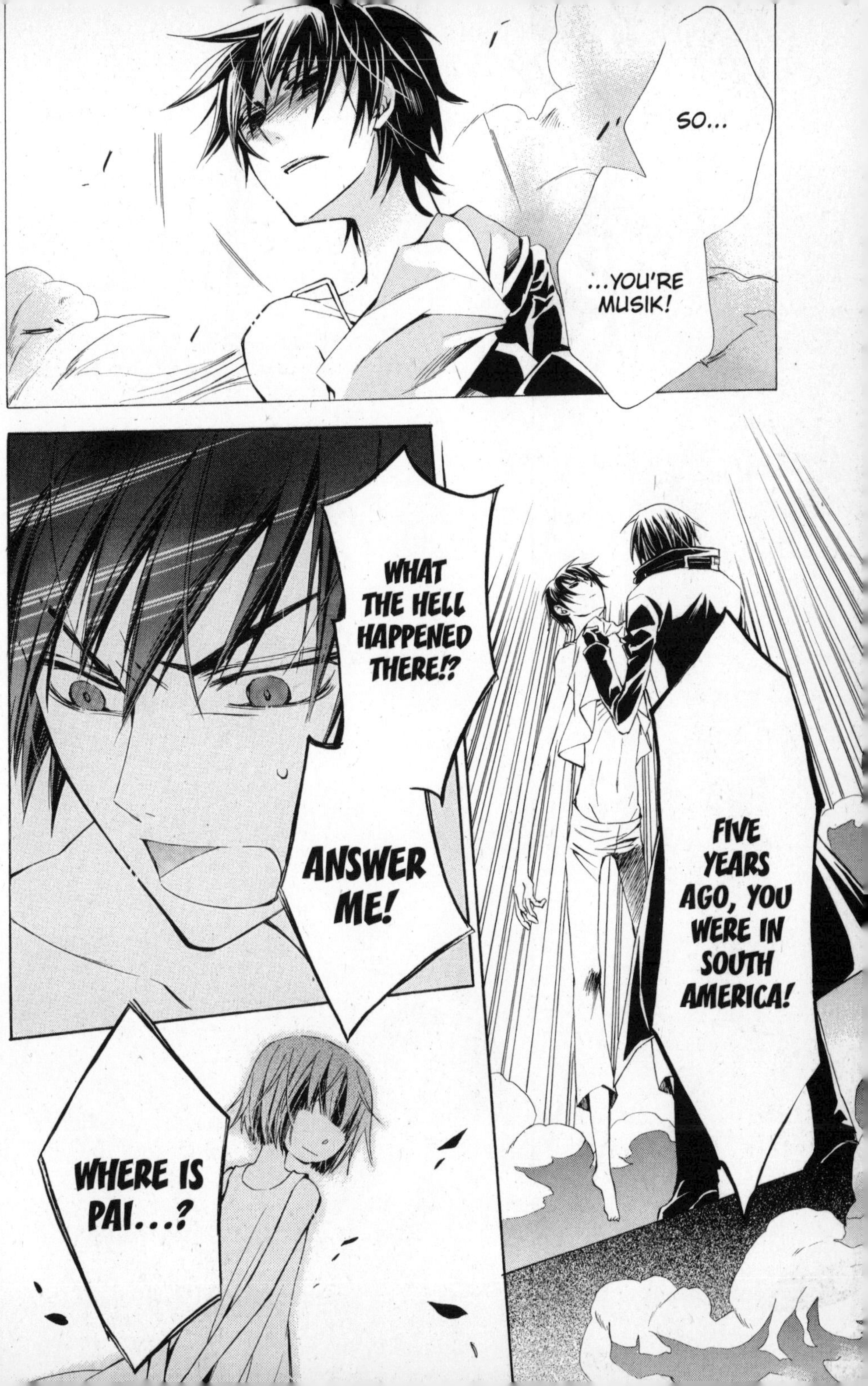
SO...
...YOU'RE MUSIK!
FIVE YEARS AGO, YOU WERE IN SOUTH AMERICA!
WHAT THE HELL HAPPENED THERE!?
ANSWER ME!
WHERE IS PAI...?

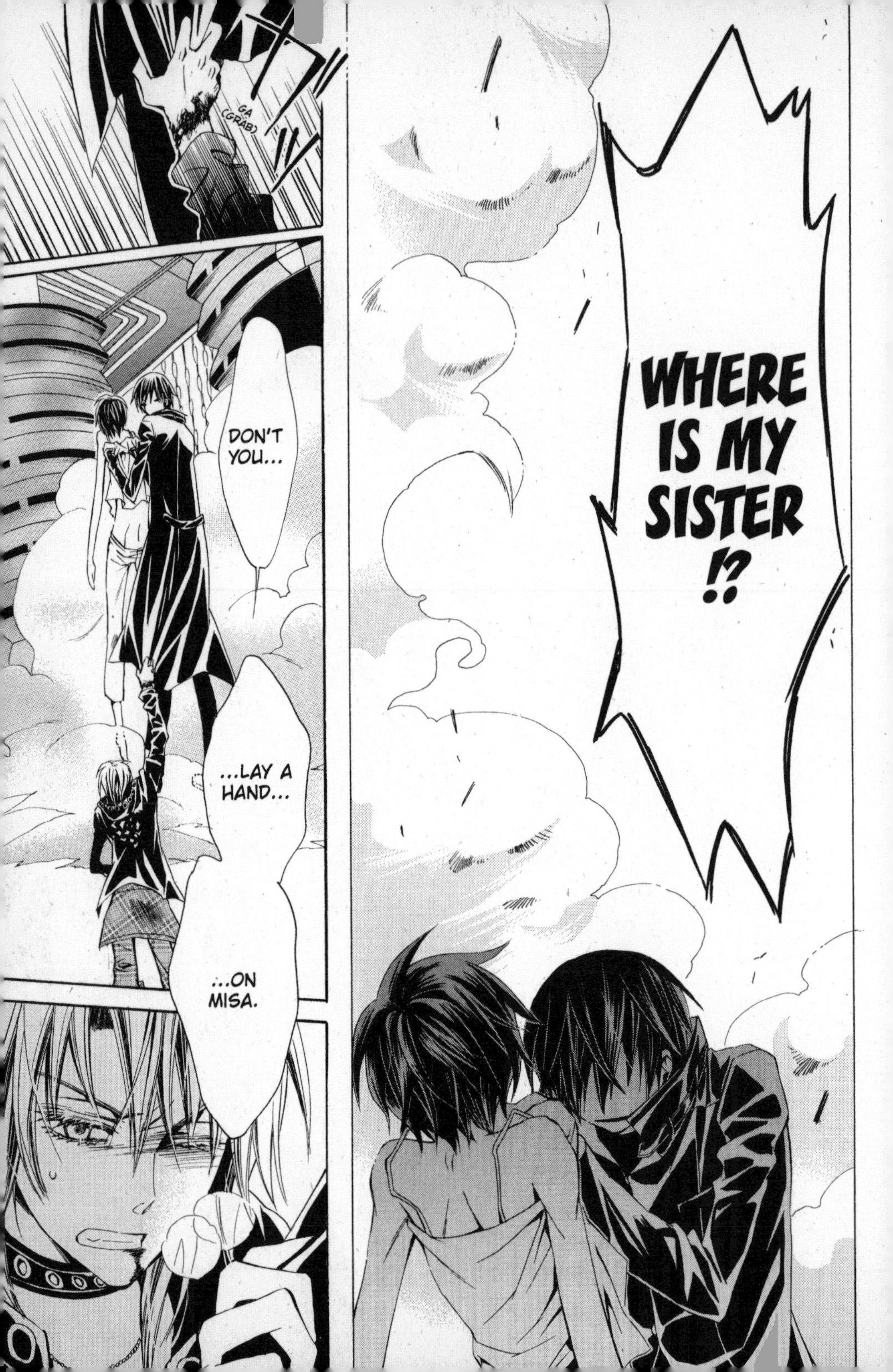
WHERE IS MY SISTER!?
GA (GRAB)
DON'T YOU...
...LAY A HAND...
...ON MISA.

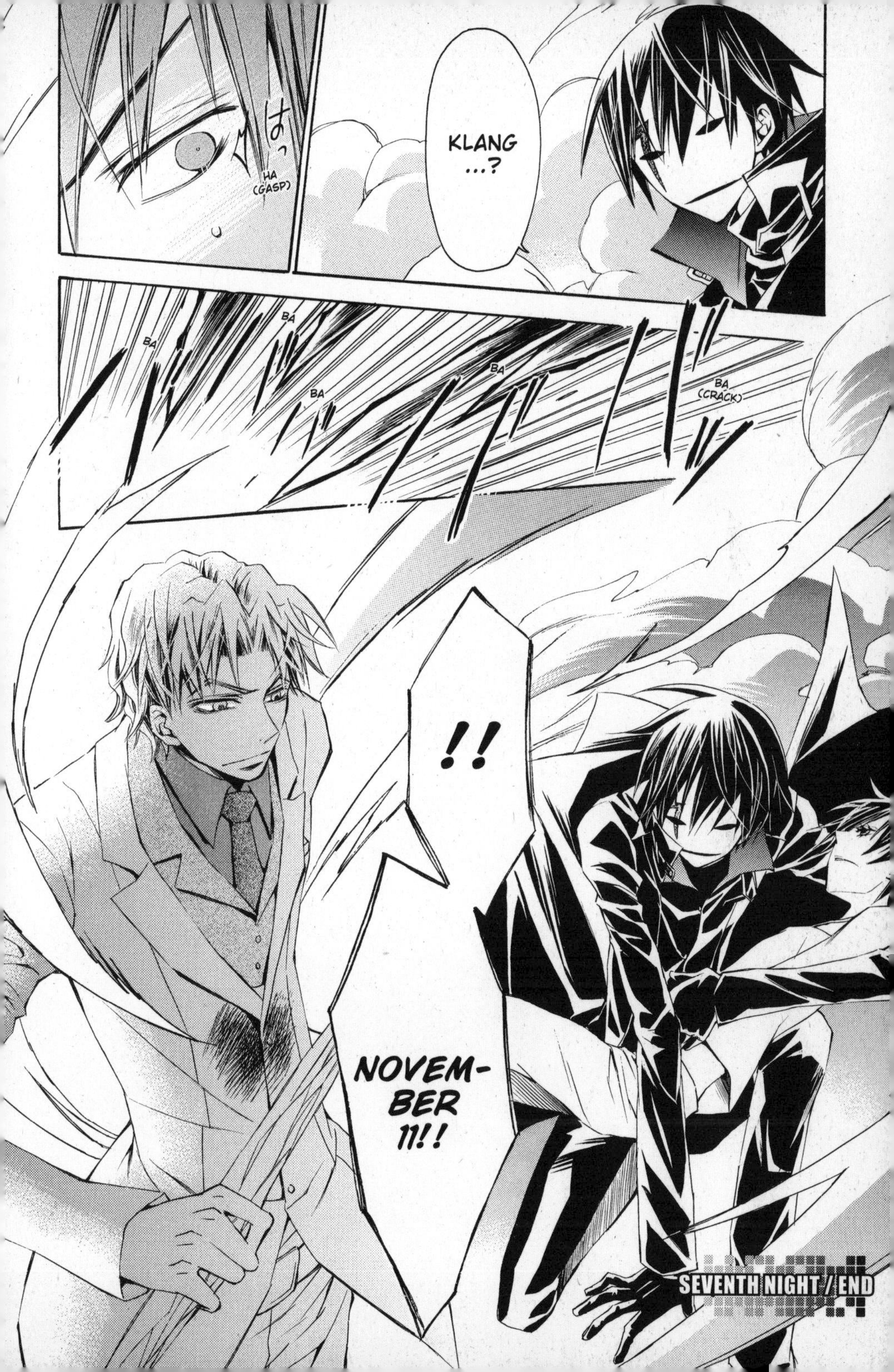
KLANG ...?
HA (GASP)
BA (CRACK)
BA
BA
BA
BA
!!
NOVEMBER 11!!
SEVENTH NIGHT / END

EIGHTH NIGHT

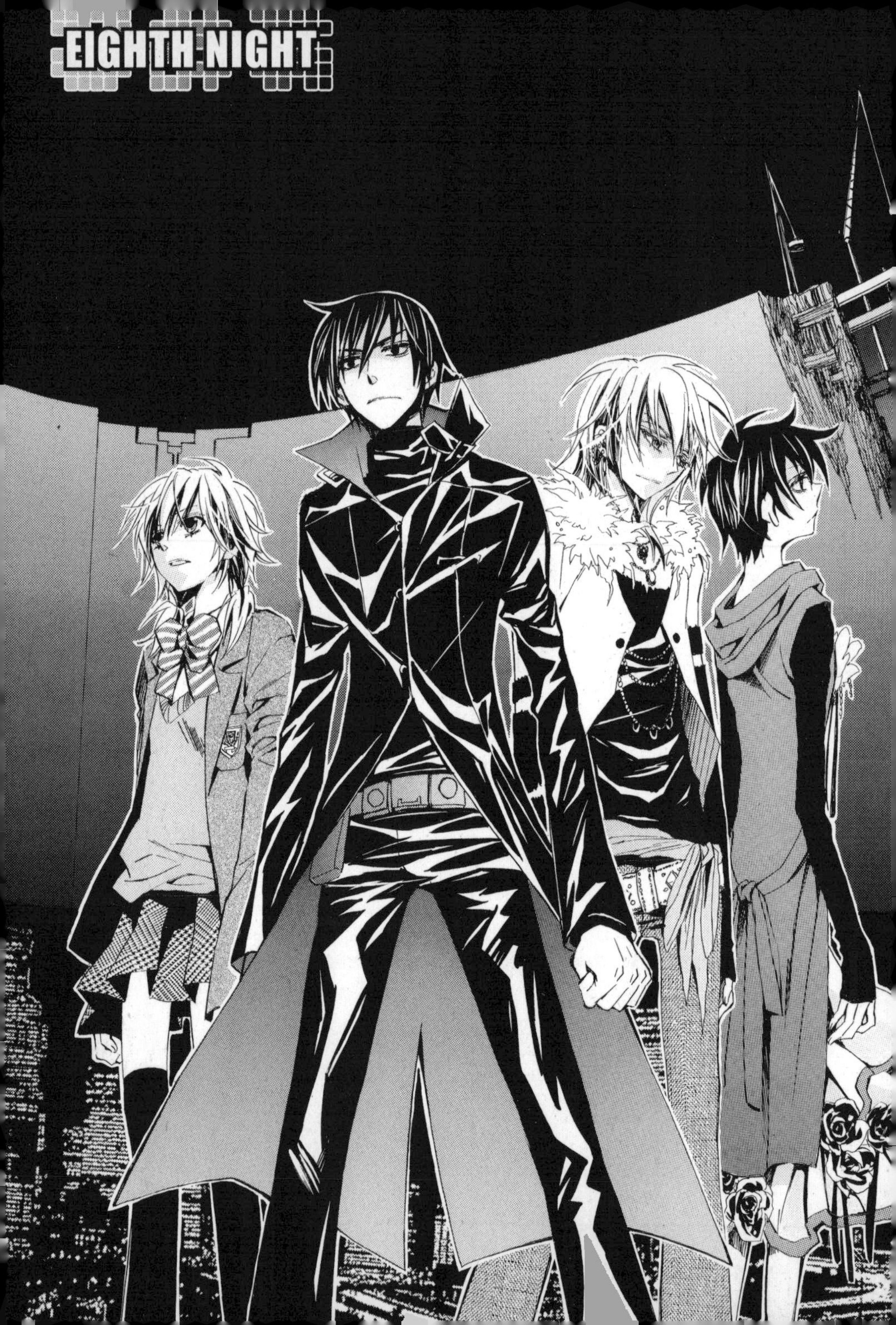

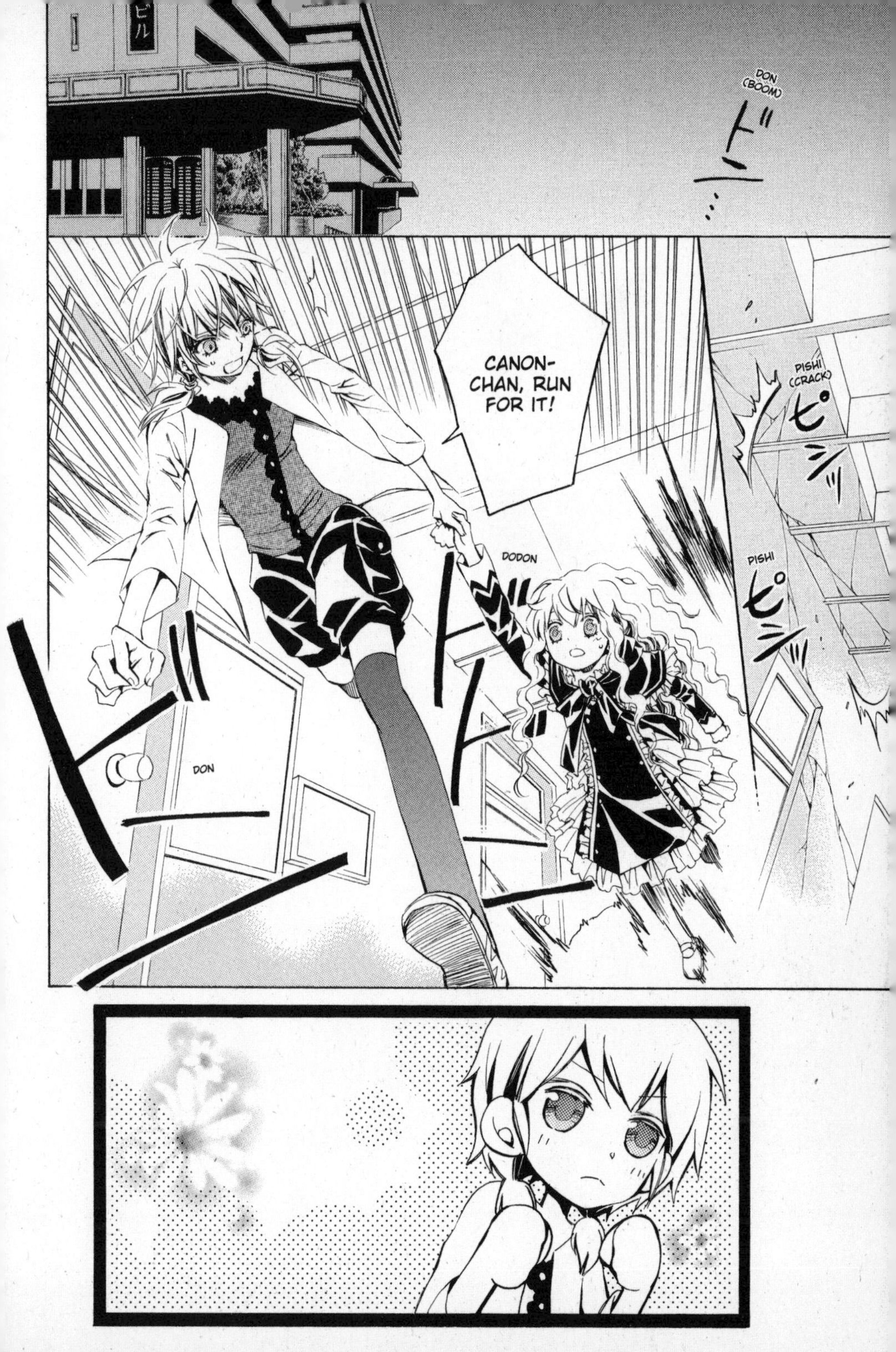
DON (BOOM)
ド…
ビル
PISHI (CRACK)
ピシッ
CANON-CHAN, RUN FOR IT!
PISHI
ピシッ
DODON
DON

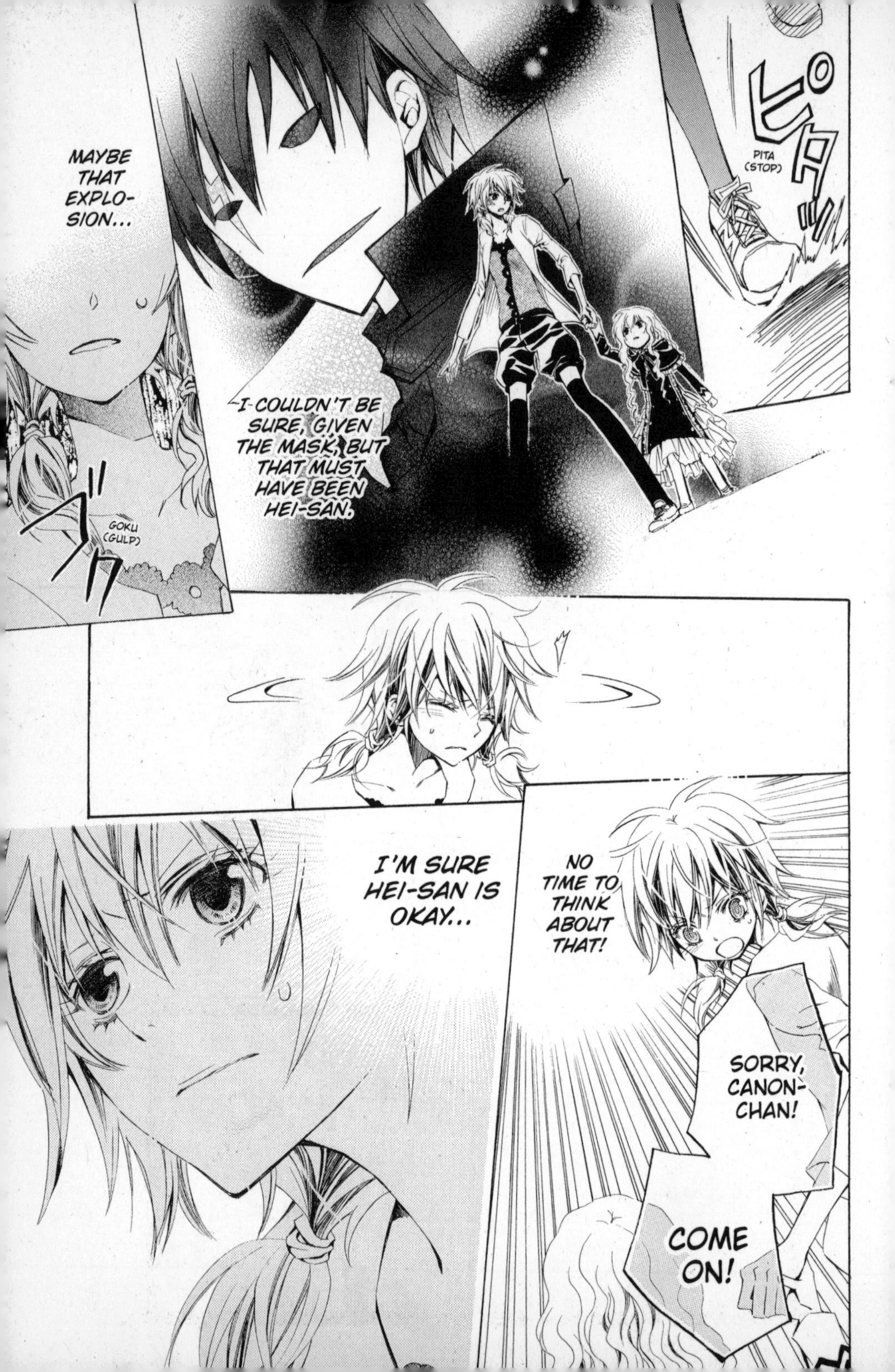
ピタッ
PITA (STOP)
—I COULDN'T BE SURE, GIVEN THE MASK, BUT THAT MUST HAVE BEEN HEI-SAN.
MAYBE THAT EXPLOSION...
ゴク
GOKU (GULP)
NO TIME TO THINK ABOUT THAT!
SORRY, CANON-CHAN!
COME ON!
I'M SURE HEI-SAN IS OKAY...

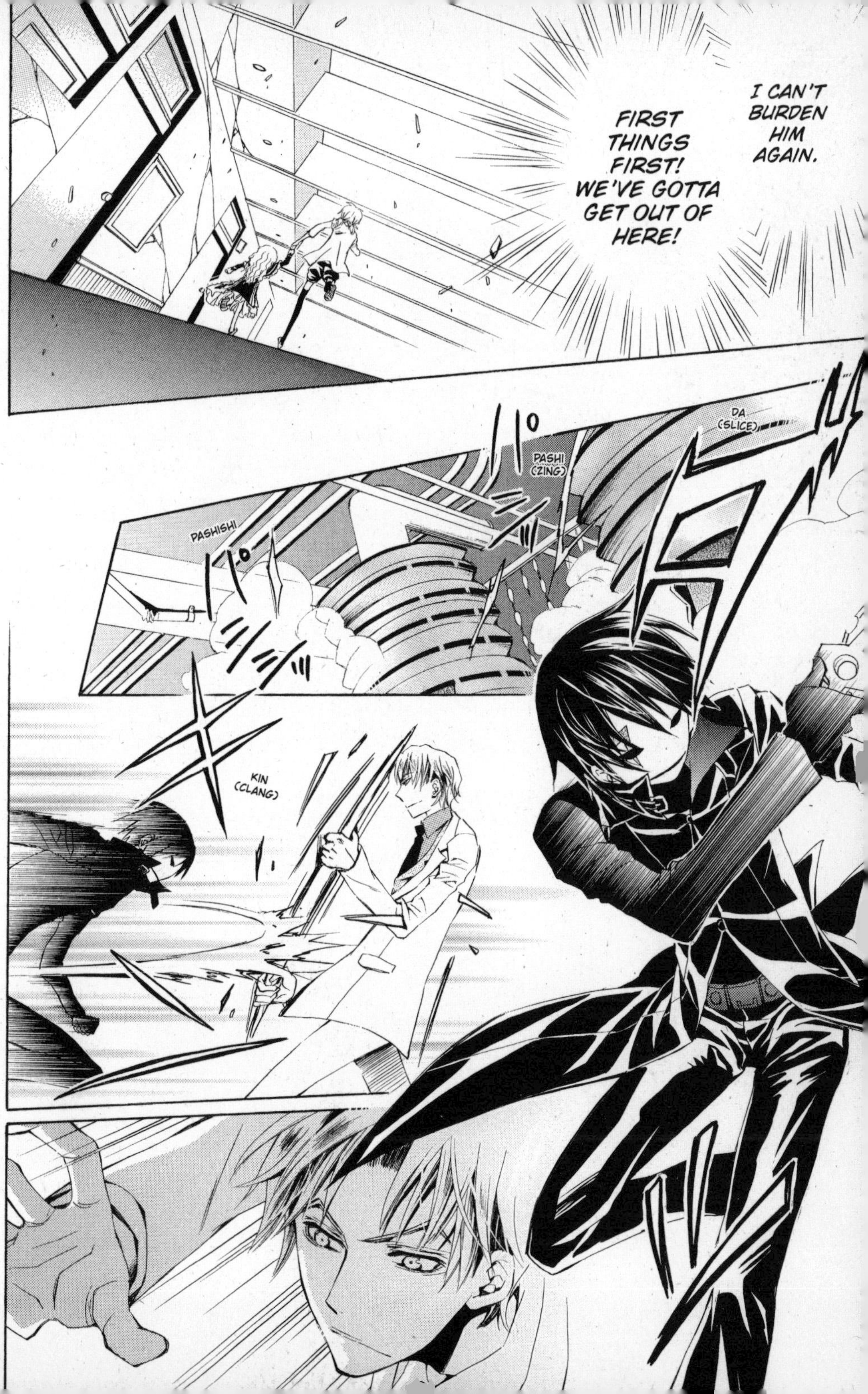
I CAN'T BURDEN HIM AGAIN.
FIRST THINGS FIRST! WE'VE GOTTA GET OUT OF HERE!
DA (SLICE)
PASHI (ZING)
PASHISHI
KIN (CLANG)

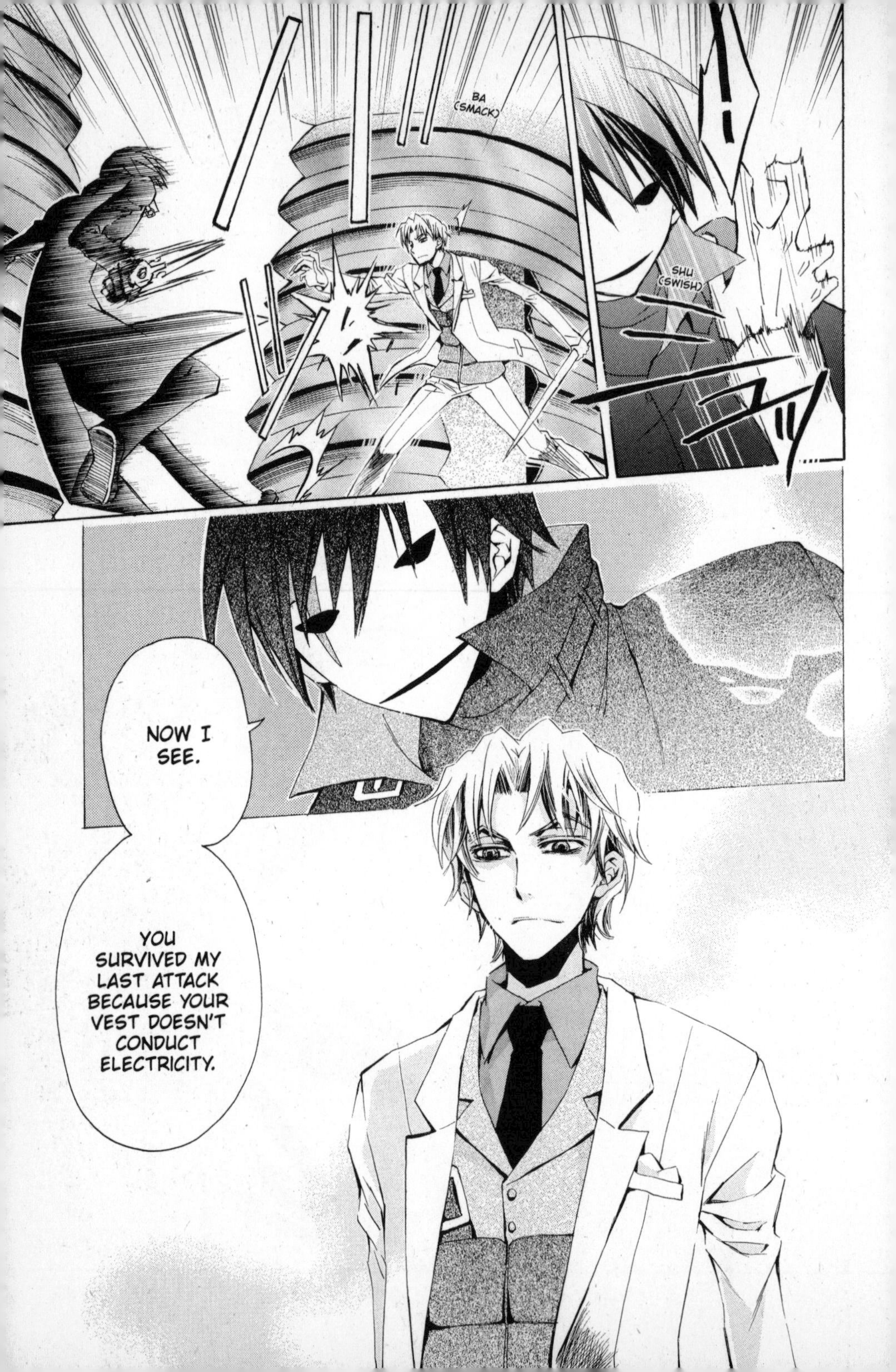
!
SHU (SWISH)
BA (SMACK)
NOW I SEE.
YOU SURVIVED MY LAST ATTACK BECAUSE YOUR VEST DOESN'T CONDUCT ELECTRICITY.

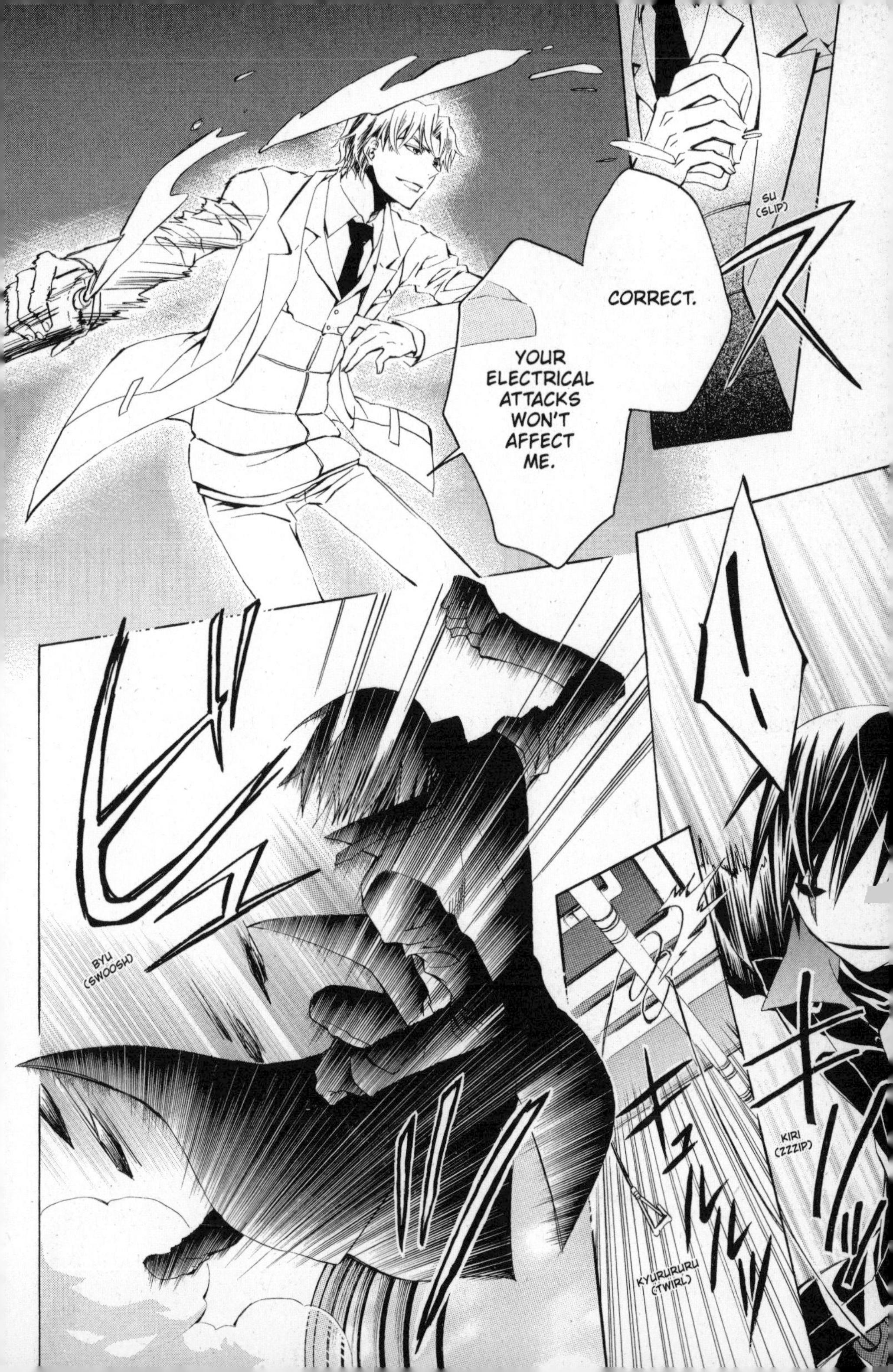
SU (SLIP)
CORRECT.
YOUR ELECTRICAL ATTACKS WON'T AFFECT ME.
!
KIRI (ZZZIP)
KYURURURU (TWIRL)
BYU (SWOOSH)

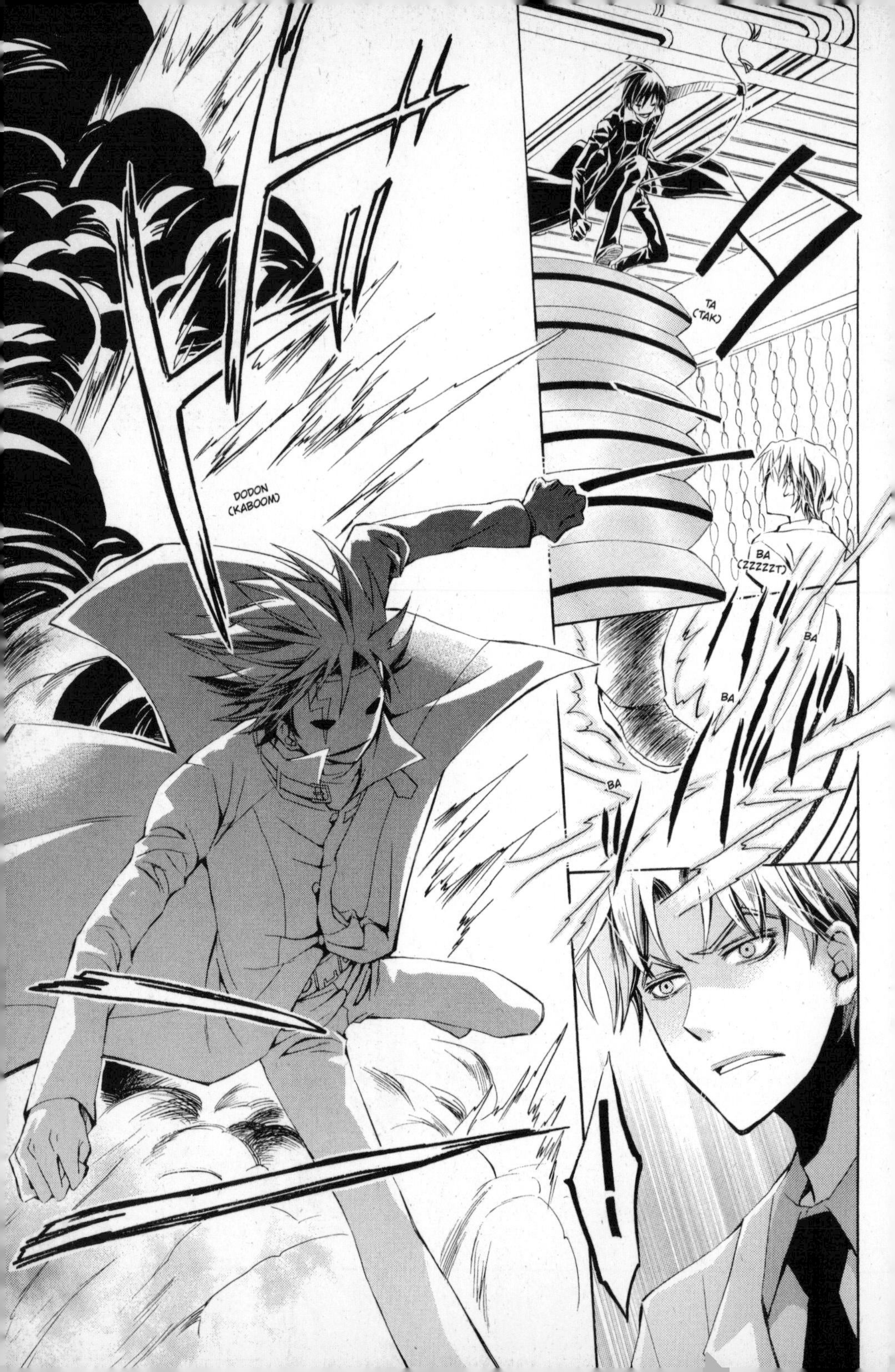
TA
(TAK)
BA
(ZZZZZT)
BA
BA
BA
!
DODON
(KABOOM)

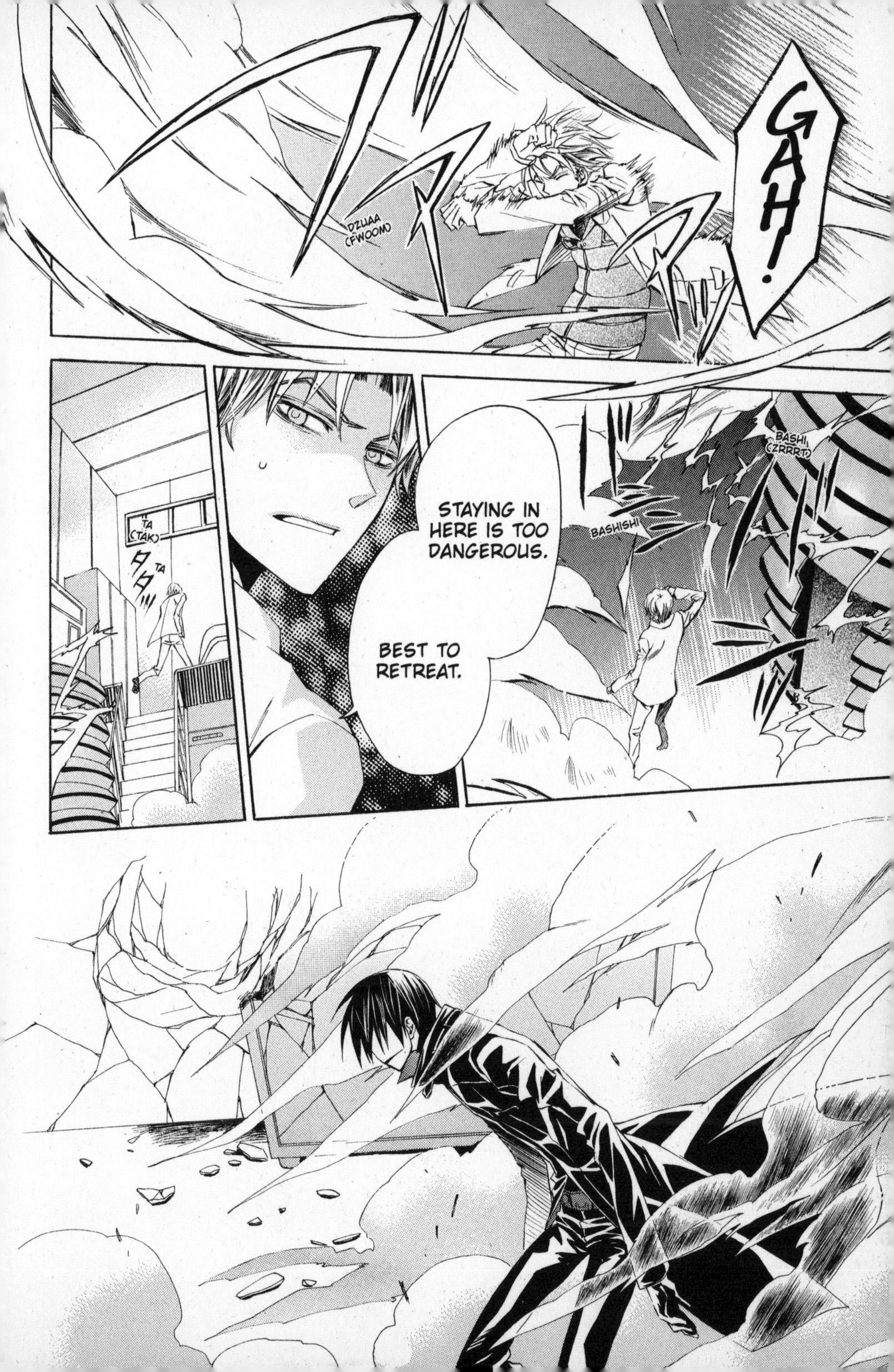
GAH!
DZUAA (FWOOM)
BASHI (ZRRRT)
BASHISHI
STAYING IN HERE IS TOO DANGEROUS.
BEST TO RETREAT.
TA (TAK)
TA

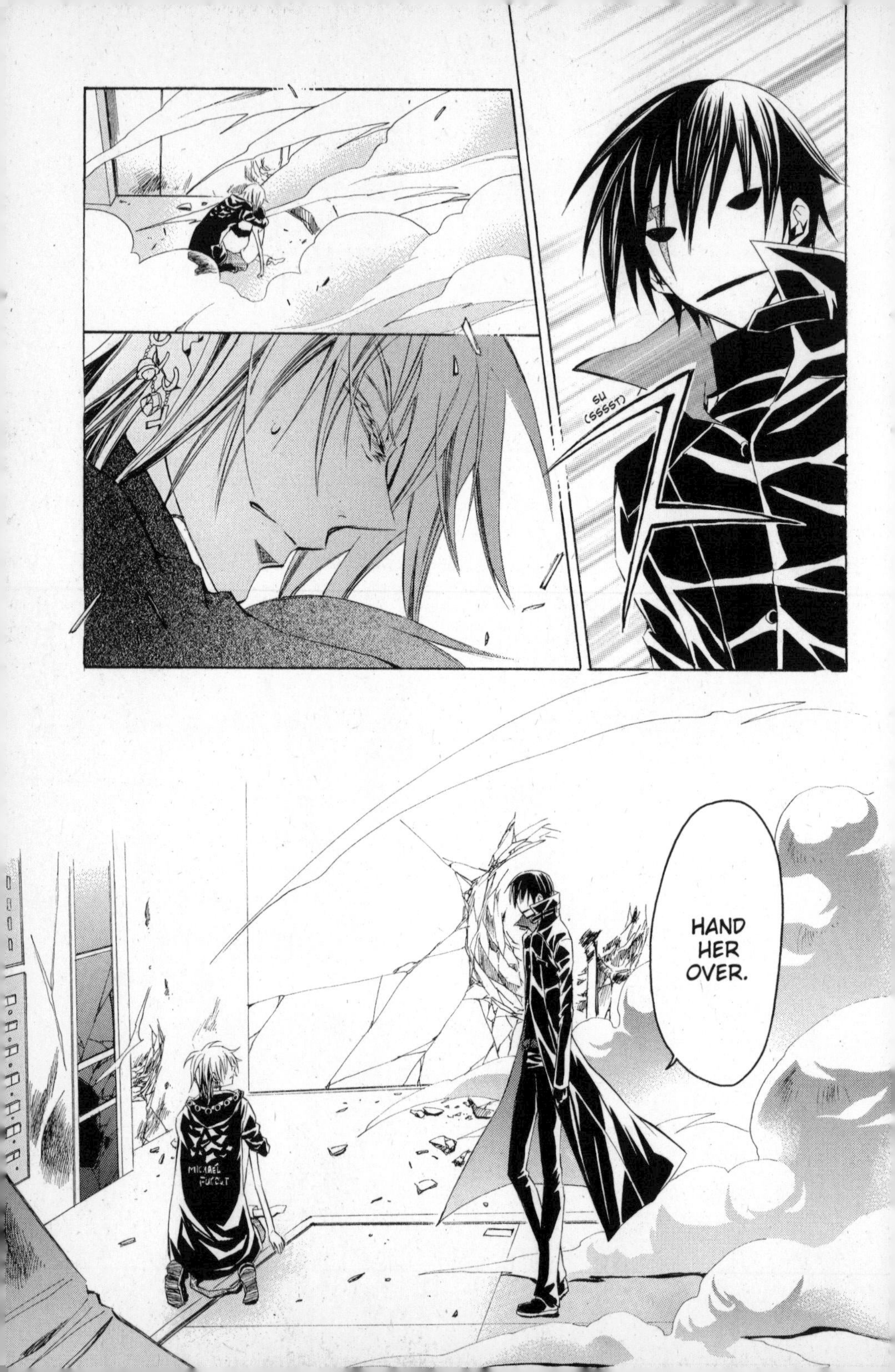
SU (SSSST)
HAND HER OVER.

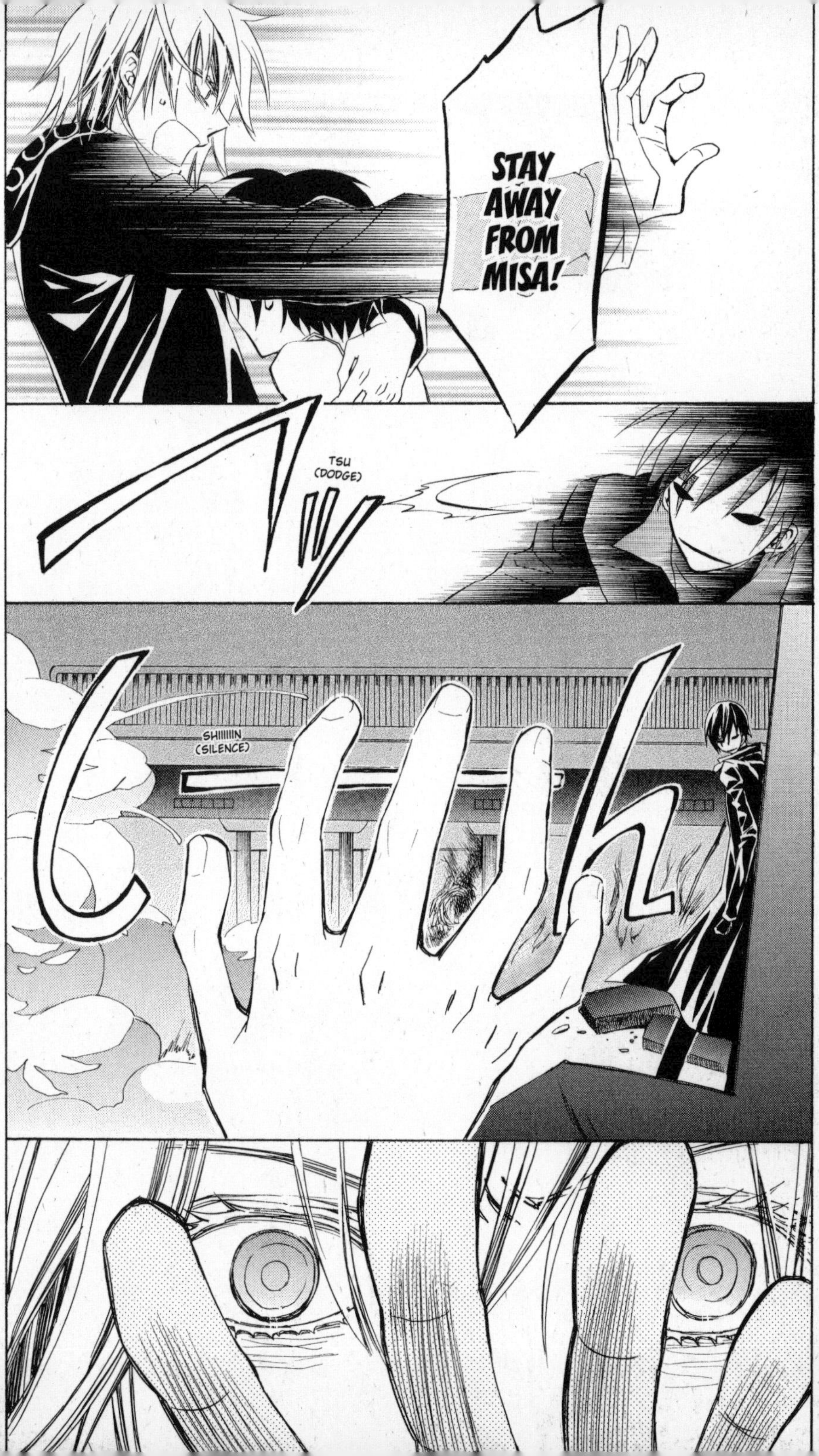
STAY AWAY FROM MISA!
TSU
(DODGE)
SHIIIIIN
(SILENCE)

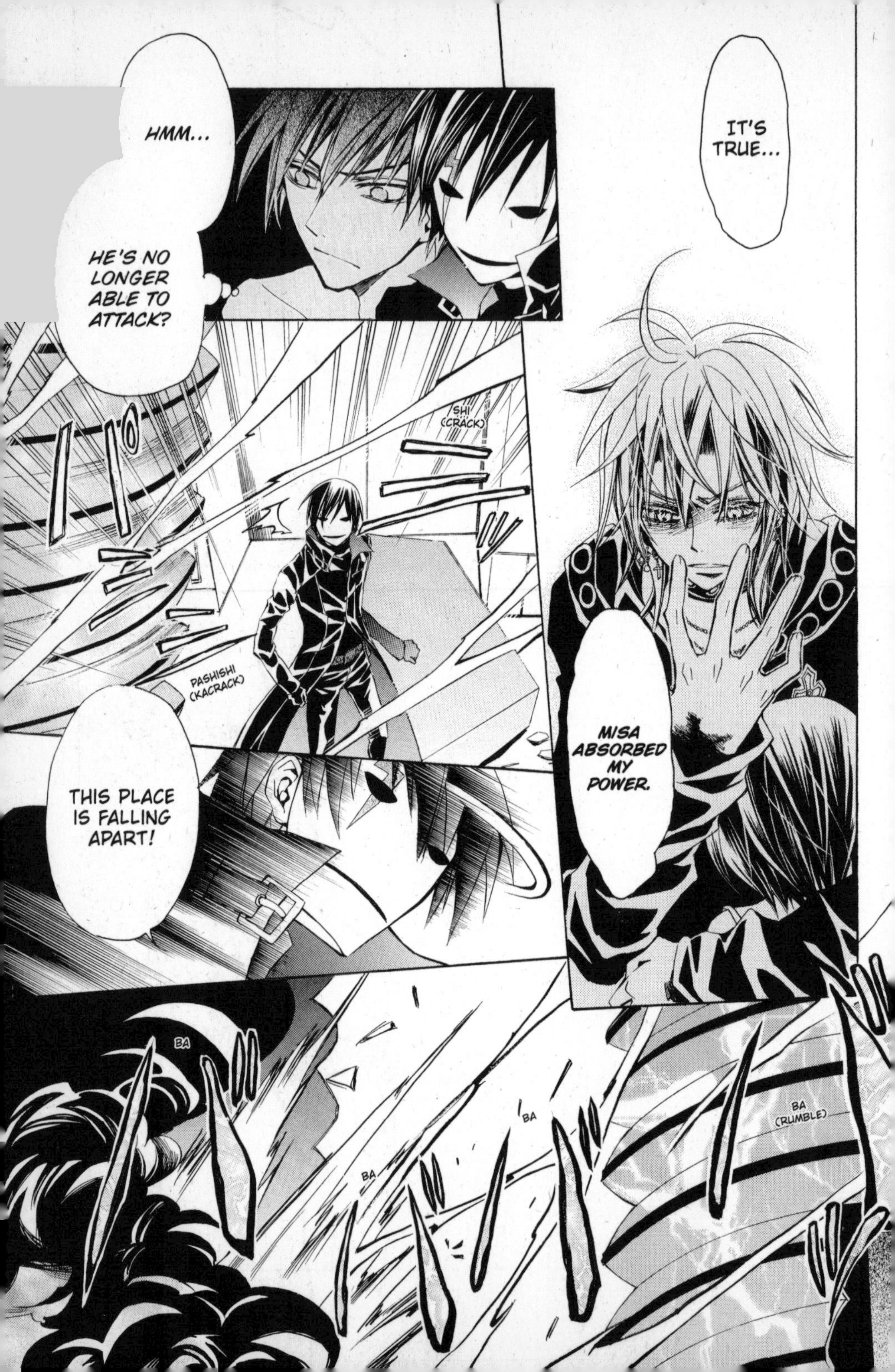
IT'S TRUE...
MISA ABSORBED MY POWER.
HMM...
HE'S NO LONGER ABLE TO ATTACK?
SHI (CRÄCK)
PASHISHI (KACRACK)
THIS PLACE IS FALLING APART!
BA (RUMBLE)
BA
BA
BA

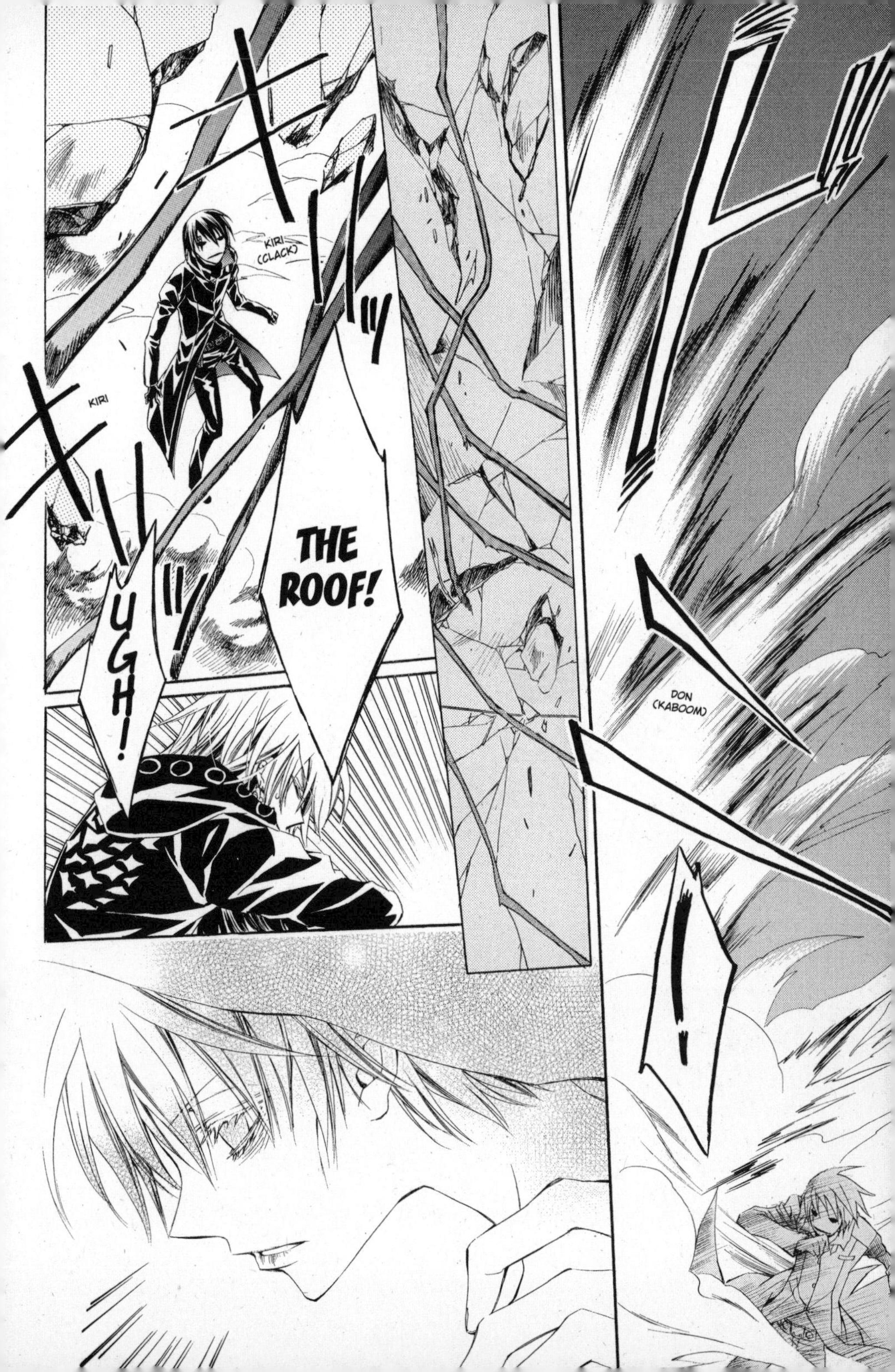
DON (KABOOM)
KIRI (CLACK)
THE ROOF!
KIRI
UGH!

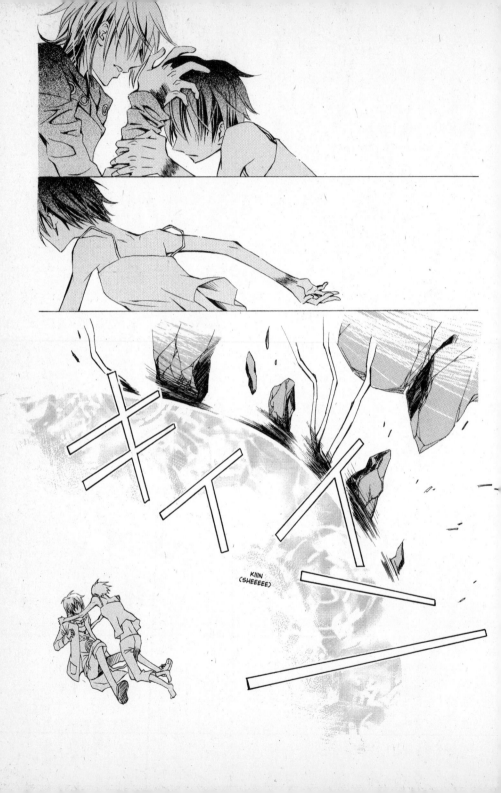

KIIIN
(SHEEEEE)

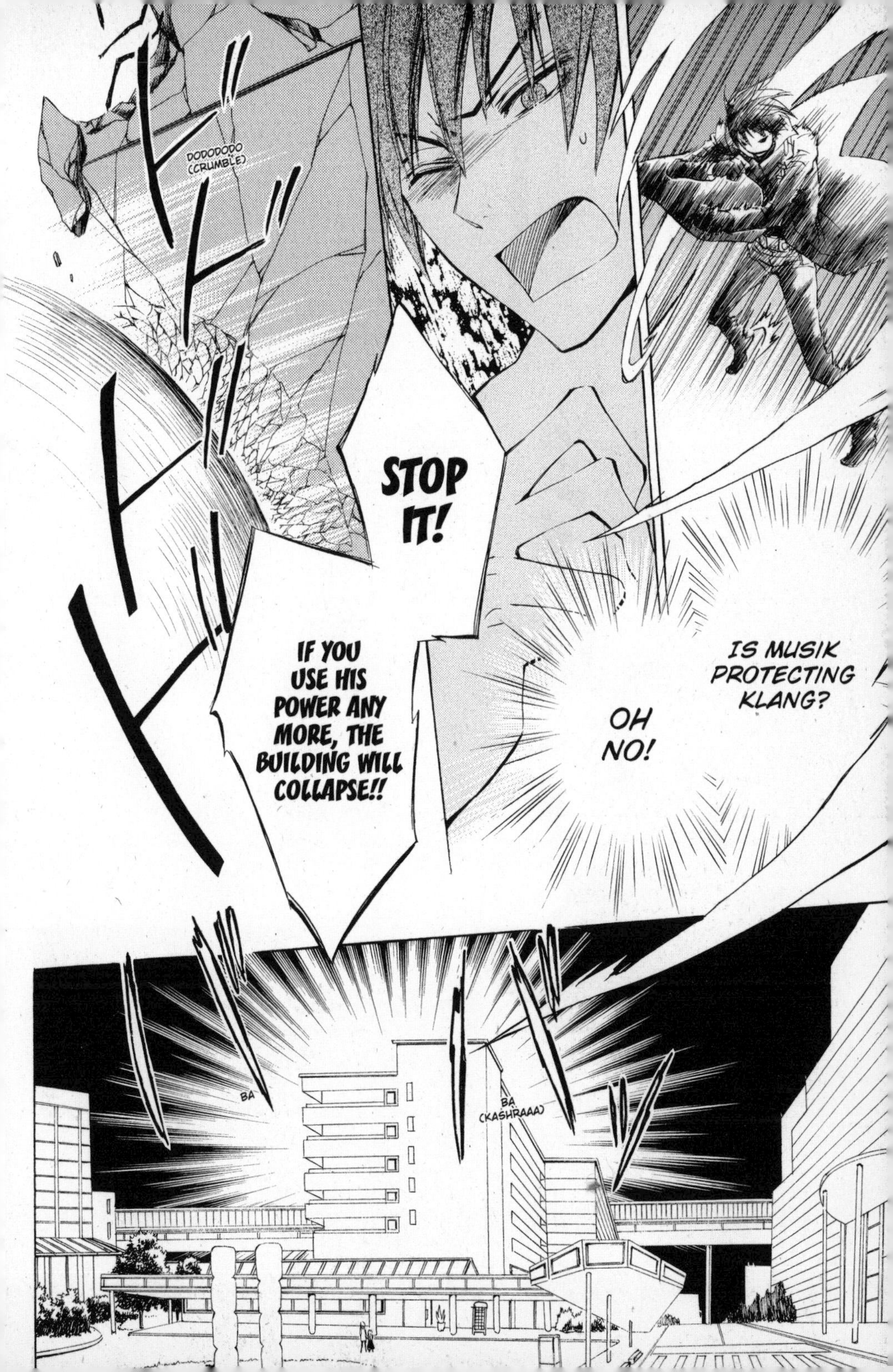
IS MUSIK PROTECTING KLANG?
OH NO!
STOP IT!
IF YOU USE HIS POWER ANY MORE, THE BUILDING WILL COLLAPSE!!
DODODODO (CRUMBLE)
BA (KASHRAAA)
BA

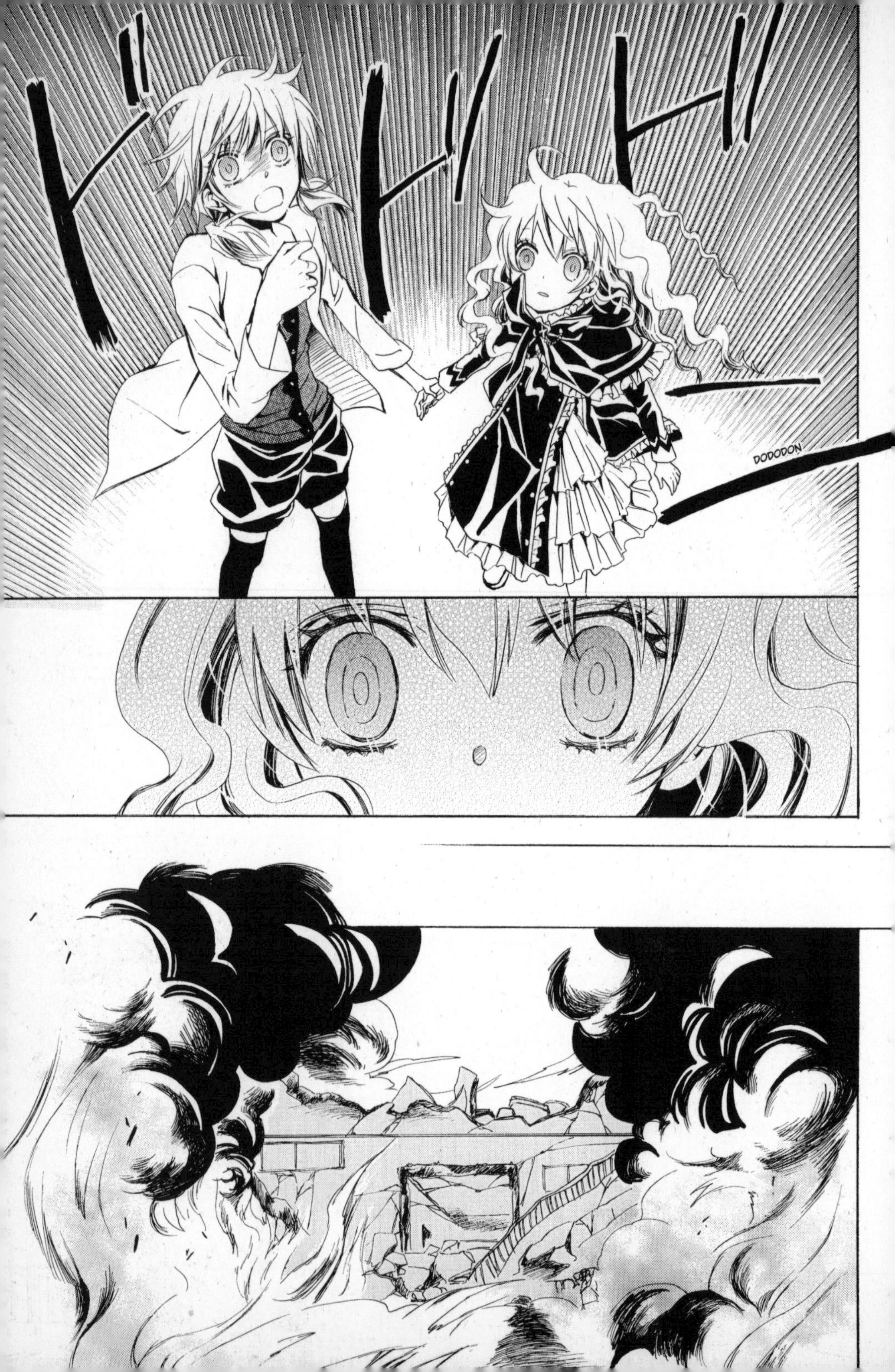
DODODON

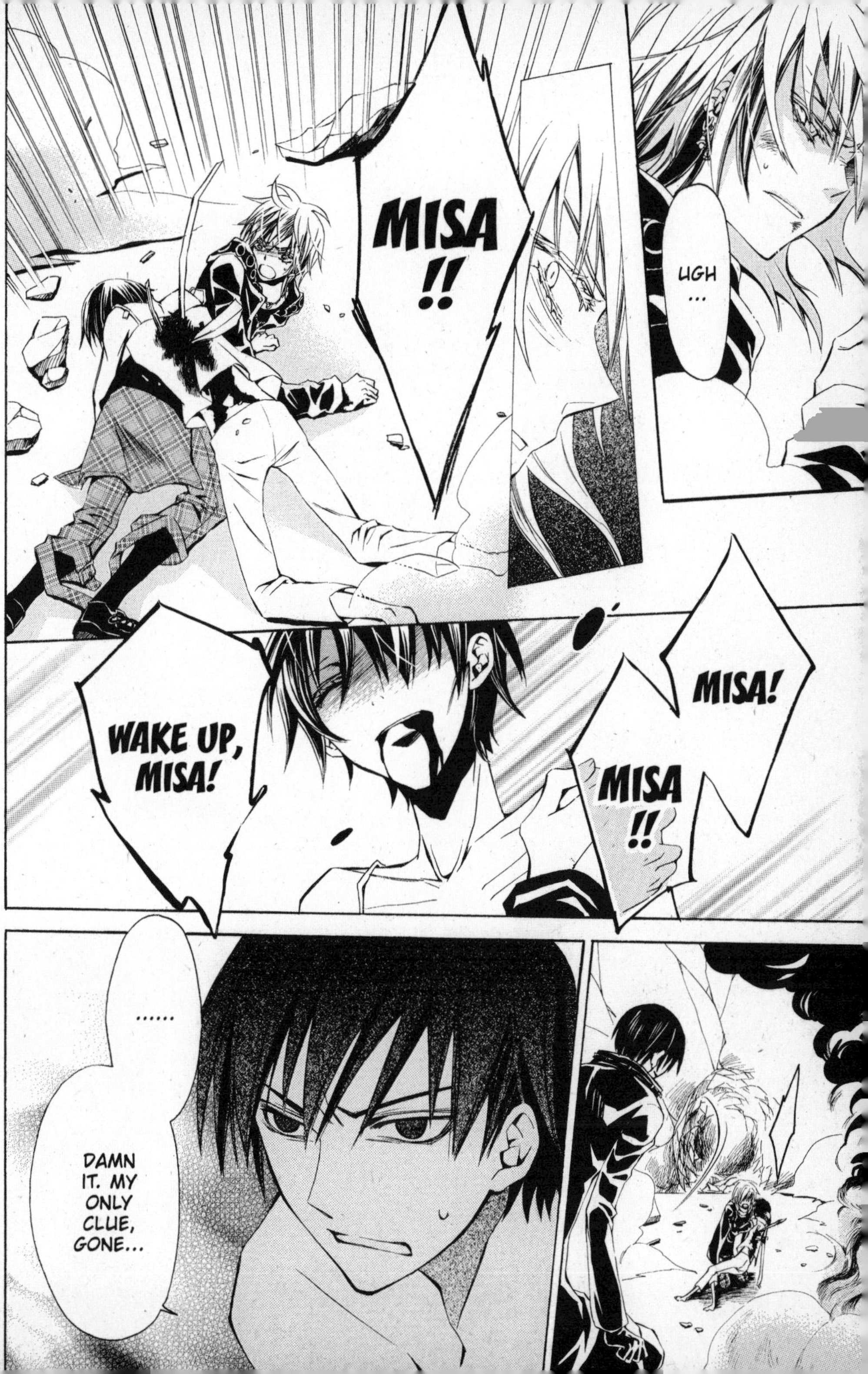
UGH ...
MISA !!
MISA!
MISA !!
WAKE UP, MISA!
......
DAMN IT. MY ONLY CLUE, GONE...

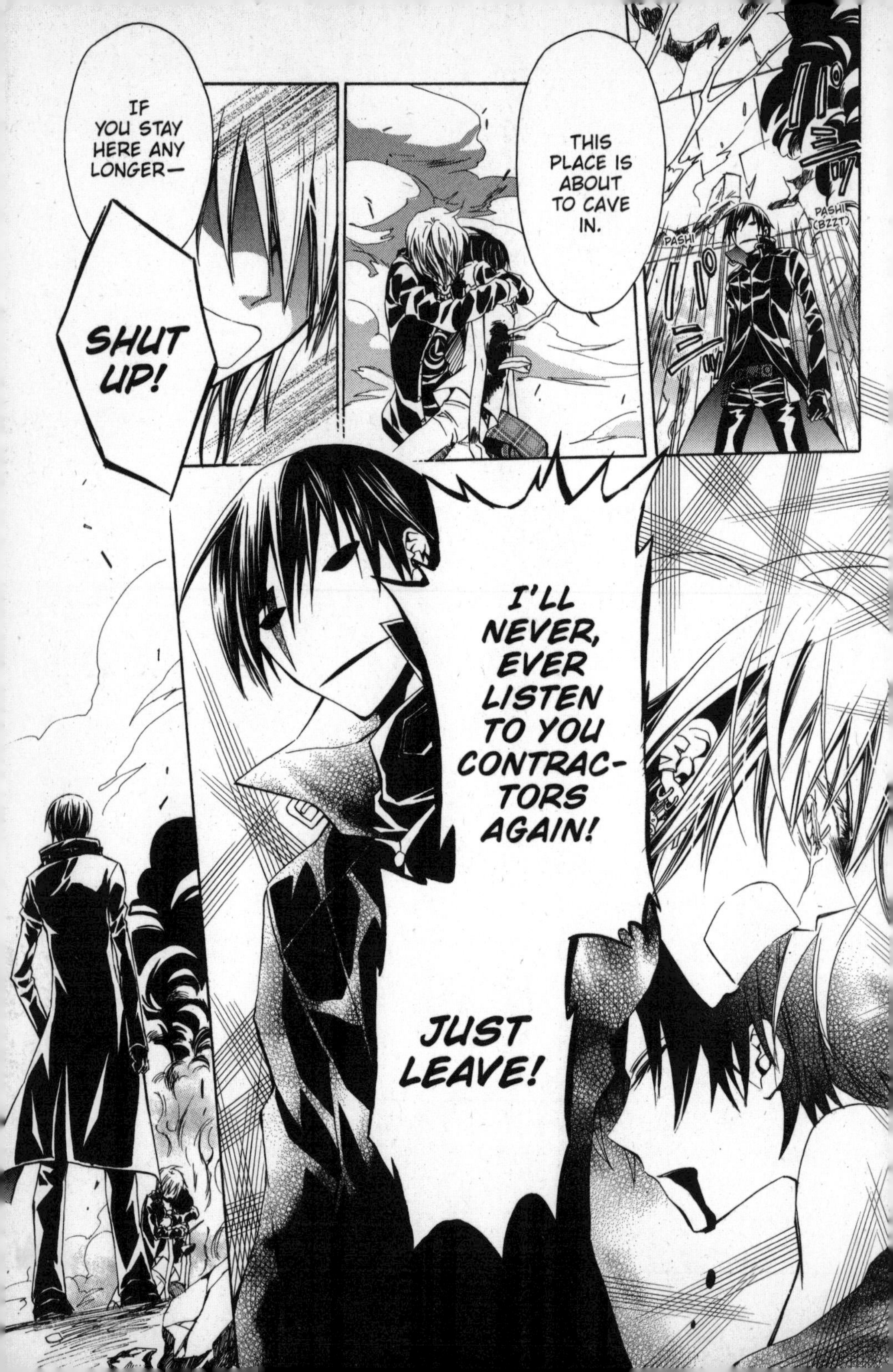
PASHI
PASHI (BZZT)
THIS PLACE IS ABOUT TO CAVE IN.
IF YOU STAY HERE ANY LONGER—
SHUT UP!
I'LL NEVER, EVER LISTEN TO YOU CONTRAC-TORS AGAIN!
JUST LEAVE!

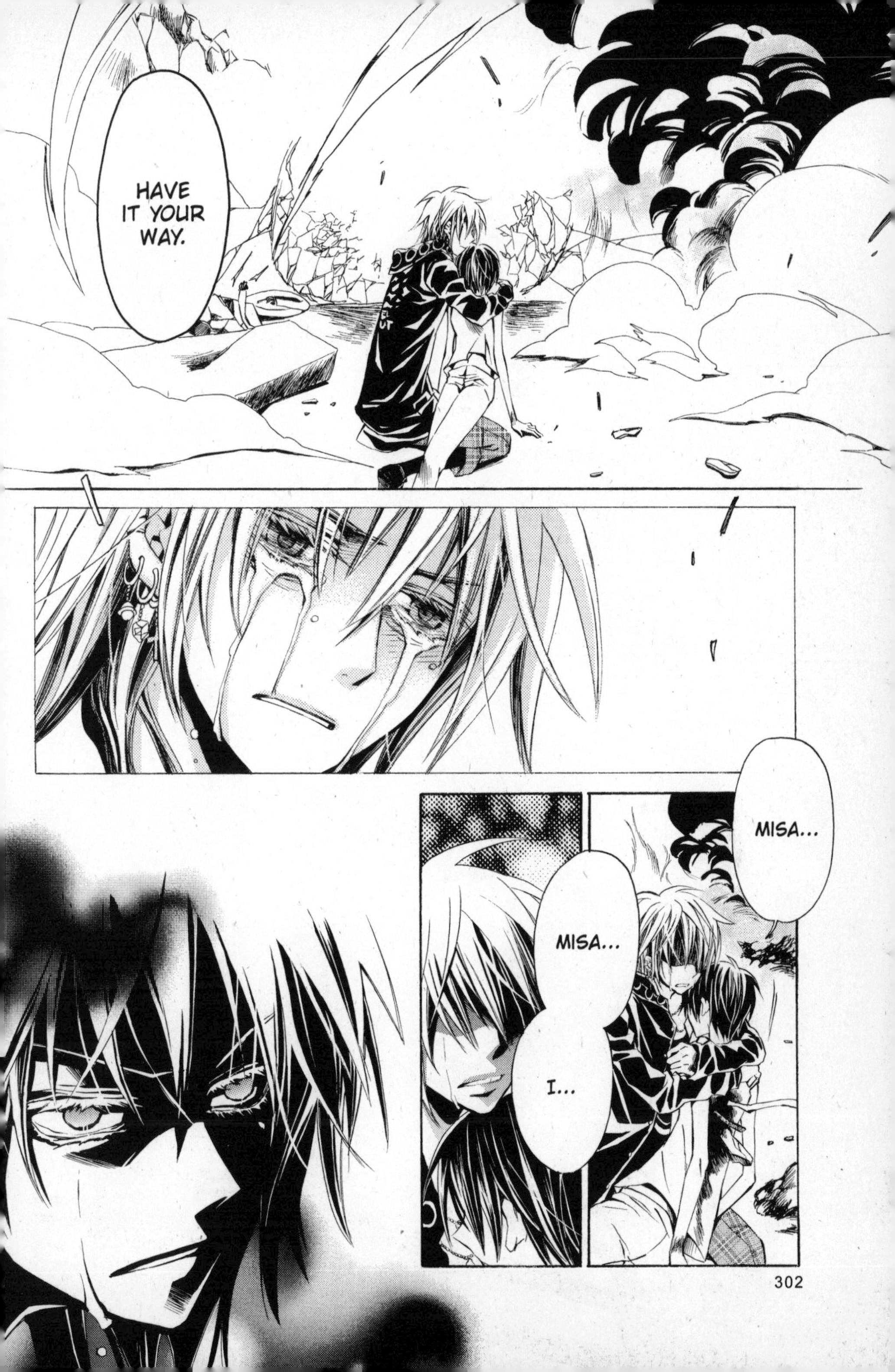
HAVE IT YOUR WAY.
MISA...
MISA...
I...

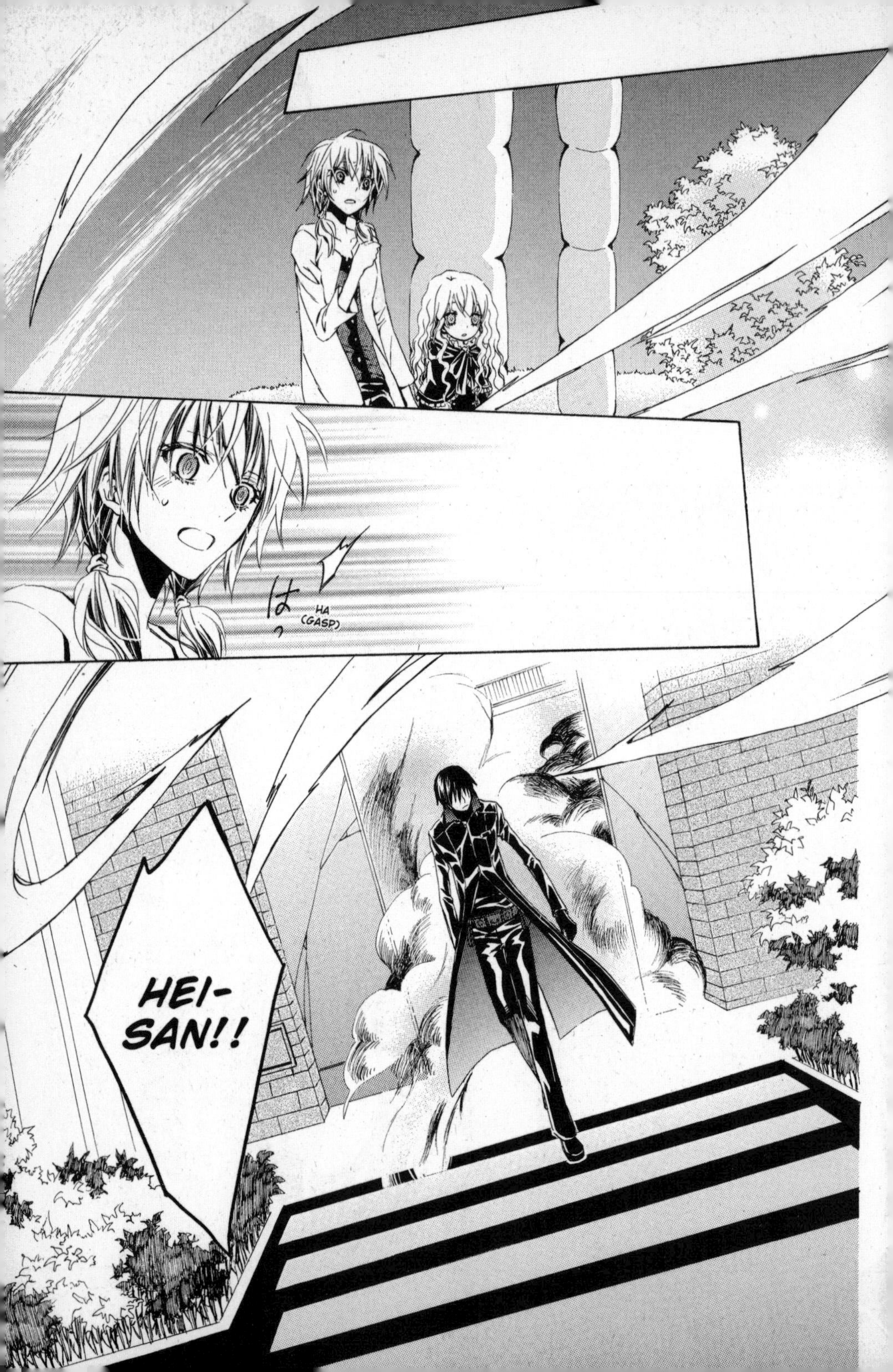

はっ
HA (GASP)
HEI-SAN!!

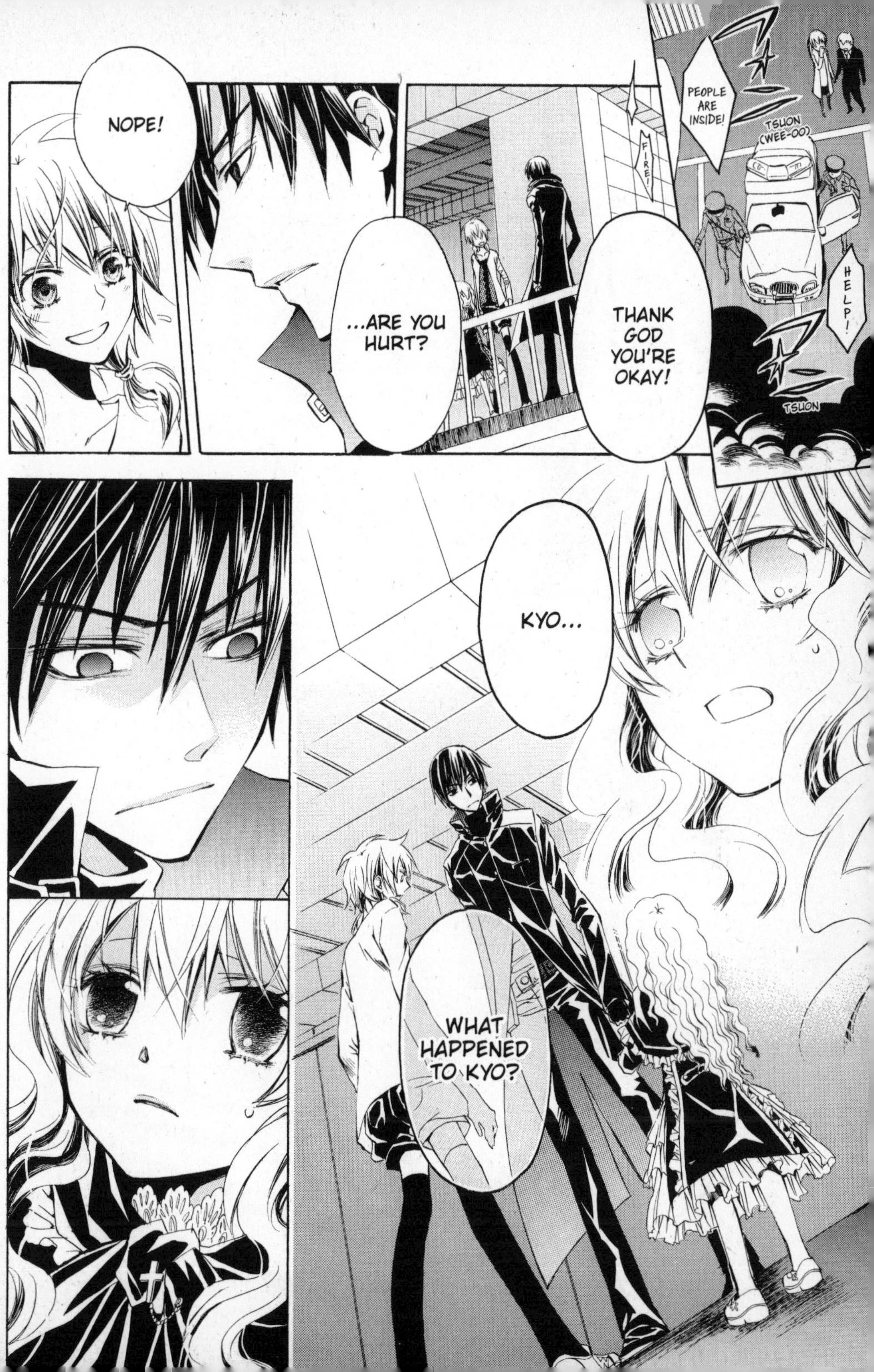
PEOPLE ARE INSIDE!
TSUON (WEE-OO)
HELP!
TSUON
FIRE!
THANK GOD YOU'RE OKAY!
...ARE YOU HURT?
NOPE!
KYO...
WHAT HAPPENED TO KYO?

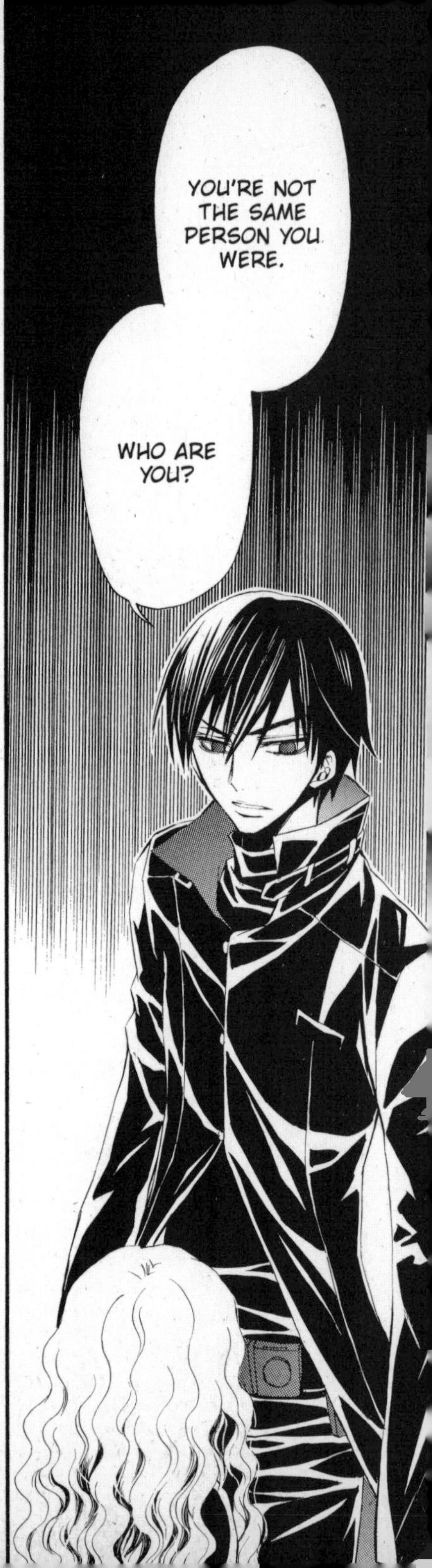
YOU'RE NOT THE SAME PERSON YOU WERE.
WHO ARE YOU?

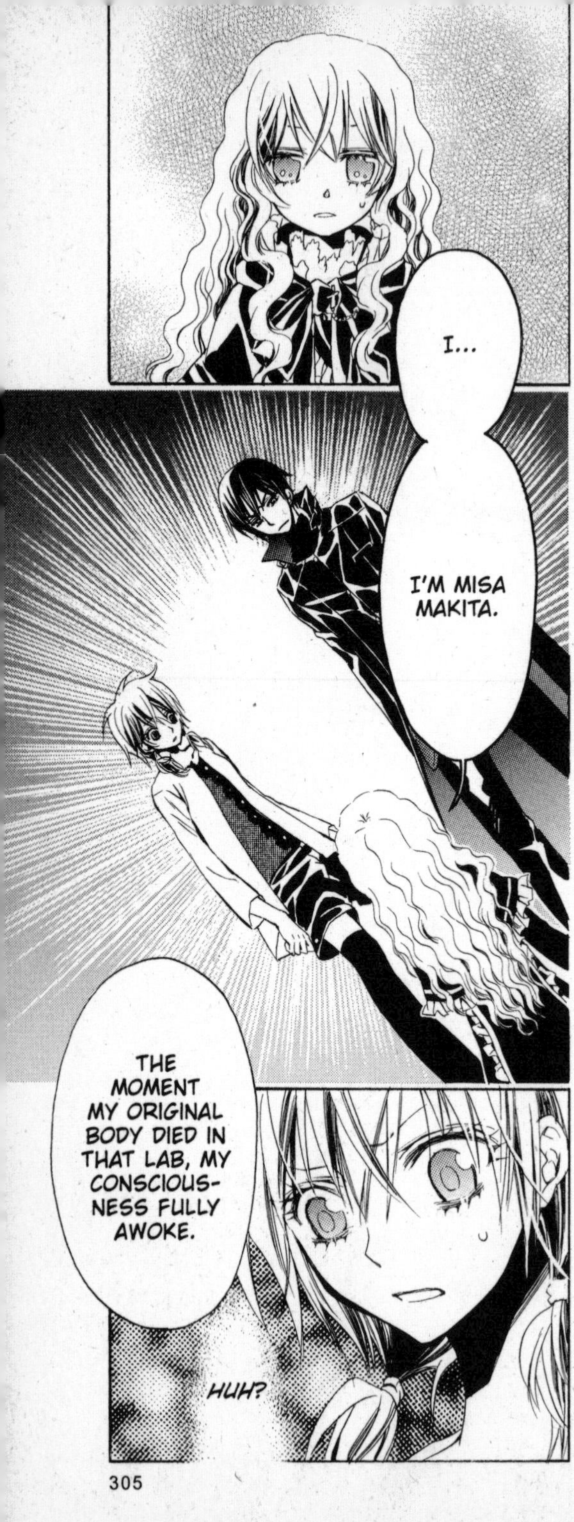
I...
I'M MISA MAKITA.
THE MOMENT MY ORIGINAL BODY DIED IN THAT LAB, MY CONSCIOUS-NESS FULLY AWOKE.
HUH?

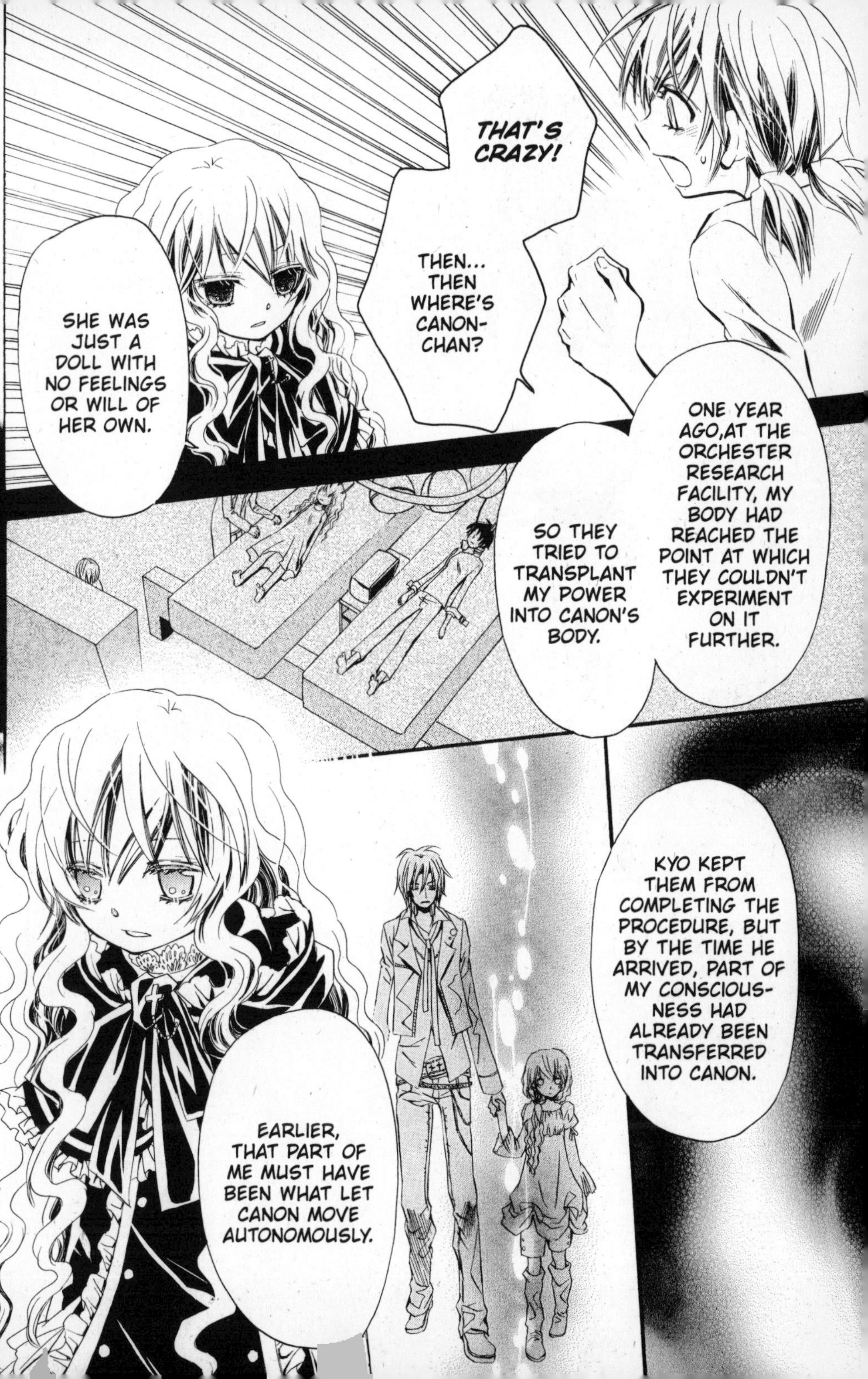
THAT'S CRAZY!
THEN... THEN WHERE'S CANON-CHAN?
SHE WAS JUST A DOLL WITH NO FEELINGS OR WILL OF HER OWN.
ONE YEAR AGO,AT THE ORCHESTER RESEARCH FACILITY, MY BODY HAD REACHED THE POINT AT WHICH THEY COULDN'T EXPERIMENT ON IT FURTHER.
SO THEY TRIED TO TRANSPLANT MY POWER INTO CANON'S BODY.
KYO KEPT THEM FROM COMPLETING THE PROCEDURE, BUT BY THE TIME HE ARRIVED, PART OF MY CONSCIOUS-NESS HAD ALREADY BEEN TRANSFERRED INTO CANON.
EARLIER, THAT PART OF ME MUST HAVE BEEN WHAT LET CANON MOVE AUTONOMOUSLY.

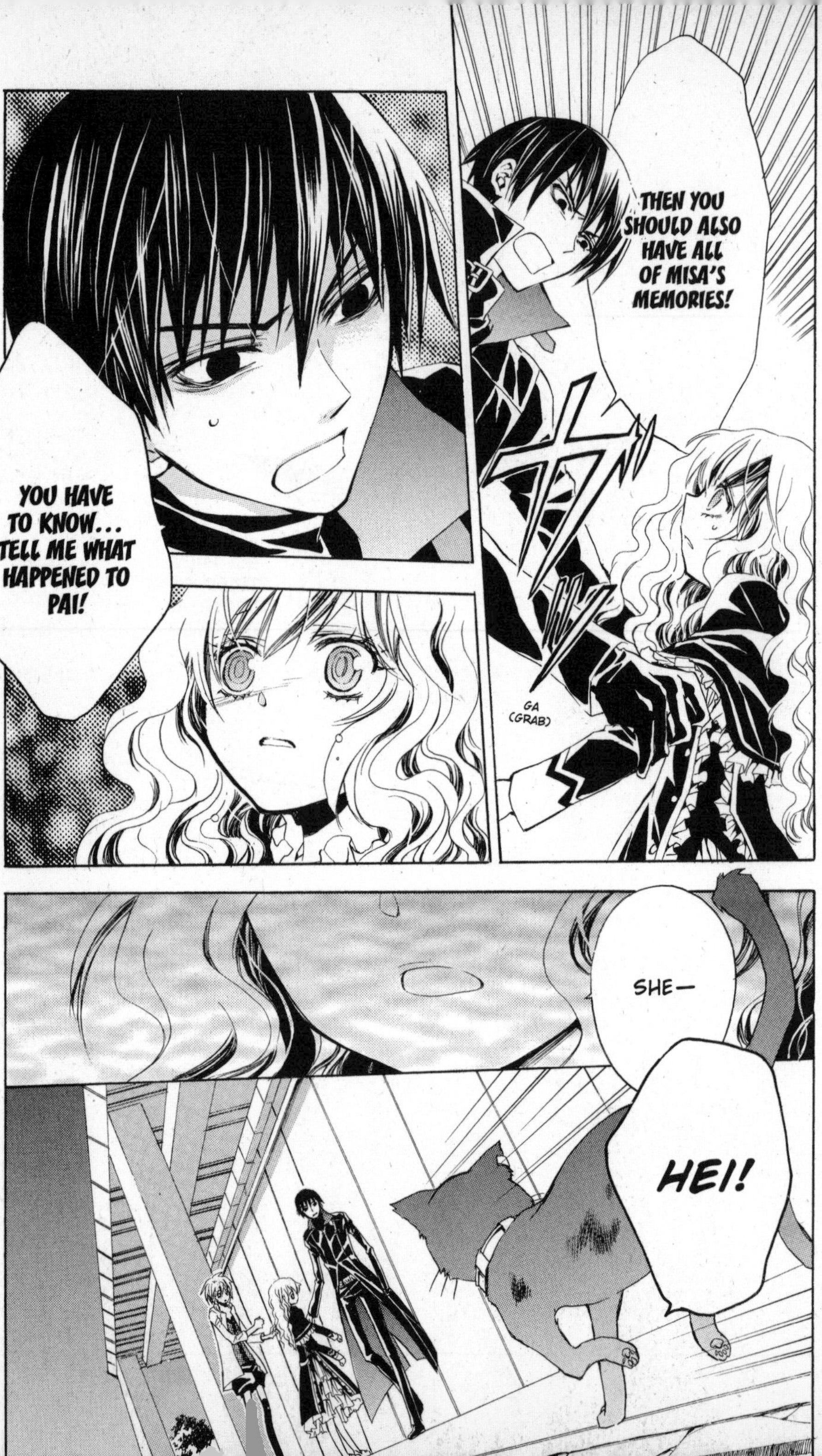
THEN YOU SHOULD ALSO HAVE ALL OF MISA'S MEMORIES!
GA (GRAB)
YOU HAVE TO KNOW... TELL ME WHAT HAPPENED TO PAI!
SHE—
HEI!

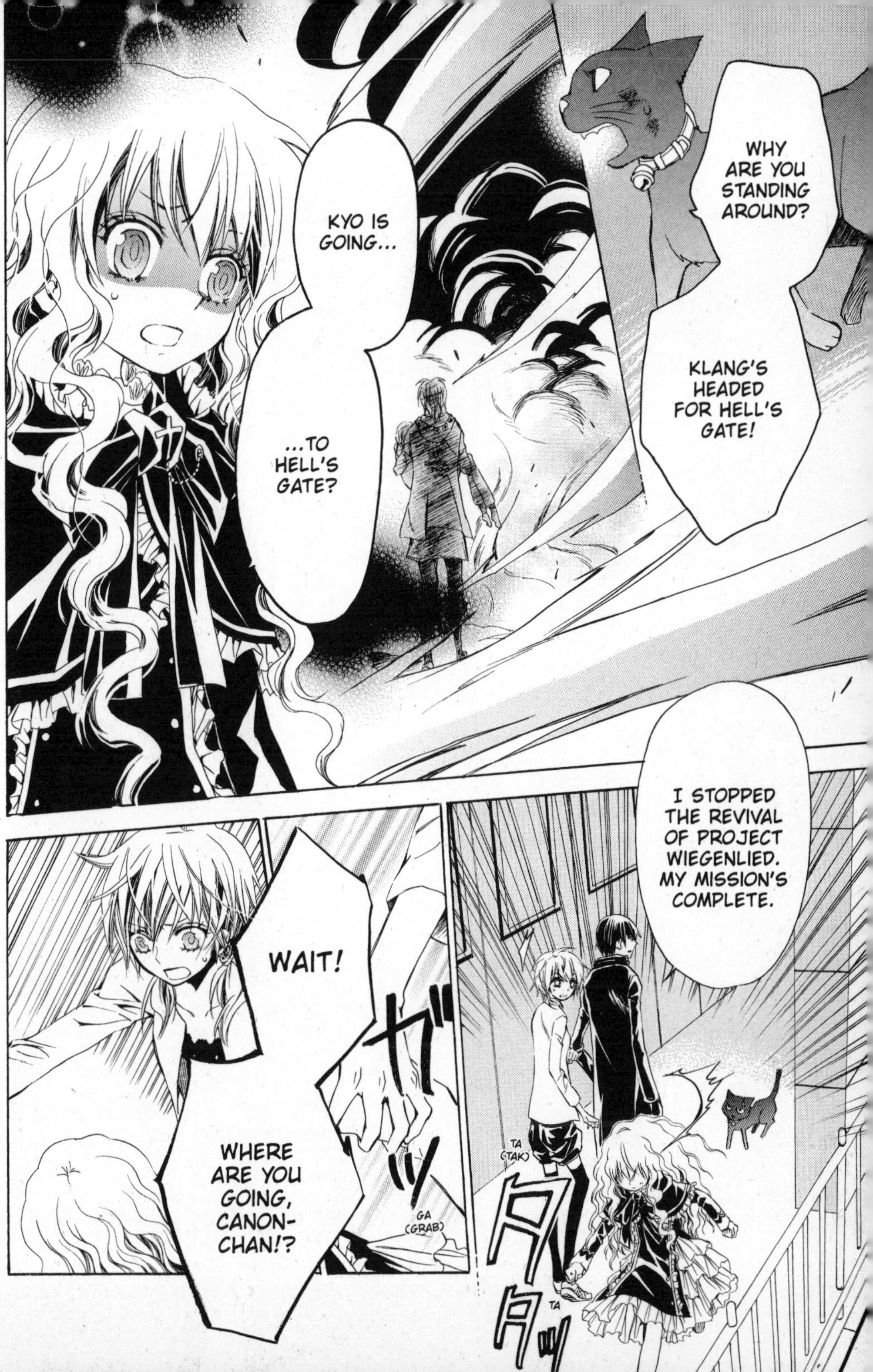
WHY ARE YOU STANDING AROUND?
KLANG'S HEADED FOR HELL'S GATE!
KYO IS GOING...
...TO HELL'S GATE?
I STOPPED THE REVIVAL OF PROJECT WIEGENLIED. MY MISSION'S COMPLETE.
TA (TAK)
TA
WAIT!
GA (GRAB)
WHERE ARE YOU GOING, CANON-CHAN!?

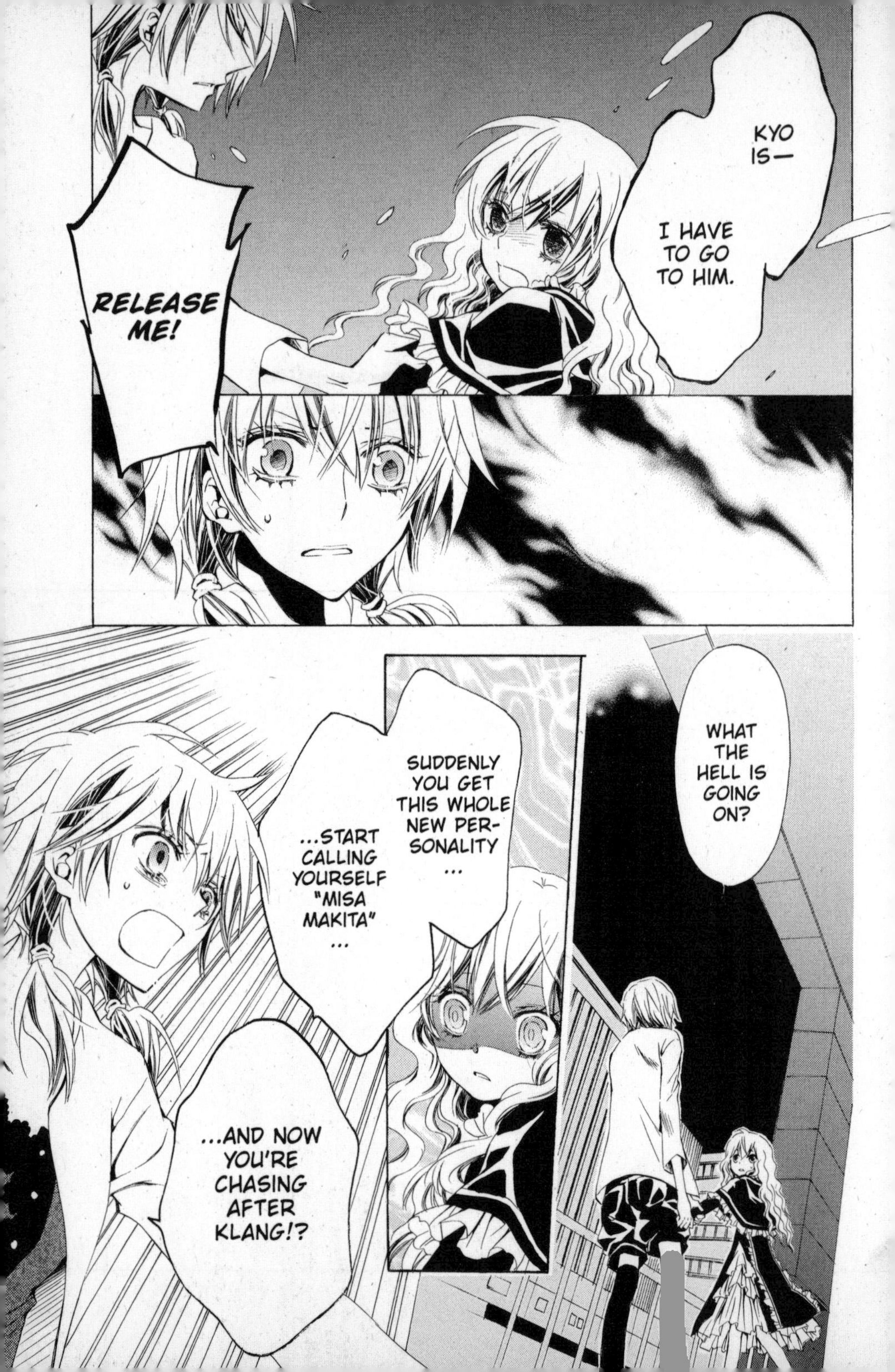
KYO IS—
I HAVE TO GO TO HIM.
RELEASE ME!
WHAT THE HELL IS GOING ON?
SUDDENLY YOU GET THIS WHOLE NEW PER-SONALITY...
...START CALLING YOURSELF "MISA MAKITA"...
...AND NOW YOU'RE CHASING AFTER KLANG!?

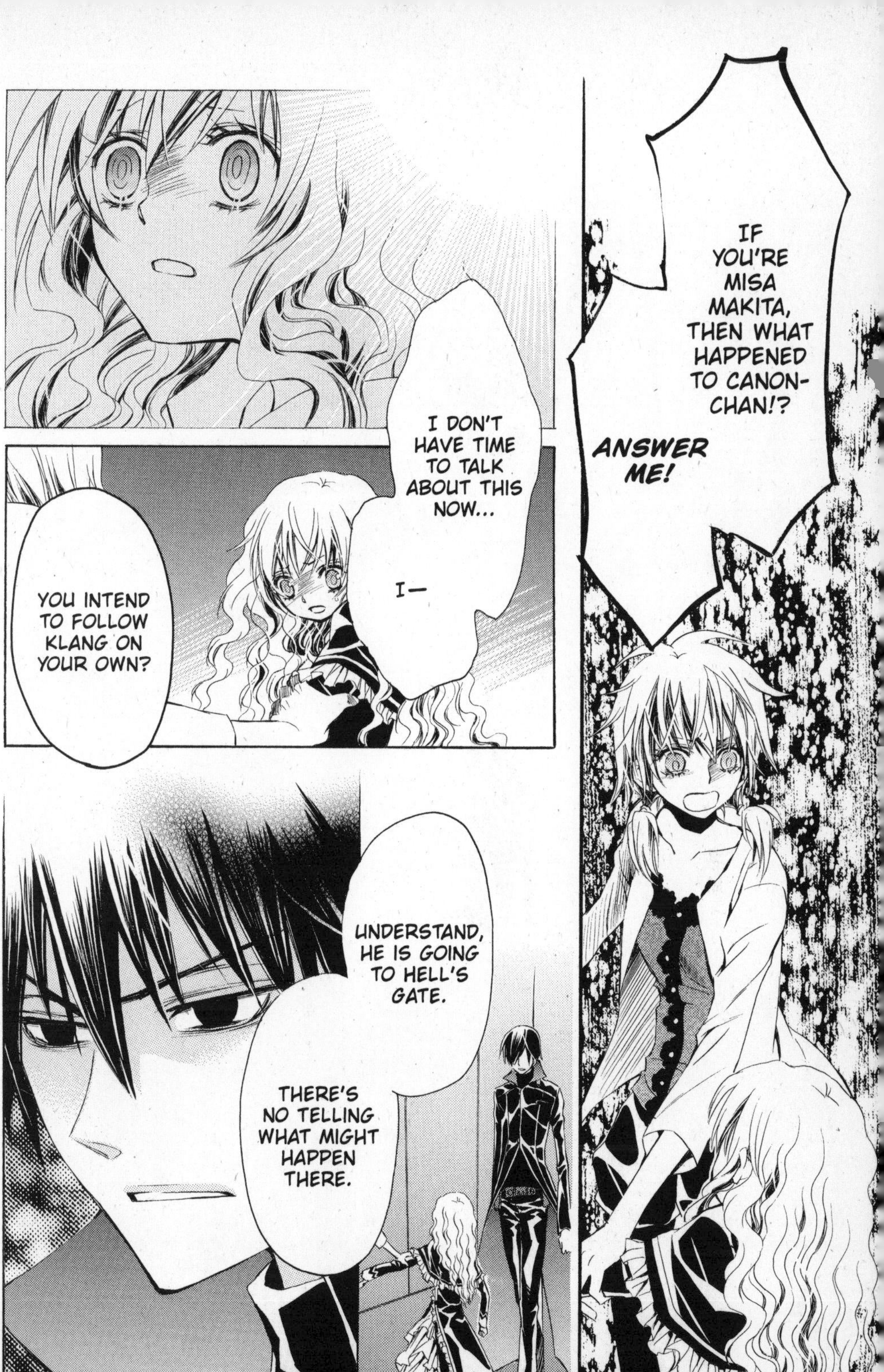
IF YOU'RE MISA MAKITA, THEN WHAT HAPPENED TO CANON-CHAN!?
ANSWER ME!
I DON'T HAVE TIME TO TALK ABOUT THIS NOW...
I—
YOU INTEND TO FOLLOW KLANG ON YOUR OWN?
UNDERSTAND, HE IS GOING TO HELL'S GATE.
THERE'S NO TELLING WHAT MIGHT HAPPEN THERE.

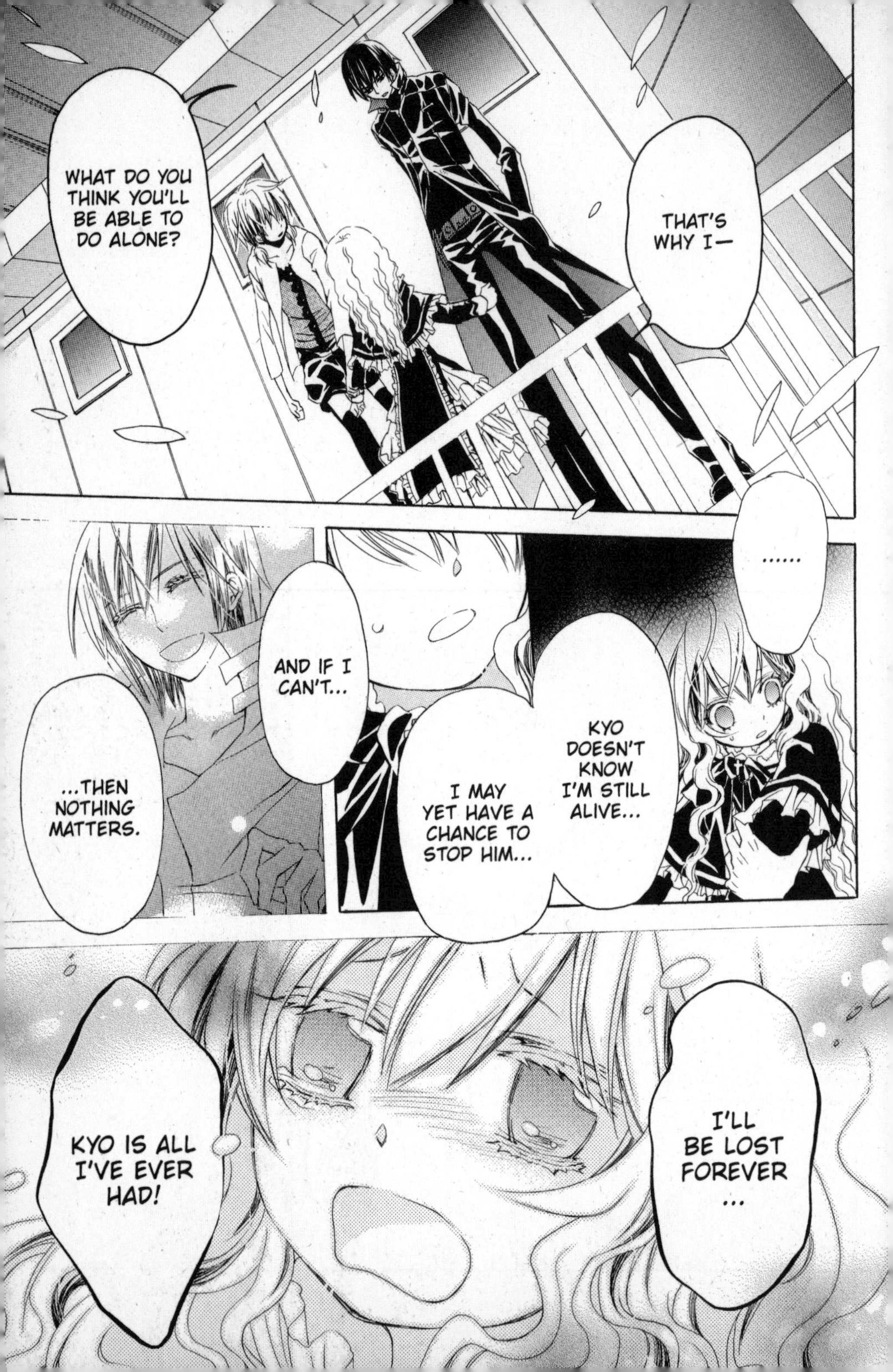
THAT'S WHY I—
WHAT DO YOU THINK YOU'LL BE ABLE TO DO ALONE?
......
KYO DOESN'T KNOW I'M STILL ALIVE...
I MAY YET HAVE A CHANCE TO STOP HIM...
AND IF I CAN'T...
...THEN NOTHING MATTERS.
I'LL BE LOST FOREVER ...
KYO IS ALL I'VE EVER HAD!

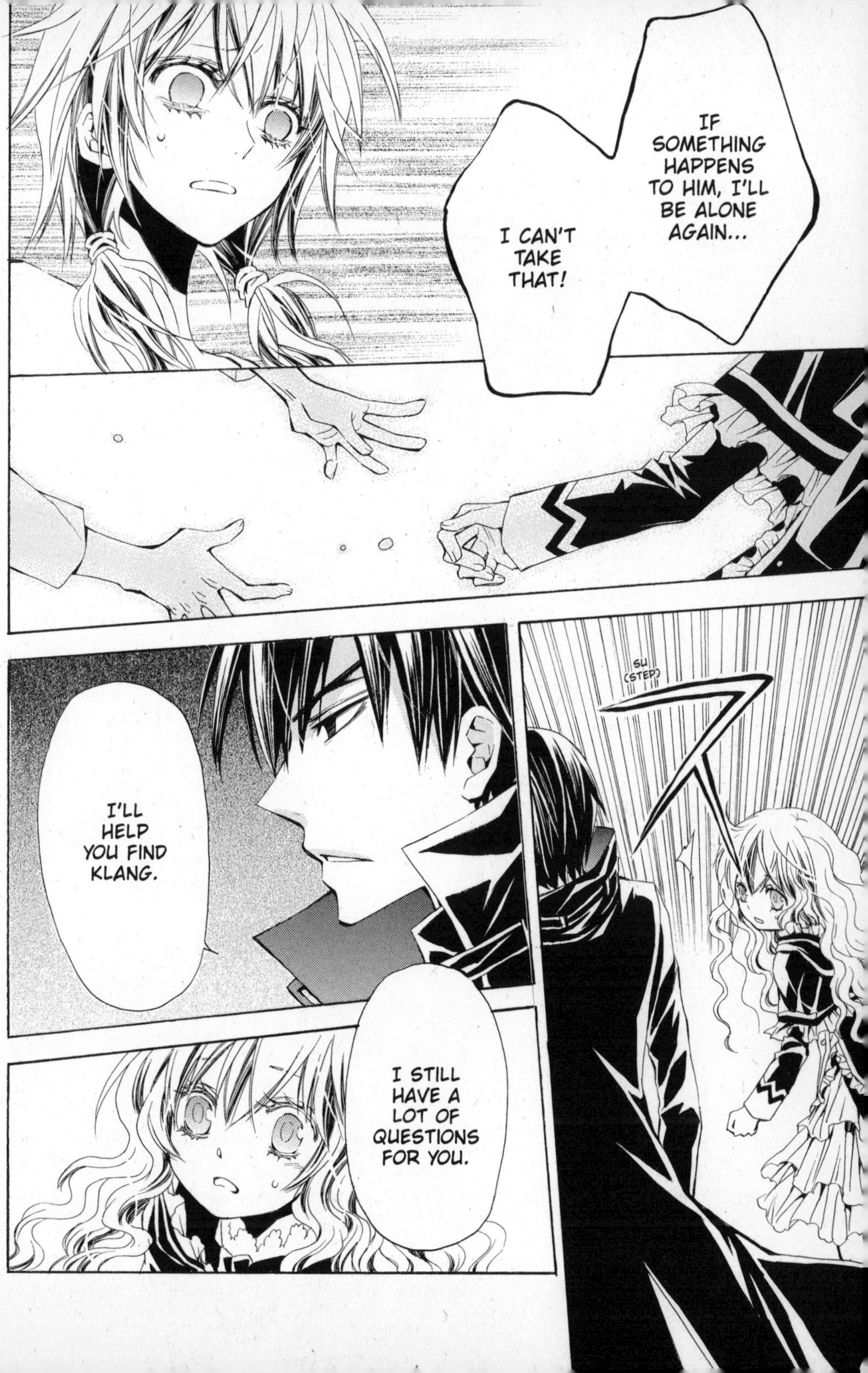
IF SOMETHING HAPPENS TO HIM, I'LL BE ALONE AGAIN...
I CAN'T TAKE THAT!
SU (STEP)
I'LL HELP YOU FIND KLANG.
I STILL HAVE A LOT OF QUESTIONS FOR YOU.

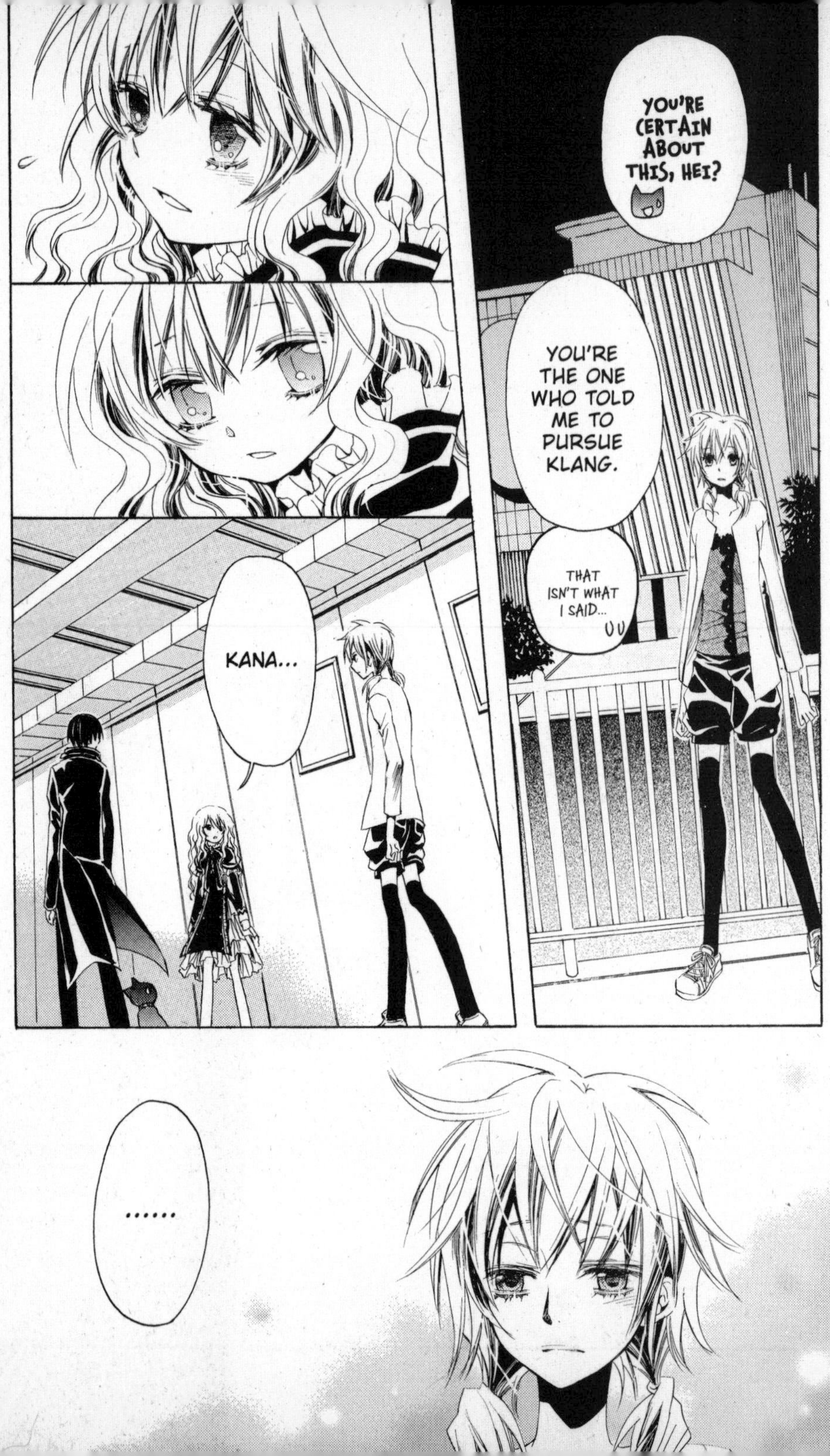
YOU'RE CERTAIN ABOUT THIS, HEI?
YOU'RE THE ONE WHO TOLD ME TO PURSUE KLANG.
THAT ISN'T WHAT I SAID...
KANA...
......

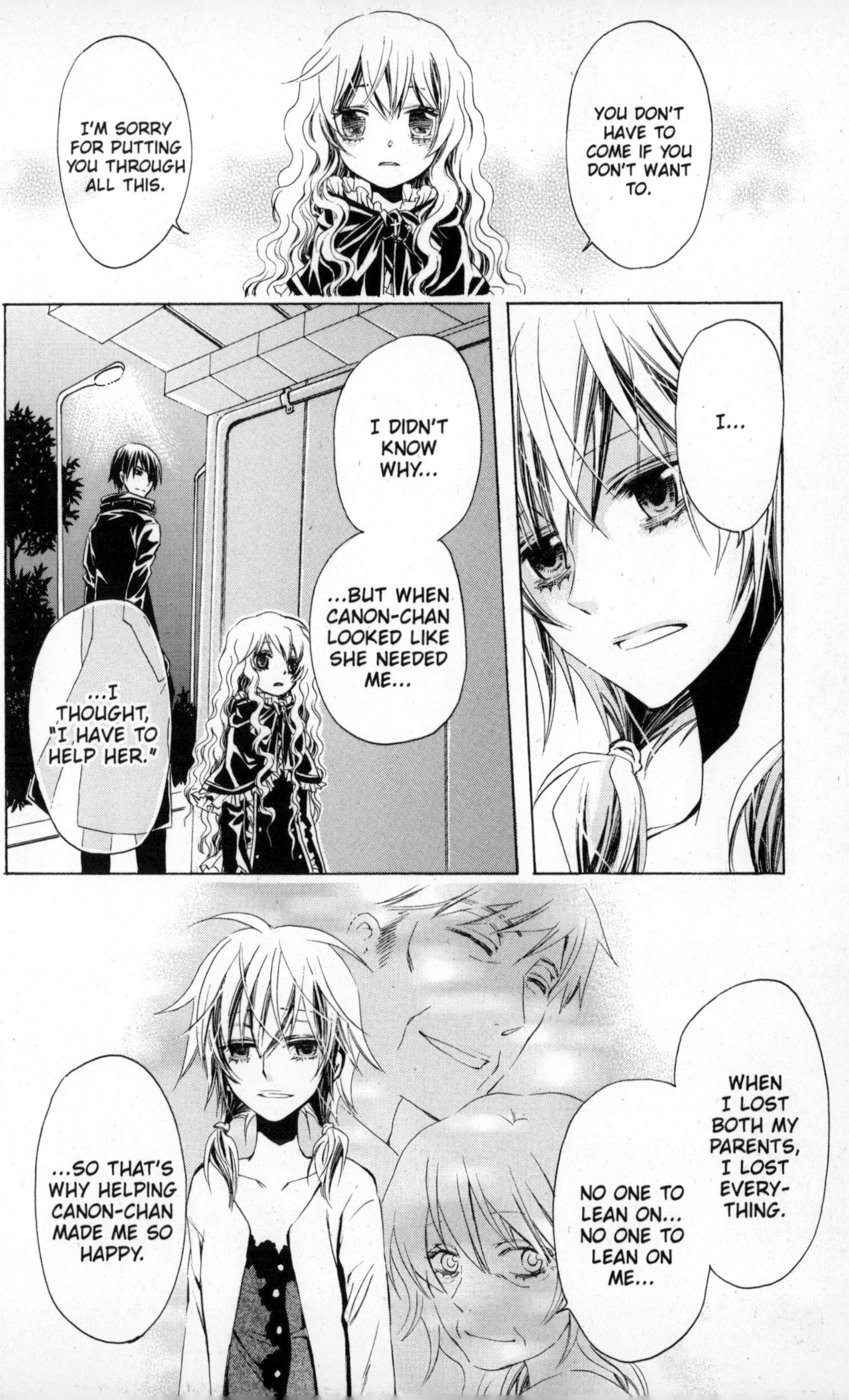
YOU DON'T HAVE TO COME IF YOU DON'T WANT TO.
I'M SORRY FOR PUTTING YOU THROUGH ALL THIS.
I...
I DIDN'T KNOW WHY...
...BUT WHEN CANON-CHAN LOOKED LIKE SHE NEEDED ME...
...I THOUGHT, "I HAVE TO HELP HER."
WHEN I LOST BOTH MY PARENTS, I LOST EVERY-THING.
NO ONE TO LEAN ON... NO ONE TO LEAN ON ME...
...SO THAT'S WHY HELPING CANON-CHAN MADE ME SO HAPPY.

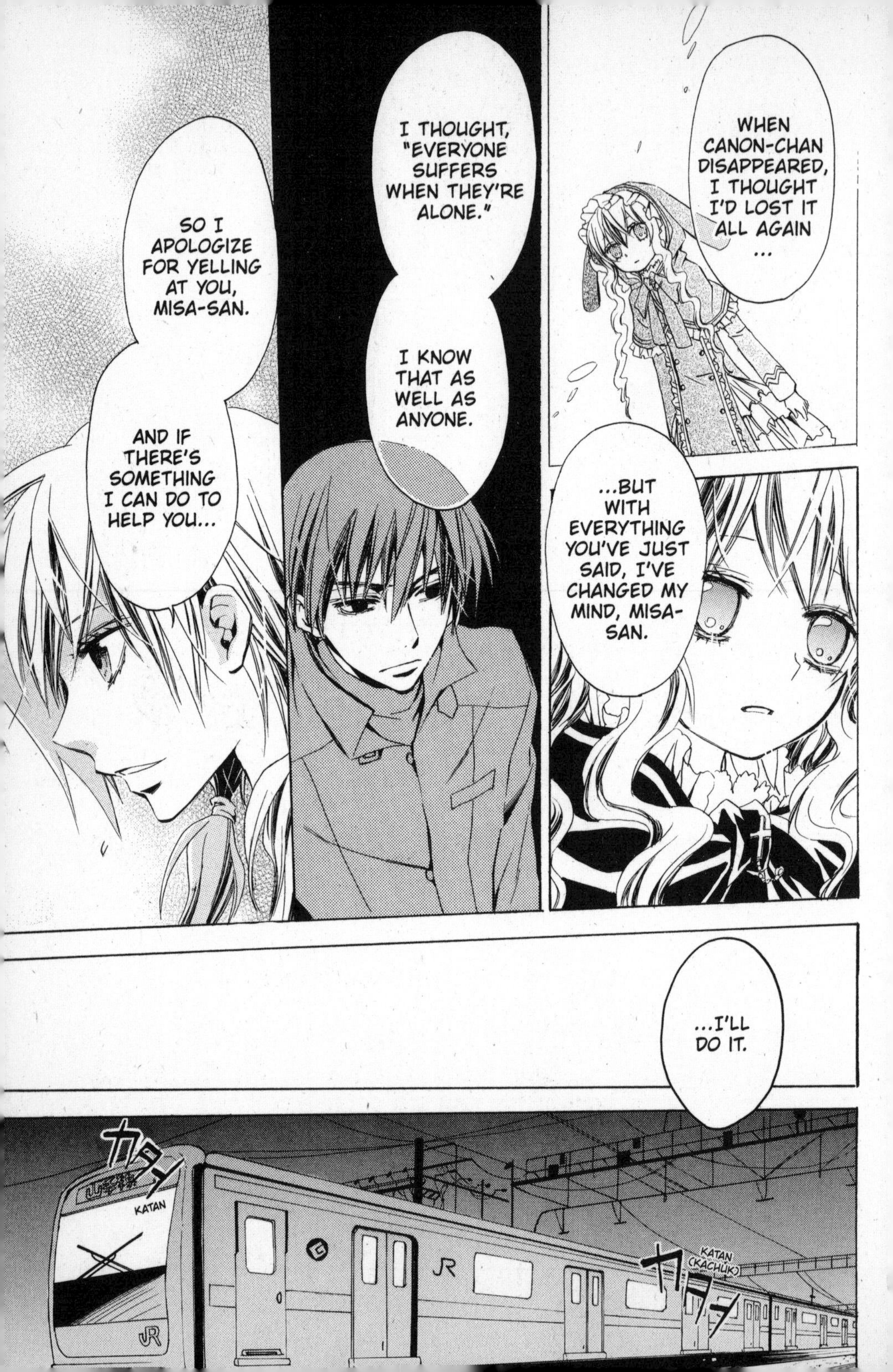

WHEN CANON-CHAN DISAPPEARED, I THOUGHT I'D LOST IT ALL AGAIN ...
...BUT WITH EVERYTHING YOU'VE JUST SAID, I'VE CHANGED MY MIND, MISA-SAN.
I THOUGHT, "EVERYONE SUFFERS WHEN THEY'RE ALONE."
I KNOW THAT AS WELL AS ANYONE.
SO I APOLOGIZE FOR YELLING AT YOU, MISA-SAN.
AND IF THERE'S SOMETHING I CAN DO TO HELP YOU...
...I'LL DO IT.
KATAN
KATAN (KACHUK)

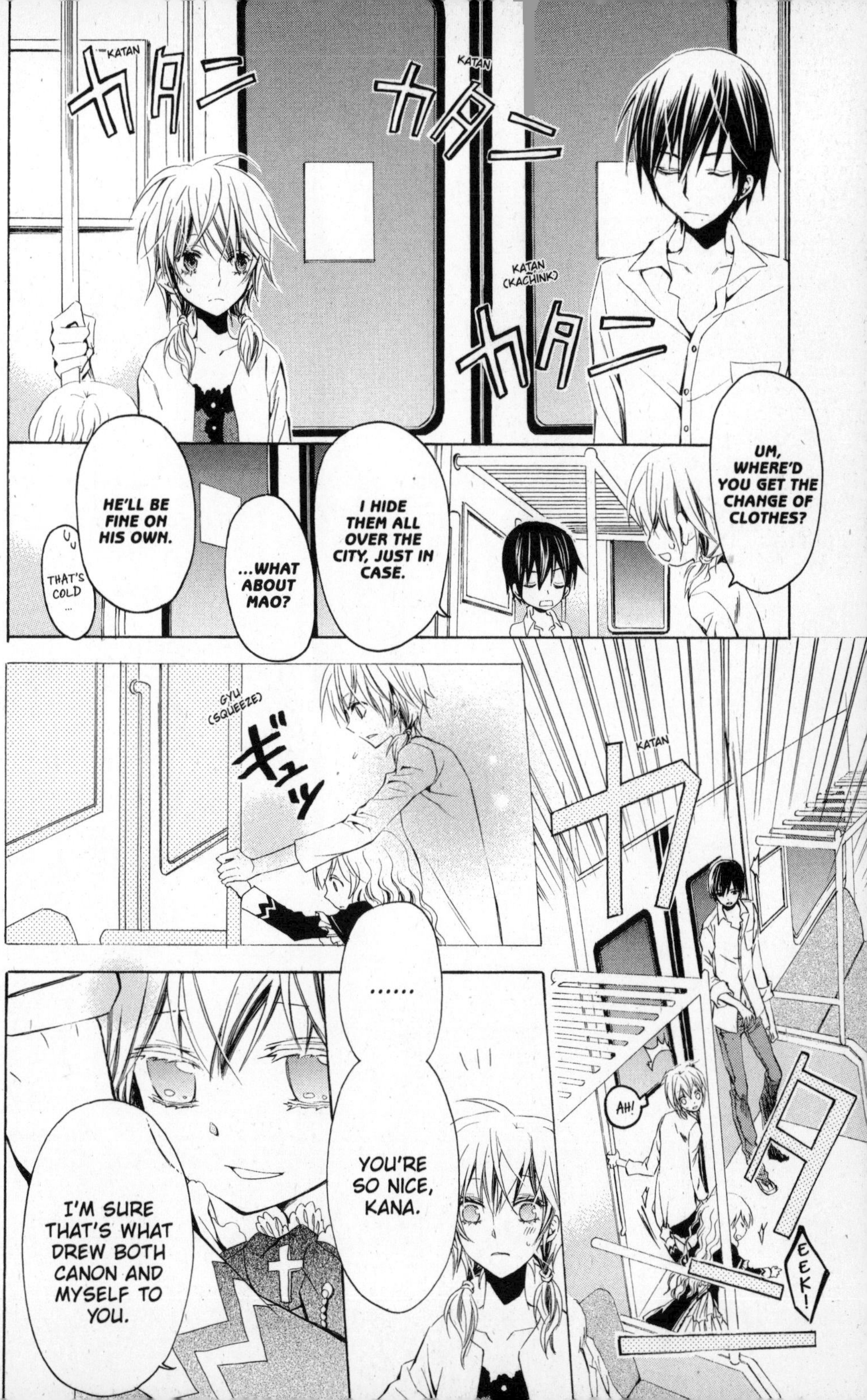
KATAN
KATAN
(KACHINK)
KATAN
UM, WHERE'D YOU GET THE CHANGE OF CLOTHES?
I HIDE THEM ALL OVER THE CITY, JUST IN CASE.
...WHAT ABOUT MAO?
HE'LL BE FINE ON HIS OWN.
THAT'S COLD ...
KATAN
AH!
EEK!
GYU (SQUEEZE)
......
YOU'RE SO NICE, KANA.
I'M SURE THAT'S WHAT DREW BOTH CANON AND MYSELF TO YOU.

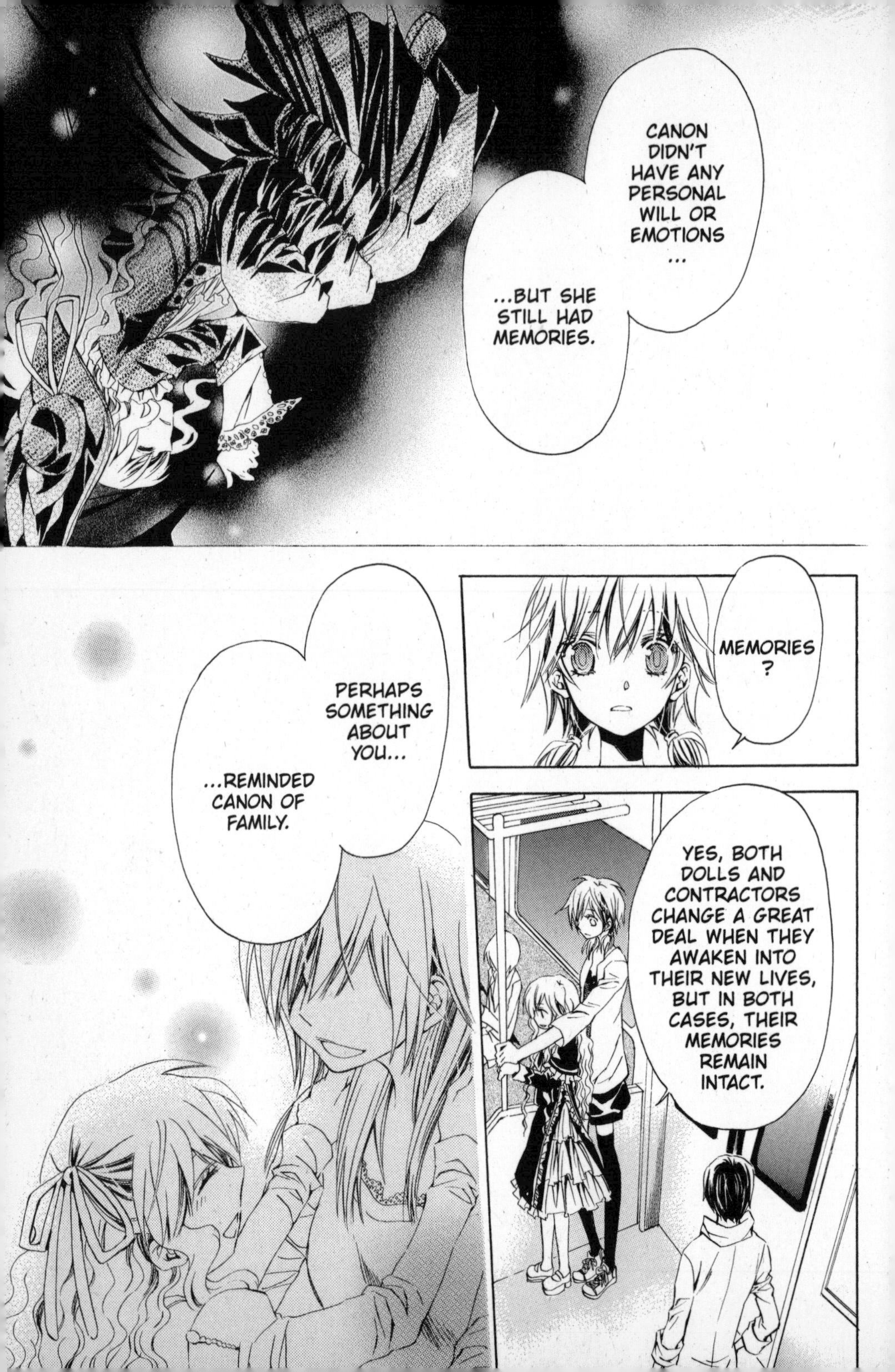
CANON DIDN'T HAVE ANY PERSONAL WILL OR EMOTIONS ...
...BUT SHE STILL HAD MEMORIES.
MEMORIES?
YES, BOTH DOLLS AND CONTRACTORS CHANGE A GREAT DEAL WHEN THEY AWAKEN INTO THEIR NEW LIVES, BUT IN BOTH CASES, THEIR MEMORIES REMAIN INTACT.
PERHAPS SOMETHING ABOUT YOU...
...REMINDED CANON OF FAMILY.

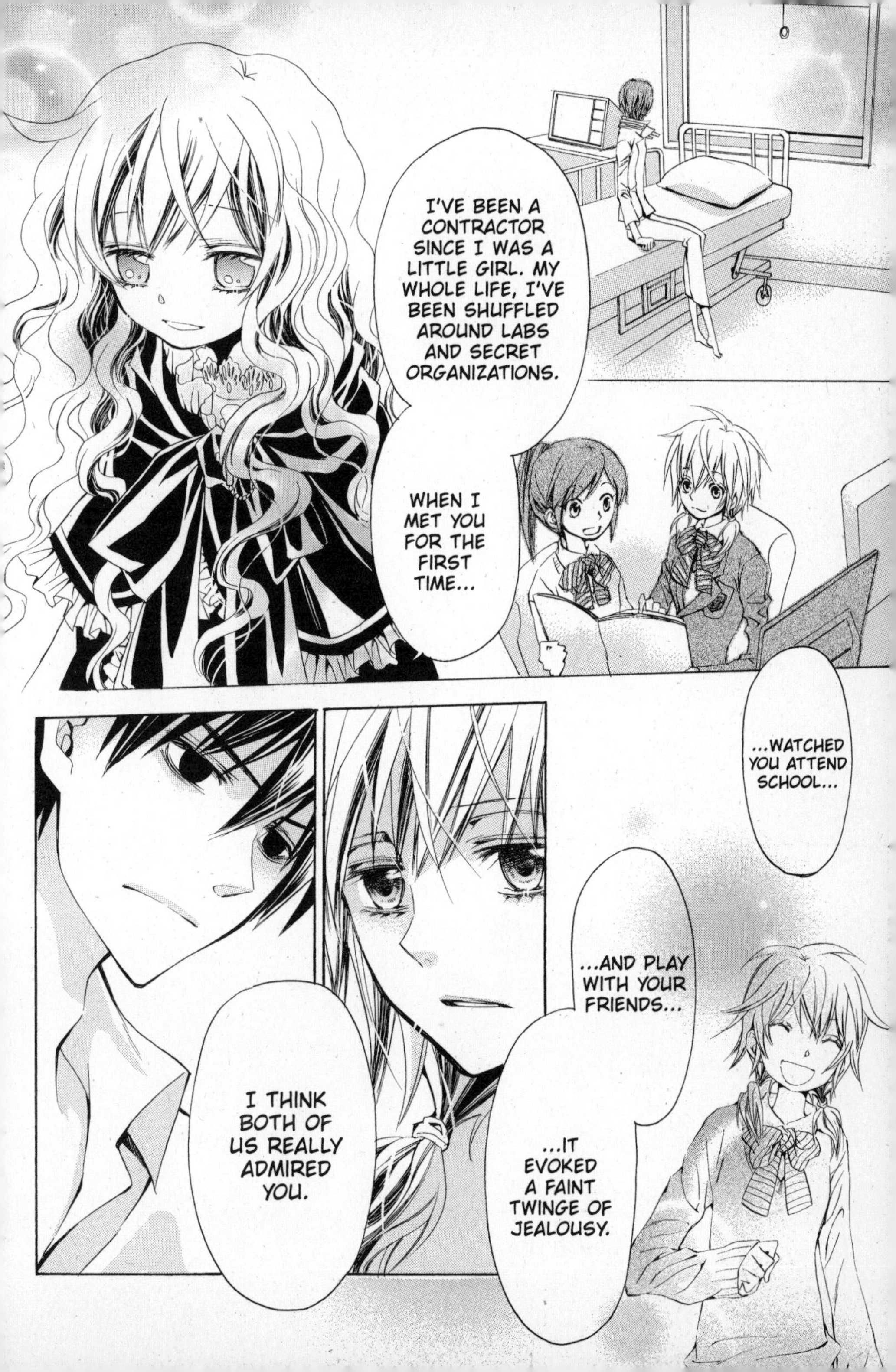
I'VE BEEN A CONTRACTOR SINCE I WAS A LITTLE GIRL. MY WHOLE LIFE, I'VE BEEN SHUFFLED AROUND LABS AND SECRET ORGANIZATIONS.
WHEN I MET YOU FOR THE FIRST TIME...
...WATCHED YOU ATTEND SCHOOL...
...AND PLAY WITH YOUR FRIENDS...
...IT EVOKED A FAINT TWINGE OF JEALOUSY.
I THINK BOTH OF US REALLY ADMIRED YOU.

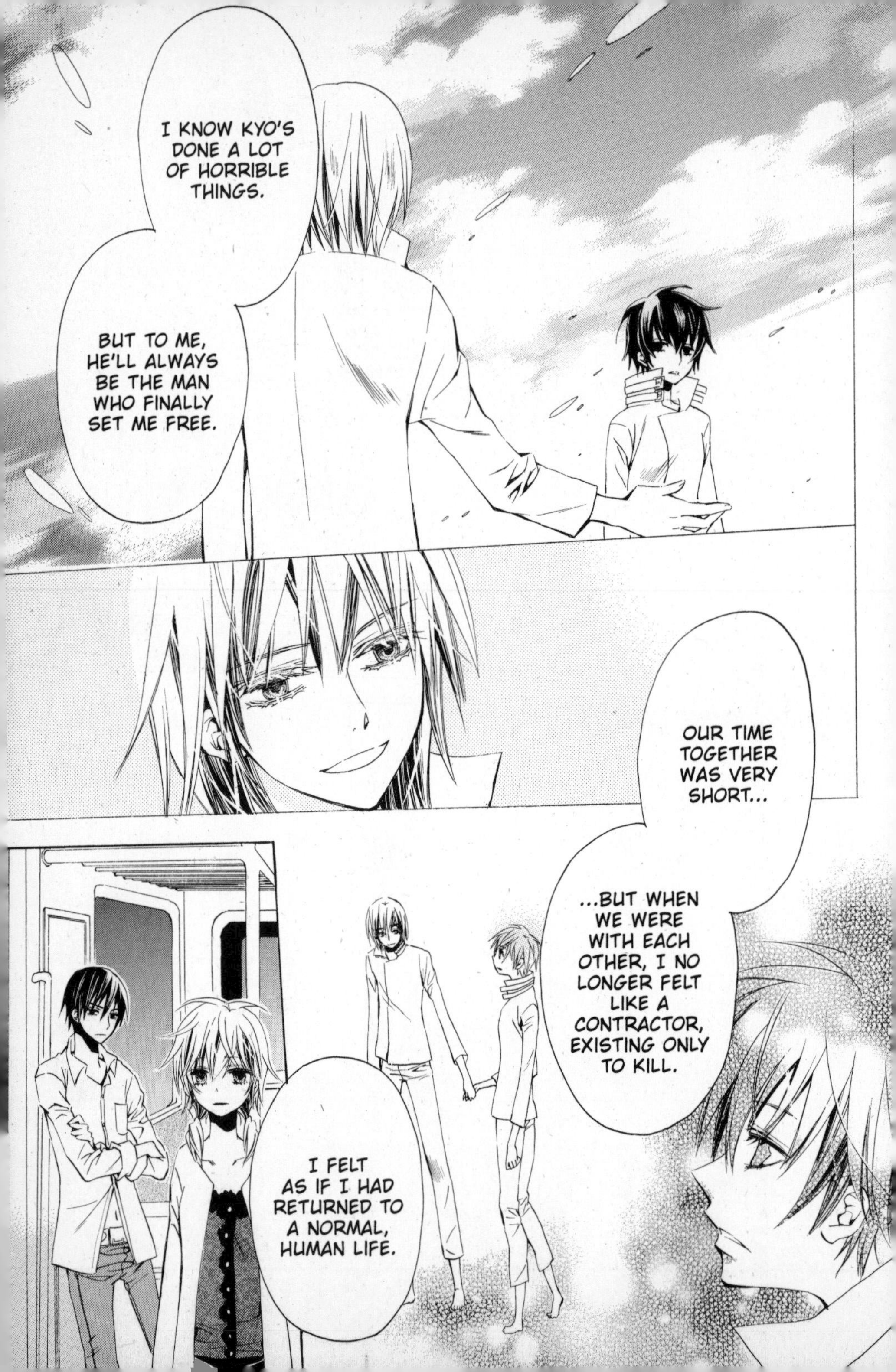
I KNOW KYO'S DONE A LOT OF HORRIBLE THINGS.
BUT TO ME, HE'LL ALWAYS BE THE MAN WHO FINALLY SET ME FREE.
OUR TIME TOGETHER WAS VERY SHORT...
...BUT WHEN WE WERE WITH EACH OTHER, I NO LONGER FELT LIKE A CONTRACTOR, EXISTING ONLY TO KILL.
I FELT AS IF I HAD RETURNED TO A NORMAL, HUMAN LIFE.

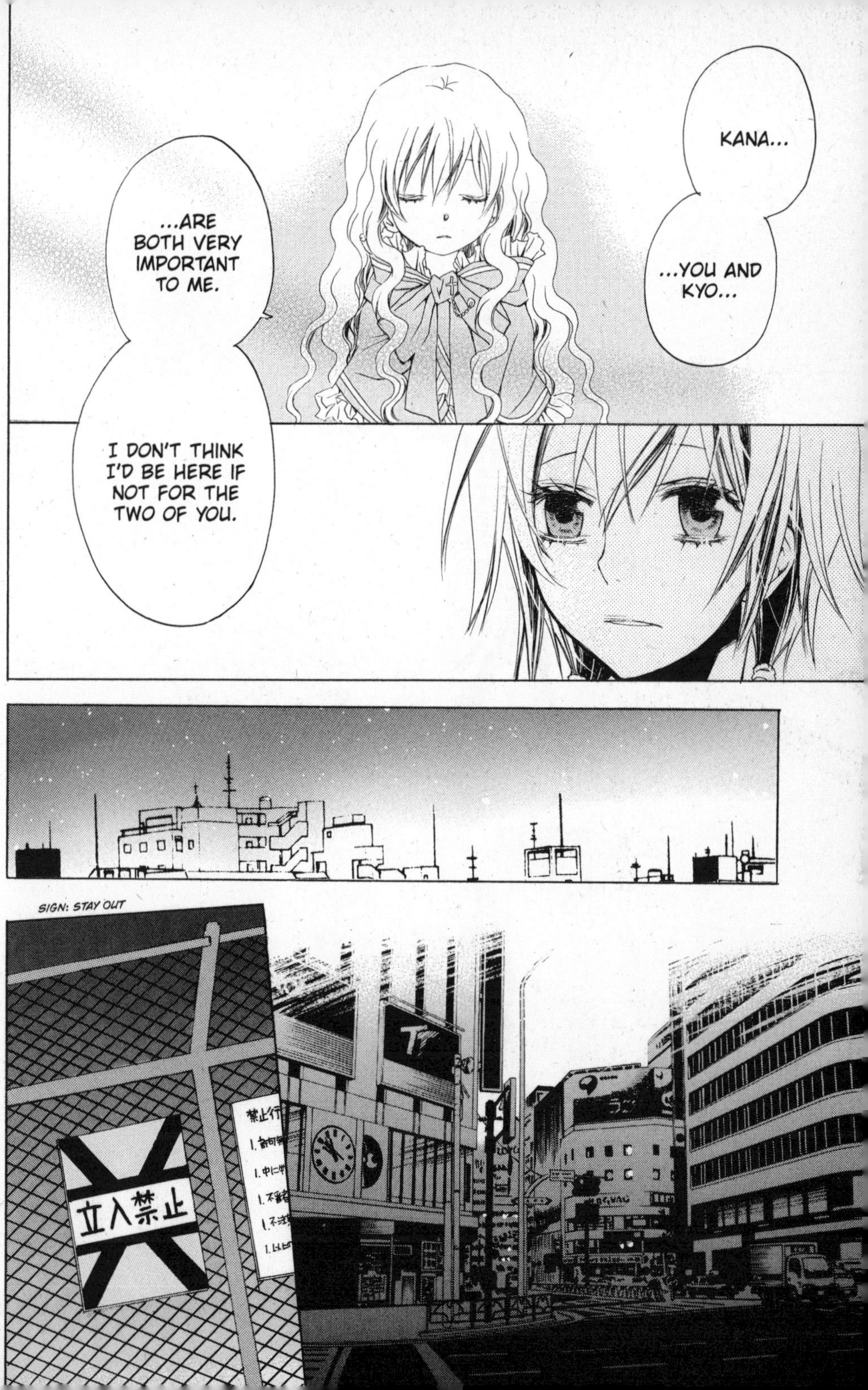
KANA...
...YOU AND KYO...
...ARE BOTH VERY IMPORTANT TO ME.
I DON'T THINK I'D BE HERE IF NOT FOR THE TWO OF YOU.
SIGN: STAY OUT
立入禁止

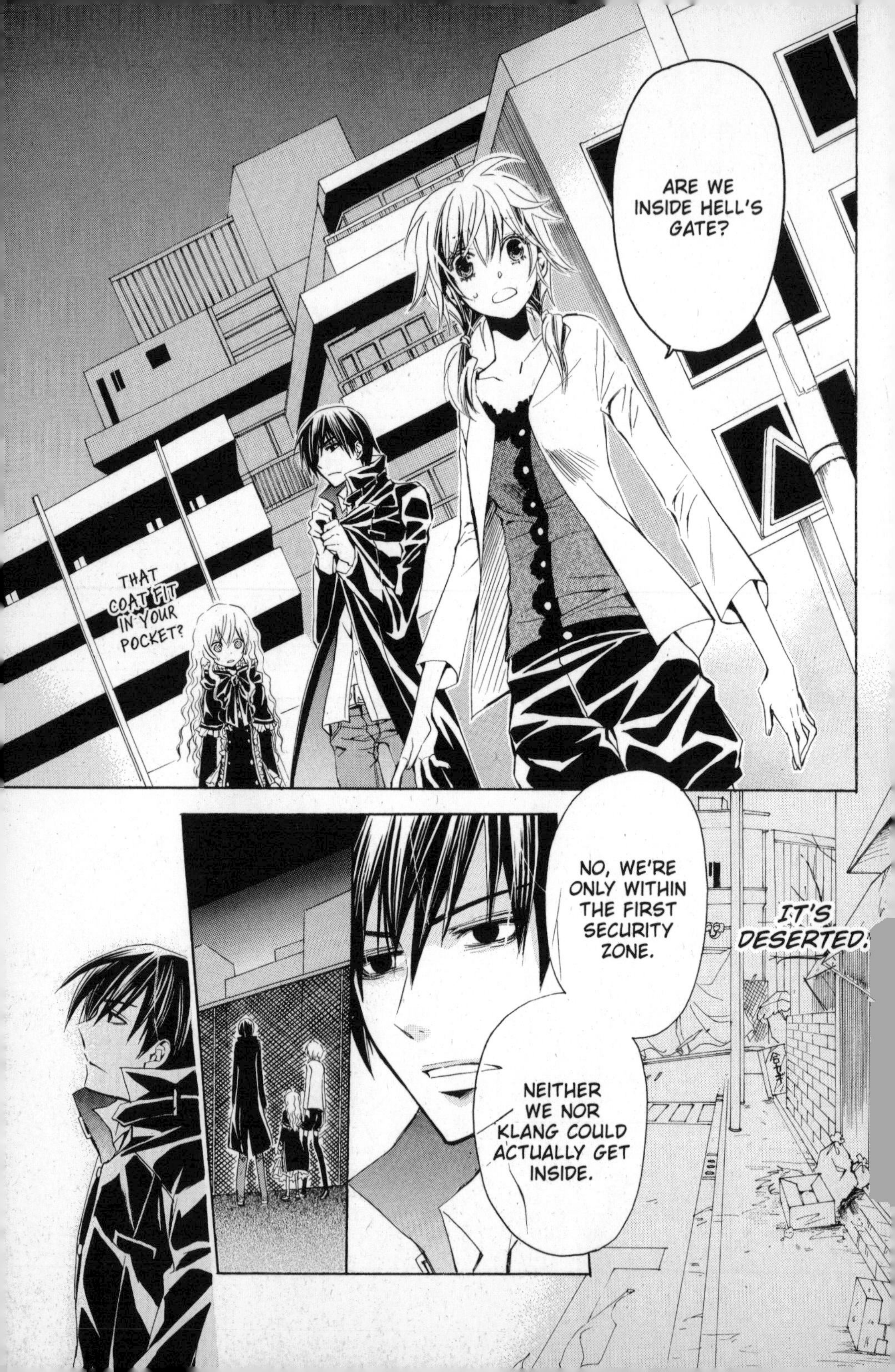
ARE WE INSIDE HELL'S GATE?
THAT COAT FIT IN YOUR POCKET?
IT'S DESERTED.
NO, WE'RE ONLY WITHIN THE FIRST SECURITY ZONE.
NEITHER WE NOR KLANG COULD ACTUALLY GET INSIDE.

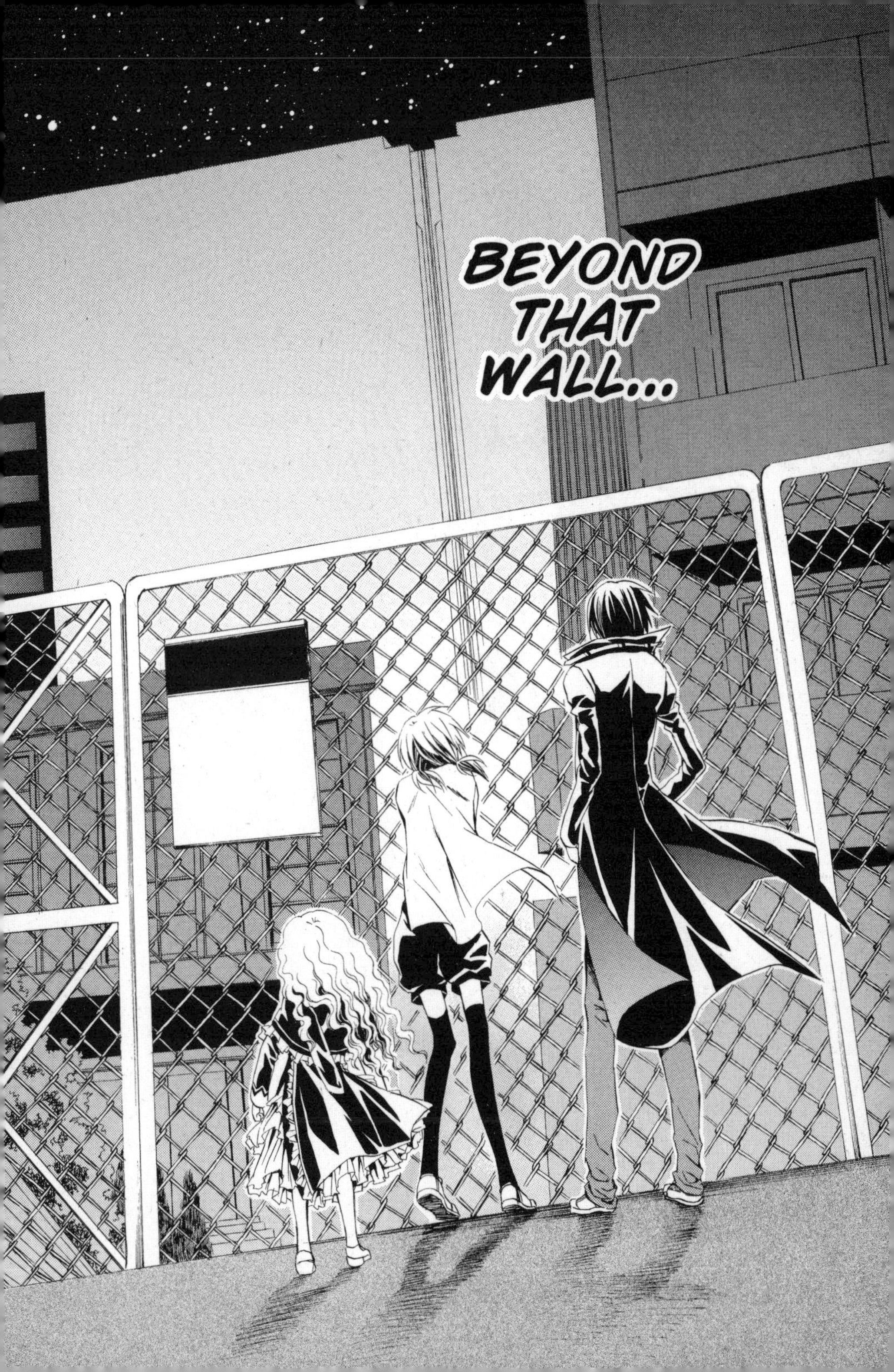
BEYOND THAT WALL...

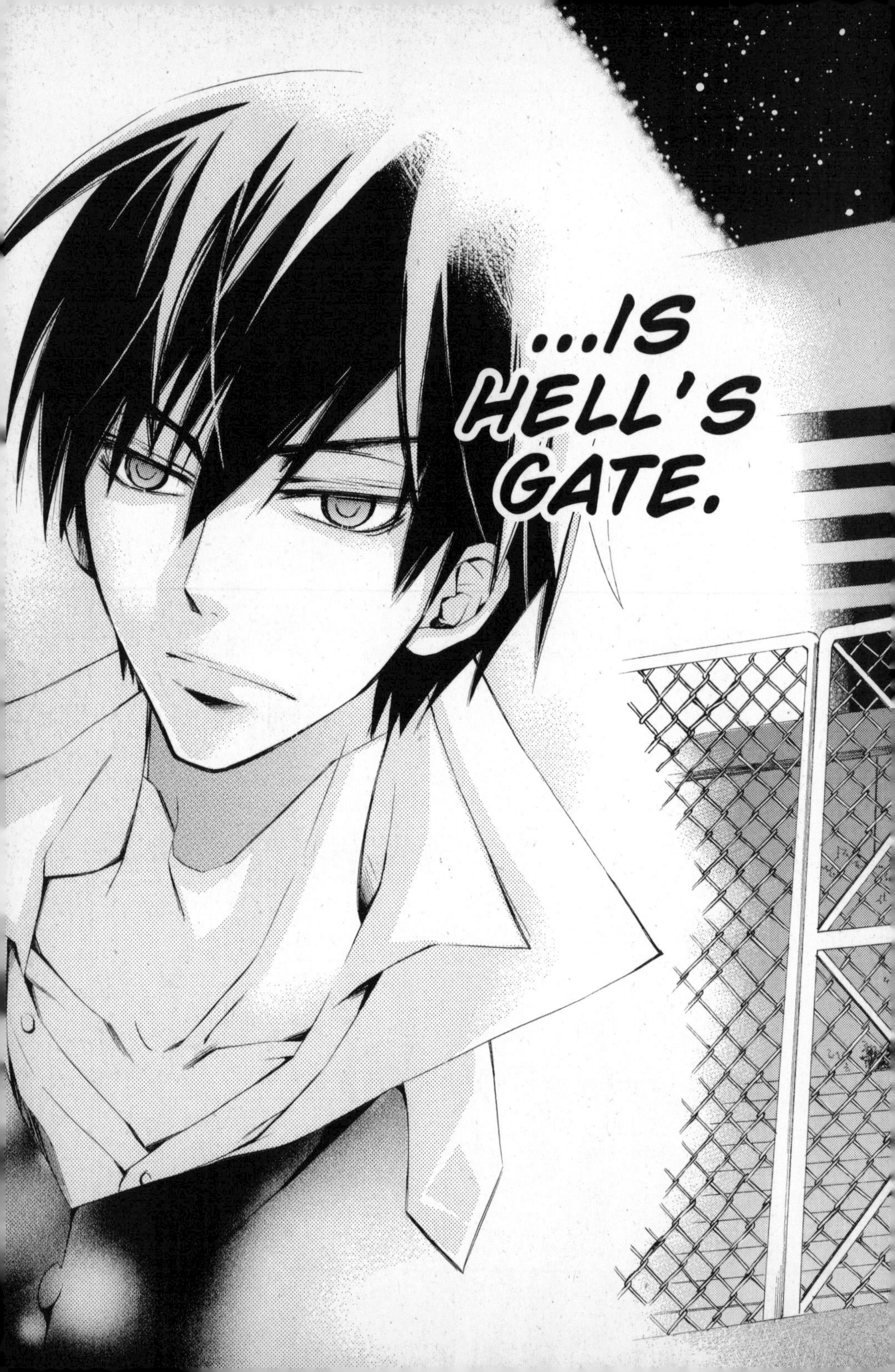
...IS HELL'S GATE.

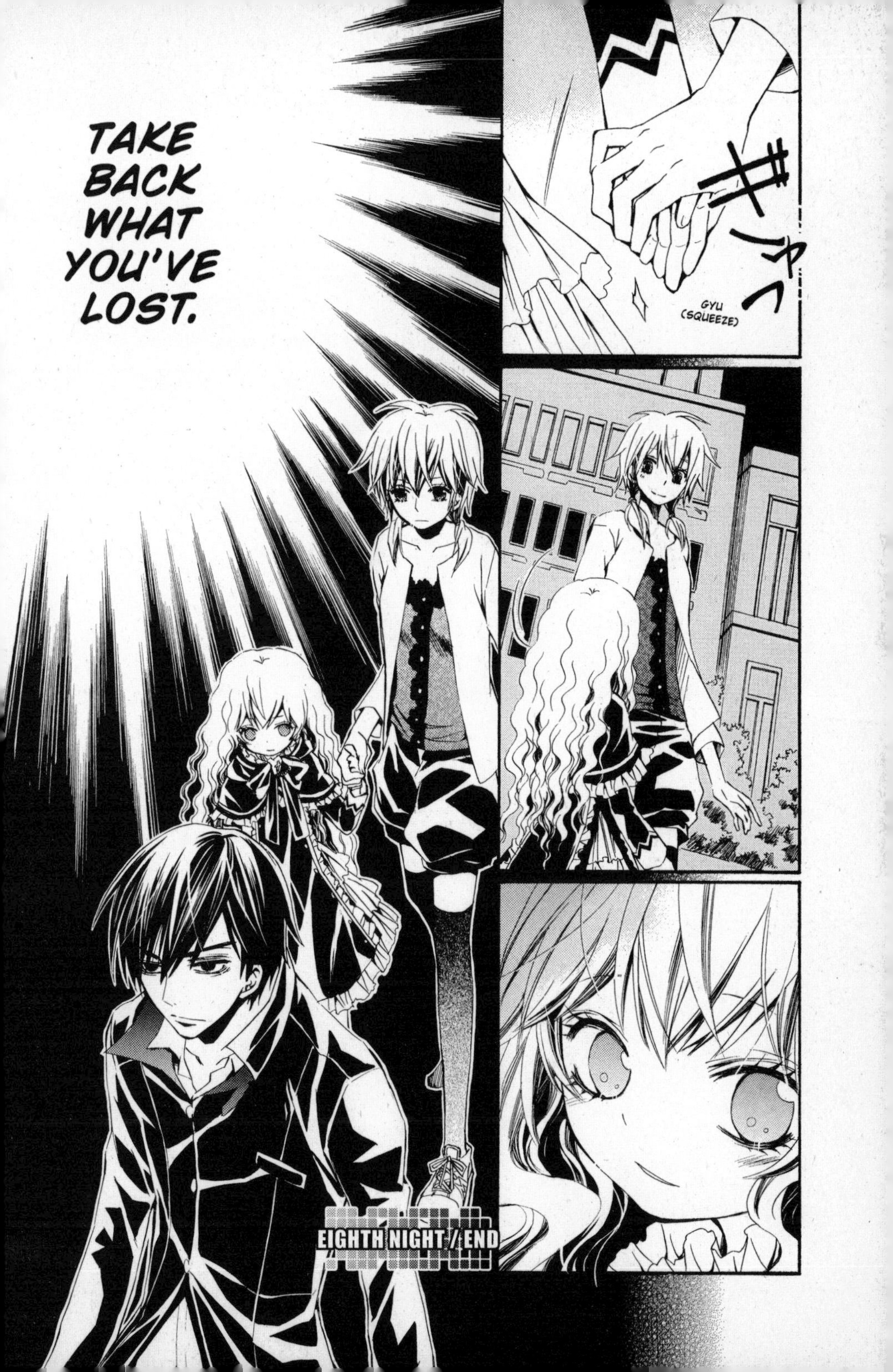

ギュッ
GYU (SQUEEZE)
TAKE BACK WHAT YOU'VE LOST.
EIGHTH NIGHT / END

FINAL NIGHT

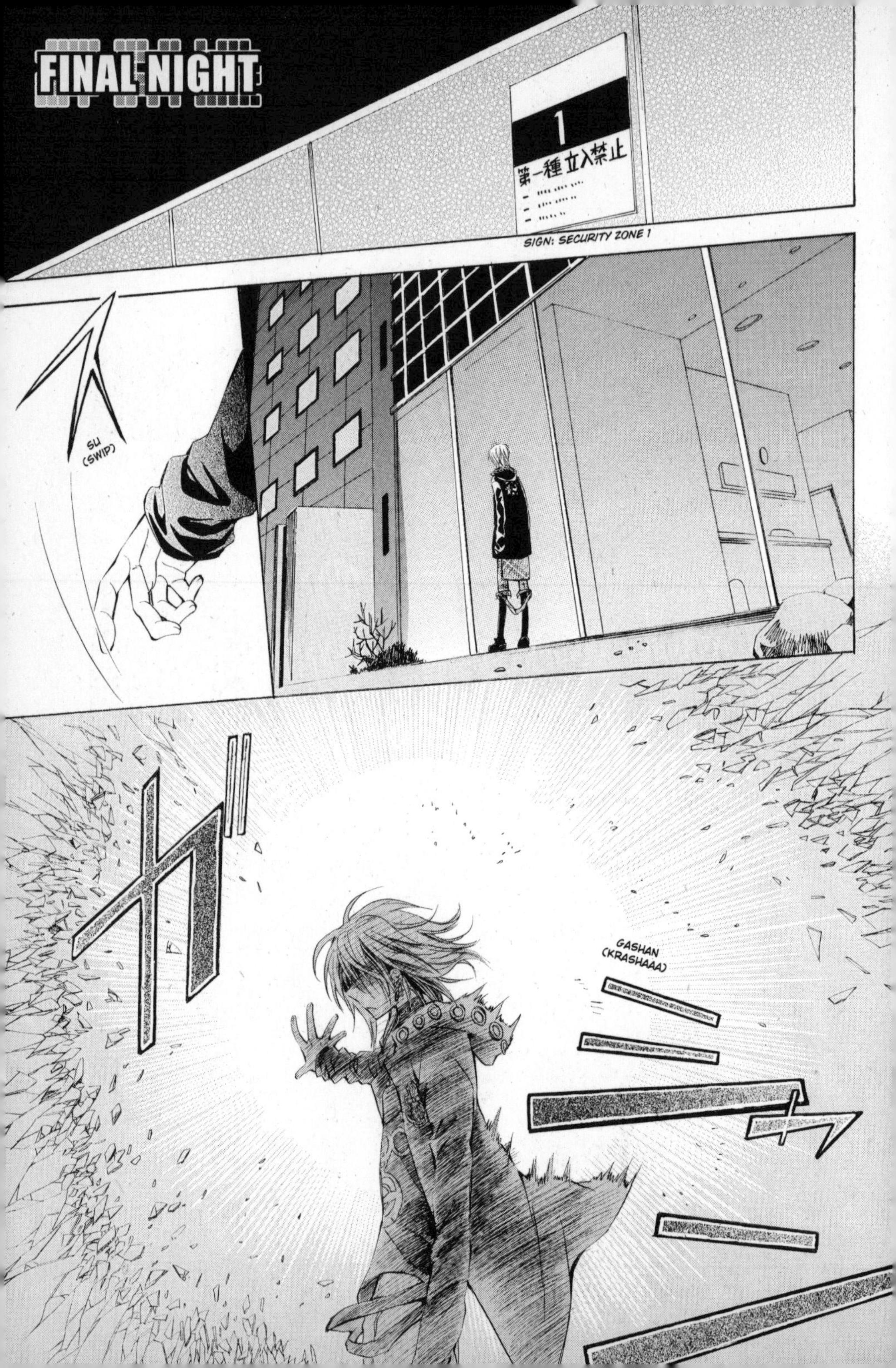
1
第一種立入禁止
SIGN: SECURITY ZONE 1
SU
(SWIP)
GASHAN
(KRASHAAA)

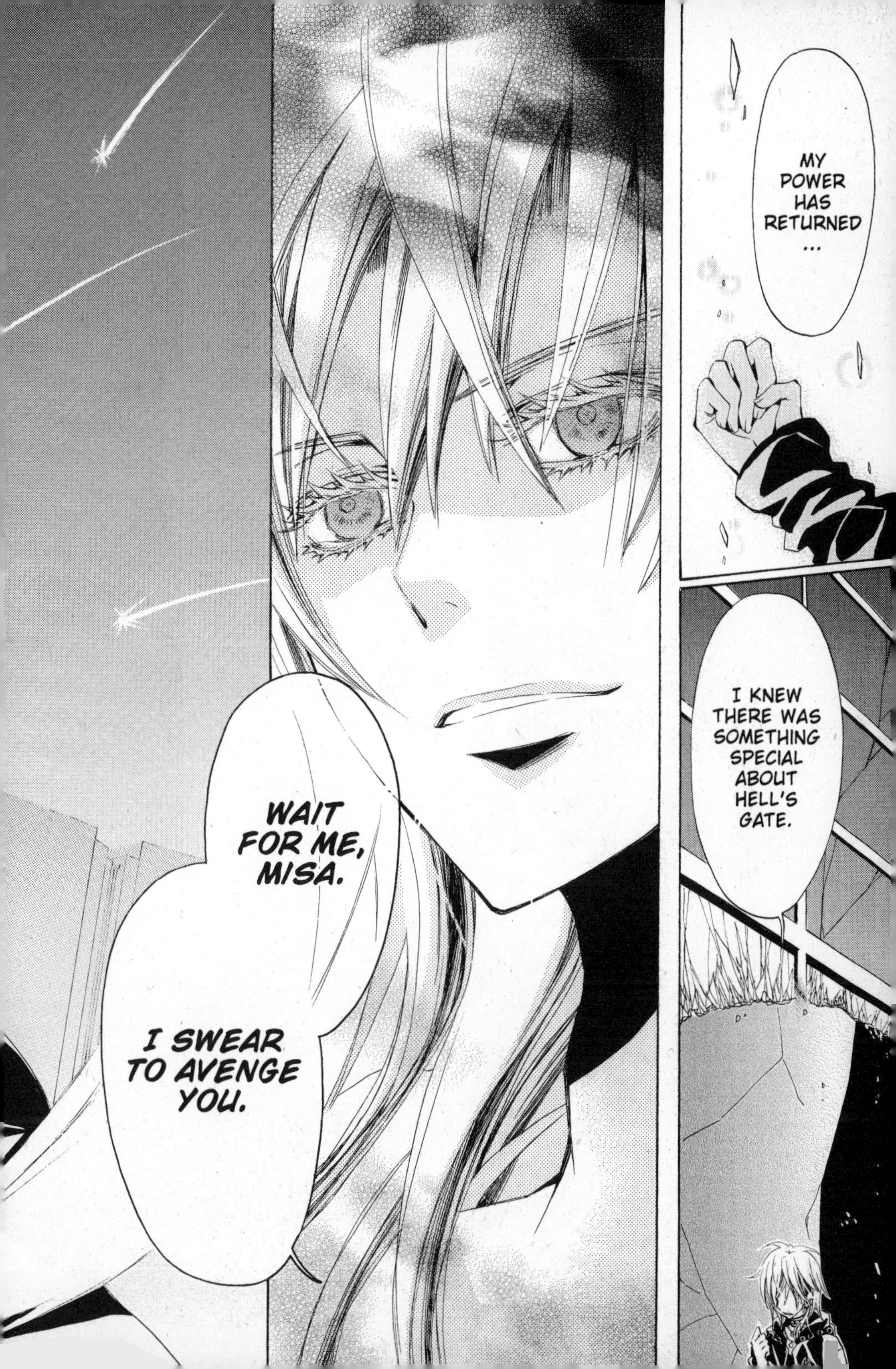
MY POWER HAS RETURNED ...
I KNEW THERE WAS SOMETHING SPECIAL ABOUT HELL'S GATE.
WAIT FOR ME, MISA.
I SWEAR TO AVENGE YOU.

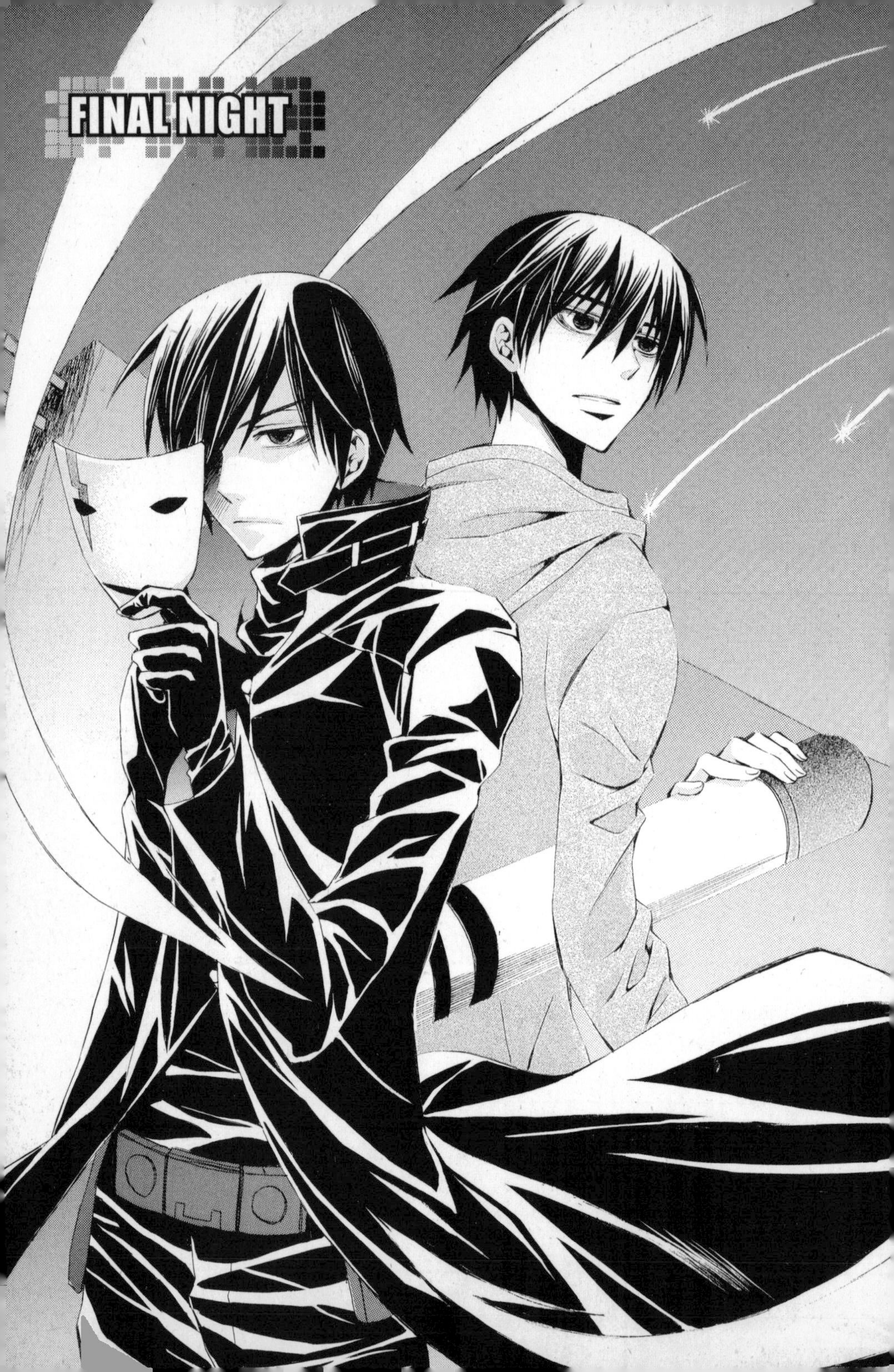
FINAL NIGHT

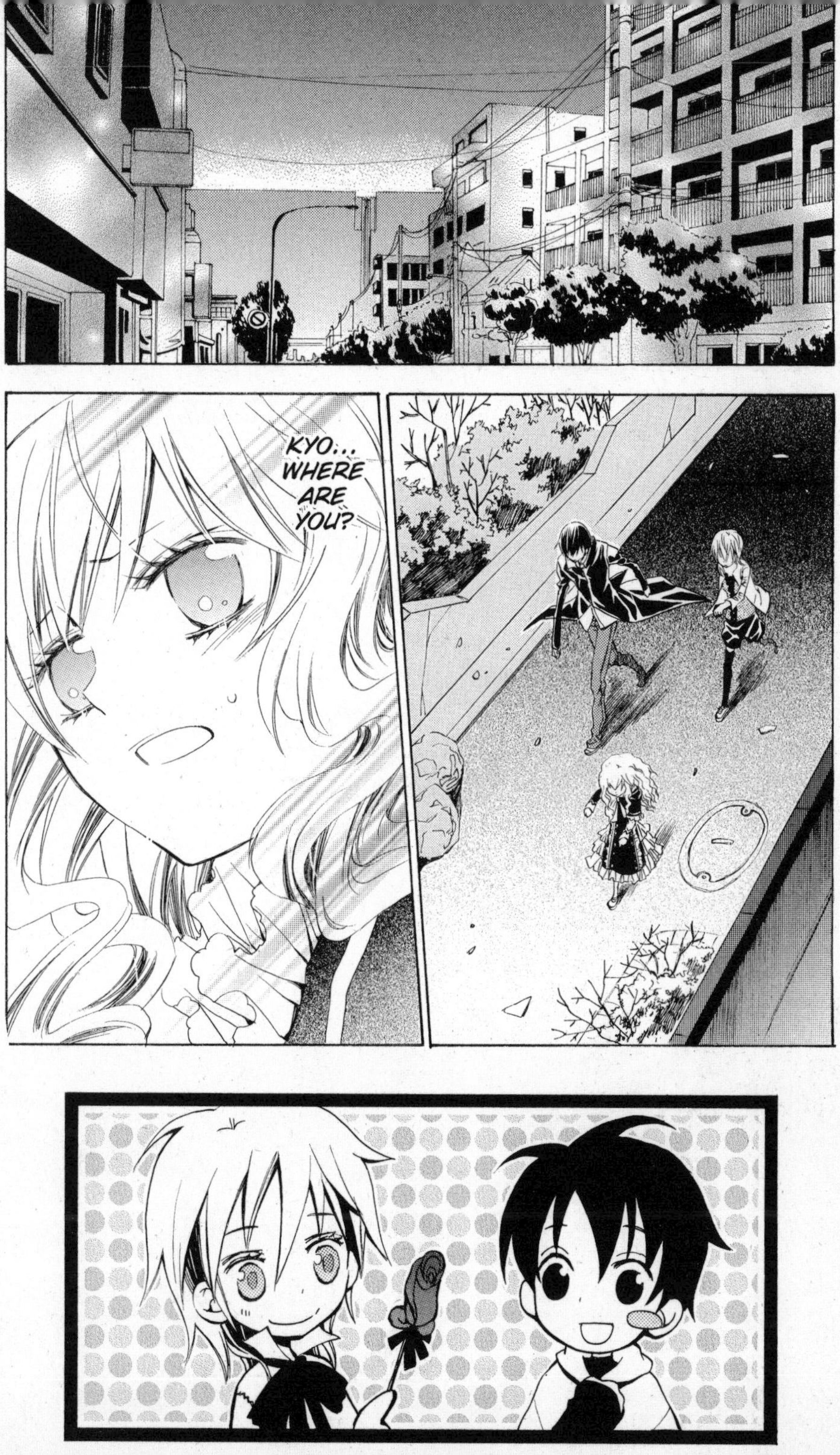
KYO... WHERE ARE YOU?

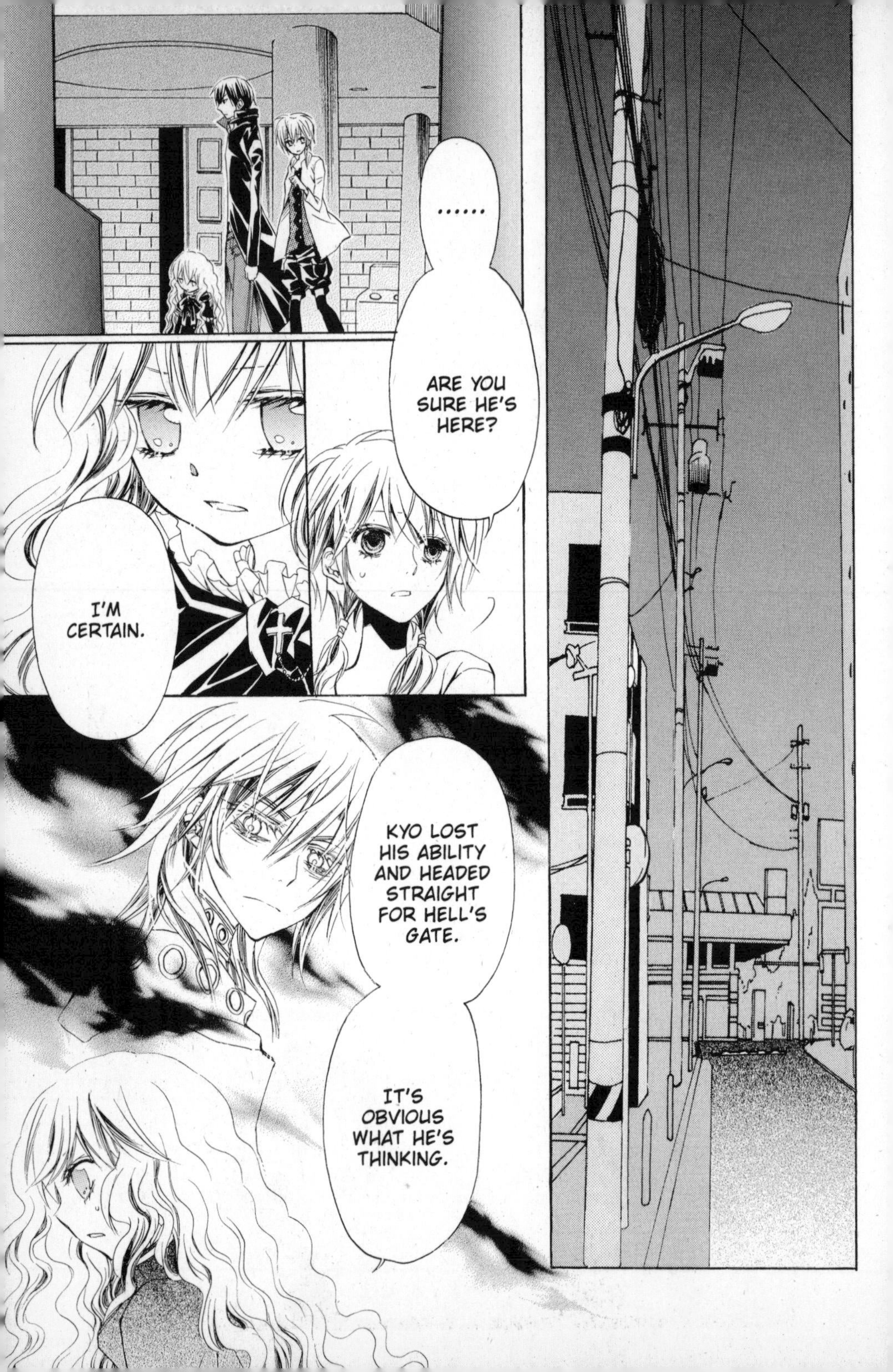
......
ARE YOU SURE HE'S HERE?
I'M CERTAIN.
KYO LOST HIS ABILITY AND HEADED STRAIGHT FOR HELL'S GATE.
IT'S OBVIOUS WHAT HE'S THINKING.

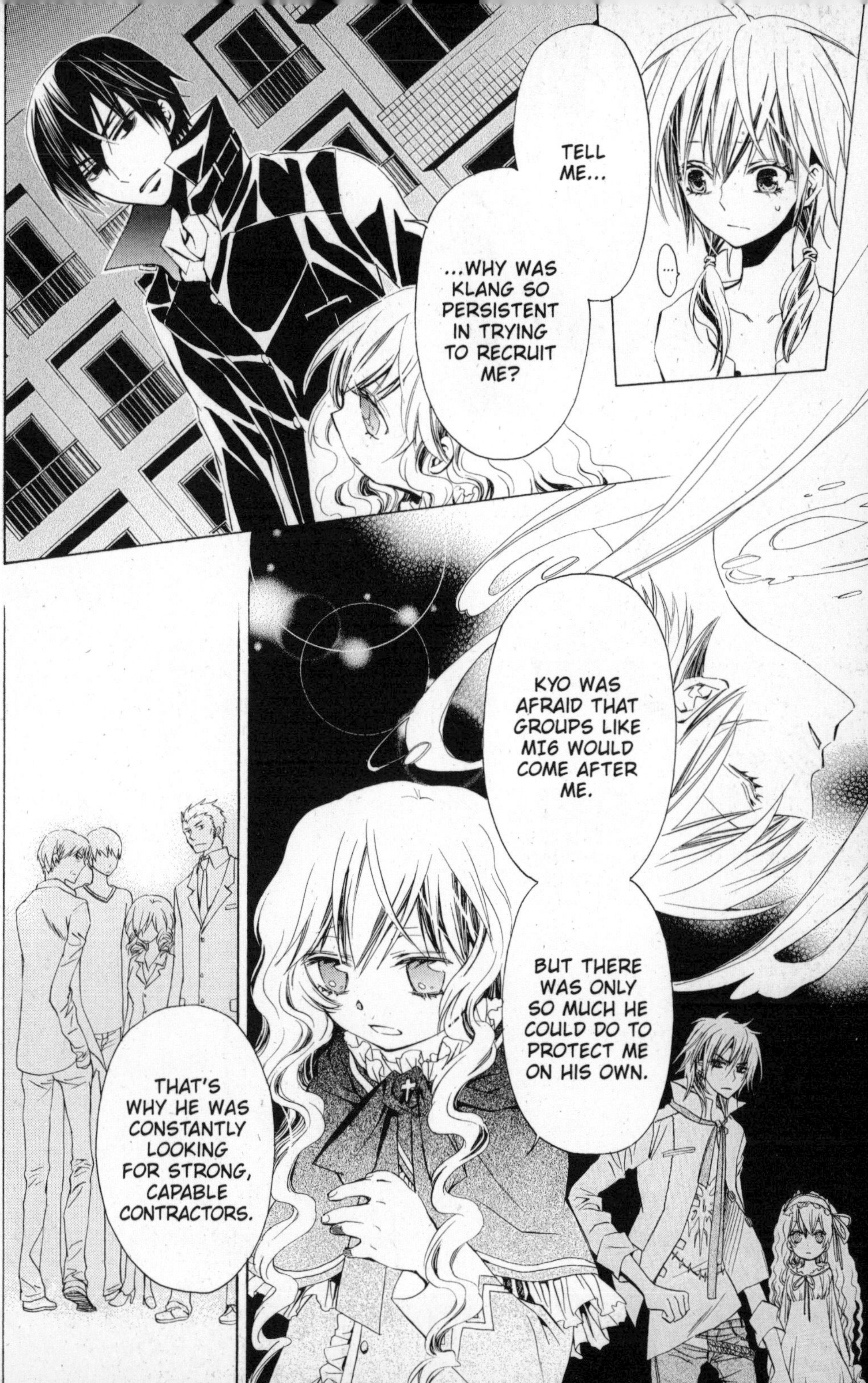
...
TELL ME...
...WHY WAS KLANG SO PERSISTENT IN TRYING TO RECRUIT ME?
KYO WAS AFRAID THAT GROUPS LIKE MI6 WOULD COME AFTER ME.
BUT THERE WAS ONLY SO MUCH HE COULD DO TO PROTECT ME ON HIS OWN.
THAT'S WHY HE WAS CONSTANTLY LOOKING FOR STRONG, CAPABLE CONTRACTORS.

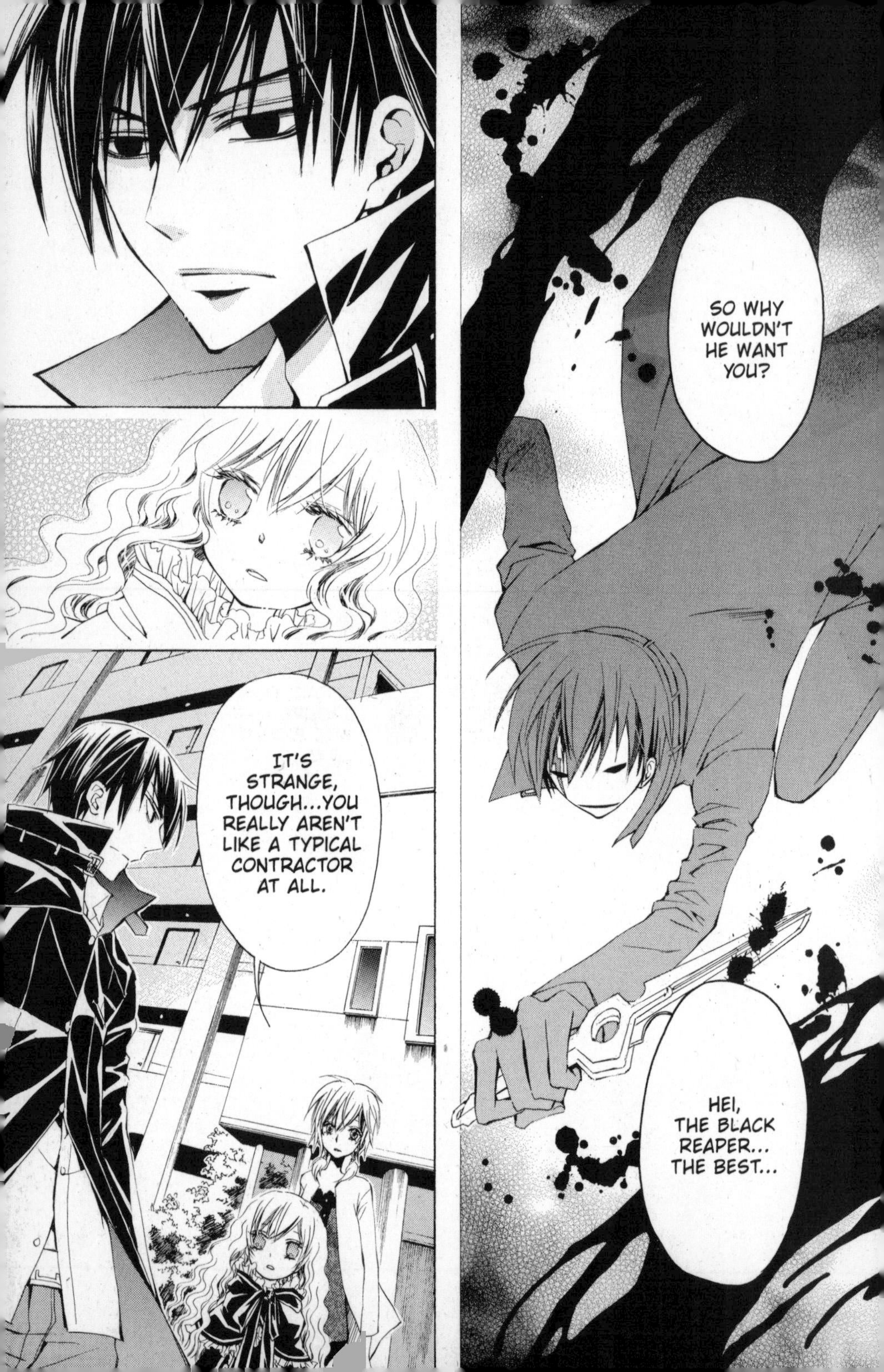
SO WHY WOULDN'T HE WANT YOU?
HEI, THE BLACK REAPER... THE BEST...
IT'S STRANGE, THOUGH...YOU REALLY AREN'T LIKE A TYPICAL CONTRACTOR AT ALL.

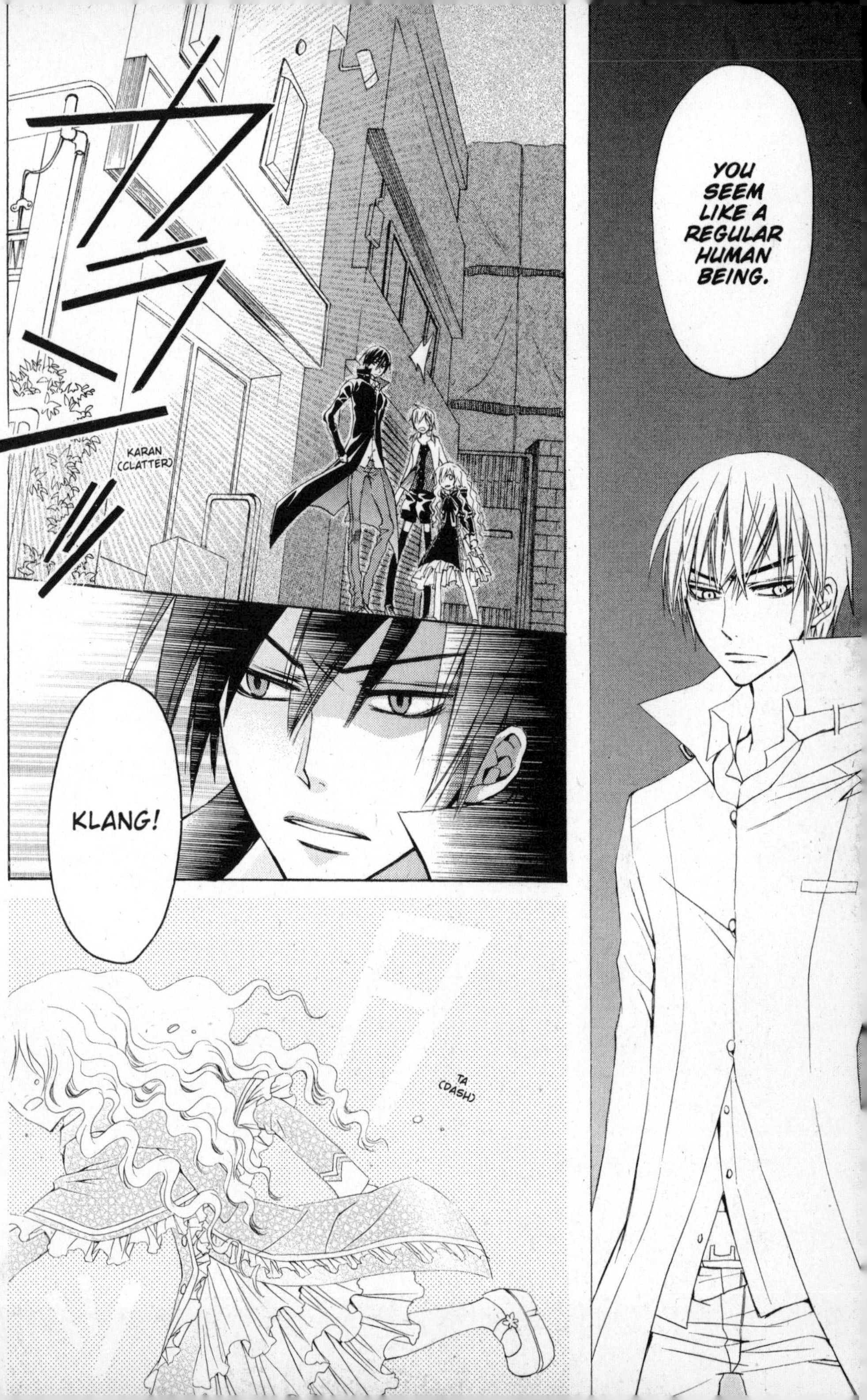
YOU SEEM LIKE A REGULAR HUMAN BEING.
KARAN (CLATTER)
KLANG!
TA (DASH)

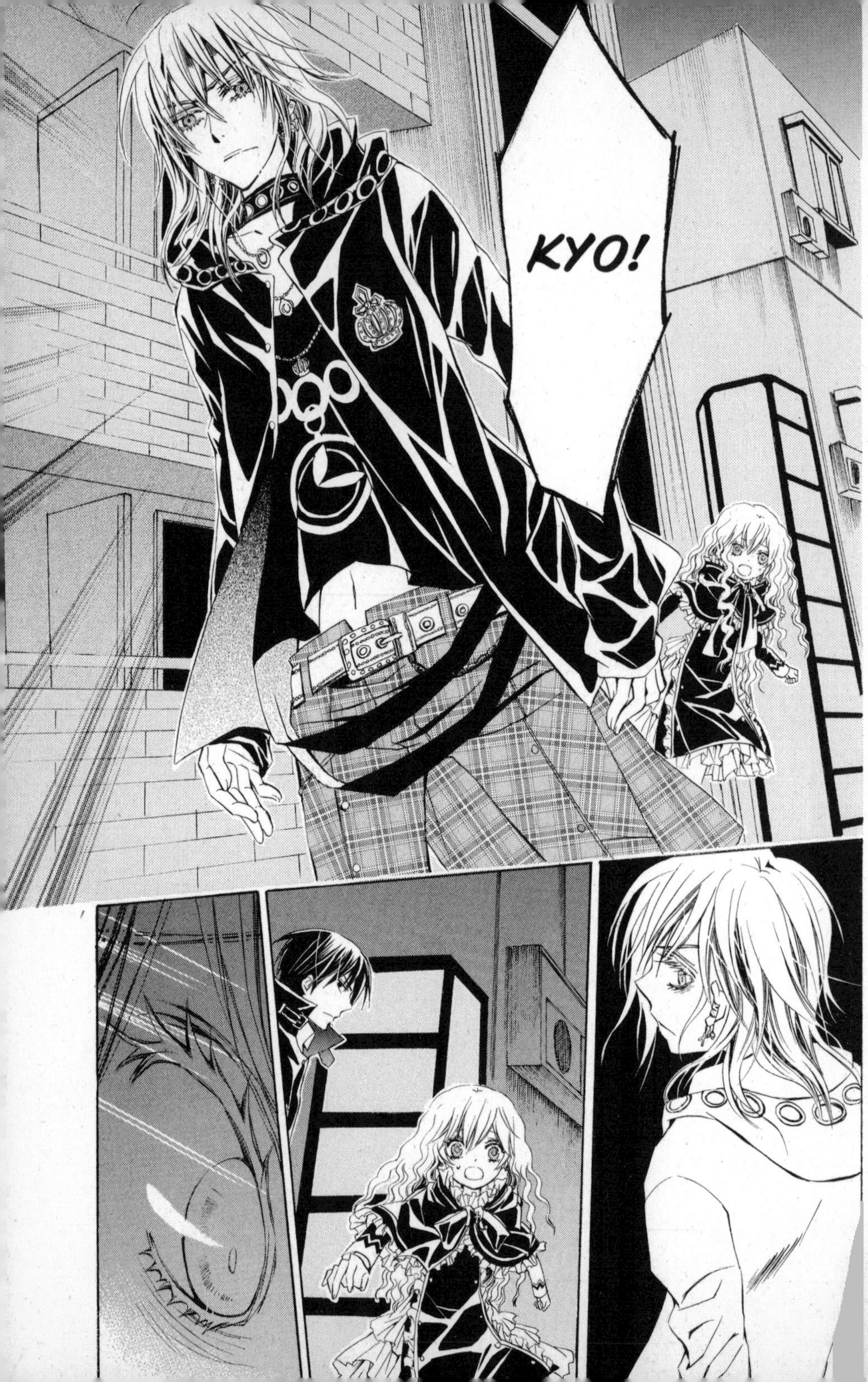
KYO!

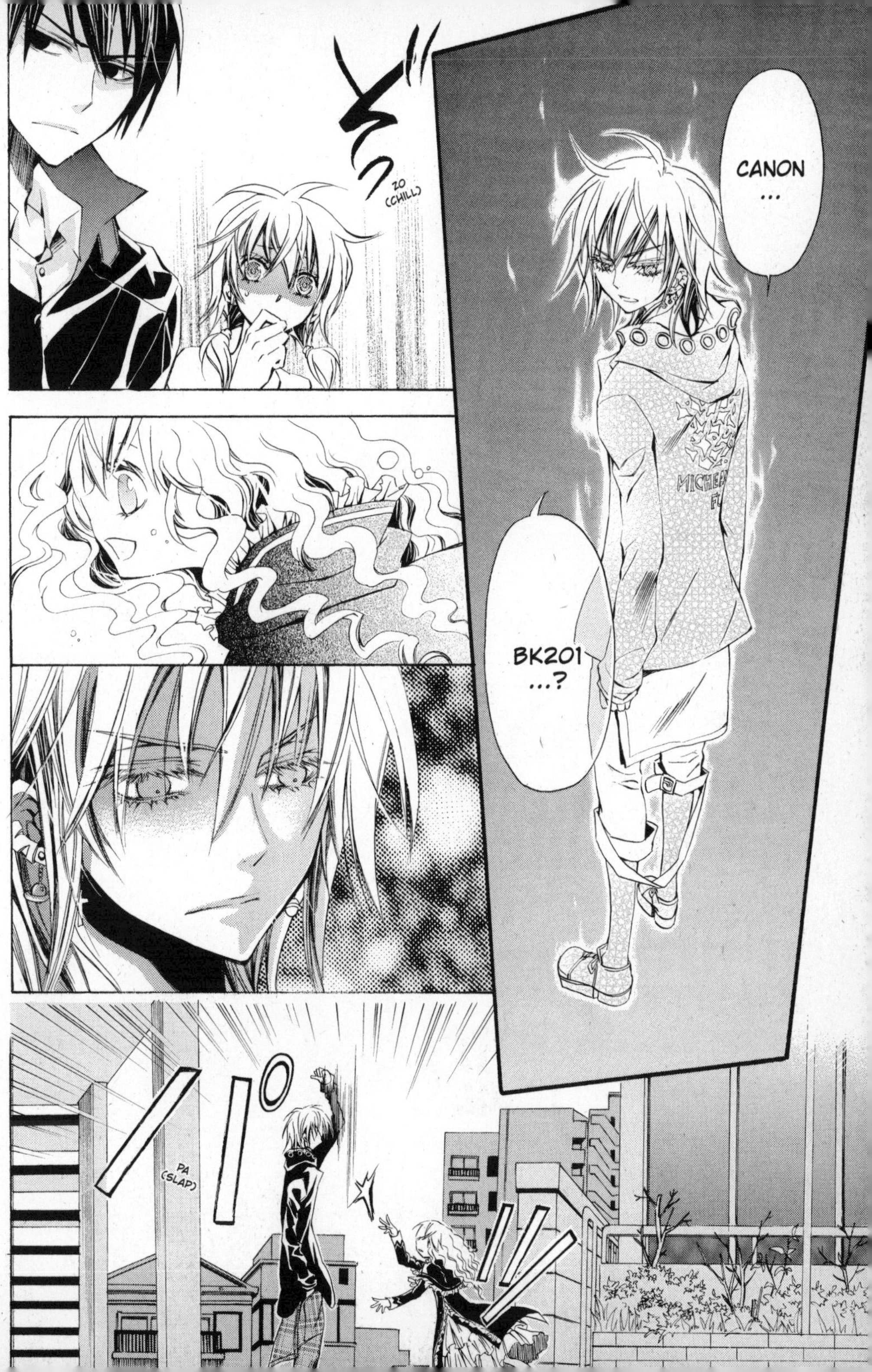
CANON ...
BK201 ...?
ZO (CHILL)
PA (SLAP)

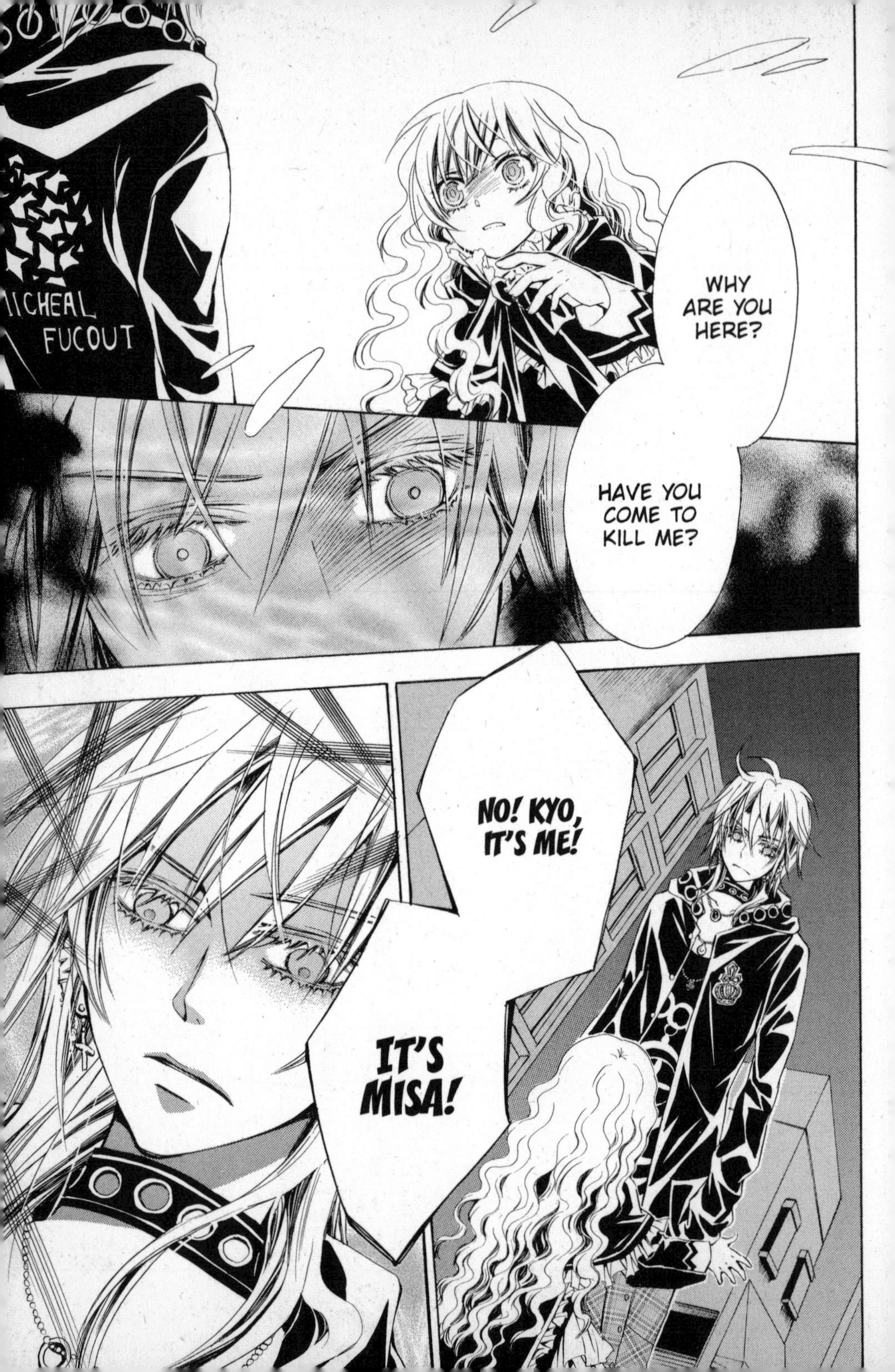
WHY ARE YOU HERE?
ICHEAL
FUCOUT
HAVE YOU COME TO KILL ME?
NO! KYO, IT'S ME!
IT'S MISA!

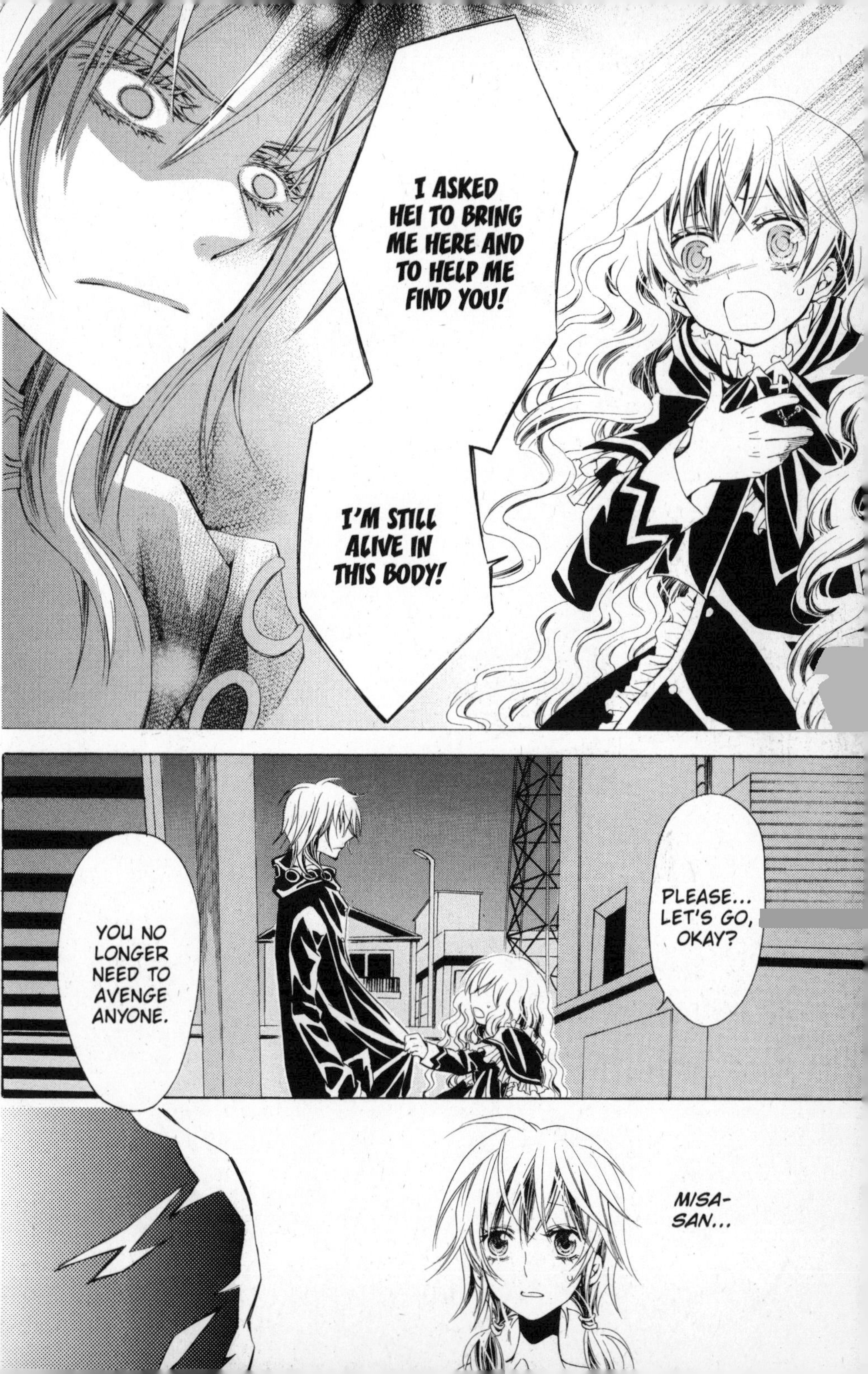
I ASKED HEI TO BRING ME HERE AND TO HELP ME FIND YOU!
I'M STILL ALIVE IN THIS BODY!
PLEASE... LET'S GO, OKAY?
YOU NO LONGER NEED TO AVENGE ANYONE.
MISA-SAN...

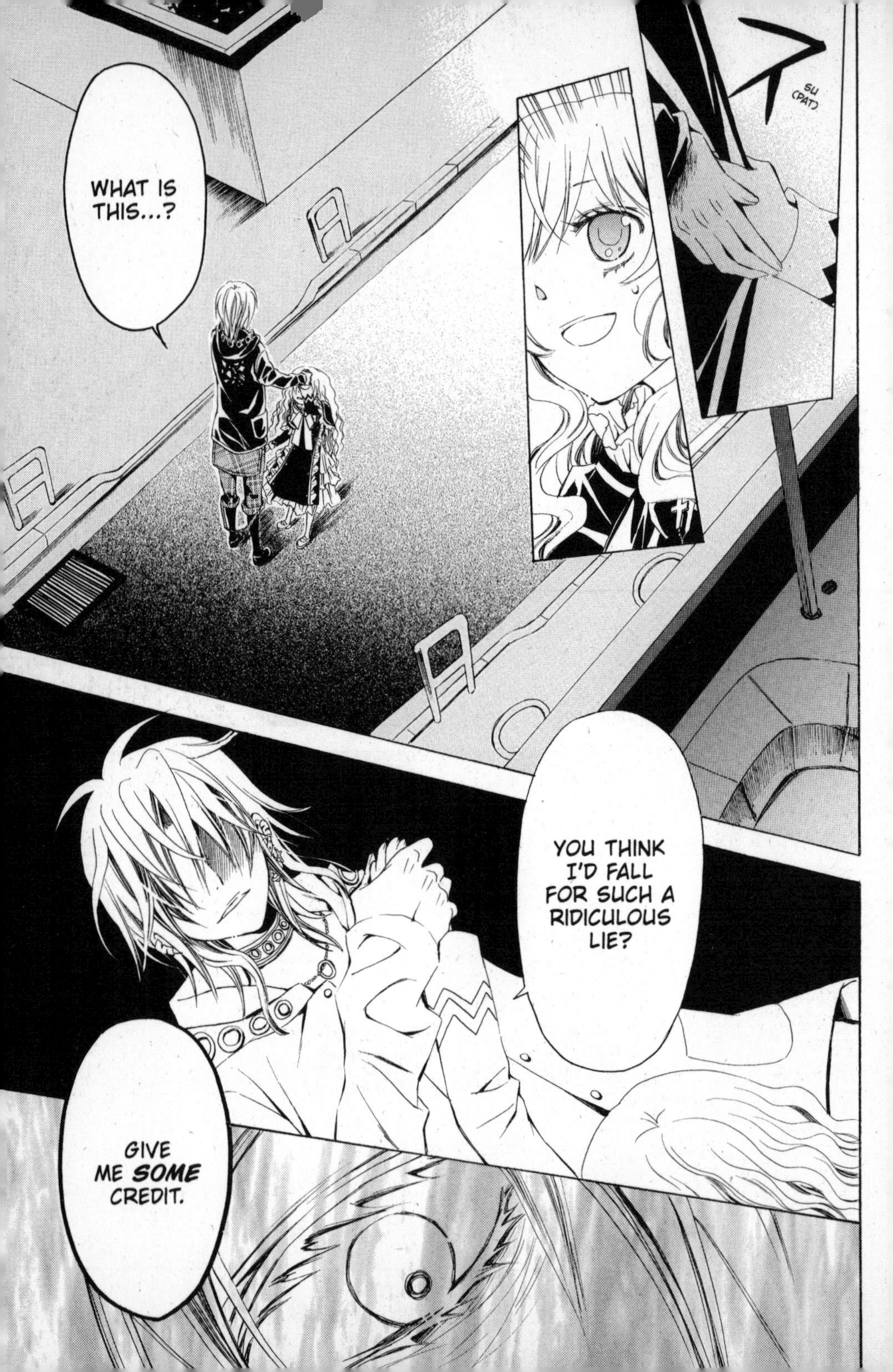
SU (PAT)
WHAT IS THIS...?
YOU THINK I'D FALL FOR SUCH A RIDICULOUS LIE?
GIVE ME **SOME** CREDIT.

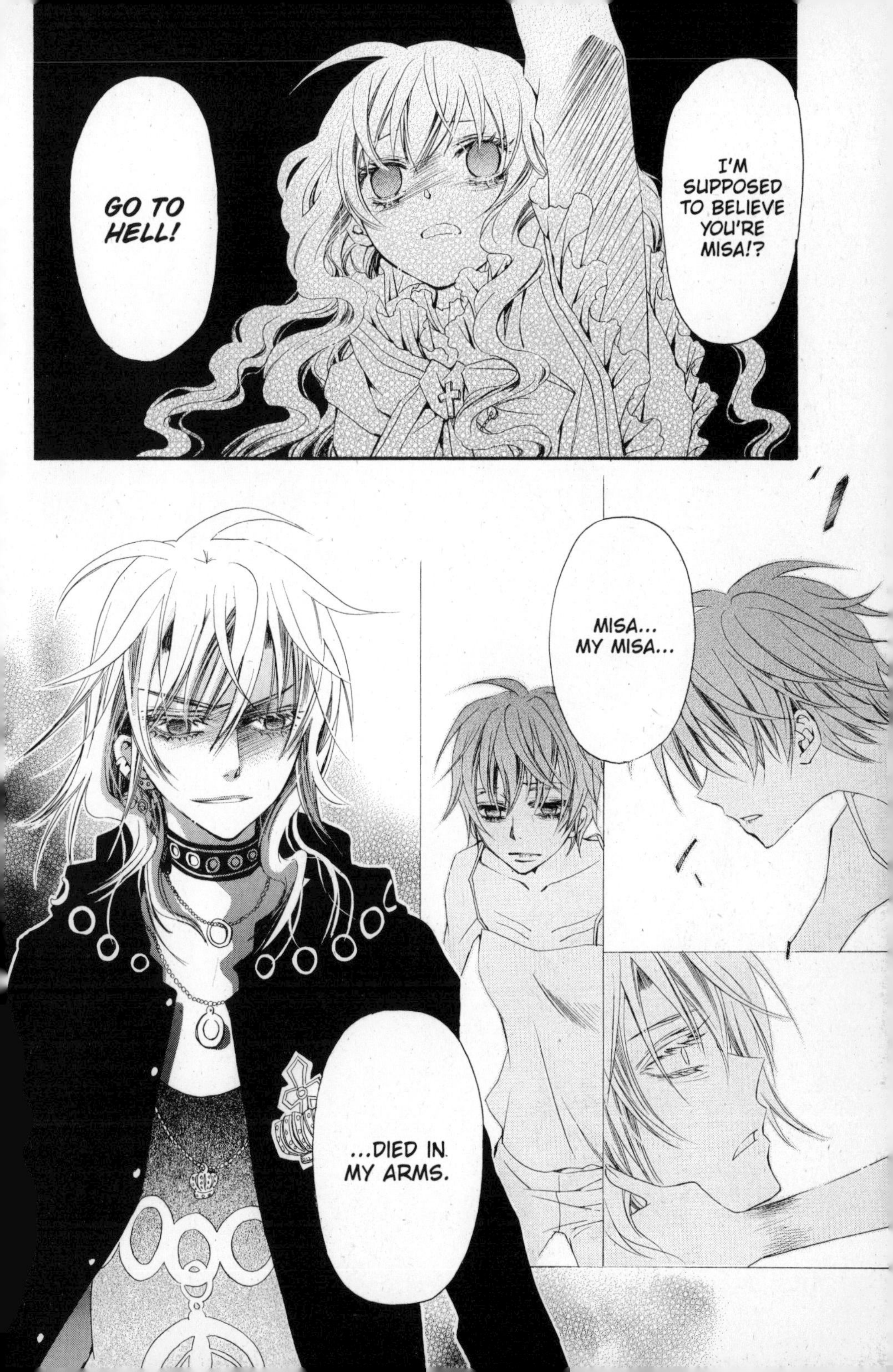
I'M SUPPOSED TO BELIEVE YOU'RE MISA!?
GO TO HELL!
MISA... MY MISA...
...DIED IN MY ARMS.

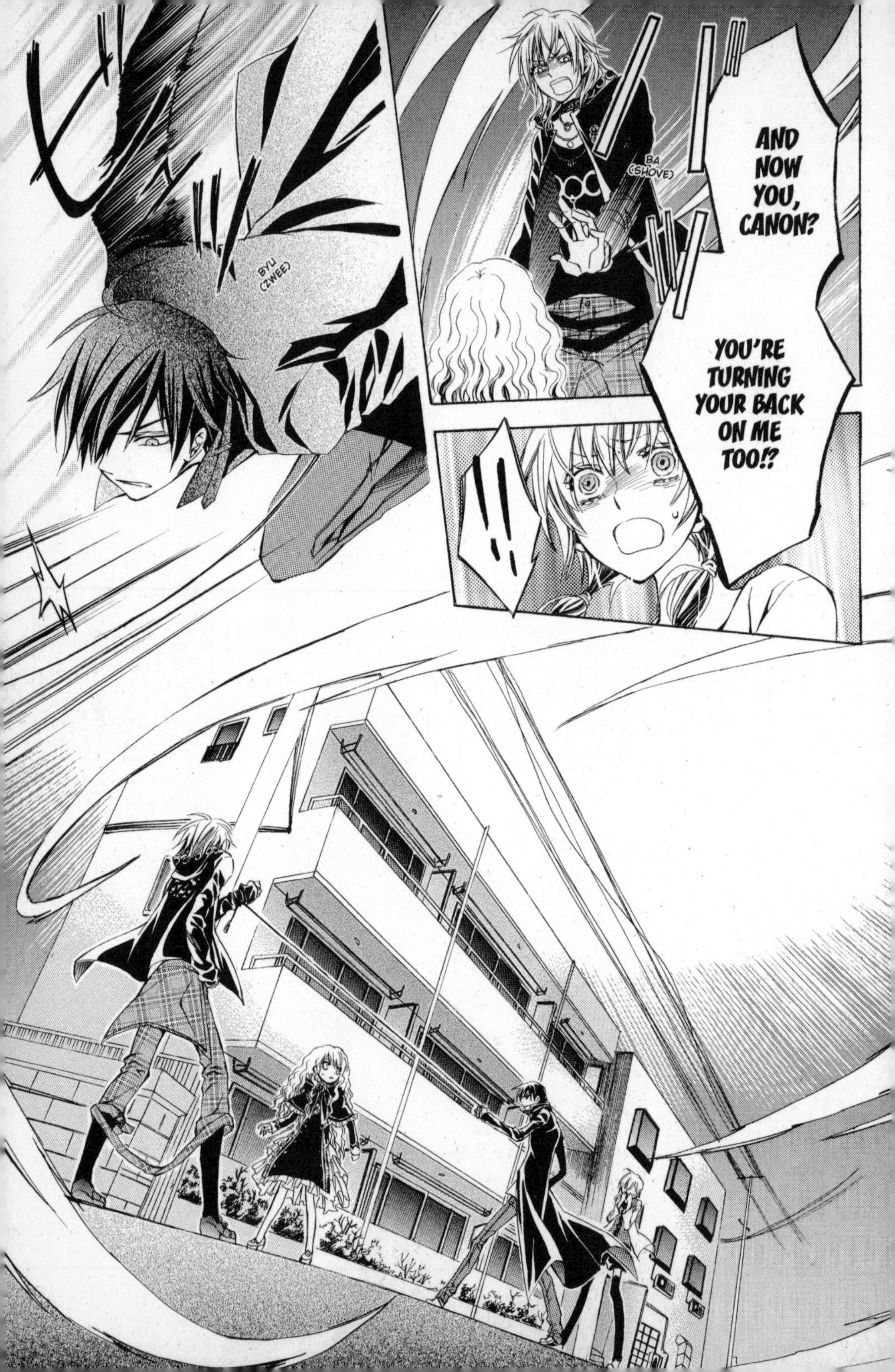
BA (SHOVE)
AND NOW YOU, CANON?
YOU'RE TURNING YOUR BACK ON ME TOO!?
!!
BYU (ZWEE)

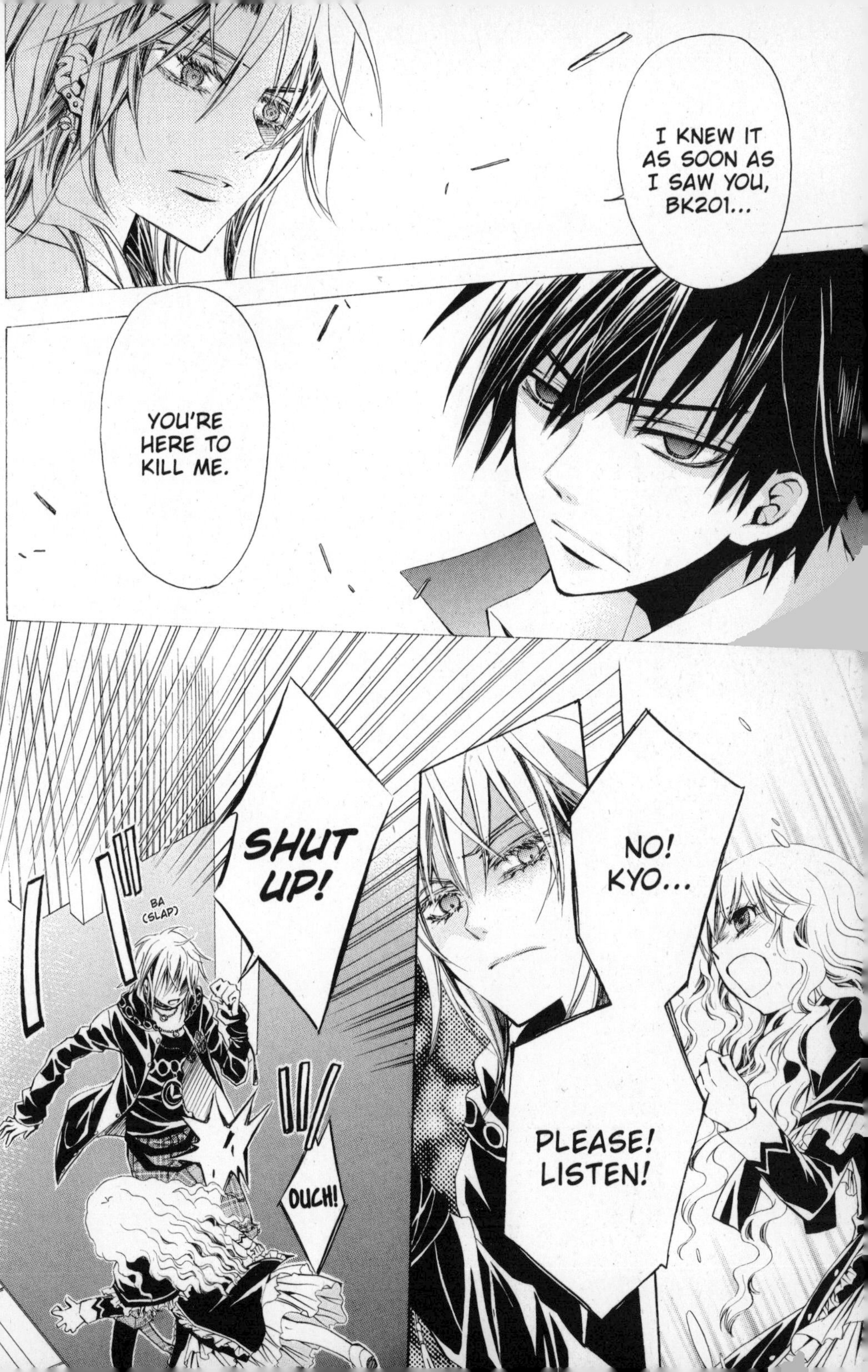
I KNEW IT AS SOON AS I SAW YOU, BK201...
YOU'RE HERE TO KILL ME.
NO! KYO...
PLEASE! LISTEN!
SHUT UP!
BA (SLAP)
OUCH!

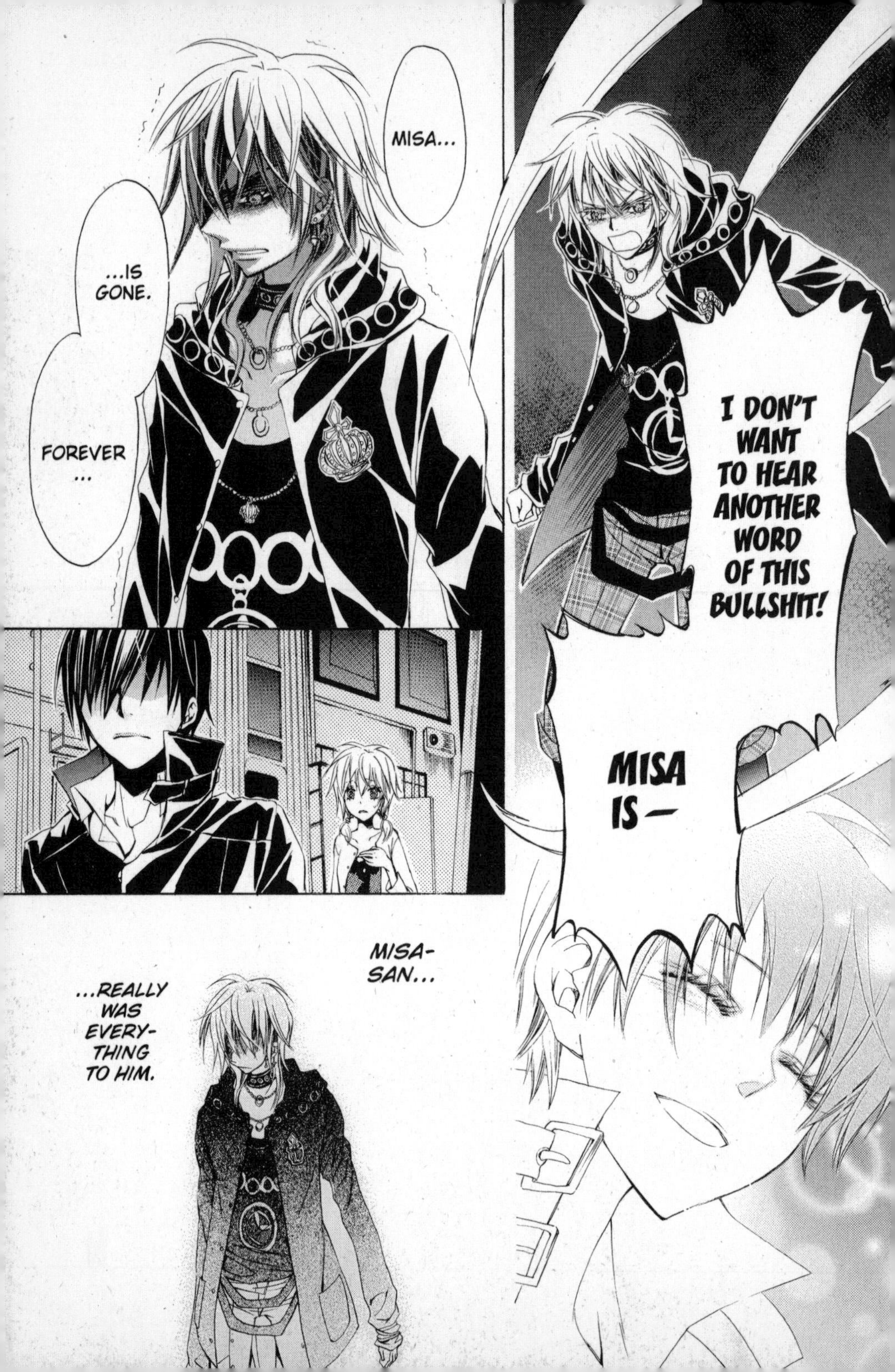
I DON'T WANT TO HEAR ANOTHER WORD OF THIS BULLSHIT!
MISA IS—
MISA...
...IS GONE.
FOREVER...
MISA-SAN...
...REALLY WAS EVERY-THING TO HIM.

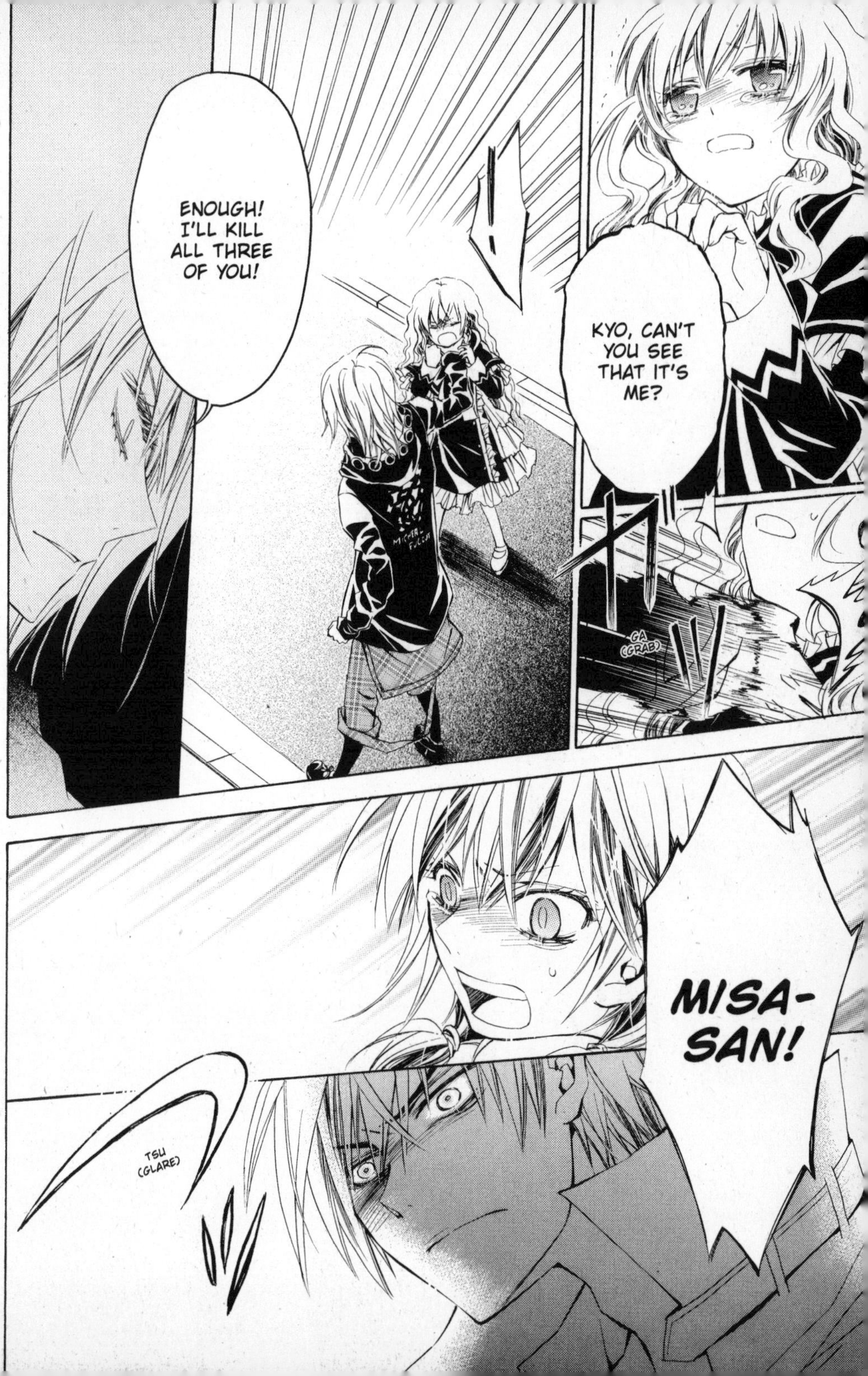
KYO, CAN'T YOU SEE THAT IT'S ME?
GA (GRAB)
!
ENOUGH! I'LL KILL ALL THREE OF YOU!
MISA-SAN!
TSU (GLARE)

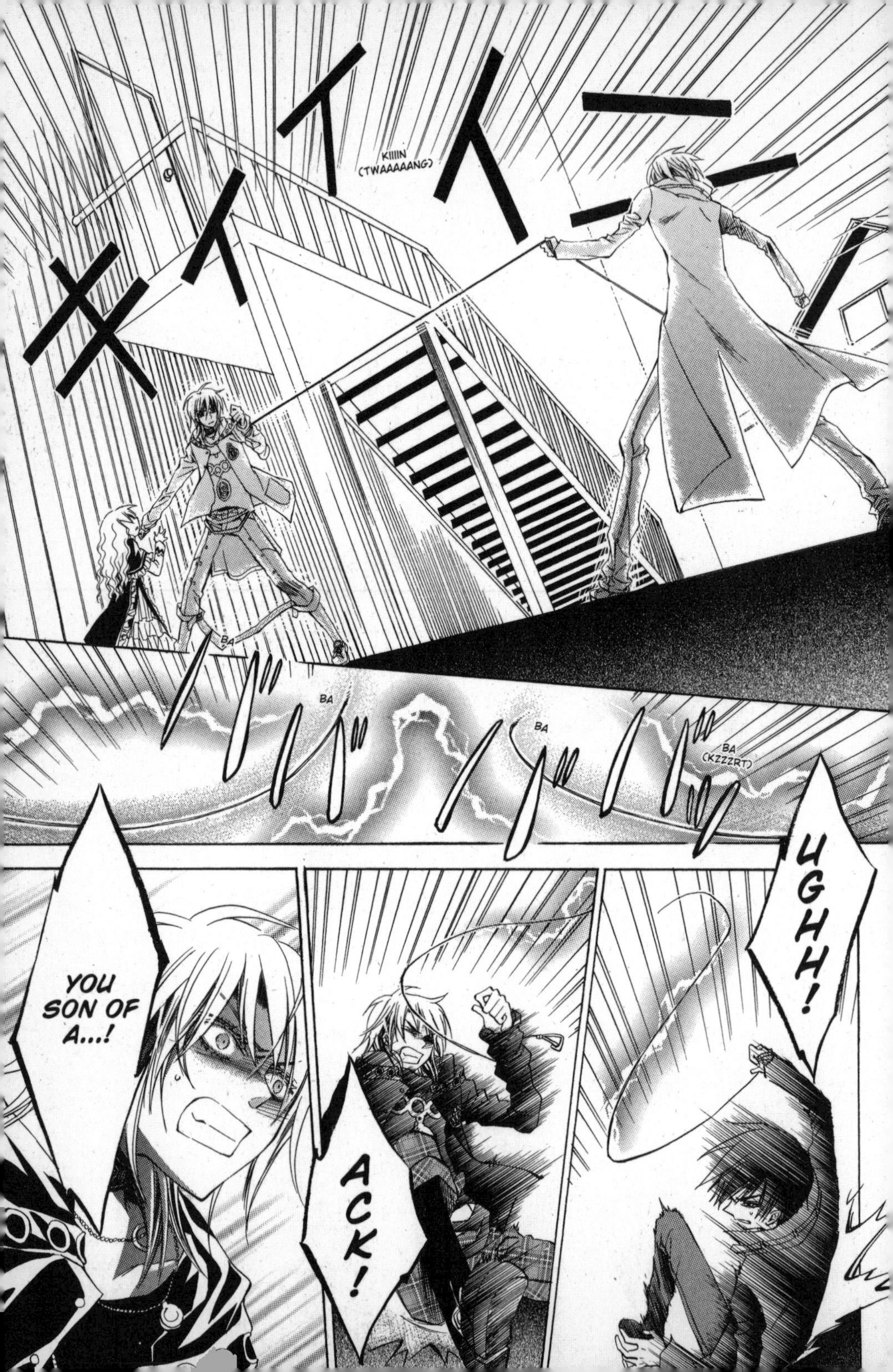
KIIIN
(TWAAAAANG)
BA
(KZZZRT)
BA
BA
BA
UGHH!
ACK!
YOU SON OF A...!

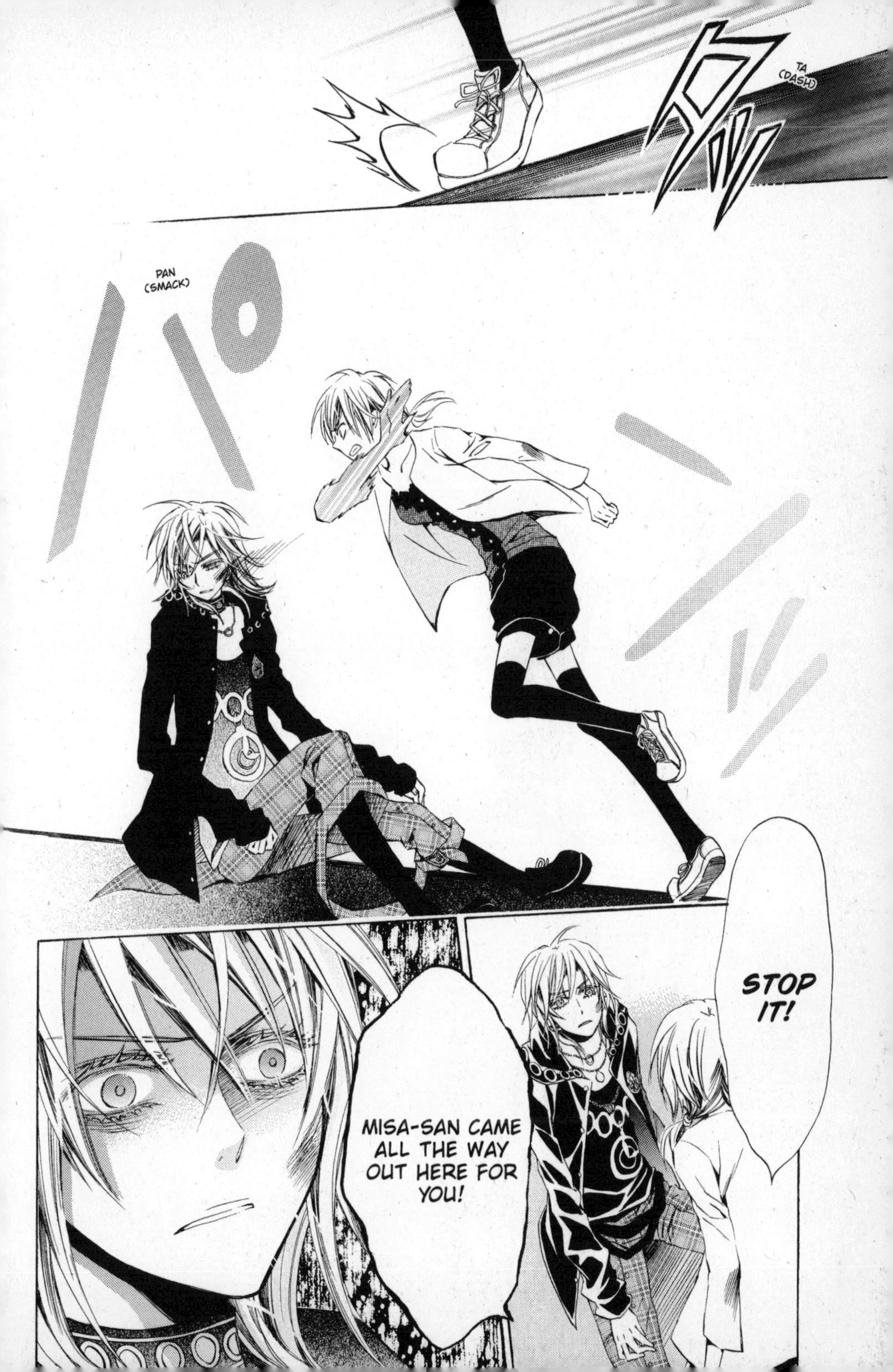
TA (DASH)
PAN (SMACK)
STOP IT!
MISA-SAN CAME ALL THE WAY OUT HERE FOR YOU!

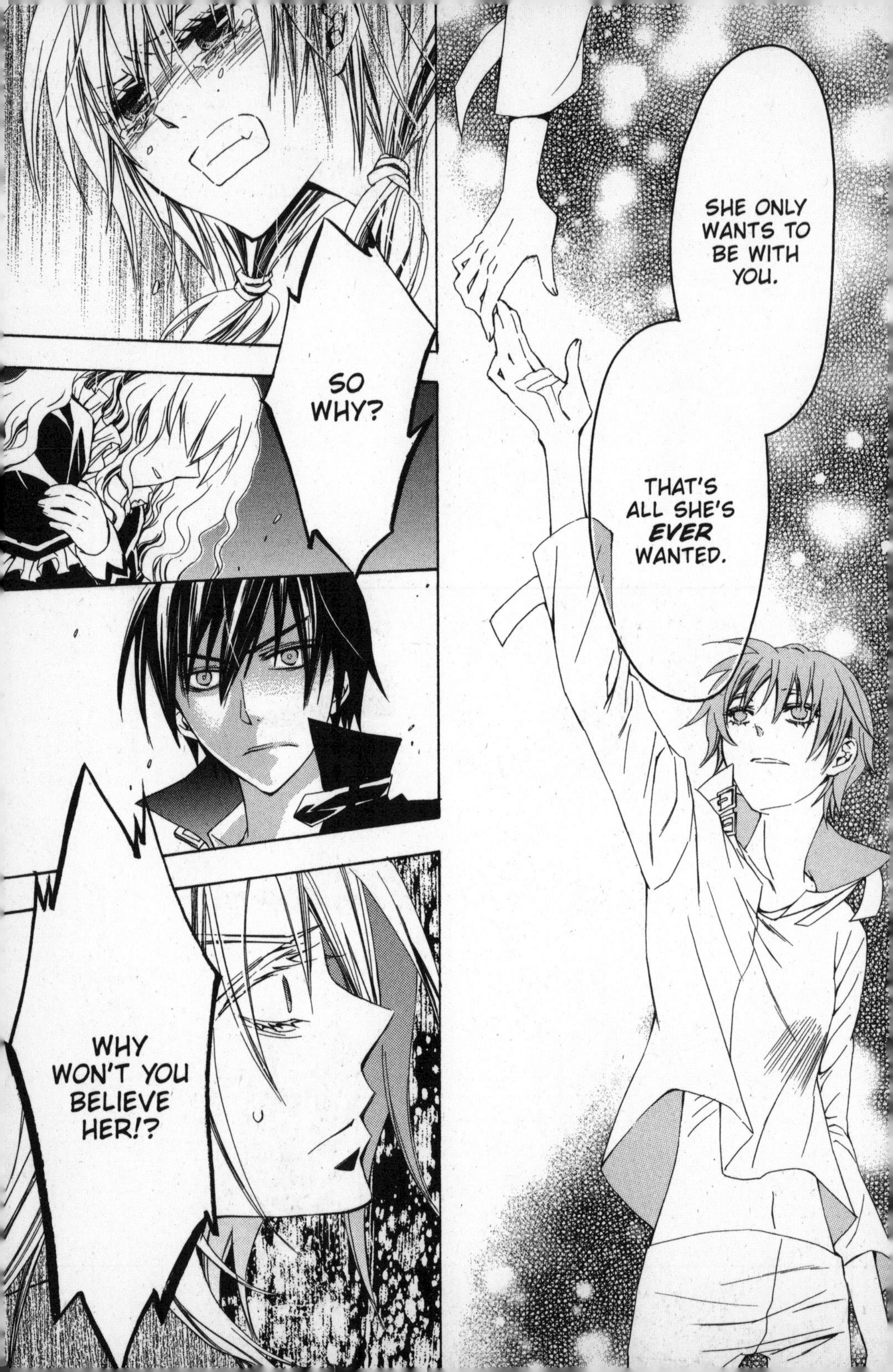
SHE ONLY WANTS TO BE WITH YOU.
THAT'S ALL SHE'S *EVER* WANTED.
SO WHY?
WHY WON'T YOU BELIEVE HER!?

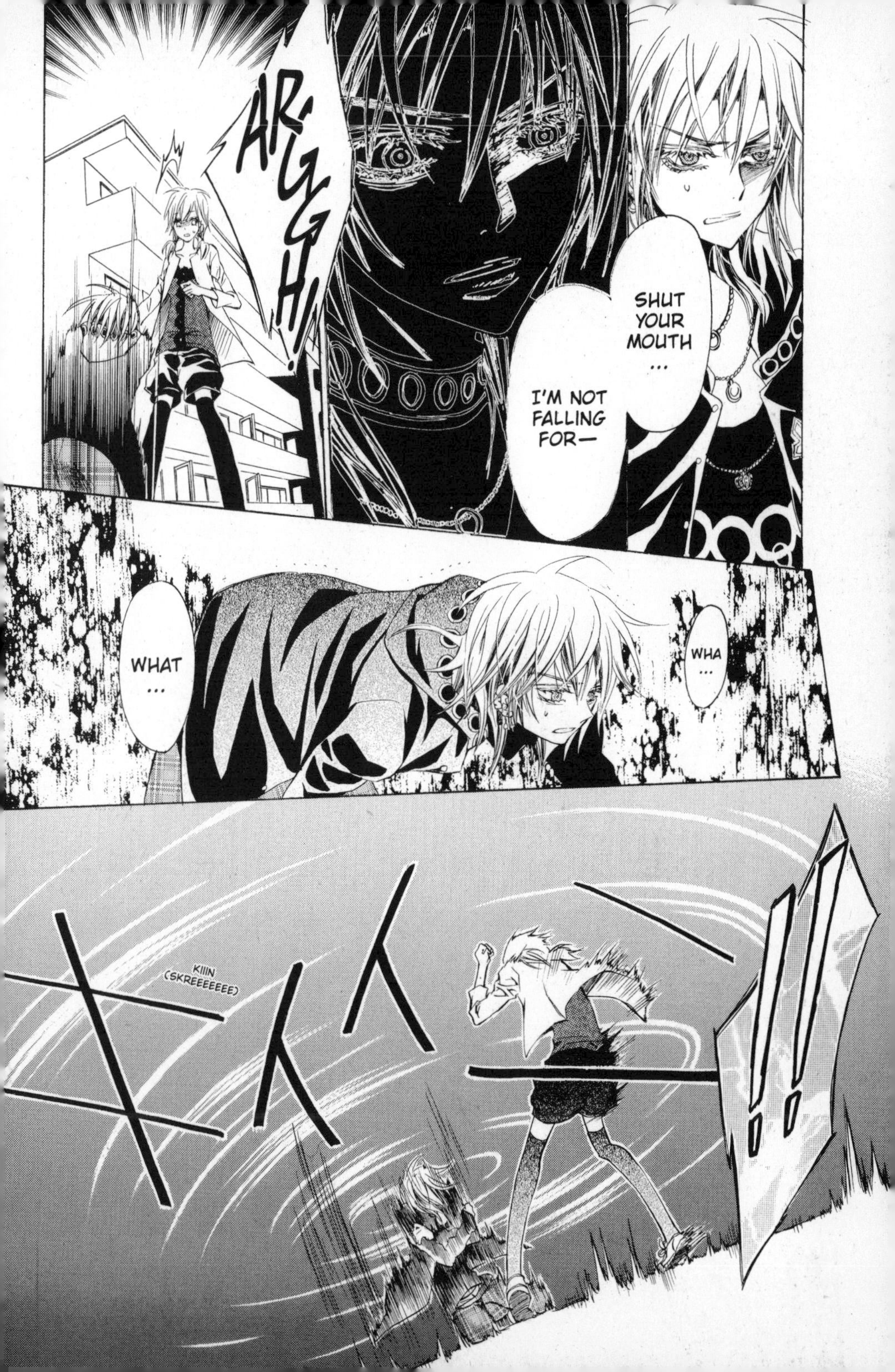
SHUT YOUR MOUTH ...
I'M NOT FALLING FOR—
ARUGH!
WHA ...
WHAT ...
KIIN (SKREEEEEEE)
!!

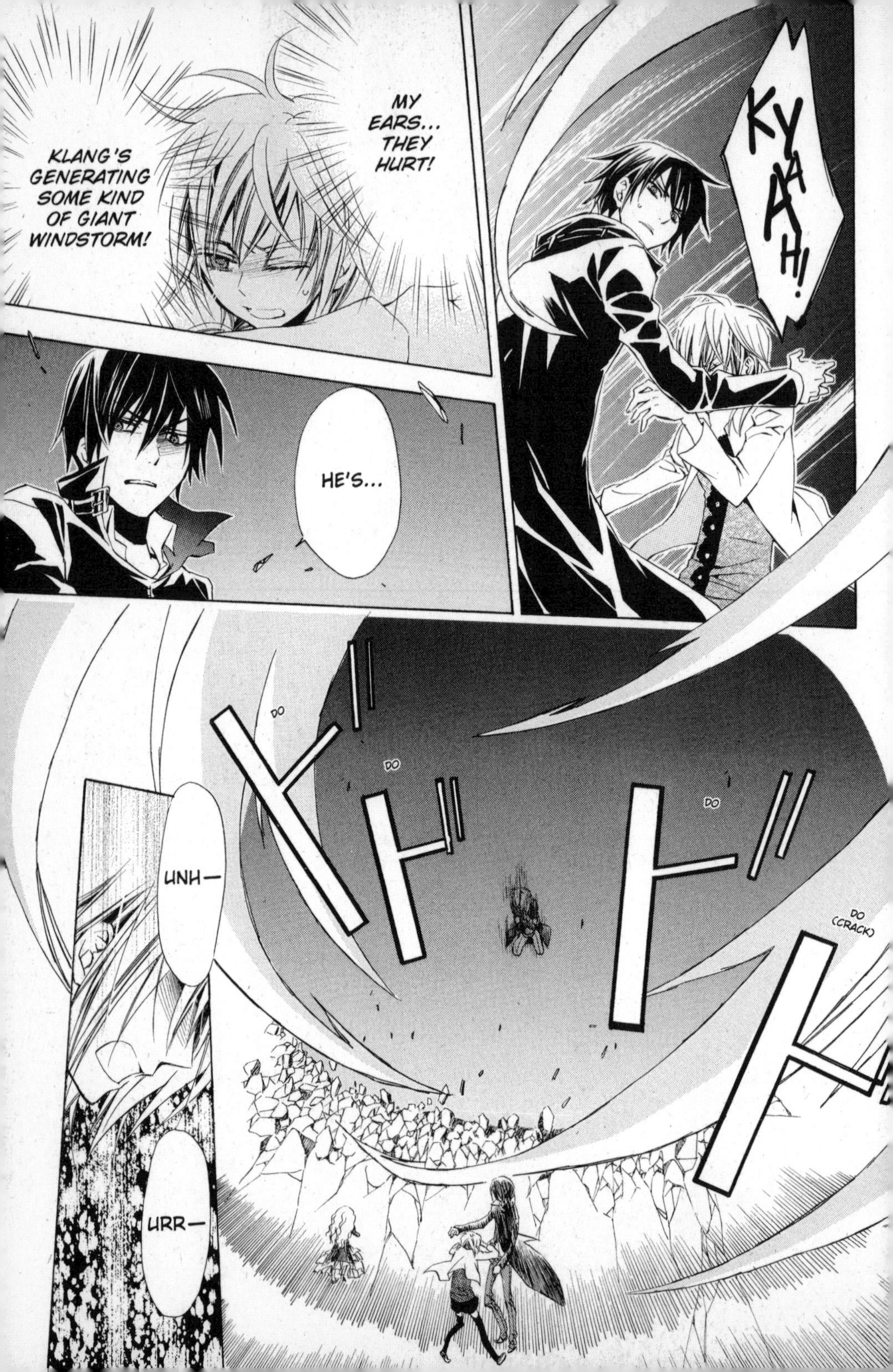
KYAAH!
MY EARS... THEY HURT!
KLANG'S GENERATING SOME KIND OF GIANT WINDSTORM!
HE'S...
DO
DO
DO
DO (CRACK)
UNH—
URR—

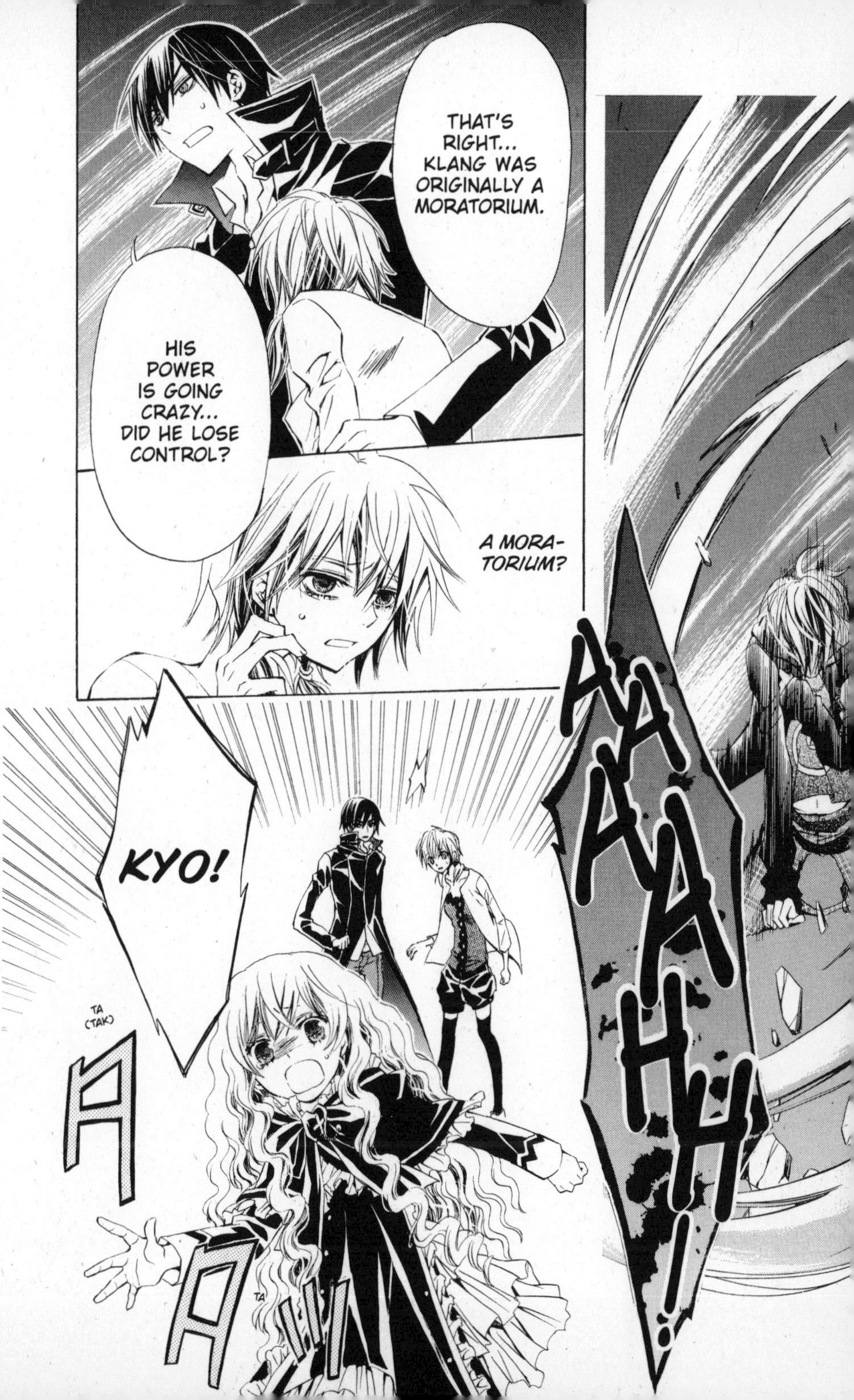
AAAHH!
THAT'S RIGHT... KLANG WAS ORIGINALLY A MORATORIUM.
HIS POWER IS GOING CRAZY... DID HE LOSE CONTROL?
A MORA-TORIUM?
KYO!
TA (TAK)
TA

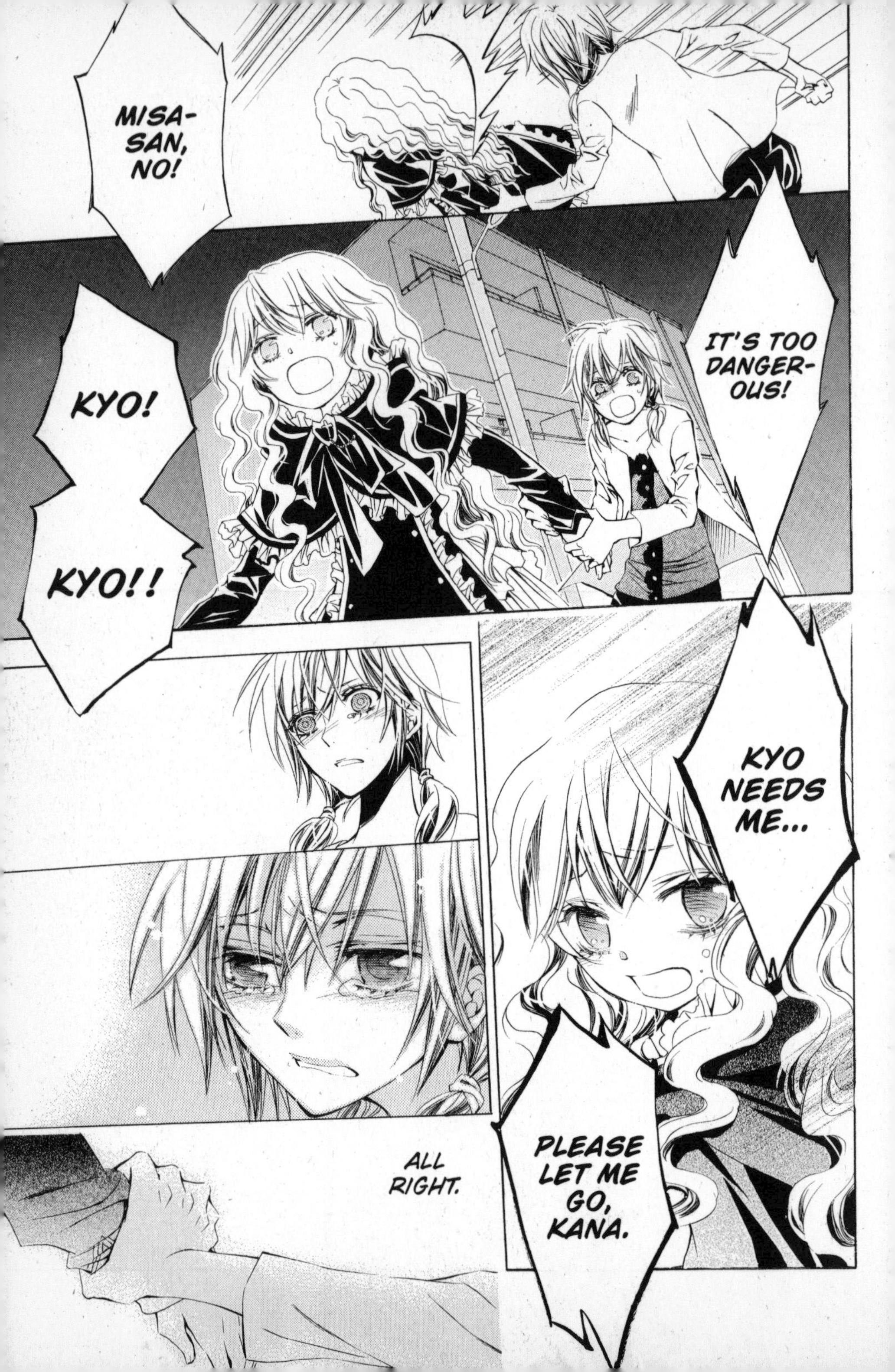

MISA-SAN, NO!
IT'S TOO DANGER-OUS!
KYO!
KYO!!
KYO NEEDS ME...
PLEASE LET ME GO, KANA.
ALL RIGHT.

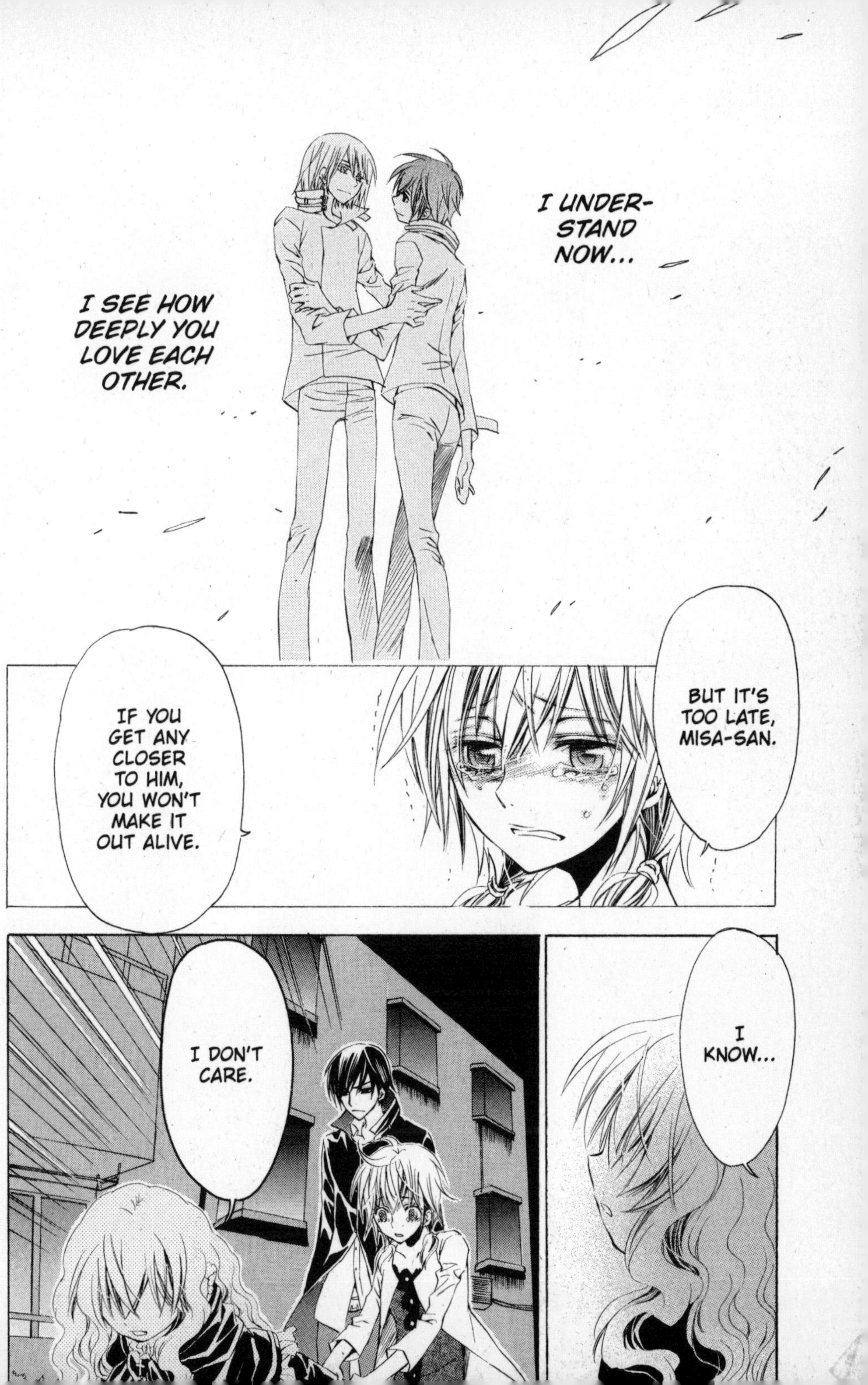
I UNDER-
STAND
NOW...
I SEE HOW DEEPLY YOU LOVE EACH OTHER.
BUT IT'S TOO LATE, MISA-SAN.
IF YOU GET ANY CLOSER TO HIM, YOU WON'T MAKE IT OUT ALIVE.
I KNOW...
I DON'T CARE.

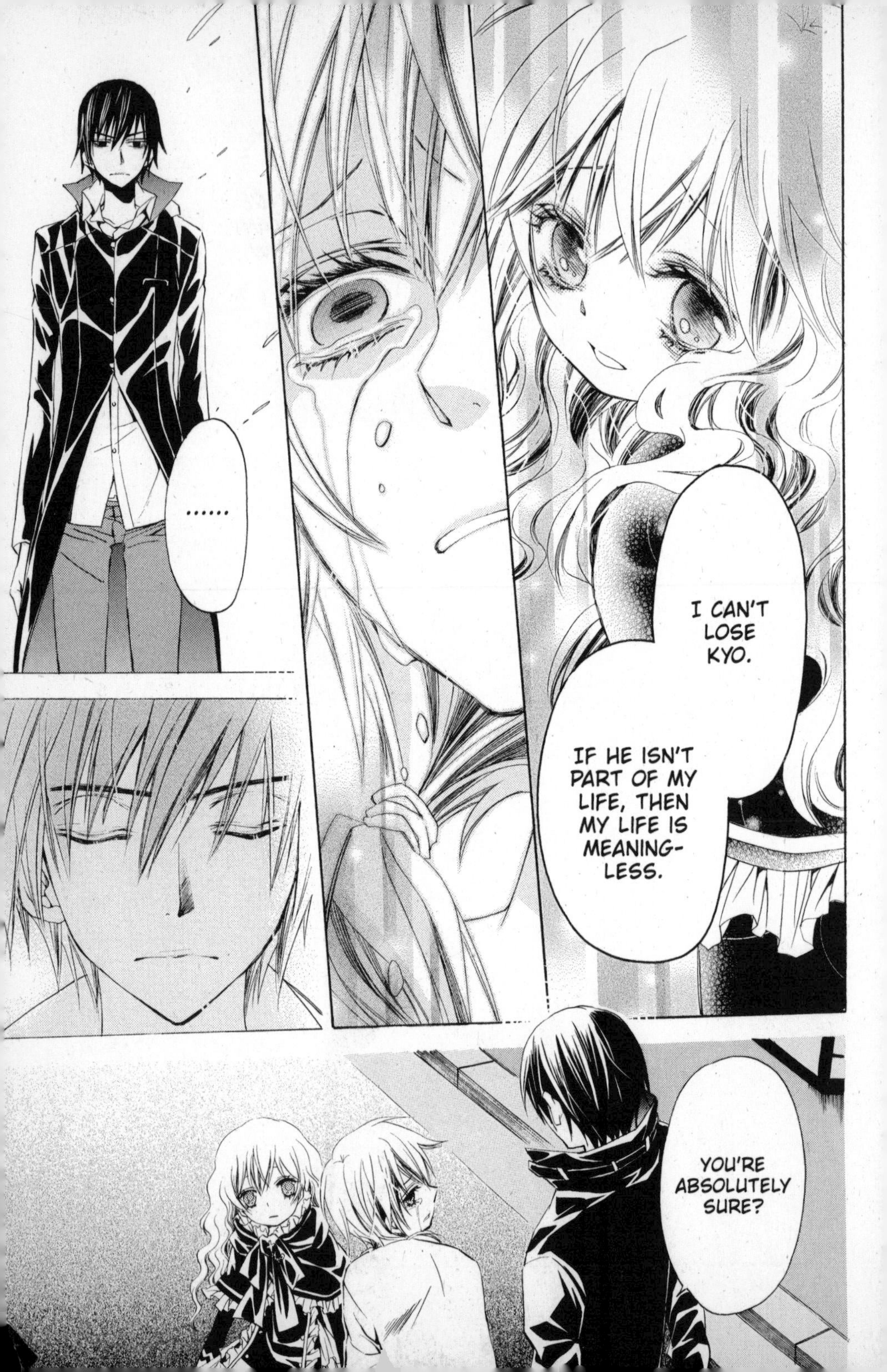
I CAN'T LOSE KYO.
IF HE ISN'T PART OF MY LIFE, THEN MY LIFE IS MEANING-LESS.
......
YOU'RE ABSOLUTELY SURE?

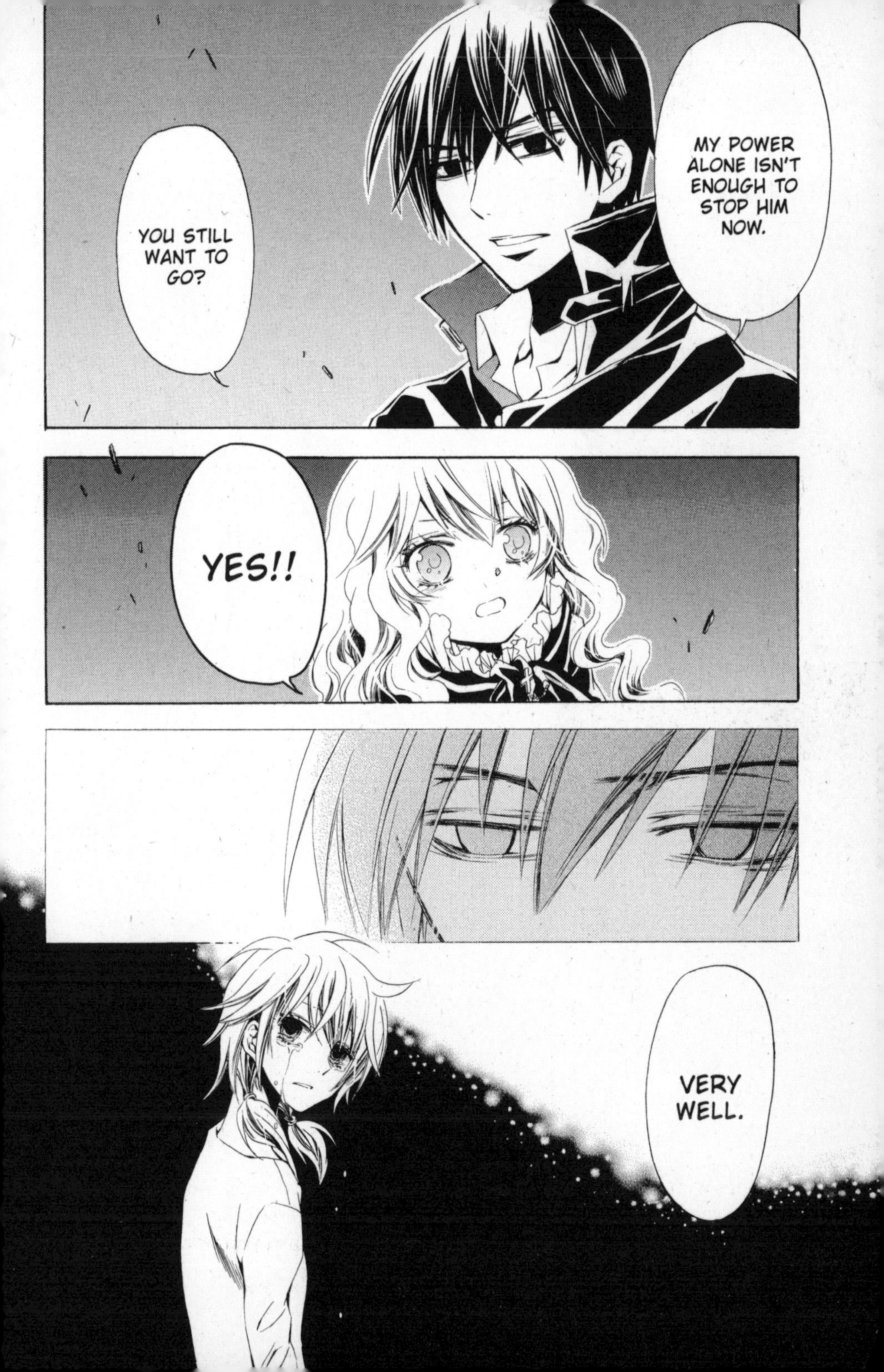
MY POWER ALONE ISN'T ENOUGH TO STOP HIM NOW.
YOU STILL WANT TO GO?
YES!!
VERY WELL.

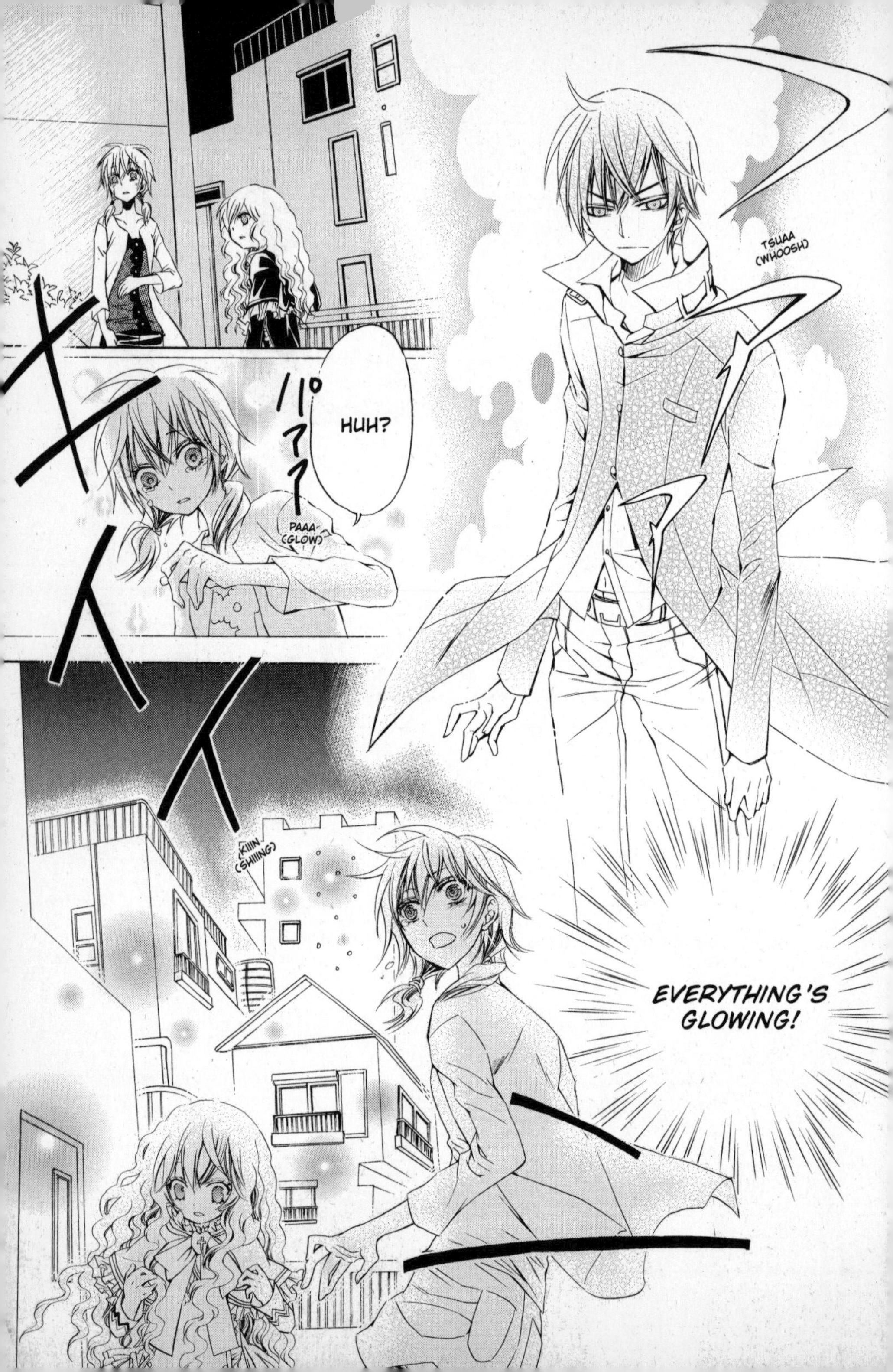

TSUAA (WHOOSH)
HUH?
パァァ
PAAA (GLOW)
キイイ
KIIIN (SHIIING)
EVERYTHING'S GLOWING!

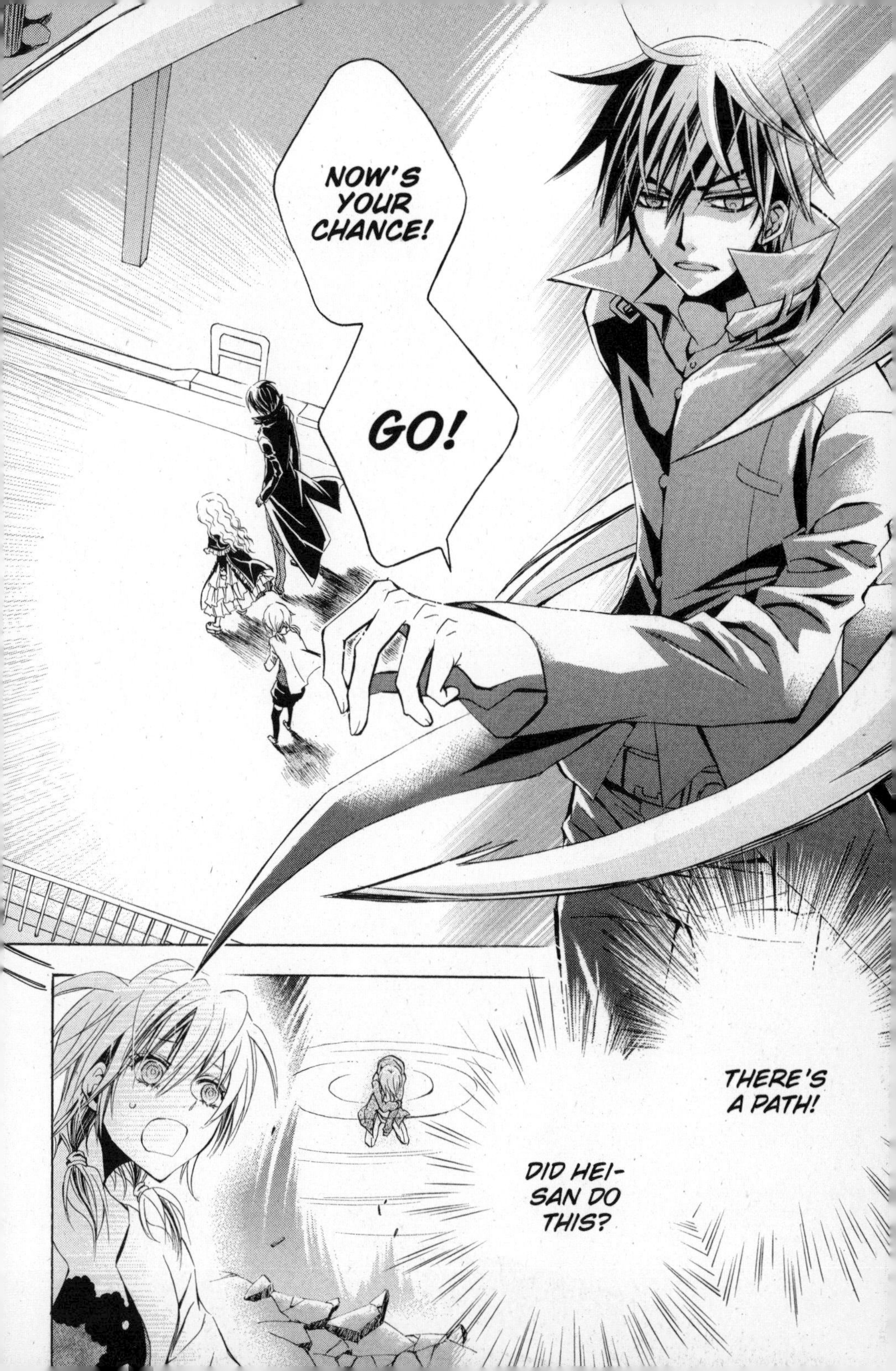
NOW'S YOUR CHANCE!
GO!
THERE'S A PATH!
DID HEI-SAN DO THIS?

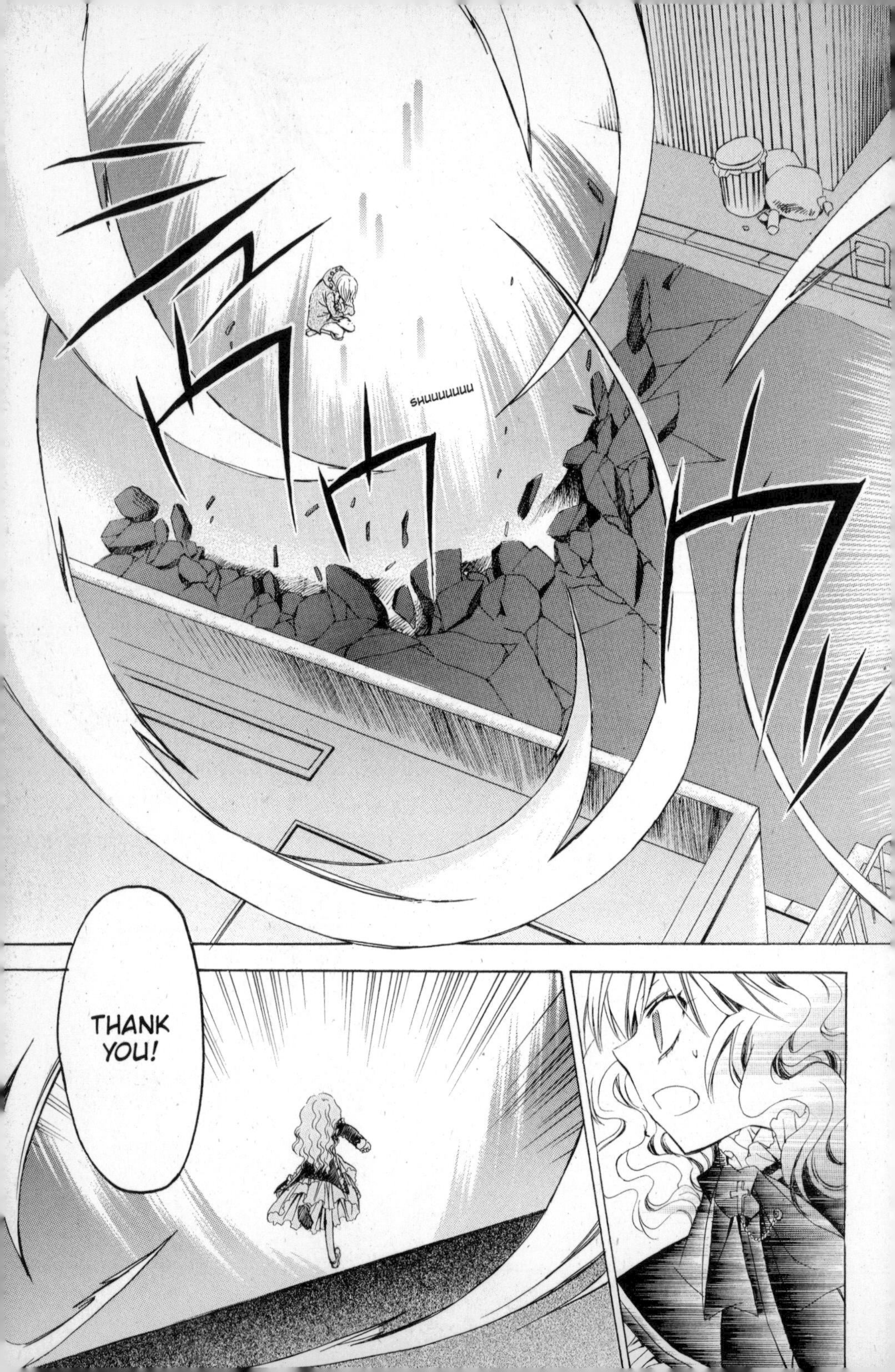

SHUUUUUUU
THANK YOU!

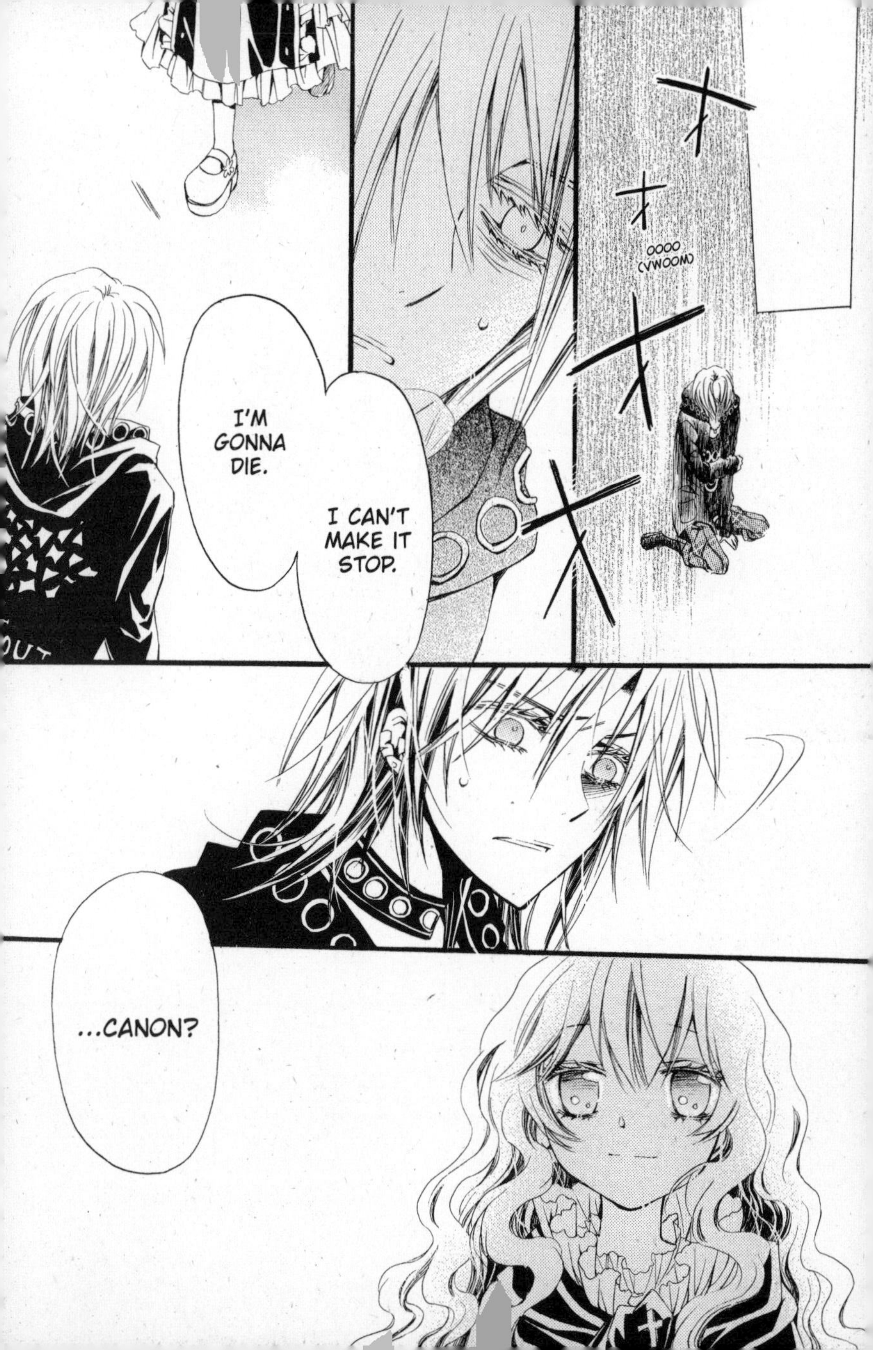
(VWOOM)
I'M GONNA DIE.
I CAN'T MAKE IT STOP.
...CANON?

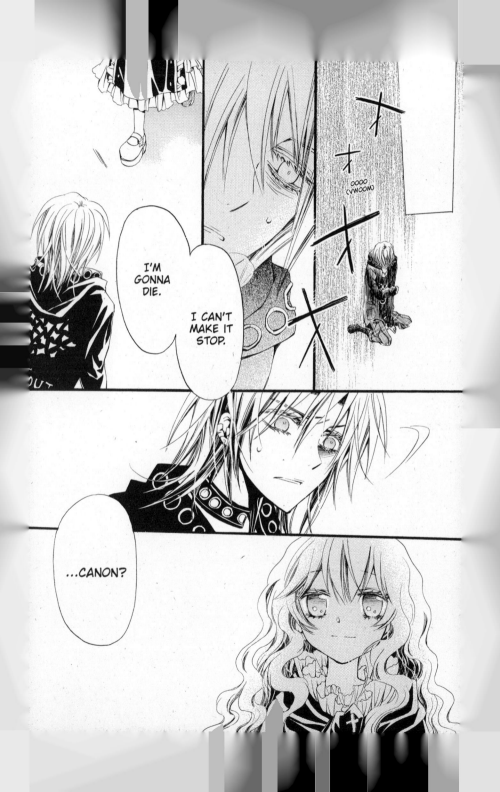

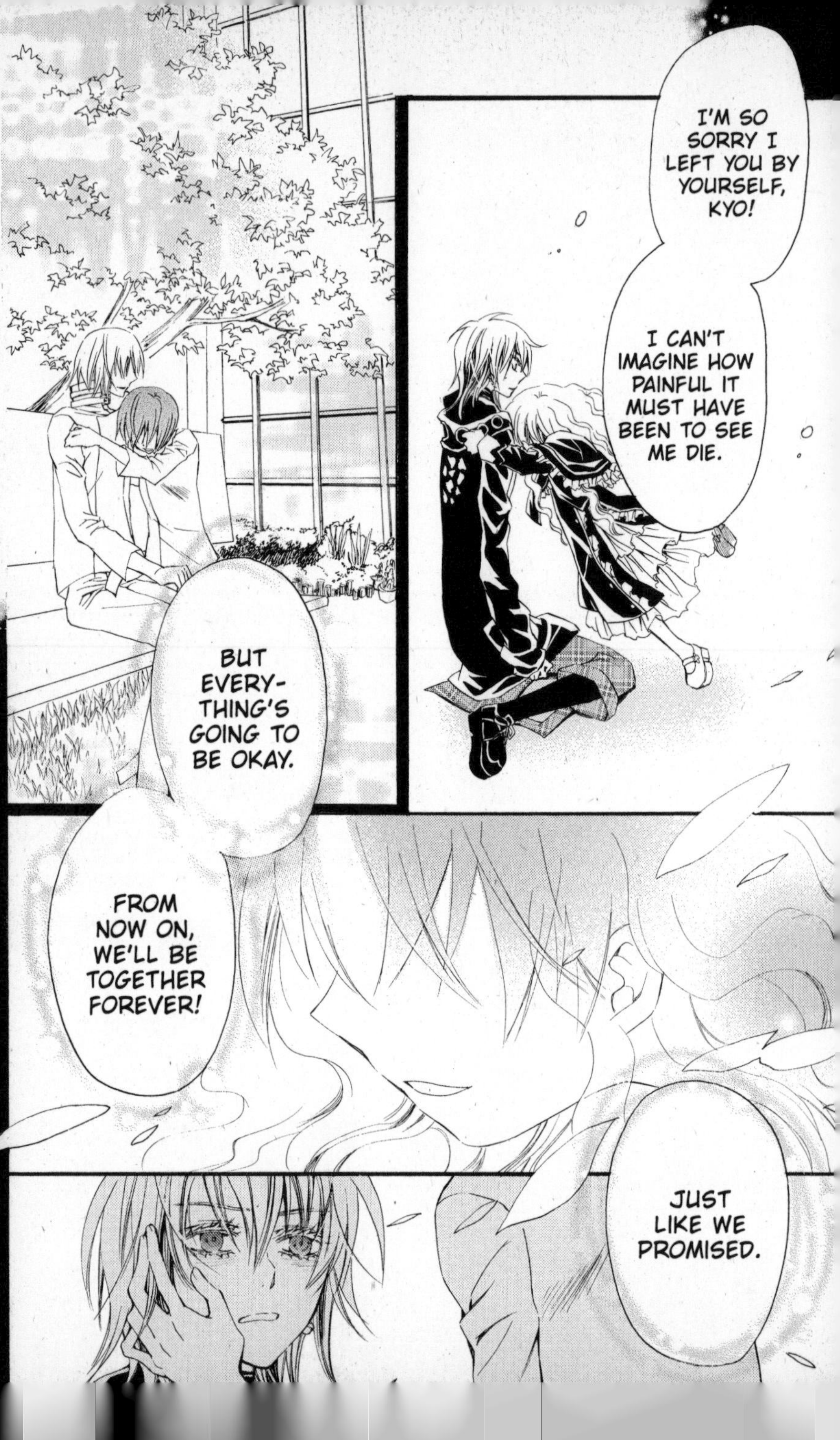
I'M SO SORRY I LEFT YOU BY YOURSELF, KYO!
I CAN'T IMAGINE HOW PAINFUL IT MUST HAVE BEEN TO SEE ME DIE.
BUT EVERY-THING'S GOING TO BE OKAY.
FROM NOW ON, WE'LL BE TOGETHER FOREVER!
JUST LIKE WE PROMISED.

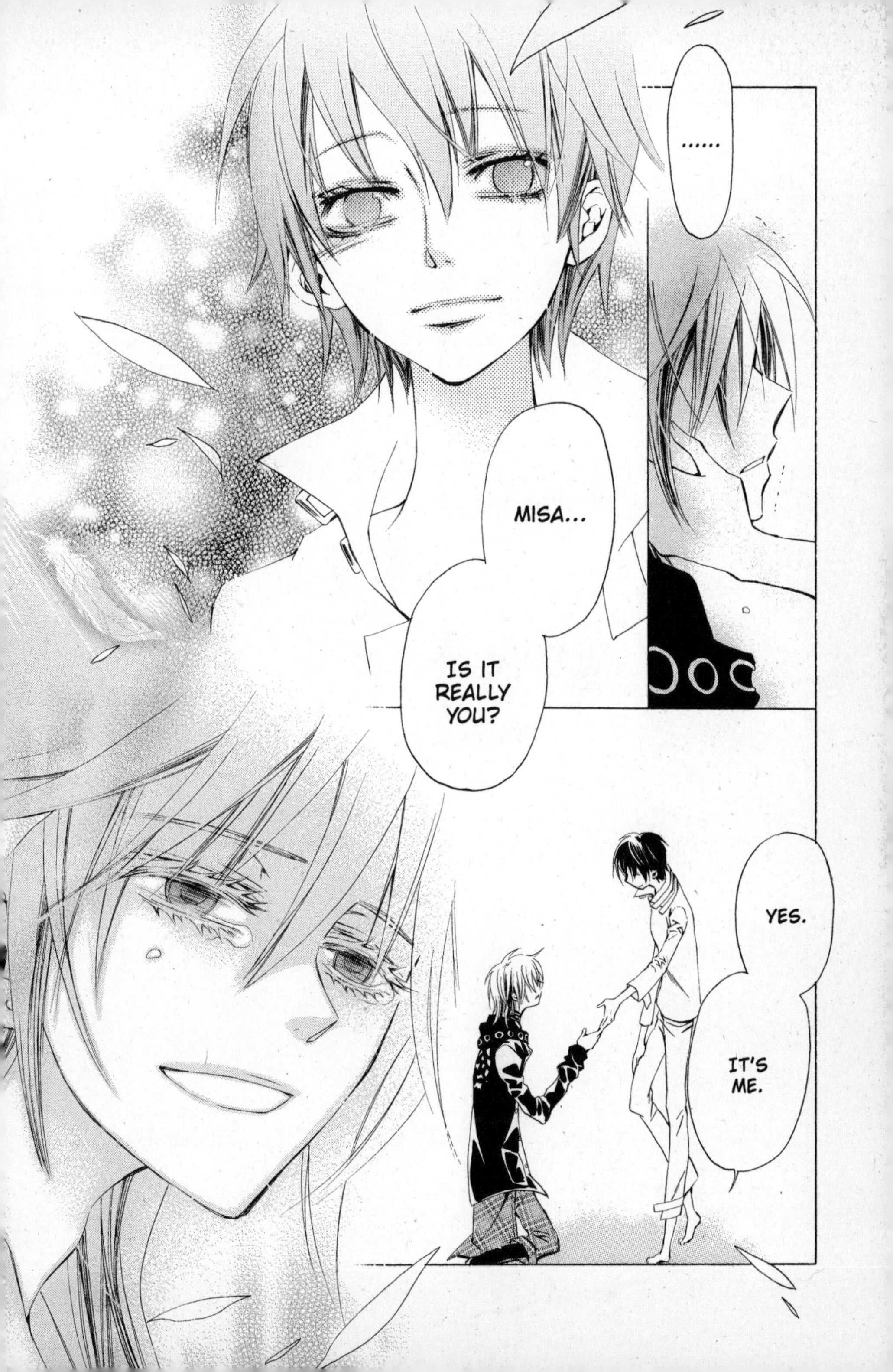
......
MISA...
IS IT REALLY YOU?
YES.
IT'S ME.

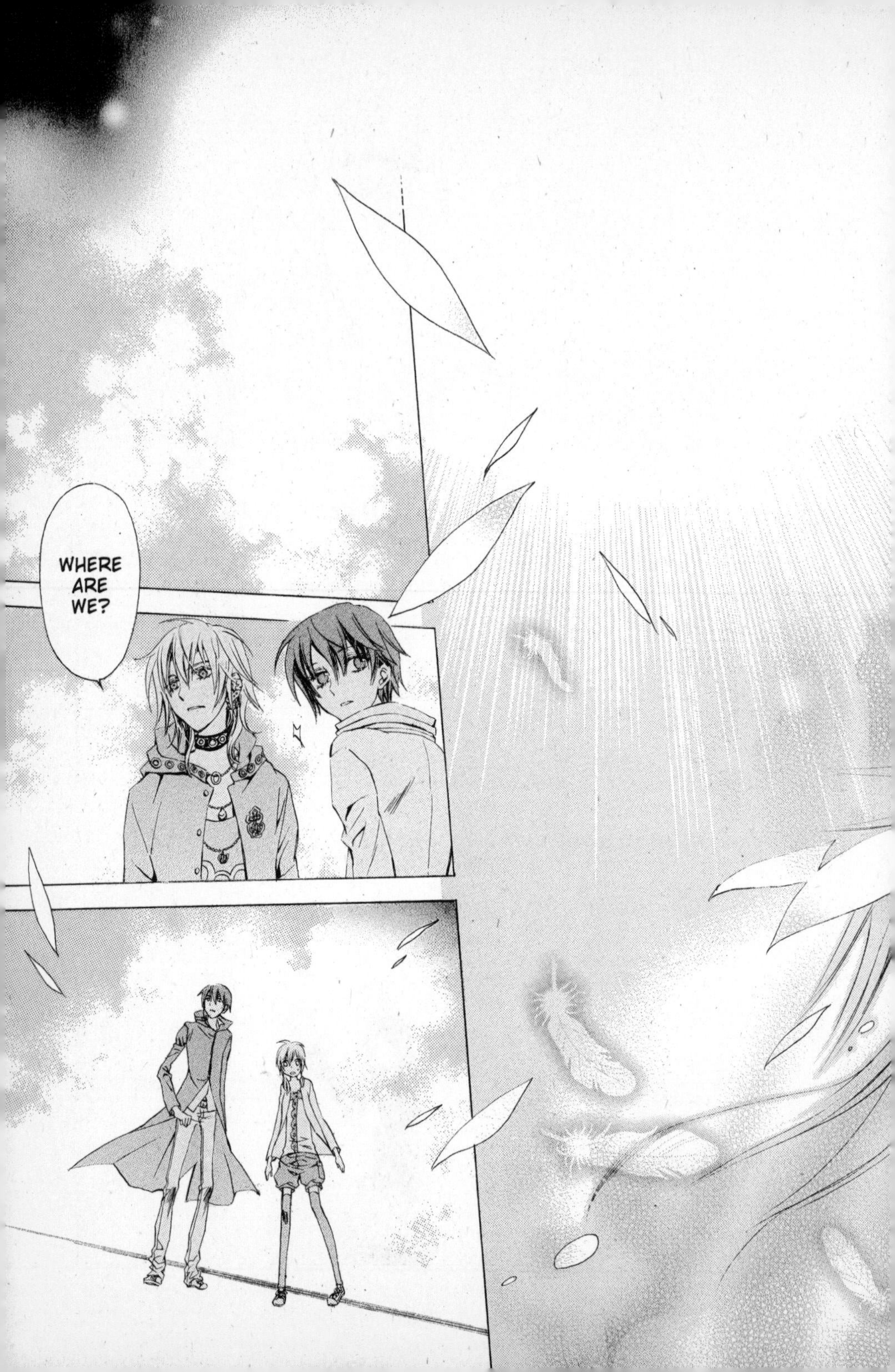
WHERE ARE WE?

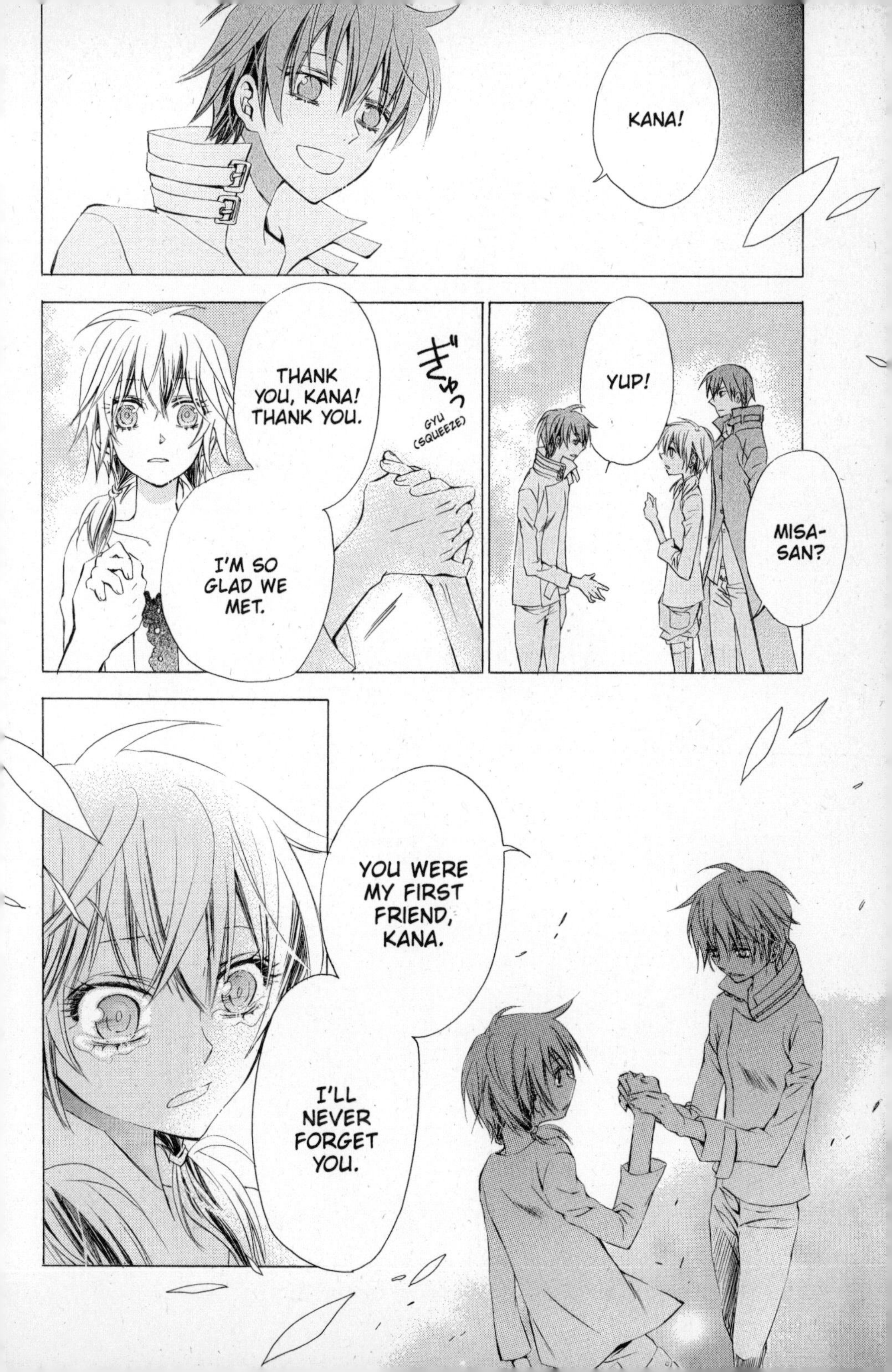
KANA!
YUP!
MISA-SAN?
THANK YOU, KANA! THANK YOU.
ぎゅっ
GYU (SQUEEZE)
I'M SO GLAD WE MET.
YOU WERE MY FIRST FRIEND, KANA.
I'LL NEVER FORGET YOU.

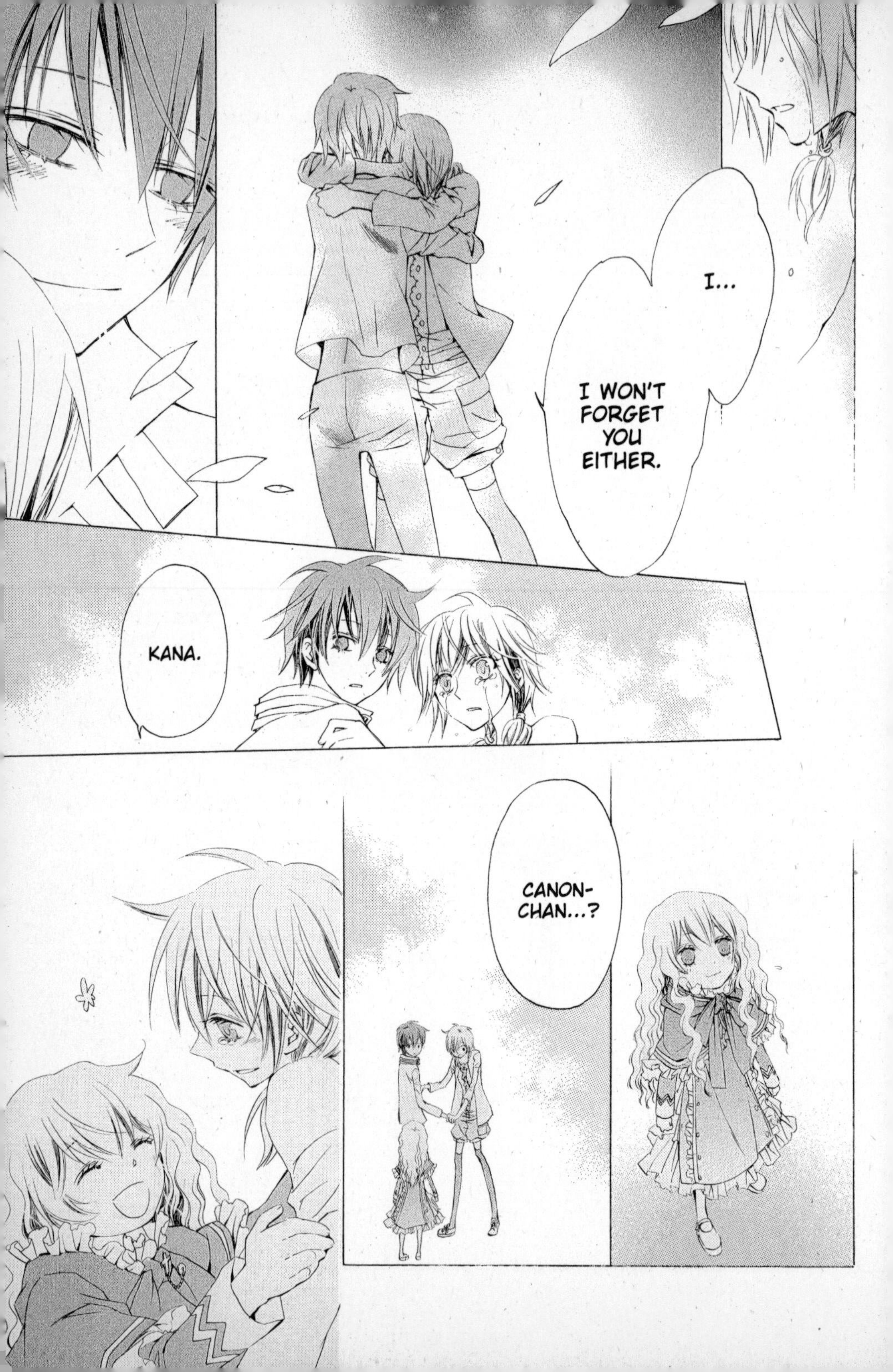
I...
I WON'T FORGET YOU EITHER.
KANA.
CANON-CHAN...?

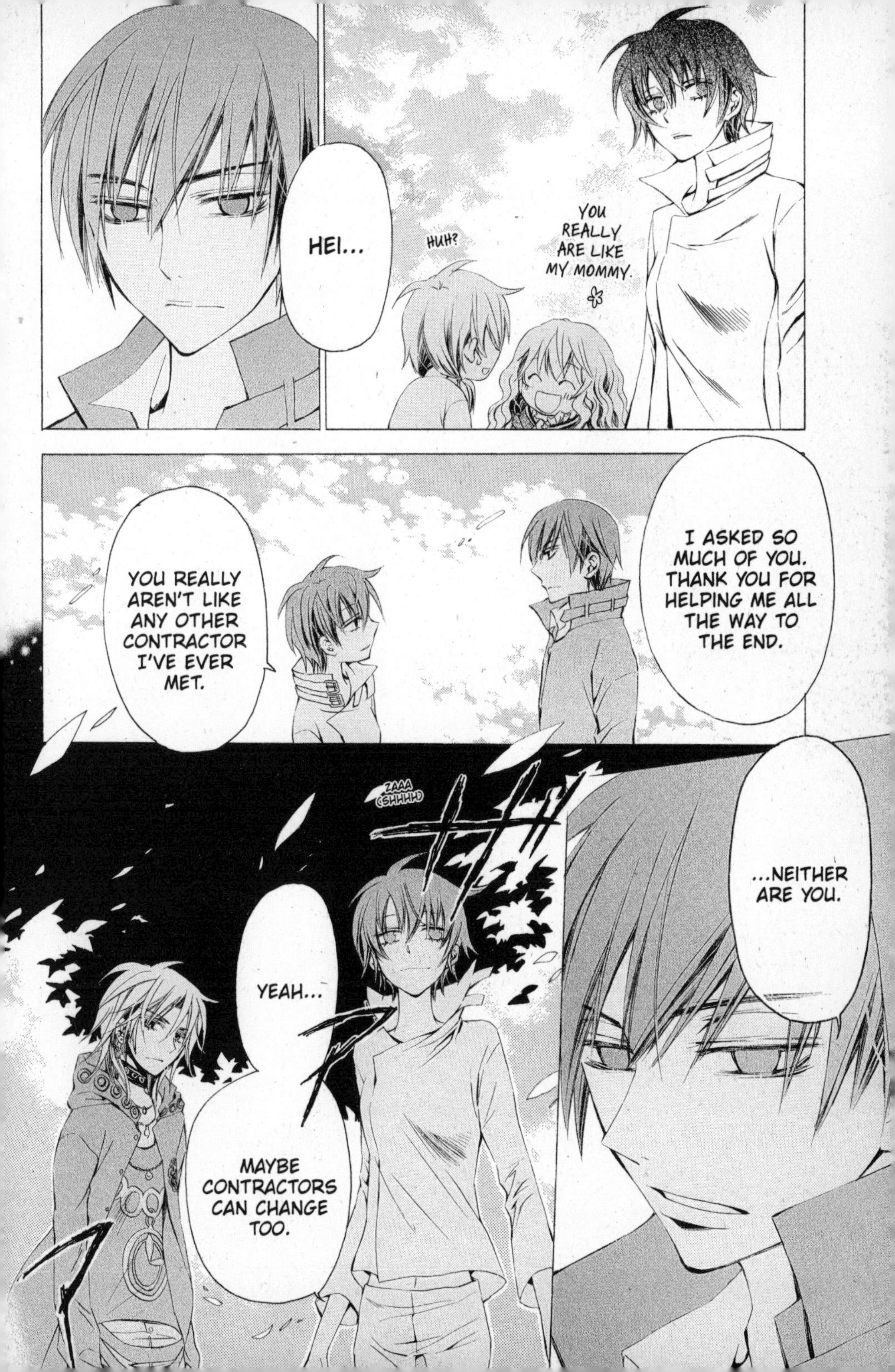

YOU REALLY ARE LIKE MY MOMMY.
HUH?
HEI...
I ASKED SO MUCH OF YOU. THANK YOU FOR HELPING ME ALL THE WAY TO THE END.
YOU REALLY AREN'T LIKE ANY OTHER CONTRACTOR I'VE EVER MET.
...NEITHER ARE YOU.
ZAAA (SHHHH)
YEAH...
MAYBE CONTRACTORS CAN CHANGE TOO.

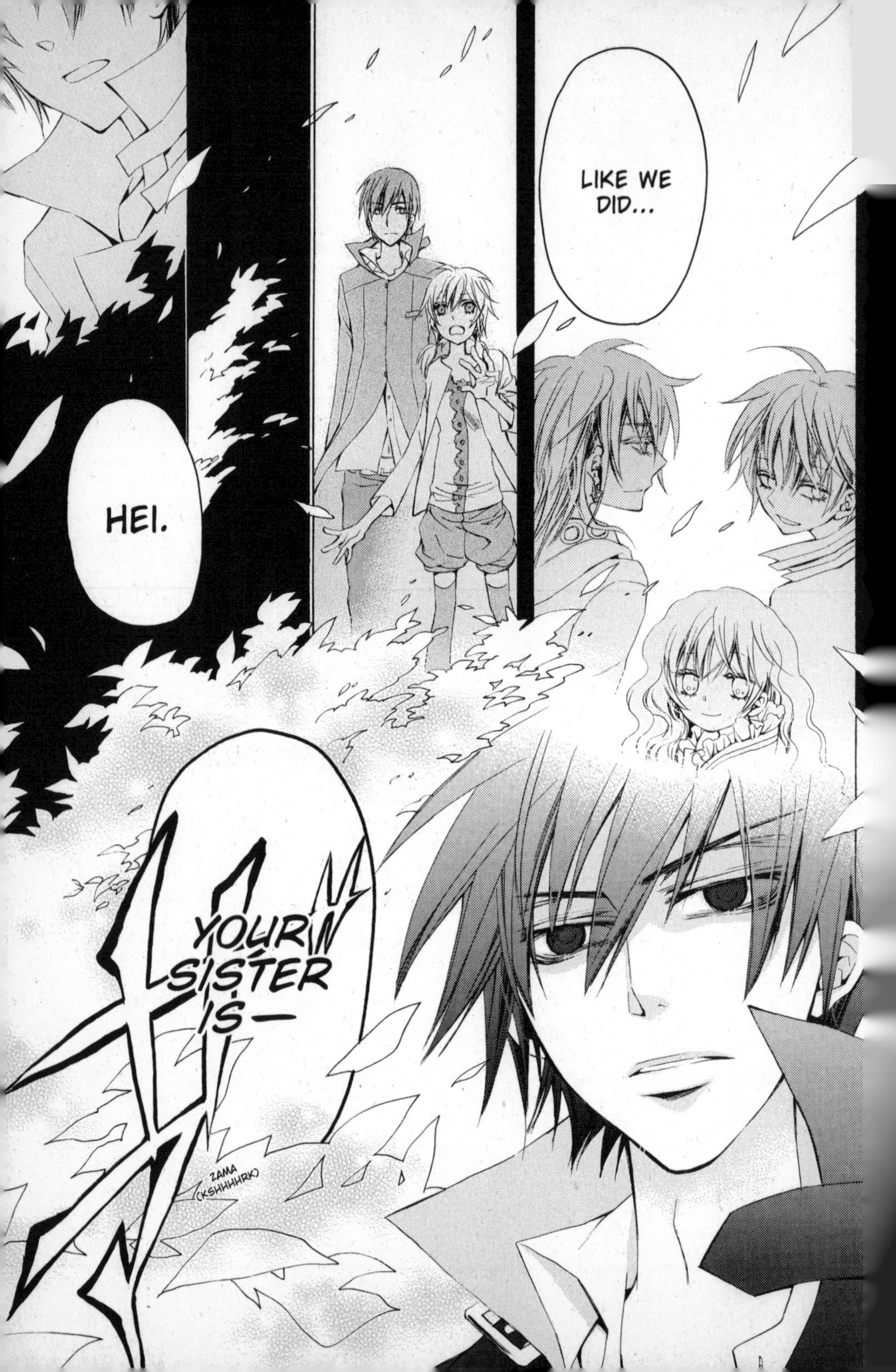
LIKE WE DID...
HEI.
YOUR SISTER IS—
ZAMA (KSHHHHRK)

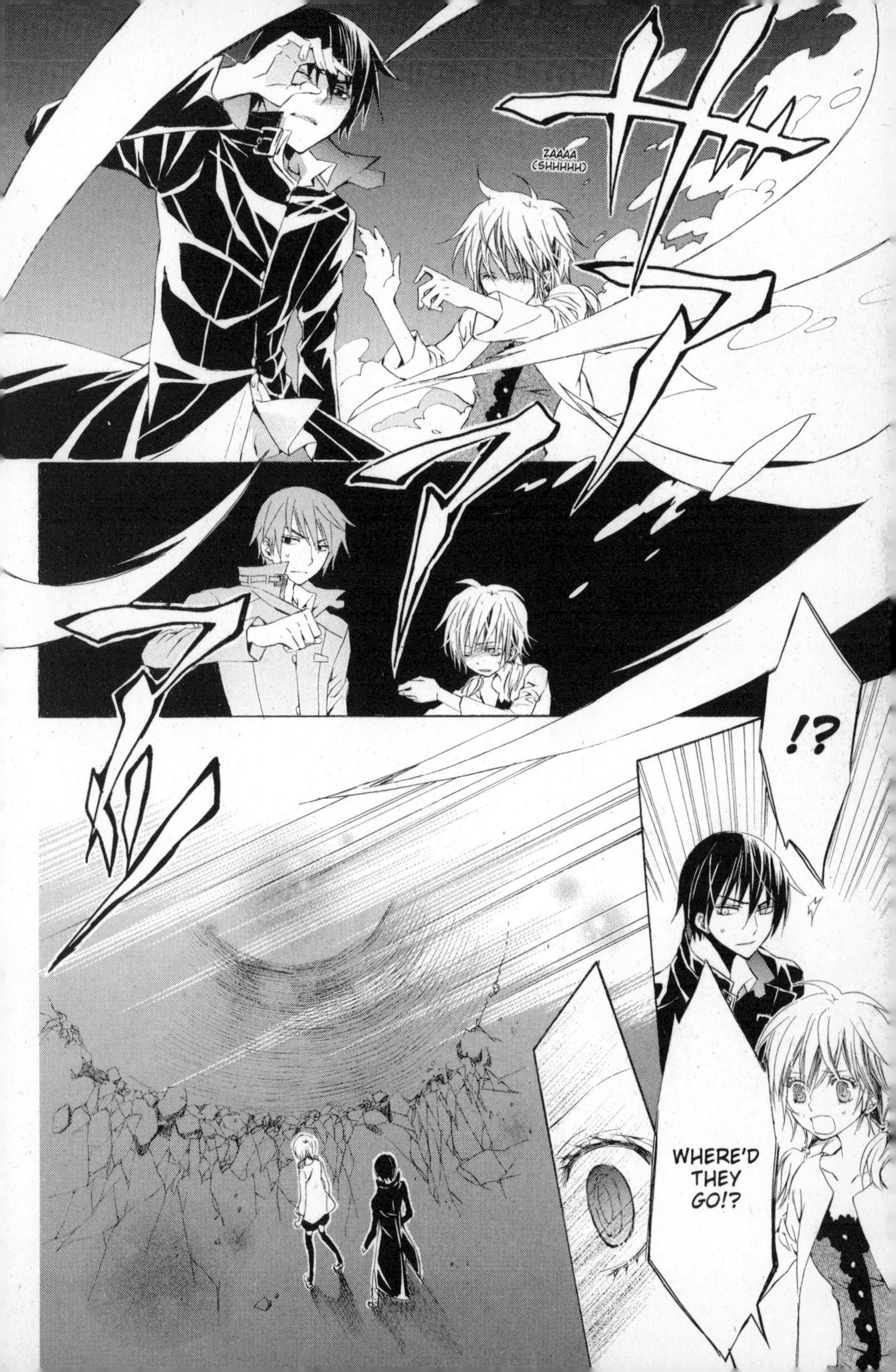
ZAAAA
(SHHHHH)
!?
WHERE'D THEY GO!?

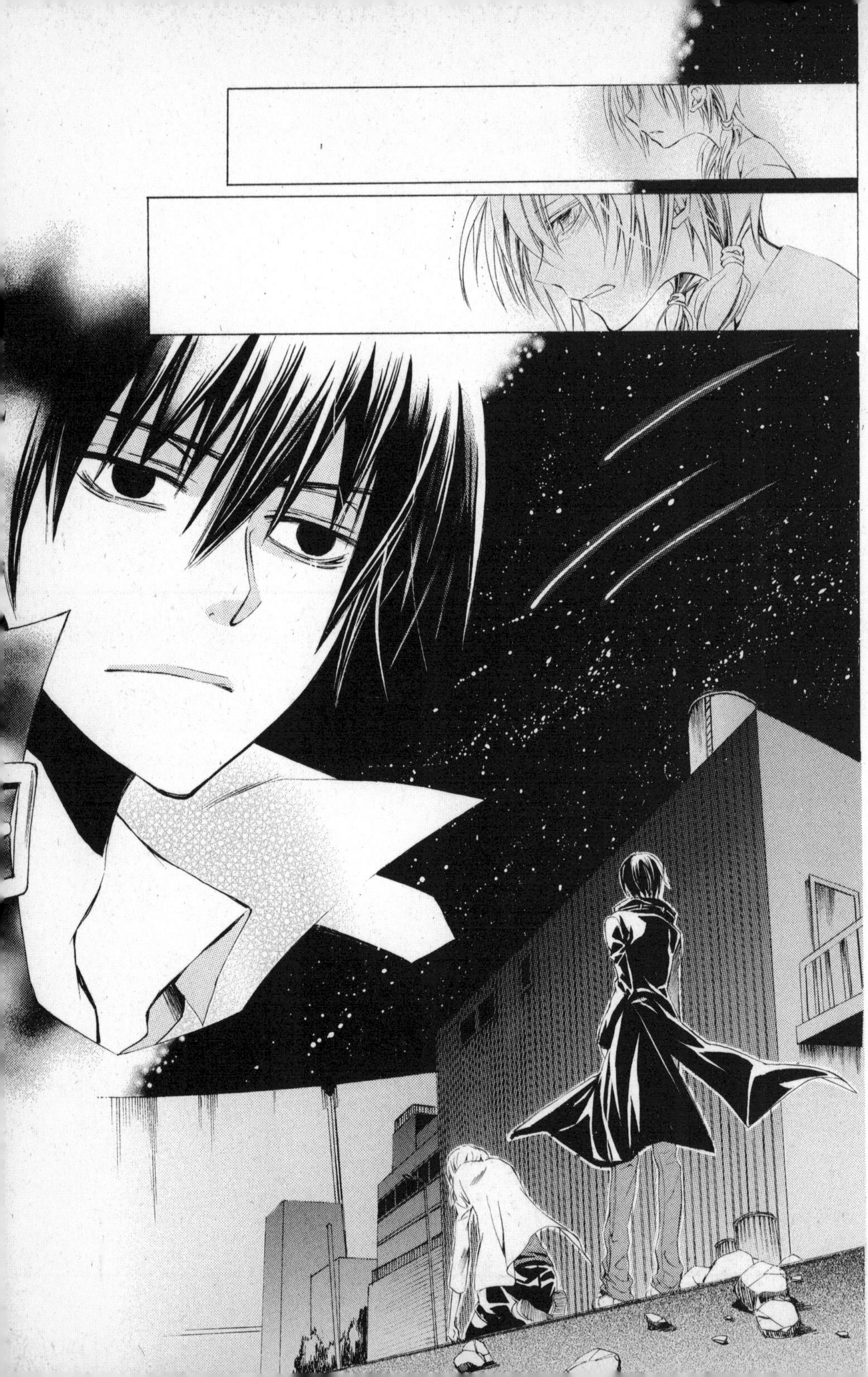

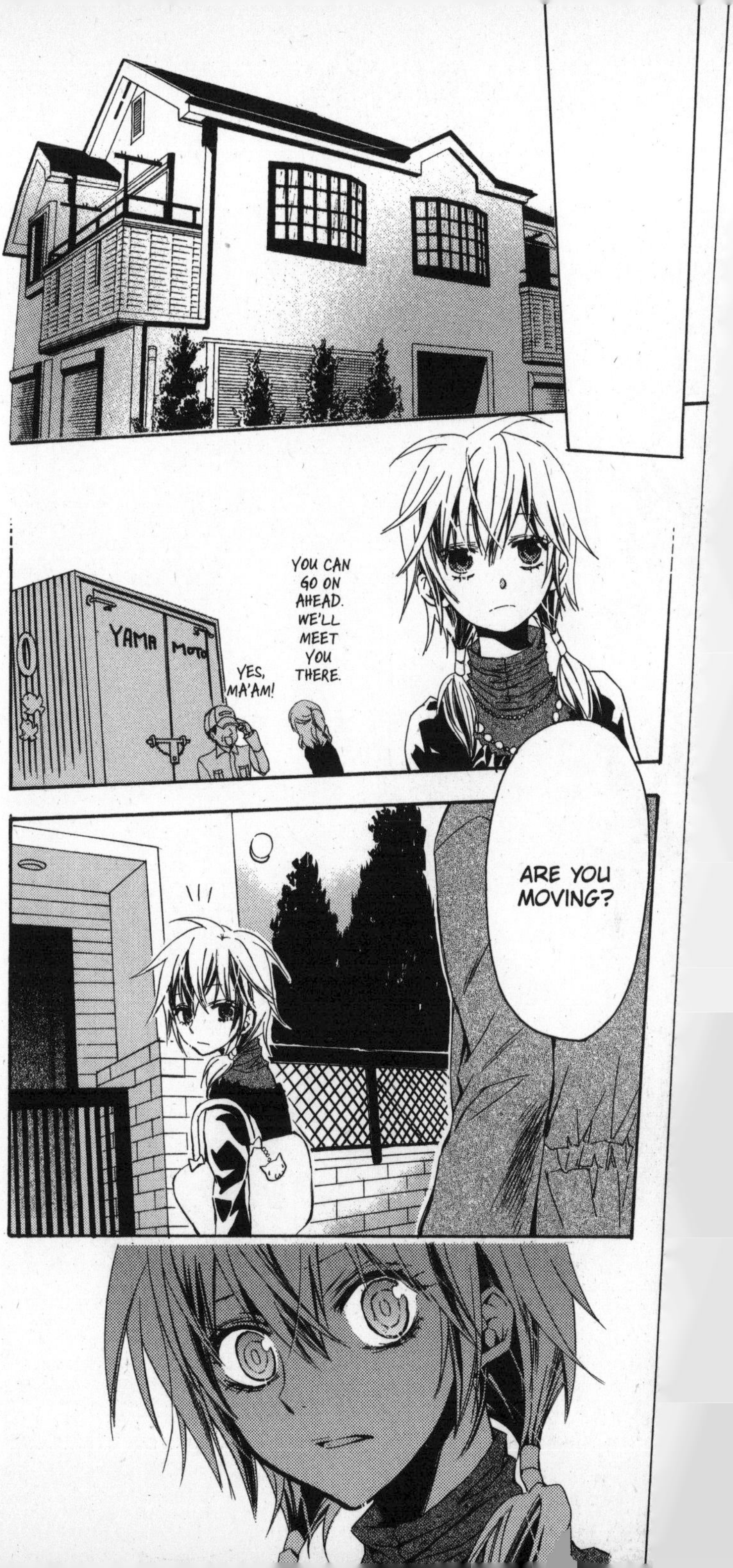
YOU CAN GO ON AHEAD. WE'LL MEET YOU THERE.
YES, MA'AM!
YAMA MOTO
ARE YOU MOVING?

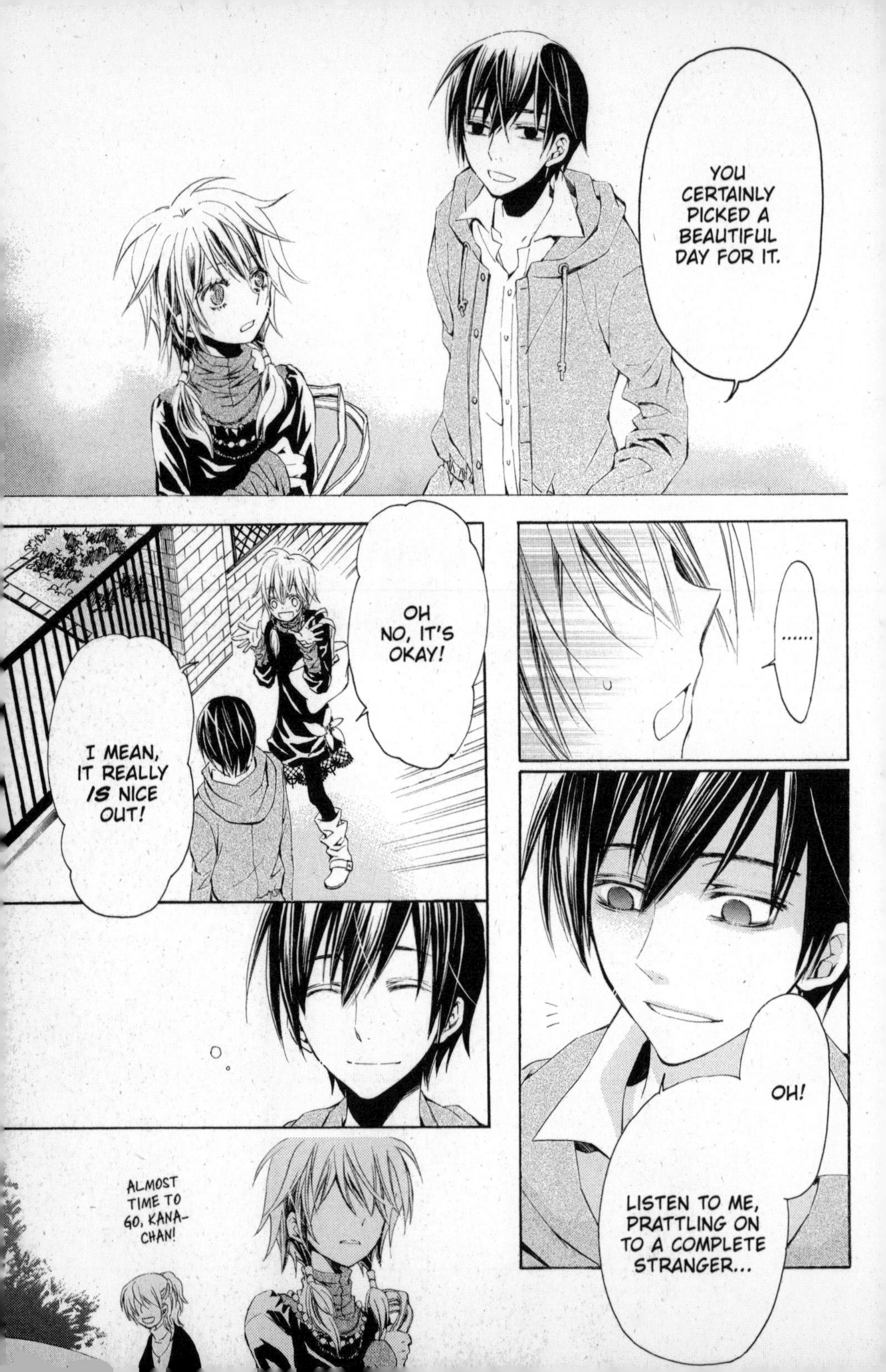
YOU CERTAINLY PICKED A BEAUTIFUL DAY FOR IT.
......
OH!
LISTEN TO ME, PRATTLING ON TO A COMPLETE STRANGER...
OH NO, IT'S OKAY!
I MEAN, IT REALLY *IS* NICE OUT!
ALMOST TIME TO GO, KANA-CHAN!

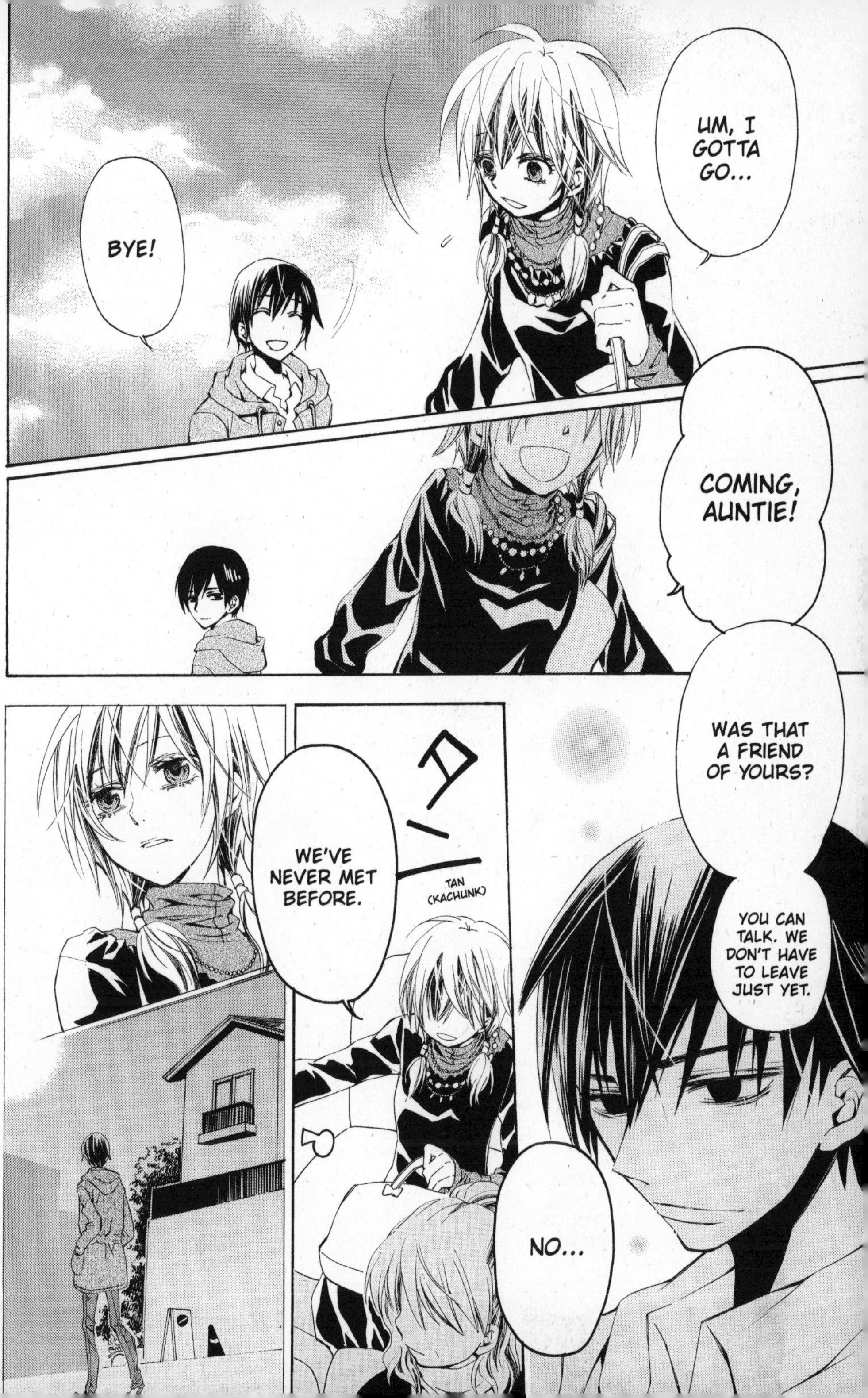
UM, I GOTTA GO...
BYE!
COMING, AUNTIE!
WAS THAT A FRIEND OF YOURS?
YOU CAN TALK. WE DON'T HAVE TO LEAVE JUST YET.
NO...
タン
TAN (KACHUNK)
WE'VE NEVER MET BEFORE.

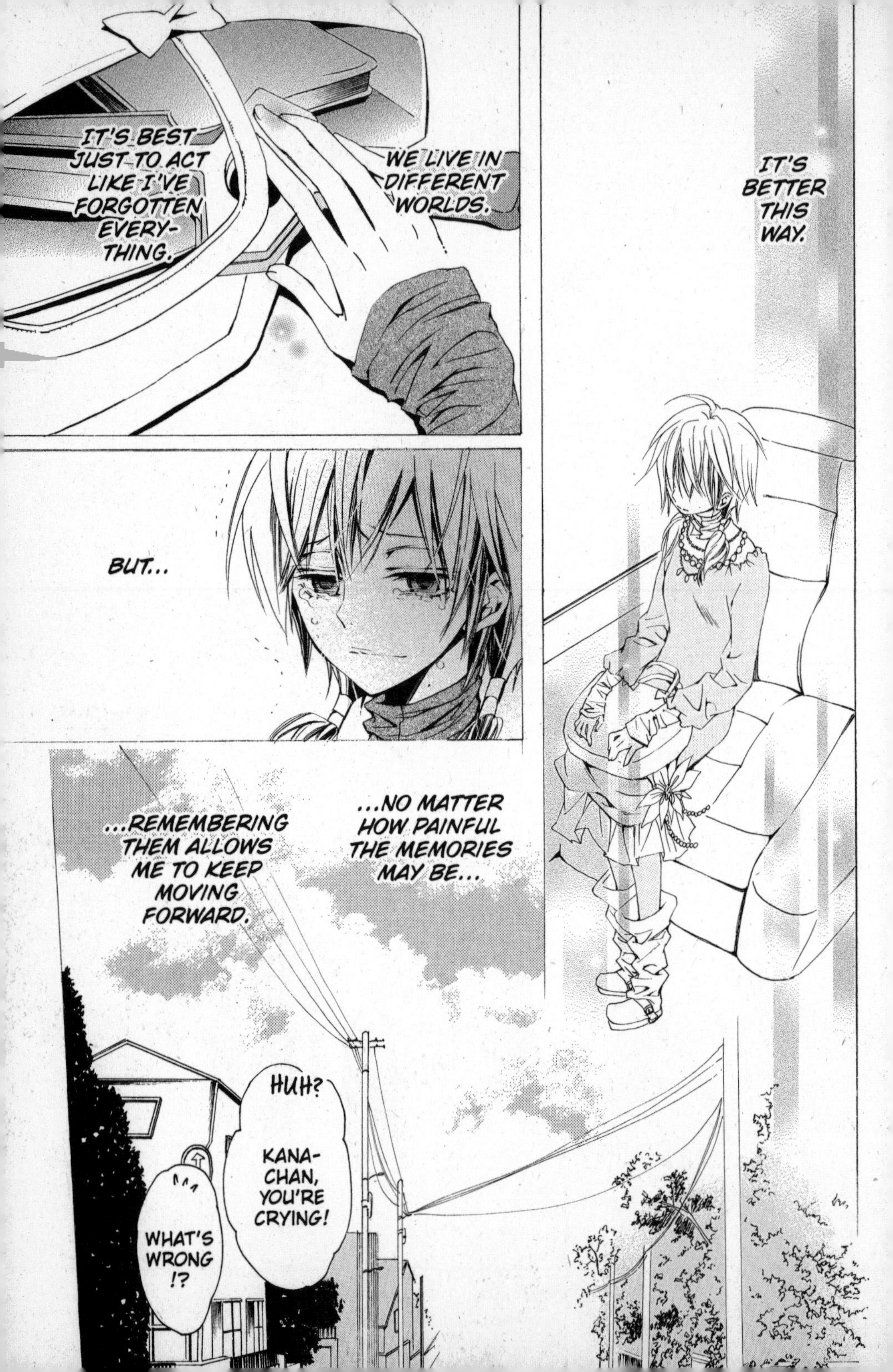
IT'S BETTER THIS WAY.
WE LIVE IN DIFFERENT WORLDS.
IT'S BEST JUST TO ACT LIKE I'VE FORGOTTEN EVERY-THING.
BUT...
...NO MATTER HOW PAINFUL THE MEMORIES MAY BE...
...REMEMBERING THEM ALLOWS ME TO KEEP MOVING FORWARD.
HUH?
KANA-CHAN, YOU'RE CRYING!
WHAT'S WRONG !?

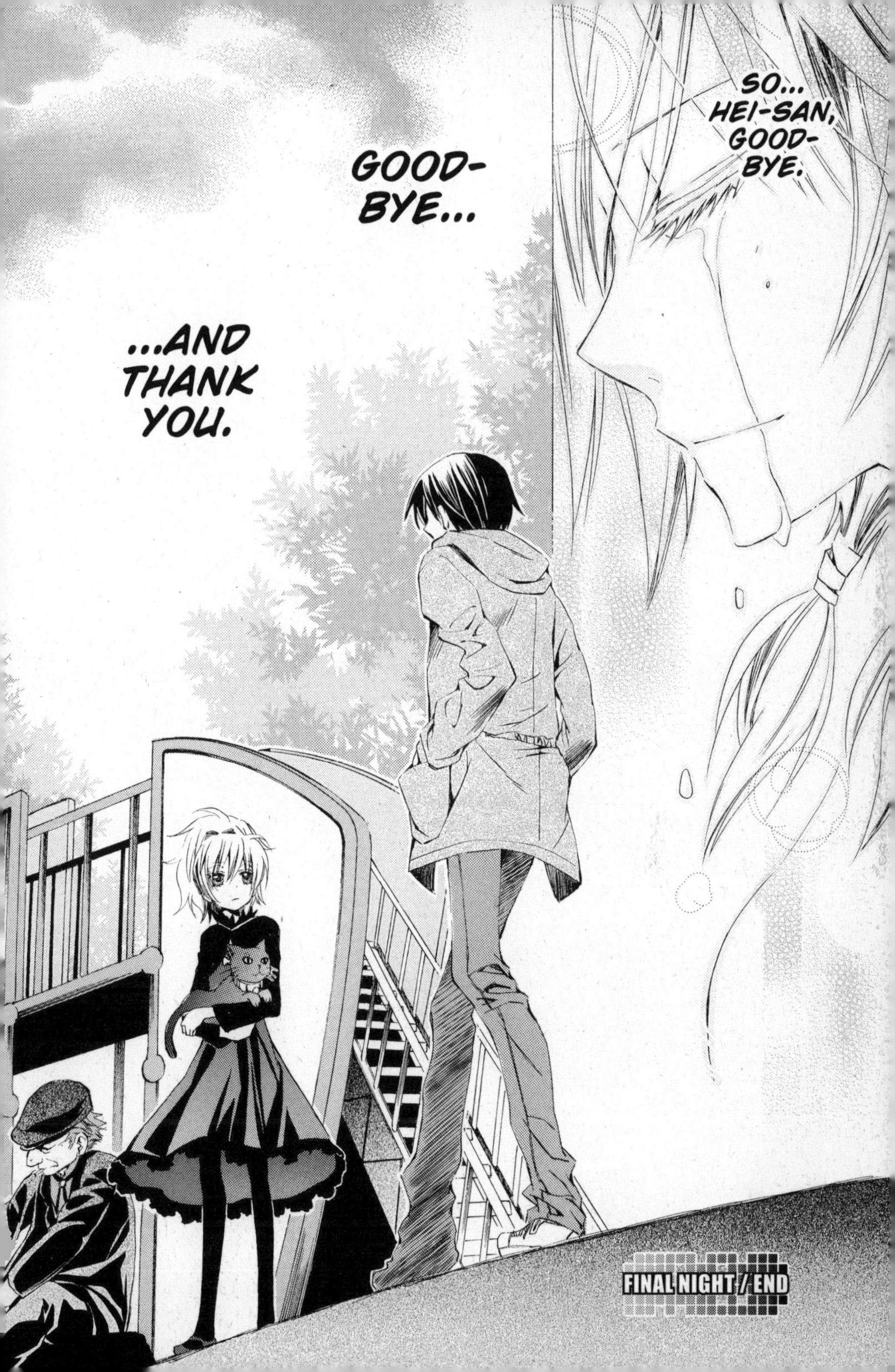
SO... HEI-SAN, GOOD-BYE.
GOOD-BYE...
...AND THANK YOU.
FINAL NIGHT / END

DARKER THAN
BLACK
THE BLACK CONTRACTOR

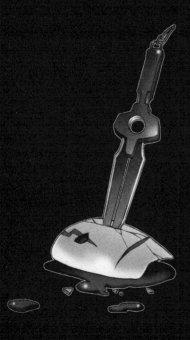

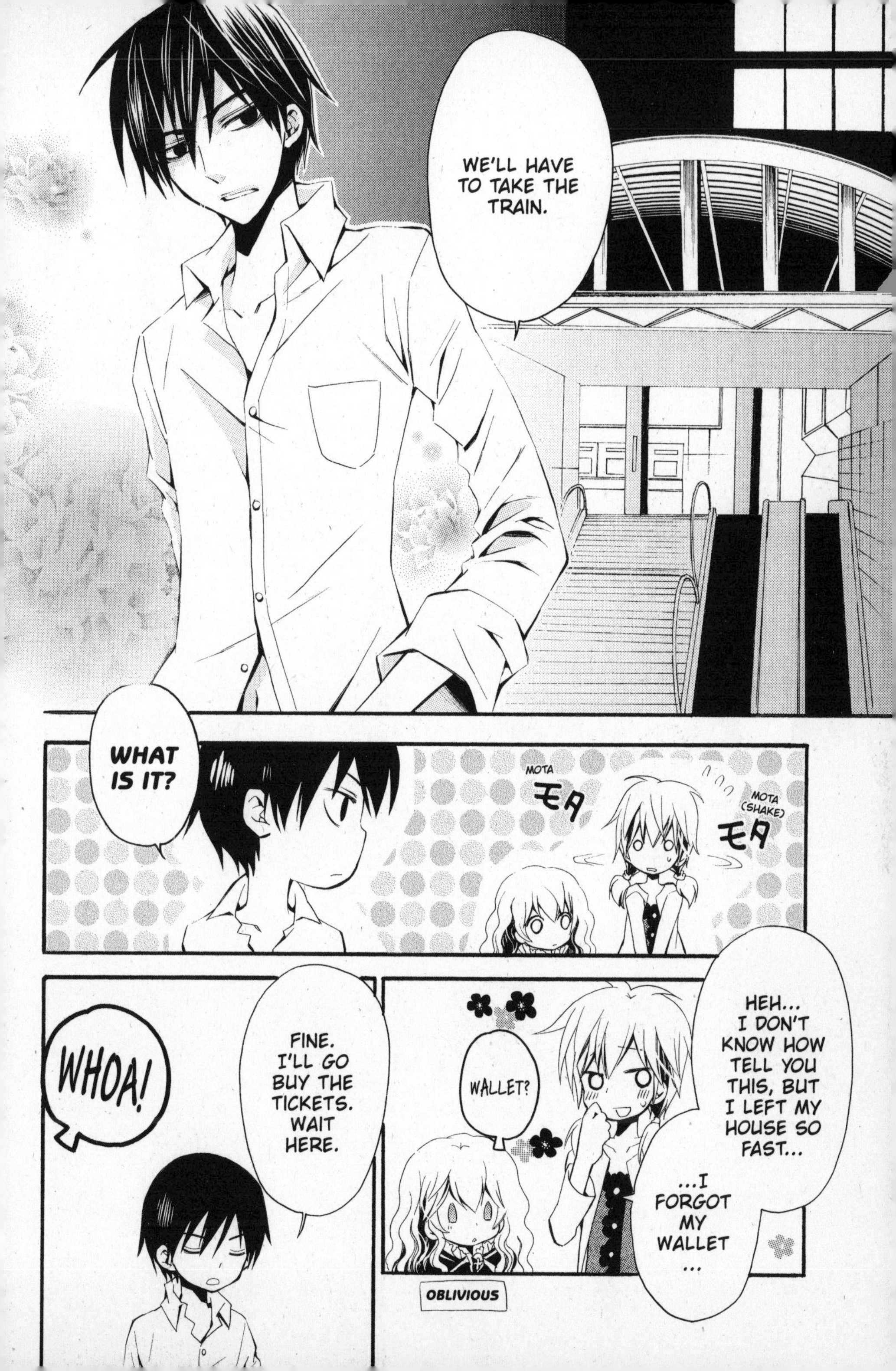
WE'LL HAVE TO TAKE THE TRAIN.
MOTA (SHAKE)
モタ
MOTA
モタ
WHAT IS IT?
HEH... I DON'T KNOW HOW TELL YOU THIS, BUT I LEFT MY HOUSE SO FAST...
...I FORGOT MY WALLET ...
WALLET?
OBLIVIOUS
FINE. I'LL GO BUY THE TICKETS. WAIT HERE.
WHOA!

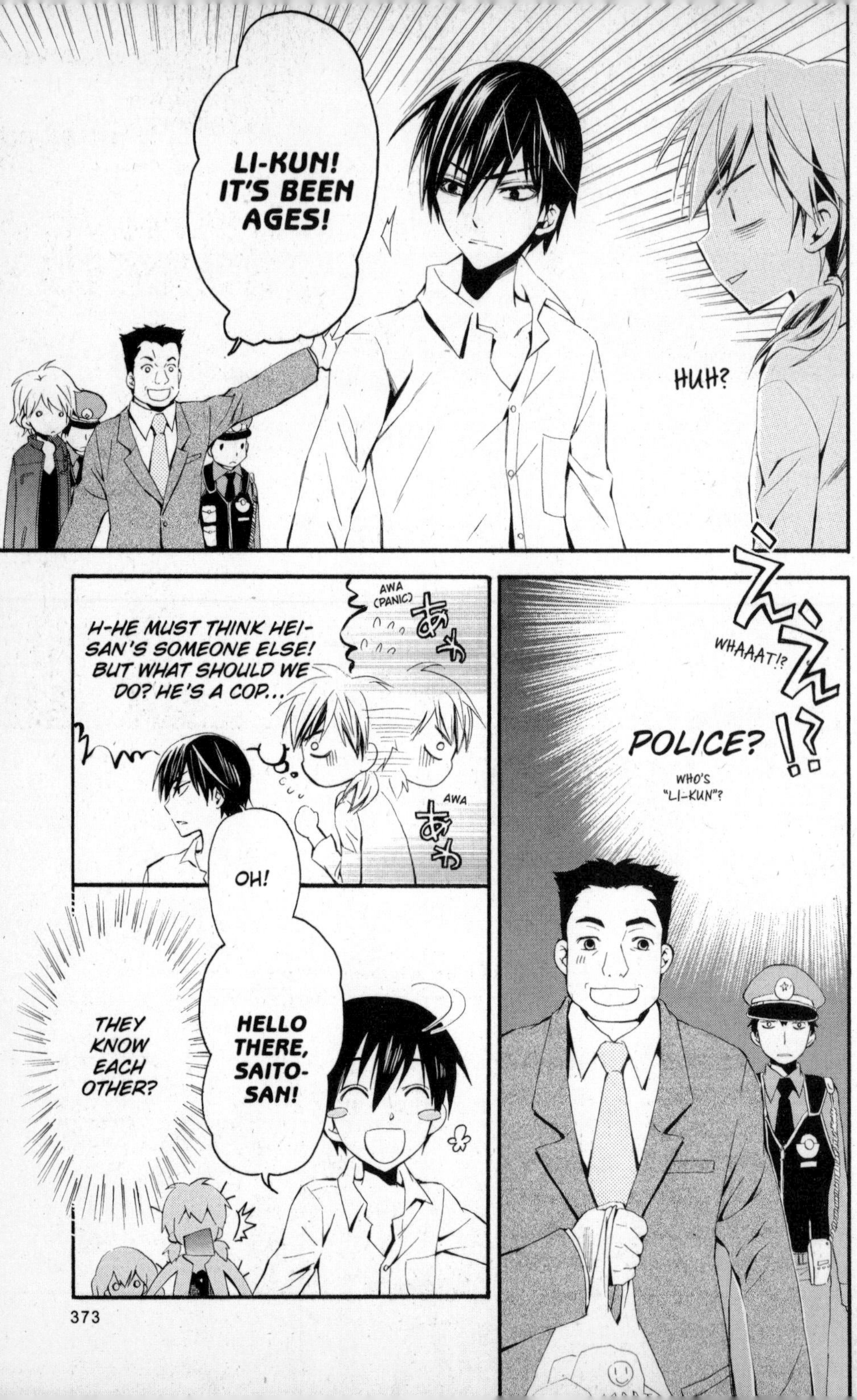
LI-KUN! IT'S BEEN AGES!
HUH?
えええ!?
WHAAAT!?
POLICE?
WHO'S "LI-KUN"?
あわ
AWA (PANIC)
H-HE MUST THINK HEI-SAN'S SOMEONE ELSE! BUT WHAT SHOULD WE DO? HE'S A COP...
あわ
AWA
OH!
HELLO THERE, SAITO-SAN!
THEY KNOW EACH OTHER?

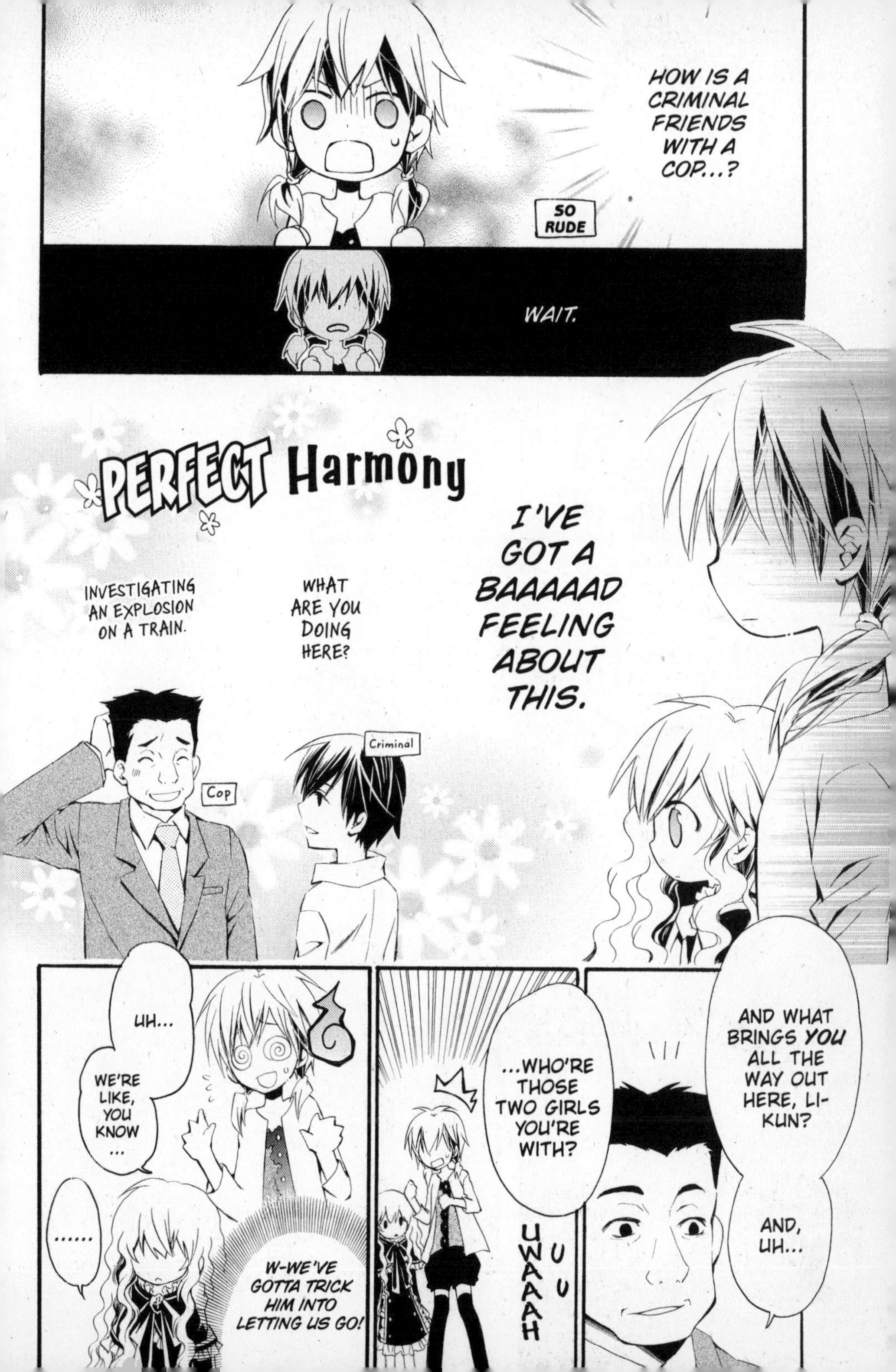

HOW IS A CRIMINAL FRIENDS WITH A COP...?
SO RUDE
WAIT.
PERFECT Harmony
I'VE GOT A BAAAAAD FEELING ABOUT THIS.
WHAT ARE YOU DOING HERE?
INVESTIGATING AN EXPLOSION ON A TRAIN.
Criminal
Cop
AND WHAT BRINGS YOU ALL THE WAY OUT HERE, LI-KUN?
AND, UH...
...WHO'RE THOSE TWO GIRLS YOU'RE WITH?
UWAAAH
UU
UH...
WE'RE LIKE, YOU KNOW...
W-WE'VE GOTTA TRICK HIM INTO LETTING US GO!
......

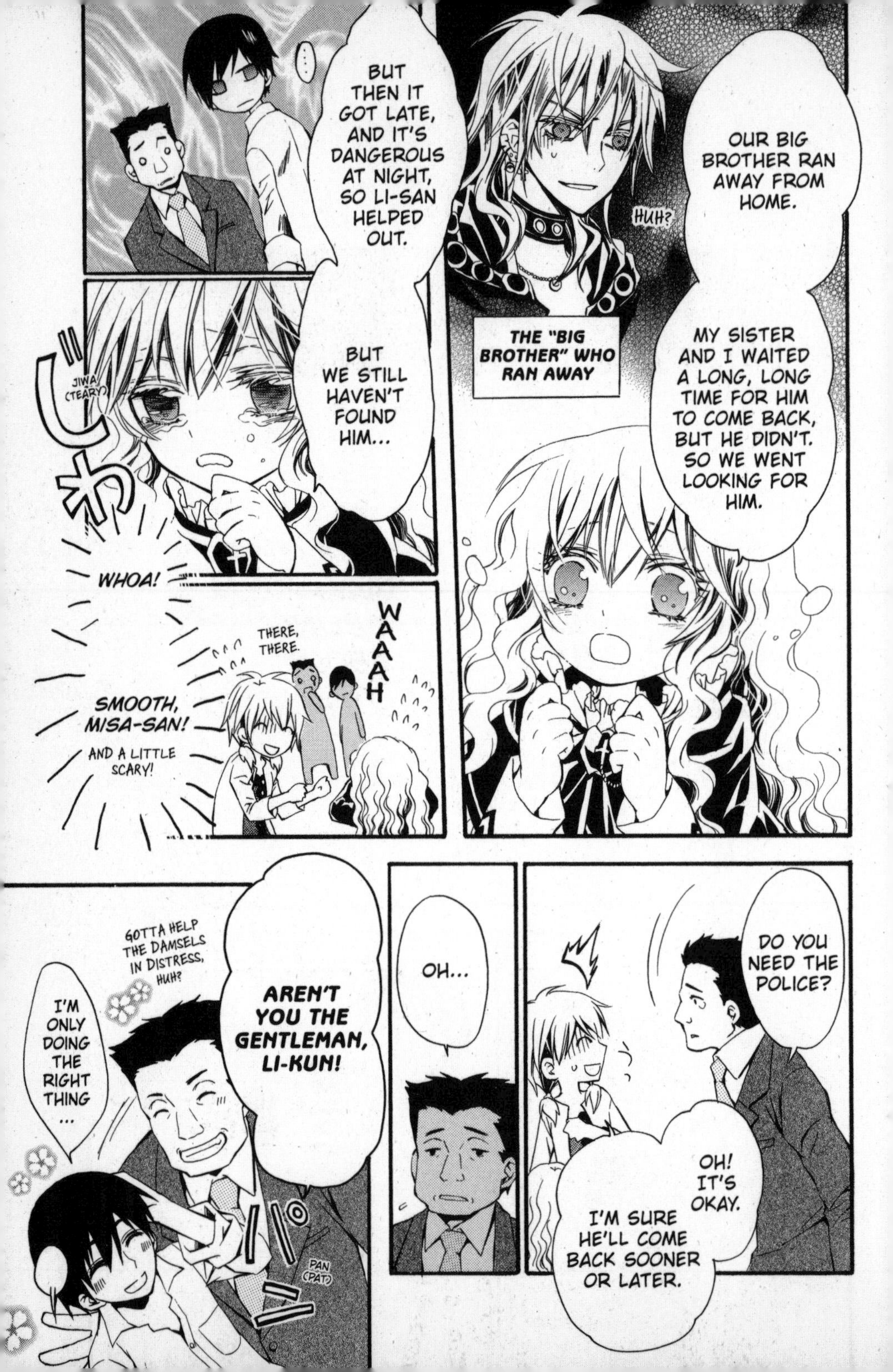

OUR BIG BROTHER RAN AWAY FROM HOME.
HUH?
THE "BIG BROTHER" WHO RAN AWAY
MY SISTER AND I WAITED A LONG, LONG TIME FOR HIM TO COME BACK, BUT HE DIDN'T. SO WE WENT LOOKING FOR HIM.
...
BUT THEN IT GOT LATE, AND IT'S DANGEROUS AT NIGHT, SO LI-SAN HELPED OUT.
BUT WE STILL HAVEN'T FOUND HIM...
JIWA (TEARY)
WHOA!
WAAAAH
THERE, THERE.
SMOOTH, MISA-SAN!
AND A LITTLE SCARY!
DO YOU NEED THE POLICE?
OH! IT'S OKAY.
I'M SURE HE'LL COME BACK SOONER OR LATER.
OH...
AREN'T YOU THE GENTLEMAN, LI-KUN!
GOTTA HELP THE DAMSELS IN DISTRESS, HUH?
I'M ONLY DOING THE RIGHT THING...
PAN (PAT)

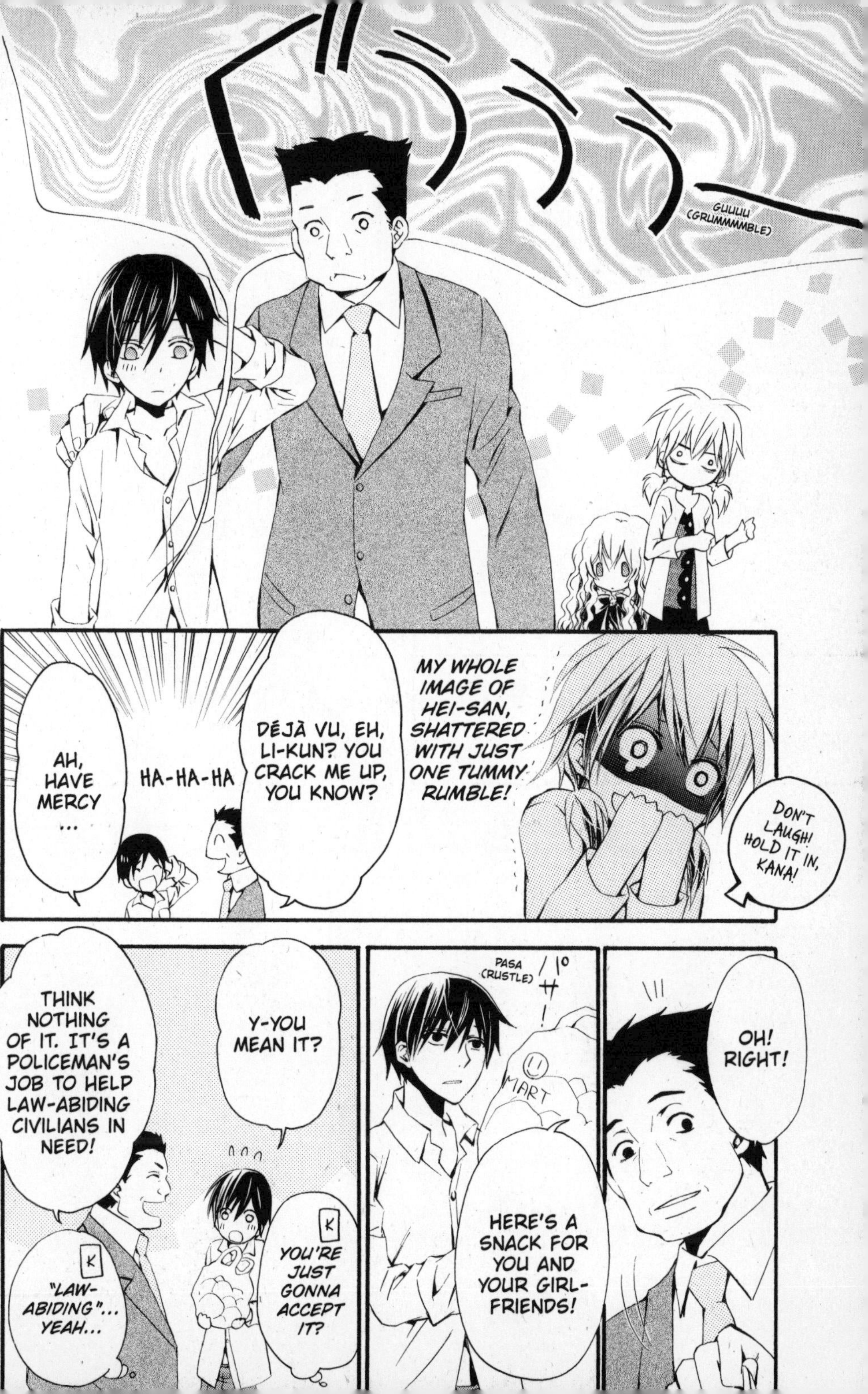
GUUUU (GRUMMMMBLE)
DON'T LAUGH! HOLD IT IN, KANA!
MY WHOLE IMAGE OF HEI-SAN, SHATTERED WITH JUST ONE TUMMY RUMBLE!
DÉJÀ VU, EH, LI-KUN? YOU CRACK ME UP, YOU KNOW?
HA-HA-HA
AH, HAVE MERCY ...
OH! RIGHT!
PASA (RUSTLE)
MART
HERE'S A SNACK FOR YOU AND YOUR GIRL-FRIENDS!
Y-YOU MEAN IT?
THINK NOTHING OF IT. IT'S A POLICEMAN'S JOB TO HELP LAW-ABIDING CIVILIANS IN NEED!
YOU'RE JUST GONNA ACCEPT IT?
"LAW-ABIDING"... YEAH...

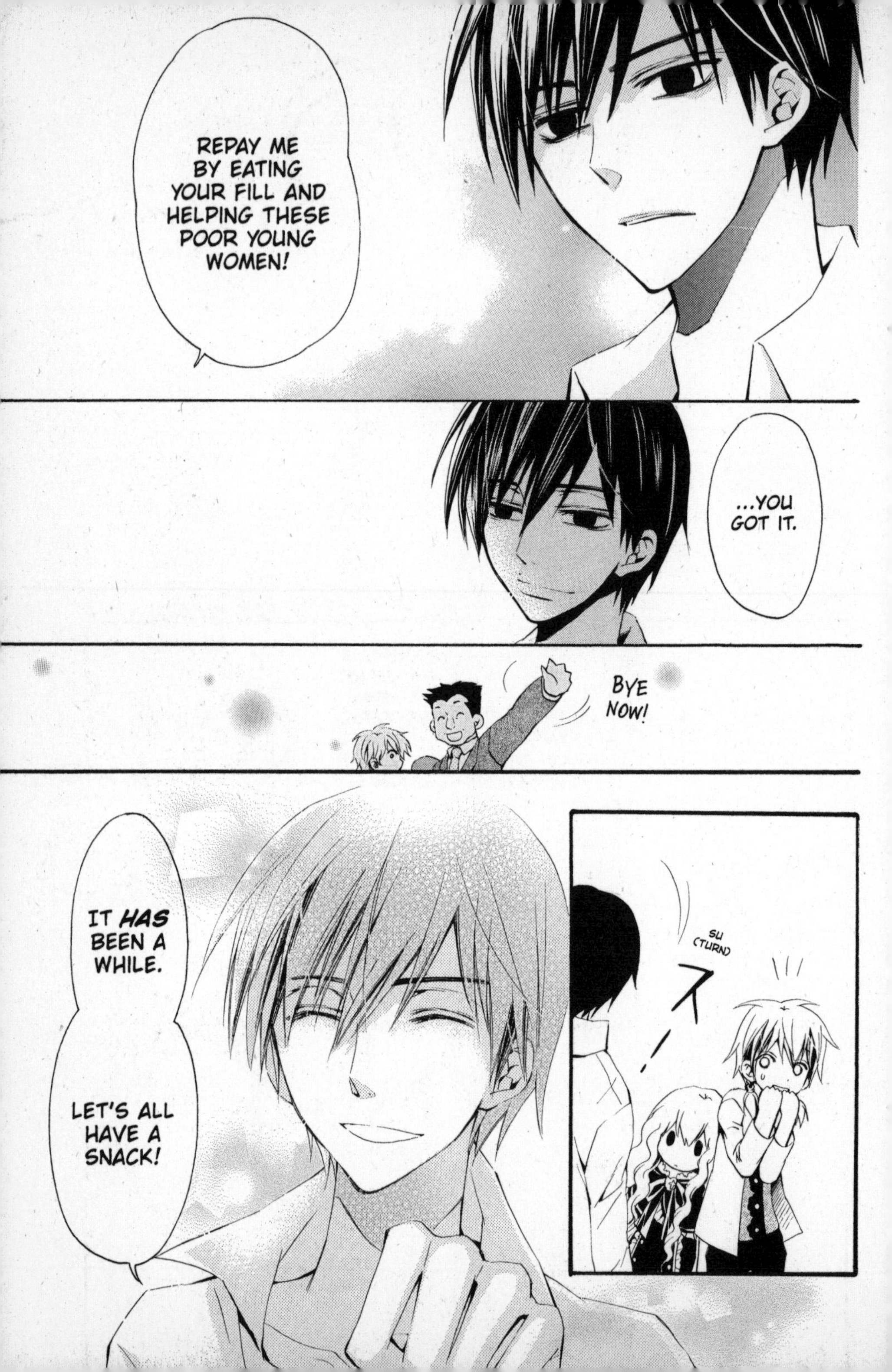
REPAY ME BY EATING YOUR FILL AND HELPING THESE POOR YOUNG WOMEN!
...YOU GOT IT.
BYE NOW!
SU (TURN)
IT *HAS* BEEN A WHILE.
LET'S ALL HAVE A SNACK!

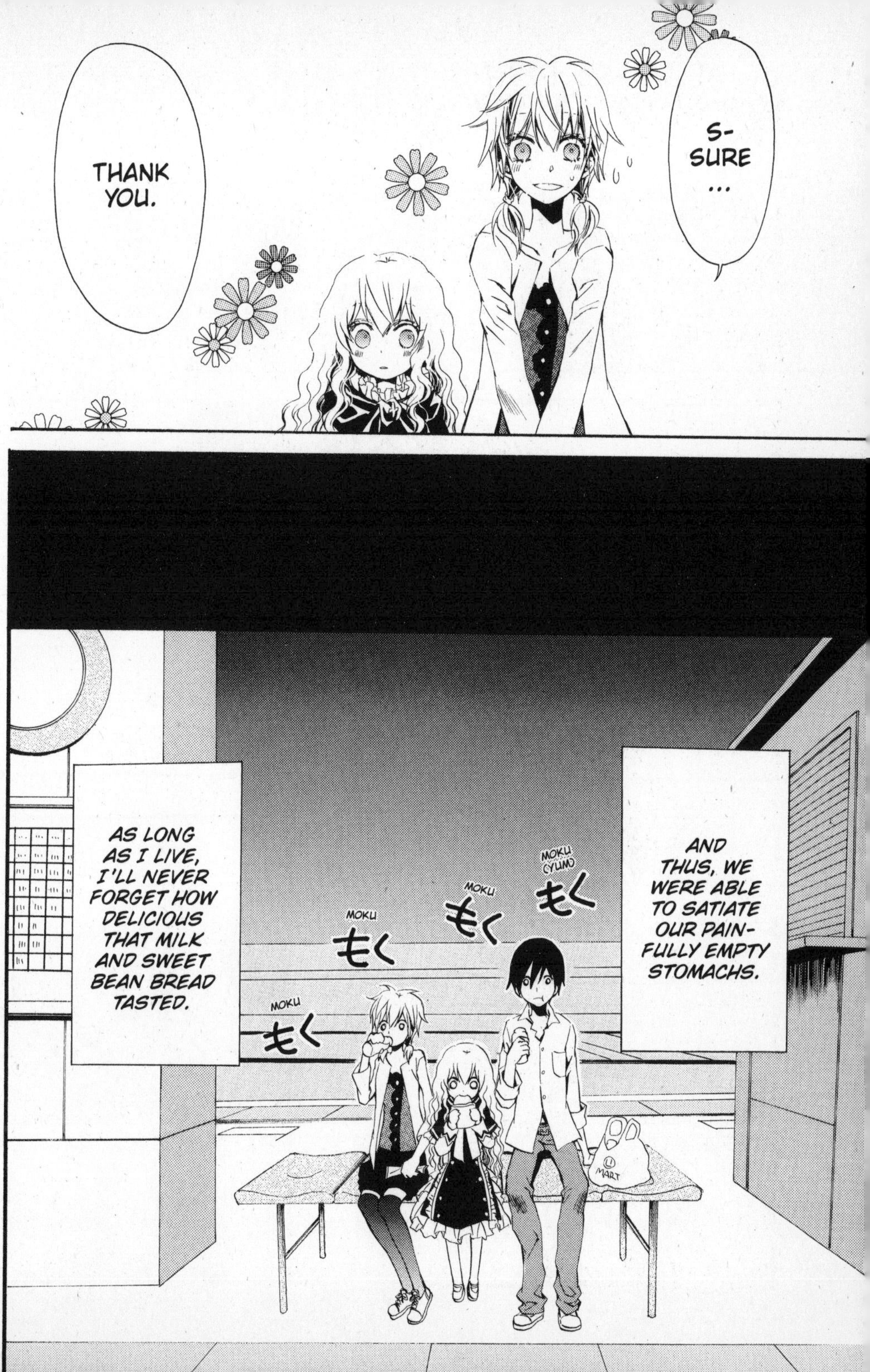
S-SURE...
THANK YOU.
AND THUS, WE WERE ABLE TO SATIATE OUR PAIN-FULLY EMPTY STOMACHS.
MOKU (YUM)
もく
MOKU
もく
MOKU
もく
MOKU
もく
MART
AS LONG AS I LIVE, I'LL NEVER FORGET HOW DELICIOUS THAT MILK AND SWEET BEAN BREAD TASTED.

Crazy Comic Strips

ピ
PIIII
(SQUEE)

HIS BEST DISH

THIS IS THE RESTAURANT THAT HEI'S INFILTRATING.
WEL-COME!
HAVE A SEAT, SIR.
SEEMS LIKE HE'S HANDLING EVERYTHING OKAY.
NO MATTER HOW MANY TIMES I SEE THAT ACT, IT WEIRDS ME OUT.
TH-THIS IS...
HMMM!?
THE FLAVOR OF ROASTED VEGETABLES PERMEATES THIS HEARTY BROTH PERFECTLY...
THIS IS THE SOUP OF THE GODS!

CONSPIRACY

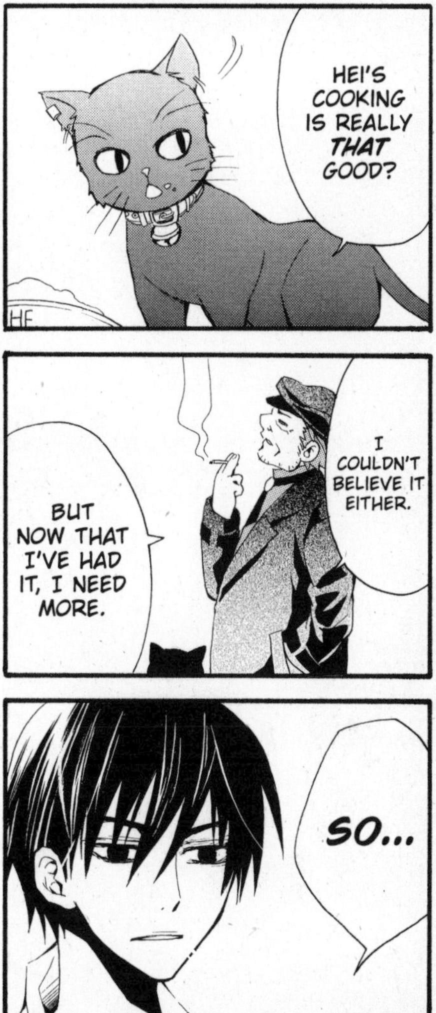
HEI'S COOKING IS REALLY *THAT* GOOD?
I COULDN'T BELIEVE IT EITHER.
BUT NOW THAT I'VE HAD IT, I NEED MORE.
SO...
YOU CALLED EVERYONE ALL THE WAY OUT HERE JUST FOR DINNER?
YOU EVEN RENTED AN APARTMENT...

SKILL

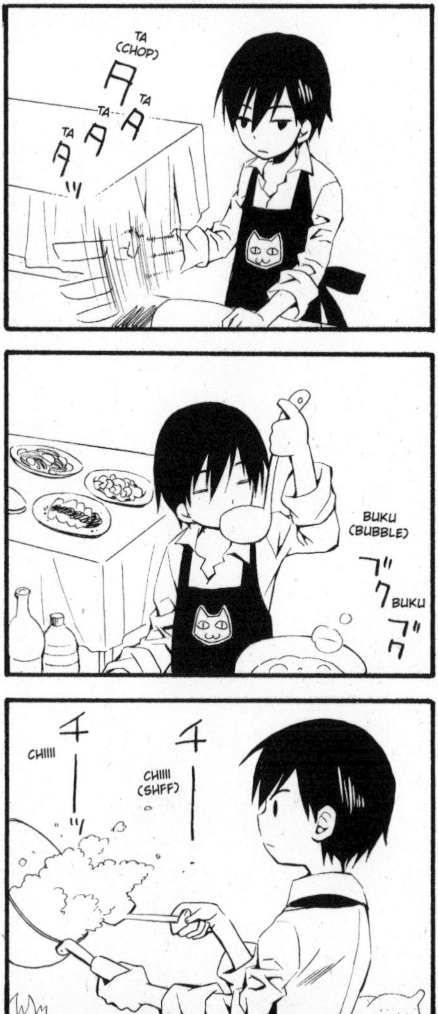
TA (CHOP)
TA
TA
TA
BUKU (BUBBLE)
BUKU
CHIIII (SHFF)
CHIIII
HEI'S AMAZING.
SO MUCH FOOD!
HE'S STILL GOING...

RATIONS

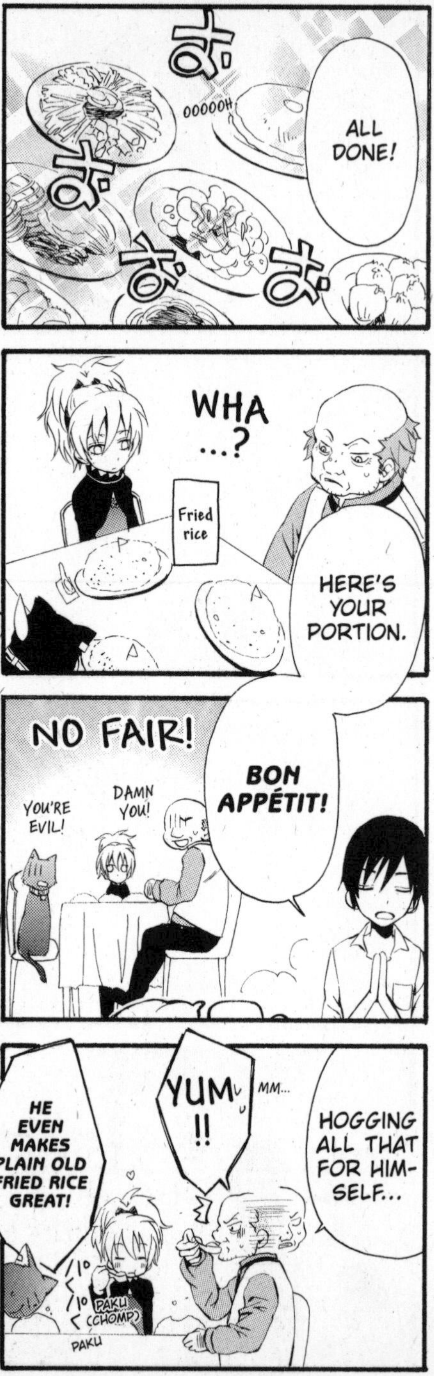
ALL DONE!
OOOOOH
おおおおお
WHA ...?
Fried rice
HERE'S YOUR PORTION.
BON APPÉTIT!
NO FAIR!
DAMN YOU!
YOU'RE EVIL!
HOGGING ALL THAT FOR HIM-SELF...
MM...
YUM!!
HE EVEN MAKES PLAIN OLD FRIED RICE GREAT!
PAKU (CHOMP)
PAKU

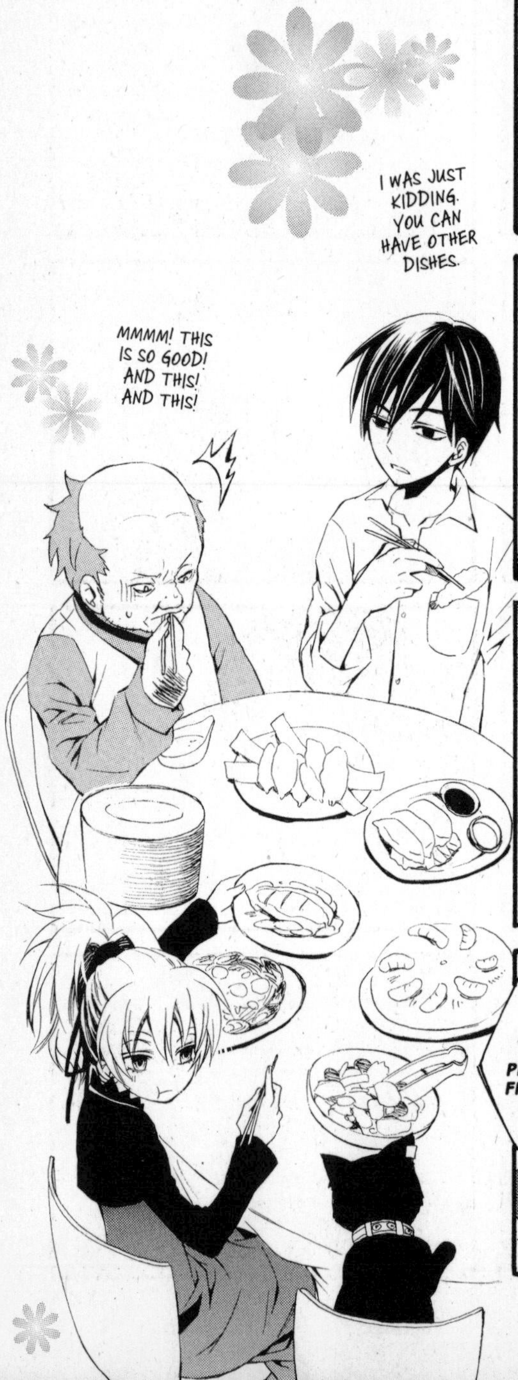
I WAS JUST KIDDING. YOU CAN HAVE OTHER DISHES.
MMMM! THIS IS SO GOOD! AND THIS! AND THIS!

OBSTACLE

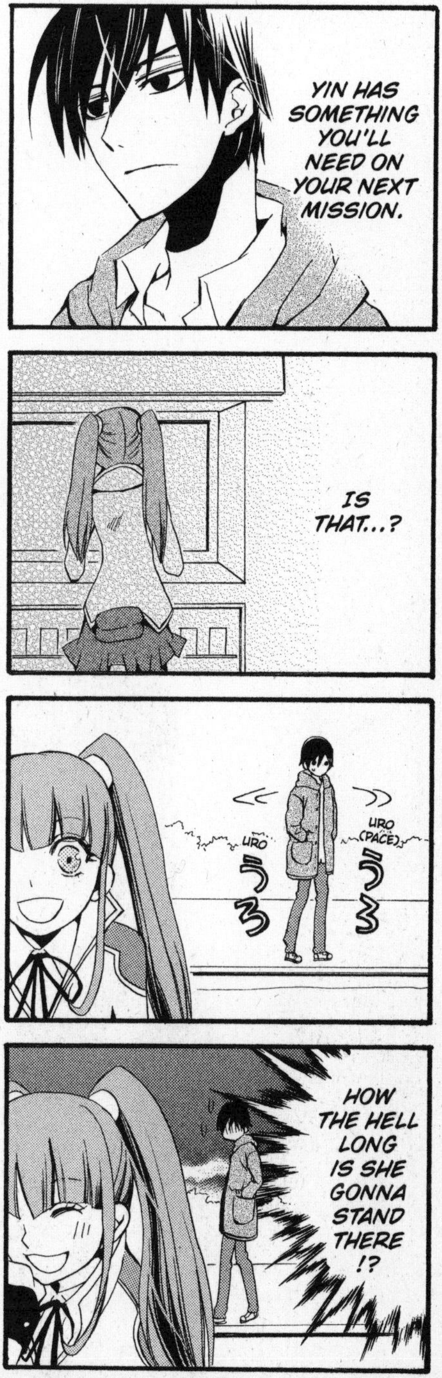
YIN HAS SOMETHING YOU'LL NEED ON YOUR NEXT MISSION.
IS THAT...?
URO (PACE)
うろ
URO
うろ
HOW THE HELL LONG IS SHE GONNA STAND THERE !?

RENDEZVOUS

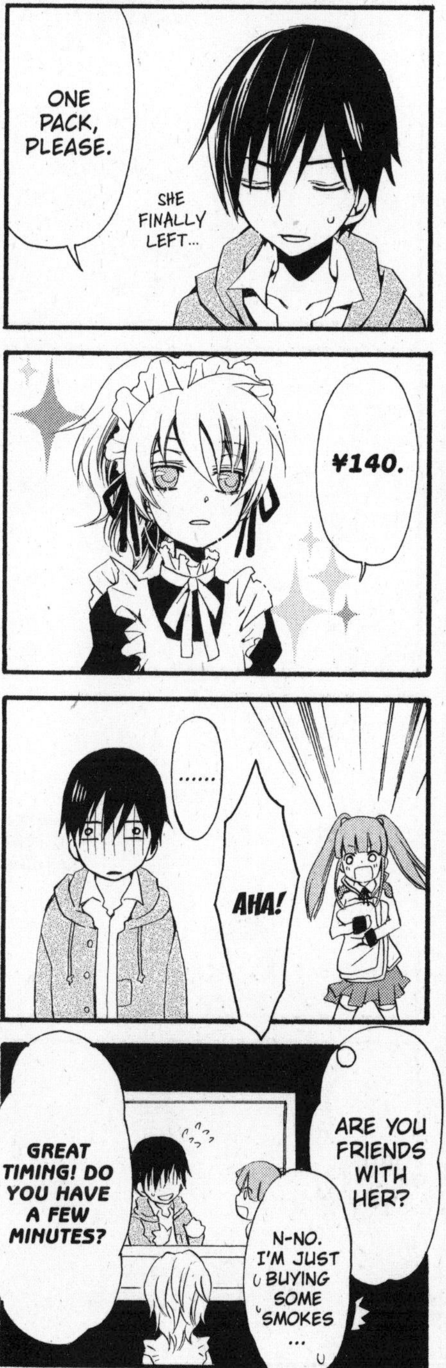
SHE FINALLY LEFT...
ONE PACK, PLEASE.
¥140.
......
AHA!
ARE YOU FRIENDS WITH HER?
GREAT TIMING! DO YOU HAVE A FEW MINUTES?
N-NO. I'M JUST BUYING SOME SMOKES ...

COSPLAY

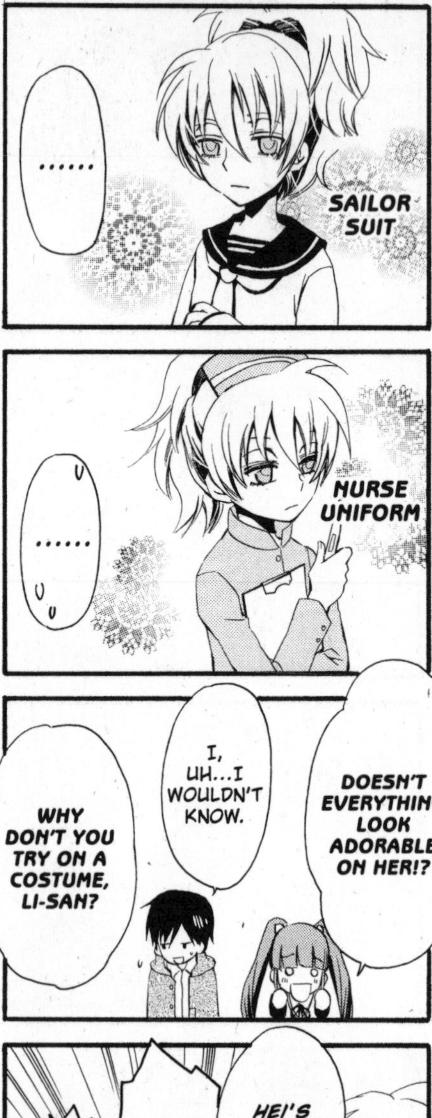

SAILOR SUIT
......
NURSE UNIFORM
......
DOESN'T EVERYTHING LOOK ADORABLE ON HER!?
I, UH...I WOULDN'T KNOW.
WHY DON'T YOU TRY ON A COSTUME, LI-SAN?
HEI'S ALREADY GOT A COSTUME.
EHHH? REALLY !?
N-NO, I DON'T!

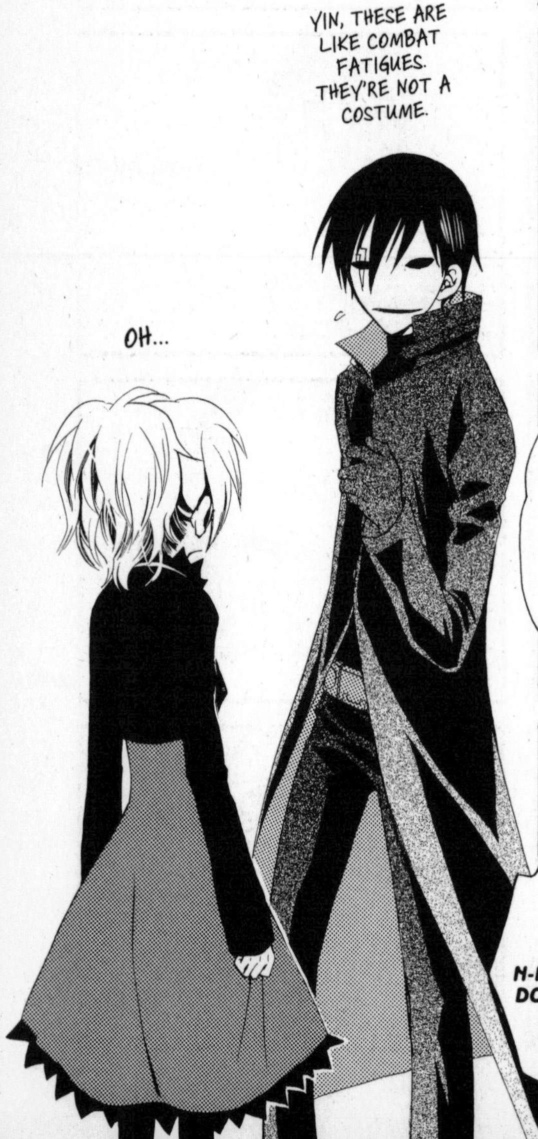

YIN, THESE ARE LIKE COMBAT FATIGUES. THEY'RE NOT A COSTUME.
OH...

BIRDS OF A FEATHER

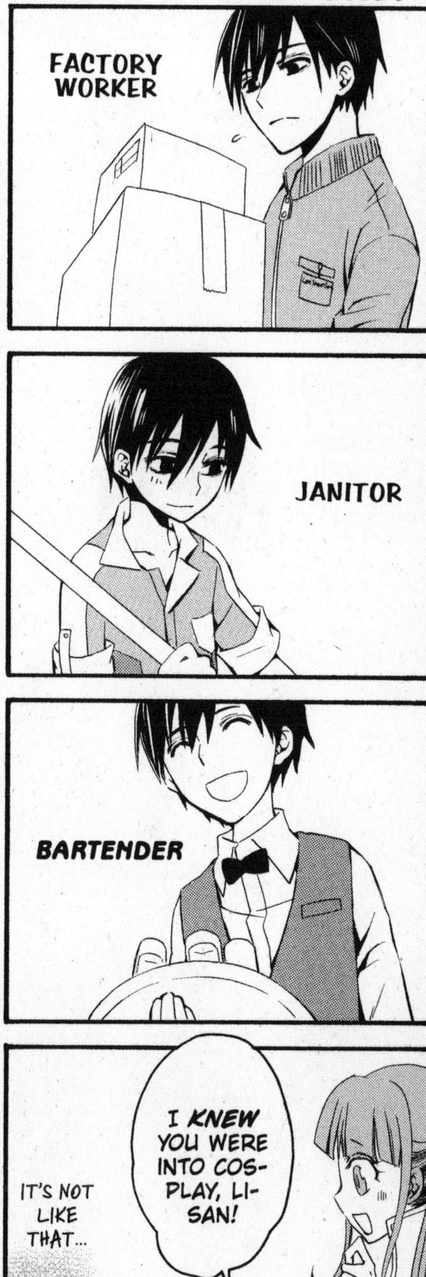
FACTORY WORKER
JANITOR
BARTENDER
I KNEW YOU WERE INTO COS-PLAY, LI-SAN!
IT'S NOT LIKE THAT...

SUSPICION

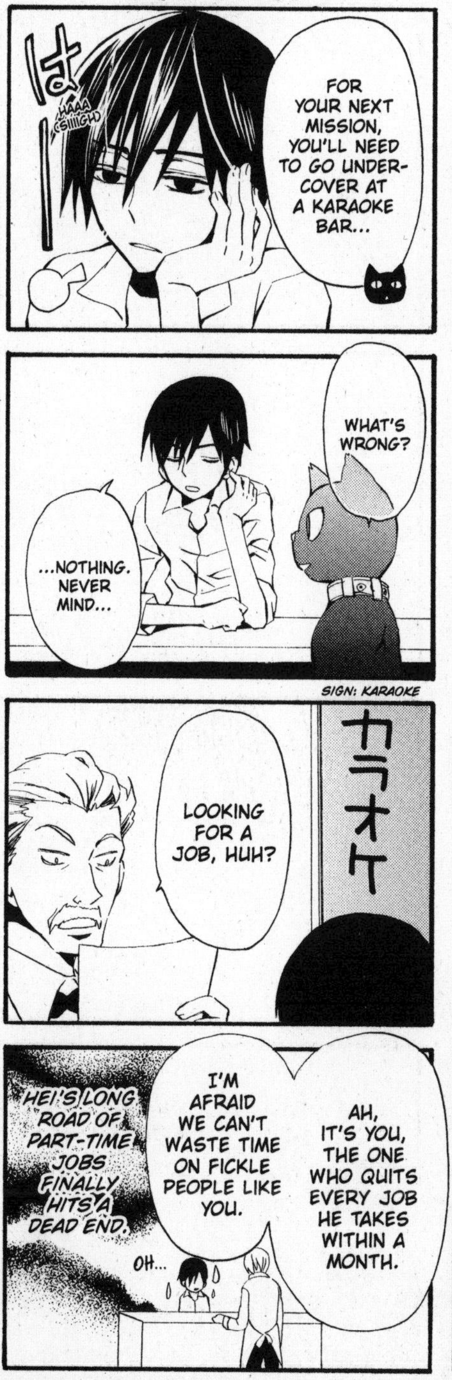
FOR YOUR NEXT MISSION, YOU'LL NEED TO GO UNDER-COVER AT A KARAOKE BAR...
は
HAAA (SIIIIGH)
WHAT'S WRONG?
...NOTHING. NEVER MIND...
SIGN: KARAOKE
カラオケ
LOOKING FOR A JOB, HUH?
AH, IT'S YOU, THE ONE WHO QUITS EVERY JOB HE TAKES WITHIN A MONTH.
I'M AFRAID WE CAN'T WASTE TIME ON FICKLE PEOPLE LIKE YOU.
HEI'S LONG ROAD OF PART-TIME JOBS FINALLY HITS A DEAD END.
OH...

DIVINE RETRIBUTION

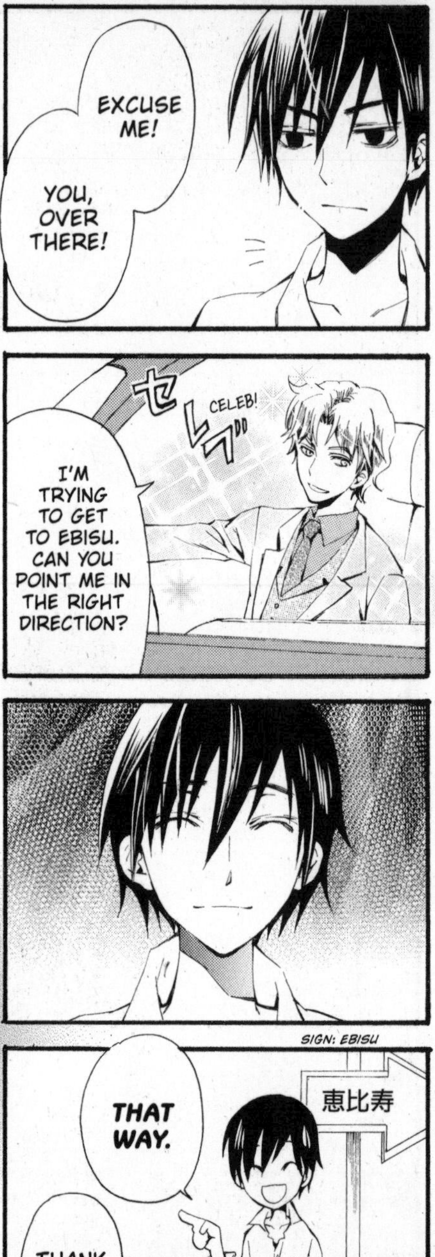
EXCUSE ME!
YOU, OVER THERE!
セレブ
CELEB!
I'M TRYING TO GET TO EBISU. CAN YOU POINT ME IN THE RIGHT DIRECTION?
SIGN: EBISU
恵比寿
THAT WAY.
THANK YOU! ♡

EXPENSE REPORT

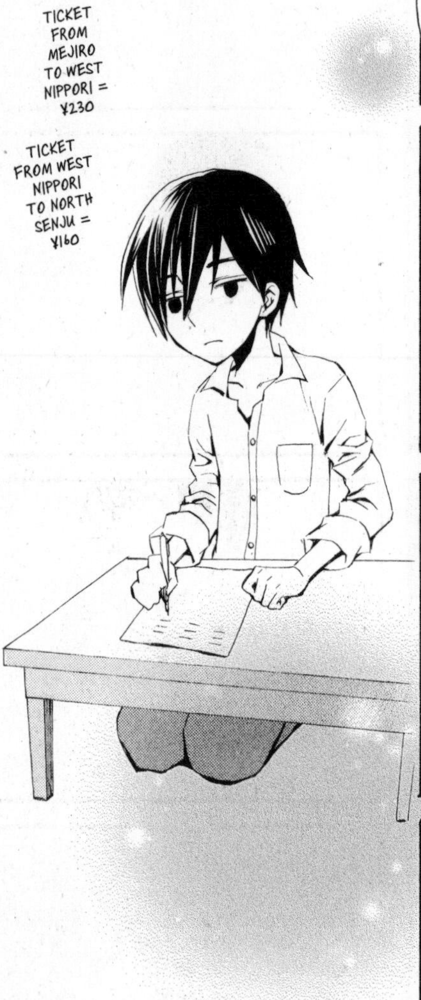
TICKET FROM MEJIRO TO WEST NIPPORI = ¥230
TICKET FROM WEST NIPPORI TO NORTH SENJU = ¥160

FINAL INTERVIEW

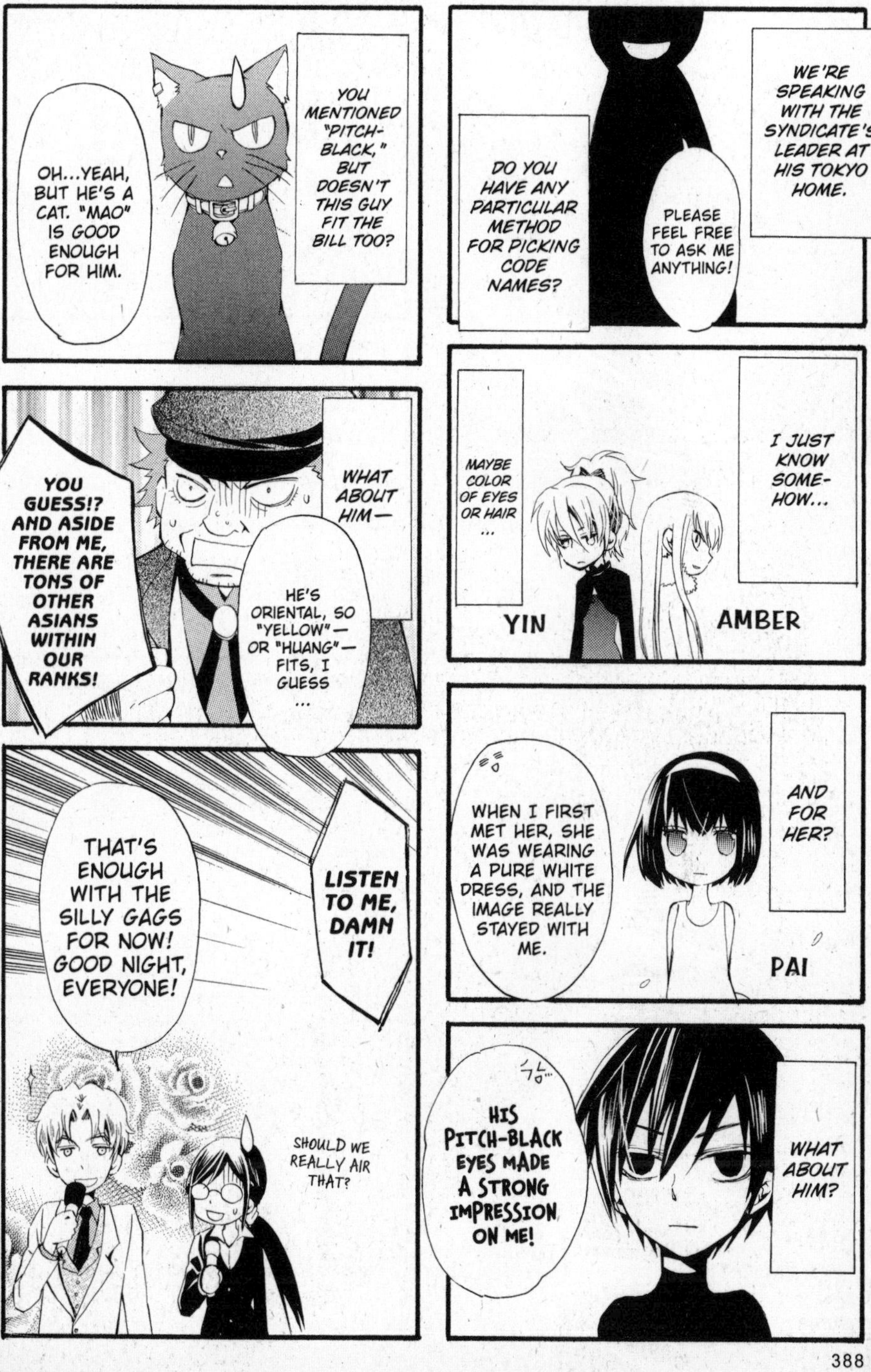
WE'RE SPEAKING WITH THE SYNDICATE'S LEADER AT HIS TOKYO HOME.
PLEASE FEEL FREE TO ASK ME ANYTHING!
DO YOU HAVE ANY PARTICULAR METHOD FOR PICKING CODE NAMES?
I JUST KNOW SOMEHOW...
AMBER
MAYBE COLOR OF EYES OR HAIR ...
YIN
AND FOR HER?
PAI
WHEN I FIRST MET HER, SHE WAS WEARING A PURE WHITE DRESS, AND THE IMAGE REALLY STAYED WITH ME.
WHAT ABOUT HIM?
HIS PITCH-BLACK EYES MADE A STRONG IMPRESSION ON ME!
YOU MENTIONED "PITCH-BLACK," BUT DOESN'T THIS GUY FIT THE BILL TOO?
OH...YEAH, BUT HE'S A CAT. "MAO" IS GOOD ENOUGH FOR HIM.
WHAT ABOUT HIM—
HE'S ORIENTAL, SO "YELLOW"—OR "HUANG"—FITS, I GUESS ...
YOU GUESS!? AND ASIDE FROM ME, THERE ARE TONS OF OTHER ASIANS WITHIN OUR RANKS!
LISTEN TO ME, DAMN IT!
THAT'S ENOUGH WITH THE SILLY GAGS FOR NOW! GOOD NIGHT, EVERYONE!
SHOULD WE REALLY AIR THAT?

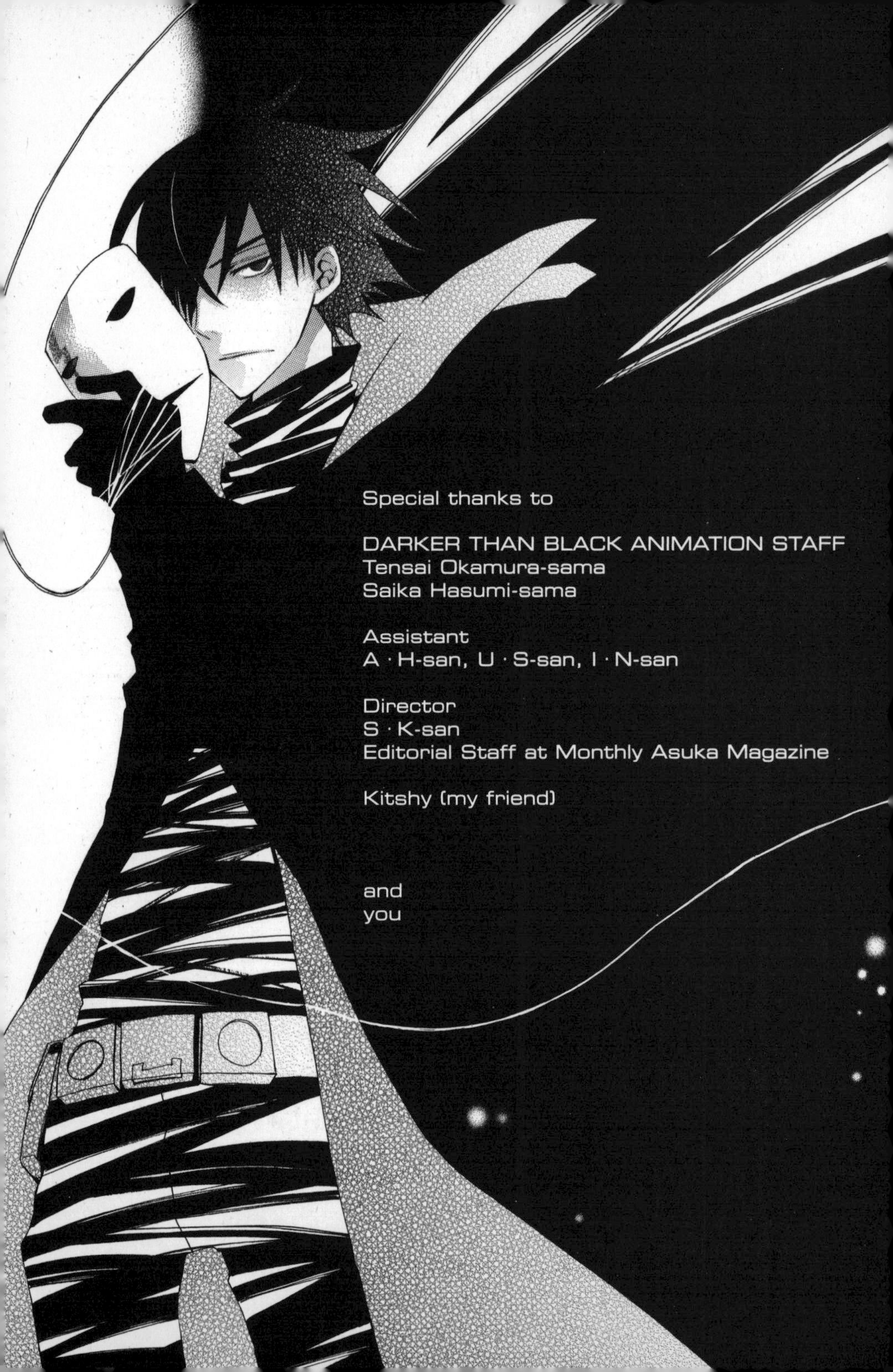

Special thanks to

DARKER THAN BLACK ANIMATION STAFF
Tensai Okamura-sama
Saika Hasumi-sama

Assistant
A · H-san, U · S-san, I · N-san

Director
S · K-san
Editorial Staff at Monthly Asuka Magazine

Kitshy (my friend)

and
you

VOLUME ONE AFTERWORD

Same old Tokyo, same old daily routine...
And with one pinch of that spice we call "variety," everything changes and the story begins. That's one my favorite things in manga and anime — the moment in which that one "if" happens, and the whole world turns upside-down. DARKER THAN BLACK is one such series: The stars disappear, the sky over Tokyo turns pitch dark...and the Contractors appear, as if it were an even trade. Normal people's daily lives become, like the title, darker than black.

Our main character, Hei, seems to have traded his emotions for his power. But beneath the cold, ruthless assassin's face, he has another expression: a sad face, full of loneliness. Hei, and all of us, keep our pain on the inside, oftentimes refusing to let it show, even in the most difficult situations. That critical human element may be what makes this book so gloomy — or so heartwarming. Perhaps that dichotomy might even give the book its own unique charm.

As one of many DARKER THAN BLACK fans, I was thrilled to be given the opportunity to work on this manga. I promise I'll keep working my tail off, and I hope you enjoy this new foray into the world of DARKER THAN BLACK. See you next time!

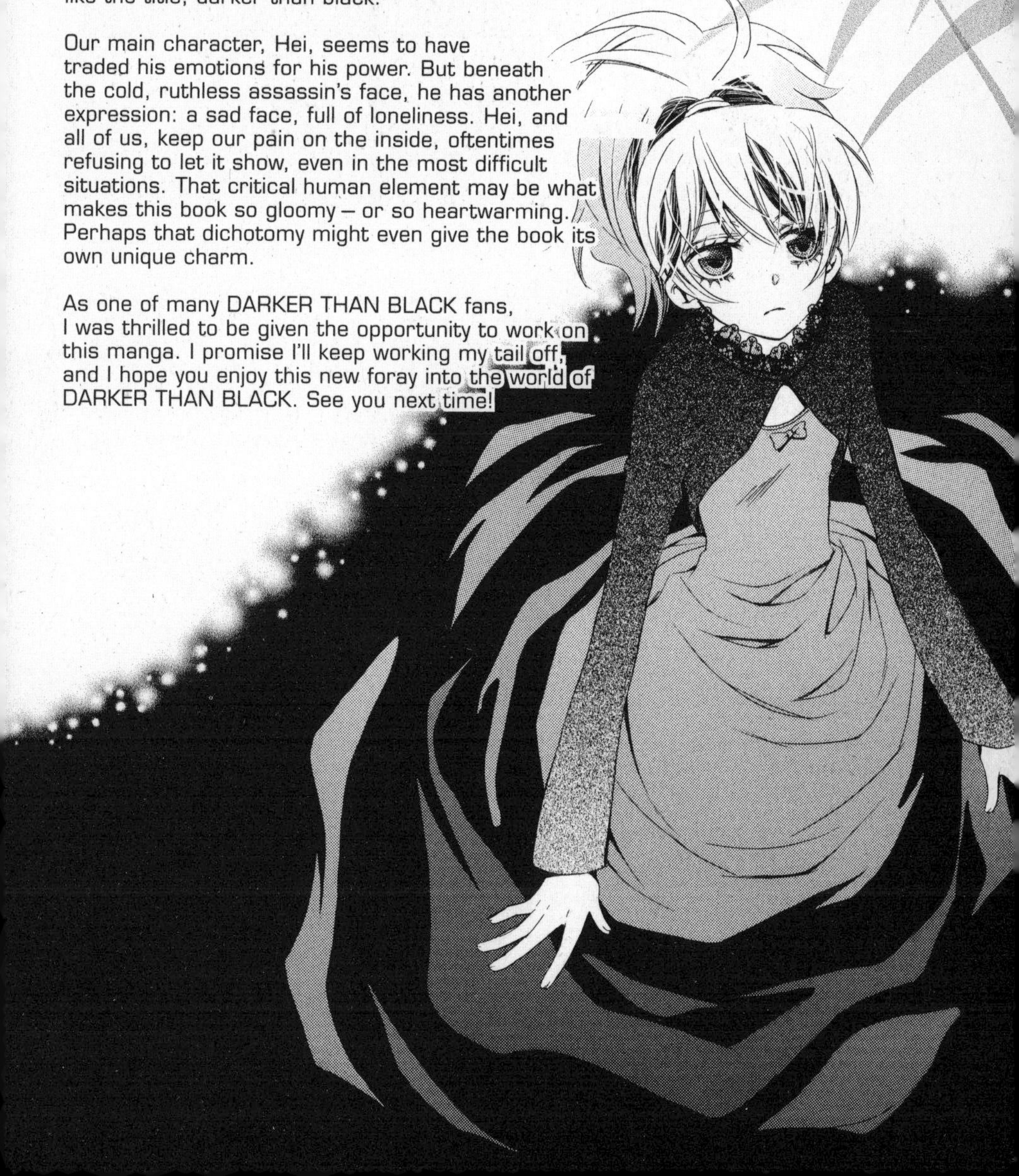

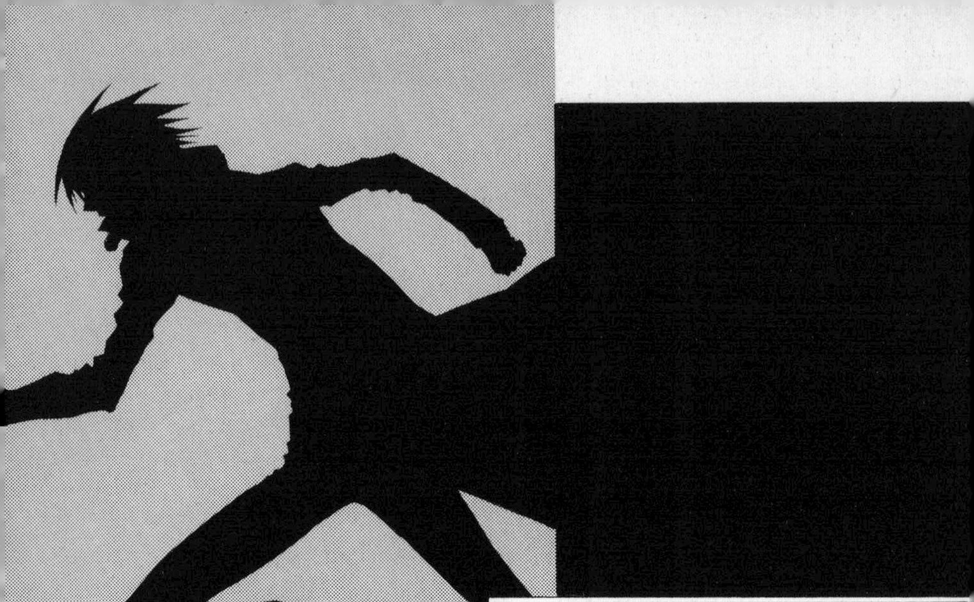

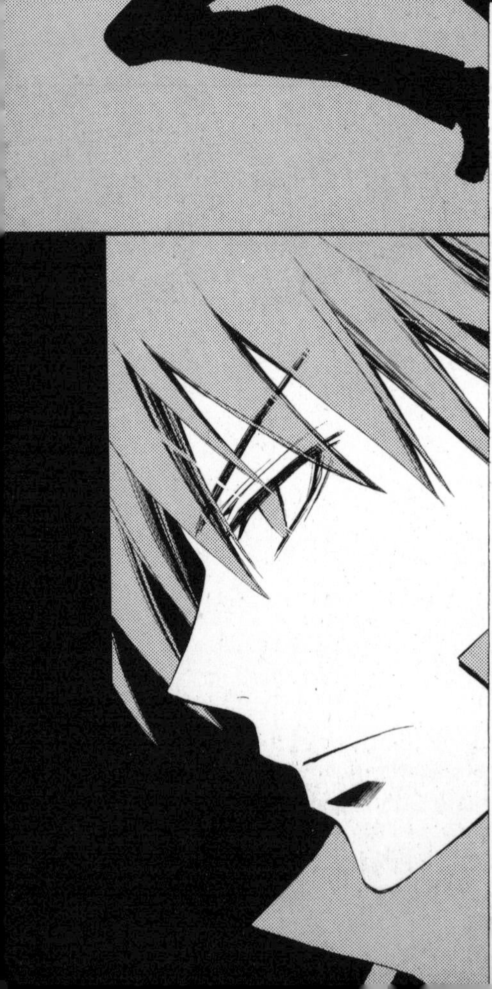

VOLUME TWO AFTERWORD

Now that everything's finally over, I'm getting nostalgic for the time before, when all I could think about was, "I won't get to draw Hei anymore!" There were so many things I wanted to say, but now that the moment's finally here, I just can't find the words.

At any rate, it honestly was a joy to spend this year with Hei. And I've learned exactly how important all these wonderful people are to me, all those who stepped up to help this inexperienced artist. More than anything, I feel truly blessed to have been introduced to the world of DARKER THAN BLACK. I hope the day comes when I'll get to meet Hei and his companions once again!

To the anime staff, Hasumi-san, the editors, my assistants, and everyone else —you all did a fantastic job! Thank you, from the bottom of my heart!

—Nokiya, 12/2007

COMMON HONORIFICS

No honorific: Indicates familiarity or closeness; if used without permission or reason, addresssing someone in this manner would constitute an insult.

-san: The Japanese equivalent of Mr./Mrs./Miss. If a situation calls for politeness, this is the fail-safe honorific.

-sama: Conveys great respect; may also indicate that the social status of the speaker is lower than that of the addressee.

-kun: Used most often when referring to boys, this indicates affection or familiarity. Occasionally used by older men among their peers, but it may also be used by anyone referring to a person of lower standing.

-chan: An affectionate honorific indicating familiarity used mostly in reference to girls; also used in reference to cute persons or animals of either gender.

PAGE 12
Wiegenlied: The German word for "lullaby," it also suggests the musical theme common to many of the proper names in this manga.

Klang: The German word for "sound."

PAGE 37
Canon: A musical term referring to a piece of music in which a common melody is repeated, as in Johann Pachelbel's famous *Canon in D major*.

PAGE 57
Hei: Chinese for "black." Fans of the anime may recall that all of the named (human) members of The Syndicate have codenames associated with color.

PAGE 58
Mao: The Chinese word for "cat."

PAGE 81
Stille: The German word for "silence."

PAGE 94
Musik: The German word for "music."

PAGE 186
201BK: When the night sky was blotted out with the emergence of Hell's Gate, a field of false stars, each tied to a particular contractor, appeared in its place. A Messier catalogue number identifies these astronomical objects with a mixture of letters and numerals. As opposed to calling Hei by his technical Messier code, BK201, November 11 reverses the numerals and letters, as was also his habit in the TV series.

PAGE 191
Orchester Research Facility: The facility tied to Project Wiegenlied, its name uses the German word for "orchestra."

PAGE 198
MI6: The name by which the British Secret Intelligence Service (SIS) is most commonly known. MI6 is the British security branch responsible for external intelligence, overseen by the Joint Intelligence Committee (JIC).

PAGE 202
Yin: The Chinese word for "silver."

Huang: The Chinese word for "yellow."

PAGE 224
Pai: The Chinese word for "white."

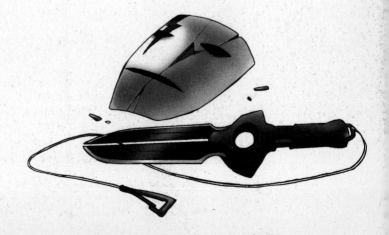

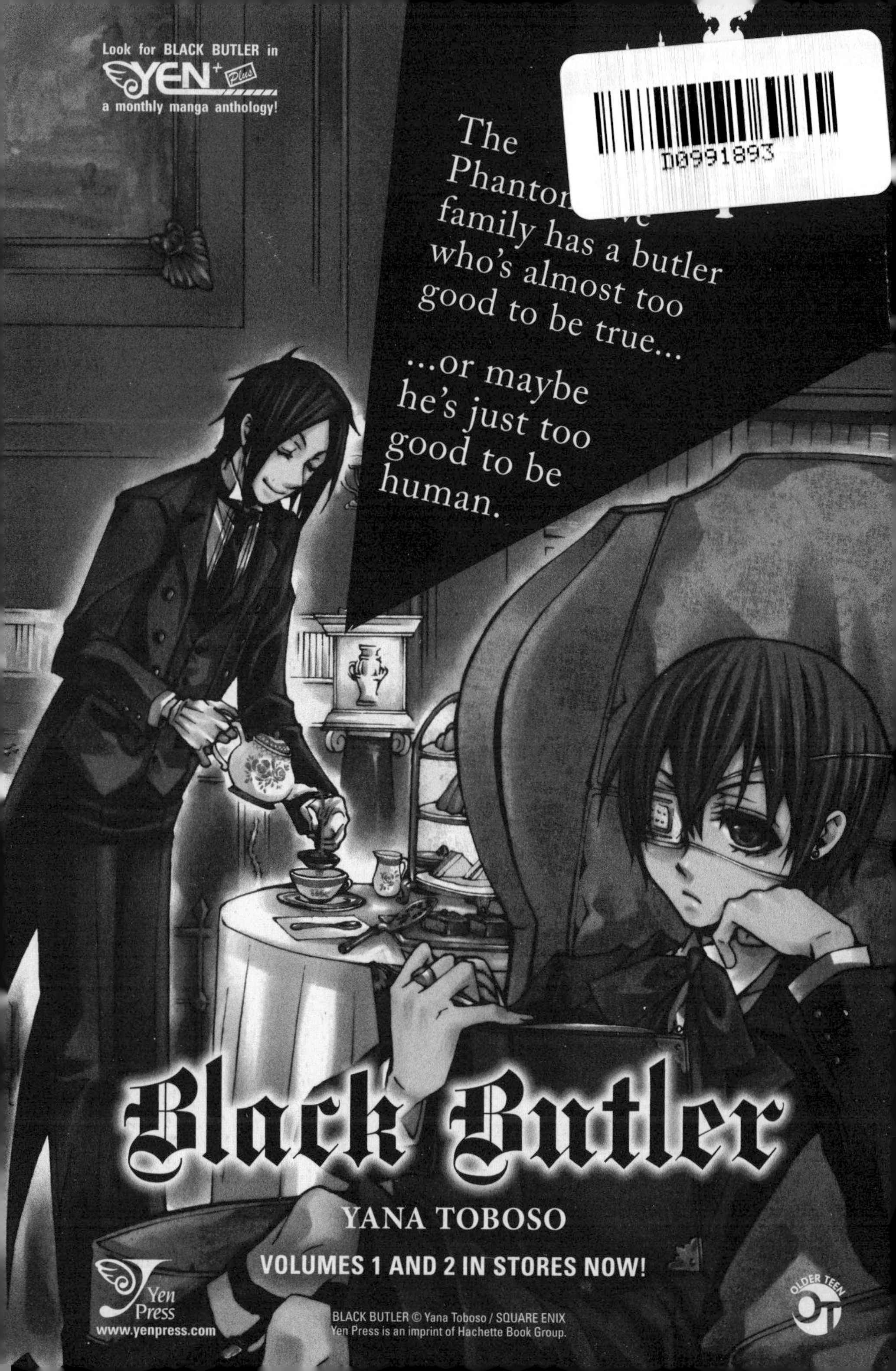
Look for BLACK BUTLER in
YEN+ Plus
a monthly manga anthology!
The
Phanton
family has a butler
who's almost too
good to be true...
...or maybe
he's just too
good to be
human.
D0991893
Black Butler
YANA TOBOSO
VOLUMES 1 AND 2 IN STORES NOW!
Yen Press
www.yenpress.com
BLACK BUTLER © Yana Toboso / SQUARE ENIX
Yen Press is an imprint of Hachette Book Group.
OLDER TEEN
OT